"No book has been more influential for n
Bible than *Discovering Biblical Equality*. 1.
developed in complementarianism, and this new third edition responds to the most
recent challenges. There are new chapters on fresh themes by new authors. Students
and pastors alike will find experts expounding Scripture and demonstrating the
Spirit's unleashing of gifts among women and men alike."

Scot McKnight, professor of New Testament at Northern Seminary

"Addressing the questions often asked, as well as introducing those that should be
asked, *Discovering Biblical Equality* covers the terrain with lucidity, verve, and gra-
ciousness. The authors give voice to that which stirs the hearts of so many: the singular commitment to the authority of Scripture and the imago Dei in all humans.
They do so by laying out their deep exegetical and theological reasoning so that
others can assess the logic for themselves. I am excited to recommend this volume
to all who wonder about the biblical foundations for equality."

Amy Peeler, associate professor of New Testament, Wheaton College and Graduate School

"This is a wonderfully thoughtful study that combines a multitude of voices on a topic
that continues to trouble churches worldwide. It demonstrates uncompromising
respect for the holy Scriptures and a determination to reconcile the genders and
celebrate the fullness of their humanity."

Myrto Theocharous, professor of Hebrew and Old Testament at Greek Bible College,
Athens, Greece

"The earlier editions of *Discovering Biblical Equality* were foundational for my understanding of men and women in the Bible. This third edition retains the best of
what came before and adds lots of fresh materials to strengthen the case for biblical
equality and mutuality. This continues to be the best all-in-one resource for understanding a Christian theology of women in ministry, family, and society."

Nijay K. Gupta, professor of New Testament at Northern Seminary

"Having found the earlier editions of *Discovering Biblical Equality* to be extremely
helpful resources in supplementing conversations within the church and the
academy concerning our shared human identity in Christ Jesus, we say 'welcome'
and 'well done' to this revised edition. With new essays from fresh (particularly
female) voices and a slightly renewed format, this volume continues to address historical and present concerns in wise, irenic, knowledgeable ways. Hence it continues
to help us discover the gift of life together as God's coequal image-bearing children.
A truly wonderful 'upgrade'!"

Cherith Fee Nordling, associate professor at the Robert E. Webber Institute for Worship
Studies, Regent College, Vancouver, and author of *Knowing God by Name*

THIRD EDITION

Discovering
BIBLICAL
EQUALITY

Biblical, Theological, Cultural & Practical Perspectives

RONALD W. PIERCE AND
CYNTHIA LONG WESTFALL, *editors*

CHRISTA L. McKIRLAND, *associate editor*

With contributions from
LYNN H. COHICK, GORDON D. FEE,
MIMI HADDAD, CRAIG S. KEENER,
AND MORE

ivp
Academic
An imprint of InterVarsity Press
Downers Grove, Illinois

InterVarsity Press
P.O. Box 1400, Downers Grove, IL 60515-1426
ivpress.com
email@ivpress.com

InterVarsity Press® is the book-publishing division of InterVarsity Christian Fellowship/USA®, a movement of students and faculty active on campus at hundreds of universities, colleges, and schools of nursing in the United States of America, and a member movement of the International Fellowship of Evangelical Students. For information about local and regional activities, visit intervarsity.org.

Scripture quotations, unless otherwise noted, are from the New Revised Standard Version Bible, copyright © 1989 National Council of the Churches of Christ in the United States of America. Used by permission. All rights reserved worldwide.

While any stories in this book are true, some names and identifying information may have been changed to protect the privacy of individuals.

The publisher cannot verify the accuracy or functionality of website URLs used in this book beyond the date of publication.

Cover design and image composite: David Fassett
Interior design: Jeanna Wiggins
Image: garden painting: © The Garden of Earthly Delights, Hieronymus Bosch / Bridgeman Images

ISBN 978-0-8308-5479-0 (print)
ISBN 978-0-8308-5480-6 (digital)

Printed in the United States of America ♾

InterVarsity Press is committed to ecological stewardship and to the conservation of natural resources in all our operations. This book was printed using sustainably sourced paper.

Library of Congress Cataloging-in-Publication Data

Names: Pierce, Ronald W., 1946- editor. | Westfall, Cynthia Long, editor.
Title: Discovering biblical equality : biblical, theological, cultural, and
    practical perspectives / Ronald W. Pierce, Cynthia Long Westfall,
    editors and Christa L. McKirland, Associate editor.
Description: Third edition. | Downers Grove, IL : InterVarsity Press,
    [2021] | Includes bibliographical references and index.
Identifiers: LCCN 2021030775 (print) | LCCN 2021030776 (ebook) | ISBN
    9780830854790 (print) | ISBN 9780830854806 (digital)
Subjects: LCSH: Sex role—Biblical teaching. | Equality—Biblical teaching.
    | Evangelicalism.
Classification: LCC BS680.S53 D57 2021 (print) | LCC BS680.S53 (ebook) |
    DDC 220.8/3053—dc23
LC record available at https://lccn.loc.gov/2021030775
LC ebook record available at https://lccn.loc.gov/2021030776

| P | 25 | 24 | 23 | 22 | 21 | 20 | 19 | 18 | 17 | 16 | 15 | 14 | 13 | 12 | 11 | 10 | 9 | 8 | 7 | 6 | 5 | 4 | 3 | 2 | 1 |
| Y | 38 | 37 | 36 | 35 | 34 | 33 | 32 | 31 | 30 | 29 | 28 | 27 | 26 | 25 | 24 | 23 | 22 | 21 |

May God bless your reading of this book.

[signature]

To Rebecca Merrill Groothuis (1954–2018):

original coeditor, dear friend, and colleague,

and beloved sister in Christ

• • • • •

Her unwavering commitment to

the inspiration and authority of Scripture,

her keen editorial eye, her razor-sharp mind,

and her deep love for Jesus laid the firm

foundation for this third edition of

Discovering Biblical Equality.

CONTENTS

PART II: THINKING IT THROUGH
Theological and Logical Perspectives

PART III: ADDRESSING THE ISSUES
Interpretive and Cultural Perspectives

PART IV: LIVING IT OUT
Practical Applications

ACKNOWLEDGMENTS

· · · · ·

AS IT WAS IN THE EARLIER EDITIONS OF *Discovering Biblical Equality*, so now this third edition is the result of the collaborative effort of a diverse group of evangelical scholars, men and women from a wide range of disciplines who are united here by two convictions: that the Bible is the fully inspired and authoritative Word of God, and that it teaches a holistic theology of gender equality in both status and function in the home, church, and society.

Original coeditors Ronald W. Pierce and Rebecca Merrill Groothuis had independently contemplated a volume like this for several years before God brought them together in 2000 to begin work on the first edition, after which Gordon D. Fee was asked to join them as contributing editor. Now more than twenty years later, it is time for a substantive revision of this resource to properly address the many new questions, arguments, and scholarly contributions that have arisen. Because of the loss of our friend Becky Groothuis through her homegoing in 2018, Ron asked Cynthia Long Westfall to join him as the new coeditor, after which they invited Christa L. McKirland to come on board as associate editor.

On behalf of all those contributing to this third edition of *Discovering Biblical Equality*, we would like to thank the following individuals and groups who, by God's grace, have made this work possible. Regrettably, space permits us to mention only a few by name.

First, we could not have accomplished this task without the sacrificial support of our families, namely Ron's wife, Pat; Cindy's husband, Glenn; and Christa's husband, Matt. They, along with numerous children and grandchildren, deserve our sincere gratitude for their patience and encouragement.

Second, the academic institutions where we serve have provided invaluable support, and sometimes resources, to support our writing and editing: Ron as Old Testament professor in Biola University's Talbot School of Theology (California), Cindy as New Testament professor at McMaster Divinity College (Ontario), and Christa as lecturer in systematic theology at Carey Baptist College (Aotearoa New Zealand). Moreover, our appreciation does not merely extend to our administrators, colleagues, and staff, but also to the many students over our respective tenures who have asked hard questions without accepting easy answers and offered fresh new ideas that give us great confidence in the next generation of leaders for Christ's church.

Third, we likewise are indebted to the leadership, staff, and members of CBE International (www.cbeinternational.org), who have championed the cause of evangelical gender equality since the organization's inception in 1987. CBE International has contributed to this book in many ways from its founder, Katherine Clark Kroeger (who originally encouraged Ron to take on this project), to its current president, Mimi Haddad, who has promoted this resource and contributed essays to it from the beginning—not to mention the many other members of CBE International who have also contributed essays.

Finally, we very much appreciate the work of the InterVarsity Press editorial staff—longtime advocates for gender equality—especially David McNutt, who readily accepted and has since then skillfully overseen the present volume. His patience, guidance, and expertise have been indispensable.

ABBREVIATIONS

• • • • •

MISHNAH, TALMUD, AND RABBINIC LITERATURE

b.	Babylonian Talmud
B. Metz.	Bava Metziʾa
B. Qam.	Bava Qamma
Ber.	Berakhot
Eruv.	Eruvin
Git.	Gittin
Hag.	Hagigah
Ketub.	Ketubbot
m.	Mishnah
Ned.	Nedarim
Qidd.	Qiddushin
Rosh Hash.	Rosh Hashanah
Sanh.	Sanhedrin
Shabb.	Shabbat
Shevu.	Sheuvuʾot
t.	Tosefta
Yevam.	Yevamot

SECONDARY SOURCES

AB	Anchor Bible
BBR	*Bulletin for Biblical Research*
BDAG	Frederick W. Danker, Walter Bauer, William F. Arndt, and F. Wilbur Gingrich. *Greek-English Lexicon of the New*

	Testament and Other Early Christian Literature. 3rd ed. Chicago: University of Chicago Press, 2000
BECNT	Baker Exegetical Commentary on the New Testament
BSac	*Bibliotheca Sacra*
CBQ	*Catholic Biblical Quarterly*
CT	*Christianity Today*
JBMW	*Journal of Biblical Manhood and Womanhood*
JETS	*Journal of the Evangelical Theological Society*
JGRChJ	*Journal of Greco-Roman Christianity and Judaism*
JSOTSup	Journal for the Study of the Old Testament Supplement Series
L&N	Johannes P. Louw and Eugene A. Nida. *Greek-English Lexicon of the New Testament Based on Semantic Domains.* 2nd ed. New York: United Bible Societies, 1989
LCL	Loeb Classical Library
LSJ	Henry George Liddell, Robert Scott, and Henry Stuart Jones. *A Greek-English Lexicon.* 9th ed. with revised supplement. Oxford: Clarendon, 1996
NA²⁸	*Novum Testamentum Graece*, Nestle-Aland, 28th ed.
NAC	New American Commentary
NCCS	New Covenant Commentary Series
NIBC	New International Biblical Commentary
NICNT	New International Commentary on the New Testament
NICOT	New International Commentary on the Old Testament
NIGTC	New International Greek Testament Commentary
NIVAC	New International Version Application Commentary
NTS	*New Testament Studies*
PriscPap	*Priscilla Papers*
RBMW	John Piper and Wayne Grudem, eds. *Recovering Biblical Manhood and Womanhood: A Response to Evangelical Feminism.* Wheaton, IL: Crossway, 1991. 2nd ed., 2006; 3rd ed., 2021. All references, unless otherwise noted, are to the 3rd ed.
TDNT	*Theological Dictionary of the New Testament.* Edited by Gerhard Kittel and Gerhard Friedrich. Translated by Geoffrey W. Bromiley. 10 vols. Grand Rapids, MI: Eerdmans, 1964–1976
UBS⁵	*The Greek New Testament*, United Bible Societies, 5th ed.
WBC	Word Biblical Commentary
WTJ	*Westminster Theological Journal*

INTRODUCTION

RONALD W. PIERCE, CYNTHIA LONG WESTFALL, AND CHRISTA L. McKIRLAND

• • • • •

IF YOU HOLD TO MY TEACHING, you are really my disciples. Then you will know the truth, and the truth will set you free" (Jn 8:31-32 NIV).[1] So promised Jesus Christ, the Lord of the church and the universe. The cause of Christ is advanced only as the "true message of the gospel" is recognized, affirmed, and lived out with wisdom and integrity, and in the power of God's Spirit (Col 1:5 NIV; see Gal 2:5, 14). This gospel truth must be brought to the church and to the world. Christian teachings that fall short of truth not only impede believers from walking in the full freedom of the gospel of grace and truth (Gal 5:1), but also hinder those who are not yet believers from coming to salvation through the person and work of Jesus in the world through those who chose to follow him.

This volume is born of the conviction that both the world and the church urgently need to hear and take to heart the message of biblical equality, because it is at once gospel-grounded, true, logical, biblical, and beneficial. The essential message of biblical equality is simple and straightforward: maleness and femaleness, in and of themselves, neither privilege nor curtail one's ability to be used to advance the kingdom, or to glorify God in any

---

[1]We are all grateful to Rebecca Merrill Groothuis (1954–2018), coeditor with Ron Pierce of the previous editions of *Discovering Biblical Equality*, who drafted the first half of this introduction twenty years ago. Much of her wording has been preserved here, even though some of the content has been updated. Her brilliant mind, her prophetic voice, her editorial skills, and her deep devotion to our Lord and the Scripture will appropriately endure as cherished fingerprints across this entire volume.

dimension of ministry, mission, society, or family. The sexual differences that exist between men and women do not justify granting men unique and perpetual prerogatives of leadership and authority that are not shared by women. Biblical equality, therefore, denies that there is any created or otherwise God-ordained hierarchy *based solely on* sexual difference.[2] Egalitarianism recognizes patterns of authority in the family, church, and society—it is not anarchistic—but rejects the notion that any office, ministry, or opportunity should be denied anyone on the grounds of being male or female. This is because women and men are made equally in God's image and likeness (Gen 1:27), equally fallen (Rom 3:23), equally redeemable through Christ's life, death, and resurrection (Jn 3:16), equally participants in the new-covenant community (Gal 3:28), equally heirs of God in Christ (1 Pet 3:7), and equally able to be filled and empowered by the Holy Spirit for life and ministry (Acts 2:17). In short, this is the essence of biblical equality.

Consequently, any limits placed on the gifts and abilities of women should be challenged through a rigorous and honest investigation of the biblical texts that is rightly interpreted in the larger context of God's Word. Biblical egalitarianism (as opposed to any brand of secular feminism) is biblically based and kingdom focused. It does not rest its arguments on secular political movements or a theologically liberal denial of the Scripture's full and discernible truth and authority for all time. Moreover, biblical egalitarians apply the basic historical-grammatical method of interpretation and the best principles of theologizing to their task. They make no appeal to "women's consciousness" or "feminine traits" as normative; neither do they feel free to dispense with or underplay any aspect of any part of sacred Scripture, since it is all equally God-breathed and profitable for all of life (2 Tim 3:15-17). Biblical equality, while concerned about the false limits and stereotypes that have fettered women, is not woman-centered but God-centered and concerned with the biblical liberation of both men and women for the cause of Christ in our day and beyond. For when women are denied their gifts and callings, men suffer from this omission as well.

---

[2]While many contributors will use the language of *gender* to refer to sexual difference, sex and gender are now commonly understood to be two distinct concepts. *Sex* refers to the chromosomal, genetic, and gonadal characteristics of males and females, whereas *gender* refers to the culturally determined scripts of masculinity and femininity.

THE PURPOSE OF THE BOOK

This comprehensive collection of scholarly essays is part of an ongoing controversy among evangelical Christians over the meaning of sexual difference for ministry and marriage. Though varying expressions of a predominantly male leadership have persisted in the church and home over the last two millennia, a remnant has always been present to speak on behalf of biblical equality between men and women. This voice became stronger and clearer around the time of the Reformation in the sixteenth century, even more so at the turn of the nineteenth to twentieth century, and during recent decades has been expressed by a host of evangelicals who hold firmly to the inspiration and authority of Scripture. This volume is built on the faithful work of all those women and men who have preceded us.

A threefold goal guides the writing and editing of this collection of essays. First, we have sought to present a positive explanation and a fresh defense of biblical equality in a format that may be useful as a resource for teachers, students, and laypersons who have a serious interest in "the gender question."[3] To this end, the book is academic and persuasive in tone, and may be read alongside similar texts that defend the male-leadership position.[4]

Second, we have sought to foster a dialogue that will draw in those who share our evangelical heritage yet disagree with or have questions about the biblical equality position. In order to offer a fuller, more informative picture of gender equality, we have widened the scope of our discussion beyond the relevant biblical texts to cover a range of theological, cultural, and practical perspectives as well. Thus, we hope that there will be something in this book that will be helpful and relevant for everyone. We are convinced that an ongoing constructive dialogue among evangelicals can lead us all to a better understanding of God's Word and God's will for our shared lives together as the body of Christ.

---

[3]This has become shorthand for women's roles in the church and home, not so much questioning what gender is and how it relates and does not relate to biological sex. While the latter is a vitally important question, it is not the focus of this work and will only be directly touched on in Elizabeth Hall and Christa McKirland's chapters in this volume.

[4]Such as *RBMW*; Robert L. Saucy and Judith K. TenElshof, eds., *Women and Men in Ministry: A Complementary Perspective* (Chicago: Moody, 2001); and Wayne Grudem, *Evangelical Feminism and Biblical Truth* (Sisters, OR: Multnomah, 2004).

Third, we wish to encourage women as well as men to celebrate God's gift of maleness and femaleness in the context of mutually shared partnerships and spiritual friendship, without the trappings of male hierarchy that traditionally have accompanied such relationships, whether in marriage, in ministry, or in the context of cross-gender friendships. Further, it is our desire that women called to ministry will be better able to discover and develop their gifts and exercise them in their callings to fruitful ministry.

EVANGELICALS AND GENDER: TWO VIEWS

While there is a spectrum of views on this topic, the most fundamental divide is over one basic question: Are there any aspects of leadership denied to women and reserved for men strictly on the basis of one's sex? Many of those who answer yes prefer to be called complementarians because they believe that "complementary" differences between men and women empower men and restrict women to some extent. While egalitarians do not argue that men and women are the same, we are less likely to define what "masculine" and "feminine" qualities are, let alone to make adherence to any given list of qualities morally binding.

It is vitally important to meaningful discussion—especially between Christians—to use terms that are accurate and respectful representations of each view. Speaking of and to each other in a Christlike manner is crucial. Toward this end, we must take a moment to offer a brief explanation of how we really differ on this issue. Though there is much common ground that we share, at the end of the day two distinctive positions emerge.

Male leadership. This position sets forth a predominantly male-leadership model that restricts women from full participation in certain ministries and decision-making responsibilities. The emphasis is on *male* leadership rather than *shared* leadership in the home and/or church. For the greater part of church history this position has been expressed in such terms as *patriarchy, hierarchy, headship* (interpreted to mean "leadership"), *authority,* and *tradition.* However, such language has been shunned recently by many proponents, due to some negative connotations and misuse of early descriptives. Despite their drawbacks, however, patriarchal terminology continues to identify most accurately the essential distinction of the position. According to this view, men are seen as responsible under

God for the leadership in the home and/or church, though they should serve in these roles with an attitude of Christlike servanthood. Women may have a limited degree of input into the leadership and decision-making processes, but in the end, they must submit to the decisions of their husbands and/or male church leaders—though significant disagreement still exists within this position as to how exactly this theory is to be worked out in practice.

The long tenure of this view as the majority opinion in society and the church has led to its being called the traditional view. But since this could be perceived to have a negative implication (being *only traditional* as opposed to being *biblical*), and because the traditional view had understood women to be ontologically inferior to men in many ways, new terminology was sought. By the end of the 1980s the idea of "biblical manhood and womanhood" expressed in terms of gender complementarity became the language of preference for a number of proponents of male leadership.[5] Concurrent with this terminology is the contention that God created male and female as equal in personhood but distinct in function (i.e., to be complements of each other) *and* that female submission to male leadership is inherent in the gender distinctions. Thus, sex and gender are typically conflated on this view, since to be a male person is to be the leader and to be a female person is to be the follower. On this view, maleness and femaleness are not simply something human persons are, but something they do.

Gender equality.[6] For those holding to gender equality, the most common descriptives have been *evangelical feminism*, *egalitarianism*, and *biblical equality*. As with the terms applied to the male-leadership view, there have been negative implications and pejorative uses of these terms in the debate. For example, though *feminism* accurately describes the aspect of a position that seeks to be more supportive of a woman's freedom and opportunity to serve alongside men in ministry and marriage, the qualifier

---

[5]Piper and Grudem, "Preface," *RBMW*, 14-15; Robert L. Saucy and Judith K. TenElshof, "A Problem in the Church," in Saucy and TenElshof, *Women and Men*, 26-30.

[6]Again, *gender equality* is a shorthand in this volume for the equality of males and females in their roles in the church and home. Given current debates on gender fluidity, and the distinction between sex and gender that is often made, this can be confusing. However, the history of this debate has used this language even though egalitarians have not always agreed on the conflation of these terms.

evangelical is helpful in distinguishing evangelical feminism from the unbiblical aspects of liberal religious and secular feminism. The term *egalitarian* has been used by some opponents to suggest that evangelicals who hold this position admit to no differences between men and women—though such an extreme egalitarianism has never been held by evangelical proponents of gender equality. Finally, *biblical* is added to the concept of gender equality in order to distinguish evangelicals from those who seek gender equality primarily because of cultural pressure, personal agendas, or equal-rights politics, rather than out of obedience to Scripture.

With regard to the idea of complementarity, it should be noted that from the time of the first wave of the modern women's movement (nineteenth to twentieth centuries), many have argued that women should participate equally with men precisely *because* they bring complementary gender qualities to marriage, ministry, and society. In fact, terminology of *complementarity* was used earlier by egalitarians before it was coined by the Council on Biblical Manhood and Womanhood in 1987 to mean "male leadership." For example, one egalitarian wrote four years before this Council on Biblical Manhood and Womanhood milestone, "The relation between men and women is presented in terms of the three principles of diversity, unity, and complementarity."[7] Although contributors to this volume are varied in their opinions on the degrees of gender-related complementarity, one thing remains distinct about the egalitarian view: regardless of differing opinions on the specifics of how sex and gender are related or how males and females should act as men and women in the world, there is consensus that males do not have unilateral leadership simply because they are males. That is the main argument of this volume.

In view of all these considerations, it is probably most fitting and accurate to refer to those who believe in restricting some leadership roles to men as advocates of male leadership, or patriarchalists, because they affirm to some degree male authority over women. The term *traditionalist* has been used in reference to this view, since the patriarchal component reflects the dominant tradition of church history.[8] However, one of

---

[7]Mary J. Evans, *Woman in the Bible* (Downers Grove, IL: InterVarsity Press, 1983), 132.
[8]Ronald and Beverly Allen, *Liberated Traditionalism: Men and Women in Balance* (Eugene, OR: Wipf & Stock, 1985).

[handwritten margin notes: so "equal authority" wasn't always a part of comp. It's what the reason was grounded in]

[handwritten margin note: when]

the hallmarks of contemporary complementarianism is the denial of women's inferiority, which was assumed in the traditional patriarchy of church history.

In the end, the debate between those who promote male leadership and those who promote gender equality cannot be rightly settled by name calling, issuing propaganda, or evading this divisive issue. Rather, it can be approached with integrity only through careful, scholarly investigation of what Scripture teaches about the nature, gifts, and callings of women and men. To that end this revised and expanded edition of *Discovering Biblical Equality* continues to function as the only multiauthored volume that comprehensively, systematically, and consistently articulates an egalitarian position based on the tenets of biblical teaching.[9] While the authors are aware of and responsive to the patriarchal alternative, the overall spirit of the book is more affirming of God's gifting of women and men than it is critical of those who dispute biblical equality.

AN OVERVIEW OF *DISCOVERING BIBLICAL EQUALITY*

As an intentionally comprehensive work, *Discovering Biblical Equality* is not meant to be read through from front to back in one or two sittings—although some will do that. Rather, it is offered primarily as a reference resource that is more likely to be accessed as selected sections or chapters by those interested in specific questions or issues related to evangelical gender equality. With this in mind, all of its sections contribute in complementary ways to one another, as well as to the broader and multifaceted area of studies in evangelicals and gender. To that end, we offer this following guide for reading and referencing *Discovering Biblical Equality*.

The first chapter, by CBE International president and church historian Mimi Haddad, stands alone in providing a crucial, historical context for the ongoing debate. In it, she sets the contemporary divide against the backdrop of early egalitarians from the first centuries of the church through the Reformation (sixteenth century), where the modern

---

[9]Two important volumes of this nature—though less comprehensive—appeared at the beginning of the second wave of the modern women's movement, edited respectively by Alvera Mickelsen, *Women, Authority and the Bible* (Downers Grove, IL: InterVarsity Press, 1986), and Kathy Keay, *Men, Women and God: Evangelicals on Feminism* (London: Marshall Pickering, 1987).

gender-equality movement was born largely out of the Reformers' conviction regarding the priesthood of all believers.

Part I, "Looking to Scripture: The Biblical Texts," includes eleven essays that zero in on the crucial topic of the biblical support for gender equality, challenging patriarchal assumptions, interpretations, and applications. First, Mary Conway explains the foundational Genesis passages that narrate God's good creation of humanity in the divine image, along with humanity's tragic fall into sin, and finds no hint of created patriarchy. This is followed by three essays, respectively by Ronald Pierce and Mary Conway (women under Old Testament law), Linda Belleville (women leaders in the Bible), and Aída Besançon Spencer (Jesus' treatment of women). These help to clarify the status and function of women across Old and New Testaments, while debunking myths that have arisen during the patriarchal cultures of church history. After this, the seven most relevant New Testament passages on singleness, marriage, and ministry are carefully considered respectively by Ronald Pierce and Elizabeth Kay (1 Cor 7:1-40), Gordon Fee (1 Cor 11:2-16), Craig Keener (1 Cor 14:34-35), Cynthia Westfall (Gal 3:26-29), Lynn Cohick (Col 3:18-19; Eph 5:21-33), Linda Belleville (1 Tim 2:11-15), and Peter Davids (1 Pet 3:1-7). Leaving virtually no stone unturned in their assessment of each of these important and often-misunderstood passages, they argue that biblical equality—rather than any form or degree of patriarchy—is advocated and indeed woven into the very fabric of Paul's one-another theology, as well as in Peter's understanding of men and women as co-heirs in marriage. These essays offer better understandings of these controversial texts as these are read in the light of the Spirit's guidance and in a way that is consistent with the whole corpus of Scripture. The authors employ sound principles of interpretation that carefully consider the literary, historical, and cultural contexts of passages that have been used to restrict women unnecessarily in the home and church. Notably, this edition of *Discovering Biblical Equality* incorporates 1 Corinthians 7 into this debate, an important passage that has been wrongfully neglected by proponents on both sides in the past.[10]

Part II, "Thinking It Though: Theological and Logical Perspectives," groups eight essays that explore critical theological dimensions of the

---

[10]Regrettably, even by earlier editors of *Discovering Biblical Equality.*

gender debate. These include Spirit gifting as the criterion for ministry (Gordon Fee), the nature of authority in the New Testament (Walter Liefeld), the image of God and gender essentialism (Christa L. McKirland), the priesthood of all believers (Stanley Grenz), the analogy of Scripture's treatment of slavery (Stanley Porter), the rise and fall of the Trinity argument for the subordination of women (Kevin Giles), and biblical metaphors of God as mother and spiritual formation (Ronald Pierce and Erin Heim). Finally, former coeditor Rebecca Merrill Groothuis offers a compelling analysis of the faulty hermeneutical principle used by complementarians to justify women's subordination, namely, that women are equal to men in being, yet permanently unequal in role *because of their being.* In this philosophical essay, she finds such an approach methodologically wanting.

Part III, "Addressing the Issues: Interpretive and Cultural Perspectives," brings together five essays that relate questions of interpretive methodology to gender equality as this concerns a wide range of related contemporary issues and debates. A foundational chapter on biblical hermeneutics appears at the head of this group (Cynthia Westfall), followed by essays on the scant evidence for gender complementarity from the social sciences (Elizabeth Hall), biblical equality and contemporary English Bible translations (Jeffrey Miller), evolving questions and evangelical arguments over same-sex marriage (Ronald Pierce), and concerns regarding egalitarian theology and the sanctity of human life (Heidi Unruh and Ronald Sider).

Part IV, "Living It Out: Practical Applications," finishes this volume with six essays that offer practical information and insights on working out the principles of biblical equality in the church, in marriage, and in our larger communities. The first essay addresses questions of how to communicate biblical gender equality in our broader church gatherings—indeed, all Christian organizations, whether large or small (Mimi Haddad). This is followed by contributions on marriage as a partnership of equals (Judith and Jack Balswick), how biblical equality can address deep concerns with intimate-partner violence (Kylie Maddox Pidgeon), connections between gender and racial injustice (Juliany González Nieves), global perspectives on human flourishing (Mimi Haddad), and persistent hopes for the possibility of meaningful reconciliation between contemporary complementarians and egalitarians (Alice Mathews).

In sum, all the contributors to this edition of *Discovering Biblical Equality* have applied their expertise to the cause of helping Christians discover the gospel truth, genuine goodness, and deep joy of biblical equality without the unnecessary trappings of patriarchy regardless of its evolving and ever-softening forms. Moreover, we do so out of our love for Jesus Christ, for God's inspired and authoritative Word, as well as our desire to see God's kingdom flourish more fully in the power and blessing of God's Spirit until our Lord and Savior returns. To the end, it is our sincere hope and prayer that the readers of this volume may be like the Berean Jews of noble character in the first century who, with open minds, hopeful hearts, and great eagerness, examined the Scriptures to test the truth of Paul's message (Acts 17:11).

HISTORY MATTERS

EVANGELICALS AND WOMEN

Mimi Haddad

• • • • •

IN HIS 1949 NOVEL, George Orwell observes that those in power perpetuate their dominance by misrepresenting the facts of history. According to Orwell, "He who controls the present, controls the past. He who controls the past, controls the future."[1] The persistence of patriarchy is due, in part, to a distorted representation of history. Those committed to male authority secure their ascendency by marginalizing, omitting, and devaluing women's accomplishments throughout history. The gender bias among evangelicals not only diminishes their own history; it also furthers a trajectory of marginalization and abuse.

Paige Patterson, former president of the Southern Baptist Convention—the largest Protestant denomination in the United States—was denounced in 2018 by thousands of Southern Baptist Convention women for his comments objectifying a young girl and for counseling an abused woman to remain with her violent spouse.[2] When she returned with two black eyes, Patterson said he was happy because her faithfulness led her husband to church.[3]

---

[1]George Orwell, *1984* (London: Secker & Warburg, 1949), 309.

[2]Beth Allison Barr, "Is There Hope for Evangelical Women?," Anxious Bench (blog), May 16, 2018, www.patheos.com/blogs/anxiousbench/2018/05/is-there-hope-for-evangelical-women-beth -moore-paige-patterson/.

[3]Sarah Pulliam Bailey, "'We Are Shocked': Thousands of Southern Baptist Women Denounce Leader's 'Objectifying' Comments, Advice to Abused Women," *Washington Post*, May 7, 2018.

These events prompted scholar Beth Allison Barr to consider how patriarchal ideas might be complicit in demeaning women. Since Patterson was also the former president of Southwestern Baptist Theological Seminary, Barr analyzed the priority of history in the school's curriculum. She found that only 5 percent of the 2018 fall courses offered were specifically on history. In "the primary source reader [*Story of Christianity*], 98% of the entries were written by men . . . [who] comprised 94% of the narrative."[4] Southwestern Baptist Theological Seminary's biased curriculum not only damages the credibility of Southwestern Baptist Theological Seminary as a center of higher education, but it reinforces the Southern Baptist Convention's sexism. Given the prominence of Southern Baptist Convention faculty in the leadership of the Evangelical Theological Society, and its journal, the dearth of historical inquiry at Evangelical Theological Society is telling.

Research suggests that women's experience at Evangelical Theological Society meetings is often one of hostility, suspicion, or ambivalence, with women reporting being ignored, heckled, and presumed the spouses of male scholars.[5] As of 2018, women comprise less than 6 percent of its members, yet the society explores gender in its journal and at annual meetings. In recent years, there has been an effort to include history among the hundreds of papers presented at each conference—though these frequently concern just a few prominent (male) figures who reappear often. At the 2017 annual meeting there was a commendable session, including four lectures on Reformation women, all presented by female scholars. However, in thirty years of quarterly journals (1988–2018), only 38 percent of the issues had one church history article, and 24 percent had none. Of all the church history articles published in the *Journal of the Evangelical Theological Society* since 1988, 2 percent concern women or women's issues, a figure that shows remarkable consistency across the *Journal of the Evangelical Theological Society* book reviews concerning history (2.7 percent about women), and the Evangelical Theological Society's history-related conference

---

[4]Barr, "Is There Hope?"

[5]Emily Zimbrick Rogers, "'A Question Mark over My Head': Experiences of Women ETS Members at the 2014 ETS Annual Meeting," *Special Edition Journal of CBE International* 9 (2015), www.cbeinternational.org/sites/default/files/ETS2015-web.pdf.

workshops (2.1 percent on women) and plenaries (0 percent on women). In all formats combined, women's history accounts for 2.3 percent of the Evangelical Theological Society's output since 1988. Of these articles, book reviews, and presentations, 80 percent are from an egalitarian perspective. In thirty years of scholarship, not a single complementarian has published an article in their journal concerning women in church history.[6]

The question is whether this neglect is due to ambivalence, ignorance, or something more intentional. Women played a more significant role in Christian history and the development of theology than presentations or published content by the Evangelical Theological Society acknowledge. If women have been, as this chapter will argue, incisive theologians, courageous reformers, and prophetic leaders since Christianity began, the notion that women's shared leadership is a liberal innovation—one that dismisses the teachings of Scripture—proves untenable.

To redress the distortion of history, this chapter will explore lesser-known women leaders from the early church to the modern era and the theological ideals that not only inspired their service but also characterized evangelicals as a whole. The neglect of women leaders in history reflects the theological distance between evangelicals today and those of the past.

WHO REPRESENTS EVANGELICALS?

As the president of CBE (Christians for Biblical Equality) International, I often speak on women's history at evangelical schools. When invited, I research the institution's female founders and leaders. Through this process, I have deepened my knowledge of women who have shaped denominations and institutions around the globe. Yet, whether through bias or neglect, this history is not well-known by the very schools that prepared women as global leaders. Once, as I preached on the first class of graduates of an evangelical college known today for its complementarian posture, the chair of Bible—after introducing me—walked out of the chapel. I learned later that he did so because he does not believe Scripture permits women to preach, *even while*

---

[6]Neither the Evangelical Theological Society nor the editor of *JETS* could provide conference information for the years 1988–1997, 2001, and 2006. Journals were available from 1988–2018. Chesna Hinkley, MDiv candidate at Princeton Theological Seminary and CBE International's 2018 intern, provided the research and summary analyzing Evangelical Theological Society scholarship, history, and women.

thousands embraced the gospel through the school's female graduates. Given the neglect of history among evangelicals today, the legacy of women pioneers seems radical, or *radix* in Latin—"a return to the *root*."[7]

In recounting the history of early evangelical women, I articulate a theology of women that seems imported and offensive *because* it challenges precisely where some have become biblically and historically feeble. The radical women of the 1800s believed that Calvary makes everything new. It is not gender but new life in Christ that equips every Christian for service. To condemn as unbiblical in women what we exalt as the work of Christ in men is not only inconsistent; it is also at odds with the facts of history and the teachings of Scripture. Compelled by Christ to "Go into all the world and preach the gospel" (Mk 16:15 NIV), women have advanced Christianity and shaped a Christian or evangelical identity since Easter morning.

Historian Mark Noll notes that the term *evangelical*, when first used by the early Christians, referred to the good news of Christ's "life, death and resurrection." During the Reformation, Luther appropriated the word *evangelical* to elevate Christ's atonement above the indulgences sold by the late medieval church. Repeatedly, the term *evangelical* was associated with renewal movements because they too prioritized Christ's victory over sin and death. Philipp Spener's *Pia Desideria* called for spiritual and social renewal, as did the revivals of the eighteenth century: these events were not only "intense periods of unusual response to gospel preaching . . . but also . . . linked with unusual efforts at godly living." Embedded in the early evangelical teachings were theological convictions that, as Noll observes, guided the faith and lives of adherents.[8] To be renewed by the gospel meant that one had crossed life's sharpest line—from spiritual death to new life in Christ. As such, one was expected to become a markedly new person in service to others.[9]

The theological distinctives of the early evangelicals reflect four qualities, summarized by "Bebbington's quadrilateral":[10]

---

[7]"Radix," Dictionary.com, www.dictionary.com/browse/radix.

[8]Mark Noll, *The Rise of Evangelicalism: The Age of Edwards, Whitefield and the Wesleys* (Downers Grove, IL: InterVarsity Press, 2003), 16-19.

[9]David Bebbington, *Evangelicalism in Modern Britain: A History from the 1730s to the 1980s* (Grand Rapids, MI: Baker, 1989), 5.

[10]Bebbington, *Evangelicalism in Modern Britain*, 2-17; Noll, *Rise of Evangelicalism*, 19.

conversionism: the "belief that lives need to be changed"
biblicism: a high regard for the Bible
activism: evangelism in word *and* deed
crucicentrism: a stress on Christ's atonement

Neither Bebbington nor Noll adequately acknowledges the many women leaders who shaped both the evangelical movement and the theological priorities that have characterized Christians throughout history.

EARLY CHURCH WOMEN: MARTYRS, MONASTICS, AND MYSTICS

Women martyrs, Bible scholars, and monastic leaders deepened the gospel's impact in communities throughout the ancient world.

Martyrs. The earliest, most extensive text by a Christian woman—the Acts of Perpetua—was written by a young mother martyred in Carthage in AD 203. A noblewoman still nursing her child, Perpetua was arrested with five others including her pregnant slave, Felicitas. Like Jesus, they endured a cruel mob, abusive guards, and a despairing family, aware that their battle was against Satan alone. Despite fierce opponents, Perpetua said, "I knew that victory was to be mine." Her biographer tells how Perpetua faced death glowing as the "darling of God." When "the right hand of the novice gladiator wavered, she herself guided it to her throat."[11]

Blandina was a slave arrested with her master. Refusing to renounce Christ, she too endured brutal torture. Like Perpetua, Blandina exhausted the gladiators in 177. Whipped, burned, tossed by wild animals, Blandina was finally killed by a gladiator's dagger. The amphitheater where she died in Lyon, France, remains largely intact.

Refusing to sacrifice to the Roman gods, Crispina from North Africa said, "I shall not do so save to the one true God and to our Lord, Jesus Christ his Son, who was born and died. . . . I refuse to sacrifice to these ridiculous deaf and dumb statues."[12] Crispina's head was shaved—a humiliation to her gender. She was beheaded in 304.

---

[11]Perpetua of Carthage, "The Passion of Saints Perpetua and Felicity," in *The Passion of Perpetua and Felicity*, ed. Thomas J. Heffernan (New York: Oxford University Press, 2012), 130-35.

[12]Herbert Musurillo, *The Acts of The Christian Martyrs* (London: Oxford University Press, 1972), 303-7.

United to Christ as martyrs and heirs of God's kingdom, women ignited a faith more powerful than Rome, one that challenged cultural expectations for them.

Monastics. During the late third century, affluent Christians fled city life and its comforts to live in the deserts. Here Christians mastered their appetites and discovered a vitality that comes from feasting on God. Many joined the desert movement, led by the ammas and abbas (mothers and fathers).

Wealthy and beautiful, Syncletica moved to the desert outside Alexandria in the fourth century. Her life of simplicity and prayer attracted a community of women, whom she taught that the path to holiness is filled with "many battles and a good deal of suffering for those who are advancing towards God and afterwards, ineffable joy." If one is able, a commitment to poverty is "a perfect good. Those who can sustain it receive suffering in the body but rest in the soul."[13]

Brilliant and wealthy, Macrina the Younger (330–379) turned her home in Turkey into a Christian community where all possessions were held in common and the poor were treated like the wealthy. She was the sister of bishops Gregory and Basil, known for their defense of the Nicene Creed, and both credit her for their education. A lover of knowledge, she insisted that humility and love are the aims of philosophy. Macrina was referred to as "the teacher," even by her bishop brothers.[14]

Leaving wealth and children in Rome, Paula (347–404) moved to the deserts of Palestine. Spending her fortune building hospitals, monasteries, and churches, Paula also purchased the ancient texts for a Latin translation of Scripture that she and Jerome—a leading Bible scholar—completed together. Jerome dedicated much of his work to Paula and her daughter Eustochium.[15]

The desert movement was shaped by ammas. Detached from materialism, ambition, and bodily appetites, women's monastic communities were

---

[13]Laura Swan, *The Forgotten Desert Mothers: Sayings, Lives and Stories of Early Christian Women* (New York: Paulist, 2001), 43, 46.

[14]Gregory of Nyssa, *The Life of Saint Macrina*, trans. and ed. Kevin Corrigan (Eugene, OR: Wipf & Stock, 2005), 7.

[15]Jerome, *Commentary on Zephaniah*, trans. Mary Catherine Beller and Thomas P. Scheck, in *Commentaries on the Twelve Prophets*, ed. Thomas P. Scheck, Ancient Christian Texts (Downers Grove, IL: InterVarsity Press, 2016), 1:114-15.

centers of intellectual life, renewal, and social reform, a practice that endured throughout the Middle Ages.

Mystics. Christian mystics were committed to simplicity, prayer, and community. Their intimacy with Christ gave women authority as theological and social leaders. Though excluded from traditional centers of learning, women mystics brought needed moral reform to the medieval church.

A Benedictine abbess over monks and nuns, Hildegard of Bingen (1098–1179) was one of the most influential leaders of her time. A physician who composed music and poetry, Hildegard was also a dominant voice in the politics of her day. She castigated corrupt clergy on a preaching tour sanctioned by the pope, and one bishop called her "a flaming torch which our Lord has lighted in His church."[16]

Hildegard claimed inferiority yet challenged human authority, believing that God spoke through her, especially her visions. She documented these in her influential book, *Scivias*, Latin for "Know the Ways of the Lord." Her *Scivias* received papal endorsement even as it shifted the blame for sin from Eve to Satan, challenged the tradition of reading Genesis that demeaned women, stressed mutuality between men and women, and showed how baptism replaced circumcision to welcome women.[17] Like mystic Julian of Norwich (1342–1416), Hildegard referred to God with feminine images.[18] She was declared a doctor of the church in 2012 by Pope Benedict XVI.

Teresa of Ávila (1515–1582) is considered "the most important woman mystic of the Christian tradition."[19] Her book *The Interior Castle* is read more than any other work by a mystic. The first woman declared doctor of the church, Teresa joined the Carmelites at age twenty. She was called to a life of prayer, yet her vocation was troubled by a two-decade struggle with sensuality. All her life, Teresa experienced visions and God encounters over which she had little control. Like with Hildegard, these guided her

---

[16]Barbara Newman, introduction to *Hildegard of Bingen: Scivias* (New York: Paulist, 1990), 20; Joyce Hollyday, *Clothed with the Sun: Biblical Women, Social Justice and Us* (Louisville, KY: Westminster John Knox, 1994), 146.

[17]Hollyday, *Clothed with the Sun*, 27.

[18]See Caroline Walker Bynum, *Jesus as Mother: Studies in the Spirituality of the High Middle Ages* (Berkeley: University of California Press, 1982).

[19]Harvey D. Egan, SJ, *An Anthology of Christian Mysticism*, 2nd ed. (Collegeville, MN: Liturgical Press, 1991), 438.

just realized only female heretics were referenced in my history books

writings. Her masterpiece *The Interior Castle* illustrates how prayer and meditation lead the soul toward God. Prayer, for Teresa, is nothing more "than an intimate sharing between friends; it means taking time frequently to be alone with Him whom we know loves us."[20] Working to return her order to its commitment to simplicity and prayer, she established sixteen convents built on her reforms.

Also declared a doctor of the church, Catherine of Siena (1347–1380) challenged immorality at the highest level. Drawn to Christ as a child, Catherine nurtured her faith with prayer and fasting. At eighteen, she became a Third Order Dominican. Her devotional life was one of visions, ecstasies, and conflict with evil, but eventually it yielded a deep trust in Christ that forged her extraordinary leadership.

Catherine's counsel was in great demand. Dictating nearly four hundred letters, she met with troubled parents, betrayed spouses, and feuding families, who sobbed in her presence but left with "their lives profoundly and permanently reversed." What had she done to bring such change? It "had everything to do with the way she looked at you, with enormous interest and understanding that glowed out of her huge, dark eyes."[21]

During the plague, Catherine nurtured the sick and dying. She comforted the imprisoned with visits and prayers. When a young man was unjustly condemned, Catherine alone spoke out against the injustice and remained with him through his execution.

Denouncing the spiritual poverty of clergy, Catherine wrote to Pope Gregory X: "[God] has given you authority and you have accepted it, you ought to be using the power and strength that is yours. If you don't intend to use it, it would be better and more to God's honor and the good of your soul to resign."[22]

Revered leaders, writers, and theological activists, women mystics were at the center of moral and social reform in the medieval church.

---

[20]Egan, *Anthology of Christian Mysticism*, 438-40; Teresa of Avila, *The Book of Her Life* 8.5, in *The Collected Works of St. Teresa of Avila*, trans. Kieran Kavanaugh, OCD, and Otilio Rodriguez, OCD (Washington, DC: Institute of Carmelite Studies, 1976), 1:67.

[21]Carol L. Flinders, *Enduring Grace: Living Portraits of Seven Women Mystics* (San Francisco: HarperSanFrancisco, 1993), 116.

[22]Catherine of Siena, "To Gregory XI," in *The Letters of Catherine of Siena*, trans. Suzanne Noffke, Medieval and Renaissance Texts and Studies (Tempe, AZ: Arizona Center for Medieval and Renaissance Studies, 2001), 193.

Catherine, Hildegard, and Teresa gave birth "to a race of [people] that hate sin and love [God] with a great and burning love."[23] All three were made doctors of the church for declaring God's truth and justice across time and culture.

REFORMATION WOMEN

As Scripture became a focal point for Protestants, women's biblical writings and speeches placed them at the forefront of the Reformation and led to their martyrdom. No longer restricted by the rules of monasticism, women gained new freedom as leaders even as they were devalued by leading theologians. Yet women advanced Protestant faith even as they navigated what Calvin and Luther never did—gender discrimination, torture, and martyrdom.

A gifted Bible scholar from Bavaria, Argula von Grumbach (ca. 1492–1564) defended Protestantism for four decades. Her prominence led to financial hardships, and her husband grew resentful and abusive. She wrote, "He does much to persecute Christ in me. . . . I cannot obey him. We are bound to forsake father, mother, brother, sister, child, body and life."[24] Her writings and pamphlets were the most widely distributed of any Reformer except Luther's.

Martyred in Britain, Lady Jane Grey (1537–1554) and Anne Askew (1521–1546) remained fearless throughout their imprisonment, brilliant throughout their interrogation, and courageous through death. Askew was the only woman ever tortured in the Tower of London; her hips were disjointed on the rack, and she was carried outside and burned at the stake.[25] As for Grey, the great-niece of Henry VIII, she was fluent in six languages. Grey's father, regent to Edward VI, manipulated the dying king to make her queen over the Catholic heir apparent, Mary Tudor. Jane was quickly deposed and imprisoned in the Tower of London, where Dr. Feckenham, her interrogator, warned her that unless she recanted, they would never meet again. She replied, "True it is that we shall never meet again, except

[23]Flinders, *Enduring Grace*, 117.

[24]Derek Wilson, *Mrs. Luther and Her Sisters: Women in the Reformation* (Oxford: Lion Books, 2016), 114.

[25]Mimi Haddad, "Egalitarian Pioneers: Betty Friedan or Catherine Booth?," *PriscPap* 20, no. 4 (2006): 55, www.cbeinternational.org/resources/article/priscilla-papers/egalitarian-pioneers.

God turn your heart."[26] The responses of Jane and Anne recorded during their inquisition reveal not only the intellectual force of the English Reformation but also the influence of women's theological leadership.

Spared martyrdom, Margaret of Navarre (1492–1549) and her daughter Jeanne d'Albret (1528–1572) supported the Prostestant Reformation in France. Margaret, queen of Navarre, never made an official break with Rome. Her palace at Nérac became a center for Protestant theologians such as Jacques Lefèvre and for Huguenots.[27] As queen, Jeanne made Protestantism the official religion of Navarre, turned churches over to the Protestants, opened a school of Reformed theology, and had the New Testament translated into Basque for the first time. Jeanne's son, as king of France, ensured religious freedom to Protestants in 1598 through the Edict of Nantes—the first law protecting religious freedom in Europe.

As biblical activists and martyrs, women proved essential in establishing Protestant faith in Europe and Britain. In the centuries that followed, the gospel flourished on every continent through women preachers, missionaries, and humanitarians.

CONVERSIONISM: AWAKENINGS AND MOVEMENTS

As pioneering evangelists, women shaped emerging denominations and were at the forefront of new movements. Two examples are Susanna Wesley (1669–1742) and Margaret Fell Fox (1614–1702). Widowed with nine children, Margaret Fell married George Fox, founder of the Quakers. Once widowed, she continued to write, speak, and lead the movement. Adamant that the Quakers would support women's equality, she published *Women's Speaking Justified* in 1666.[28]

Like Fell Fox, Susanna Wesley was the spiritual leader of her family and eventually her community. Homeschooling her nineteen children, including John, the father of Methodism, and Charles, the great hymn writer, Wesley also led Sunday home meetings, first for her family but eventually for overflowing crowds in her community. Disturbed by her influence, she

---

[26]Paul F. M. Zahl, *Five Women of the English Reformation* (Grand Rapids, MI: Eerdmans, 2001), 70.

[27]Sarah Towne Martyn, *Margaret, The Pearl of Navarre* (London: Hamilton, Adams, 1867), 178.

[28]Margaret Fell Fox, *Women's Speaking Justified, Proved and Allowed by the Scriptures* (London, 1666).

responded to her husband: "Your objections against our Sunday evening meetings are, first, that it will look particular; secondly, my sex. . . . As to its looking particular, I grant it does; and so does almost everything that is serious, or that may any way advance the glory of God, or the salvation of souls."[29]

The best defense for women pastors was women, such as African American Methodist preacher Jarena Lee (ca. 1783–1850). Lee located God's approval for women preachers in the example of biblical women. Her autobiography recounts: "Did not Mary first preach the risen Savior, and is not the doctrine of the resurrection the very climax of Christianity—hangs not all our hope on this, as argued by St. Paul? Then did not Mary, a woman, preach the gospel?"[30] Lee's was the first autobiography by a woman of color, but it inspired others, such as Julia A. J. Foote (1823–1901), for whom spiritual experiences gave women of color the "very real sense of freedom from a prior 'self' and a growing awareness of unrealized, unexploited powers within."[31] African American Zilpha Elaw (1790–1846?) enjoyed spiritual experiences that resembled those of women mystics. Elaw believed God alone called her as a preacher. She "durst not confer with flesh and blood."[32]

Another prominent Methodist, Phoebe Palmer (1807–1874), not only launched the Third Great Awakening, but she also guided nineteenth-century holiness theology and modeled leadership for holiness women. Serving the infamous Tombs prisoners, Palmer also established the Five Points Mission. An international evangelist, Palmer was certain that God had called her preach. So "truly has He set His seal upon it . . . in the conversion of thousands of precious souls, and the sanctification of a multitude of believers, that even Satan does not seem to question that my call is divine." She "attributed the long-standing prohibitions against women in the church to two things in particular: a faulty interpretation of the Bible

---

[29]Charles Wallace Jr., ed., *Susanna Wesley: The Complete Writings* (Oxford: Oxford University Press, 1997), 79-81.

[30]Jarena Lee, *The Life and Religious Experience of Jarena Lee, a Coloured Lady* (self-published, 1849), 11.

[31]William Andrews, *Sisters of the Spirit: Three Black Women's Autobiographies of the Nineteenth Century* (Bloomington: Indiana University Press, 1986), 12.

[32]Paul W. Chilcote, *The Methodist Defense of Women in Ministry* (Eugene, OR: Cascade Books, 2016), 86.

and a distorted and unchristian view most men had of women." She defended women's call to preach in *Promise of the Father*.[33]

EVANGELISM: A GOLDEN ERA

Women's impact as evangelists reached its zenith in the 1800s, a golden era of missions. Outnumbering men two to one as missionaries globally, women pursued new opportunities that demonstrated their gifts and calling. Founding mission organizations, funding their work, and working at all levels, women served in regions where males seldom went.[34] The priority women placed on evangelism was embedded in the early evangelical ethos.

African American Amanda Berry Smith (1837–1915) achieved world acclaim as a missionary and leader. Smith served in England, India, Sierra Leone, and Liberia, and Methodist bishop and noted missionary William Taylor said that she "had done more for the cause of missions and temperance in Africa than the combined efforts of all missionaries before her." Preaching in White and Black communities, Smith was the first African American woman to receive invitations to preach internationally. At a Keswick convention in England, Smith said, "You may not know it, but I am a princess in disguise. I am a child of the King." Smith realized that "if she was a child, she was an heir of God!" Her confidence in Christ was indomitable.[35]

A pioneering missionary like Smith, Charlotte "Lottie" Moon (1840–1912) served the people of China for forty years. Lottie's mother not only preached to her household, since there was no Southern Baptist church in their area, but she also read to them from the writings of noted Baptist missionary Ann Hasseltine Judson (1789–1826). In 1872, Lottie Moon's

---

[33]Richard Wheatley, *The Life and Letters of Mrs. Phoebe Palmer* (New York: W. C. Palmer Jr., 1876), 83; Chilcote, *Methodist Defense*, 110; Phoebe Palmer, *Promise of the Father* (repr., Eugene, OR: Wipf & Stock, 2015).

[34]Wendy Murray Zorba, "A Woman's Place: Women Reaching Women Is Key to the Future of Missions," *CT*, August 4, 2000, www.christianitytoday.com/ct/2000/august7/1.40.html. See also Dana Robert, ed., *Gospel Bearers, Gender Barriers: Missionary Women in the Twentieth Century* (Maryknoll, NY: Orbis, 2002); Mimi Haddad, "Egalitarians: A New Path to Liberalism? Or Integral to Evangelical DNA?," *Special Edition Journal of CBE International* (2013), www.cbe international.org/blogs/egalitarian-history.

[35]William Taylor, as quoted by Hallie Quinn Brown, *Homespun Heroines and Other Women of Distinction* (New York: Oxford University Press, 1988), 131; W. B. Sloan, *These Sixty Years: The Story of the Keswick Convention* (London: Pickering & Inglis, 1935), 91; Amanda Smith, *An Autobiography*, electronic ed. (1999), https://docsouth.unc.edu/neh/smitham/smith.html.

sister sailed to China as a missionary, and Lottie joined her in 1873. Adapting rapidly to Chinese culture and language, Lottie moved north to Pingtu to plant and pastor a Baptist Church in 1889. As famines devastated China, she begged family and friends to give generously in gratitude for God's gift of Christ at Christmas. In response, she received enough money for three more women missionaries, launching the North China Woman's Missionary Union. As poverty persisted, Moon used all her money to feed her community but died of starvation herself. She said she wished she had a thousand lives to give to the people of China. The year after her death saw the first Lottie Moon Christmas offering—a tradition that continues among Southern Baptists. As of June 2016, more than $168 million has been raised in memory of Moon, a Southern Baptist missionary pastor and church planter.

The church in China exists today because of women evangelists. Dora Yu (1873–1931), a medical doctor and preacher's daughter, preached in Korea and at revival meetings in China. It was Yu who introduced China's noted church planter Watchman Nee to Christ.[36]

Serving Christ in India, Amy Carmichael (1867–1951) devoted more than fifty years to prostituted children. Born in Northern Ireland, she worked initially as an itinerant evangelist, but upon learning of children enslaved as Hindu temple prostitutes, Carmichael intercepted two thousand children and raised nine hundred at her orphanage. Carmichael, an author of more than thirty books, is one of the best-known missionaries of her era.

Single and fearless like Yu, Carmichael, and Moon, Mary Slessor (1848–1915) served over two thousand miles in Calabar (Nigeria) for thirty-eight years. Known affectionately by thousands of Africans as "White Ma," Slessor built schools, taught trade classes, opened churches, and preached. She adopted abandoned twins, who continued her work after she died. Slessor said her life was

> one long daily, hourly, record of answered prayer. For physical health, for mental overstrain, for guidance given marvelously, for errors and dangers

---

[36] Alexander Chow, "The Remarkable Story of China's 'Bible Women,'" *CT*, May 23, 2017, www .christianitytoday.com/history/2018/march/christian-china-bible-women.html.

averted, for enmity to the Gospel subdued, for food provided at the exact hour needed, for everything that goes to make up life and my poor service, I can testify with a full and often wonder-stricken awe that I believe God answers prayers.[37]

Surrounded by danger, women missionaries planted churches, schools, and orphanages. They preached, married, buried, trained their successors, and suffered beside their communities. Their character and calling were manifest on mission fields around the world, and even more as they championed the great humanitarian causes of their day.

ACTIVISM

Confronting entrenched injustices, the early evangelicals were decisive leaders in abolition, temperance, and suffrage. The vast majority, 88 percent of evangelical Christians, were abolitionists. Evangelical institutions were stations along the Underground Railroad, and evangelical women not only strategically championed abolition and suffrage, but they also exposed domestic violence, human trafficking, and the sexual abuse of girls and women—key priorities of organizations such as the Women's Christian Temperance Union and its leaders, Frances Willard and Katharine Bushnell.

Leading abolition were women such as Quaker Sarah Grimké (1792–1873), who gained a national platform for her abolitionist writings. She offered biblical support for women's equality in public preaching and speaking.[38] Quaker Elizabeth Coltman Heyrick (1789–1831) launched a successful boycott of slave-produced goods; a British runaway slave, Mary Prince (1788–1833), was the first woman to present an abolitionist petition to Parliament; and Quaker Mary Ann Shadd Cary (1823–1893) was an African American lawyer who launched *The Provincial Freemen*, a weekly newspaper devoted to abolition.[39]

An activist of the highest order, American slave, abolitionist, and suffragist Sojourner Truth (ca. 1797–1883) was one of the most gifted speakers

---

[37]W. P. Livingstone, *Mary Slessor of Calabar: A Pioneer Missionary* (London: Hodder & Stoughton, 1917), 316.

[38]Sarah Grimké, *Letters on the Equality of the Sexes* (Boston: Isaac Knapp, 1838).

[39]Mary Prince, *The History of Mary Prince, a West Indian Slave* (repr., Mineola, NY: Dover, 2004), http://docsouth.unc.edu/neh/prince/prince.html.

of her day. Revered by Frederick Douglass, William Lloyd Garrison, and Abraham Lincoln, Truth used piercing logic to challenge racial and gender prejudice. At an 1852 suffrage meeting in Ohio, Truth observed that denying women the right to vote or preach because Christ was male ignored the fact (articulated by fourth-century theologians) that <u>it was Christ's humanity, not his maleness, that made Jesus an atonement for all people</u>.[40]

Like Truth, Pandita Ramabai (1858–1922) gained international renown as an activist. Having become a Christian through a revival in Calcutta, Ramabai founded the Mukti Mission, a humanitarian compound for eight hundred abandoned women, children, and disabled persons. Pandita translated the Bible from Greek and Hebrew into Marathi—a translation solely the work of women. Her book, *The High Caste Hindu Woman*, exposed the abuses of females in India.[41]

An international leader like Ramabai, Frances Willard (1839–1898) was president of the Women's Christian Temperance Union, the largest Christian women's organization of its day. Promoting evangelism, suffrage, temperance, and abolition, the Women's Christian Temperance Union was at the forefront of dismantling the sex industry. Willard's activism mobilized global women such as Wang Liming (1896–1970), who led Women's Christian Temperance Union work in China, later dying in a labor camp for her faith.[42]

BIBLICISM

The biblicism that once opposed patriarchy, racism, and their global consequences gave way to an anti-intellectual critique of evangelical social activism and women's leadership, judging these as liberal. Addressing issues biblically, the early evangelicals published more than fifty documents defending women evangelists and preachers.[43] Distinguished pastor

---

[40]Gregory of Nazianzen, "To Cledonius the Priest Against Apollinarius," *NPNF²*, vol. 7, trans. Charles Gordon Browne and James Edward Swallow, ed. Philip Schaff and Henry Wace (Buffalo, NY: Christian Literature, 1894). He writes: "For that which He has not assumed He has not healed." For Nazianzen, healing, or redemption, requires representation. For Sojourner Truth, born of a woman, Christ represented women on Calvary.

[41]Pandita Ramabai, *The High Caste Hindu Woman* (Philadelphia: Tenth Thousand, 1888).

[42]John Barwick, "Wang Liming: Promoting a Protestant Vision of the Modern Chinese Woman," in *Salt and Light 3: More Lives of Faith that Shaped Modern China*, ed. Carol Lee Hamrin and Stacey Bieler (Eugene, OR: Pickwick, 2011), 136-57.

[43]Charles O. Knowles, *Let Her Be: Right Relationships and the Southern Baptist Conundrum over Woman's Role* (Columbia, MO: KnoWell, 2002), 85.

A. J. Gordon (1836–1895) insisted that in Christ, God's favor is no longer limited to the "favored few, but upon the many, without regard to race, or age, or sex." Gordon said that all "texts that prohibit a practice in one place, while allowing it in another, must be considered in the light of the entire New Testament teaching."[44]

Cofounder of the Salvation Army, Catherine Booth (1829–1890) also exposed inconsistencies when interpreting passages concerning women. She wrote:

> If commentators had dealt with the Bible on other subjects as they have dealt with it on this, taking isolated passages, separated from their explanatory connections, and insisting on the literal interpretation of the words of our version, what errors and contractions would have been forced upon the acceptance of the Church, and what terrible results would have accrued to the world.[45]

The most systematic egalitarian critique of Scripture and women was published by American Katharine Bushnell (1856–1946). After working briefly as a physician in China, Bushnell returned home to lead the Women's Christian Temperance Union's Social Purity Department. After decades of exposing sex slavery in the United States and abroad, Bushnell argued that a misreading of Scripture fueled the abuse of girls and women. She wrote:

> So long as [Christians] imagine that a system of caste is taught in the Word of God, and that [men] belong to the upper caste while women are of the lower caste; and just so long as [we] believe that mere FLESH—fate— determines the caste to which one belongs; and just so long as [we] believe that . . . the "he will rule over you" [Genesis 3:16 is prescriptive] . . . the destruction of young women into a prostitute class will continue.[46]

For Bushnell, Paul supported women's public teaching provided they were not domineering, distracting, or teaching error. "[We] cannot, for women, put the 'new wine' of the Gospel into the old wine-skins of 'condemnation.'"[47]

---

[44]A. J. Gordon, "The Ministry of Women," *Missionary Review of the World* 17, no. 4 (1894): 911, 913.

[45]Catherine Booth, "Female Ministry; or, Women's Right to Preach the Gospel," in *Terms of Empowerment: Salvation Army Women in Ministry* (West Nyack, NY: Salvation Army, USA Eastern Territory, 2001), 19-20.

[46]Katharine Bushnell, *Dr. Katharine C. Bushnell: A Brief Sketch of Her Life and Work* (Hertford, UK: Rose and Sons, 1930), 14. See also Katharine Bushnell, *God's Word to Women: One Hundred Bible Studies on Women's Place in the Divine Economy* (Mossville, IL: God's Word to Women, 1999), 10-64.

[47]Bushnell, *God's Word to Women*, 169.

Turning to Scripture as their highest authority, the early evangelicals exposed interpretative errors that [devalued] females and [justified] their [marginalization] and [abuse.]

CRUCICENTRISM

Passionate about Calvary, the early evangelicals published extensively on the cross and preached on Galatians 2:20 more than any other Christian movement.[48] Their high Christology forged an egalitarian worldview, insisting that Calvary created a new humanity in which Jew and Greek, slave and free, male and female are grafted into God's family, made one in Christ, and called to equal service in the church. Their crucicentrism gave theological teeth to their egalitarian worldview, which challenged spiritual and social barriers for slaves and women.

Jessie Penn-Lewis (1861–1927), a prominent Welsh revivalist, writer, and international speaker, popularized early evangelical crucicentrism. For Penn-Lewis, Christians were united to Christ on Calvary and joined as equal members of Christ's body, where hostilities that had formerly separated and marginalized believers were overcome by the sanctifying power of the cross. Penn-Lewis wrote: "Christ upon the Cross of Calvary broke down the middle wall of partition between man and man, as well as between man and God. He died that in Him there might be a new creation, one new man, [in which] all divisions caused by sin cease in Him."[49] Penn-Lewis's cross theology cast vision for personal and corporate holiness that challenged racial and gender bias in the church and beyond.

EVANGELICALS TODAY

Women opened new global centers of Christian faith in the nineteenth and early twentieth centuries, but as their churches and organizations became institutionalized, women were pressed out of leadership.[50]

---

[48]Bebbington, *Evangelicalism in Modern Britain*, 13. Galatians 2:20 reads, "I have been crucified with Christ and I no longer live, but Christ lives in me. The life I live in the body, I live by faith in the Son of God, who loved me and gave himself for me" (NIV).

[49]Jessie Penn-Lewis, *Thy Hidden Ones: Union with Christ, Traced in the Song of Songs* (London: Marshall Brothers, 1899), 30.

[50]Stanley J. Grenz and Denise Muir Kjesbo, *Women in the Church: A Biblical Theology of Women in Ministry* (Downers Grove, IL: InterVarsity Press, 1995), 37-62.

Further, following the fundamentalist-modernist controversy in the mid-twentieth century, mission organizations, Bible institutes, and denominations moved women into support roles to distinguish them-selves from a growing secularization of feminism.[51] Early evangelical biblicism, which supported abolition, suffrage, and pressing humanitarian work worldwide, gave way to an anti-intellectualism that judged social activism and women's leadership as liberal. Responding to the threat of liberalism, Bible institutes such as Northwestern Bible Training School terminated courses on "archaeology, history, and the ancient languages." Willam Bell Riley, founder of the World Christian Fundamentals Association, helped lead fundamentalists toward the "plain reading of the Scriptures."[52] *can they really be called fundamental?*

As a result, fundamentalists abandoned their leadership in these and other fields. They also lost respected positions in the academy and culture, as noted in Charles Malik's inaugural address at Wheaton's Billy Graham Center in 1980.[53] According to Malik, it would take many decades to recover the intellectual and cultural leadership surrendered by fundamentalists and evangelicals after 1950. Since then, evangelicals have not only become estranged from the theological priorities that drove social activism and women's leadership in an earlier generation, but also alienated from their own history and theology.[54] Because of this, after 1950, evangelical women could preach, teach, plant churches, and train men on mission fields, but never in their sending churches in the West.[55]

---

[51]The fundamentalist-modernist controversy began in the United States as modernists accommodated to scientific inquiry by challenging the "fundamentals of Christianity," such as the inspiration of Scripture, the miracles cited in Scripture, the virgin birth, the resurrection, and the atonement of Christ. See Ernest R. Sandeen, "Christian Fundamentalism," Britannica, 2000, www.britannica.com/topic/Christian-fundamentalism.

[52]William Vance Trollinger Jr., *God's Empire: William Bell Riley and Midwestern Fundamentalism* (Madison: University of Wisconsin Press, 1990), 94.

[53]Charles Malik, "Graham Center Dedication" (presentation, Wheaton, IL, September 13, 1980), https://media.wheaton.edu/hapi/v1/contents/permalinks/a9W3NoSf/view.

[54]As noted, the Southwestern Baptist Theological Seminary's curriculum minimizes the history of women's leadership while also failing to adequately expose its support of slavery at its formation in 1845. See Allan Cross, "Southern Baptists Have a History Problem: Let's Stop Saying We Started over Missions," SBC Voices, February 12, 2015, https://sbcvoices.com/southern -baptists-have-a-history-problem-lets-stop-saying-we-started-over-missions.

[55]My in-laws were career missionaries in Brazil, where my mother-in-law and her female colleagues enjoyed using their teaching, preaching, and administrating gifts, which they quietly hid from view when visiting their sending churches on furlough in the United States.

After World War II, evangelicals celebrated women's work in domestic spheres, a stereotype explored in Betty Friedan's *The Feminine Mystique* (1963) and declared biblical by Charles Ryrie's *The Place of Woman*.[56] In response, writers affiliated with the Evangelical Women's Caucus (incorporated in 1975) supported the biblical foundations for women's leadership in harmony with earlier evangelical traditions, such as those evident in the writings of pastor Lee Anna Starr (1853–1937). Patricia Gundry challenged the misrepresentation of post-1970s egalitarians as theologically and socially liberal. Her 1977 book, *Woman Be Free!: The Clear Message of Scripture*, resulted in her husband's dismissal from Moody Bible Institute, representing the divide among evangelicals concerning the biblical basis for women's leadership.[57]

By 1984, two volumes were pivotal in demonstrating how egalitarians honor the authority of Scripture but arrive at different conclusions from complementarians—*Women, Authority and the Bible* and *No Time for Silence*.[58] In 1986, the Evangelical Theological Society convention considered the theme "Men and Women in Biblical and Theological Perspective," sponsoring the largest conversation on gender among evangelicals in history.[59] Each camp formed an organization in 1987 to host events, publish resources, and advocate in churches, denominations, and educational institutions, and at events such as Evangelical Theological Society meetings. The Council on Biblical Manhood and Womanhood defended male authority in the church and home in John Piper and Wayne Grudem's *Recovering Biblical Manhood: A Response to Evangelical Feminism*. CBE International promoted the shared authority of men and women in books such as *I Suffer Not a Woman: Rethinking 1 Timothy 2:11-15 in Light of Ancient Evidence*, by Richard and Catherine Kroeger.[60]

---

[56]Betty Friedan, *The Feminine Mystique* (New York: W. W. Norton, 1963); Charles Ryrie, *The Place of Woman* (London: Macmillan: 1958); Ron Pierce, "Contemporary Evangelicals for Gender Equality," in *Discovering Biblical Equality: Complementarity Without Hierarchy*, ed. Ronald W. Pierce, Rebecca Merrill Groothuis, and Gordon Fee (Downers Grove, IL: InterVarsity Press, 2004), 59. What follows is a summary of Pierce's excellent chapter.

[57]Lee Anna Starr, *The Bible Status of Women* (New York: Fleming H. Revell, 1926); Patricia Gundry, *Woman Be Free!: The Clear Message of Scripture* (Grand Rapids, MI: Zondervan, 1977).

[58]Alvera Mickelsen, ed., *Women, Authority and the Bible* (Downers Grove, IL: InterVarsity Press, 1986); Janette Hassey, *No Time for Silence: Evangelical Women in Public Ministry Around the Turn of the Century* (repr., Grand Rapids, MI: Zondervan, 1986).

[59]Pierce, "Contemporary Evangelicals for Gender Equality," 63-64.

[60]Richard Kroeger and Catherine Kroeger, *I Suffer Not a Woman: Rethinking 1 Timothy 2:11-15 in Light of Ancient Evidence* (Grand Rapids, MI: Baker, 1992).

In the publications that followed, the meaning of words such as *head* (Greek *kephalē*) and *authority* (Greek *authentein)* were debated, as were themes in systematic theology such as whether the Trinity supports male headship.[61] Sociologists explored the impact of nature and culture on gender.[62] The topic of abuse gained attention as evangelicals considered the consequences of male authority in *Women, Abuse and the Bible* by Catherine Kroeger and James Beck.[63] The topic of homosexuality surfaced in 1998.[64] Accused of slippery-slope hermeneutics, egalitarians responded with theologically provocative works, while ontological gender essentialism deepened among complementarians with Bruce Ware's advocacy for hierarchy in the Trinity as the basis for male authority and Piper's "masculine feel" Christianity.[65]

In 2003, a third way was published by Steven Tracy, for whom male headship should reflect Christ's sacrifice and service.[66] Michelle Lee-Barnewall also proposed an alternative position in 2016. While Tracy is concerned for abused women, Lee-Barnewall never mentions the topic. She too understands headship as self-sacrifice, which, in her view, initiates unity, love, and oneness not only between husband and wife but also in Christ's body, the church. Further, Lee-Barnewall critiques post-1970s egalitarianism's focus on rights and equality as out of step with first-wave

---

[61]See Richard S. Cervin, "Does Kephale Mean 'Source' or 'Authority Over' in Greek Literature? A Rebuttal," *Trinity Journal* 10 (1989): 85-112; Kevin Giles, *The Trinity and Subordinationism: The Doctrine of God and the Contemporary Gender Debate* (Downers Grove, IL: InterVarsity Press, 2002).

[62]Mary Stewart Van Leeuwen, *Gender and Grace: Love, Work and Parenting in a Changing World* (Downers Grove, IL: InterVarsity Press, 1990); Elaine Storkey, *Origins of Difference: The Gender Debate Revisited* (Grand Rapids, MI: Baker, 2001).

[63]Catherine Kroeger and James Beck, *Women, Abuse and the Bible* (Grand Rapids: Baker, 1996).

[64]Stanley J. Grenz, *Welcoming but Not Affirming: An Evangelical Response to Homosexuality* (Louisville, KY: Westminster John Knox, 1998).

[65]Such egalitarian works include William J. Webb, *Slaves, Women and Homosexuals: Exploring the Hermeneutics of Cultural Analysis* (Downers Grove, IL: InterVarsity Press, 2001). See also Megan DeFranza, *Sex Difference in Christian Theology: Male, Female, and Intersex in the Image of God* (Grand Rapids, MI: Eerdmans, 2015); Wesley Hill, *Washed and Waiting: Reflections on Christian Faithfulness and Homosexuality* (Grand Rapids, MI: Zondervan, 2016). Complementarian works include Bruce Ware, *Father, Son and Holy Spirit: Relationships, Roles and, Relevance* (Wheaton, IL: Crossway, 2005); John Piper, "'The Frank and Manly Mr. Ryle'—the Value of a Masculine Ministry," Desiring God Conference for Pastors, Minneapolis, September 28-30, 2012, www .desiringgod.org/messages/the-frank-and-manly-mr-ryle-the-value-of-a-masculine-ministry.

[66]Steven Tracy, "Headship with a Heart: How Biblical Patriarchy Actually Prevents Abuse," *CT*, February 1, 2003, www.christianitytoday.com/ct/2003/february/5.50.html.

feminists whose aim was serving others.[67] But is this the case? Consider that in 1970, women's full-time annual income was 59 percent of men's.[68] The median income for women (including part-time workers and stay-at-home women) was only 33 percent of the median income for men, and women of color were paid even less.[69] Most women also shouldered a second shift at home. Prior to the 1994 Violence Against Women Act, domestic-violence data was almost nonexistent. Thanks to the activism of second-wave feminists and post-1970s egalitarians, violence against women declined 48.2 percent between 1994 and 2000.[70] To address these and other injustices, post-1970s egalitarians published the Chicago Declaration of Evangelical Social Concern of 1975 and inaugurated an advocacy organization, Evangelicals for Social Action, in 1978, led by Ron Sider. Gretchen Gaebelein Hull served on Evangelicals for Social Action's board and was also a founding board member of CBE International.

While complementarians rarely address abuse biblically or socially, it remains paramount for egalitarians. Since 1994, CBE International has addressed abuse at events, in research and publications beside its partners, and through nongovernmental-organization projects. Male headship construed as control and dominance leads not only to marital dissatisfaction but also to violence; hence egalitarians (first-wave and post-70s) interpret *headship* as mutual submission (Eph 5:21) and Christian service as shared authority (Gen 1:26-29).[71]

The tension between third-way proponents and post-'70s egalitarians persists. Just as third-way proslavery Christians attempted to address the abuses of slavery, insisting the system was God-approved, third-wave

---

[67]Michelle Lee-Barnewall, *Neither Complementarian nor Egalitarian: A Kingdom Corrective to the Evangelical Gender Debate* (Grand Rapids, MI: Baker Academic, 2016), 63, 84-145.

[68]"Table P-40: Women's Earnings as a Percentage of Men's Earnings by Race and Hispanic Origin," United States Census Bureau, September 15, 2020, www.census.gov/data/tables/time-series /demo/income-poverty/historical-income-people.html.

[69]"Median Annual Earnings," Institute for Women's Policy Research, https://iwpr.org/wp-content /uploads/2020/08/C478_Gender-Wage-Gap-in-2018.pdf.

[70]Shannan Catalano, "Special Report: Intimate Partner Violence, 1993–2010," US Department of Justice Office of Justice Programs, Bureau of Justice Statistics, September 29, 2015, www.bjs.gov /content/pub/pdf/ipv9310.pdf.

[71]Shuji G. Asai and David H. Olson, "Spouse Abuse & Marital System Based on ENRICH," www .prepare-enrich.com/pe/pdf/research/abuse.pdf, accessed June 11, 2018. See also Mimi Haddad, "Human Flourishing: Global Perspectives" in this volume.

complementarians oppose the abuses of patriarchy but wish to retain forms of male headship. In contrast, egalitarians (first-wave and post-'70s) oppose slavery and Christian patriarchy as biblically and socially flawed. As Richard Hays observes, the New Testament calls those with

> power and privilege to [*surrender it*] for the sake of the weak. . . . It is *husbands* (not wives) who are called to emulate Christ's example of giving themselves up in obedience for the sake of the other (Eph. 5:25). . . . [Interpreting this] as though it somehow warranted a husband's domination or physical abuse of his wife can only be regarded as a bizarre—indeed, blasphemous—misreading. . . . The followers of Jesus—men and women alike—must read the New Testament as a call to renounce violence and coercion.[72]

Post-1970s egalitarians focused on political and legal rights [*as a means of*] serving women who were abused physically and also economically. In this way, post-1970s egalitarians today are perfectly in step with the first wave, who also advanced suffrage and laws against rape and trafficking in order to protect the vulnerable of their day.

CONCLUSION

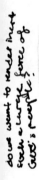

Throughout history, women were the hands and feet of Jesus in the desert, amphitheaters, abbeys, brothels, prisons, and hospitals. Planting churches, launching movements, denominations, mission, and humanitarian organizations, women mastered biblical languages and produced more accurate Bible translations. As gospel activists on every continent, they led spiritual and social reform in the church and beyond. Their life and work constituted an egalitarian worldview to challenge theology and practices that devalued and marginalized the dignity and gifts of humankind created in God's image. Scripture calls us to remember our leaders and those who have spoken God's word to us. In honoring their legacy, we strengthen our own faith and work as well. May we always remember women leaders and celebrate "the outcome of their way of life and imitate their faith" (Heb 13:7 NIV).

---

[72]Richard Hays, *The Moral Vision of the New Testament* (San Francisco: HarperSanFrancisco, 1996), 197. It is confusing that Lee-Barnewall's citation of Hays omits his clear affirmation of women's equality as biblical. See Lee-Barnewall, *Neither Complementarian nor Egalitarian*, 176.

PART I

LOOKING TO SCRIPTURE

The Biblical Texts

2

GENDER IN CREATION AND FALL

GENESIS 1–3

Mary L. Conway

• • • • •

THE CREATION ACCOUNTS IN GENESIS 1–3 constitute the theological foundation for the relationship between men and women.[1] These chapters are significant in their own right but are also an essential basis for the interpretation of later passages, especially a number of passages in the New Testament. There seem to be two narratives, and indeed Genesis 1:1–2:3 and Genesis 2:4-25 have differing focuses, genres, and functions; however, they are closely related to each other and together form a complete account.[2] Unlike the expositional letters of Paul, Genesis conveys theology through story. Narrative does not rely exclusively on "propositional statements of truth" in the modern sense; however, the stories convey many significant principles that arise from the events, plot, characterization, and dialogue.[3]

---

[1] It is impossible in the space of this chapter to deal with the many interpretive issues related to Gen 1–3; the focus here will be exclusively on issues with specific relevance to the role of men and women.

[2] See, for example, Iain W. Provan, *Discovering Genesis: Content, Interpretation, Reception* (Grand Rapids, MI: Eerdmans, 2015), 69-71.

[3] For a discussion of narrative and its interpretation, see Shimeon Bar-Efrat, *Narrative Art in the Bible* (New York: T&T Clark, 2004); Yairah Amit, *Reading Biblical Narratives: Literary Criticism and the Hebrew Bible* (Minneapolis: Fortress, 2001); Adele Berlin, *Poetics and Interpretation of Biblical Narrative*, Bible and Literature (Sheffield: Almond, 1983); Meir Sternberg, *The Poetics of*

GENESIS 1:1–2:3: AN OVERVIEW OF
THE CREATION OF HUMANITY

The nature of humanity. The first narrative, Genesis 1:1–2:3, gives a broad overview of the creation of the physical world and its biological life. The creative activity of Yahweh is celebrated as he forms and fills the earth, bringing order from disorder (e.g., bringing light to darkness, gathering dry land together), setting boundaries (e.g., separating the waters from the waters, day from night), naming (e.g., calling the dry land earth, and the gathered waters seas), and establishing functions (e.g., the two great lights to govern the day and the night, humanity to have dominion over the animals).[4]

Human beings are created in Genesis 1:26-27: "Let us make humanity in our image."[5] This passage clearly shows that when 'adam, "humanity," is created, *both* men and women are equally created in the image and likeness of God. It is important to note that the Hebrew lexis 'adam is most often a nongendered/collective term for a specific human or humanity in general, male and/or female, unless its meaning is restricted by context.[6] In older books and translations, the gendered term *man* was used to indicate humanity in general, but this term obscures the Hebrew meaning and is no longer accepted in most contemporary contexts.[7] I prefer to use the transliterated term 'adam (humanity, a gender-inclusive term) instead of *man* in this section. This avoids confusion with both the later term '*ish*, which means "man" in contrast to woman ('*ishah*) and which emphasizes sexual distinctions, and the specific individual *ha'adam* ("the man" or "Adam") described in Genesis 2.[8] Here, in Genesis 1:26, God creates 'adam and then

---

Biblical Narrative: Ideological Literature and the Drama of Reading, Indiana Literary Biblical Series (Bloomington: Indiana University Press, 1985).

[4]The focus is not so much on order in terms of sequence as it is on order as the opposite of chaos. See Gordon J. Wenham, *Genesis*, WBC (Waco, TX: Word, 1987), 1:39-40; John H. Walton, *The Lost World of Adam and Eve: Genesis 2–3 and the Human Origins Debate* (Downers Grove, IL: IVP Academic, 2015), 35-45; J. Richard Middleton, *The Liberating Image: The Imago Dei in Genesis 1* (Grand Rapids, MI: Brazos, 2005), 74-75.

[5]Translations are my own unless otherwise specified.

[6]David J. A. Clines, David M. Stec, and Jacqueline C. R. De Roo, eds., *The Dictionary of Classical Hebrew* (Sheffield: Sheffield Academic, 1993–2011), 1:123.

[7]Even the term *mankind* is misleading.

[8]Note that the use of the article *the* with 'adam tends to refer to Adam, but the use of the definite article is not totally consistent in Hebrew. See James Barr, "'Determination' and the Definite

says, "And let *them* have dominion" using a plural verb; thus, 'adam does not refer here to a specific single male but to humanity, both male and female, collectively.[9] However, in passages such as Genesis 2:25, where "*The man* and his wife were both naked," *ha'adam* is used in a context that indicates a reference to a specifically male person, in that case, "the man/Adam" and his wife.

According to Genesis 1:27: "So God created humanity in his image, in the image of God he created him [third-person masculine singular suffix], male [*zakar*] and female [*neqebah*] he created them [third-person masculine plural suffix]." Some translate: "in the image of God he created *them*, male and female he created them," referring to humanity in general rather than specific individual humans.[10] Since the third-person masculine plural suffix "him" can be a collective singular and may include both men and women (i.e., "in the image of God he created humanity"), this translation is appropriate. The change in the number of the suffix may be suggestive, however, of a two-stage process where the female was created second, as detailed in Genesis 2. In any case, the parallelism here makes it clear once again that both male and female are created equally in the image of Yahweh. It is significant that this information is reiterated in Genesis 5:1-2, *after* the fall of humanity: "In the day God created humanity, he made them in the likeness of God. Male and female he created them, and he blessed them and named them 'humanity' in the day they were created." This repetition seems to imply that not even judgment has altered the significance of the status of both men and women in the eyes of God.

The function of humanity. Humanity's creation in the *imago Dei* makes a powerful statement about the nature and worth of both men and women; however, this truth has functional implications.[11] The

---

Article in Biblical Hebrew," *Journal of Semitic Studies* 34, no. 2 (1989): 307-35; Peter Bekins, "Non-prototypical Uses of the Definite Article in Biblical Hebrew," *Journal of Semitic Studies* 58, no. 2 (2013): 225-40.

[9]It should be noted that in Hebrew there is usually no neutral verb form even in the plural, as in English. Most verbs are either masculine or feminine, with only a few common (i.e., can refer to either) forms. Gender in verbs is grammatical, not biological, and the masculine plural form may refer to both men and women as a group. Note also that I will use the term 'adam when referring to humanity and Adam/"the man" when referring to the specific male human in the narrative.

[10]E.g., NRSV, NASB, NIV.

[11]For an excellent extended discussion of what it means to be made in the image and likeness of God, see Middleton, *Liberating Image*.

significance of being created in God's image has been taken by interpreters variously throughout history to imply humanity's physical appearance, will, intellect, or relationality, among other traits.[12] Some claim that being "male and female" constitutes being in the image of God, but this is not a valid reading. Phyllis Bird effectively argues that the sexuate nature of humanity is not part of the *divine* image but relates to the blessing and instruction to multiply and fill the earth in Genesis 1:28.[13] Sexual distinction thus constitutes part of humanity's *creatureliness* in distinction to God.[14] Middleton has shown definitively that the implications of being created in Yahweh's image are functional: "the *imago dei* refers to human rule, that is, the exercise of power on God's behalf in creation."[15] Humans—both male and female, since both are created in his image—are to act as regents of Yahweh, carrying out his purposes for creation as his representatives.[16]

The specification of *ha'adam* as *zakar uneqebah*, "male and female," in Genesis 1:27 explicitly defines the division of humanity into two biological

---

[12]See, for an overview, Wenham, *Genesis*, 1:29-31; Claus Westermann, *Genesis 1–11: A Commentary*, trans. John J. Scullion (Minneapolis: Augsburg, 1984), 148-55.

[13]See Phyllis A. Bird, "Sexual Differentiation and Divine Image in the Genesis Creation Texts," in *Image of God and Gender Models in Judaeo-Christian Tradition* (Oslo: Solum Forlag, 1991), 11-34. See also Middleton, *Liberating Image*, 49-50.

[14]This is not to deny that feminine as well as masculine imagery is used meaningfully of God. See, e.g., Job 38:8-9; Is 49:15; 66:13; Hos 13:8. See also Jesus' lament in Mt 23:37-38; Lk 13:34-35.

[15]Middleton, *Liberating Image*, 88.

[16]Scholars have argued that the Garden of Eden was a sanctuary, with Adam/humanity as priest, that replicated the heavenly sanctuary and foreshadowed the temple. See, e.g., Richard M. Davidson, "Earth's First Sanctuary: Genesis 1–3 and Parallel Creation Accounts," *Andrews University Seminary Studies* 53, no. 1 (2015): 65-89; Gordon J. Wenham, "Sanctuary Symbolism in the Garden of Eden Story," in *"I Studied Inscriptions Before the Flood": Ancient Near Eastern, Literary, and Linguistic Approaches to Genesis 1–11*, ed. Richard S. Hess and David Toshio Tsumura (Winona Lake, IN: Eisenbrauns, 1994), 399-404; Wenham, *Genesis*, 61, 74; John H. Walton, *Ancient Near Eastern Thought and the Old Testament: Introducing the Conceptual World of the Hebrew Bible* (Grand Rapids, MI: Baker Academic, 2006), 197-99. Note that the terms *'bd* (work/serve) and *shmr* (guard/keep) are also used for priestly service, and there are many other parallels. However, this idea is sometimes extrapolated to justify the submission of women by claiming that since Levitical priests (and even Christ's apostles) were men, only men can serve as leaders in the church. See, e.g., Adam Hensley, "Redressing the Serpent's Cunning: A Closer Look at Genesis 3:1," *Logia* 27, no. 3 (2018): 42-43. This, however, is to illegitimately read the consequences of the fall back into creation. As Davidson remarks, "From the very beginning, woman, as well as man, is welcomed into the priestly function in the Eden sanctuary, to be a leader in worship and to serve in other priestly functions alongside her male counterpart" ("Earth's First Sanctuary," 73).

sexes.[17] It is important to note, however, that the terms *zakar* and *neqebah* are biological descriptions, not social/cultural categories.[18] Therefore, the specification does not indicate any social or functional superiority or inferiority of either male or female, since both have dominion over creation before the fall. This is detailed in Genesis 1:28 immediately after the identification of "them" as male (*zakar*) and female (*neqebah*): "God blessed them [plural], and God said to them [plural], 'Be fruitful [plural] and multiply [plural], and fill [plural] the earth and subdue [plural] it; and have dominion [plural] over . . . every living thing.'" The pronouns and imperative verbs are all plural, and therefore include both the man and the woman, who are given the same functions.[19] There is no indication that any of these activities is restricted to either the man or the woman, including "to have dominion," which derives from the Hebrew root *rdh*: "have dominion (over), rule (over), be in charge of."[20]

It is clear that there is nothing in the first creation narrative to indicate that the subordination of women, whether in regard to their nature or function, was part of Yahweh's original intention for humanity.

GENESIS 2:4-25: A DETAILED VIEW OF THE CREATION OF HUMANITY

The meaning of ha'adam *in Genesis 2:4-25.* The second creation account is not necessarily in strict temporal sequence with the first; it overlaps the first, extends it, and unpacks events in more detail, especially in regard to the creation of humanity. The Hebrew term *ha'adam* is identical to that used in Genesis 1:1–2:4. Since its definition is determined by context, it is not meaningful to understand *ha'adam* as "male/man" in terms of male/female opposition before the creation of the woman, when there is no female to whom the male/man is in juxtaposition. However, since in the current narrative there is a close-up focus on a specific *ha'adam* leading up

---

[17]This is not to deny the existence of intersex individuals, who have the physical characteristics of both males and females. However, a meaningful discussion of this issue is beyond the mandate of this chapter.

[18]Middleton, *Liberating Image*, 50. Compare Gen 6:19; 7:2-3, 9, 16; Lev 12:7; Deut 4:16; etc.

[19]Note again that there is usually no neuter form of verbs or pronouns in Hebrew. The masculine plural is used when it is necessary to refer to both males and females.

[20]Clines, Stec, and De Roo, *Dictionary of Classical Hebrew* 7:419.

to the creation of a specific woman, and the deliberate placing of male and female in juxtaposition to each other, the use of the translation of *ha'adam* as "man" or "the man" in this section is justified.[21]

This *ha'adam* is treated *literarily* in Genesis 2 as an individual—whether as a literal individual human or as a representative or archetypical human—not as general/collective humanity.[22] Unfortunately, in the English language "man" also translates the specifically male Hebrew term *'ish*, which is used of humans. To avoid confusion with *'ish*, the Hebrew will be included in brackets after the English word *man* where necessary to distinguish the terms.

Ha'adam *in the Garden.* In this section the narrative alludes back to the creation of the physical earth, and Yahweh plants a garden in Eden, to the east (Gen 2:8).[23] The reader is told that originally there was no human (*'adam)* to till the ground (Gen 2:5). Therefore Yahweh forms a *specific* human, a man (*ha'adam)*, and places him in the garden "to till it and to watch over it" (Gen 2:15).[24] On placing him there, God gives a command to this man (*ha'adam)*, forbidding the consumption of fruit from the tree in the middle of the garden, the tree of the knowledge of good and evil: "And the Lord God commanded the man [*ha'adam*], 'You may freely eat [second-person masculine singular] of every tree of the garden; but of the tree of the knowledge of good and evil you shall not eat [second-person masculine singular], for in the day that you [second-person masculine singular suffix] eat of it you shall die [second-person masculine singular].'" Note that the forms here are second-person

---

[21]For more on the translation of *'adam*, see Walton, *Lost World*, 58-62; John Ellington, "Man and Adam in Genesis 1–5," *Bible Translator* 30, no. 2 (1979): 201-5.

[22]See, e.g., Walton, *Lost World*, 70-103.

[23]It is beyond the scope of this paper to describe the significance of the garden in detail. For a brief introduction, see Walton, *Ancient Near Eastern Thought*, 123-24.

[24]Although guarding/keeping/watching over and tilling/working may seem like stereotypically male activities, they would most likely have been carried out by both husband and wife after the creation of the woman. In early societies based on subsistence agriculture, men carried out most of the agricultural work, while women focused on equally valuable economic tasks, including childbearing and rearing, health care, food processing, and textile production. See Carol L. Meyers, *Rediscovering Eve: Ancient Israelite Women in Context* (New York: Oxford University Press, 2013), 125-70. However, women were also "a vital part of the labor force of Israelite households, especially at harvest time. . . . Women's harvesting tasks were in addition to their arduous regular work load" (Meyers, *Rediscovering Eve*, 51). Note that these terms may also refer to activities of the priesthood (see note 17).

woman's partnership with them in the garden as specific tasks

masculine singular; this is significant since the *specific* woman, Eve, has not yet been formed.[25]

A "helper corresponding to him": The beginning of biological sex. In Genesis 2:18 Yahweh points out that it is "not good" for the man (*ha'adam*) to be alone (Gen 2:18). This does not imply that this individual human was "not good" or did not bear God's image, but that *being alone* was not good. There is a need for a partner—the man (*ha'adam*) is incomplete—although the actual reason for the need is not specified here. It may be for companionship or shared responsibility, or it may be because the man (*ha'adam*) is unable to reproduce alone; this is suggested by the call to "be fruitful and multiply" in Genesis 1:28 immediately after the first mention of male (*zakar*) and female (*neqebah*).[26] Therefore, Yahweh makes him an *'ezer kenegdo*, a "help(er) corresponding to him" (Gen 2:18, 20). The use of the term *helper* does not imply subordination or inferiority, since Yahweh himself often "helps" or provides "help" (e.g., Gen 49:25; Ex 18:4; Deut 33:7; Ps 20:3; 21:1-2; 115:9-11; 146:5). In fact, in life it is often the older, more skilled, or wiser person who helps the younger, less skilled, or more naive. The phrase *kenegdo* is best translated as "corresponding to him," a term that implies competence and equality, rather than subordination or inferiority.[27] In his article "Woman, a Power Equal to Man," R. David Freedman notes that the term *'ezer* may well derive from a related root, originally spelled with a *ghayyin*, whose spelling became conflated with a similar Semitic root spelled with an *ayin*.[28] Although the meanings remained separate, the roots became homonyms or "homomorphs."[29] *The Hebrew and Aramaic Lexicon of the Old Testament* and *The Dictionary of Classical Hebrew* recognize this possibility in their inclusion of a third root, *'ezer* III,

---

[25]Or "built" (*bnh*). Recall that even Gen 1:27 may hint at a two-stage process.

[26]On companionship, see Wenham, *Genesis*, 68; John Chrysostom: "For it was for the consolation of this man that this woman was created." See John Chrysostom, *Homilies on Genesis 1–17*, trans. Robert C. Hill, Fathers of the Church (Washington, DC: Catholic University of America Press, 1986), 200.

[27]See John H. Walton, *Genesis*, NIVAC (Grand Rapids, MI: Zondervan, 2001), 175-77.

[28]R. David Freedman, "Woman, a Power Equal to Man: Translation of Woman as a 'Fit Helpmate' for Man Is Questioned," *Biblical Archaeology Review* 9, no. 1 (1983): 56. Note that there are some problems with the way this idea is expressed in the article; however, the basic argument is valid.

[29]A term coined by Mark Boda, professor of Old Testament, McMaster Divinity College (personal communication).

glossed as "strength," "might," or "valor." This supports a translation of "a strength/power equivalent to him," equally able to carry out the creation mandate assigned to humanity.

That the woman is formed after the man (ha'adam) does not imply subordination or inferiority either, since there are numerous examples in Scripture of a younger child being given preference (e.g., Joseph, Gen 37:5-11; Jacob, Gen 25:22-23; David, 1 Sam 16:1-13; Gideon, Judg 6:11-16).[30] The term *firstborn* is often associated with the concept of preeminence, however, and this that may be relevant in regard to some New Testament passages (e.g., Ex 13:1; Deut 21:15-17; Num 3:13; 1 Chron 5:1-2; see also Rom 8:28; Col 1:15).[31] The term traditionally translated as the man's (ha'adam) "rib," from which the woman is formed, is *tsela'* (Gen 2:21, 22), which has often been interpreted as implying subordination. However, this is more of an architectural than anatomical word, as in Exodus 26:26-27, where it indicates the sides of the tabernacle; Exodus 25:14, the sides of the ark; and Exodus 38:7, the sides of the altar. It is better translated "side" (see, e.g., Ex 25:12; 26:20), which implies equality rather than subordination.[32]

The woman is physically taken out of the man (ha'adam; Gen 2:21), but the narrative makes clear that she has a distinct consciousness and identity; she is a newly formed person.[33] Here in Genesis 2:23, the use of *'ish* and *'ishah*—"this one shall be called woman ['ishah], for out of man ['ish] this one was taken"—is the first actual evidence in the second narrative of meaningful sexual distinction; however, in many translations both *'adam* and *'ish* are confusingly translated "man."[34] That the woman is taken out

---

[30]Cynthia Long Westfall, *Paul and Gender: Reclaiming the Apostle's Vision for Men and Women in Christ* (Grand Rapids, MI: Baker Academic, 2016), 76-78.

[31]Westfall, *Paul and Gender*, 71-79.

[32]Interpreters as early as John Chrysostom drew this conclusion: "'Let us make him a helpmate like himself,' meaning of his kind, with the same properties as himself, of equal esteem, in no way inferior to him" (Chrysostom, *Homilies on Genesis 1–17*, 197). See also Victor P. Hamilton, *The Book of Genesis: Chapters 1–17*, NICOT (Grand Rapids, MI: Eerdmans, 1990), 178.

[33]See Bird, "Sexual Differentiation," 18: "It does not presuppose an original androgyne [i.e., a creature consisting of both male and female aspects] (the progressive specification of attributes is logical, not temporal) but a bisexual order of creatures as the crown of creation."

[34]See Clines, Stec, and De Roo, *Dictionary of Classical Hebrew* 1:222: "3. man, husband, as distinct from woman." For meaningful sexual distinction in the first narrative, see the mention of *zakar unqebah*, "male and female," in Gen 1:27.

of the man (*ha'adam*) by God will become relevant later in reference to Genesis 3:20. Although something ("one of his sides," Gen 2:21) is removed from the man, the narrative is clear that the identity—consciousness and personality—of the man before and after the creation of Eve is continuous. He is referred to as *'ish* in Genesis 2:23 to focus on his new identity as male in contrast to the femaleness of Eve (see also Gen 2:24; 3:6, 16). He is still, however, sometimes referred to as *ha'adam* (e.g., Gen 2:25; 3:8, *ha'adam we'ishto*, "the man and his wife") where the context constrains the more general semantic range of *ha'adam* as it was used in Genesis 1. In cases such as Genesis 3:22, 24, however, it is unconstrained and may refer to humanity/the human. This usage contributes to the sense of continuity between the specific individual *ha'adam* of Genesis 2:5-20 and the specific individual *ha'adam* in Genesis 2:21–3:24 *after* the woman is formed from him. This individual is also called Adam (*'adam*) as early as Genesis 2:20 (NASB 1995, NIV, ESV, NET, NLT), in Genesis 3:17 in most translations, and in Genesis 4:25 in other translations (NRSV, LEB), where the context suggests a personal name.

I suggested above that the man (*ha'adam*) is unable to reproduce by himself and that this is one reason it is not good for the man to be alone; he needs the help of Yahweh, who forms Eve from the man's side. That is, the man needs the woman to reproduce, in order that together they can become co-creators with God of all subsequent humanity, fulfilling the mandate to be fruitful, multiply, fill the earth, subdue it, and have dominion (Gen 1:28). Marriage in Genesis 2:24 is described as the man (*'ish*) and the woman (*'ishah*) returning to "one flesh" again, a re-union and completion of their shared humanity after the separation of the woman from the man. It also emphasizes the similarity and equality between men and women. Indeed, that the man (*ha'adam*) calls the woman "bone of my bone and flesh of my flesh" (Gen 2:23) implies equality and similarity, not subordination or inferiority. Genesis 2 ends with the positive statement, "And the man and his wife were both naked and were not ashamed" (Gen 2:25). The picture is one of innocence, harmony, and purity—but unfortunately, it does not last.

GENESIS 3:1-24: THE FALL AND ITS CONSEQUENCES

Genesis 3:1-7: Gender and the fall. Two issues need to be addressed in this section. The first is that of false teaching. The narrative of what is commonly termed "the fall" begins with a description of the serpent, and it is important to note that the creature is not depicted as evil personified. The reader is told that it "was more *'arum* than any beast of the field" (Gen 3:1). The Hebrew term *'arum* means crafty, prudent, subtle, or shrewd.[35] The serpent does not appear to the woman, as in some old paintings, as a perverse, evil creature—Satan personified, with horns, no less—but as a concerned, wise, logical teacher, eager to help and advise Eve.[36] It is also important to note that the woman is at this point innocent; she has had no exposure to evil, and no experience of manipulation or deception. It is not as if she knowingly and willingly cooperates with the devil himself, as some understand Satan today. She encounters what appears to be a subtle, appealing teacher; however, the serpent is a false teacher of false doctrine.

At first, Eve responds appropriately, correcting the serpent's erroneous assumption that *all* the trees are forbidden to the humans. She is well aware that the tree in the middle of the garden is the prohibited tree. The woman seems somewhat confused, however, since she thinks they must not eat *or touch* the fruit (Gen 3:3). It is unclear where she picked up this idea; she may have made up the extra information herself, exaggerating the situation, or she may have been told this. Since the man (*ha'adam*) is the only other human that the narrative mentions, perhaps she has been insufficiently taught by her husband.[37] Although these reasons are admittedly speculative, recall that Eve had not yet been formed when Yahweh gave the instructions to Adam. However it happened, her theology is now demonstrably inadequate.

The serpent immediately challenges her, not by correcting her actual error, but by denying that eating the fruit of the forbidden tree would cause them to die, as Yahweh clearly said it would in Genesis 2:17, before Eve was

---

[35]Clines, Stec, and De Roo, *Dictionary of Classical Hebrew* 6:556.

[36]See J. Richard Middleton, "Reading Genesis 3 Attentive to Human Evolution," in *Evolution and the Fall*, ed. William T. Cavanaugh and James K. A. Smith (Grand Rapids, MI: Eerdmans, 2017), 84-86.

[37]The teaching of Eve by Adam would not imply subordination but would simply reflect the sequence of events in the narrative.

formed. The false teacher proceeds in Genesis 3:4-6 to give the woman apparently good reasons to eat the fruit: their eyes will be opened, and they will be like God, knowing good and evil (Gen 3:5).[38] There is no evidence that Eve is pressured to defy God by committing acts that she fully knows are evil; it is more probable that she is misled by false teaching that sounds good and convincing. Nevertheless, Eve disobeys God; her own speech shows that she knows that she and her husband are not to eat from the tree in the middle of the garden. She is guilty, and excuses cannot exonerate her, even if in part they explain her motivation.

The woman is gullible; however, there is no evidence that she is more gullible or more easily deceived than the man, her husband (*'ish*), for he is actually present with her during the conversation (Gen 3:6). The text specifically tells the reader that she took the fruit, ate, and gave it "to her husband with her." Why he does not object, or intervene to clarify the situation to his wife, or stop her, is unknown. Either he also is convinced by the serpent's argument, or he sees through the serpent's reasoning but for some reason chooses not to get involved. He too eats the fruit of the forbidden tree, and there is no evidence that he was forced.

The second issue that needs to be addressed is what the Old Testament refers to as sinning with a "high hand." That the man (*'ish*) is with the woman is also suggested by the use of plural verbs and pronouns by the serpent: "You [masculine plural] shall not eat" (Gen 3:1), "you [masculine plural] will not die" (Gen 3:4), "you [masculine plural] eat," "your [masculine plural] eyes," "you [masculine plural] will be like God" (Gen 3:5). The man (*ha'adam*) had his instructions directly from Yahweh before the woman was formed (Gen 2:15-17), yet he does not try to correct the woman or contradict the serpent. In terms of relative culpability, an argument could be made that the woman's sin is inadvertent sin. Even if not—since she does know, after all, that they are not to eat—she appears less guilty than the man, who sins defiantly.

Numbers 15:22-31 explains the difference between inadvertent and defiant sin. Inadvertent or unwitting sin (from the root *shgh*, "to stray, do

---

[38]There are various interpretations of this phrase. Some say they will understand God's stance on good and evil, but others say that they will be able to determine what constitutes good and evil themselves. See Walton, *Genesis*, 170-72.

wrong unintentionally") could be atoned for by making an offering, and the offender could be forgiven, for it was a *shegagah*, an "error, inadvertent sin, in which one is conscious of one's act but not of its consequences."[39] It is not premeditated (see Josh 20:3). Defiant sin, however, which is referred to in the text as acting "with a high hand," *beyad ramah*, as if one is shaking one's fist in the face of God, is very different. Defiant sinners were reviling or blaspheming Yahweh and were to be completely cut off from their people; there was no atonement available.

There is some evidence that Eve was not fully aware of the consequences of her action—that she acted without full knowledge—although she did nevertheless sin. Adam, however, was fully informed by Yahweh himself about the ban on the tree and is without excuse. As 1 Timothy 2:14 states, "Adam was not deceived, but the woman was deceived and became a transgressor." Some commentators read this as an exoneration of Adam, but it is actually a condemnation, since it does not offer Adam the extenuation that Eve is given.

Adam and Eve had dwelled in Eden "naked and unashamed," in innocence, harmony, and purity, but now the serpent's predictions come at least partly true. Their eyes are opened to the true nature of the serpent and the consequences of their actions, and they do know good and evil in an experiential way; however, they now face death.

Genesis 3:8-24: The impact of the fall on male-female relations. Again, two issues need to be addressed in this section. The first is that of the consequences of sin. That God addresses the man (*ha'adam*) first in Genesis 3:9 need not be an example of his greater responsibility or superior status as representative of the family. It could equally well be because he is more culpable, or because he was the first to have received the prohibition. In Genesis 3:12, however, the man (*ha'adam*) evades responsibility and passes on the guilt to the woman and, with considerable chutzpah, to Yahweh himself. His accusation of Eve is not fully justified; the woman is *not* solely to blame, since Adam heard the instructions directly from Yahweh and should not have eaten the fruit, regardless of what Eve and the serpent said. There is no record that he was forced to

---

[39]Clines, Stec, and De Roo, *Dictionary of Classical Hebrew* 8:262.

eat; he did so willingly. In Genesis 3:13, the woman admits that the serpent tricked her. This is partly an admission of responsibility for allowing herself to be tricked, but also partly an attempt to mitigate her own guilt. Note that the woman is given the results of her sin, but her specific sin is not mentioned. In Genesis 3:17, however, the man's/Adam's specific sin is detailed and stressed.[40]

The consequences of the sins of the couple are, in part, a destruction of the previously harmonious relationship between men and women, husband and wife; what was characterized by mutuality is now characterized by male domination: "Your desire will be for your husband ['*ish*] and he shall rule over you" (Gen 3:16).[41] In Genesis 3:16, the consequence for the woman is an intensification of "her pain/toil ['*itsabon*] in childbearing," probably implying an increase in risk during childbirth, for it was a dangerous event for women until very recently and still is in many places today. The consequence for the man (Gen 3:17-19) is the cursing of the ground and increased toil ('*itsabon*), as well as death: ultimately a return to the ground from which he was taken. Although the first birth apparently occurred after the fall (Gen 4:1), this situation is not the result of the fall, since humans were told to reproduce and multiply before sin entered the situation (Gen 1:28).[42] Both Adam and Eve (now treated as specific individuals) are driven out of the garden and suffer separation from the presence of God. The tree of life is also forbidden to them.

---

[40]In *ul'adam* the Hebrew vowel *qamets*, indicating the definite article, may be obscured by the addition of the *lamed* prefix, as suggested by the apparatus; in the consonantal text there is no difference between "to the man" and "to Adam."

[41]The term often translated "desire" is widely contested and occurs only three times in the Old Testament. The suggestion that this verse should be "your desire will be against your husband" (see, e.g., Wayne A. Grudem, *Biblical Foundations for Manhood and Womanhood*, Foundations for the Family Series [Wheaton, IL: Crossway, 2002], 35) is untenable for a number of reasons that are too technical to delve into here. For an introduction to the issue, see Chenxin Jiang, "Rewriting the Biblical 'Curse' on Womanhood," *The Atlantic*, November 20, 2016, www.theatlantic.com/politics/archive/2016/11/bible-evangelicals-womanhood-marriage/508076/. Susan T. Foh equates the phrase with a desire to dominate. See Foh, "What Is the Woman's Desire?," *WTJ* 37 (1975): 376-83. However, her argument is heavily biased by her unsupported assumption that creation itself mandates the husband's rule over his wife, what she calls "the husband's God-ordained headship" (379). Other interpretations include sexual desire, based on Song 7:10 and a desire to have children. For the former, see Wenham, *Genesis*, 1:81; for the latter, see Walton, *Genesis*, 228-29.

[42]The *qatal* verb, found in Gen 4:1, may be rendered in English as a perfect or a pluperfect.

The second issue to be addressed in this section is the naming of Eve. Although being the firstborn does not imply dominance, the sequencing of creation in Genesis is relevant to an understanding of New Testament references, including 1 Corinthians 11:3 (see further below), which will be dealt with in other chapters of this book.[43] Yahweh was the source of life for the man (*ha'adam*). It is significant that the man was the source of life for Eve, since she was "birthed" from the man by Yahweh as a distinctly female human. Genesis 3:20 states that "the man called his wife Eve, because she was the mother of all living." Consequently, Eve is the source of life for all subsequent humans, both male and female. Humanity is now to fulfill its mandate to reproduce and fill the earth (1 Cor 11:11-12).

That the man (*ha'adam*) names the woman, as he previously did the animals, however, is also not a sign of the man's superiority or dominance. Naming in the Old Testament is an act of discerning a trait or function or ability that already exists in the person being named, not a sign of authority over that person.[44] An example is Hagar's naming of God *el ro'i*, "God who sees me" (Gen 16:13); another is the name of Gideon's son, Abimelech, which in Hebrew means "my father is king" (Judg 8:31). Eve's name is revealed in Genesis 3:20: "Now the man called his wife's name Eve [*hawwah*], because she was the mother of all the living."[45] Her Hebrew name is related to the verb "to live," *hayah*.[46]

GENESIS 1–3 AND THE NEW TESTAMENT

The narrative of the creation and fall in Genesis 1–3 forms the foundation of a number of New Testament texts dealing with headship, such as Romans 5; 1 Corinthians 15; and Ephesians 5:31.[47] Although these passages

---

[43]See Westfall, *Paul and Gender*, 38, 80-90.

[44]See George W. Ramsey, "Is Name-Giving an Act of Domination in Genesis 2:23 and Elsewhere," *CBQ* 50, no. 1 (1988): 24-35.

[45]In modern Hebrew, the letter *waw* (transliterated as *w*) is pronounced as the English *v* and is called *vav*, hence the pronunciation *havva*.

[46]See Scott C. Layton, "Remarks on the Canaanite Origin of Eve," *CBQ* 59, no. 1 (1997), esp. 31, for a convincing argument in support of this derivation.

[47]Obviously much more can be said about the New Testament passages. I am only making suggestions here of the specific relevance of Genesis to them. For a detailed study of biblical passages relating to gender, especially in the New Testament, see Westfall, *Paul and Gender*.

will be dealt with more fully in other chapters, a few points are worth mentioning here. For example, in 1 Corinthians 11:8-12, gender reciprocity is assumed:

> Indeed, man was not made from woman, but woman from man. Neither was man created for the sake of woman, but woman for the sake of man. For this reason, a woman ought to have authority over her head/freedom of choice in regard to her head, because of the angels. Nevertheless, in the Lord woman is not independent of man or man independent of woman. For just as woman came from man, so man comes through woman; but all things come from God. (NRSV modified)

In the Old Testament, woman/Eve was originally made from the man (*ha'adam*)/Adam by God.[48] This was "for the sake of man," who was unable to fulfill his purpose—to reproduce and fill the earth—alone. This remains true in the New Testament even after the fall and the redemption offered in Christ. Woman is the source of life and produces both male and female children. Just as Eve was taken from Adam, so male and female children are taken from woman. Nevertheless, male and female are not independent of each other; both are necessary for life and for service to God. This is significant in the understanding of headship in the New Testament.[49]

GENESIS 1-3 AS A BASIS FOR 1 TIMOTHY 2

A particularly clear intertextual link occurs with the book of 1 Timothy. Although this passage will be dealt with in depth by a New Testament scholar in chapter eleven, a few comments are relevant here due to the direct reference to the Genesis 1–3 narrative:

> Let a woman learn undisturbed with full submission. I permit no woman to teach or to usurp authority over a man; she is to be undisturbed. For Adam was formed first, then Eve; and Adam was not deceived, but the woman was deceived and became a transgressor. Yet she will be saved through childbearing, provided they continue in faith and love and holiness, with self-control. (1 Tim 2:11-15 NRSV modified)

---

[48]Note that the continuity between *ha'adam* and Adam was stressed above.

[49]See above under "A 'Helper Corresponding to Him': The Beginning of Biological Sex." See also Westfall, *Paul and Gender*, 71-79.

Although women in that time and culture could be well educated, many were less literate and educated in matters of religion, and therefore more likely to hold wrong ideas.[50] This was certainly the case in Ephesus, where the prevalence of "profane myths and old wives' tales" (1 Tim 4:7 NRSV) needed to be addressed by the author of 1 Timothy.[51] Indeed, the primary issue in 1 Timothy is false teaching.[52] The women, exercising their new freedom in Christ, were outspokenly causing an issue by questioning or challenging the more informed men. Paul instructs them to submit, *not* to men as men, but to Yahweh and to the sound teaching of those who *at the time and in that place* were better informed, that is, men. The Greek *en hēsychia*, often translated "in silence" or "quietly" and implying that the *women* should not speak or cause disruption, is more legitimately translated as "undisturbed," meaning that the women should not be disrupted by the intervention of *others* who might try to prevent them from learning.[53] The solution to this aspect of the problem of false teaching was to allow women to learn, undisturbed by those who would prevent them.[54] The striking thing in this passage is that women, contrary to much of the culture of the time, are actually encouraged to learn.

The link to Genesis 3 in 1 Timothy 2:13-15 is relevant to the argument here because the issue in Genesis was that Eve was *also* inadequately informed and had mistaken theology, as discussed above. Her apparently confused understanding of God's instructions, passed on to her by Adam, resulted in her being deceived by the false—but appealing—teaching of the serpent. She passed the fruit on to her husband, and Adam—who was also there listening to the serpent's argument—ate, although he did not have the same excuse. He had heard the instructions directly from Yahweh himself, but did not even interrupt with a question, let alone a challenge

---

[50]On well-educated women, see Lynn H. Cohick, *Women in the World of the Earliest Christians: Illuminating Ancient Ways of Life* (Grand Rapids, MI: Baker Academic, 2009), 206-9, 242-49.

[51]See Westfall, *Paul and Gender*, 127 (including n51), 239-40. Contra William D. Mounce, *Pastoral Epistles*, WBC 46 (Dallas, TX: Word, 2000), 139.

[52]Note that throughout the letter *both* men and women are upbraided for false teaching and warned against its dangers. See 1 Tim 1:3-7; 3:1; 4:1-6, 6-7; 6:2-5, 20. In fact, Paul says that he himself was once a blasphemer and acted ignorantly in unbelief (1 Tim 1:13) but was later appointed a herald, apostle, and teacher (1 Tim 2:7).

[53]Personal communication with Stanley E. Porter, president, dean, and professor of New Testament, McMaster Divinity College.

[54]Probably in her own home, taught by her husband. See Westfall, *Paul and Gender*, 305-9.

or correction.[55] According to William Mounce in his commentary on the verse, such explanations do not take into account the statement that Adam was not deceived, the "emphatic teaching of Adam's prior creation," or the parallelism of 1 Timothy 2:13 and 1 Timothy 2:14, or that of 1 Timothy 2:14a with 1 Timothy 2:14b.[56] However, these factors are all accounted for in this interpretation: "Adam heard the command directly; Eve did not since she was not yet created // Adam was not deceived (defiant sin); Eve was deceived (inadvertent sin)."

The issue here is not whether someone is a man or a woman, but inadequate teaching. The point is not that women should be excluded from teaching or having authority, but that *anyone* who is inadequately taught and is inappropriately usurping authority over those who have had a better education and possess better understanding should not teach others, at least temporarily until their understanding has improved.[57] In Paul's day, in Ephesus, it was primarily women who were in this situation, but in our culture it may be equally men or women, and men and women may be equally educated. Therefore, there is no longer any reason to deny women the full role of teaching and preaching in the church.

The following statement that the woman "will be preserved through childbearing" does not mean that having children will result in the salvation of women's souls. It may well, however, indicate a corrective of the women's reliance on Artemis, a goddess associated with midwifery, for protection during childbirth—part of their false understanding.[58] These misconceptions were likely influenced by the dominating presence of the temple of Artemis in Ephesus. After all, the primary cause of death for

---

[55]See Craig S. Keener, *Paul, Women and Wives: Marriage and Women's Ministry in the Letters of Paul* (Grand Rapids, MI: Baker Academic, 2012), 133: "The third possibility is that Paul intends to connect Eve's later creation to why she was deceived: she was not present when God gave the commandment, and thus was dependent on Adam for the teaching. In other words, she was inadequately educated like the women in the Ephesian church."

[56]Mounce, *Pastoral Epistles*, 139-41. See also Westfall, *Paul and Gender*, 127-28.

[57]See Sandra Glahn, "The First-Century Ephesian Artemis: Ramifications of Her Identity," *BSac* 172, no. 688 (2015): 642.

[58]Sandra Glahn, "The Identity of Artemis in First-Century Ephesus," *BSac* 172, no. 687 (2015): 316-34, argues effectively that the Ephesian manifestation of Artemis was associated specifically with midwifery, and that she was not "a fertility goddess, a sex goddess, or a mother figure" (333). Glahn demonstrates that the Ephesian version of Artemis was closely associated with protection (321, 331-32).

women in this culture was childbirth.[59] What the statement does mean is that, in spite of the dangers inherent in childbearing that often resulted in death, women who trust in God, not Artemis, can be assured that God is able to preserve them through it in this life, and ultimately to eternal life.[60] This statement is actually about the undoing of part of Eve's punishment in Genesis 3:16—"I will greatly increase your pangs in childbearing; in pain you shall bring forth children"—for those women who persevere in faith, love, holiness, and self-control: the Christian virtues.

CONCLUSION

In Genesis, before the fall, there was mutuality, equality, and harmony between men and women. Incorrect understanding and false teaching were influences contributing to the sin of Adam and Eve, although deliberate disobedience was certainly a major factor. The fall destroyed the mutuality and harmony between men and women, resulting in millennia of male domination in both the church and in marriage. In Christ, that consequence is undone, and the mutuality and harmony of marriage is potentially restored . . . if the church allows it. With appropriate teaching—combined with faith, love, holiness, and self-control—both men and women can now be full participants in the ministry of the church.

---

[59]Glahn, "First-Century Ephesian Artemis," 451.
[60]See Glahn, "First-Century Ephesian Artemis," 466; Westfall, *Paul and Gender*, 279-312, especially 309-11.

3

THE TREATMENT OF WOMEN UNDER THE MOSAIC LAW

Ronald W. Pierce and Mary L. Conway

• • • • •

BECAUSE THE LAW OF MOSES REFLECTS a male-centered social environment, many view its statements regarding women as morally offensive. For example, critics argue that women frequently appear in the Pentateuch as dependent on, or even inferior to, men, and that legal rulings either ignore women or are negative toward them. Women are normally subject to the authority of a father, husband, or brother, except when widowed or divorced. Further, a woman's legal rights are usually stated in terms of her relation to a man—or lack thereof. Even though such laws do not compose a large portion of the Pentateuch, they remain troubling to many readers today.

Two general errors occur in attempting to deal with this situation: either the Old Testament law is ignored as antiquated, or cherry-picked laws are applied mechanically with little sensitivity to context. In an effort to seek understanding of these passages in the broader context of the Bible's teaching regarding men and women, this chapter has a threefold emphasis. First, it will give an overview of the nature of Old Testament law, giving examples that reflect its purpose and function, and clarifying the differences between it and modern law codes. Second, it will give examples of the positive, regulatory character of the law, given that it was designed (in part) to expose and restrain sinful behavior. In other words, the law not only showed us our need for redemption but also functioned as a guardian and disciplinarian until that redemption was more fully realized.[1] Its function was character building in response to, and in imitation of, Yahweh's own gracious character.[2]

Third, this chapter will demonstrate a redemptive movement, of which the law is but one stage.[3] This process begins with (1) God's good creation, which was (2) marred by humanity's sin, which in turn was (3) regulated by the Mosaic law, a structure that was (4) fulfilled in the gospel. Thus, just as the law took humanity beyond the judgments of Genesis 3:14-19, the New Testament believer is called to go beyond the law to the fullness of the gospel. This process is confirmed by comments of Jesus (Mt 5:17-48; 19:1-20) and Paul (Gal 3:19, 23; 4:4). Jesus explains the implications already inherent in the law, yet adds his own clarification of what the Old Testament law was always intended to be and do. Likewise, Paul argues that the law was added because of transgressions, guarding those under its care, while serving as their disciplinarian or guardian until the set time had fully come when a Redeemer would appear, born of a woman, born under the law, and giving humanity an actual embodiment of the character of God for Christians to emulate. The law is honored yet understood as part of a redemptive process that leads to something more fully realized in the New Testament.

THE NATURE OF OLD TESTAMENT LAW

It is important to understand the nature of Old Testament law and how it differs from a modern understanding of a law code. Some Christians today try to enforce Old Testament laws in contemporary society. However, many of the individual laws, if enforced literally, would seem inappropriate (Deut 21:11: do not wear cloth made of mixed wool and linen), immoral

---

[1]See Carolyn Pressler, *The View of Women Found in the Deuteronomic Family Laws*, Beiheft zur Zeitschrift fur die Alttestamentliche Wissenschaft (Berlin: de Gruyter, 1993), as well as Victor H. Matthews, Bernard M. Levinson, and Tikva Frymer-Kensky, eds., *Gender and Law in the Hebrew Bible and the Ancient Near East*, JSOTSup 262 (Sheffield: Sheffield Academic, 1998).

[2]As Bruce C. Birch notes, "In Christian ethics we are being called to attend more carefully to the character of God alongside the conduct of God." See Birch, "Moral Agency, Community, and the Character of God in the Hebrew Bible," *Semeia* 66 (1994): 30.

[3]This is similar to William J. Webb's model developed in *Slaves, Women, and Homosexuals: Exploring the Hermeneutics of Cultural Analysis* (Downers Grove, IL: InterVarsity Press, 2001). However, we are not suggesting that this movement need go beyond the New Testament to arrive at gender equality for men and women in Christ, since this is accomplished *within* the New Testament.

(Lev 25:44: you may keep slaves), or even illegal (Lev 20:9: a rebellious son should be put to death). Consequently, other Christians deem Old Testament laws to be outdated or superseded by the New Testament and ignore them, arguing that the law has been replaced by grace; however, this distorts the character of the gracious God depicted in the Old Testament.

The traditional translation of *torah*, Torah—the five books of Moses or the Pentateuch—as "law" can be somewhat misleading, implying that it consists entirely of a rigid legal code. The better translation is "instruction," "decisions," or "teaching."[4] Traditionally, the Torah is considered to contain 613 individual laws touching on almost every aspect of the Israelites' lives. Many of these are gathered into collections commonly referred to as law codes: the Ten Words (Ex 20:1-17; Deut 5:1-21), the Holiness Code (Lev 17–26), the Covenant Code (Ex 20:19–23:33), and the Deuteronomic Code (12–26).[5] These, however, are not law codes in the modern sense and are not intended to be definitive, comprehensive, and centralized. In fact, the Old Testament law was never intended as a template for God's ideal society, but rather guidelines for how an imperfect Israel was to live within an ancient, flawed society that was, among other things, polytheistic, patriarchal, and authoritarian. As John Walton argues, the law "does not endorse those systems; it addresses the people who live in those systems. There is no ideal social system because all systems are populated by fallen people."[6] Jesus himself implies this when he comments on Moses' law concerning divorce: "'It was because your hearts were hard that Moses wrote you this law,' Jesus replied. 'But at the beginning of creation God "made them male and female"'" (Mk 10:5-6 NIV). Therefore, the laws are not intended to be absolute, timeless, universal regulations.

M. Daniel Carroll R., for example, notes that even within the Old Testament, laws showed evidence of change from one time to another and from

---

[4]See David J. A. Clines, David M. Stec, and Jacqueline C. R. De Roo, eds., *The Dictionary of Classical Hebrew* (Sheffield: Sheffield Academic, 1993–2011), 8:612.

[5]The term "Ten Commandments" is a misnomer. These are not necessarily phrased as imperatives (the verbs are negated imperfects), and the root *tswh*, "command," is not used. The Hebrew *hadbarim* means "the words/statements" or "the matters."

[6]John H. Walton, "Understanding Torah: Ancient Legal Text, Covenant Stipulation, and Christian Scripture" (paper presented at the Institute for Biblical Research Annual Meeting, Boston, 2017). See also Walton, *The Lost World of the Israelite Conquest* (Downers Grove, IL: InterVarsity Press, 2017), 121-22.

one situation to another.[7] Exodus 21:2, in the context of the giving of the law at Sinai, states, "If you buy a Hebrew servant, he is to serve you for six years. But in the seventh year, he shall go free, without paying anything" (NIV). In Deuteronomy 15:12, however, a generation later on the border of the Promised Land, the law reads, "If any of your people—Hebrew men or women—sell themselves to you and serve you six years, in the seventh year you must let them go free" (NIV). Although we cannot know what motivated the inclusion of women in the regulation in its new context, it suggests both a fluidity in the law and a more explicit focus on the value of women.[8]

This understanding of Old Testament law can be illustrated by a very brief and selective overview of the work of key scholars. A seminal article by Albrecht Alt in 1934 attempted to clarify the role of law by distinguishing "apodictic" law from "casuistic" law.[9] Apodictic laws, he said, were unconditional, absolute, and timeless; casuistic laws were the application of those general principles to individual situations, and they might vary due to time and place. Although the specific criteria for Alt's categories have been rightly criticized, there seems to be considerable truth in his claims.[10] Whereas apodictic law consists of overarching general statements, casuistic law details specific applications and might serve a similar purpose as modern legal precedent, that is, a collection of specific legal cases intended to guide people in reaching appropriate legal decisions in analogous situations. Edward Campbell calls the Old Testament law "a collection of precedents which have arisen from specific experiences preserved as references for settling similar cases, especially the difficult ones." They are not intended to be exhaustive, but "illustrative and didactic."[11]

---

[7]See M. Daniel Carroll R., "An Introduction to the Ethics of John Rogerson," in *Theory and Practice in Old Testament Ethics*, ed. John W. Rogerson and M. Daniel Carroll R., JSOTSup 405 (New York: T&T Clark, 2004), 10-11.

[8]In the Hebrew, all the other grammatical elements in the verse are masculine singular, suggesting that the phrase "a Hebrew man or a Hebrew woman" was added later as a gloss.

[9]Albrecht Alt, "The Origins of Israelite Law," in *Essays on Old Testament History and Religion* (Garden City, NY: Doubleday, 1968), 101-71.

[10]See Rifat Sonsino, "Law: Forms of Biblical Law," in *The Anchor Yale Bible Dictionary*, ed. David Noel Freedman (New York: Doubleday, 1992), 252-53.

[11]Edward F. Campbell, *Ruth: A New Translation with Introduction, Notes, and Commentary*, AB 7 (Garden City, NY: Doubleday, 1975), 133, 134.

According to Joshua Berman, the misunderstanding of Old Testament law as a comprehensive and universal legal code originated as recently as the late nineteenth century, when a statutory approach replaced the former common-law approach to jurisprudence.[12] In statutory law, the laws themselves are codified in text, the law emanates from a sovereign or official legislative body, and the law is a finite and complete system. Should there be situations for which the individual laws do not provide explicit guidance, the judges were nevertheless to extrapolate from the existing laws in rendering decisions. In the earlier system of common law, however,

> adjudication is a process whereby the judge concludes the correct judgment based on the mores and spirit of the community and its customs. Law gradually develops through the distillation and continual restatement of legal doctrine through the decisions of courts. When a judge decides a particular case, he or she is empowered to reconstruct the general thrust of the law in consultation with previous judicial formulations. Critically, the judicial decision itself does not create binding law. No particular formulation of the law is final. As a system of legal thought, the common law is consciously and inherently incomplete, fluid, and vague.[13]

Legal texts, in this approach, did not become a final, immutable law code, but acted as a resource, a body of precedents, or a "system of reasoning" for judges to consider.[14] Denise Réaume describes these approaches as the "top down" (statutory) and "bottom up" (common law) methods, and makes interesting suggestions as to how the common-law system may work better even today in the area of discrimination law.[15] This common-law system changed, however, in the nineteenth century when small, formerly homogenous communities with common values were replaced by larger, more diverse and mobile societies. In this situation, the law codes provided a means of political and social unification. The Torah, however,

---

[12]Joshua Berman, "The History of Legal Theory and the Study of Biblical Law," *CBQ* 76, no. 1 (2014): 20. Thanks are due to Ryder Wishart for pointing out this article. See also Ryder Wishart, "Paul and the Law: Mark Nanos, Brian Rosner, and the Common-Law Tradition," *JGRChJ* 11 (2015): 153-77.

[13]Berman, "History of Legal Theory," 21.

[14]Berman, "History of Legal Theory," 22.

[15]Denise G. Réaume, "Of Pigeonholes and Principles, a Reconsideration of Discrimination Law," *Osgood Hall Law Journal* 40, no. 2 (2002): 115-16.

follows the common-law approach, which includes sources of law such as narrative, poetry, and sayings as well as typical laws.[16] From a common-law perspective, the so-called contradictions in the various law codes would not be contradictions at all, but rather alternatives to consider, supplements to previous texts, or adaptations of law to changing circumstances.

As noted above, statutory law emanates from a sovereign, whereas common law emanates from the mores of the community.[17] This does not imply, however, that biblical law is merely a product of ancient community values or of humanistic ideals, as common law might be in modern secular societies. Israel was a theocracy, and, as Waldemar Janzen notes, "Theology and ethics cannot be separated from each other in the Old Testament." The ethics of the Old Testament are inseparably embedded in its narrative of Yahweh's covenant relationship with Israel. Janzen also points out that in the Old Testament stories there is "a deeper dimension than even the maintenance of justice, namely, subjection to the sovereign leading of God."[18]

Thus, Old Testament laws are not freestanding legal statements or documents; they are contained within, and depend on, a *narrative* framework. As Janzen notes:

> A very different understanding of such laws emerges when one sees them . . . as shorthand formulations of ethical values and imperatives emerging from a particular story—Israel's story—and as continuing to be defined by that story. Then they can no longer be seen as self-contained universal maxims, nor can they be loosened from the story in which they are embedded.[19]

Mark Boda explains further: "These legal codes are carefully placed within a *covenantal and redemptive framework*. . . . Yahweh declares that the Torah is to guide their covenantal response to his redemptive act in delivering them from slavery in Egypt. This redemptive act was not just a deliverance from Egypt but a deliverance to himself ([Ex] 19:4)."[20] The ultimate purpose of the law was not simply to regulate external behavior but to

---

[16]Berman, "History of Legal Theory," 23-26.

[17]Berman, "History of Legal Theory," 21.

[18]Waldemar Janzen, *Old Testament Ethics: A Paradigmatic Approach* (Louisville, KY: Westminster John Knox, 1994), 11, 17.

[19]Janzen, *Old Testament Ethics*, 58.

[20]Mark J. Boda, *A Severe Mercy: Sin and Its Remedy in the Old Testament*, Siphrut 1 (Winona Lake, IN: Eisenbrauns, 2009), 47, emphasis original. See also Janzen, *Old Testament Ethics*, 2, 11, 17.

form human *character* in the likeness of Yahweh's character (see Gen 1:26-27; Rom 8:29; Phil 3:10).[21] Carroll points out that "ethical attitudes and behavior, in other words, are not generated in a vacuum. They should be motivated by gratitude to God and the desire to reflect his character in the world."[22] This is reinforced in the New Testament, where Jesus emphasizes that the law was intended to incorporate underlying *attitudes* as well as external expression, as when he expands the law against adultery to include everyone who looks on a woman with lust (Mt 5:27).

In recent years, this understanding of the law as embedded in narrative and contributive to character has challenged a mechanical, legalistic application of individual rules to external behavior. One change has been the shift in focus from specific regulations to the overarching principles they reflect. The term *principle* must be used with care, however, for it is often used for abstract morals or self-interpreting truths such as compassion, justice, or faithfulness. This is a reductionist approach unless the principles are fully understood as shorthand for the contextualized stories themselves.[23] Walter Kaiser is one scholar who emphasizes principles; he argues that the specificity of biblical law is no obstacle to its universal application, and concludes that "while there are fewer general principles than there are specific commands, this should not affect the eventual usefulness of most, if not all, of the injunctions."[24] In his approach to interpretation, he recommends moving up the "ladder of abstraction," which bridges the ancient and modern contexts until a general principle has been determined.[25] This can then be applied to new situations. The abstraction must never replace the narrative, however, and Kaiser's principalizing methodology has been critiqued. For example, Daniel Doriani points out that "principalizing treats the particularity and cultural embeddedness of Scripture more as a

---

[21]See Janzen, *Old Testament Ethics*, 62.

[22]Carroll, "Introduction to the Ethics," 10. See also Gordon J. Wenham, *Story as Torah: Reading the Old Testament Ethically* (Edinburgh: T&T Clark, 2000), 106. Of course, the distinction in roles and nature between the created and the Creator must be maintained. See Janzen, *Old Testament Ethics*, 115.

[23]See Janzen, *Old Testament Ethics*, 29, 55-58, especially 58, for an excellent discussion of the advantages of paradigm over principle. See also Christopher J. H. Wright, *Old Testament Ethics for the People of God* (Downers Grove, IL: InterVarsity Press, 2004), 62-74.

[24]Walter C. Kaiser, *Toward Old Testament Ethics* (Grand Rapids, MI: Zondervan, 1983), 42.

[25]Walter C. Kaiser, *Toward Rediscovering the Old Testament* (Grand Rapids, MI: Zondervan, 1987), 166.

problem to be overcome than as something essential to the givenness of the Bible."[26]

The search for general principles certainly makes the application of Old Testament law to contemporary society much easier, but it can also raise significant concerns. The focus on abstract principles has even led to the search for one supreme, overarching principle that, it is argued, guides all Christian behavior and eliminates the need for laws; one such widely accepted principle is love. Unfortunately, love as an abstract idea is subject to a variety of individual interpretations, and it can be used to justify a lax approach to godliness in which love makes anything justifiable. The biblical image of love, however, is not one of self-indulgent emotion but of self-sacrificing commitment. Only when the principle remains embedded in the narrative does this become clear.[27]

Janzen prefers to speak of paradigms; he defines a paradigm as a "personally and holistically conceived image of a model (e.g., a wise person, good king) that imprints itself immediately and non-conceptually on the characters and actions of those who hold it."[28] Christopher Wright uses a similar methodology, and John Rogerson speaks of the value of "example rather than precept."[29] Gordon Wenham argues that the Scriptures "are not demanding a minimalist conformity to the demands of the law in their storytelling, rather, they have an ideal of godly behavior that they hoped their heroes and heroines would typify."[30] Thus, as 1 Corinthians 10:11 states, "These things happened to them as examples and were written down as warnings for us, on whom the culmination of the ages has come" (NIV). These approaches have the advantage of keeping the particular laws contextualized and relevant to specific life situations. In no way does the paradigm approach minimize the value of the Old Testament laws, encouraging an ambiguous form of situation ethics in which we can apply the

---

[26]Daniel M. Doriani, "A Response to Walter C. Kaiser Jr.," in *Four Views on Moving Beyond the Bible to Theology*, ed. Stanley N. Gundry and Gary T. Meadors, Counterpoints (Grand Rapids, MI: Zondervan, 2009), 53. See also the responses in this volume by Kevin J. Vanhoozer (57-63) and William J. Webb (64-73).

[27]See Janzen, *Old Testament Ethics*, 68-70.

[28]Janzen, *Old Testament Ethics*, 27-28.

[29]Wright, *Old Testament Ethics for the People of God*, 62-74; Rogerson and Carroll, *Theory and Practice*, 36.

[30]Wenham, *Story as Torah*, 3.

laws selectively or not at all. This application of principles or paradigms to specific cultural and historical situations does not *relativize the law; it* merely makes the law *relevant*. Due to the radically different cultural situation of the church today, distanced by thousands of miles and years from the ancient Near Eastern context, some particular applications of law are no longer meaningful, and some must be reinterpreted in order to achieve a similar result in their present context.

This is not an issue unique to contemporary Western culture. A key example of contextualized law occurs within the Old Testament itself in the book of Ruth. The law in Deuteronomy 23:3-4, 6 clearly states,

> No Ammonite or Moabite or any of their descendants may enter the assembly of the LORD, not even in the tenth generation. For they did not come to meet you with bread and water on your way when you came out of Egypt, and they hired Balaam son of Beor from Pethor in Aram Naharaim to pronounce a curse on you. . . . Do not seek a treaty of friendship with them as long as you live. (NIV)

Nevertheless, Boaz generously promotes the welfare of Ruth, a Moabite woman, and admits her into the Israelite community by marrying her. The many efforts to explain this "contradiction" only serve to emphasize it: some say the law only refers to the offspring of such unions, or that it is a "divinely given exception," or that the term *qahal*, "assembly," refers only to cultic contexts, or that it only applied to the male line, among other explanations.[31] However, if one understands that specific laws were not intended to be contextless, timeless, universal, and absolute, the problem is resolved. In Deuteronomy 23:4, Moses tells Israel that the Moabites are condemned because they refused to aid Israel and cursed them. Ruth, on the other hand, has taken refuge under the wings of Yahweh, the God of Israel (Ruth

---

[31]The law only refers to the offspring of such unions: K. Lawson Younger, *Judges and Ruth*, NIVAC (Grand Rapids, MI: Zondervan, 2002), 417. It is a "divinely given exception": Robert L. Hubbard, *The Book of Ruth*, NICOT (Grand Rapids, MI: Eerdmans, 1988), 152; see also Robert B. Chisholm Jr., *A Commentary on Judges and Ruth*, Kregel Exegetical Library (Grand Rapids, MI: Kregel Academic, 2013), 597-98. It only applied to the male line: Bruce K. Waltke and Charles Yu, *An Old Testament Theology: An Exegetical, Canonical, and Thematic Approach* (Grand Rapids, MI: Zondervan, 2007), 853n7; Walton, *Lost World of the Israelite Conquest*, 187; Kirsten Nielsen, *Ruth: A Commentary*, Old Testament Library (Louisville, KY: Westminster John Knox, 1997), 44. Note that even though masculine forms are used in the grammar, in Hebrew masculine terms are often used in an inclusive sense, as was formerly common in English.

2:12). She has demonstrated loyalty and support to Naomi, an Israelite woman, in her journey, and brought blessing to Boaz as well.[32] As Boaz states, "The LORD bless you, my daughter. . . . This kindness [*hesed*] is greater than that which you showed earlier" (Ruth 3:10 NIV). He refers to her respectfully as a strong or worthy (*hayil*) woman. Ruth the Moabite's context and behavior were different, and therefore the law did not apply. Again, this does not *relativize* the law; it merely makes the law *relevant*.

There are other examples of the application of law in the same narrative. Boaz refers to the law of the "guardian-redeemer" (Ruth 3:13 NIV), but the obligations of this *go'el* covered issues such as property inheritance, redeeming slaves, and legal restitution of crimes, not marriage (Lev 25:25-55; Num 5:8; 35:12, 19-27; etc.). The levirate law, on the other hand, did involve marriage to a widow, but it applied to the husband's brother, not distant relatives (Deut 25:5-10).[33] Various property laws also enter the mix. Thus, Boaz seems to be breaking or reinterpreting numerous laws; nevertheless, in the context of the narrative, no one would doubt that his behavior toward a destitute and widowed alien woman is commended.

Boaz does not mechanically follow abstract laws and principles in his interaction with Ruth; he *embodies* the values of compassion to the homeless, the widows, and the marginalized that he has internalized from Yahweh himself:

> For the LORD your God is God of gods and Lord of lords, the great God, mighty and awesome, who shows no partiality and accepts no bribes. He defends the cause of the fatherless and the widow, and loves the foreigner residing among you, giving them food and clothing. And you are to love those who are foreigners, for you yourselves were foreigners in Egypt. (Deut 10:17-19 NIV)

As discussed above, ethical attitudes result in ethical behavior, and both should be undertaken in grateful response to the God who has graciously redeemed us. Bruce Birch notes that ethics

---

[32]Irmtraud Fischer, "The Book of Ruth: A 'Feminist' Commentary to the Torah?," in *A Feminist Companion to Ruth and Esther*, ed. Athalya Brenner, Feminist Companion to the Bible: Second Series (Sheffield: Sheffield Academic, 1999), 36.

[33]For the role of law in Ruth, see Hubbard, *Book of Ruth*, 48-51, or the more detailed analysis in Daniel I. Block, *Judges, Ruth*, NAC 6 (Nashville: Broadman & Holman, 1999), 196-243.

arises in *response* to the experience of the presence and activity of God. To have experienced the deliverance from bondage in Egypt may have some effects in imitating divine behavior (e.g., in providing for the freedom of slaves), but its far greater moral impact is in engendering responses of humility and praise for the gift of God's grace and in fostering reflection on what it means to live as God's delivered people in the world.[34]

This is the ultimate purpose of the Old Testament law, and it is confirmed in the New Testament. We are not to be mechanically legalistic; rather, we are to be conformed to the image of Christ, the ultimate embodiment of the will and character of God (Rom 8:29; Col 1:15; 3:10) through his indwelling Spirit (Rom 8:5-11; Gal 4:1-7).

THE LAW AS GUARDIAN AND DISCIPLINARIAN

This section will take a closer look at a few representative laws concerning women within the Old Testament corpus in order to show that these laws dealt with the reality of a less-than-ideal patriarchal society while offering protections to women and controlling sin.[35]

Adultery in the Old Testament and other ancient societies appears as a sin or crime against the adulteress's husband (Ex 20:14; Deut 5:18) but not against the adulterer's wife/wives. Consequences were less severe for a married man having sexual relations with an unmarried/unbetrothed woman than with a married/betrothed woman. The concern here seems to be the identity of the father and the protection of the male line. Old Testament law implicitly assumes, without endorsing, the premise of polygamy, namely, that a wife does not have exclusive sexual rights to her husband, though a husband has exclusive sexual rights to his wife/wives.[36]

---

[34]Bruce C. Birch, *Let Justice Roll Down: The Old Testament, Ethics, and Christian Life* (Louisville, KY: Westminster John Knox, 1991), 39, emphasis original. See also Birch, "Moral Agency, Community," 29-33.

[35]For a more detailed overview of the individual Old Testament laws relating to women, see Ronald W. Pierce, "From Old Testament Law to New Testament Gospel," in *Discovering Biblical Equality: Complementarity Without Hierarchy* (Downers Grove, IL: InterVarsity Press, 2004), 96-109.

[36]See the discussion of this thorny problem in Gordon J. Wenham, *Leviticus*, NICOT (Grand Rapids, MI: Eerdmans, 1979), 258. Also on Leviticus, see the three-volume commentary by Jacob Milgrom, *Leviticus 1-16, Leviticus 17-22,* and *Leviticus 23-27,* AB (New York: Doubleday, 1991–2001). There was no need for the Torah to address the hypothetical question of polyandry (multiple husbands) since the practice did not exist in a patriarchal culture.

However, the Old Testament narratives do suggest that this can lead to strife among wives and preferential treatment by husbands, such as with Rachel and Leah (Gen 30) and Hannah (1 Sam 1). Nevertheless, in ancient Near Eastern culture, polygamy could actually serve to protect women who would be at risk without a father or husband, and ensured the continuation of the family line, as in the case of levirate responsibility.

Both men and women were held accountable under the law, though in different ways. For example, in Numbers 5:11-31 a man suspects his wife of infidelity and subjects her to a trial by ordeal in which she drinks "bitter water." If found guilty, she will never again bear children; otherwise she is vindicated. This law permits the husband to put his wife through the ordeal, but only within a legal framework, preventing him from taking the matter into his own hands without a trial. Thus, although Torah does not reverse the judgment of male dominance (Gen 3:16) in this case, it guards and protects the woman within the situation.[37]

Deuteronomy deals with the situation in which a married or betrothed woman has sex with another man "in a town" (Deut 22:23 NIV). If caught, they both must die. The man and the woman bear the responsibility together because the act was consensual; she could have cried out and been heard "in a town" but did not. However, if the same case occurs "out in the country" (Deut 22:25-29 NIV), where the woman could not be heard if she cried out, a presumption of innocence is given to the woman. If she is married or betrothed, her assailant must die, while she incurs no penalty. If she is an unbetrothed virgin, the man must pay the bride price (a valuable marriage present) to her parents and marry her without the option of divorce in the future. Thus, he is required to support her, since her lack of virginity would make it unlikely that another suitable marriage could be arranged.

Moses neither instituted nor encouraged divorce, although the law recognizes and allows for its existence. Yet Moses did not allow a husband to divorce his wife for just any reason; thus, the law gives women a greater sense of dignity and emphasizes the Lawgiver's concern for justice on their

---

[37]This is not to say that a woman could call for a formal trial if she suspected her husband of adultery, as he could for her. On this the text is silent, and the patriarchal culture suggests that she most likely could not.

behalf.[38] Moreover, the law limited the practice of divorce and precluded some of its abuses, thus protecting women from irresponsible accusations by their husbands and the resultant social risk, defending the honor of the household, and ensuring the ceremonial purity of the land.[39]

Deuteronomy 25:5-10 involves the situation where a woman's husband has died without their having had children, discussed above in relation to Ruth. In this case the law required the husband's brother to marry the widow and father a child on his behalf in order to establish a memorial for the man and his family, protect the widow, and guard the orderly succession of property.[40] Although the man remains the primary actor, concern for the widow leads to a limitation of his authority and prerogatives.[41] The *duty* of the man is emphasized, and the *desire* of the woman to remarry and have a child in memory of her deceased husband is assumed.

Because widows occupied a vulnerable position in Israel, legislation is solicitous on their behalf (Ex 22:22-24; Deut 14:29; 24:17).[42] In fact, if the brother of the deceased is reluctant to marry the widow, she becomes "the plaintiff in the local court," carrying out "the symbolic legal acts against the obstinate *levir.*"[43] In addition, the solidarity of the family guarantees the continuation of the tribe, as well as that of the nation in the land.[44]

In summary, the law's guardianship and discipline are discernible for both women and men in the regulations regarding marriage, despite the patriarchal influence of the ancient culture. The intention of the Torah was

---

[38]See Eckart Otto, "False Weights in the Scales of Biblical Justice? Different Views of Women from Patriarchal Hierarchy to Religious Equality in the Book of Deuteronomy," in Matthews, Levinson, and Frymer-Kensky, *Gender and Law*, 133-38; Jacob J. Finkelstein, "Sex Offenses in Sumerian Laws," *Journal of the American Oriental Society* 86 (1966): 367.

[39]Pressler, *View of Women*, 15; S. R. Driver, *A Critical and Exegetical Commentary on Deuteronomy,* 3rd ed., International Critical Commentary (Edinburgh: T&T Clark, 1895), 272. See also Kaiser's response, *Toward Old Testament Ethics,* 200.

[40]For a discussion of the management of property in the Old Testament, see Raymond Westbrook, *Property and the Family in Biblical Law*, JSOTSup 113 (Sheffield: Sheffield Academic, 1991). The term *levirate* derives from the Latin *levir*, the husband's brother who is to marry his deceased brother's widow.

[41]Pressler provides a useful discussion of the literary features of this text (*View of Women*, 63-73).

[42]See Susan T. Foh, *Women and the Word of God: A Response to Biblical Feminism* (Grand Rapids, MI: Baker, 1979), 73.

[43]Otto, "False Weights," 140.

[44]Inger Lyung, *Silence or Suppression: Attitudes Towards Women in the Old Testament* (Stockholm: Almqvist & Wiksell, 1989), 47.

"neither to create nor to perpetuate patriarchy."[45] The law's limitation on male authority was an improvement of woman's status at that time, though the situation remained less than ideal. The Mosaic law does not endorse patriarchy, yet works within this framework and regulates it, providing a degree of care and protection for women and limiting the rights of men.[46] Eckart Otto may judge the law's success in overcoming "the patrilineal and patriarchal pattern" of Hebrew society as being "too little and by no means enough."[47] But for women living at that time, it was at the least beneficial. It meant the difference between an ordered society and a chaotic anarchy with unrestrained male dominance.

MOVING FROM LAW TO GOSPEL

It would be wrong to confuse the Mosaic law with an exhaustive statement of God's will for humanity or to assume that mere compliance with it could satisfy the righteousness God requires.[48] When Jesus declared that he came to fulfill the law without abolishing it (Mt 5:17), he called his disciples to move beyond what had become a legalistic and external understanding of Torah observance to an attitude and way of life that embodied the will and character of God. He defended and illustrated this call with six antithetical rulings regarding adultery, divorce, murder, swearing falsely and keeping a vow, retaliation, and hatred (Mt 5:21-48).[49] Jesus' teaching suggests that one must move *beyond a mechanical application of the law*. His response to the question on divorce (Mt 19:1-12) and his treatment of the same subject in the legal rulings found in Matthew 5:21-48 (specifically Mt 5:27-32) serve as an example of this point.

Divorce was not instituted or encouraged by the law of Moses, although the Torah recognized and tolerated its existence, accommodating humanity's hardness of heart by providing for the orderly dissolution of a marriage when it was the lesser of the evils.[50] This is why Jesus could both

---

[45]Phyllis Trible, "Depatriarchalizing in Biblical Interpretation," *Journal of the American Academy of Religions* 41 (1973): 31.

[46]Pressler, *View of Women*, 41-42.

[47]Otto, "False Weights," 140.

[48]Stephen Westerholm, "The Law in the Sermon on the Mount: Matt 5:17-48," *Criswell Theological Review* 6 (1992): 49.

[49]Westerholm, "Law in the Sermon," 44-47.

[50]Westerholm, "Law in the Sermon," 53.

underscore the sanctity of marriage and allow for divorce (though only in extreme cases such as adultery; Mt 5:31-32; 19:3-9). In his letters, Paul also emphasizes the sanctity of marriage. However, based on Exodus 21:10-11, divorce was allowed in the case of emotional and physical neglect, which in its extreme forms constituted abuse.[51]

But consider also the words of Malachi and Ezra (the latter being a "teacher well versed in the Law of Moses"; Ezra 7:6 NIV). While Malachi was *criticizing* the returned Judeans for divorcing their Jewish wives ("You have been unfaithful to her, though she is your partner, the wife of your marriage covenant"; Mal 2:14 NIV), Ezra was *commanding* them to divorce their foreign wives ("You have been unfaithful; you have married foreign women, adding to Israel's guilt. . . . Separate yourselves"; Ezra 10:10-11 NIV). Both easy divorce and pagan religion threatened family purity within the covenant community; neither reflected an ideal situation.

However, Jesus goes beyond mere regulation of behavior by calling his disciples not only to avoid adultery but also to address the lustful desires that lead to the act (Mt 5:27-30). Passionately, and in contrast to the outward regulatory character of the law, Jesus places the intent of the heart in sharper focus (a concept already inherent in the giving of the law; see Deut 30:11-14). Viewing others as opportunities for one's own gratification deeply offends the love that respects and delights in their otherness. The point is that love (in contrast to lust) transcends the law without dismissing it.[52]

In Matthew 19:1-12 the rationale for Jesus' treatment of the law becomes even clearer, revealing an approach similar to that discussed by the apostle Paul, who declares that the law was "added because of transgressions" and guarded us until the Messiah had come (Gal 3:19 NIV; see Gal 3:23; 4:4-5). Jesus states that Moses allowed divorce because of the people's "hardness of heart," even though "it was not this way from the beginning" (Mt 19:8 NIV). However, Jesus' position on divorce reveals the progression: creation→judgment→law→gospel. The way it was "from the beginning" (creation) is contrasted with "hardness of heart" (sin and the resultant

---

[51]See David Instone-Brewer, *Divorce and Remarriage in the Bible: The Social and Literary Context* (Grand Rapids, MI: Eerdmans, 2002), 26, 196, 212. Instone-Brewer considers that Paul reaffirms these grounds in passages such as 1 Cor 7:3-5, 33-34. See Instone-Brewer, "What God Has Joined: What Does the Bible Really Teach About Divorce?," *CT* (October 2007): 29.

[52]Westerholm, "Law in the Sermon," 53.

judgment). One of the functions of the law was to regulate human behavior while facing the harsh reality of the fallen state, which included a dominating, patriarchal culture. Finally, the fulfillment of the law in the redemptive era of the Messiah goes beyond the law by focusing on the attitude of the heart. In this, however, the law was neither changed nor abolished (i.e., it was still a good thing to be orderly about divorce when it occurred). Rather, the emphasis shifted from a negative restriction to a positive initiative, carrying forward the divine intention that was present from the beginning: that men and women should be mutually supportive and function equally as caretakers of God's good creation as they follow God's instruction to "be fruitful and increase in number; fill the earth and subdue it. Rule over the fish in the sea and the birds in the sky and over every living creature that moves on the ground" (Gen 1:28 NIV).[53]

CONCLUSION

The situation in which women found themselves under the Old Testament law was less than perfect. Clearly, they continued to suffer under the heavy hand of male dominance as a result of the fall and judgment. Nevertheless, laws—including and in addition to those discussed above—regulated to a certain extent the severity of their plight. Adultery was forbidden to both men and women. A woman accused of sexual promiscuity or infidelity by her husband had the benefit of a trial. A man who raped a woman was held responsible for his actions. Divorce and remarriage were discouraged. Widowed women were to be cared for by near relatives. Punishment of women was proportionate to their offenses. Women could participate in the covenant life of the community, including festivals and the making of vows. Thus, it can be argued that the law neither created nor perpetuated patriarchy but rather reflected a progressive and protective attitude toward women. It was beneficial to women in its time, bringing order to the society in which they lived.

However, the gospel transcended a legalistic application of the law and emphasized more than the mere restriction of sinful behavior, as illustrated in Jesus' treatment of the laws regarding adultery, divorce, murder,

---

[53]See the previous chapter, "Gender in Creation and Fall: Genesis 1–3," for a fuller discussion of God's intent for humanity.

swearing falsely, keeping a vow, and traditional understandings of retaliation and hatred. It demonstrated the next step in the progression from creation marred by sin (and resultant judgment), by temporary way of the law, to the redemption inaugurated by the Messiah in the gospel. However, to a degree even the New Testament situation is incomplete: creation still waits for the *full* redemption found in the contrast of our here and now with the "then and there" of New Testament eschatology.

Jesus treated women with dignity and respect. Women, as part of the priesthood of believers, were permitted to learn (1 Tim 2:11), teach (Acts 18:26), lead in worship (1 Cor 11:4-16), and even serve as apostles (Junia, Rom 16:7). Husbands were called to mutually love and serve their wives, who, along with their children and slaves, were no longer to be treated as property (Eph 5:21-28). Thus, believers have the joyful privilege of implementing this redemptive message while living in hope of the full redemption that is to come at the Messiah's return.

4

WOMEN LEADERS
IN THE BIBLE

Linda L. Belleville

• • • • •

ONE CAN READILY FIND STUDIES of women leaders in the Bible.
Yet three research tools are now in hand that make revisiting the topic
both prudent and worthwhile. First, there are recently published Qumran
papyri and Greco-Roman inscriptions that challenge considerably the
common stereotype of women in both Jewish and Greco-Roman circles
as little more than chattel.[1] Second, there are current sociohistorical studies that show that there were more women leaders in antiquity, particularly in formerly male-dominated arenas, than has commonly been
acknowledged.[2] Third, Greek computer databases permit a more informed

---

[1]The Babata documents from Qumran, in particular, show the legal capabilities of women in
the most religiously conservative Judean circles. Here is a woman who inherits the properties
of two husbands, buys and sells properties, and supervises her holdings. The number of legal
transactions that Babata handled is remarkable even by modern standards. Thirty-five legal
documents were found in her possession. This accords with what is found in early mishnaic
legal materials. A woman of independent means could bring suit for damages (m. B. Qam. 1:3),
sell property in her possession (m. Ketub. 11:2), testify in court (m. Ketub. 2:5-6), swear an
oath (m. Shevu. 5:1; m. Ketub. 9:4; m. Ned. 11:9), manage her earnings (m. B. Metz. 1:5), and
arrange her own marriage (m. Qidd. 2:1). Greco-Roman inscriptions show that women under
Roman law enjoyed more freedoms and privileges than has traditionally been supposed. These
privileges included ownership and disposal of property, terminating a marriage, suing for
child support and custody, making a will, holding office, swearing an oath, and giving testimony. For further discussion of women's roles in Jewish and Greco-Roman first-century society, see Linda L. Belleville, *Women Leaders and the Church* (Grand Rapids, MI: Baker, 2000),
71-96.

[2]Literature on women in antiquity has mushroomed since the 1960s. For an overview and bibliography, see Belleville, *Women Leaders and the Church*, 71-96.

and accurate understanding of women's roles in Scripture than was attainable previously.[3]

WOMEN LEADERS IN THE OLD TESTAMENT

Few today contest the fact that women appear in a variety of ministry roles in the Old Testament. The key questions are, Were these *leadership* roles? Did the community of faith affirm women in such positions? The biblical record yields a yes on both accounts.

From early on, women were affirmed as leaders. Miriam is a good example. She is portrayed in the Exodus narratives as a leader in and of her own right, and is accorded a level of respect similar to that of Aaron and Moses. The congregation of Israel viewed her role as essential to its mission, refusing to move ahead on one occasion until she was restored to leadership after her criticism of Moses (Num 12:15).

Her impact can be gauged by the affirmation she received from subsequent generations. Tradition commends her as a *prophet* sent by God to join her brothers in *leading* Israel out of Egypt and *redeeming* them from the land of slavery. Her memory is celebrated by the community of faith for the leadership she provided at this crucial juncture in Israel's history (Mic 6:4; cf. Ex 15:20).

Women proved to be capable leaders during Israel's subsequent history. During the period of the judges, Deborah particularly comes to mind. She assumed a variety of leadership roles, including prophet (Judg 4:4, 6-7), judge (Judg 4:5), and mother of Israel (Judg 5:7).[4] In the role of prophet, her leadership was accepted without dispute as from "the LORD, the God of Israel," indicated by Barak's response to her summons (Judg 4:6).[5] This is due, in part, to cultural familiarity. Archaeological

---

The decision whether the Greek name Junia(s) in Rom 16:7 is the masculine Junias or the feminine "Junia . . . outstanding among the apostles" (NIV) can now be determined with relative ease and confidence. See the second section of this chapter, "Women Leaders in the New Testament."

[3]E.g., Thesaurus Linguae Graecae (ancient literary works), the Packard Humanities Institute (ancient papyri and inscriptions), and the Perseus Project (archaic and classical texts and artifacts).

[4]The Hebrew terms *shaphat* (verb; Judg 4:4) and *mishpat* (participle; Judg 4:5) connote the work of a "law-giver, judge, or governor" as their primary meaning. See Francis Brown, S. R. Driver, and Charles A. Briggs, *A Hebrew and English Lexicon of the Old Testament* (1906). The twofold usage in this text renders Deborah's judgeship beyond dispute.

[5]Barak's submission to a woman has sometimes been construed as a sign of weakness for two reasons: his insistence on her presence in battle, and Deborah's reply (Judg 4:8-9). In response

finds show that female prophets, both professional and lay, were well known in antiquity.[6]

Deborah's stature as a judge is confirmed by the types of cases she handled. Intertribal disputes too difficult for the local judges fell to her (Deut 17:8).[7] She held court in the hill country of Ephraim between Ramah and Bethel, where men and women alike came to her to have their disputes settled (Judg 4:4-5; a similar itinerant route to that of the prophet Samuel; see 1 Sam 7:16).[8]

Deborah's ability as a commander in chief is also clear. When the tribes were incapable of standing together against their oppressors, Deborah not only united them but led them to victory. This is underscored by the placement of her name ahead of that of Israel's general: "Deborah and Barak . . . sang [a victory song] on that day" (Judg 5:1).

---

to the first issue, it should be noted that Barak's demand that Deborah go with him most likely meant that he valued her leadership as a prophet so greatly that he would not fight without her. In response to the second, it should be noted that the NIV's "*Very well* . . . I will go with you" (changed to "*Certainly* I will" in TNIV) and the TEV's "All right" (Judg 4:9) are misleading. The Hebrew participle used along with a finite form of the same verb serves to intensify rather than suggest a grudging agreement: "*Surely* [or 'Indeed'] I will go with you" (most translations). The LXX translator reflects this understanding by rendering it with the intensive: *poreuomenē poreusomai*. See Bruce K. Waltke and M. O'Connor, *An Introduction to Biblical Hebrew Syntax* (Winona Lake, IN: Eisenbrauns, 1990), 35.3.1-2; E. Kautzsche, *Gesenius' Hebrew Grammar*, trans. A. E. Cowley (Oxford: Oxford University Press, 1910), no. 133L; and F. C. Conybeare and St. George Stock, *A Grammar of Septuagint Greek* (repr., Grand Rapids, MI: Zondervan, 1980), no. 81.

The NIV's "*but because* of the way you are going about this, the honor will not be yours" is also questionable (Judg 4:9). *'Epes* with a noun clause introduced by *ki* is restrictive, not causative: "*However,* you will have no glory on the enterprise" (most translations). See Ronald J. Williams, *Hebrew Syntax*, 2nd ed. (Toronto: University of Toronto Press, 1976), nos. 427, 558, "a restrictive clause"; cf. Waltke and O'Connor, *Introduction to Biblical Hebrew Syntax*, 35.3.5e: "but [contrary to your expectations], there will be no glory for you."

[6]For instance, there were a large number of female prophets (lay and professional) at Mari, Syria, during the third and second millennia BC who were contemporaries of Israel's patriarchs and judges. This included King Zimrilim's own daughter. See Abraham Malamat, "A Forerunner of Biblical Prophecy: The Mari Documents," in *Ancient Israelite Religion*, ed. P. D. Miller, P. D. Hanson, and S. D. McBride (Philadelphia: Fortress, 1987), 33-47.

[7]"If a judicial decision is too difficult for you to make between one kind of bloodshed and another, one kind of legal right and another, or one kind of assault and another—any such matters of dispute in your towns—then you shall immediately go up to the place the LORD your God will choose" (Deut 17:8). Deborah's legal role is sometimes disputed. See, e.g., Paul R. House, *1, 2 Kings*, NAC 8 (Nashville: Broadman, 1995), 197. This, however, overlooks legal language such as *ham-mishpat*, which has to do with decisions made in response to particular legal inquiries. See Robert Boling, *Judges*, AB 6A (New York: Doubleday, 1975), 95n5.

[8]The political involvement of female prophets in antiquity is well documented. See Herbert Huffmon, "Prophecy in the Mari Letters," *Biblical Archaeologist* 31 (1968): 101-24.

Deborah's overall leadership skills are highlighted in several ways. Her gender is placed first for emphasis: "Now Deborah, a woman prophet" (Judg 4:4 Bible in Basic English). Her judicial role is expressed in the participial form ("judging Israel"), thereby emphasizing her ongoing activity (Judg 4:4). Her posture ("she used to sit under the palm," Judg 4:5) is that of an official exercising her duties. As a judge, she made a profound difference. Before her tenure "the roads were abandoned; travelers took to winding paths. Village life in Israel ceased" (Judg 5:6-7 NIV 1984). With Deborah's ascendancy came a return of security in the countryside.

In her honor, the site was named "the palm of Deborah" (Judg 4:5), and the title "mother in Israel" was bestowed on her (Judg 5:7). The phrase "in Israel" commends her as a national leader. "Mother in Israel" is comparable today to an honorary doctorate bestowed in recognition of national leadership contributions.[9]

Similarly, the prophet Huldah provided leadership during the time that prophets of the stature of Jeremiah (Jer 1:2), Zephaniah (Zeph 1:1), Nahum (Nah 3:8-10), and Habakkuk (Hab 1:6) were active. Huldah was related by marriage to a court official, which placed her at the center of public affairs (along with Zephaniah). Her renown as a religious counselor was such that when King Josiah commanded his advisers to "go, inquire of the LORD . . . concerning the words of this book that has been found [the book of the law]," they sought out Huldah (2 Kings 22:13).

The size and prestige of the embassy that sought her counsel indicates something about not only the seriousness of the situation but also Huldah's professional stature: the high priest (Hilkiah), the father of a future governor (Ahikam), the son of a prophet (Achbor), the secretary of state (Shaphan), and the king's officer (Asaiah). Huldah's counsel was immediately heeded, and sweeping religious reforms resulted (2 Kings 22:8-20; 23:1-25).

Some speculate that the king's advisers picked Huldah because she was a political insider. Yet the prophet Zephaniah was more closely identified with the ruling class as a descendant of King Hezekiah (715–686 BC; Zeph 1:1). More likely Huldah was approached because of her track record of

---

[9]See Roman codes, such as Theodosian Code 16.8.4.

prophetic leadership and expert counsel. The narrator calls attention to
the fact that the whole people of God (including "the prophets") pledged
themselves afresh to the covenant as a result of her counsel (2 Kings 23:1-3).
Indeed, Huldah's role in Josiah's reforms may have helped elevate all the
true prophets to their rightful place in Judah's religious community.

It is sometimes remarked that God permitted women to lead at times
when Israel lacked adequate male leadership. But the examples of Miriam,
Deborah, and Huldah, who ministered in the context of other renowned
male figures (Moses, Barak, Josiah, Jeremiah, etc.), demonstrate the opposite. Others plead exceptional circumstances. They argue that Israel's
nomadic existence during the wilderness years and a leadership vacuum
after years of slavery in Egypt called for exceptional measures. The period
of the judges, they point out, was a unique time when everyone did whatever was deemed right in their own eyes. Yet if there was any time when
wise spiritual counsel was in evidence, strong leadership was in place, and
the nation was on an even keel, it was during King Josiah's reign—and
Huldah's tenure. The prophet Jeremiah speaks highly of Josiah (Jer 22:15-16),
as does the author of 2 Kings 22:2.

Why, though, were there so few women leaders? The lack of a comprehensive history of the period makes it difficult to know actual percentages.
Matter-of-fact references to female prophets may indicate that women
such as Miriam, Deborah, and Huldah were only the tip of the leadership
iceberg. There are a number of unnamed women that suggest as much: the
female prophet whom Isaiah is instructed to marry (Is 8:3), the female
prophets Ezekiel speaks against (Ezek 13:17- 23), and Noadiah, mentioned
by Nehemiah (Neh 6:14). Some, like their male counterparts, were lured
by fame and fortune. The prophet Ezekiel pronounced judgment against
both the sons of Israel and the daughters of Judah, who prophesied "out of
their own imagination" (Ezek 13:2, 17; cf. Jer 28:1-17).

There were women who served as advisers to heads of state. One example is the "wise woman" from Tekoa during David's reign who advised the
king regarding Absalom (2 Sam 14:1-33). Another example is the "wise
woman" of Abel-beth-maacah who saved her city from destruction at the
hand of David's troops by giving expert counsel (2 Sam 20:16-22). Such

would not have been the case had these women not had significant standing and authority within their local setting.[10]

Women leaders are also well attested in the political arena. City records and inscriptions give ample evidence of their civic-mindedness. Women's names appear in connection with the underwriting of temples, theaters, gymnasiums, public baths, and other civic projects.[11] From time to time women even served as heads of state. Athaliah ruled Judah 842–836 BC, albeit unwisely (2 Kings 11:1-3; 2 Chron 22:10-12); Salome Alexandra, honored queen of the Hasmonean dynasty, reigned 76–67 BC; and Cleopatra was the effective ruler of Egypt from 51 to 31 BC.

Though there appear to have been more men than women in the political spotlight, it was not due to a lack of intelligence, temperament, or political savvy. Nor is there any notion in the Old Testament that women leaders were inappropriate. The only exception is the Levitical priesthood, where purity laws precluded Jewish women's serving in certain ceremonial roles due to uncleanness related to childbirth and menstruation. Men too were excluded, but for different reasons (e.g., not being a Levite, sexual uncleanness, or physical defect). Other roles, however, show women and men serving side by side. Women were involved in building and furnishing the tabernacle (Ex 35:22-26) and standing watch at its entrance (Ex 38:8; 1 Sam 2:22).[12] They played musical instruments in public processions (Ps 68:25), danced and sang at communal and national festivals (Judg 21:19-23), and chanted at victory celebrations (1 Sam 18:7). Women brought offerings, performed rituals prescribed for purification and pardon, performed vows (Lev 12:1-8; 13:29-39; 15:19-29; 1 Sam 1:11, 24-28), and were recipients of divine communication (Judg 13:2-7; 8-20).[13] There is also

---

[10]See Claudia Camp, "The Wise Women of 2 Samuel: A Role Model for Women in Early Israel?," *CBQ* 43 (1981): 14-29.

[11]For example, Phile, the first woman magistrate in Priene, Asia Minor, dedicated at her own expense a cistern and the water pipes (Epigraphica 2.5.G; first century BC). Another woman, Eumachia, was public priestess of Pompeii, Italy, and patron of the guild of fullers, one of the most influential trade guilds of the city (Corpus Inscriptionum Latinarum 10.810, first century AD). See H. W. Pleket, *Epigraphica II: Texts on the Social History of the Greek World* (Leiden: Brill, 1969).

[12]The Hebrew *sebo'* (to serve) is used elsewhere of the Levites to describe their role in the tabernacle (Num 4:23; 8:24) and of Israel's warriors (Num 31:7, 42).

[13]In these respects they functioned in a parallel fashion to women in the pagan cults. See Phyllis Bird, "The Place of Women in the Israelite Cultus," in Miller, Hanson, and McBride, *Ancient Israelite Religion*, 397-411.

every indication that women and men worshiped and ministered side by side. Together they sang in the choir (2 Chron 35:25; Ezra 2:65; Neh 7:67) and offered sacrifices (1 Sam 1:24-25).

WOMEN LEADERS IN THE NEW TESTAMENT

Women leaders come to the fore with the advent of the apostolic period. Several factors explain this. One is the Spirit's empowerment of both women and men for ministry. The outpouring of the Spirit at Pentecost was an equal-opportunity event. The women among Jesus' disciples were enabled for witness just as the men were (Acts 1:8, 14-15; 2:17-18). The result was a major paradigm shift from the male priesthood of the Jewish cult to the charismatic worship format and gender-inclusive leadership of the early church.[14] "When you assemble," Paul states, "each one has a psalm, has a teaching, has a revelation, has a tongue, has an interpretation" (1 Cor 14:26 NASB).

Another factor was the involvement of women in leadership positions in Greco-Roman religion and politics.[15] Recent sociohistorical studies have shown that official religion in the Roman Empire was gender inclusive and that women leaders were a known phenomenon. For example, while Paul was planting the Ephesian church, Iuliane served as high priestess of the imperial cult in Magnesia, a city fifteen miles southeast of Ephesus.[16] Also, because religion and society were inseparable, to lead in one arena was often to lead in the other. Mendora, for example, served at one time or another during Paul's tenure as magistrate, priestess, and chief financial officer of Sillyon, a town in Pisidia, Asia.[17]

Women in the Roman church. The more Romanized the area, the more visible were women leaders. Since Paul's missionary efforts focused on the urban areas of the Roman Empire, it should come as no surprise that most of the women named as church leaders in the New Testament surface in his letters.

---

[14]See Stanley Grenz's "Biblical Priesthood and Women in Ministry."

[15]There were some political exclusions. Women were not present in the Roman assemblies and did not hold positions of command in the military. Public speaking roles were also scarce. Although this restriction was increasingly a formality, women continued to need a male guardian for performing important transactions such as making a will, selling a piece of land, freeing a slave, entering into a contract, or accepting an inheritance.

[16]Die Inschriften von Magnesia am Maeander, 158.

[17]Inscriptiones Graecae ad res Romanas pertinentes 3.800-902.

This is especially true of his letter to the Roman church. The letter carrier was a woman (Rom 16:1-2), and at least five of the nine women Paul greets were ministry colleagues ("coworkers"; Rom 16:3, 6-7, 12). English translations stemming from the 1940s to the 1980s tend to obscure this fact. A hierarchical, noninclusive understanding of leadership during this period is partly to blame: women cannot be leaders, so the language of leadership must be eliminated. Phoebe becomes a "servant" and Paul's "helper" (instead of a church deacon and Paul's patron; Rom 16:1-2), and the esteemed apostle Junia becomes the masculine "Junias" (Rom 16:7).[18]

Junia is especially to be noted. Among the leaders recognized at Rome, she receives highest marks. Paul greets her and a coworker named Andronicus as "my fellow Jews who have been in prison with me. They are outstanding among the apostles" (Rom 16:7 NIV). Andronicus and Junia could have been among "all the apostles" (beyond the Twelve) or among the five hundred to whom Christ appeared (1 Cor 15:6-7).[19] But the facts better fit their having been among the visitors from Rome who responded to Peter's preaching at Pentecost (Acts 2). Both were Jewish, both had Greek (Hellenized) names, and both preceded Paul "in Christ" (Rom 16:7). This would place them most naturally during the early years of the church's outreach in Jerusalem (Acts 2–7).

Some try to circumvent the attribution of apostleship to a woman by changing the gender. The majority of English translations done from the 1940s to the early 1970s translate *Iounian* as the masculine name Junias.[20]

---

[18]Concerning Phoebe, the translation "deaconess" in Rom 16:1 (RSV, JB, NJB, Phillips) is anachronistic, for the feminine *diakonissa* was not used during the apostolic period. The first clear instance is about the time of the Council of Nicaea in AD 325 (canon 19).

[19]Paul uses *apostolos* more broadly than "the Twelve." James, Andronicus, Junia, Barnabas, Silas, Timothy, and Apollos are all called apostles (Rom 16:7; 1 Cor 4:6, 9; 9:5-6; Gal 1:19; 2:9; 1 Thess 1:1; 2:7).

[20]This requires that *Iounias* be understood as a contraction of the masculine name *Iounianus*. In this case, the masculine accusative ending of *Iounias* would be the same as the feminine accusative ending of *Iounia*—except for the accent. The contracted (or shortened) form would have a circumflex. The feminine would have an acute accent. Ancient manuscripts typically did not contain accents, so the Greek technically can go either way.

Even so, from the time accents were added to the text until the early decades of the twentieth century, editions of the Greek New Testament printed the acute accent and not the circumflex. The reasons for this are clear. The shortened form of Junianus would be Junas, not Junias. Also, while it is true that Greek nicknames were abbreviations of longer names, Latin nicknames were typically formed by lengthening the name, not shortening it—hence Priscilla for Prisca (Acts 18:2,

On the other hand, older translations (e.g., Wycliffe Bible, Tyndale New Testament, Geneva Bible, KJV, Weymouth), more recent revisions (NKJV, NRSV, NAB, REB, NIV), and newer translations (e.g., God's Word, NLT, Holman Christian Standard, NET, ESV) render *Iounian* as the feminine Junia. They do so for good reasons. The masculine name Junias does not occur in any inscription, letterhead, piece of writing, epitaph, or literary work of the New Testament period. The feminine Junia, however, appears widely and frequently. Perhaps the best-known Junia is the half-sister of famed Roman general Brutus.[21] The name Junia also appears in first-century inscriptions from such familiar New Testament locales as Ephesus, Didyma, Lydia, Troas and Bithynia.[22] Junia is found as well on tombstones—especially in and around Rome.[23]

Others attempt to get around Paul's apostolic acknowledgment by translating the Greek prepositional phrase as "esteemed *by*" or "*in the sight of* the apostles" rather than "outstanding *among* the apostles." To do this, however, is to introduce a strange thought for Paul. In Paul's writings there are "*us* apostles" (1 Cor 4:9), *Christ's* apostles (1 Thess 2:6-7), "*his [God's]* holy apostles" (Eph 3:5), "*the other* apostles" (1 Cor 9:5), those "who were *already apostles*" (Gal 1:17), and "any *other* apostle" (Gal 1:19). There are also the "pillars" (Gal 2:9) and the "super-apostles" (2 Cor 12:11), but not "*the* apostles." The terminology appears in the kerygma that preceded Paul. Paul states in 1 Corinthians 15:3-7 that he was faithful in transmitting to his converts and church plants "as of first importance" what he himself had received—"that he [Christ] appeared . . . to all the apostles." But "the apostles" is not native to Paul's own thinking or speaking.

18, 26; cf. Rom 16:3; 1 Cor 16:19; 2 Tim 4:19). See John Thorley, "Junia a Woman Apostle," *Novum Testamentum* 38 (1996): 24-26.

[21]Plutarch, *Marcus Brutus* 7.1.4.

[22]The inscription evidence includes Ephesos Ionia 627.1; 788.1; 822.1; 2373.1; Didyma Ionia 225.1; Tituli Asiae Minoris V.1403.5; Kyzikene Propontiskueste Mysia/Troas 2077.11; Die Inschriften von Prusias ad Hypium 93.1.

[23]E.g., "Here lie infants [*Anu*]nia *Iounia Noeta*," Corpus inscriptionum Judaicarum 10.1; cf. 303.1. For additional primary sources, see Peter Lampe, *Die stadtrömischen Christen in den ersten beiden Jahrhunderten*, Wissenschaftliche Untersuchungen zum Neuen Testament 2/18 (Tübingen: Mohr, 1987), 156-64. The evidence for *Junia* is so compelling that even the most traditional scholars are now conceding that *Iounian* in Rom 16:7 is feminine. See, e.g., Thomas Schreiner, "Women in Ministry," in *Two Views on Women in Ministry*, ed. James R. Beck and Craig L. Blomberg (Grand Rapids, MI: Zondervan, 2001), 198.

To say that Junia was "esteemed *by*" or "prominent *in the sight of* the apostles" is to ignore early Greek translations and commentaries. For example, the Vulgate, the standard Latin translation of the Western church, has "Junia . . . notable *among* the apostles" (*nobiles in apostolis*). John Chrysostom, bishop of Constantinople in the fourth century, states, "To be even *amongst these of note*, just consider what a great enconium this is! . . . Oh how great is the devotion of this woman [Junia] that she should be even counted worthy of the appellation of apostle!"[24]

More recently the translation "outstanding among the apostles" has been challenged on the basis of usage outside the Bible. It is argued that every known instance of the adjective *episēmos* with the preposition *en* and the personal dative bears the exclusive sense of "well-known *to*" rather than the inclusive "notable *among*."[25] The first implies that Junia was outside the group of apostles but esteemed *by* them; the second implies that she was honored *as one of* them.

But all considerations support the latter. For one, *episēmos* is the adjective "notable" and not the passive verb "well known to."[26] Two, it is a compound of *epi* (upon) and *sēma* (mark), yielding the literal sense "having a mark, inscription," "bearing the marks of," and the metaphorical sense "remarkable, notable."[27] This would make Junia a "distinguished" or "remarkable" *member of* (not simply *known to*) the apostles. Three, overwhelming usage of the preposition *en* and the personal dative (inside and outside the New Testament) bears the local meaning "in/among."[28]

---

[24]John Chrysostom, *Homilies on Romans* 31 (on Rom 16:7). Subsequent Greek commentators echo the attribution (Theodoret, *Epistles* 82.2 [fourth century]; *Catena on the Epistle to the Romans* 519.32 [fifth century]; *Chronicon Paschale* [seventh century]; John of Damascus, *Epistles* 95.565 [seventh century]).

[25]E.g., Michael Burer and Daniel B. Wallace, "Was Junia Really an Apostle? A Re-examination of Rom 16.7," *NTS* 47 (2001): 76-91.

[26]None of the standard Greek lexicons support such a meaning. L&N, no. 28.31, has "pertaining to being well known or outstanding, either because of positive or negative characteristics— 'outstanding,' 'famous,' 'notorious,' 'infamous.'" Indeed, L&N render Rom 16:7 as "they are outstanding among the apostles" (contra Burer and Wallace, "Was Junia Really an Apostle?," 84n39).

[27]LSJ s.v.

[28]A. T. Robertson lists numerous examples of an adjective followed by *en* plus the personal plural dative as "inclusive" (i.e., a member of the larger group). See Robertson, *A Grammar of the Greek New Testament in the Light of Historical Research* (Nashville: Broadman, 1934), 587. See, e.g., Mt 2:6, "But you, Bethlehem, . . . are by no means least among the rulers of Judah [*en tois hēgemosin Iouda*]"; Acts 4:34, "There was not a needy person among them [*en autois*]."

While dative personal nouns often designate the recipients (to/for), this is not the case for the preposition *en*. In fact, the standard grammars and lexicons lack salient examples of it bearing the sense "to."[29] On the other hand, *episēmos en* with either a personal or impersonal object in each case yields the meaning "notable *among*," not "well known *to*."

> Additions to Esther 16:22 (NRSV): "Therefore, you shall observe this with all good cheer as *a notable day among* your commemorative festivals."

> Josephus, *Jewish Wars* 2.418: "So the men of power . . . sent ambassadors; some to Florus . . . and others to Agrippa, *eminent among* whom were Saul, Antipas, and Costobarus."

> Lucian, *On Salaried Posts* 28: "So you must raise your thirsty voice like a stranded frog, taking pains to be *conspicuous among* those who praise [the mistress' page]."

> Lucian, *Dialogues of the Dead* 438: "We had quite a crowd with us on our way down, *most distinguished among whom* were our rich countryman Ismenodorus [and others]."

 Thus the clearest reading of this reference to Junia yields an example of a woman not only functioning as an apostle in the New Testament church but being highly esteemed as such by Paul and his apostolic colleagues.

---

[29]Burer and Wallace's study ("Was Junia Really an Apostle?") assumes a conclusion not found in the evidence. Despite their assertions to the contrary, they fail to offer one clear biblical or extrabiblical parallel to support their position that in this idiom the *en* phrase is exclusive, not inclusive. First, it should be noted that evidence for this construction (*episēmos* as an adjective modified by *en*) is exceedingly rare, much too rare to support their sweeping conclusions. They do concede, somewhat grudgingly, that the one certain instance (Lucian, *On Salaried Posts* 28) in fact supports the traditional view of Rom 16:7. On the other hand, what *they* perceive as the closest parallel to Rom 16:7 becomes so only because it is not cited accurately. When citing Psalms of Solomon 2.6, which reads *en episēmō en tois ethnesin*, they drop the preposition *en*, permitting *episēmos* to be read as a straight adjective modifying the preceding "seal" (thus "with a seal, a spectacle among the Gentiles"). But that strains the plain sense of the grammar in every way; much more likely it is a neuter noun ("with a mark," "brand"). Thus: "Their [captive Jews'] neck was *with* a seal [*en sphragidi*], *with* a slave-brand [*en episēmō*] among the Gentiles [*en tois ethnesin*]" (i.e., describing what made "their captivity" in Babylon "grievous"). "Aphrodite, glorious to mortals" (Euripides, *Hippolytus* 103) looks to be an exclusive example. But translators (e.g., Rex Warner, 1949; Michael R. Halleran, 1995) and scholars on this text typically define *episēmos* as "renowned, notorious among" and not "glorious to." See Richard Hamilton, *Euripides' Hippolytus: Commentary* (Bryn Mawr, PA: Bryn Mawr Greek Commentaries, 1980–1982), 8, line 103. Moreover, the Greek of Euripides predates Paul's by five centuries, when the adjective had not yet acquired a comparative sense, and thus does not offer a contemporary parallel.

This flies in the face of arguments that Jesus excluded women from the Twelve because their gender precluded their functioning as apostles.[30]

Women in the Philippian church. Euodia and Syntyche are singled out as leaders of the Philippian church. That Paul does this is significant. It is not his practice to name names in letters to his churches. In part, the public nature of his letters precluded it. They were written to be read aloud and concerned matters that affected the whole church (Col 4:16). When Paul does mention someone by name, it is with decided intentionality.

Paul's initial evangelistic foray in Philippi took place among a group of Jewish women during Sabbath prayers (Acts 16:13-15). Some, such as Euodia and Syntyche, then partnered with Paul in the preaching of the gospel, as well as in leading the congregation. Paul's public appeal to a "loyal companion" to "help these women" to "be of the same mind in the Lord" says something about their stature within the Christian community (Phil 4:2-3).

Euodia's and Syntyche's differences were not of a petty or personal nature. Paul speaks to the issue of conflict in the church, spending significant time exhorting the church to stand firm in "one spirit" (Phil 1:27), to be of the "same mind" (Phil 2:2, 5; 3:15), "striving side by side" for "the faith of the gospel" and in no way intimidated by their opponents (Phil 1:27-28). Much of this same language is used of Euodia and Syntyche. They too are called to be of "the same mind," having "struggled beside" Paul in "the work of the gospel" (Phil 4:2-3). Their role so clearly involves leadership that their disagreement put the unity of the church in jeopardy.

There is no hint that these or any other women should not be in leadership roles. If this had been so, Paul would have said as much. He is not shy to do so elsewhere (e.g., 1 Tim 1:19-20). Nor is the disagreement an indication that women are not well suited for leadership. Paul himself sharply disagreed with a colleague on at least one occasion (Acts 15:36-41). At issue is simply two leaders not seeing things the same way in the context of outside opposition to the church.

Women in the Cenchreaen church. Phoebe is commended as "a deacon of the church at Cenchreae" (Rom 16:1). Some translations obscure this

---

[30]Contra Michael J. Wilkins, "Women in the Teaching and Example of Jesus," in *Women and Men in Ministry: A Complementary Perspective*, ed. Robert L. Saucy and Judith TenElshof (Chicago: Moody, 2001), 91-112, esp. 105-6; on this matter see chapter five in this volume.

fact by rendering *diakonos* as "servant" (e.g., NKJV, NASU, NIV). To do so is to miss the official character of Paul's commendation. Phoebe was Paul's designated letter carrier to the Roman church (Rom 16:2).

A church's welcome was based on the presentation of credentials. This is why Paul routinely provided credentials for his letter carriers (e.g., 2 Cor 8:16-24; Eph 6:21-22; Phil 2:25-30; Col 4:7-9). Since Phoebe was a virtual unknown, strong credentials would have been critical in her case. "Servant" would hardly have sufficed in the imperial capital. "A *deacon* of the church in Cenchreae" is what was needed (NIV, NRSV; cf. NLT, NEB, CEV).

Here we do well to take our cue from the early church fathers. "Deacon" is how they universally understood Phoebe's role. Origen cites Romans 16:7 as an example of the fact that "even women are instituted deacons in the church." John Chrysostom understands *diakonos* to be a term of "rank."[31]

Paul instructs the Roman church to "receive [Phoebe] in the Lord" and to "give her any help she may need" (Rom 16:2). Elsewhere this is technical language for an itinerant missionary (e.g., 1 Cor 16:10-11; 2 Cor 7:15). In Phoebe's case it indicates that Paul entrusted her with a mission beyond carrying his letter. This was certainly within the scope of a deacon's job description. Ignatius, bishop of Rome at the turn of the century, twice refers to a deacon of one church serving as an ambassador to another church.[32]

Women in the Lycus Valley churches. Priscilla and Aquila are twice greeted by Paul as "co-workers" (Rom 16:3-5; 2 Tim 4:19). It is a common misconception within evangelical circles that Greco-Roman women rarely left their house and that when they did go out they did not speak to members of the opposite sex. There was no stratum of Roman society where this was the case. Even the wives of Roman artisans worked side by side with their husbands (Acts 18:3). Priscilla and Aquila were no exception. They are recognized throughout the New Testament as a team.

The language Paul uses of both Priscilla and Aquila points to the equivalent of today's church planter, a role very much like his own. They are Paul's "co-workers in Christ Jesus," "they risked their lives" for him, and "all the churches of the Gentiles are grateful to them" (Rom 16:3-4).

---

[31]Origen, *Homilies on Romans* 10.17 (third century); John Chrysostom, *Homilies on Romans* 31 (on Rom 16:1; late fourth century).

[32]Ignatius, *Letter to the Philadelphians* 10.1; *Letter to the Ephesians* 2.1.

What is unusual is the order of their names. As in our "Mr. and Mrs." nomenclature, the Roman husband's name typically appeared first. When New Testament writers refer to their occupation of tentmakers and to "their house," the order is "Aquila and Priscilla" (Acts 18:2; 1 Cor 16:19). But when ministry is in view, the order is "Priscilla and Aquila" (Acts 18:18; Rom 16:3; cf. 2 Tim 4:19). This is also the case with the instruction of Apollos (Acts 18:26), suggesting that Priscilla possessed the dominant ministry and leadership skills of the duo.[33]

Women were also among the ranks of deacons in the Ephesian church: "Women [deacons], likewise, are to be worthy of respect, not slanderers, temperate, and trustworthy in everything" (1 Tim 3:11, my translation). That Paul is speaking of women in a recognized leadership role is apparent not only from the listing of credentials but also from the fact that these credentials are duplicates of those listed for male deacons in 1 Timothy 3:8-10. Also, the Greek word order of 1 Timothy 3:8, 11 is identical: "[Male] deacons likewise [*diakonous hōsautōs*] must be serious, not double-tongued, not indulging in much wine. . . . Women likewise [*gynaikas hōsautōs*] must be serious, not slanderers, but temperate" (1 Tim 3:8, 11).

It is commonly assumed that despite the meaning of *authentein*, the prohibition "I do not permit a woman to *teach*" is absolute because authority resides in the act of teaching (or in the person who teaches) and women cannot exercise authority in the church. It is also assumed that by the time of the Pastorals teaching was something "official" and what "elders" did, and women were not permitted to hold office or be an elder.

There are several difficulties with this line of argument. For one, it is anachronistic. Teaching in the New Testament period was an activity and not an office. All are called to "go . . . and make disciples of all nations, baptizing . . . and *teaching* them to obey everything that [Christ] commanded" (Mt 28:19-20). It was also a spiritual gift that was given to women

---

[33]Luke is precise throughout Acts about the order of names in ministry teams. For example, when the famous missionaries are commissioned by the church at Antioch, the order is "Barnabas and Saul" (Acts 11:30; 12:25; 13:2-7). But when Saul takes the lead, the order becomes "Paul and Barnabas" (Acts 13:9-12, 43; 14:12, 20; 15:2, 22, 35). The two exceptions are Acts 15:12, 25, where political diplomacy and expediency dictated the order. Andreas Köstenberger claims that 1 Cor 16:19 proves otherwise: "Aquila and Prisca, together with the church that meets in their house, greet you warmly." See Köstenberger, "Book Review," *JETS* 44 (2001): 346. But "their house" is a statement of ownership, not ministry, thus warranting the order.

and men alike. Teaching is found in all of the Pauline lists of gifts and was an integral part of every facet of church life (Rom 12:6-8; 1 Cor 12:28-31; Eph 4:11). When the church at Corinth gathered in worship, it was presumed that there would be those with a "word of knowledge" (1 Cor 12:8 NASB) and that each would have a psalm, *a teaching*, a revelation, a tongue, or an interpretation (1 Cor 14:26). Both men and women publicly prayed and prophesied during worship (1 Cor 11:5). Prophecy, Paul states, *instructs* the congregations (1 Cor 14:19; *katēchēsō*) and results in "all learning" (*pante manthanōsin*; 1 Cor 14:31, my translation). Indeed, the whole congregation at Colossae was called to "teach and admonish one another" (Col 3:16).

Some counter with the claim that teaching in the Pastorals involved teaching doctrine, which women could not do. The flaw here lies in translating the Greek phrase *tē hygiainousē didaskalia* as "sound doctrine" instead of "sound teaching" (1 Tim 1:10; 4:6; cf. 1 Tim 6:1, 3; 2 Tim 4:3; Titus 1:9; 2:1). Doctrine as a system of thought (i.e., dogma) is foreign to Paul's letters. In contrast, Paul urges Timothy to avoid "profane myths and old wives' tales" (1 Tim 4:7), to practice godliness (1 Tim 4:7-8), to honor God as the one true Savior of all people (1 Tim 4:9-11), and to encourage slaves to treat their earthly masters with full respect (1 Tim 6:1-2). He is teaching Christian living—not doctrine. Teaching was subject to evaluation just like any other gift. This is why Paul instructed Timothy to publicly rebuke anyone who departed from "the sound words of our Lord Jesus Christ" (1 Tim 6:3; see 1 Tim 5:20).

Others claim that the leadership qualifications of an overseer in 1 Timothy 3:1-7 exclude women. An "overseer" (the Greek is *episkopēs*, "overseer," and not *presbyteros*, "elder") was to be "faithful to his wife" and "apt to teach."[34]

---

[34]What is to be avoided is anachronism. Some translate the term *episkopos* as "elder" or "bishop." Yet bishops did not emerge in the church until much later. Then too Greco-Roman elders were the equivalent of city council members (Lk 7:3; Mk 11:27), while Jewish elders were civic leaders. It is clear that the church did not follow the cultural model, whether Roman or Jewish. This means an understanding of the church elder, overseer, and deacon is solely New Testament-based. To be noted is that *overseer* and *deacon* in 1 Timothy and Titus are singular, have qualifications, and have a descriptive role. *Elder*, on the other hand, is plural and has no qualifications. That the leadership of the Philippian church consisted of "overseers and deacons" with no mention of elders, and that Paul appointed elders in each planted local church (Acts 14:23), and Titus is told to do the same in Crete (Titus 1:5), suggests that *elder* is the umbrella term for both overseer and deacon.

Although "faithful to his wife" is commonly thought to make the role of overseer an exclusively male one, the standard is not exclusively so. It is also a qualification of widowed women leaders (*faithful to her husband*; 1 Tim 5:9). It is true that qualifications are the same for male and female deacons except when related to family. Qualifications for male deacons include being faithful to his wife (1 Tim 5:12), while qualifications for female deacons omit it (1 Tim 3:11).[35] A reasonable explanation is that Paul adds qualifications that simply do not apply to women. It could be that women deacons were drawn from the ranks of the unmarried (in which case there would be no need to list qualifications having to do with marital status and providing for one's family). First Corinthians 7 certainly attests to the presence of virgins in the congregation. Another possibility is that marital faithfulness was a greater challenge for men in that society. In a Greek city such as Ephesus, where men were still by and large the initiators in matters of divorce and philandering, Paul could have considered a husband's faithfulness to be a critical part of his Christian witness. He certainly highlights this need in his list of qualifications for overseers: "[An overseer] must also have a good reputation with outsiders, so that he will not fall into disgrace and into the devil's trap" (1 Tim 3:7 NIV). "Disgrace" and "the devil's trap" are suggestive of marital unfaithfulness.

It is also important to note that it is "apt to teach" and not "gifted to teach." Aptitude is different from gifting. Paul is not saying that one must possess a teaching gift to be an overseer. It is competency that is in view—*able* to teach. The need for overseers to be competent to teach makes particular sense in the context of false teaching, especially because "they [false teachers] are turning whole families away from the truth" (Titus 1:11 NLT).

It is further claimed that *tou idiou oikou kalōs prohistamenon*, translated by the NIV as "he must manage his own family well and see that his children obey him. . . . (If anyone does not know how to manage his own

[35]Some translations have "in the same way *their wives*." While the Greek word can mean either "woman" or "wife," syntax makes "wife" improbable. If Paul were turning to the wives of deacons, he would have written "their women likewise" or have included some other spousal linkage. This also begs the question of the lack of "their wives likewise" for overseers. Why include the wives of one group of leaders and exclude the wives of the other? "Their wives likewise" further indicates that a married couples had the same gifts. But to assume that they do conflicts with Paul's teaching elsewhere about spiritual gifting (e.g., 1 Cor 12:11).

family, how can he take care of God's church?)," excludes women as overseers. However, the Greek terms *prohistamenon* and *epimelēsetai* have to
do with providing assistance or guidance. This is clear from the language
that follows: "If a man cannot *prohistamenon* his own household, how can
he *care for* [*epimelēsetai*] God's church?" This is also clear from New Testament usage elsewhere. In Romans 12 *prohistēmi* is grouped with the spiritual gifts of generous giving and showing mercy, and suggests a translation
such as "offering practical assistance to those in need" (Rom 12:8). In
Romans 16:1 it is used of Phoebe's provision of patronage and protection
of both Paul and the broader Christian community. The same goes for
epimelēsetai. *Epimelemai* elsewhere involves providing for the need at
hand. The Samaritan took the battered man to an inn, where he *cared for*
him (Lk 10:34-35). While he was under house arrest, Paul's friends *provided* what he needed (Acts 27:3). It is common to construe the overseer's
role in an authoritarian and hierarchical way. But there is a world of difference between the parent who *protects and cares well for* his family and
the one who *rules and manages* his household.

Not to be overlooked is the fact that both men and women served as
church leaders. In spelling out qualifications for both male and female
deacons, there is an acknowledgment that the church at Ephesus had
women in at least one of its key leadership positions. Nor was Ephesus the
exception. Paul makes mention of female deacons in Philippi and
Cenchreae. Phoebe is commended by Paul as a "deacon in the church at
Cenchreae" (Rom 16:1), and Euodia and Syntyche are spoken of in language that places them in the ranks of the Philippian church leadership of
"overseers and deacons" (Phil 1:1 NIV).

Postapostolic writers understood Paul to be speaking of women deacons.
Clement of Alexandria (second to third century), for instance, says, "For
we know what the honorable Paul in one of his letters to Timothy prescribed regarding women deacons." And John Chrysostom (fourth century) talks of women who held the rank of deacon in the apostolic church.[36]

Among the Lycus Valley churches, Nympha surfaces as another woman
leader. Paul greets her at the close of Colossians: "Give my greetings to the

---

[36]Clement of Alexandria, *Stromateis* 3.6.53; John Chrysostom, *Homilies on Timothy* 11 (on 1 Tim 3:11).

brothers and sisters in Laodicea, and to Nympha and the church in her house" (Col 4:15). While the reference is brief, the implications are noteworthy. Patronage of a house church was an authoritative role. The householder in Greco-Roman times was automatically in charge of any group that met in his or her domicile. Households in the first century included not only the immediate family and relatives but also slaves, freedmen and freedwomen, hired workers, and even tenants and partners in a trade or craft. This meant that the female head of household had to have good administrative and management skills (see *oikodespotein*, "to rule one's household," in 1 Tim 5:14). Paul thus places great emphasis on a person's track record as a family leader, as it is a definite indicator of church leadership potential (1 Tim 3:4-5; 5:14).

Women in the Caesarean church. Luke commends Philip's four daughters as prophets in the Caesarean church (Acts 21:9). They belong to a tradition of women prophets stretching back to Mosaic times. In fact, if there was one gift that women consistently possessed and exercised throughout the history of God's people, it is this one. (Anna also continued this tradition in New Testament times; Lk 2:36-38.)

Luke's reference to Philip's daughters is brief. No further commentary was necessary, because women prophets were likely well established as church leaders. Postapostolic authors confirm this. Papias tells how he heard a wonderful story from the lips of Philip's prophetic daughters. Proclus (third-century leader of the Phrygian Montanists) places their later prophetic ministry in Hierapolis, Asia. Eusebius ranks them "among the first stage in the apostolic succession."[37]

Philip's daughters were not lone exceptions. A woman named Ammia in the Philadelphian church is also said to have prophesied during New Testament times. In fact, second-century Montanists Priscilla and Maximilla used women such as Ammia to justify their own prophetic office.[38]

Some argue that early church prophecy was merely an impromptu movement of the Spirit and not a recognized leadership role in the church. Yet Luke makes it clear that the prophet was just such, when he identifies the leaders of the church at Antioch as "prophets and teachers" (Acts 13:1).

---

[37]Eusebius, *Ecclesiastical History* 3.39; 3.37.1.
[38]Eusebius, *Ecclesiastical History* 5.17.2-4.

Nor was prophecy, as some would claim, an activity valued less than other forms of ministry. This is evident from Paul's identification of prophetic speaking with "revelation" (*apokalyphthē*; 1 Cor 14:29-30) and his naming apostles and prophets together as the "foundation" of the church when speaking of it metaphorically (Eph 2:20). Paul even goes further and puts apostles and prophets in a category by themselves. It is to "[God's] holy apostles and prophets" that "the mystery of Christ . . . has now been revealed . . . by the Spirit" (Eph 3:4-5). In a very real sense, therefore, the New Testament prophet carries on the "Thus saith the LORD" task of the Old Testament prophet.

CONCLUSION

Recent studies have focused appropriately on Paul's language for male and female leaders. The uniform conclusion is that Paul uses exactly the same language of colleagues in ministry whether they are male or female. The men are described as fellow prisoners, fellow workers, and hard workers who risked their necks for Paul and labored side by side with him in the gospel (Rom 16:3, 7, 9, 21; 1 Cor 3:9; 4:12; 16:16-17; 2 Cor 8:23; Phil 2:25; 4:3; Col 4:10-11; 1 Thess 3:2; 5:12; Philem 1, 24). The women are equally described as fellow prisoners, fellow workers, and hard workers who risked their necks for Paul and labored side by side with him in the gospel (Rom 16:3-4, 6, 12; Phil 4:2-3).

Parallel language reveals the same pattern in Greco-Roman society. Epigraphical data shows that terms such as *magistrate, chief officer, prophet, priest/priestess, patron/protectress, overseer,* and the like are used equally of women and men in the religious cults and civic associations of the day.

What is too often overlooked is that women as well as men are named without qualification or geographical boundaries, and in commensurate numbers for each leadership role. Junia was "outstanding *among the apostles*" at Rome (Rom 16:7 NIV). Phoebe was a *deacon* of the Cenchreaen church (Rom 16:1-2). Syntyche and Euodia were leaders of the Philippian church and *evangelists* alongside Paul himself (Phil 4:3; cf. Phil 1:1). Philip's four daughters were *prophets* at Caesarea (Acts 21:9). Priscilla was a *church planter* alongside Paul (Rom 16:3-4) and a *teacher* at Ephesus who expounded "the way of God" to a man in exactly the same way Paul expounded the gospel to men and women in Rome (*exethento*, from *ektithēmi*; Acts 18:26; cf. Acts 28:23). Under Roman law, Nympha had legal responsibility for and hence *authority over* the church that met in her house (Col 4:15).

These are facts hardly open to debate—although some remain eager and willing to attempt to circumvent them. To do so, however, one must dismiss the evidence of women leaders in the culture at large, deny the impact of the union of religion and life on the church, or impose on the biblical women the image of a cloistered, domestic female that did not exist in the Greco-Roman world of antiquity. If anything, the matter-of-fact mention and listing of women in ministry permits us to conclude there was a substantially wider and well-established early Christian praxis of women leaders.[39]

There is no indication that men and women functioned within any hierarchical leadership framework in the New Testament church. Indeed, that Paul calls women "laborers" and "fellow workers" means that what is said of other leaders must apply also to them. Paul urges the Corinthian church to "submit to such people [who have devoted themselves to the service of God's people] and to *everyone* who joins in the work and labors at it" (1 Cor 16:16 NIV). And he asks the Thessalonians "to acknowledge those who work hard among you, who care for you in the Lord and admonish you. Hold them in the highest regard in love because of their work" (1 Thess 5:12-13 NIV). It follows that Paul would presume such respect and esteem should also be shown toward the women who work and labor in the Lord—proclaiming, admonishing, teaching, and leading.[40]

---

[39]Stefan Schreiber, "Arbeit mit der Gemeinde (Röm 16.6, 12): Zur versunkenen Möglichkeit der Gemeindeleitung durch Frauen," *NTS* 46 (2000): 204-26.

[40]Keith A. Gerberding, "Women Who Toil in Ministry, Even as Paul," *Currents in Theology and Mission* 18 (1991): 285-91.

5

JESUS' TREATMENT OF WOMEN IN THE GOSPELS

Aída Besançon Spencer

• • • • •

IN 1667 QUAKER MARGARET Fell declared that "women's speaking" was "justified, proved and allowed of by the Scriptures" because "women were the first that preached the tidings of the Resurrection of Jesus, and were sent by Christ's own command, before He ascended to the Father, John 20:17."[1] In this she was echoing John Chrysostom's (fourth-century) sentiments that women carried on the race that "apostles and evangelists ran." About Andronicus and Junia, Chrysostom wrote: "Indeed to be apostles at all is a great thing. But to be even amongst these of note, just consider what a great encomium this is! But they were of note owing to their works, to their achievements. Oh! How great is the devotion of this woman, that she should be even counted worthy of the appellation of apostle!"[2] Christian writers have long marveled at the impact of Jesus' words and deeds on the status of women, even when they have differed on the roles women and men were to have in the later church.

The purpose of this chapter is to look at the data in the Gospels once again, because even though many scholars view positively Jesus' affirmations of women, some are reluctant to see this as bearing on women's

---

[1]Margaret Fell (Fox), *Women's Speaking Justified* (1667; repr., Los Angeles: University of California Press, 1979). See also Ruth A. Tucker and Walter L. Liefeld, *Daughters of the Church: Women and Ministry from New Testament Times to the Present* (Grand Rapids, MI: Zondervan, 1987), 230-31.
[2]John Chrysostom, *Epistle to the Romans* 31.

possible leadership roles in the church.[3] After an overview of what is generally accepted by all, that Jesus both affirmed and elevated women, I will examine more closely how Jesus' actions affect the priorities in women's lives. The chapter will conclude with a reexamination of the key point of disagreement: the significance of Jesus' choosing twelve males to form the so-called inner circle of his disciples.

JESUS AFFIRMS WOMEN

Recognizing that Jesus both affirmed and elevated the status of women has now become commonplace on both sides of the women-in-leadership divide. Among those opposed to women in senior leadership roles in the church, Michael Wilkins states that

> Jesus restored and affirmed the worth and dignity of women. . . . [He] did not make a distinction between women and men in this ministry of restoration. . . . Women were called to be Jesus' disciples. . . . As disciples of Jesus, women have restored to them the full dignity that was theirs in the creation, when men and women were both created in the image of God. . . . Women received instruction and nurture as Jesus' disciples.

He adds, "Jesus restored and affirmed women to his ministry team" as "colaborers with men."[4]

Wilkins follows the positive tone set earlier by James Borland: "Christ placed a high value on women" by "recognizing their intrinsic value as persons," by "ministering to women," and by "according them dignity in his ministry."[5] Wayne House agrees: "Jesus treated women with kindness and respect and considered them equal before God," and he assumed women were "of equal intelligence, equal spiritual discernment, and equal religious acumen."[6] Samuele Bacchiocchi further reiterates this perspective. Jesus was unique in contrast to first-century Judaism. He viewed women as "*persons* for whom He had come . . . not in terms of sex, age or

---

[3]See, e.g., Michael J. Wilkins, "Women in the Teaching and Example of Jesus," in *Women and Men in Ministry: A Complementary Perspective,* ed. Robert L. Saucy and Judith K. TenElshof (Chicago: Moody, 2001), 91-112.

[4]Wilkins, "Women in the Teaching," 95, 97-98, 100.

[5]James A. Borland, "Women in the Life and Teachings of Jesus," in *RBMW*, 144, 146, 148. See also James B. Hurley, *Man and Woman in Biblical Perspective* (Grand Rapids, MI: Zondervan, 1981), 82-111.

[6]H. Wayne House, *The Role of Women in Ministry Today* (Grand Rapids, MI: Baker, 1995), 21, 82.

marital status." He appreciated their "intelligence and faith," accepted women as "treasured members of the human family," admitted them "into His fellowship," and took "time to teach them the truths of the Kingdom of God."[7]

The ways Jesus affirmed women can be summarized under four broad categories. First, Jesus' conversations with women indicate his esteem for them. Jesus openly conversed with women despite the ancient Jewish practice of discouraging men from speaking with women in public.[8] For example, in John's Gospel Jesus has a deep theological discussion with a man, Nicodemus (Jn 3:1-21), followed by a deep theological discussion with a woman, a Samaritan, at Jacob's well (Jn 4:4-42). She is the first person to whom Jesus discloses that he is the Messiah (Jn 4:25-26), and she becomes an evangelist to her people (Jn 4:28-29, 39-42). Later in the same Gospel, Martha affirms the key doctrines about Jesus: Jesus is "the Messiah, the Son of God, who is to come into the world" (Jn 11:27 NIV).[9]

Second, Jesus' teachings are favorable to women. Jesus is firm that marriage entails commitment between one man and one woman for life, whereas rabbinic teaching allowed polygamy and divorce for many reasons other than adultery.[10] As well, women, like men, were to place obedience to God as most important (Mt 12:46-50; Mk 3:31-35; Lk 8:19-21; 11:27-28).

---

[7]Samuele Bacchiocchi, *Women in the Church: A Biblical Study on the Role of Women in the Church* (Berrien Springs, MI: Biblical Perspectives, 1987), 47-50.

[8]We are explicitly told that Jesus' disciples were "surprised" that he spoke "with a woman" (Jn 4:27 NIV). According to rabbinic teaching, if a woman spoke with a man in public she could be divorced without having her dowry repaid (m. Ketub. 1:8; 7:6). Earlier ben Sirach asserted, "Do not let [your daughter] parade her beauty before any man" (Ecclesiasticus 42:12).

[9]For extended descriptions of Jesus' special treatment of women, see Gilbert Bilezikian, *Beyond Sex Roles: A Guide for the Study of Female Roles in the Bible* (Grand Rapids, MI: Baker, 1985), chap. 4; Leonard Swidler, *Biblical Affirmations of Woman* (Philadelphia: Westminster, 1979), 164-290; Linda L. Belleville, *Women Leaders and the Church* (Grand Rapids, MI: Baker, 2000), 48-60, 109-11.

[10]See, e.g., Mt 5:31-32; note that this is preceded by his extending adultery to include even looking at another woman lustfully (Mt 5:27-30). See further Mt 19:3-9; Mk 10:2-12; Lk 16:18. For polygamy see m. Sanh. 2:4. The schools of Hillel and Shammai debated the allowable grounds for divorce on the basis of the phrase "something objectionable about her" (Deut 24:1). The Hillelites took the extreme view (see esp. m. Git. 9:10), which allowed divorce even for a spoiled dish or a facial blemish (b. Ketub. 75a) or if the husband found someone more attractive. See also m. Yevam. 14:1; m. Ketub. 7:1-10; m. Qidd. 2:5. On the Greek side, even though Epictetus argues for monogamy, he begins with the presupposition that "women by nature" are "common property" (*Discourses* 2.4.8-10).

3.   Third, women form an important part of Jesus' ministry, helping usher in the time of God's rule. Five women are included in his messianic pedigree: Tamar, Rahab, Ruth, Bathsheba, and of course Mary (Mt 1:3-16). Many women serve as positive models of faith. Mary's role, as a virgin who conceived by the Holy Spirit, is highlighted. She is presented as a thinker of great faith (Mt 1:18; Lk 1:26-56; 2:19, 34-35, 51). A Canaanite woman is also extolled for her great faith (Mt 15:28; cf. Lk 4:25-26), similar to the way a Roman soldier is praised (Mt 8:10). Likewise, a restored immoral woman who is allowed to touch Jesus is commended for her faith, greater than that of the rude Simon and his Pharisee friends (Lk 7:36-50).[11] A healed woman is called "a daughter of Abraham" (Lk 13:16) in the same way as a male tax collector is called a restored "son of Abraham" (Lk 19:9-10); thus, both women and men are included in the newly formed people of God that Christ himself both represents and gathers. And Mary of Bethany is commended for her insight into Jesus' coming crucifixion—insight that went far beyond that of the Twelve (Jn 12:1-8).

Besides these, Luke singles out Elizabeth, who names John (Lk 1:60); the prophet Anna (Lk 2:36-38); the named women who are among his disciples (Lk 8:1-3); an only daughter whom Jesus heals (Lk 8:40-42, 49-56); a woman with constant bleeding who, by touching Jesus' cloak, makes him "unclean" (Lk 8:43-48); Martha and Mary (Lk 10:38-42); the women who mourn his impending death (Lk 23:27-28); and the women who come to anoint the buried Jesus but instead are the first to hear and tell of the resurrection (Lk 23:55–24:12).

4.   Fourth, Jesus' teachings and comments often take into consideration a woman's perspective. He uses female images for himself—a hen desiring to gather her chicks under her wings (Mt 23:37; Lk 13:34). Similarly, God's care for the lost, exemplified in Jesus' eating with sinners, is pictured not only as a father with lost sons (Lk 15:11-32) but also as a woman with a lost coin (Lk 15:8-9). Humanity is described as those "born of women" (Mt 11:11). Both father and mother are to be honored (Mk 7:10-11).

---

[11]Many scholars consider the woman is called a "sinner" because Jesus and Simon agree that she had done "many" sins, unlike when *sinner* is used as a general term for Jews who did not comply with all the rabbinic regulations of ritual cleanliness (e.g., Lk 5:34). Mary Magdalene, in contrast, is not called a sinner (Lk 8:2).

In his analogies[Jesus uses household activities common to women] such as sewing (Lk 5:36) and cooking (Lk 6:38; 13:21). Household service is a key to understanding genuine obedience to God: feeding and clothing the hungry, the stranger, the ill, the inmate, and the wounded (Mt 25:37-39, 42-43; Lk 10:34). The church becomes a loving family (Mt 23:8; Jn 19:25-27). Jesus shows special concern for pregnant and nursing women and widows (Mt 24:19; Mk 12:40; 13:17; Lk 7:12-17; 18:3; 20:47; 21:2-4, 23; 23:29; Jn 16:21). Pressure against Christ's followers will come from both male and female relatives (Mt 10:35-37; 19:29; Mk 10:29-30; Lk 12:53; 14:26; 18:29; 21:16). And of course, marriage has a significant place in representing God's reign (Mt 25:1; Mk 2:19; Lk 5:34-35; Jn 2:1).

Thus, most scholars would agree that Jesus' teachings and actions are favorable to women and that women are an important part of his ministry. Nonetheless, advocates of male-only leadership do not always develop the implications of Jesus' actions toward women—actions that stood in remarkable contrast to his own culture and society.

JESUS' ACTIONS AFFECT WOMEN'S PRIORITIES

Rather than simply reassert, as many continue to do, that "the woman's place is in the home"—as though that were a *biblical* (and not merely cultural) viewpoint—one needs to ask such questions as: Why were first-century Jewish women discouraged from having formal higher education in biblical law? Why were women not required to pursue religious training at all or given merit if they did study? Why was no one required or encouraged to teach them?[12] Why were women not admitted into Jewish schools? Why even in the synagogue service were they not encouraged to study fully? Of course, they could attend worship services, but they were not welcome to the place of further study ("the place of men") or were required to sit at the back of the worship area.

These restrictions for women were made for two reasons: (1) women were primarily to be homemakers, and (2) they were to be protected

---

[12]Wilkins suggests that m. Ned. 4:3 implies that a father could teach his sons *and* daughters Scripture ("Women in the Teaching," 351n18). But this is not referring to formal training in the Torah but to the training a husband/father was expected to give to his whole household so that they all might walk in the ways of the Lord. See further Aída Besançon Spencer, *Beyond the Curse: Women Called to Ministry* (repr., Grand Rapids, MI: Baker, 2010), 47-56.

against unchastity. Philo of Alexandria, a slightly older contemporary of Jesus, described what was considered the ideal for Jewish women in the Diaspora:

> Market-places and council-halls and law-courts and gatherings and meetings, where a large number of people are assembled, and open-air life with full scope for discussion and action—all these are suitable to men in both war and peace. The women are best suited to the indoor life which never strays from the house, within which the middle door is taken by the maidens as their boundary, and the outer door by those who have reached full womanhood. Organized communities are of two sorts, the greater which we call cities and the smaller which we call households. Both of these have their governors; the government of the greater is assigned to men under the name of statesmanship, that of the lesser, known as household management, to women.[13]

Similarly, rabbinic laws were constructed to ensure that women were not encouraged to leave their homes. As in Philo, the location of women seems to be the underlying concern.[14] Indeed, Jewish law consistently assumed the necessity for women to be centered on their household. If women spent time in study of the law, it was feared, their care of the household would suffer.

Wives were required to sustain a household's economy, unless they had servants to direct. For instance, in the Mishnah a wife is required to grind flour, bake bread, wash clothes, cook food, nurse her child, make ready her husband's bed, oversee Sabbath celebrations, and spin wool.[15] Women were so integrally associated with the house and homemaking that Rabbi

---

[13]Philo of Alexandria, *On the Special Laws* 3.169-70, LCL (Cambridge, MA: Harvard University Press, 1941), 583-85. Cf. Philo, *Flaccus* 89, LCL (Cambridge, MA: Harvard University Press, 1941), 51, where this is expressed in a more abbreviated form.

[14]Women were exempt from leaving the home for any period of time. Thus, they were exempt from attending synagogue school as well as traveling to Jerusalem for the feasts of Passover, Pentecost, and Tabernacles (m. Qidd. 1:7; m. Hag. 1:1; m. Sukkah 2:8). The rabbis concluded that the Torah was applicable to men who traveled about daily, since they considered the Torah comparable to phylacteries (small leather boxes) worn on the head and left arm during prayer by men only. A woman instead had a *mezuzah* on her doorpost (m. Ber. 3:3; b. Qidd. 34a-35a). At a later time, Rabbi Jeremiah upheld an ancient tradition when he said, "A woman generally stays at home, whereas a man goes out into the streets and learns understanding from men" (Midrash Rabbah Genesis 1, 18.1).

[15]m. Ketub. 5:5, 9.

Judah said that "his house" (in Lev 16:6) is a synonym for "his wife."[16] Rabbi Jose, commenting on Yoma 1:1, proudly adds: "Never have I called my wife by that word ['my wife'], but always 'my home.'" Even a woman's body came to be perceived as constructed for homemaking. Rabbi Hisda thus interprets Genesis 2:22, wherein God takes Adam's rib and "builds (it) into a woman": "This teaches that the Holy One, blessed be He, built Eve in the shape of a storehouse. As a storehouse is [made] wide below and narrow above so that it may contain the produce, so was [the womb of] a woman [made] wide below and narrow above so that it may contain the embryo."[17]

However, this emphasis on women's remaining in the household as much as economically possible does not flow from any clear teaching in the Old Testament. (According to Deut 31:12 and Josh 8:35, all people— Hebrew men, women, children, and foreigners—were exhorted to attend regularly the reading of the law.) Rather, it reflects an inculturation from the larger pagan society that goes far back in time. For instance, Xenophon (fourth century BC) creates an ideal gentleman, Ischomachus, who explains to his wife that God

> from the first adapted the woman's nature, I think, to the indoor and man's
> to the outdoor tasks and cares. For he made the man's body and mind more
> capable of enduring cold and heat, and journeys and campaigns; and there-
> fore imposed on him the outdoor tasks. To the woman, since he has made
> her body less capable of such endurance, I take it that God has assigned the
> indoor tasks. And knowing that he had created in the woman and had
> imposed on her the nourishment of the infants, he meted out to her a larger
> portion of affection for new-born babes than to the man. And since he
> imposed on the woman the protection of the stores also, knowing that for
> protection a fearful disposition is no disadvantage, God meted out a larger
> share of fear to the woman than to the man; and knowing that he who deals
> with the outdoor tasks will have to be their defender against any wrong-doer,

---

[16]m. Yoma 1:1.

[17]b. Eruv. 18a-b; b. Shabb. 118b; see Spencer, *Beyond the Curse*, 47-57. The Constitutions of the Holy Apostles (which is semi-Arian) also relegates women to indoor tasks: "Let the widow therefore own herself to be the 'altar of God,' and let her sit in her house, and not enter into the houses of the faithful, under any pretence, to receive anything; for the altar of God never runs about, but is fixed in one place" (3.1.6).

he meted out to him again a larger share of courage. . . . Thus, to the woman it is more honorable to stay indoors than to abide in the fields, but to the man it is unseemly rather to stay indoors than to attend to the work outside.[18]

Jesus, in contrast, does not treat women primarily as homemakers. A woman calls out in Jesus' hearing: "Blessed is the mother who gave you birth and nursed you!" Here we see this principle of woman primarily as mother voiced before Jesus. And what is his reply? "Blessed rather are those who hear the word of God and obey it!" (Lk 11:27-28 NIV). What Jesus states here explicitly, he models earlier in his actions. Thus, when Mary sits as a pupil in rabbinic fashion before Jesus (Lk 10:38-42) while Martha follows the cultural mandate to serve as homemaker, Jesus declares that Mary is the one who has selected the good share—to sit at a rabbi's feet in learning. She has made the right choice, and he will not allow anyone to take learning away from those who sit at his feet.[19]

Despite all this, many evangelicals today still see homemaking as women's primary role. For instance, Thomas Schreiner writes that childbearing "represents the fulfillment of the woman's domestic role as a mother in distinction from the man. Childbearing, then, is probably selected by synecdoche [in 1 Tim 2:15] as representing the appropriate role for women."[20] James Hurley agrees: "Women in general (and most women in [Paul's] day) will be kept safe from seizing men's roles by participating in marital life (symbolized by childbirth)." Similarly, Dorothy Patterson asserts: "Keeping the home is God's assignment to the wife."[21]

I am by no means suggesting that bearing and rearing children are not essential and honorable tasks. Rather, obeying and learning from God have a *higher* priority for men as well as for women. Moreover, rearing children is a significant ministry for men as well as women. Godly overseers and deacons need to govern well their own household before

---

[18]Xenophon, *Oeconomicus* 7.22-25, 30.

[19]See Spencer, *Beyond the Curse*, 57-63; Hurley, *Man and Woman*, 88-89; and most contemporary commentaries on Luke.

[20]Thomas R. Schreiner, "An Interpretation of 1 Timothy 2:9-15: A Dialogue with Scholarship," in *Women in the Church: A Fresh Analysis of 1 Timothy 2:9-15*, ed. Andreas J. Köstenberger, Thomas R. Schreiner, and H. Scott Baldwin (Grand Rapids, MI: Baker, 1995), 150-51.

[21]Hurley, *Man and Woman*, 223; Dorothy Patterson, "The High Calling of Wife and Mother in Biblical Perspective," in *RBMW*, 2nd ed., 366.

becoming church leaders (1 Tim 3:4-5, 12), just as godly widows do (1 Tim 5:10). Indeed, how can they say they love God if they do not love, and therefore care for, their neighbors and family (e.g., 1 Jn 4:8)?

JESUS' APOSTLES AFFIRM THE JEWISH FOUNDATION OF HIS COVENANT

Despite noting Jesus' affirmation of women as people, many supporters of male-only leadership today use the same "evidence" to restrict women's roles as did the influential fourth-century Constitutions of the Holy Apostles, which declares: "We do not permit our 'women to teach in the Church,' but only to pray and hear those that teach; for our Master and Lord, Jesus Himself, when He sent us the twelve to make disciples of the people and of the nations, did nowhere send out women to preach, although He did not want such."[22]

This argument has several levels. First, it assumes that gender is the abiding precedent but does not extend this precedent to race or political state; thereby it selectively eliminates "male and female" from the basis for equality in Christ established in Galatians 3:28. The same argumentative strategy could be used to exclude all Gentiles from leadership. Second, it assumes that what the biblical model does not establish it thereby prohibits. Yet although the biblical model establishes that men *can* be apostles, it does not establish that women *cannot* be. The hermeneutical presupposition of the Constitutions, and that of some contemporary evangelicals, seems to be that the Bible's teaching is limited to whatever is explicitly stated. In effect, if the text does not specifically say you *may* do something, then you may not. Thus House, for example, states: "The biblical record says nothing at all about Christ considering a woman's role in ministry leadership or spiritual headship indistinguishable from a man's. There is no evidence that any woman was commissioned as one of the seventy-two or the Twelve."[23] Silence on this matter means that women may not be ordained as overseers.

What makes this hermeneutical stance more valid than its opposite, except assertion pure and simple? Why not take a less limited view of the

---

[22]Constitutions 3.1.6.
[23]House, *Role of Women*, 21.

text? If the text does not actually prohibit something, either explicitly or in principle, one may well choose to do it—especially given the way Jesus explicitly affirms women. Nowhere does Jesus ever say—or even imply in anything he says—that only men can be leaders in the church. Similarly, neither of the two ecumenical councils at Nicaea and Chalcedon (AD 325 and 451) limits church leadership to men.[24]

Wilkins takes the male-only argument a step further by mapping out concentric circles to locate the various followers of Jesus: the "large number of disciples who believed in Jesus"; the Seventy-Two who were "sent out on a preaching tour" (Lk 10:1-17); the women (not included in the Seventy[-Two]) who "traveled with Jesus and the Twelve to support Jesus' missionary tour (Luke 8:1-3)"; the Twelve, "who were called to be trained as apostles"; and the inner circle of "Peter, James, John, and sometimes Andrew (e.g., Mark 13:3)." Under this scenario, women can be among the disciples "who have believed on Jesus" and are "called into ministry with and to Him." But their absence from the two inner circles means that they were not among those being trained "to be the leadership of the church."[25]

In order to evaluate this recent reconstruction of the Constitutions' argument, we need to reconsider what may appear obvious but is often neglected: the emphasis in Jesus' own teachings. He does not teach that we will advance God's reign by maintaining male-female distinctions in leadership. For example, in Mark's Gospel we learn that Jesus has authority on earth to forgive (Mk 2:10, 17) and is Lord of the Sabbath (Mk 2:27; 3:3-5); his family is composed of those who do God's will (Mk 3:31-35); he is merciful and compassionate (Mk 5:19; 6:34), the Messiah, the crucified one, God's beloved Son who will return (Mk 8:29, 31; 9:7, 31; 14:61-62). Explicit teachings such as these, which have the same meaning for both men and

---

[24]It was the Synod of Laodicea in Phrygia (AD 343–381) that began a process of restricting women, deacons, laity, artists, and Messianic Jews. For example, female elders are not to be appointed in the church (canon 11), women may not approach the altar (canon 44), a deacon may not sit in the presence of an elder (canon 20), only the canonical singers may sing in the church (canon 15), and Christians may not rest but must work on the Sabbath so as not to "judaize" (canon 29). Ironically, as the church became more anti-Semitic, it also became more legalistic. The Council of Trullo explains one reason women could not speak during the divine liturgy: their monthly flux of blood was polluting (canon 70)—a total collapsing of new-covenant ministry into that of the old.

[25]Wilkins, "Women in the Teaching," 96-99, 101-2.

women, are the focus of the Gospels. Jesus' teachings do not focus on gender or race for Christian leaders.

In the same vein, the authority given to the apostles by Jesus is not over other people but rather over demons or unclean spirits (to drive them out) and over illness and death—that is, against nonhuman enemies of God's reign (Mt 10:1, 8; Mk 3:14-15; 6:7-30; Lk 9:1).[26] Thus Jesus' apostles were to be distinct from false apostles who, like Gentile leaders, took authority to dominate others (Mk 10:42-45; 2 Cor 11:20-21). When some argue today that only men are to have authority in the church, they appear still to be arguing in this pagan vein of who is the greatest (Mk 9:34)—in this case, men or women. When the truly "greatest" welcomes the little child in Jesus' name, leadership no longer is a question of power but rather of service.[27] These instructions to the Twelve are important for all Christians, especially leaders, setting forth the Christlike character traits they should have. Leaders are to be like Jesus, who came to serve and to give his life as a ransom for many, not like the Gentiles who "lord it over" others (Mk 10:42-45).[28]

Furthermore, apostleship is not synonymous with church leadership as such. At a very early stage in the church, apostles and elders were distinguishable categories (Acts 15:2, 4, 6, 22, 23; 16:4). A little later (1 Cor 12:28), along with apostle, Paul lists other gifts such as prophet (one who confronts and builds up the church; see 1 Cor 14:4), teacher (one who leads by instructing), and leadership (*kybernēsis* = "guidance"). Moreover, *apostle* is never linked directly to *overseer* (e.g., 1 Tim 3:1).

So why did Jesus choose twelve Jewish men as the first apostles? First, he chose twelve Jews to serve as a synecdoche, representing the twelve tribes of Israel (Mt 19:28; Lk 22:30; Rev 21:12). Jesus' call to ministry was focused on reaching Israel (Mt 10:5-6; 15:24; Lk 7:9; Jn 1:11; Rom 15:8; 13:1) because the earlier covenant was made with Israel (e.g., Gen 35:10-12;

---

[26]See the discussion in chapter fifteen below.

[27]Leadership established according to the principles of a crucified Messiah is the difficult lesson Paul tries to explain to the Corinthians (in both letters).

[28]See also Mt 18:1-5; 19:14; 20:20-27; 21:15-16; Mk 9:35-37; 10:13-16; 12:14, 38-40; Lk 9:46-48; 10:21; 18:16-17; 20:21; 22:24-27; Jn 13:12-17. See Gilbert Bilezikian, "Biblical Community Versus Gender-Based Hierarchy," *PriscPap* 16 (2002): 3-10; and Aída Besançon Spencer and William David Spencer, eds., *Christian Egalitarian Leadership: Empowering the Whole Church According to the Scriptures* (Eugene, OR: Wipf & Stock, 2020).

If this opposition argument is the case then I should have as much angst over being a Gentile as I do over being a woman.

Jesus' Treatment of Women in the Gospels 101

1 Kings 18:31).[29] Jesus' choice of the Twelve indicates the importance of the new covenant's being founded on the old covenant. That is why, at the end of the New Testament, the two covenant peoples are symbolically joined in the new Jerusalem, on whose twelve foundations are the names of the twelve apostles of the Lamb and whose twelve gates bear the names of the twelve tribes of Israel (Rev 21:12-14). Gentile inclusion in God's household rests on the earlier witness of Jewish apostles and prophets (Eph 2:20). Many of the original twelve focused their ministries in Jerusalem and to the Jews (Acts 8:1, 14; cf. Gal 1:17; 2:8).

The Twelve, who represent the twelve tribes, do so because they also represent the twelve patriarchs.[30] Thus the Twelve could not have been other than Jewish free males. If there had been Gentiles or women or slaves among them, the deliberate reconstitution of Israel in Jesus himself, signaled by the Father at his baptism (Mt 3:13-17), simply would not have worked.[31] As an integral part of the ministry of Jesus, the Twelve represented not only the twelve patriarchs/tribes of Israel but also the newly constituted Israel under the new covenant in Christ. Consequently, the Twelve cannot serve as precedents for *Gentile* leadership, which is what prevails in the church today.[32]

the statements are for covenant and approbation not male leadership

---

[29]See also Eusebius, *Ecclesiastical History* 6.14.

[30]Richard Bauckham cites Num 1:4-16 as important because it shows the Twelve are the symbolic heads of the new Israel, corresponding to the twelve patriarchs of Israel's founding generation. See Bauckham, *Gospel Women: Studies of the Named Women in the Gospels* (Grand Rapids, MI: Eerdmans, 2002), 188. Scot McKnight also notes the importance of the Twelve as a symbol of the leadership characteristics of Jesus' new nation, so the land could be reclaimed for God's covenant. See McKnight, "Jesus and the Twelve," *BBR* 11 (2001): 229-31.

[31]I am indebted to Gordon Fee for some of these observations. Fee further notes that during the whole of his ministry Jesus himself symbolically steps into the role of Israel, from his baptism (= Red Sea) and forty days in the desert to be tested (he overcame precisely where Israel failed), to his assuming the role both of Israel's King-Messiah (Son of God; Ps 2:7) and of Isaiah's Suffering Servant, articulated for him in the voice from heaven at his baptism. And at the end he symbolically cleanses the temple and offers his own resurrection as the new locus of God's presence among his people (Jn 2:22). With the Twelve about him at the final meal, he reconstitutes the bread and wine of Passover to become a meal in which they will recall his death as effecting the new covenant. At the same time, the one certain instruction he gives to the Twelve is about their eschatological role in judging Israel (Lk 22:13-30).

[32]Some evangelicals (e.g., Borland, "Women in the Life," 154-55) have observed that even after the resurrection Peter specifies that Judas's replacement has to be male. However, Acts 1:21-22 literally reads: "Therefore, it is necessary that of those having accompanied us, one of these men, who all the time that the Lord Jesus went in and out among us—beginning from John's baptism until the day he was taken up from us—one of these should become a witness of his resurrection with us" (my translation). The emphasis of the text is on someone who had been with the Twelve

apostolic criteria?

Nevertheless, the first set of twelve apostles had certain other defining
1. criteria in common with the rest of the apostles. First, <u>an apostle by definition is a messenger, someone sent off with orders</u>. What makes Christ's
apostles distinct from other apostles is that they were sent by and represented Jesus himself (Mt 10:5; Mk 3:14). Paul also was sent by Christ (Acts
26:16-18) and preached a gospel not of human origin (Gal 1:11-12). By way
of contrast, Epaphroditus was an apostle/messenger sent off from and representing the church at Philippi to Paul (Phil 2:25), and the "brothers" who
carried the monetary gift to Corinth were "representatives [messengers]"
of the churches" (2 Cor 8:23 NIV).

2.   Second, <u>the first apostles had to have been with Jesus</u>. Indeed, the first
reason for his appointing the Twelve is for them to "be with" him (Mk 3:14;
cf. Lk 8:1; Acts 1:21-22). Being with Jesus was a key component of
their training.

3.   Third, <u>an apostle is an eyewitness of the resurrected Christ</u>. When Paul
exclaims to the Corinthians, "Am I not an apostle?" he first follows that
rhetorical question with the defense, "Have I not seen Jesus our Lord?"
(1 Cor 9:1 NIV). Having seen the risen Lord is crucial in the Gospels
(Mt 28:18-20; Jn 20:21-22), in Acts (Acts 1:21-22; 4:33), and in the letters
(1 Cor 15:5-8; Gal 1:11-12). As eyewitnesses to the resurrection, apostles are
listed first among God's gifts to the church (1 Cor 12:28-29).[33]

4.   Fourth, <u>an apostle is commissioned to preach God's reign</u>: "As you go,
proclaim this message: 'The kingdom of heaven has come near'" (Mt 10:7;
Mk 3:14; Lk 9:2 NIV). <u>Preaching</u> (*kēryssō*) <u>is never an action prohibited
to women</u>.

---

throughout Jesus' ministry ("of those who accompanied us"). The sentence structure highlights
not the candidate's gender but rather the candidate's function as an eyewitness to Jesus' life,
resurrection, and ascension. In addition, even though Peter uses the plural of *anēr* ("men") in
Acts 1:21, he also employs this term when speaking to a crowd including men and women. At
Pentecost women are present (Acts 1:14) and spoken about ("your sons and daughters will
prophesy," Acts 2:17); nevertheless, Peter addresses the crowd with the plural of *anēr*, "fellow
Jews" (Acts 2:14; see also Acts 17:22, 34; 25:23-24). Moreover, even if Peter were being gender
specific in Acts 1:21-22 but not in Acts 2:14, the Twelve were not replaced at all after their deaths
(e.g., James in Acts 12:2), which suggests that by then they had served their purpose of symbolically representing Israel at the start of the new covenant.

[33]It is doubtful that today's church planter is a New Testament apostle of Jesus Christ, since being
a witness of the resurrection is a key aspect of the latter. It is also doubtful whether Timothy
should be included as an apostle, despite the "we" in 1 Thess 2:6-7; he is called an evangelist in
2 Tim 4:5.

Thus, *apostolos* in the Gospels clearly includes the twelve who were chosen from a larger group of disciples for the first commission (Mt 10:1-2; Lk 6:13). After Jesus' death and resurrection, *apostle* was broadened to refer to other disciples who had been with Jesus and now were sent off as witnesses to the resurrection. And in the new-covenant era the apostolic witness includes both women and men.

This larger group of apostles explicitly includes Paul (Rom 1:1; 1 Cor 1:1; 2 Cor 1:1; Eph 1:1; Col 1:1; 1 Tim 1:1; 2:7; 2 Tim 1:1; Titus 1:1), Barnabas (Acts 14:4, 14), James (Gal 1:1, 12-19), and Andronicus and Junia (Rom 16:7).[34] Paul and James the brother of Jesus are included in the list of apostles because they were eyewitnesses to the Messiah's resurrection (1 Cor 15:7-8). Then how might Junia, Barnabas, and Andronicus have been included? They may have been among the "more than five hundred of the brothers and sisters" who witnessed the risen Lord (1 Cor 15:6-7 NIV).[35] Or, being part of the larger group of "all the apostles," perhaps they had been among the Seventy-Two (Lk 10:1).[36] Clement of Rome calls Apollos an apostle.[37] Eusebius suggests that Barnabas, Sosthenes, Matthias, and Justus were part of the Seventy-Two and that the more than five hundred witnesses and James the Lord's brother were apostles as well. Eusebius explains that these other apostles were "patterned on the Twelve."[38]

This understanding of the New Testament data means that the female disciples, like the males, had spent time with Jesus and were sent out to preach God's reign. They were *with* Jesus, learning from his teachings to seek God's reign, selling their possessions, and giving all to the Lord's ministry, as they were taught by Jesus (Lk 12:31-34; 18:22). The women

---

[34]In Gal 1:17 Paul also refers to "those who were apostles before I was" (NIV), presumably the Twelve and James. Junia is "outstanding among the apostles" (Rom 16:7 NIV); see the discussion of this matter in chapter four above.

[35]"Brothers and sisters" is an accurate translation of the plural of *adelphos*. See *LSJ*, 20. See also Aída Besançon Spencer, "Exclusive Language—Is It Accurate?," *Review & Expositor* 95 (1998): 388-89. Women are included clearly in the plural of *adelphos* in Acts 16:40; Phil 4:1-2.

[36]The seventy-two disciples most likely are a deliberate echo of the seventy-two elders who helped Moses (Num 11:16-17, 26-29). They model the premise that all the Lord's people can be filled with God's Spirit and prophesy, as would happen at Pentecost (Acts 2:17-18). On the textual question favoring seventy-two over seventy (as in the TNIV), see Kurt Aland's argument in *A Textual Commentary on the Greek New Testament*, 2nd ed., ed. Bruce M. Metzger (Stuttgart: United Bible Societies, 2002), 127.

[37]1 Clement 47.3-4.

[38]Eusebius, *Ecclesiastical History* 1.12; 3.5, 7.

from Galilee may not have been part of the Twelve, but they certainly were part of an inner circle that was trained in all ways as the twelve men were. They had been with Jesus since Galilee (Mt 4:23; 27:55; Mk 15:40-41; Lk 23:49, 55). The angels remind the women that in Galilee Jesus told them he would suffer, be crucified, and be raised (Lk 24:6-8), which suggests they were present in Matthew 17:22; Mark 9:31; and Luke 9:18-22. Mark tells us Jesus wanted to be separated from the crowds because "he was teaching his disciples" (Mk 9:31 NIV). These women would have heard Jesus' teaching to "deny themselves and take up their cross daily" (Lk 9:23 NIV); thus they denied themselves by giving generously to Jesus' mission (Lk 8:2-3; Mt 27:55). They recognized, accepted, and honored the forthcoming suffering of the Messiah by anointing Jesus before the crucifixion and being present at the crucifixion (Mt 26:6-13; 27:61; Mk 14:3-9; Lk 23:55; Jn 11:2; 12:3-8). Mary anointed Jesus' feet, having understood that the Messiah would be crucified (Jn 12:3-7), a lesson Peter did not understand until later (Mt 16:21-23; Lk 24:33- 49; cf. 1 Pet 2:19-24).

The women did not understand everything perfectly. They too were surprised by the empty tomb, the angelic messengers, and the resurrected Messiah (Mk 16:8). Nevertheless, as the eleven male disciples were in Jerusalem to hear Jesus' final revelations, so too very likely were some early women disciples (Mk 8:31-33; Lk 24:33).[39]

As witnesses of the resurrection, women were *sent* by Jesus to proclaim the good news. Jesus sends Mary Magdalene to "go" to "my brothers [and sisters] and tell them, 'I am ascending to my Father and your Father'" (Jn 20:17 NIV).[40] Similarly, in the Synoptic accounts the angel first tells the women (Mary Magdalene, the "other Mary," Salome), "Go quickly and tell [Jesus'] disciples: 'He has risen from the dead and is going ahead of you

---

[39]It is possible that Cleopas's companion was his wife—after all, the two travelers invite Jesus into their home to stay with them (two single men living alone in a village dwelling seems most highly unlikely). Almost certainly Luke intends women to be included in his statement "They found the eleven *and those with them.*" See Bauckham, *Gospel Women,* 112-15, 165-94, 282, who explains exhaustively how the Galilean women were discipled by Jesus and present at Jesus' preascension teachings, as well as part of the seventy-two disciples. The women might also be included in "apostles" in Acts 1:2, 14. See also Lee Anna Starr, *The Bible Status of Women* (1926; repr., New York: Garland, 1987), 172-73.

[40]Some in the early church regarded Mary Magdalene as "an apostle to the apostles." See Swidler, *Biblical Affirmations,* 209-10; Esther de Boer, *Mary Magdalene* (Harrisburg, PA: Trinity Press International, 1996), 60-61.

[Faith]

into Galilee. There you will see him'" (Mt 28:7 NIV; cf. Mk 16:1, 7; Lk 24:1-10). Then Jesus himself appears to the two Marys and commissions them: "Do not be afraid. Go and tell my brothers [and sisters] to go to Galilee; there they will see me" (Mt 28:10 NIV).

Jesus certainly broke convention by choosing women as the first witnesses for the greatest event of all time, the resurrection, even though women were not considered valid witnesses in court. Roman law treated women as "weak" and "light-minded."[41] First-century Jewish thinkers repeat this perspective. For instance, Philo declares that "the judgments of women as a rule are weaker." Josephus proclaims that Jewish law states, "Let no evidence be accepted" from women because of their "levity and temerity." Rabbinic law stated that women did not have to testify; they were ineligible to declare the new year and to speak for ownerless property. Women as witnesses were in the same class as dice players, usurers, pigeon flyers, traffickers in seventh-year produce, and slaves.[42] Generally, rabbinic tradition disqualified women as witnesses.[43] Even some of the male disciples reflected such views when they did not at first believe the women who gave witness to the resurrection (Lk 24:11).

In contrast, for Jesus faith is the key determiner of one's place in the new covenant—as it originally was of the old covenant. Thus, women functioned as witnesses or apostles who had been with Jesus, were eyewitnesses of the resurrection, and were sent by Jesus to proclaim the good news.[44] As apostles sent by God, the twelve Jewish men looked back to the old covenant, whereas the multinumbered women and men looked forward, beyond the resurrection, to the new covenant.

When scholars disqualify women from church leadership by using the twelve male apostles as precedents, they ignore the significance both of

---

[41]Spencer, *Beyond the Curse*, 62; Sarah B. Pomeroy, *Goddesses, Whores, Wives and Slaves: Women in Classical Antiquity* (New York: Schocken, 1975), 150. In contrast, when Peter calls wives a "weaker partner" (referring most likely to physical strength), his call is for husbands to bestow "honor" on "heirs with you of the gracious gift of life" (1 Pet 3:7 NIV).

[42]Philo, *Embassy* 40.319; Josephus, *Antiquities of the Jews* 4.8.15.219; m. Shevu. 4:1, 3; m. Sanh. 3:3; m. Rosh Hash. 1:8.

[43]For an explanation of the general rules and the exceptions, see Tal Ilan, *Jewish Women in Greco-Roman Palestine* (Peabody, MA: Hendrickson, 1996), 163-66.

[44]Similarly, Philip's four daughters "prophesied" (Acts 21:9 NIV). The early church had no hesitation in calling them prophets (Eusebius, *Ecclesiastical History* 3.31).

their number (twelve) and of their Jewishness, and they dismiss the importance of women's functioning as apostles and of Junia's being titled an
apostle. Why choose the Twelve as paradigmatic of all leadership, since
after Pentecost the rest of the Twelve (after Judas) are not replaced after
their deaths in Acts (e.g., Acts 12:2)? If their particular ministry was
not perpetuated, how can the Twelve serve as a precedent for church
leadership today?

We do, however, have the precedents of men *and* women who were
commissioned to preach the gospel. Therefore, we should emphasize what
Jesus emphasized in his teachings: humble mutual service, not male-
female distinctions in leadership. In our applications we need to keep in
mind what Jesus commanded and modeled and explicitly prohibited, not
what we *assume* he implied by his actions.

CONCLUSION

Jesus was "the light of *all* people" that "*all* might believe through him"
(Jn 1:4, 7). Scholars agree that Jesus' ministry of salvation, restoration, and
transformation included men and women, without distinction. As their
Creator, Jesus treated women as intrinsically valuable; he respected them
as intelligent and faithful, and as disciples and laborers along with men.

Since we are agreed on these points, why are some churches not following the example of Jesus? Sometimes today the church and academia
are not instructing women as disciples, not listening to their spiritual
discernment, and not treating them equally as colaborers.

Instead, some still separate women for the indoor tasks of homemaking and men for the outdoor tasks of worldmaking. Jesus' practice
undermined this scheme when he talked with women, instructed them
along with men, and sent them out on mission. If the Bible and ecumenical councils did not hold back women who wanted to lead others
in serving Christ, why should we?[45] We should act out of grace, not
from an unwritten law. Maintaining male-leadership role distinctions

---

[45]For evidence of early church female leadership, see Kevin Madigan and Carolyn Osiek, *Ordained Women in the Early Church: A Documentary History* (Baltimore, MD: Johns Hopkins University Press, 2005), and arguments for female elders in Aída Besançon Spencer, *1 Timothy*, NCCS (Eugene, OR: Cascade, 2013), 57-85, and *2 Timothy and Titus*, NCCS (Eugene, OR: Cascade, 2014), 10-14, 33-41, 44.

is not the best way to save, restore, and transform our church families and society.

John's heavenly vision is of "a great multitude that no one could count, from every nation, tribe, people and language" (Rev 7:9 NIV). In the postresurrection, post-Pentecost new covenant, apostles are no longer limited to twelve but are multinumbered, because Jesus' ministry has refocused from the Jewish people (the twelve tribes, the old covenant) to the Gentiles (the nations, the many tribes, the new covenant). At Pentecost the Holy Spirit equipped every believer to be a priest and proclaimer before God. As Jesus had reminded the disciples earlier, Spirit-gifted leaders must be servants enabling *all* other new-covenant priests to function fully.

- Big argument for male leadership is male 12 apostles, which is not a proper framework for multiple reasons
- Women were considered apostles
- requirements for leadership are faith and attribute based
- women's place in the home is a pagan, cultural practice that is undermined by Jesus' treatment of women

6

MUTUALITY IN MARRIAGE AND SINGLENESS

1 CORINTHIANS 7:1-40

Ronald W. Pierce and Elizabeth A. Kay

• • • • •

INTRODUCTION

One searches in vain for an extended and focused study of 1 Corinthians 7:1-40 by an evangelical scholar addressing Paul's sweeping call here for mutuality in marriage and singleness, specifically as it relates to the contemporary evangelical gender debate.[1] Instead, both sides of this controversy—those advocating for male leadership and those advocating for shared leadership—make only brief and occasional references to individual sections of this chapter, and usually with little to no reference to its larger context.[2] For example, the two standard, evangelical anthologies on the gender debate—*Recovering Biblical Manhood and Womanhood* and

---

[1] The earliest and most extensive discussion is in Gordon D. Fee, *The First Epistle to the Corinthians*, NICNT (Grand Rapids, MI: Eerdmans, 1987), 266-356. Two other egalitarians address this chapter's significance in a few pages each: Philip B. Payne, "1 Corinthians 7: The Equal Rights of Man and Woman in Marriage," in *Man and Woman, One in Christ: An Exegetical and Theological Study of Paul's Letters* (Grand Rapids, MI: Zondervan, 2009), 105-8; and Lucy Peppiatt, *Rediscovering Scripture's Vision for Women: Fresh Perspectives on Disputed Texts* (Downers Grove, IL: IVP Academic, 2019), 95-96. These are, of course, aside from efforts to reconstruct the theological and cultural backdrop of this text and address its numerous exegetical challenges. See Anthony C. Thiselton, *The First Epistle to the Corinthians*, NIGTC (Grand Rapids, MI: Eerdmans, 2000), 484-87, 545-46, and 566-67 for working.

[2] *RBMW*; Ronald W. Pierce and Rebecca Merrill Groothuis, eds., *Discovering Biblical Equality: Complementarity Without Hierarchy*, 2nd ed. (Downers Grove, IL: InterVarsity Press, 2005).

Discovering Biblical Equality—comment only on 1 Corinthians 7:3-5 while ignoring their relevance to the chapter's larger context. John Piper and Wayne Grudem acknowledge Paul's emphasis on "mutuality," yet ignore the force of this chapter as a whole by claiming this emphasis does not "nullify the husband's responsibility for general leadership"—a concept that appears nowhere in the text.[3] In comparison, seven contributors over five chapters in earlier editions of *Discovering Biblical Equality* address these verses in a way that is consistent with the chapter's overall tone—though still only briefly. Out of these, Gordon Fee is the only one who alludes to the chapter's coherent argument by noting, "The mutuality argued for in 1 Corinthians 7:1-16 stands all by itself in the literature of the ancient world."[4]

As evangelicals, we have wrongly neglected this text on many counts. First, Paul's remarks here are three times longer than any gender-related passage in his other letters—in fact, roughly equal to the length of all of his other comments on this subject taken together.[5] Second, he addresses no fewer than twelve related, yet distinct, issues regarding mutuality for men and women in marriage and singleness—again, more than in any other text.[6] Third, his rhetoric is explicitly, consistently, and intentionally gender inclusive, meaning that the language used seeks to include both genders in each statement or principle—while at the same time reflecting a carefully balanced sense of mutuality.[7] Fourth, Paul wrote 1 Corinthians 7 in AD 55, around the time of his Galatians letter (AD 49–55), in which he declares that race, class, and gender are irrelevant for how we value one

---

[3] *RBMW*, 109-10.

[4] In *Discovering Biblical Equality*, see Gordon Fee, 181; Walter Liefeld, 262; Judith and Jack Balswick, 460; Mimi Haddad and Alvera Mickelsen, 490; and Alice Mathews, 500.

[5] In the Greek text, 1 Cor 7:1-40 includes approximately 687 words, in comparison to a combined total of 680 words in 1 Cor 11:2-16 (227); Eph 5:21-33 (196); 1 Tim 2:8-15 (97); Titus 2:2-6 (52); Gal 3:26-29 (53); 1 Cor 14:34-35 (36); and Col 3:18-19 (19).

[6] The number of distinct issues was first noted by Fee, *First Epistle to the Corinthians*, 288, and acknowledged more recently by Thiselton, *First Epistle to the Corinthians*, 515. Compare ten virtues and vices in Titus 2, two prescriptions in Eph 5 and Col 3, four admonitions in 1 Tim 2, two issues addressed in 1 Cor 11, two concerns in 1 Cor 14, and the single principle of practicing Christian oneness in Gal 3.

[7] This is remarkable considering its cultural context. Paul always includes specific reference to both men and women, yet varies the sequence. Men are mentioned first seven times (1 Cor 7:2, 12-15, 17), women, four times (1 Cor 7:3-4, 10-11, 16), and "each other" language is used once (1 Cor 7:5). It is a kind of gender symmetry or parallelism. See Glen G. Scorgie, *The Journey Back to Eden: Restoring the Creator's Design for Women and Men* (Grand Rapids, MI: Zondervan, 2005), 120, 142-44.

another regarding both status in Christ (Gal 3:28) and relationships in the church community (Gal 3:3; 5:1, 7, 16, 25), though they remain salient features of personal identity and interpersonal relationships.[8]

Therefore, it seems prudent to consider 1 Corinthians 7 as an important point of reference for other—and mostly later—New Testament gender texts (1 Cor 11; 14; Eph 5; Col 3; 1 Pet 3; 1 Tim 3; Titus 2), serving as a more comprehensive statement against which these may be interpreted. It is a collection of "seed ideas" that grow into Paul's larger theology of gender.[9] To be clear, 1 Corinthians 7 should not be used to nullify or diminish the teachings of other texts. However, this text must be afforded its own important voice in the evangelical dialogue.

PRINCIPLES OF MUTUALITY IN MARRIAGE (1 COR 7:1-16)

In response to an earlier letter from the Corinthian church, Paul writes to confront a distorted view of spirituality, celibacy, marriage, and the end of the age.[10] He advises his readers to remain as they were when first called to Christ, because being single or married is irrelevant for personal spirituality and devotion to ministry.[11] But Paul also appends to this advice twelve marriage-related principles for practical living by which it becomes clear that the occasion of his remarks is not fully the same as his purpose.[12]

---

[8]Paul does not distinguish biological sex from the concept of gender as a social construct.

[9]William J. Webb, "A Redemptive Movement Hermeneutic," in Pierce and Groothuis, *Discovering Biblical Equality*, 391.

[10]Perhaps he has in mind Jesus' words about living "like God's angels in heaven" (Mt 22:30); see Fee, *First Epistle to the Corinthians*, 12, 269, 290, 330. Celibacy at the time was skewed by the idea that human sexuality was a part of the fallen nature of humanity. As sexual activity became to be seen as fallen, it led Christians in Corinth to believe that celibacy was the better path, not because they were called into this lifestyle but because they were being led to believe that marriage and sexuality would alienate them "from God on an anthropological level." This line of thought came to be known as asceticism. See Will Deming, *Paul on Marriage and Celibacy: The Hellenistic Background of 1 Corinthians 7* (Grand Rapids, MI: Eerdmans, 2004), 214-19.

[11]Throughout 1 Cor 7, Paul reveals his personal preference for singleness (1 Cor 7:1, 6-8, 32-35, 38) to serve God with an undivided heart in a world that is passing away (1 Cor 7:26, 29-31). At the same time, he acknowledges that each believer has his or her own "gift from God" (1 Cor 7:7), which means for some getting married to avoid immorality (1 Cor 7:2, 5, 9, 36) and for others celibate singleness.

[12]This is not the "complete Pauline teaching concerning marriage" (Thiselton, *First Epistle to the Corinthians*, 493-95). However, all twelve issues relate either to marriage or singleness (Fee, *First Epistle to the Corinthians*, 270). Thus, the entire context might be viewed as a discussion about the question of marriage.

More specifically, it is Paul's way of framing these twelve principles that catches the eye of the careful reader. Here, he does not address the man as "head" of the women, as he does in 1 Corinthians 11:3 and Ephesians 5:23. Nor does he refer to believers in the generic masculine (e.g., 1 Cor 7:24, 29, and many other instances)—though this was a common convention of his time. Instead, his rhetoric is at the same time gender specific (he addresses men and women individually) and gender inclusive (the principles clearly apply to both genders). It is never gender exclusive in the sense of a principle applying to one gender and not the other. Such an emphasis on mutuality is striking given the general assumptions toward patriarchy in both the Roman and Jewish traditions of Paul's day.

1. Fidelity in marriage: Each man should have sexual relations with his own wife, and each woman with her own husband (1 Cor 7:2).[13] Although sexual immorality is the stated occasion for Paul's first principle, he says more than is necessary to address this concern. With explicit and precisely mirrored language (*anēr/andros* and *gynē*), he addresses the husband and the wife individually. Although Paul later addresses men and women regarding this matter in separate contexts (that is, husbands in 1 Tim 3:2, 12; wives in 1 Tim 5:9), his commitment to mutual fidelity in marriage remains the common denominator.

By calling each man to be faithful to his own wife and each woman to her own husband, Paul condemns in principle a broad range of unbiblical sexual activity, such as fornication (sexual intercourse outside marriage), adultery, homosexuality—and, by extension, polygamy.[14] Even though men have more commonly perpetuated some of these behaviors

---

[13]These twelve numbered headers contain representative and condensed paraphrases of the texts under consideration.

[14]The practice of a man having multiple wives (also known as polygyny) has been far more common across ancient and modern cultures than that of a woman having multiple husbands (polyandry). Moreover, in the Greco-Roman culture of Paul's day, abuse of marital fidelity was rampant. Demosthenes, a Greek statesman and orator from Athens, summed it up this way: "Courtesans were for companionship, concubines to meet every-day sexual needs, and wives to tend the house and bear legitimate children." Cited by Alison Le Cornu in *The IVP Women's Bible Commentary*, ed. Catherine Clark Kroeger and Mary J. Evans (Downers Grove, IL: InterVarsity Press, 2002), 653.

The lexical meaning of *exetō* (NRSV "sexual immorality") is "to stand in a close relationship to someone." See *A Greek-English Lexicon of the New Testament and Other Early Christian Literature*, rev. and ed. Fredrick William Danker, electronic version 1.3 (Chicago: University of Chicago Press, 2001), 420.

throughout history, Paul is committed here to addressing men and women in a mutual way.

2. Spousal obligations: *The husband should give to his wife sexual intimacy, and likewise the wife also to her husband (1 Cor 7:3).* Paul's concern with sexual immorality continues as he calls believers to offer to their spouses what is rightfully theirs: regular and voluntary sexual intimacy. They are to give generously, not depriving each other. The longer statement addresses the husband's obligation first; then a shorter, mirrored statement speaks to wives.[15] However, the inclusive, compound conjunction "and likewise also" (*homoiōs de kai*) makes it clear that the same obligation evenhandedly applies to both.

The Greek phrase *opheilēn apodidotō*, "to fulfill one's duty," connotes a voluntary repaying of a debt or obligation to another. In the most intimate aspect of marriage, Paul emphasizes surrendering to one another, not exercising or asserting one's own rights.[16] In this case, the husband—the one with greater power and social status—is called on first to yield by giving what rightfully belongs to his wife. Then, to be complete, the wife is told the same obligation applies to her. Such mutuality regarding marital rights is remarkable in a predominantly patriarchal world.

Paul's language here reflects what is often seen in marriage contracts in both Jewish and Roman cultures. In a marriage certificate from 92 BC, the husband is obliged to give the wife what she is owed, in this case, clothing and "the rest."[17] Likewise, the wife's family had to give to the husband what was owed (e.g., a dowry). So, while Paul broadly says that the husband and the wife are each to fulfill their marital duty, there is an undertone of a marriage contract that would have been evident to the Corinthian church. Paul may here be referring to a specific aspect the Corinthians were inquiring about in their letter to him, or he may be speaking generally in that each should give to the other what is owed.

---

[15]The Greek word order in 1 Cor 7:3 puts the wife first in both clauses, though in the first clause she is the object of the preposition, while the husband is the subject of the sentence.

[16]Ephesians 5 shows this is done out of a place of love.

[17]Marriage certificate from 92 BC in Tebtunis Egypt (Tebtunis Papyri 1.104.G), see David Instone-Brewer, "1 Corinthians 7 in the Light of the Graeco-Roman Marriage and Divorce Papyri," *Tyndale Bulletin* 52 (2001): 108. See also Instone-Brewer, *Divorce and Remarriage in the Church: Biblical Solutions for Pastoral Realities* (Downers Grove, IL: InterVarsity Press, 2003), chap. 5.

As the passage progresses, Paul further expands on what it means to fulfill their marital duty.

3. Yielding authority: Neither the wife nor the husband has authority over their own body—that goes to the other (1 Cor 7:4). Much debate has occurred during the last few decades among evangelicals regarding the notion of men's authority or leadership over women in society, church, and home.[18] In this context, it is imperative to point out that 1 Corinthians 7:4 is the only biblical text that directly and explicitly addresses the question of "authority" (*exousia*) in marriage—and here it is clearly mutual.[19] Paul first balances personal rights with a model of giving what is due the recipient: sexual intimacy (1 Cor 7:3). Then, he broadens his call to include the principle of *yielding* the presumed "authority" of a marriage partner rather than *yielding* it (1 Cor 7:4). Like his call to fidelity in 1 Corinthians 7:2, the dual commands here are set in precisely mirrored language. By doing so, Paul goes out of his way to be gender inclusive, by calling for "functional unity and mutual submission" in "the most patriarchal of settings in the ancient world—the bedroom."[20]

The uniqueness, content, and tone of this verse make it more important in the gender-role debate than most have been inclined to acknowledge. Paul's point is that neither spouse should claim authority even over their

---

[18]The usual point of reference for male-leadership arguments is Wayne Grudem's "The Meaning of *kephalē* ('Head'): An Evaluation of New Evidence Real and Alleged," in *Evangelical Feminism and Biblical Truth: An Analysis of More Than One Hundred Disputed Questions* (Portland, OR: Multnomah, 2004), 552-99. In addition, Robert L. Saucy and Clinton B. Arnold argue that "subordination" is "inherent" in Paul's references to "order" (*hypotassō*): see Saucy and Arnold, "Woman and Man in Apostolic Teaching," in *Women and Men in Ministry: A Complementary Perspective*, ed. Robert L. Saucy and Judith K. TenElshof (Chicago: Moody, 2001), 114-21. The most thorough egalitarian response to Grudem's work is Payne, *Man and Woman: One in Christ*, 117-37, 271-90. On the debate over headship and the Trinity, see the chapter by Kevin Giles in this volume.

[19]Paul addresses women teaching men in 1 Tim 2:12 but uses *authentein* instead of the more common *exousia*, found here and in 1 Cor 11:10. However, its meaning in 1 Tim 2 is uncertain as it is the only occurrence of the word in the New Testament. It could connote "exercising authority, usurping authority, or a domineering style of teaching." See Linda L. Belleville, "Teaching and Usurping Authority in the Assemblies: 1 Timothy 2:11-15," in this volume.

[20]Michelle Lee-Barnewall, *Neither Complementarian nor Egalitarian: A Kingdom Corrective to the Evangelical Gender Debate* (Grand Rapids, MI: Baker, 2016), 183. Piper and Grudem's only comment is that 1 Cor 7:4 does not "nullify the husband's [alleged] responsibility for general leadership in marriage" (which is never mentioned in the Bible). They acknowledge the emphasis on mutuality in this passage, but then go on to diminish this principle by insisting that the husband as head should be the one to develop "the pattern of intimacy" for both himself and his wife (*Recovering Biblical Manhood and Womanhood*, 109-10). Scripture nowhere suggests such a qualification.

own body. Instead, each should yield that authority to the other. Such radical servanthood was modeled by Jesus, who enjoys equal power and authority within the Trinity, yet chose a life of sacrificial service (Mt 23:8-12; Phil 2:5-8). In the same way, Paul calls for mutual yielding of authority among human beings—especially spouses. One might say that he stands the traditional notion of male headship on its head (as he is inclined to do elsewhere; see 1 Cor 11:8-9, 11-12; Eph 5:21, 25-28).[21] Just as Jesus chose to yield his rights, so both men and women should do the same.

Such a radical call to yield authority in marital intimacy could possibly serve as a paradigm for surrendering authority in other areas of marriage, since it is the only explicit statement regarding authority in marriage in Scripture. David Garland goes so far as to suggest that "body" (*sōma*) in 1 Corinthians 7:4 "does not refer simply to the physical body . . . but to their whole physical-spiritual existence."[22] Further, the notion of a husband "exercising" authority over his wife runs counter to the direction and force of this statement. Yet still many reject this idea based on two texts where the metaphorical use of "head" (*kephalē*) appears regarding husbands.

First, Paul uses the same noun for "authority" (*exousia*) in 1 Corinthians 11:10, where he declares that "a woman ought to have authority over her head" when praying or prophesying in the assembly. However, it is not clear there whether Paul is referring to the abstract idea of authority (the woman choosing how she might cover her head) or a tangible symbol of authority (some kind of head covering). Nor is it clear whether the woman's authority should be over her literal head (topmost part of her body) or over her figurative head (her husband, who is called her head in 1 Cor 11:2). In addition, the term translated "head" (*kephalē*) can carry the force of "authority over," but also can connote "preeminence, ground of being, or life-giving source." In contrast to this maze of interpretive challenges, the command to yield authority over one's body in 1 Corinthians 7:4 is relatively straightforward.[23] Such clarity should help readers

---

[21]The inverted head imagery is suggested by Lee-Barnewall in her insightful chapter "Marriage, Part 2: Husbands and Wives in Ephesians 5," in *Neither Complementarian nor Egalitarian*.

[22]David E. Garland, *1 Corinthians*, BECNT (Grand Rapids, MI: Baker, 2003), 259.

[23]On exegetical difficulties in 1 Cor 11:2-16, see Gordon D. Fee's essay in this volume, "Praying and Prophesying in the Assemblies: 1 Corinthians 11:2-16," as well as the comprehensive treatise by Payne, *Man and Woman: One in Christ*, chaps. 6-13.

avoid the mistake of imposing an unbiblical prescription of a husband's authority over his wife on other New Testament texts.

Second, though Paul does not explicitly mention authority in Ephesians 5, he instructs the wife to "submit herself" to her husband (who was construed culturally as the head of the Roman household) as part of the apostle's principle of "submitting to one another" in the church (Eph 5:21-22, 24).[24] Though *kephalē* ("head") in the head-body metaphor may connote "authority over" or "source of provision" in the larger contexts of both Ephesians (Eph 1:20-23; 4:15-16) and Colossians (Col 1:18-32; 2:9-15, 18-19), Paul only reinforces the idea of "source of provision" for husbands to wives.[25] Moreover, he calls husbands to love their wives sacrificially as Christ did for the church (Eph 5:25-30)—again, standing *kephalē* on its head. As "head" of his wife, the husband is commanded to love her—not to exercise leadership or authority over her—however benevolent that might be.

In the end, 1 Corinthians 7:4 remains the only explicit statement in all of Scripture about authority (*exousia*) within marriage—and here both the husband and the wife are called to yield it to the other in the deeply personal context of sexual intimacy. Again, as Paul's earliest statement about marriage relations, this text should serve as a reference point for later texts—not to nullify those that are equally clear but to help clarify those that are not.

4. Consent for abstinence: Do not deprive one another, except consensually and for a limited time of focused prayer, then come together again to avoid temptation (1 Cor 7:5). On occasion, personal devotion to extended times of fasting, study, and prayer can disrupt marital intimacy. When this happens, Paul insists that mutual consent be reached first with one's spouse. Though his "one another" language here is more concise than before, he once again emphasizes mutual yielding rather than the notion that either spouse should exercise a leadership role.[26] This undermines the

---

[24]The eldest male bears the title *paterfamilias*, denoting him as head of the Roman household. It is often the case that this would be the husband or grandfather within a family.

[25]Clinton E. Arnold, "Jesus Christ: 'Head' of the Church," in *Jesus of Nazareth, Lord and Christ: Essays on the Historical Jesus and New Testament Christology*, ed. J. B. Green and M. Turner (Grand Rapids, MI: Eerdmans, 1994), 346-66.

[26]Although the exact phrases vary slightly, the same "one another" idea is expressed with regard to at least eighteen different applications of Paul's essential principle of mutuality: unity, kindness, honor, humility, grace, strength, attitude, hospitality, accountability (Rom 12:5, 10, 16; 14:13,

dysfunctional behavior in many patriarchal marriages today where the husband exercises authority over his wife, who counters with more manipulative forms of control such as withholding sexual intimacy.

Taken as a larger thought unit, 1 Corinthians 7:3-5 presents mutual partnership as a model for marriage relationships—one that includes, among other things, mutual consent in processing marital decisions. At the same time, it militates against the long-standing and culturally endorsed notion that Paul's call for the wife to submit to her husband in Ephesians 5:22-24 should be interpreted to mandate the responsibility for a husband to exercise authority—however gracious or self-sacrificing—as head over his wife.[27] Whereas Paul clearly calls for voluntary and mutual submission in marriage (including that of the wife), nowhere does he or any other biblical writer instruct a husband to exercise authority over his wife.[28]

5. Loss of a spouse through death: It is good for widowers and widows to remain single as I am. But if they cannot exercise self-control, let them remarry (1 Cor 7:8-9). Paul addresses the human inclination toward "sensual desires" (see 1 Tim 5:11-14) throughout this text, but not in an exclusive way. The terms for widowed men and women differ slightly, yet are virtually synonymous in this context—clearly implying that the same principle of remaining as one was when called applies to both.[29] At the same time, the variance reveals a contrast in the persistent cultural reality for men and women who have lost spouses to death. The change for women has generally been much more dramatic throughout history, while that for men has been relatively minimal. However, though Paul certainly recognizes these differences, his advice is the same to both regardless of gender.

19; 15:5, 7, 14; 16:16), intimate generosity, care (1 Cor 7:5; 12:25), service, help (Gal 5:13; 6:2), patience, truth telling, forgiveness, submission (Eph 4:2, 25, 32; 5:21), love, and comfort (1 Thess 3:12; 4:18). A Christian model of mutuality plays a significant role in Pauline theology.

[27]See this argument in George W. Knight III, "Husbands and Wives as Analogues of Christ and the Church," in Piper and Grudem, *Recovering Biblical Manhood and Womanhood,* 231.

[28]Contrary to those who argue that wives should be "ordered under" husbands in a "subordinate position," while husbands are to exercise "authority over" their wives as benevolent "leaders and providers." See Saucy and Arnold, "Woman and Man in Apostolic Teaching," 117-19, 133-38.

[29]The alternate NIV translation has "widowers" for men; also see Thiselton's argument (*First Epistle to the Corinthians,* 515-16). The variance between the generic term "unmarried men/widowers" (similar to "unmarried women/widows" in 1 Cor 7:34) and the more explicit term "widows" in 1 Cor 7:8 is not as great as it may seem. The context of this chapter, as well as the specific parallel in this verse, confirms the meaning of "widowers" in 1 Cor 7:8a.

6. Initiating divorce with a believing spouse: *The wife should not separate from her husband, and the husband should not divorce his wife (1 Cor 7:10-11).* Here, the wife is addressed first, more extensively, and with slightly different language. She should not "separate from" her husband, whereas he is not to "send away or divorce" his wife. Yet again, the variance may reflect the reality of Paul's day, when a man generally had greater power to bring about a divorce than a woman. But the difference is not substantive, as evidenced by Paul's inclusive use of the stronger term for divorce for both marriage partners in 1 Corinthians 7:12-13. In the end, the actions he prohibits, left unchecked with either spouse, could lead to the dissolution of the marriage.

In addition, Paul tells the wife that, if she leaves her husband, she must remain unmarried or else be reconciled. Yet, given the larger context of this chapter, the wife's call to reconciliation should be understood to apply equally to the husband. Though Paul's reason for addressing the wife first and more extensively is not clear, it continues to serve his apparent interests in constructing a balanced theology of gender roles. By doing so, Paul empowers the woman in the relationship as she is called to exercise her will in the matter, while still encouraging her to stay in the marriage. In contrast, there is no greater responsibility or burden placed on the man. Instead, wives and husbands must share the challenge of staying together.

7. Initiating divorce with an unbelieving spouse: *If any brother has a nonbelieving wife who consents to stay in the marriage, he should not divorce her. If any woman has an unbelieving husband who consents to stay in the marriage, she should not divorce him (1 Cor 7:12-13).* Paul continues his emphasis on mutuality in sustaining and nurturing a marriage, though here he addresses the problem of already-existing marriages with nonbelievers. Once again, his language of "brother" (*adelphos*) versus "wife" (*gynē*) varies slightly, yet the difference remains insignificant, as the woman being addressed is certainly a sister in Christ (see 1 Cor 7:15).

Scripture makes it clear that God opposes a believer marrying outside the faith, as well as initiating divorce with one's spouse (1 Cor 7:10-13)—though the latter is permitted in extreme circumstances.[30] With this larger

---

[30]Instructive examples of God's opposition to a believer marrying outside the faith include Abraham's search for a bride for Isaac (Gen 24), Samson's escapades with Philistine women (Judg 13–16),

backdrop in mind, Paul calls the believing spouse (husband or wife) to extend grace to the one who does not yet believe. Again, the decision is not presented as the primary responsibility of the husband or wife, but that of the believing spouse. This is similar to Paul's principle that spiritually mature believers are to help restore those who have sinned (Gal 6:1).

In Paul's day, as multiple cultures were converging, there was some consistency regarding marriage and divorce contracts and traditions, but there were also variants between the cultures. For example, Greek and Roman marriage contracts allowed for the possibility that marriage might end in separation or divorce, so stipulations regarding this were built into the contract itself. In contrast, Jewish marriages contracts generally assumed that a marriage would not end until the death of one of the partners. So, in Corinth, where there was a strong Gentile population, divorce would have been seen as an acceptable way to deal with marital differences. Therefore, it was relatively easier for a divorce to take place. Paul is fighting against this understanding of divorce and encourages those who are in marriages with a nonbeliever to hold strong. Since the culture permitted the husband to leave without notice, Paul is intentional in noting that one should not be held accountable for a separation or divorce if one was not the initiator.

8. Sanctification of a nonbelieving spouse: The nonbelieving husband is made holy because of the believing wife, and the nonbelieving wife is made holy because of the believing brother. Otherwise your children would be unclean, but as it is, they are holy (1 Cor 7:14). Again, the language of "wife" (*gynē*) versus "husband/brother" (*anēr/adelphos*) appears, as it did in 1 Corinthians 7:12-13. Yet, again, the difference is not significant for two reasons: Paul is clearly equating the "brother" (1 Cor 7:14b) with

---

Solomon's pagan wives who turned his heart from Yahweh (1 Kings 11), the infamous Jezebel (1 Kings 16–2 Kings 9), and, especially, Paul's prohibition against being unequally yoked (2 Cor 6). The law of Moses prohibits divorce under certain circumstances (Deut 22:19, 29), yet allows for a "certificate of divorce" in other cases (Deut 24:1, 3). Later, Malachi asserts, "God hates divorce" (Mal 2:16). Regarding divorce initiated by an abused spouse, see the helpful discussion by Instone-Brewer, *Divorce and Remarriage*, 93-106. Ironically, Ezra actually insists that the postexilic Jews send away their pagan wives from the Judean community (Ezra 9–10). Later, Jesus grants exceptions for divorce in cases of "sexual immorality" (compare the identical language in Mt 19:9 NIV with 1 Cor 7:2). Jesus' ruling indicates that Moses' original exception was because of the hardness of human hearts (Mt 19:7-8). Such exceptions may suggest the possibility of separation or divorce under other unusually severe circumstances, such as spousal abuse.

the "husband" in the previous clause (1 Cor 7:14a), and the idea of a spouse who does not yet believe being "made holy" (*hagiastai*) by the other spouse is applied mutually to both husband and wife.

Though it falls outside the scope of this chapter to speculate on all Paul means by the "sanctification" of spouses and children, at the least, an unbelieving spouse remaining with a believer sets himself or herself aside (along with their children) for holy purposes.[31] That is to say, they remain under the sanctifying influence of the believing spouse—regardless of their gender. Moreover, it is clear that to whatever extent one can be sanctified through one's spouse, such sanctification is mutual for both the husband and the wife.

Further, this text must be allowed to inform our interpretation of Paul's instructions to husbands to love their wives "just as Christ loved the church and gave himself up for her to make her holy [*hagiasē*]" (Eph 5:25-26 NIV). Paul implies that husbands can have a sanctifying influence on their wives. However, such gender-specific language should not be read as gender exclusive.[32] On the contrary, 1 Corinthians 7:14 makes it clear with explicit, gender-inclusive language that spiritual benefit to a nonbelieving spouse can come from the wife to the husband as well. Keeping both texts in conversation can bring greater clarity to this aspect of the evangelical gender-role debate.

9. Responsibility when the nonbelieving spouse leaves: If the nonbeliever leaves, let it be so. In such cases a brother or sister is not bound. God has called you to peace (1 Cor 7:15). Paul's admonitions above regarding separation and divorce are now softened to words of grace as he addresses believing spouses in mixed marriages as "brother" (*adelphos*) and "sister" (*adelphē*) respectively. Such gender-inclusive language also clarifies the broader range of meaning in the generic masculine *apistos* for the nonbelieving spouse at the beginning of this verse. If the marriage

---

[31]In Paul's writings, the term *hagiastai* usually carries "moral/ethical implications" and can even function as a metaphor for salvation (1 Cor 1:30; 6:11), though the force of the word is certainly not that strong here (Fee, *First Epistle to the Corinthians*, 299-302).

[32]Contra Talley, who argues for a benevolent-patriarchy model of sanctification in marriage based on implications drawn from Christ's sanctification of the church in Eph 5:25-27, yet without reference to the more explicit and gender-inclusive mention of sanctification in the context of marriage in 1 Cor 7:14. See David L. Talley, "Gender and Sanctification: From Creation to Transformation," *JBMW* (Spring 2003): 6-16.

between the believer and the nonbeliever were based on a Greco-Roman standard, there would be nothing that the believing spouse could do to in order to keep the marriage together.[33] It was the custom that simply leaving the home, separating, would have been seen as a divorce, and the stipulations of an impending divorce would have been built into one's marriage contract. Based on this, Paul encourages the believing partner to be at peace, for they have done what they were able to do.

Each of the eight principles discussed previously has reflected the idea of mutual responsibility of a spouse *to* his or her partner, whereas this verse makes it clear that neither is responsible *for* the other. When a nonbeliever chooses to leave, believers who have tried their best to keep the marriage together are under no further obligation, for "God has called us to live in peace." This could mean the peace to remain within a religiously mixed marriage or the peace to let go of the relationship if the nonbelieving spouse insists.[34] Context suggests the latter.[35]

10. Salvation of a nonbelieving spouse: How do you know, wife, whether you will save your husband? Or how do you know, husband, whether you will save your wife? (1 Cor 7:16). Keeping in mind the principle of being responsible *to*, but not *for*, Paul asks a rhetorical question with the same mirrored language of mutuality employed at the beginning of this chapter. In this way, he explores the possibility that the marital commitment of a believer (male or female) to a nonbeliever might lead to that person's salvation.

Surely, the spiritual benefit one human being can give to another only goes so far. It certainly falls short of Christ's effective benefit to save and sanctify the church. Yet, this passage suggests that we can partner with Christ as we aid nonbelieving spouses on their journey toward salvation and sanctification. At the same time, however, Paul makes it equally clear that neither of these potential benefits is limited to a husband or wife based on gender. On the contrary, with his consistent and explicitly inclusive

---

[33]Instone-Brewer, "1 Corinthians 7 in the Light," 241.

[34]See Fee, *First Epistle to the Corinthians*, 304-5; Thiselton, *First Epistle to the Corinthians*, 537-40.

[35]This is also consistent with Paul's earlier exhortation (based on a gospel of grace) that believers should stand firm in the liberty in which Christ has made them free (Gal 5:1, 13). It is reinforced by his later admonition, "If it is possible, as far as it depends on you, live at peace with everyone" (Rom 12:18 NIV). *stand firm in liberty*

language, Paul insists that these are mutually beneficial influences that either Christian spouse may have toward a partner who has not yet come to faith.

THE COMPARATIVE ISSUES OF RACIAL AND SOCIOECONOMIC STATUS (1 COR 7:17-24)

The "interactive significance" of race and slavery mentioned in these verses is essential to the larger discussion of Paul's twelve principles for mutuality in marriage and singleness in 1 Corinthians 7.[36] It is not coincidental that he mentions Jew and Gentile (1 Cor 7:17-20), as well as slave and free (1 Cor 7:21-24), given his grouping of these categories with that of male and female in his foundational statement in Galatians 3:26-29 (especially Gal 3:28). In Galatians his focus is on the former, whereas in Philemon it is on the latter. Here, it is on humanity as male and female.[37] The link that connects the three groups is the principle that believers do not need to change their status in order to live holy lives or to serve Christ better.

It is not at all certain that the Corinthians would have been aware of Paul's circulating letter to the churches in the Galatian province; yet, the times of writing the two letters are close enough that the reader can assume Paul still has the essential concern of Galatians: that the old categories of race, socioeconomic status, and gender are irrelevant in determining one's spiritual *and* functional equality in the new-covenant community.[38] To the Corinthians he argues, "circumcision is nothing and uncircumcision is nothing" (1 Cor 7:19 NIV); and the slave is "the Lord's freed person," and "the one who was free when called is Christ's slave" (1 Cor 7:22 NIV). A robust theology of mutuality ties these three representative groups together, making the principled statement in Galatians 3:28 a point of reference for reading 1 Corinthians 7.

---

[36]See Thiselton, *First Epistle to the Corinthians*, 545-65.

[37]When Paul speaks of "male and female," he is not excluding intersex persons but rather simply not referring to them. Elsewhere, Jesus mentions "eunuchs" (Mt 19:12), though these are not the equivalent to intersex persons, along with the goodness of celibate singleness. Further, eunuchs are explicitly honored by God in Is 56:4-5.

[38]This perspective allows for the range of opinions on the dating of Galatians (AD 48–55) and agrees with the near consensus on the date of 1 Corinthians (AD 55).

PRINCIPLES OF MUTUALITY IN SINGLENESS
(1 COR 7:25-40)

1. Thinking carefully before marriage: In view of the present distress it is good for a man or woman to remain as they are—single or married (1 Cor 7:26-28a). This section may be addressing those men and women who have never been married, those who are already engaged, or both.[39] Consistent with one of his recurring themes in this chapter, Paul admonishes believers not to make a radical change in status because of the perceived nearness of the end of the age. Whether a man or woman is single, engaged, or married is irrelevant to functioning as a productive member of the new-covenant community.

In contrast to Paul's more balanced statements above, here he addresses the man more extensively. One cannot be sure whether this reflects a greater concern for the men than women at Corinth on this matter. Moreover, the woman is addressed here (as well as in 1 Cor 7:34) as *parthenos* ("virgin") and *gynē* ("woman"), whereas the man is referred to simply by the generic *anthropos* ("man"). The difference in terminology seems negligible, though it serves once more as an example of the diverse language used to describe gender mutuality that Paul paints across these twelve principles—the latter being a common thread throughout.

2. Ministry and spiritual calling: Those who choose to marry—men or women—will face worldly problems, as well as distractions from undivided devotion to Christ (1 Cor 7:28b, 32-34).[40] It is ironic—though not entirely surprising—that Paul ends his larger discussion of gender mutuality in marriage with a statement regarding singleness. He has woven the thread of his preference for celibate singleness throughout the chapter with the purpose of serving Christ more efficiently (1 Cor 7:1, 6-8, 26, 29-35, 38).

---

[39]Again, see Thiselton's discussion of the various options for the subjects of this section (*First Epistle to the Corinthians*, 565-71) and Fee's (*First Epistle to the Corinthians*, 322-34). The argument of this chapter, however, does not depend on answering this question.

[40]Over time, the church has begun to raise marriage to such a high value that as a result it has begun to undervalue singleness. As Paul points out in this chapter, though, singleness is a calling, and there are certain things that make it more beneficial when it comes to looking at kingdom values. Those who remain single are able to serve God without their heart being pulled in different directions, and they also have the freedom to serve the church in ways that those who are married are unable to do.

Often Paul's focus in this chapter is perceived as being aimed toward those who are married. Though this passage contains prescriptions for marriage, the intent is not only this. Nor is the apostle merely pitting marriage against singleness. Rather, he follows his remarks on marriage to focus more broadly on the church family by showing how marriage relates to God's larger purposes.[41] Too often, it is mistakenly concluded that marriage is the ultimate goal for a Christian, and singleness is for a season, or a lesser position, or for those especially gifted. But Paul negates these thoughts, stating that singleness is ultimately more favorable than marriage in regard to God's kingdom plan.[42]

Therefore, the focus of this essay has not been on marriage as opposed to singleness—though an equally important topic. Rather, the issue at hand has been the remarkable, gender-inclusive way that Paul goes about his task, correcting the Corinthian church's view on both singleness and marriage. His closing statements remind the reader that ministry priorities, responsibilities, and privileges apply mutually to both men and women, whether devotion to prayer that distracts from sexual intimacy (1 Cor 7:5) or devotion to ministry that avoids the distractions of marriage altogether (1 Cor 7:28).

One last time in his concluding thoughts, Paul addresses women shoulder-to-shoulder alongside men, making it clear that either may choose devotion to ministry instead of marriage. This runs contrary to the stubbornly persistent cultural tradition that a young woman should have as her goal in life to find a good husband who will lead and care for her—in fact radically countercultural, because women, in Paul's day, were greatly dependent on marriage. Their livelihood was based on their family or that of their husband. So as Paul encourages singleness, he also calls for a radical change in lifestyle. Women would have to be dependent on themselves or on the church if they were to remain unmarried.[43] So, whether it concerns the question of marriage or singleness in faithful service to Christ and the church, one of Paul's clear themes in this chapter is an equal sense of gender mutuality.

---

[41]See Joseph H. Hellerman, *When the Church Was a Family* (Nashville: B&H, 2009), 90.
[42]Hellerman, *When the Church Was*, 91.
[43]Conversely, Paul encourages young widows to remarry so that their "sensual desires" do not "overcome their dedication to Christ" (1 Tim 5:11-14).

CONCLUSIONS

This brief survey of 1 Corinthians 7 is intended to begin a dialogue that will reframe the discussion of this important yet neglected text. Perhaps it will provide some fresh thinking toward a fresh approach to this passage in the context of the evangelical gender debate. Hopefully, a more extensive study of 1 Corinthians 7 with a focus on its relevance to the evangelical gender-role debate will emerge in the near future. Until then, a few tentative conclusions can be drawn.

First, both celibate singleness and faithful marriage should have legitimate and honored places in our churches. Paul's argument is: "If you're not ready to embrace a godly and mutual marriage relationship, perhaps you should stay single. And, if you're not ready to embrace godly celibate singleness, perhaps you should consider marriage. But remember, godly devotion to Christ is more important than either!"

Second, by writing 1 Corinthians 7 around the same time as his letter to the Galatians, Paul's language of even-handed gender mutuality contrasts sharply with what one might expect from a first-century writer—Jewish or Roman. Yet, it coheres with the cryptic—though more famous—declaration in Galatians 3:28, being most likely his first occasional expansion on the "new creation" model of radical oneness in Christ (see Gal 6:15; 2 Cor 5:17).[44] Though Paul's words do not address every aspect of marriage, this twelve-part statement is the most comprehensive made on the subject in Scripture—and, as such, it deserves much more attention in the contemporary evangelical dialogue on gender.

Third, as an early point of reference, this text shines the positive light of gender-inclusive mutuality on other statements in both contemporary and later gender texts in the Bible (1 Cor 11; 14; Eph 5; Col 3; 1 Pet 3; 1 Tim 3; Titus 2). By doing so, it helps to clarify important issues in this debate—such as yielding of authority (otherwise referred to by Paul in Eph 5:21 as "submitting to one another") and the giving of spiritual benefits (leading to sanctification and salvation) that a believer may give to a spouse in marriage.

In sum, this chapter paints a portrait of the beauty of mutuality in intimate, personal relationships—sexual or not, and whether one remains

---

[44]Thiselton, *First Epistle to the Corinthians*, 527.

single or chooses to marry.[45] It is the fully inclusive complementarity that was intended when God first said of Adam, "It is not good for the man to be alone. I will make a helper corresponding to him" (Gen 2:18, author's translation). Of course, for the sake of being fruitful, multiplying, and filling the earth, that narrative involved what later came to be known as marriage. Yet, Paul extends it to mutuality in singleness as well here in 1 Corinthians 7. In both we can find God's gift of mutuality in "a covenantal, God-imaging, self-sacrificial relationship of faithfulness and love" in the service of Christ.[46]

---

[45]On the challenges related to finding intimate, nonerotic relationships in the spiritual family of God, see Wesley Hill, *Spiritual Friendship: Finding Love in the Church as a Celibate Gay Christian* (Grand Rapids, MI: Brazos, 2015).

[46]Paul Gardner, *1 Corinthians*, Zondervan Exegetical Commentary on the New Testament (Grand Rapids, MI: Zondervan, 2018), 306.

7

PRAYING AND PROPHESYING IN THE ASSEMBLIES

1 CORINTHIANS 11:2-16

Gordon D. Fee

• • • • •

THE INTERPRETATION OF 1 CORINTHIANS 11:2-16 has long been a major crux in the study of Paul's letters.[1] This is mostly because several key aspects of the passage are shrouded in mystery, including the specific nature of the sociocultural issue Paul is addressing, what the Corinthian women (presumably) were doing that called forth this response, how Paul's response works as an argument, and especially the meaning of several crucial terms.[2] At the same time, the argumentation as a whole is especially uncharacteristic of Paul, both in terms of his generally relaxed attitude to

---

[1]This is illustrated in part by the considerable differences of interpretation to be found in three recent major commentaries in English: Gordon D. Fee, *The First Epistle to the Corinthians*, NICNT (Grand Rapids, MI: Eerdmans, 1987); R. F. Collins, *First Corinthians*, Sacra Pagina (Collegeville, MN: Liturgical Press, 1999); Anthony C. Thiselton, *The First Epistle to the Corinthians*, NIGTC (Grand Rapids, MI: Eerdmans, 2000). Necessary limitations of space for each chapter in this book prohibit lengthy interaction with the wide range of options available. I apologize in advance to some scholars who will feel slighted by what I have done—but this is written as an essay rather than an academic piece that would give proper recognition to the work of others.

[2]Including (1) the meaning of *head*, which seems to fluctuate between the literal physical head on one's body and the (not totally clear) metaphorical use posited in 1 Cor 11:3; (2) the phrase in 1 Cor 11:4-5 translated "head covered" in most English versions, literally "having down the head"; (3) the word for "uncovered" in 1 Cor 11:5, 13; (4) the phrase "authority over her head" in 1 Cor 11:10; (5) the prepositional phrase "because of the angels" in 1 Cor 11:10; (6) the preposition *anti* in 1 Cor 11:15, which ordinarily means "in place of"; and (7) the clause "we have no such custom" in 1 Cor 11:16, which most English translations (illegitimately?) render "we have no *other* custom."

the presenting issue itself and of his arguing primarily on the basis of cultural shame rather than from the person and work of Christ. And finally, the basic datum in 1 Corinthians 11:5, that women are here assumed to pray and prophesy in the gathered community, stands in stark contrast to the requirement of absolute silence "in church" in 1 Corinthians 14:34-35.[3]

Yet despite these many uncertainties, acknowledged in part by almost everyone who has written on this passage, one may still find some who are bold to assert that this passage teaches "that women should pray and prophesy in a manner that makes it clear that they submit to male leadership."[4] In light of what Paul actually says—or does not say—such an assertion is made with a great deal more confidence than a straightforward exegesis of the passage would seem to allow.

Limitations of space do not permit me to deal with all the issues raised above. For our present purposes, five matters will be addressed: (1) the nature of the issue that called forth this response, (2) the structure of Paul's argument as a whole, (3) the significance of "praying and prophesying," (4) the meaning of the metaphorical use of *head* in 1 Corinthians 11:3, and (5) the meaning of 1 Corinthians 11:10 in the argument of 1 Corinthians 11:7-12.

THE PRESENTING ISSUE IN CORINTH

In 1 Corinthians Paul is responding both to issues reported to him (1 Cor 1:11; cf. 1 Cor 5:1) and to the Corinthians' letter to him (1 Cor 7:1). With the formula "now concerning the matters you wrote about" in 1 Corinthians 7:1, he begins to pick up a series of items from their letter.[5] This formula recurs in 1 Corinthians 7:25 and then at the beginning of the extended argument of 1 Corinthians 8:1–11:1.[6] Since the latter deals with matters of worship—pagan worship in this case—it appears that Paul moves on next to deal with three matters of worship within the believing

---

[3]This, of course, is a problem only for those who consider 1 Cor 14:34-35 authentic. For an argument against its authenticity, with some rejoinder to those who have objected to this view as presented in my commentary, see Gordon D. Fee, *God's Empowering Presence: The Holy Spirit in the Letters of Paul* (Peabody, MA: Hendrickson, 1994), 272-81.

[4]Thomas R. Schreiner, "Head Coverings, Prophecies and the Trinity: 1 Corinthians 11:2-16," in *RBMW*, 176.

[5]Translations of 1 Corinthians in this chapter are my own.

[6]In some of these instances he is clearly quoting from their letter itself (1 Cor 7:1; 8:1, 4); see Fee, *First Epistle to the Corinthians*, 275-77, 362.

community itself. The final one of these (1 Cor 12–14) again picks up the formula "now about" and therefore most likely emerges from their letter. But the source of the two items addressed in 1 Corinthians 11 is much less certain. They are tied together by intentionally contrasting introductions in 1 Corinthians 11:2, 17, the first as commendatory as the second is confrontational. The second matter at least has surely been reported to him.[7] It probably sits in its present context—between items from their letter rather than in 1 Corinthians 1–6—because of the overarching theme of "worship matters" in 1 Corinthians 8–14.

The placement of this section in the letter is thus easily explained. It too takes up a matter of worship; at the same time, it is not a problem of such serious consequence as is the potential destruction of the community when the rich abuse the poor at the Lord's Table (see 1 Cor 11:20-22). Most likely the present issue (1 Cor 11:2-16) has been reported to Paul as well; and although he feels strongly enough about it to speak to it, his repeated, basically cultural appeals make it clear that even though the Corinthian believers are not being commended with respect to the head-covering issue, neither are they being scolded as they were in 1 Corinthians 1:10–4:21; 5:1-13; 6:1-11, 12-20; 8:1–10:22 and will be in 1 Corinthians 11:17-34; 14:36-38.[8] Thus, the passage serves as a useful, contrasting lead-in to the major issue to be taken up next.

But what exactly is the issue in our text? Here there is a division of the house—in four ways: (1) whether both men and women were involved in the behavior Paul seeks to correct; (2) what exactly the women were doing, whether they were discarding an (assumed) external head covering or simply letting down their hair in this semipublic setting; (3) whether the covering was always to be in place or only when they prayed or prophesied (no clear decision can be made here, but at least it included the latter); and (4) whether the men and women involved were (only) husbands and wives or all women in relation to all men (it is usually assumed that Paul is dealing with husband-wife relationships because of 1 Corinthians 11:3-4, but in

---

[7]This is indicated both by the clear "I hear" statement in 1 Cor 11:18 and the confrontational nature of the whole.

[8]Although there are theological and biblical moments expressed in 1 Cor 11:3 and 1 Cor 11:7-9, all the rest is based on "shame" (1 Cor 11:5-6), what is "fitting/proper" (1 Cor 11:13), "nature" (1 Cor 11:14), and "custom" (1 Cor 11:16), none of which is implied as bringing shame on Christ!

fact everything that is said could be addressed generically to all women in relationship to all men).[9]

In any case, even though much of this discussion is fraught with uncertainty regarding details, determining the precise nature of the presenting problem does not seem to be absolutely essential to an understanding of Paul's argumentation as a whole, nor will it greatly affect how one views the relational issues involved—except at one crucial point, which will be taken up at the end: *Why* were they doing whatever they were doing, so that Paul addresses the issue in terms of male-female *relationships*?

PAUL'S RESPONSE: AN OVERVIEW

The place to begin one's discussion of any of the details is to have some sense of how Paul's argument works and how its various parts relate to one another. Thus, after the commendation in 1 Corinthians 11:2, Paul sets out to correct a matter regarding appropriate head apparel/appearance, which, even though not especially disturbing to him, apparently still had the potential of causing a measure of distress within the community.

The complexity of the argument begins with 1 Corinthians 11:3, where Paul anticipates what he will say about their heads *literally*, by using "head" (Greek *kephalē*) *metaphorically* with regard to three sets of relationships: "Christ" and "every man," "man" and "woman," and "Christ" and "God." Although the meaning of this metaphor is hotly debated, the concern here is to point out how this statement works in the argument itself. For the very next thing Paul says in 1 Corinthians 11:4 picks up the first set of relationships in 1 Corinthians 11:3: "every man praying or prophesying 'having down the head' brings shame to [*kataischynei*] his 'head.'" This seems to

---

[9]Concerning (1), it is sometimes argued (most recently by Collins and Thiselton) that the issue is with the behavior of both. While the passage most certainly has to do with both, in terms of relationships within the community, the structure of the three parts to the argument (1 Cor 11:3-6, 7-12, 13-15) makes a double-sided behavioral issue highly improbable. In the first two cases Paul starts with the man but shows interest primarily in the woman (note esp. the "therefore" regarding the woman in 1 Cor 11:10), while in the final section he starts with, and deals mostly with, the woman (the man is mentioned in 1 Cor 1:14 merely to serve as a contrast to the woman in 1 Cor 11:15).

Concerning (2), see the helpful summary discussions in Thiselton, *First Epistle to the Corinthians*, 823-26, 828-33. Although most scholars continue to believe that it involves some kind of external head covering on the women, deciding this issue is ultimately irrelevant for our present purpose.

refer at least to bringing shame on his metaphorical "head" (Christ) in 1 Corinthians 11:3.[10]

A similar thing is then said about the woman, that if she does the opposite of the man ("prays or prophesies *uncovered* as to the head"), she brings shame to her head. But in her case Paul elaborates on the theme of shame. An uncovered head when prophesying is equal to her being "shaved" or "shorn"; and if these are shameful—and the supposition is that they are indeed—then let her be covered.[11] The unexpected turn in the argument is that the shame is now her own, with no mention of the relationship to the man.[12] The upshot is that the meaning of the crucial phrase in 1 Corinthians 11:5 ("shame on her head") now seems to be a toss-up: is "her head" "the man" of 1 Corinthians 11:3-4 or her own head? The most likely resolution lies in a form of double entendre; that is, by shaming her *own* head in this way, she also brings shame on "her head = man" in some way.

The next two parts of the argument seem intended to elaborate on the man-woman relationship. The first (1 Cor 11:7-12) is full of intrigue. The structure of the argument and the reason for it are clear enough, while the content and intent of the two key sentences (1 Cor 11:7, 10) are filled with mystery. Paul begins with the man, initially simply repeating the point of 1 Corinthians 11:4: "A man ought not to cover his head."[13] This is then qualified by a participial phrase that seems to require a causal or explanatory sense: "since he is the image and glory of God." But here there are further difficulties.

That Paul is appealing to Genesis 1–2 can scarcely be doubted, especially in light of the double explanation given in 1 Corinthians 11:8-9: that woman

---

[10]Those who see the problem as having to do with the behavior of both men and women also argue that the head referred to in this instance is first of all the man's own head (see, e.g., Thiselton, *First Epistle to the Corinthians*, 827-28); but this seems to put 1 Cor 11:3 on the back burner altogether.

[11]Although one cannot be sure precisely why being shaved or shorn would be shameful. There is some evidence for the use of verbs to refer to a woman who wanted to appear "mannish." See Fee, *First Epistle to the Corinthians*, 511n81. An older view, which has no support from the literature, suggested that "shorn" women were prostitutes.

[12]The Greek text makes the woman's shame being her own quite clear: *ei de aischron gynaiki*, "if it is shameful to/for a woman to . . ."

[13]These are two sentences (1 Cor 11:4, 7) that have led some to see the problem as dealing as much with the man as the woman. But in fact, things are not equal. Paul offers no elaboration to these sentences, nor does he make a further point of them. Indeed, in the present instance (1 Cor 11:7) he concludes by saying something about the woman's relationship to the man, and that is what is elaborated in the rest of the section.

is "from the man" and was "created for his sake." But because Paul is alluding to the Genesis creation narrative, he does two things. First, he abandons the relationship expressed in 1 Corinthians 11:3 for the one narrated in Genesis 1–2 (that is, between man and God, not man and Christ), thereby suggesting that the relationships expressed in 1 Corinthians 11:3 probably do not control the whole passage. At the same time, he restates the nature of the relationship between man and woman in terms of her being his "glory."[14] His point seems to be that she who was created to be man's glory is behaving in a way that is causing shame. With this turn in the argument the metaphorical use of *head* now disappears altogether—at least in terms of actual usage.

The real puzzle comes with 1 Corinthians 11:10. The "for this reason" with which the new sentence begins probably picks up what is said about the man-woman relationship in 1 Corinthians 11:7-9.[15] But after that there is neither what is expected, given the way the argument has unfolded to this point, nor what is in any way clear. What is expected, in light of the argument of 1 Corinthians 11:4-5 and to correspond fully with 1 Corinthians 11:7, is "Therefore the woman ought to have her head covered." What is present instead is the most obscure clause in the whole passage: "[She] ought to have authority over her head because of the angels." This sentence in turn is followed by an adversative "nonetheless" (or "in any case"), which introduces two sentences intended (at least) to modify in reverse order the relational statements based on creation in 1 Corinthians 11:8-9, while at the same time also modifying 1 Corinthians 11:10 in some way.[16]

As the woman was created for the man's sake (1 Cor 11:9), so now "in the Lord" neither is to live without the other (1 Cor 11:11); and as the woman

---

[14]After all, the Old Testament narrative is clear that man and woman together were created in God's image, which is why Paul adds the phrase not found in Genesis that man, who is indeed "in the image of God," is at the same time "God's glory," a phrase that Paul will pick up in 2 Cor 4:4-6 to refer to Christ in his humanity as being in both the image and glory of God.

[15]I say probably because this inferential conjunction (*dia touto*) functions in Paul's letters either backward or forward, or, in many cases, as is most likely the case here, simultaneously in both directions.

[16]"Nonetheless" is Greek *plēn*, a "marker of someth[ing] that is contrastingly added for consideration" (BDAG). It seems highly probable that it has a double function: to limit the degree of "authority over her head" that a woman possesses (if that is in fact the meaning of this verse—see below) and to sharply qualify 1 Cor 11:8-9 so that they will *not* be understood in the subordinating fashion that so many are prone to read into them.

originally came from the man (1 Cor 11:8), the man subsequently is born "through the woman," so "all things come from God" (1 Cor 11:12).

The final section (1 Cor 11:13-15) appeals only to what is "fitting" and to "nature itself." In another very complex set of sentences, Paul urges that the very fact that "nature" has given a man short hair and a woman long hair argues for her need to keep with the traditional covering.[17] Then the whole is wrapped up in 1 Corinthians 11:16 with a final appeal: "Anyone who might appear to be contentious" over this matter should acknowledge that "we have no such custom, nor do the churches of God."[18] In this way Paul appeals to what is true of his own churches as well as of the church universal.

In the end, it is plain that Paul wants the woman to maintain the tradition (whatever it is) and to do so primarily for reasons of "shame" and "honor" in a culture where this is the primary sociological value.[19] He is prepared to base this argument also on some basic matters regarding the relationship between men and women that goes back to creation, but he is equally prepared to qualify the latter by appealing to what it means for both to be "in the Lord" and to the fact that subsequent to creation the "order of creation" is reversed. But that still leaves us with several unresolved matters, which the rest of this essay speaks to.

It is of interest to note that the metaphorical use of *head* in 1 Corinthians 11:3 simply disappears from the argument after 1 Corinthians 11:5. And while the relational dimension of the argument regarding men and women continues through 1 Corinthians 11:7-12, it is not found at all at the end, nor is it picked up in any way at the conclusion.

---

[17]This is too easy an answer to a very complex issue, offering a conclusion without argumentation; but settling this exegetical issue is not crucial for the purposes of this paper and is a rat's nest for people on all sides of the sociocultural issue (for a fuller argument, see Fee, *First Epistle to the Corinthians*, 526-29).

"Nature" means, as the NIV rightly has it, "the very nature of things." After all, nature in the case of the man comes about by an *un*natural act, namely a haircut.

[18]The Greek adjective *toiautēn* means "of such a kind, such as this" (BDAG); to stretch it, as most English translations tend to do, to equal *allos*, "other," is to make it conform to what one thinks Paul ought to have said. Most likely he is referring back to what the women are doing, as indicated in 1 Cor 11:5, 13. That is, the churches have no such custom as the women are promoting by their behavior—although earlier commentators thought the custom referred to was to be contentious itself (so also Collins, *First Corinthians*, 414).

[19]See, e.g., David A. deSilva, *Honor, Patronage, Kinship and Purity: Unlocking New Testament Culture* (Downers Grove, IL: InterVarsity Press, 2000), 23-93, and the literature cited in his notes.

ON WOMEN PRAYING AND PROPHESYING

Despite an occasional demurral, the text is quite clear that women were regular participants in the "praying and prophesying" that were part of the worship in churches under Paul's oversight.[20] This is fully in keeping with what comes later in 1 Corinthians 14, where Paul variously says that "*all* speak in tongues" (1 Cor 14:23), that "*all* may prophesy, one by one" (1 Cor 14:29), and that when they assemble, "*each one* of you has [some participatory role]" (1 Cor 14:26). No distinction is made between men and women in these matters, and the present text makes it certain that the *all* means what it is expected it to mean: that women and men alike participated in verbalized expressions of worship in the early house churches.

It is also likely that the present passage anticipates the argument of 1 Corinthians 14 in yet another way: in the distinction Paul will make there between "speaking in tongues" and "prophesying." What is certain in 1 Corinthians 14 is that Paul is trying to cool the Corinthians' ardor for tongues. To do this he sets it in a context of edification in the gathered assembly. Thus, he argues, first, that only intelligible utterances can edify the community (1 Cor 14:1-19) or bear witness to outsiders (1 Cor 14:20-25), and second, that everything must be orderly, since God is a God of shalom, not chaos (1 Cor 14:26-33). In the process he clearly denominates "tongues speaking" a form of prayer (1 Cor 14:2, 14, 28), while "prophecy" represents all forms of Spirit-inspired intelligible speech, capable of edifying the whole community (1 Cor 14:6). Thus *tongues* equals speech that is God-directed (prayer), and *prophecy* equals speech that is community-directed.

In light of this later distinction, it seems altogether likely that Paul intends "praying and prophesying" to be not exclusive of other forms of ministry but representative of ministry in general. And since *prophets* precedes *teachers* in the ranking in 1 Corinthians 12:28, and prophesying is grouped with teaching, revelation, and knowledge in 1 Corinthians 14:6, one may legitimately assume that women and men together shared in all these expressions of Spirit gifting, including teaching, in the gathered assembly.[21]

---

[20]See Fee, *First Epistle to the Corinthians*, 497n22.
[21]See Fee, *God's Empowering Presence*, 144-46.

THE PROBABLE MEANING OF "HEAD" AS A METAPHOR

Kephalē *in 1 Corinthians 11:3.* Paul's metaphorical use of "head" in 1 Corinthians 11:3 has set off an unfortunate, but massive, debate that has often produced as much heat as light.[22] Without rehashing that debate, we may safely isolate several things about Paul's usage here.

1. This is both the first occurrence of *kephalē* in Paul's writings and its only appearance in a context where "the body" is not mentioned or assumed. Later when Paul speaks of Christ as head in relationship to the church (Eph 4:15-16; Col 2:19), it is a metaphor not for lordship but for the supporting, life-giving role that in ancient Greek thought the (literal) head was understood to have in relationship to the physical body.

2. In this passage it is not Christ's relationship to the church that is in view but specifically his relationship to the man (= male human being). And whatever the relationship of Christ to the man envisioned by the metaphor in this context, it must be viewed in a way that is similar to Paul's understanding of the relationship of God the Father to Christ. That is, it is highly unlikely that Paul has set up the whole argument with a relational metaphor that would change meaning from pair to pair. So at issue, finally, in this whole passage is the nature of the relationship perceived between God and Christ.[23]

3. What we also know from the evidence is that when the Jewish community used this metaphor, as they did frequently in the Old Testament, it most often referred to a leader or clan chieftain. On the other hand, although something close to this sense can be found

---

[22]See the especially helpful overview, with bibliography, in Thiselton, *First Epistle to the Corinthians*, 812-22.

[23]It should perhaps be noted that John Chrysostom, who assumed the metaphor in the case of man and woman to express a hierarchical relationship based on the fall, felt compelled to argue against the "heretics" (Arians) that of necessity it had to have a different sense in the God-Christ pair (*Homilies on the Epistles of Paul to the Corinthians*, Homily 26 on 1 Cor 11:2-16). But in either case, he utterly rejects that the metaphor includes the notion of "rule and subjection"; otherwise Paul would "not have brought forward the instance of a wife, but rather of a slave and master." With regard to Christ and man, and God and Christ, he resorts to the language "authors of their being." His reason for abandoning that meaning for the man-woman relationship (which he understands as husband-wife) is that he imports here his understanding of Eph 5:22 as supporting a hierarchical relationship.

among Greeks, they had a broader range of uses, all of which can be shown to arise out of their anatomical understanding of the relationship of the head to the body (its most prominent or important part; the source of the body's working systems, etc.).[24]

4. The earliest extant consistent interpretation of the metaphor in this passage is to be found in a younger contemporary of Chrysostom, Cyril of Alexandria (d. 444?), who explicitly interprets in terms of the Greek metaphor: "Thus we can say that 'the head of every man is Christ.' For he was made by [*dia*] him . . . as God; 'but the head of the woman is the man,' because she was taken out of his flesh. . . . Likewise, 'the head of Christ is God,' because he is of him [*ex autou*] by nature."[25] That is, as with Chrysostom's understanding of the two pairs (God-Christ, Christ-man), Cyril is ready to go this way with all three pairs because of what is said in 1 Corinthians 11:8: that the woman was created from the man. Not only was the idea that the head is the source of supply and support for all the body's systems a natural metaphor in the Greek world, but in this case, it also

---

[24]Thus Chrysostom, with regard to the two pairs Christ-man and God-Christ, understands the metaphor in a very anatomical way: "the head is of like passions with the body, and liable to the same things."

On *kephalē*, note, e.g., Thiselton's caption for his excursus "*Kephalē* and Its Multiple Meanings" (*First Epistle to the Corinthians*, 812). There is no known instance where *kephalē* is used as a metaphor for the husband-and-wife relationship; this seems to be unique to Paul. The closest thing to metaphorical *kephalē* = "lord over" is found in Aristotle (*Politics* 1255b): "The rule of the household is a monarchy; for every house is under one head." But here *head* does not mean "male human being," since Aristotle's observations would apply, e.g., to Lydia (Acts 16:15) and Nympha (Col 4:15), as well as to Philemon (Philem 1). There is a similar usage (apparently) in Plutarch (*Pelopidas* 2.1; *Galba* 4.3), in both cases to refer to a general and his troops. But in the second instance, one of the rare instances where *head* and *body* occur together, he refers to the army as "a vigorous body [= the Gallic provinces with 100,000 men in arms] in need of a head." While this certainly refers to their need of a commander, the metaphor in this case seems more to call for someone with brains to lead them.

The clearest evidence for the real differences between the Jewish and Greek metaphorical uses is to be found in the Septuagint (LXX). In the hundreds of places where the Hebrew *rosh* is used for the literal head on a body, the translators invariably used the only word in Greek that means the same thing, *kephalē*. But in the approximately 180 times it appears as a metaphor for leader or chieftain, they almost always eliminate the metaphor altogether and translate it *archē* (leader), which is evidence that they were uncomfortable with (unfamiliar with?) the Jewish metaphor and simply translated it out. The few instances (six in all) where they do not do this (Judg 11:11; 2 Sam 22:44; Ps 18:43; Is 7:8-9; Lam 1:5) are simply the exceptions that prove the rule.

[25]Cyril of Alexandria, *Ad Arcadiam et Marinam* 5.6.

supported Cyril's christological concern (not to have Christ "under" God in a hierarchy), just as it did for Chrysostom.

The question for us, then, is whether Paul was speaking out of his Jewish heritage or whether in speaking into the Corinthians' Greek setting he used a metaphor that would have been more familiar to them.[26] At issue, of course, is what kind of relationship between the man and the woman is envisaged in 1 Corinthians 11:3 and how this plays out in the discussion that follows. For several reasons, it seems most likely that something very much like Cyril's understanding was in Paul's mind.

1. Despite repeated assertions to the contrary, nothing that is said following this verse hints at an authority-subordination relationship. Most often those who advocate this view have either a husband-wife or a "church order" relationship in view. But the latter is to read something into the text that simply is not there, and while it is possible that the former may be intended, nothing inherent in the discussion that follows requires such a view. The final wrap-up in 1 Corinthians 11:13-15 is about men and women in general and therefore offers no further help for understanding the metaphor.

2. In the one instance in our passage where Paul might be picking up some dimension of the metaphor (1 Cor 11:8-9), the relationship envisaged is clearly not one of subordination to the man as "leader." Paul is setting out to explain his assertion that "the woman is the *glory* of man." The answer lies in the Genesis narrative: she came from man (in the sense that she was taken from his side) and was created for his sake; this is what makes her the man's glory. If this is an extension of the metaphor in 1 Corinthians 11:3, then it clearly points to "man" as metaphorical head in the sense Cyril maintains. Moreover, there is no usage of *glory* anywhere in Scripture that would suggest that Paul is here advocating a subordinating relationship by means of this word.[27] On the other hand, in a context where

---

[26]And, of course, one cannot appeal to the Old Testament usage as a place of familiarity for them, since they would not know Hebrew and their Greek Bible already had the metaphorical usage basically translated out.

[27]See Fee, *First Epistle to the Corinthians*, 571: "Paul is really reflecting the sense of the Old Testament text to which he is alluding. Man, by himself, is not complete; he is alone, without a

women are bringing shame on themselves and thus on their husbands, this appeal makes perfectly good sense. She who is to be his glory is behaving in a way that turns that glory into shame.

3. One of the ongoing puzzles for all interpreters is why Paul should include the third member in his opening sentence, since "God as the head of Christ" is not picked up again in any way. Most likely this is because the saying had prior existence and Paul is simply appealing to it. But if so, what was its point? Although one cannot be certain here, most likely it was a useful metaphor to express something of a chronology of salvation history. According to 1 Corinthians 8:6, all things (including Adam) were created "through Christ"; the man then became the "source" of the woman's being, while God was the "source" of Christ's incarnation. In any case, this view of the saying can make sense of all three members, in a way that seeing the metaphor as expressing subordination does not seem to—unless one wants to embrace a heterodox Christology.[28]

Kephalē *Elsewhere in Paul.* Nonetheless, it is common to appeal to Paul's later use of this metaphor in Colossians and Ephesians, as Chrysostom did, and then to import here a hierarchical meaning from there.[29] But much confusion seems to be at work here, since in these two later (companion) letters the metaphor is used in three distinct ways: to point to

---

companion or helper suitable to him. The animals will not do; he needs one who is bone of his bone, one who is like him but different from him, one who is uniquely his own 'glory.' In fact, when the man in the Old Testament narrative sees the woman he 'glories' in her by bursting into song. . . . She is not thereby subordinate to him, but necessary for him. She exists to his honor as the one who having come from man is the one companion suitable to him, so that he might be complete and that together they might form humanity."

[28]See the chapter by Kevin Giles in this volume.

[29]One of the problems with much of the debate regarding the metaphorical use of *kephalē* in Paul is the tacit assumption that the resolution lies in deciding once and for all what the metaphor meant in Greek sources outside the New Testament. This seems especially evident in the debate between Wayne Grudem and Richard Cervin, carried on first in the *Trinity Journal* (Grudem, vol. 6 [1985]: 38-59; Cervin, vol. 10 [1989]: 85-112; Grudem, vol. 11 [1990]: 3-72) and in a final rejoinder by Cervin that was distributed as an unpublished paper (ca. 1991) by CBE International. But what Cervin has especially demonstrated in his survey of the literature is the diversity of options to be found there—even though he wants finally to narrow it to a primary meaning of "prominent" or "topmost." The problem with this narrowing of things is that while there can be no question that Christ as head of the church is the most prominent part of the body, this can hardly be Paul's point. Rather, Paul's meaning is the Greek anatomical one, that the body is sustained by its relationship to its most prominent part.

(1) Christ's relationship with the church (Eph 4:15-16; 5:23; Col 1:18; 2:19), (2) Christ's relationship to the powers (Eph 1:22; Col 2:10), and (3) a householder's relationship to his wife (Eph 5:23).[30]

The imagery in its first instance (Col 1:18; 2:19) seems to stem ultimately from Paul's view of the church as the body of Christ, celebrated at every Lord's Supper according to 1 Corinthians 10:16-17; 11:29. What is at issue in Colossians are some people who are moving in clearly heretical directions, who are "not holding fast to the head" (Col 2:19) but are cutting themselves off from the body altogether and, by implication, being "joined" to the "powers" to whom they now give undue significance. This concern is anticipated in the earlier occurrence of the metaphor in Colossians 1:18, where it appears in a clause that serves as the janus between the two stanzas of the hymn in Colossians 1:15-20: "And he [the Son of God] is the head of the body, the church."[31] This otherwise unnecessary insertion into the hymn/poem of Colossians 1:15-20 seems clearly intended—as does the whole hymn/poem itself—to set the stage for some things that will be said later about Christ's relationship both to the powers and to the church in the main argument of Colossians 2:6-19.

First, Paul claims that Christ is "head of [= over] every power and authority" (Col 2:10) and is so, he adds in Ephesians 1:22, *for the sake of* the church. These two instances are in fact the only certain places where Paul uses the imagery in this more specifically Jewish way. Although he will go

---

[30]I use the term *householder* here because the entire passage in Ephesians (Eph 5:21–6:9) assumes the Greco-Roman villa, not relationships within other settings. After all, Colossians (a companion letter to Ephesians) was written at the same time as Philemon and assumes the reading of both letters in the context of that household. For example, if there were a married slave couple in the household, Philemon would be the head of the slave wife in the same way he would be of Apphia. Paul's point in using the metaphor in Ephesians is that the householder is the savior of his wife, in the sense of being the one on whom the entire household is dependent for their well-being. See further Gordon D. Fee, "The Cultural Context of Ephesians 5:18–6:9," *PriscPap* 16 (Winter 2002): 3-8.

[31]I say "janus" here because this clause is otherwise unrelated to the content of the first stanza (Col 1:15-17), where the emphasis is on the Son as the firstborn over the whole created order; in him all things, including the powers, were created; indeed, they were created by him and for him; and in him all things hold together. The balancing second stanza begins in the second part of Col 1:18—"he [the Son] is the beginning, the firstborn from the dead"—and moves on to speak of his redemptive work that makes him so. The beginning of Col 1:18, "the Son is the head of the body, the church," joins these two stanzas. Thus, with Paul's later use of this metaphor, the church is dependent on its life-giving, life-sustaining "head" (Col 2:19); at the same time Christ is head over "the powers" (Col 2:10).

on to speak of Christ as head of the body, here the metaphor stands alone without connection to a body and clearly refers to Christ's authority over all the powers. Thus, Paul appears in this usage to be making a play on the metaphorical options. Christ is "head over the powers"—whom he has conquered through his death, resurrection, and ascension.

Second, when the imagery is used in relationship to the church, the key to its intended meaning is the elaboration in Colossians 2:19, where the false teachers have lost connection with the head. This is obviously not a metaphor for subordination or lordship but for the maintenance of life, as the rest of the sentence makes plain. To lose connection with the head means to lose life itself, since the church functions as Christ's body only as it maintains connection with the head. This is also how the head-body imagery is elaborated in Ephesians 4:15-16. Now in a positive context, the imagery encourages the life and growth of the church as a unity, which is why in Colossians those who cease to "hold fast" to the head cease to live—and in fact are moving the church itself toward death.

This relationship between head and body seems also to be the point of the analogical use of the metaphor in Ephesians 5:22-24.[32] Precisely because Paul is deliberately using an analogy, not offering a literal description of reality, the point of the analogy takes us back to Ephesians 4:15-16, *not* to the relationship of Christ to "the powers."[33] And this point is the apt one: just as the church is totally dependent on Christ for life and growth, so the wife in the first-century household was totally dependent on her husband as her "savior," in the sense of being dependent on him for her life in the world.

In view of all this, the importation into 1 Corinthians of *any* of Paul's later uses of the imagery is probably suspect at best. That is, Paul surely does not intend here that the first member of each pair is "head over" the other in the same sense in which Paul asserts that Christ is "head over the

---

[32]It should be pointed out that the metaphor is *not* used for the other two relationships with the householder (children and slaves), where lordship is plainly expressed. The change of verbs from *hypotassō* (where the middle suggests a form of volunteerism that is expected of all, but in a special way of wives) to *hypakouō* for children and slaves (in both Colossians and Ephesians) suggests that Paul simply would never have used the latter for wives and that there is therefore a basic difference between them, despite occasional semantic overlap.

[33]That is, the husband is *not* the savior of his wife in the same way as Christ is of the church.

powers," having disarmed and triumphed over them (Col 2:10, 15). More-over, since there is no head-body relationship expressed in our passage, neither does it seem appropriate to think of the second member as "sus-tained and built up by" its relationship to the first (as in Eph 4:15-16; 5:22-33; Col 2:19). That leaves us, then, with Cyril's view—the first member as the source/ground of the other's being—as the most likely meaning here. This, after all, is the one relationship actually spelled out in our pas-sage (the woman coming from the man, 1 Cor 11:8; the man now coming from the woman, 1 Cor 11:12).

THE MEANING OF 1 CORINTHIANS 11:10

First Corinthians 11:10 is the most puzzling sentence in the entire passage—for three reasons: (1) what is said is not what is expected on the basis of 1 Corinthians 11:7, (2) the sudden use of the word *authority* in relation to the woman's head is both unexpected and seemingly unrelated to anything that has been said heretofore, and (3) the second reason offered, "because of the angels," is shrouded in obscurity.

1. The unexpected nature of this sentence is in part due to what is actu-ally said; but in part it is also due to the way it begins, "for this reason." If the connector in this case points both backward and forward, then the forward look would probably be anticipating the phrase "because of the angels"; thus, "for this reason, namely, because of the angels." But a backward look is more likely the primary intent. If so, then even though it would embrace the content of 1 Corinthians 11:8-9, Paul most likely intends to draw an inference from the end of 1 Cor-inthians 11:7: "but the woman is the glory of man." This, after all, is what 1 Corinthians 11:8-9 are setting out to justify. But it is this very reality that makes the *content* of 1 Corinthians 11:10 so puzzling, since not a single word that follows has any immediately apparent relationship to what has been said up to this point.

2. The most puzzling moment in the entire passage is Paul's use of the word *exousia* ("authority/right to act") at the very place where 1 Cor-inthians 11:7 has set us up the expectation of "ought to have *her head covered.*" For this reason the church has historically assumed, and

many continue to assert, that what Paul does write should in fact be understood as standing in for what we are led to expect. But this historic position is full of difficulties, bluntly expressed a century ago by Archibald Robertson and Alfred Plummer: "The difficulty is to see why Paul has expressed himself in this extraordinary manner. That 'authority' (*exousia*) has been put for 'sign of authority' is not difficult; but why does St Paul say 'authority' when he means 'subjection'?"[34] Precisely! But the problems are far more substantial than his simply saying one thing when he meant another.

First, the only way one can come to this view is by a particular reading of the context. If we were to come across this sentence in a free-standing setting, no one would interpret it in this passive sense. This construction (subject, the verb *echein* ["has/have"], with *exousia* as the object followed by the preposition *epi*) would be read in the only way it is known to occur in the language: the subject has the authority "over" the object of the preposition. This does not mean that in context a passive sense could not occur; but in fact, such an occurrence is otherwise unknown.

Second, this is simply not a case of one word's standing for another. Because a passive relationship of the subject (woman) to the object (*exousia*) is required, one must make two jumps to get to the assumed meaning (as Robertson and Plummer clearly recognized). That is, the word *exousia* would stand in for the covering itself (a "veil"—so some early versions and English translations), which in turn stands in for a "sign of" the authority a man presumably has over her (see NRSV, NEB). But this double jump is not easy to come to from a straight reading of the text.

Third, the word *exousia* has already occurred several times in 1 Corinthians, most of them in the immediately preceding argument, where it is used in a strictly pejorative way. It emerges first in 1 Corinthians 8:9 (surprisingly, but absolutely straightforwardly), where Paul warns that those who are acting on the basis of "this *exousia* of

---

[34]Archibald Robertson and Alfred Plummer, *A Critical and Exegetical Commentary on the First Epistle of St Paul to the Corinthians,* 2nd ed., International Critical Commentary (Edinburgh: T&T Clark, 1914), 232.

yours" are thereby putting a stumbling block in the way of others. The word is then picked up again in the extended defense of Paul's apostolic "rights" to the Corinthians' material support (1 Cor 9:1-23), where the context indicates that they are rejecting his apostleship precisely because he does not make use of his rightful *exousia* (see 2 Cor 12:13). He argues in defense (see 1 Cor 9:1-3) that he has the *exousia*, all right, but has freely curtailed it (1 Cor 9:12-19) for the sake of the gospel ("so that by all possible means I might save some," 1 Cor 9:22). His ultimate point is that the Corinthians themselves should act accordingly. It is precisely this faulty/arrogant use of their *exousia* that is the cause of the warnings in 1 Corinthians 10:1-13. Given this immediate context to our passage, it would seem likely that this is also how we should understand the present sentence in context: that the women do indeed have *exousia*, but at issue again is the use they would make of it.

3. The equally puzzling "because of the angels" has been the bane of all interpreters, and any number of suggestions have been brought forward.[35] A good case can made for at least starting with the evidence from 1 Corinthians itself, where, besides this passage, angels are mentioned three other times (1 Cor 4:9; 6:2-3; 13:1). There is good reason to believe that the Corinthians understood speaking in tongues to be speaking the language of the angels (1 Cor 13:1) and thus to be evidence of a superior spirituality.[36] If so, then the earlier two occurrences make sense in terms of Paul's trying to help the Corinthians gain perspective on this matter: he designates the angels as witnesses to his apostolic weaknesses (1 Cor 4:9), and he asserts that the Corinthians themselves will be involved in the eschatological judgment of angels (1 Cor 6:2-3). In keeping with this suggestion, "because of the angels" in this passage may thus reflect the Corinthians' own positive view of being like the angels.

---

[35]For example, that the angels were understood to be the guardians (or overseers or assistants) of Christian worship and would be offended by impropriety, or that the angels would lust after women who were uncovered. See further Fee, *First Epistle to the Corinthians*, 521-22; Thiselton, *First Epistle to the Corinthians*, 839-41.

[36]See the discussion in Fee, *First Epistle to the Corinthians*, 630-31.

Within this scenario, this sentence could be yet another instance in the letter where Paul is reflecting their own point of view—in this case, of some Corinthian women.[37] As elsewhere, Paul would be agreeing with them in principle, but then he sets out qualifications so that his agreement ends up being in principle only. If this is the case, then Paul is here momentarily allowing the rightness of the Corinthian women's perspective: that because of their "angelic" status they have the right to put what they please (or not) on their own heads.

But this also means the *plēn* ("nevertheless") that immediately follows is a very important qualifier. First, Paul is not backing down from what he has affirmed in 1 Corinthians 11:8-9 on the basis of the Genesis story, which explains how the woman is man's glory. But neither will he allow that to be taken in a subordinating way. The first set of realities is not reversed "in the Lord," but neither is it to be understood wrongly. At the same time, if 1 Corinthians 11:10 is his (ostensible) agreement with the reasons the women are discarding the normal covering, then 1 Corinthians 11:11-12 also functions as a rejoinder to their position. Being "in the Lord" does not mean *exousia* to be as the angels now, where distinctions between male and female are understood no longer to exist; rather, it means that in the present age neither man nor woman can exist without the other, and gender distinctions are part of the "all things [that] are from God."

A POSSIBLE EXPLANATION

That leads to a final suggestion as to *what* was going on in the church gatherings in Corinth and *why* some women had both abandoned the cultural norm and perhaps argued for the right to do so. The most common answer to this question, either expressed or assumed, is that it was an act of insubordination on the part of some wives toward their husbands. The problem with this answer, of course, is that nothing else in 1 Corinthians seems to support it. But by gathering up all the evidence in the letter, including what Paul says here, one may reconstruct a fairly consistent point of view that covers most of the letter.

---

[37] As would also be true of 1 Cor 7:1 (cf. 1 Cor 6:12-13 for the perspective of some men and 1 Cor 8:1, 4, 8 for the perspective of those in the know).

Beginning at the end (1 Cor 12–14), there is a community that has put a considerable emphasis on speaking in tongues, and Paul's reference to "speaking the language of angels" (1 Cor 13:1) probably has direct bearing on their reasons for it.[38] Speaking in an angelic tongue gave these new believers, the majority of whom were not among the Corinthian elite (1 Cor 1:26-28), a new sense of status. With that also came a sense that they had begun to move in a spirituality that resembled the existence of the angels themselves. Moreover, such a viewpoint could have been attributed in part to Paul himself, since whatever else is true, he had a thoroughly eschatological view of being in Christ—that the basic moments of the future (resurrection and the outpoured Spirit) have already taken place, even though their final expression was yet to be.

If this understanding of spirituality prevailed in Corinth, and especially if some of the women were deeply into it, then one can account for several other matters in our letter, including the church's basically negative attitude toward the apostle (1 Cor 1:10-12; 4:1-21; 9:1-19). His bodily weaknesses, combined with his not using his *exousia* regarding their support, serves as evidence for the Corinthians that Paul lacks true *exousia*—the right to choose one's behavior for oneself.[39] But even more important, such a view can especially account for some women's (apparent) rejection of the marriage bed (1 Cor 7:1-7; because they are already as the angels), so much so that they could even argue for divorce if need be (1 Cor 7:10-16). It also accounts for their (possibly) discouraging some virgins already promised in marriage from following through (1 Cor 7:25-38) and for some men's resorting to prostitutes as a result (1 Cor 6:12-20). This also explains in part the denial of a future bodily existence on the part of some (1 Cor 15:12, 35) and very likely lies behind their fascination with wisdom (1 Cor 1–4) and knowledge (1 Cor 8–10). These views are generally shared by both men and women in the community, but they especially find expression in the behavior of the women in 1 Corinthians 7; 11:2-16.

If this is a reasonable explanation for the women's behavior in this passage, then what lies behind it is not so much an act of insubordination as

---

[38]See Fee, *First Epistle to the Corinthians*, 630-31.
[39]Paul's not using his *exousia* regarding their support is such an obvious source of contention between them that he picks it up again very sarcastically in 2 Cor 11:7-9; 12:13.

a deliberate casting aside of an external marker that distinguished women from men.[40] That is, the issue in Corinth is very likely a subtle movement toward androgyny, where distinctions between men and women are of little value "because of the angels"; they have already experienced a form of angelic life where there is neither marrying nor giving in marriage (Lk 20:35-36).[41]

For Paul this is not only a betrayal of the gospel but also a denial of the "not yet" dimension of our present eschatological existence. Above all, it puts considerable strain on present relationships between men and women. Paul begins his answer with a metaphorical appeal to one's head because the problem lies squarely on the head. In a culture where the vast majority of women are dependent on a man for life in the world, a woman who brings shame on her own head by getting rid of one of the cultural markers of distinction also brings shame on her metaphorical head, the one on whom the woman is primarily dependent and to whom she is responsible in the Greco-Roman household (which also serves as the nucleus expression of the house church that meets in the household).

While none of this is certain, it does offer a view of 1 Corinthians 11:2-16 that can make sense of all its parts and at the same time fits well into the larger perspective of the letter. Paul's intent, therefore, is not to put women in their place, as it were, but to maintain a cultural tradition that has the effect of serving as a gender distinctive, even while "in the Lord" neither is independent of the other (1 Cor 11:11).

---

[40]This at least explains the one moment of vigor in the whole argument, 1 Cor 11:5-6, where Paul expostulates that if they are going to remove the external marking of gender difference then they might as well go all the way and have their hair cut in a mannish style. For the evidence for this meaning of these verbs, see Fee, *First Epistle to the Corinthians*, 511n81.

[41]The significance of Luke's expression of this periscope is that Luke's Gospel most likely gave written form to the Jesus tradition as it circulated in Paul's churches, for which their common tradition of the words of institution (1 Cor 11:24-25; Lk 22:19-20) serves as ample evidence.

8

LEARNING IN THE ASSEMBLIES

1 CORINTHIANS 14:34-35

Craig S. Keener

• • • • •

VERY FEW CHURCHES TODAY take 1 Corinthians 14:34-35 to mean all that it could possibly mean. Indeed, any church that permits women to participate in congregational singing recognizes that Paul was not demanding what a face-value reading of his words seems to imply: complete silence as a sign of women's subordination. Thus, almost *everyone* has a problem with pressing this text literally, and interpreters must explain the divergence between what it states and what they believe it means. But beyond this near consensus, church traditions and interpreters diverge: Just how silent must women be?

VARIOUS INTERPRETATIONS

Interpretations vary considerably. Some scholars, for example, argue that Paul cites a Corinthian position here, which he then refutes, as he sometimes did earlier in the letter (e.g., 1 Cor 6:12-14). First Corinthians 14:36 does not, however, read easily like a refutation of preceding verses.[1] Others propose that, following synagogue practice, husbands and wives met in

---

[1] I cite documentation for all these positions in Craig S. Keener, *Paul, Women and Wives* (Peabody, MA: Hendrickson, 1993), 74-80; for the sake of space I omit most documentation here. See also Craig S. Keener, *1–2 Corinthians*, New Cambridge Bible Commentary (Cambridge: Cambridge University Press, 2005), 117-21.

different parts of the church, so that women who asked questions could not avoid disrupting the worship. This proposal fails on two counts. First, synagogues were probably not segregated in this period.[2] Second, although the Corinthian church started in a synagogue (Acts 18:4), it now met in homes (Acts 18:7)—which would hardly afford the space for such gender segregation.

Some scholars question whether Paul even wrote the passage, noting both textual evidence and its contrast with its context and Paul's usual teaching.[3] There is no question that it sounds intrusive. For example, the opening "or" of 1 Corinthians 14:36, in light of Paul's usage elsewhere in 1 Corinthians, most naturally follows "as in all the churches of the saints" in 1 Corinthians 14:33 (which itself naturally reads as concluding what precedes it, as in the similar appeal of 1 Cor 11:16).[4] The early Western textual tradition has 1 Corinthians 14:34-35 in a different location, which may mean that early scribes were still debating the best place in Paul's writings to insert them. These scholars point out that such relocation in ancient texts usually suggests an interpolation and that this is the only passage in Paul's writings where scribes changed the sequence of his argument. The earliest evidence, including from the church fathers, treats 1 Corinthians 14:34-35 as a unit distinct from the context.

But though the passage certainly does interrupt the context, none of the ancient manuscripts lack these verses. That the verses do not seem to fit the context could explain why scribes struggled with where to locate them. Brief digressions were common both in Paul and other ancient writers.[5] It is thus possible that Paul himself inserted this brief digression into a

---

[2]Shemuel Safrai, "The Synagogue," in *The Jewish People in the First Century*, 2 vols., ed. Shemuel Safrai and M. Stern (Philadelphia: Fortress, 1974–1976), 939; Bernadette J. Brooten, *Women Leaders in the Ancient Synagogue* (Chico, CA: Scholars Press, 1982), 103-38.

[3]Argued by F. F. Bruce, Wayne Meeks, and others; but the most persuasive exponent of this position is Gordon D. Fee, *The First Epistle to the Corinthians*, NICNT (Grand Rapids, MI: Eerdmans, 1987), 699-705; most fully, Gordon D. Fee, *God's Empowering Presence* (Peabody, MA: Hendrickson, 1994), 272-81. In a series of articles Philip Barton Payne has also argued the likelihood that some earlier manuscripts omitted these verses, though this evidence remains disputed.

[4]Translations of 1 Corinthians are my own.

[5]See D. A. Carson, "'Silent in the Churches': On the Role of Women in 1 Corinthians 14:33b-36," in *RBMW*, 193-94. For digressions, see, e.g., Josephus, *Against Apion* 1.57; *Life of Flavius Josephus* 336-67; Livy, *History of Rome* 9.17.1–9.19.17; Cicero, *Finibus* 2.32.104; *De Oratore* 43.148; *Ad Atticus* 7.2; Arrian, *Indica* 6.1; Sallust, *Bellum Catilinae* 5.9–13.5.

context involving order in church meetings to address a problem with some Corinthian women's behavior, of which he had been informed.

Still, trying to fit the passage into the immediate context is not simple, as the variety of context-based interpretations suggests. Some suppose that Paul is silencing women's practice of spiritual gifts such as prophecy or prayer in tongues. While this proposal does pay attention to the context (which regulates public use of the gifts), it is difficult to square with Paul's acceptance of women's praying and prophesying in church earlier in the same letter (1 Cor 11:5).

Some readers interpret this passage as prohibiting women's teaching the Bible publicly, based on their understanding of 1 Timothy 2:11-12. Unfortunately, the Corinthians could not simply flip in their Bibles to 1 Timothy (which had not been written yet) to figure out what Paul meant, and unlike prophecy and tongues, teaching is not even mentioned directly in the present context. Of course, if Paul enjoins complete silence on women, that silence would necessarily preclude teaching; but it would also preclude public prophecy and prayer (contradicting Paul's earlier remarks) as well as even modern congregational singing.

One proposal that is no more persuasive, yet has gained a wide hearing, is that Paul simply prohibits women from *judging* prophecy (1 Cor 14:29).[6] Most of the supporters of this proposal are nonegalitarians, though even if the proposal were correct, one is hard-pressed to see why restricting women from judging prophecies in Corinth would thereby restrict women from teaching (yet not prophesying or praying) then or today. Judging prophecy is a task assigned to all who prophesy (1 Cor 14:29), perhaps (given the use of the cognate term) part of the gift of discerning spirits (1 Cor 12:10); and again, women can prophesy (1 Cor 11:5). The only kind of speech specifically mentioned here (asking questions) seems little related to evaluating prophecies' accuracy.[7] Perhaps the greatest weakness of the position is that

---

[6]E.g., Carson, "Silent in the Churches," 194-97; James B. Hurley, "Did Paul Require Veils or the Silence of Women? A Consideration of I Cor. 11:2-16 and I Cor. 14:33b-36," *WTJ* 35 (1973): 217; also, some egalitarians: Walter L. Liefeld, "Women, Submission and Ministry in 1 Corinthians," in *Women, Authority and the Bible*, ed. Alvera Mickelsen (Downers Grove, IL: InterVarsity Press, 1986), 150.

[7]Although people asked questions of oracles (Oxyrhynchus Papyri 1148-49, 1477; Maximus of Tyre, *Orations* 8.3) or "inquired of the Lord" (e.g., 1 Sam 9:9), this was not a method of *evaluating* prophecy.

there is nothing in the text that specifically leads us to suppose that judging prophecies is the particular sort of speech in view; if the previous proposal about limiting women's involvement in spiritual gifts fails because it contradicts 1 Corinthians 11:4-5, at least it was a specific *emphasis* in the preceding context (and not simply one activity among many others in the context, like evaluating prophecies in 1 Cor 14:29).[8] What in 1 Corinthians 14:34-35 specifies judging prophecies? And where does the text suggest that judging prophecies reveals a higher degree of authority than prophesying God's message itself? That many nonegalitarians support this reading (rather than a more explicit argument against teaching) shows how difficult it is to target Bible teaching or pastoral ministry without eliminating prophecy or prayer, and ultimately suggests that this is a difficult text for all modern interpreters, including nonegalitarians.

WHAT SITUATION WAS PAUL ADDRESSING?

When Paul named various people in the church in Corinth, he did not have to explain to his readers who these people were (e.g., 1 Cor 1:11, 14, 16; 16:17). The Corinthian Christians already knew them. Likewise, he could refer to practices such as food offered to idols and women wearing head coverings with no concern that twenty-first-century readers might struggle to reconstruct the situation. After all, the verse that tells us that Paul was writing to the Corinthians (1 Cor 1:2) is just as inspired as more popular parts of the letter, and the letter genre itself invites us to consider his readers' situation.

Some readers today reject any interpretation of a passage that requires us to take the particular situation into account. Such readers are never consistent, however: few, for example, provide offerings for the Jerusalem church every Sunday (1 Cor 16:1-4). Likewise, many do not require head coverings or holy kisses (1 Cor 11:2-16; 16:20), recognizing that these practices meant something different to first-century readers from what they would mean to us today.[9] We cannot simply cite the present passage and

---

[8]D. A. Carson, *Exegetical Fallacies* (Grand Rapids, MI: Baker, 1984), 115, offers one of the classic warnings against the danger of interpretive overspecification.

[9]For the cultural practices involved here, see Craig S. Keener, "Head Coverings" and "Kissing," in *Dictionary of New Testament Background*, ed. C. A. Evans and S. E. Porter (Downers Grove, IL: InterVarsity Press, 2000), 442-47, 628-29. For further examples of the need for cultural

claim that it applies to all situations without begging the question. In any case, the first task of the reader of Scripture is the exegetical one: understanding the text on its own terms in its own context. Only after we have understood it contextually can we apply it appropriately.

Paul can hardly mean that all women in all churches must be completely silent all the time; that would contradict Paul's earlier words in the same letter (1 Cor 11:5), not to mention his valuing of women laborers in the gospel (Rom 16:1-7, 12). As mentioned above, it would also contradict the practice of the majority of even the most conservative churches today. Since those who allow women to participate in congregational singing do not apply this text any more literally than egalitarians do, all could benefit from further discussion of the background. Tongues speakers (1 Cor 14:30) also were to remain silent, but only under particular circumstances. What clues does Paul offer us in the text itself concerning the reasons for the silence? The context addresses not simply spiritual gifts but order and propriety in house-church meetings (1 Cor 14:27-33).

Two things are absolutely central to a proper understanding of this passage. First, and most important, our verses themselves *specify only one particular kind of speech* that we can be certain Paul addresses here. Unless Paul changes the subject from women's submissive silence (1 Cor 14:34) to asking questions privately (1 Cor 14:35a) and back again to silence (1 Cor 14:35b), asking questions is at least a primary example of the sort of speech he seeks to forbid. In fact, Paul explicitly bases his injunction to ask questions privately on his demand for silence (1 Cor 14:35, "for"). Second, and related to the first, Paul explicitly ties the women's speech in this case to shame. And since honor and shame are areas in which cultures differ considerably, it is worth our while to determine the source of shame in this particular instance.

Why would women have been tempted to ask questions during the service? And what problems would these interruptions have posed? Here it is helpful to note that questions were standard fare in all ancient lecture settings—except when asked by those insufficiently learned, who were

---

sensitivity in interpreting these passages, see Craig S. Keener, "Women in Ministry," in *Two Views on Women in Ministry*, ed. James R. Beck and Craig L. Blomberg (Grand Rapids, MI: Zondervan, 2001), 46-49, 55-57.

expected to keep quiet, at least so long as they remained novices. There is good reason to suppose that most of the women in the Corinthian church—even those raised in the synagogue—were insufficiently learned. Further, their gender itself would have rendered their outspokenness offensive to conservative Roman and Greek men, probably even in the familial setting of a Corinthian house church.

WOMEN'S SILENCE AND QUESTIONS IN PUBLIC SETTINGS

Reading our passage on its own terms, I had always found most plausible the view that women were interrupting the service with questions.[10] But I never could imagine what circumstances provoked these public questions until I read Plutarch's essay *On Lectures*. Then I realized that listeners regularly interrupted lectures with questions, whether to learn more about the subject or to compete intellectually with an inadequately prepared lecturer. I quickly realized that questions were common in Jewish settings as well and were a regular part of ancient Mediterranean lecture settings in general.[11] House churches were undoubtedly less formal than larger settings but apparently included, when possible, a teaching element that would probably follow many practices familiar from similarly sized learning gatherings in the culture (see 1 Cor 12:28-29; 14:6, 26; Rom 12:7).

But why would Paul have restricted questions coming specifically from women? The questions could be an example of a broader kind of speech in the assembly prohibited to women; but then why does Paul permit the women to pray and prophesy in 1 Corinthians 11:5? Two possibilities make good sense.

The first is that ancient Mediterranean protocol would disapprove of an otherwise honorable woman addressing unrelated men.[12] Thus, for

---

[10]Also, e.g., Don Williams, *The Apostle Paul and Women in the Church* (Glendale, CA: Gospel Light, 1977), 70; Kevin Giles, *Created Woman: A Fresh Study of the Biblical Teaching* (Canberra, Australia: Acorn, 1985), 56.

[11]See, e.g., Plutarch, *Lectures* 11; *Moralia* 43B; Aulus Gellius, *Attic Nights* 1.26.2; 8.10; 12.5.4; 16.6.1-12; 18.13.7-8; 20.10.1-6; Seneca, *Epistles to Lucilius* 108.3; t. Sanh. 7:10; Avot de Rabbi Nathan 6A; Martin Goodman, *State and Society in Roman Galilee* (Totowa, NJ: Rowman & Allanheld, 1983), 79; also, intellectual conversation, e.g., Polybius, *Histories* 31.23.9; Plutarch, *Table-Talk* 2.1.2; *Moralia* 630BC.

[12]E.g., Valerius Maximus, *Memorable Doings and Sayings* 3.8.6; cf. 8.3.2. This principle is often acknowledged here; e.g., Christopher Forbes, *Prophecy and Inspired Speech in Early Christianity*

example, in one novel a noble woman protests that it is proper for only a man to speak when men are present, explaining that she speaks only under duress.[13] Speech to "their own husbands" here may thus contrast with speaking to other men—a practice Greek men permitted for "inspired" speech but rejected as shameful for casual conversation. This sort of situation could easily arise in the ambiguous boundaries between private and public spheres experienced in a house church.[14]

In current Western society, it is nearly impossible for anyone who engages in any activity in public—working, attending university, shopping—to avoid some casual cross-gender conversation, but this was not the case in the first century. Although many men considered women prone to gossip, social convention particularly respected women who were socially retiring and did not talk much with men outside their household.[15] Many men questioned women's judgment.[16] Women who conversed with men laid themselves open to gossipers' complaints about their morality.[17] Traditional Romans regarded wives' speaking publicly with others' husbands as horrible behavior, reflecting possible flirtatious designs and subverting the moral order of the state.[18] By contrast, meekness and shyness in women were

---

and Its Hellenistic Environment (Peabody, MA: Hendrickson, 1997), 274, 277; cf. James D. G. Dunn, *The Theology of Paul the Apostle* (Grand Rapids, MI: Eerdmans, 1998), 589, 592.

[13]Heliodorus, *Ethiopica* 1.21-22, especially 1.22 (probably third century AD).

[14]See especially Terence Paige, "The Social Matrix of Women's Speech at Corinth: The Context and Meaning of the Command to Silence in 1 Corinthians 14:33b-36," *BBR* 12 (2002): 217-42, published during the editing of this essay's original version. Ancient literature led us to very similar conclusions independently.

[15]See Plutarch, *Bride* 31-32; *Moralia* 142CD; Heliodorus, *Ethiopica* 1.21. Later rabbis felt Jewish men should avoid unnecessary conversation with women (m. Avot 1:5; t. Shabb. 1:14; t. Ber. 43b, bar.; b. Eruv. 53b), and the strictest felt that a wife who spoke with a man in the street could be divorced with no marriage settlement (m. Ketub. 7:6). Some felt that such verbal intercourse could ultimately lead to sin (Ecclesiasticus 9:9; 42:12; Testament of Reuben 6.1-2). Traditional Middle Eastern societies still view social intercourse as nearly the moral equivalent of sexual infidelity. See Carol Delaney, "Seeds of Honor, Fields of Shame," in *Honor and Shame and the Unity of the Mediterranean*, ed. D. D. Gilmore (Washington, DC: American Anthropological Association, 1987), 43.

[16]See Cicero, *Pro Murena* 12.27; Philo, *Qui Omnis Probus Liber Sit* 117; *Hypothetica* 11.14-17; Josephus, *Antiquities of the Jews* 1.49; 4.219; Craig S. Keener, "Marriage," in Evans and Porter, *Dictionary of New Testament Background*, 688.

[17]Theophrastus, *Characters* 28.3—also if they (rather than a husband or porter) answer the door (this suggests they have a paramour; see Tibullus, 1.2.7, 15-24, 41, 55-56).

[18]Livy, *History of Rome* 34.2.9; 34.4.18. A more progressive speaker argues that this behavior is acceptable under some circumstances (34.5.7-10).

considered honorable.[19] First-century Romans, including many in Corinth, had generally become more tolerant, but enough traditional sentiments remained to create tension in the house-church setting, especially with various cultures present. (Corinth was officially Roman in this period, but Paul's writing in Greek and presupposing Jewish customs suggests a mixed church.)

Because women's public speech was sometimes shameful in Corinth, one cannot simply assume that Paul's claim that it is shameful for a woman to speak in the assembly (1 Cor 14:35) is meant to be transcultural, any more than his earlier injunction to cover their heads (related to shame in 1 Cor 11:5-6) or his later one to greet with a holy kiss.[20] When applied to gender relations, "shameful" often involved a woman's reputation in sexual matters.[21] Conservative Greek culture, for example, regarded a wife's talking with a young man as "shameful" (the same Greek term).[22] While Paul challenges some social conventions of his day, he supports others (including gender-related conventions such as head coverings). Presumably he often does this for strategic reasons (especially where different passages in his writings offer different approaches, as they clearly do on women's roles; see, e.g., Rom 16:1-2; 1 Cor 11:5; Phil 4:2-3).[23] A wife's behavior reflected on her husband's status, and certainly neither spouse should risk shaming the other (see 1 Cor 11:3-9; Prov 12:4; 31:23, 28).

---

[19]E.g., Sophocles, *Ajax* 293; Demosthenes, *Against Meidias* 79; Valerius Maximus, *Memorable Doings and Sayings* 7.1.1; Ecclesiasticus 22:5; 26:14; see further Keener, "Marriage," 687-90.

[20]Liefeld finds here the idea of glory and disgrace, as in 1 Cor 11:7, related to decorum or "order" (cf. 1 Cor 12:23; 11:34; 14:40); he rightly notes that unnecessary social criticism could hinder the spread of Christianity ("Women, Submission and Ministry," 140-42). Speaking was "shameful" when inappropriate (e.g., in the case of a shameful speaker; Aeschines, *Timarchus* 28-29).

[21]The designation *shameful* often applied to sexual immorality (e.g., Dionysius of Halicarnassus, *Roman Antiquities* 1.78.5; Diodorus Siculus, *Library of History* 5.55.6-7; 10.31.1; 12.15.2; 12.21.2; 32.10.9; 33.15.2; Christians would agree here), which was the opposite of appropriate womanly meekness (Arrian, *Indica* 17.3), or to women being in male company (Diodorus Siculus, *Library of History* 4.4.1; on women's relative seclusion in earlier traditional Greek society, see further Keener, "Head Coverings," 443). But some observed that not all cultures shared the same sense of shame on such matters (Arrian, *Indica* 17.3; Diodorus Siculus, *Library of History* 5.32.7). See further Paige, "Social Matrix of Women's Speech," 223-24 (also noting that Paul never applies such a designation to abuse of gifts, evaluating prophecy, or other traditional proposals).

[22]E.g., Euripides, *Electra* 343-44 (though there are two men). Liefeld points out that Plutarch and Livy viewed it as disgraceful for women to "express themselves visually or vocally in public" ("Women, Submission and Ministry," 142).

[23]For Paul's strategic approach, see, e.g., Craig S. Keener, "Paul: Subversive Conservative," *Christian History* 14, no. 3 (1995): 35-37.

Paul also has reason to be concerned for the church's reputation in the larger society (1 Cor 6:6; 14:23), a concern that, incidentally, becomes all the more prominent in his later writings, often specifically concerning household relationships (1 Tim 3:7; 5:14; 6:1; Titus 2:5, 10).[24] It seems likely that in 1 Corinthians 14:34-35 he supports the cultural expectation of honorable matrons' verbal self-restraint. Exceptions could be made, as they were even in pagan religion, for divinely inspired utterances, and perhaps Paul regarded freedom to pray in house-church meetings as a nonnegotiable right of all believers (1 Cor 11:4-5; cf. Judg 4:4).[25] But the general cultural expectation was dominant, and Paul is usually reticent to divide Christians over cultural or personal issues (see Rom 14:15; 1 Cor 8:9, 13; 9:12).

Ancient culture reflects this general expectation of women's restraint far more pervasively than the suggestion to which I now turn. Indeed, even on its own this general expectation in antiquity could explain Paul's prohibition. Nevertheless, the specific circumstances probably implied in the text suggest an additional problem (for which I argue in *Paul, Women and Wives*). The second possibility, therefore, is that some kinds of questions were considered inappropriate, particularly questions that revealed that the questioner had failed to master the topic sufficiently.[26] I sometimes compare this to students whose questions reveal that they have not done the assigned reading before class.

This suggestion, however, raises an issue: Why would women be less likely to ask learned questions than men would? One could argue that this

---

[24]See Keener, *Paul, Women and Wives*, 139-48; Alan Padgett, "The Pauline Rationale for Submission: Biblical Feminism and the *Hina* Clauses of Titus 2:1-10," *Evangelical Quarterly* 59 (1987): 39-52.

[25]Pagan Greco-Roman society also respected the speech of prophetesses. Most abundant are references to the inspiration of the mythical Sibyl (e.g., Ovid, *Metamorphoses* 14.129-53; Virgil, *Aeneid* 6.77-102; Juvenal, *Satirae* 3.3; Heraclitus, *Epistulae* 8; throughout Sibylline Oracles, and also in her historic successors in Diodorus Siculus, *Bibliotheca historica* 4.66.6) and the historic Delphic priestess (e.g., Longinus, *Sublime* 13.2; Callimachus, *Hymn* 4.89-90; Valerius Maximus, *Memorable Doings and Sayings* 1.8.10; Cicero, *Divinatione* 1.36.79; Plutarch, *Oracles at Delphi* 21; *Moralia* 404E; *Dialogue on Love* 16; *Moralia* 759B; Dio Chrysostom, *Personal Appearance* 12; Pausanias, *Description of Greece* 2.2.7).

[26]See, e.g., Plutarch, *Lectures* 18; *Moralia* 48AB; Diogenes Laertius, *Lives of Eminent Philosophers* 7.1.19. Plutarch's essay is the best source for the conduct of lectures in this period. Distracting others from a lecture by one's conversation was also considered rude (Plutarch, *Lectures* 13; *Moralia* 45D). Concerning silence for novices, see, e.g., the extreme example of the Pythagoreans in Seneca, *Epistles to Lucilius* 52:10; Aulus Gellius, *Attic Nights* 1.9.3-4; Philostratus, *Vita Apollonii* 1.1.

unlearned behavior reflects a transcultural, genetic limitation in women's ability to interpret Scripture. I have been a Bible professor of enough students of both genders over the years, however, to state unequivocally that such a claim is by empirical standards demonstrably false.[27]

More reasonably, women on average were less educated than men, an assertion that no one genuinely conversant with ancient literature would doubt. To be sure, one can collect examples of many educated women in antiquity (normally from wealthier families), but on average women were far less likely to be educated than men.[28] More to the point, even among the Jews and God-fearers who constituted the initial nucleus of the Corinthian congregation (Acts 18:4-5), women would have less opportunities than men for training in Scripture. Although they learned alongside men in the synagogues, they lacked the special training that some of the men would have. More critically here, whereas most Jewish boys were taught to recite the Torah growing up, the same was not true for Jewish girls.[29] Teachers and primary questioners in the house churches probably were mostly men who had been part of the synagogue.[30]

That Paul appeals to the law as confirming his case raises the question of what statement in biblical law he may have in mind (1 Cor 14:34). Paul cites the law as teaching that women or wives should submit themselves (presumably to their husbands) and possibly also that it enjoins their silence. Josephus seems to have understood the law in the same way, though as part of his apologetic appeal to the broader Greco-Roman world.[31] What is surprising in light of this—problematic for all interpretations except the view that Paul did not write it—is that the law nowhere

---

[27]Scientific studies would also undermine this claim; see Mary Stewart Van Leeuwen, *Gender and Grace: Love, Work and Parenting in a Changing World* (Downers Grove, IL: InterVarsity Press, 1990), 75-105, as well as M. Elizabeth Lewis Hall's chapter in this edition; also note the averages in Gregg Johnson, "The Biological Basis for Gender Specific Behavior," in *RBMW*, 358-61.

[28]See, e.g., Forbes, *Prophecy and Inspired Speech*, 277; James S. Jeffers, *The Greco-Roman World of the New Testament* (Downers Grove, IL: InterVarsity Press, 1999), 249, 255-56.

[29]See, e.g., Keener, *Paul, Women and Wives*, 83-84; for women and the law in general, see, e.g., Josephus, *Antiquities of the Jews* 4.219; m. Avot 5:21; m. Hag. 1:1; m. Sukkah 2:8; t. Ber. 6:18; b. Qidd. 34a.

[30]Ancient writers could state general rules with the understanding that these sometimes permitted specific exceptions. See Quintilian, *The Orator's Education* 7.6.5; Craig S. Keener, *And Marries Another* (Peabody, MA: Hendrickson, 1991), 24-28.

[31]Josephus, *Against Apion* 2.201.

specifically commands either women's silence or their submission. Interpreters differ as to whether Paul appeals to a particular passage in the law, perhaps to the verdict at the fall (Gen 3:16), or to the general status of women in the period treated in the Pentateuch (see 1 Pet 3:5). In either case, the texts *describe* women's subordination rather than prescribe it, and Paul could uphold the law to avoid offense (1 Cor 9:20).

Though inspired, biblical law worked within a broader cultural milieu and, like any civil law, limited sin rather than creating the kingdom ideal. Because it often represents concessions to human weakness enshrined in existing culture, very few would argue that it represents God's highest ideal (see, e.g., Ex 21:21; Lev 19:20; Mk 10:5).[32]

Paul might well appeal to the creation order, as in 1 Corinthians 11:8-9 (though only those who press transculturally Paul's mandate concerning head coverings in this earlier chapter should press transculturally the claims of 1 Cor 14:34). But the creation narrative itself does not teach women's subordination, and when Paul appeals to the creation narrative, his appeals do not force us to read it this way, especially given his application of Scripture (including some texts related to the creation of man and woman) elsewhere in his writings.[33]

Assuming (as I do) that Paul would have known this, it seems easier to believe that he appeals to the law as allowing rather than mandating this situation. God challenged some aspects of ancient Near Eastern patriarchal tradition but nevertheless worked within patriarchal societies (see also 1 Pet 3:5-6), including the modified Greco-Roman patriarchalism of Paul's day. This hardly mandates the continuance of such structures today when the spirit of Paul's teaching militates against them, any more than we would maintain slavery today (e.g., Eph 6:5-9).

---

[32]Cf. Keener, *Paul, Women and Wives*, 188-93. All students of the Old Testament are familiar with the repetition of many of the categories of casuistic law found in earlier Mesopotamian legal collections.

[33]See in much more detail in Keener, "Women in Ministry," 58-63; Joy Elasky Fleming, "A Rhetorical Analysis of Genesis 2–3 with Implication for a Theology of Man and Women" (PhD diss., University of Strasbourg, 1987). See also Mary Conway's chapter on Genesis in this volume.

PAUL'S SOLUTION

Rather than let the women learn by asking questions in the church, Paul admonishes them to ask their husbands at home. From what we know of the culture, most of the women would have been married, and most such statements can address the general group without denying the existence of exceptions.[34]

To most modern ears this proposal sounds sexist, but if we read Paul less anachronistically, in his own social context it would have helped the women as well as established order. Paul implicitly makes husbands responsible for their wives' tutoring, but Plutarch tells us that most men did not believe that their wives could learn anything. (This would be especially true of Greek men, who on average were a decade or more older than their wives.) Plutarch regards himself as one of the most progressive voices of his day because he instructs a young man to take an interest in his wife's education—though Plutarch goes on to note that this is necessary because if left to themselves women produce only base passions and folly.[35] Happily, Paul's concern for women's private tutoring does not cite such grounds.

Paul avoids social impropriety by advising the women to avoid questioning other men during the Christian-education component of the gathering, but he is not against their learning. Yet, as noted above, their lack of learning may have been precisely part of the problem. With greater understanding, they might become better able to articulate themselves intellectually in the same assemblies in which they could pray and prophesy. Viewed in this light, the real issues are not gender but propriety and learning—neither of which need restrain women's voices in the church today.

CONCLUSION

Scholars have read this passage from various angles. Most likely the passage addresses disruptive questions in an environment where silence was expected of new learners—which most women were. It also addresses a

---

[34]For the married status of most women, see Keener, *And Marries Another*, 68-74; Keener, "Marriage," 680-81; for general statements allowing exceptions, see *And Marries Another*, 24-28.

[35]Plutarch, *Advice to Bride and Groom* 48; *Moralia* 145BE. Earlier, see similarly Xenophon, *Oeconomicus* 3.10-16; 7.4-5, 10-22; 9.1.

broader social context in which women were expected not to speak much with men to whom they were not related, as a matter of propriety. As in some other parts of the chapter (such as 1 Cor 14:23), Paul is concerned with the church's witness to society. Paul thus upholds church order and avoids appearances of social impropriety (as he did with head coverings in 1 Cor 11:2-16); he also supports learning before speaking. None of these principles prohibits women in very different cultural settings from speaking God's word.

9

MALE AND FEMALE, ONE IN CHRIST

GALATIANS 3:26-29

Cynthia Long Westfall

• • • • •

IN GALATIANS 3:28, Paul writes, "There is no longer Jew or Greek, there is no longer slave or free, there is no longer male and female; for all of you are one in Christ Jesus." This verse has played a major role in the discussion about the nature of biblical equality between men and women.[1] Predictably, the verse's meaning has been heavily debated. On the one hand, feminists and egalitarians claim that the verse removes religious and social disadvantages as well as boundaries in unequal racial, social, and gender power relationships.[2] Paul Jewett even refers to it as the Magna Carta for humanity.[3] On the other hand, complementarians and proponents of patriarchy tend to delimit the scope to a theological or abstract "spiritual" status (such as

---

[1]Tolmie states that Gal 3:28 has received the most attention of any verse in Galatians by far in D. Francis Tolmie, "Tendencies in the Interpretation of Galatians 3:8 since 1990," *Acta Theologica* 34, supplement 19 (2014): 105.

[2]For example, Rebecca Merrill Groothuis stated that Gal 3:28 was the most important text in the Bible that supports biblical equality in *Good News for Women: A Biblical Picture of Gender Equality* (Grand Rapids, MI: Baker Books, 1997), 25. David Scholer argues that it is one of four evidences that promote the full participation of women in the church in "Galatians 3:28 and the Ministry of Women in the Church," *Theology News and Notes* (June 1998): 19-22.

[3]Paul K. Jewett, *Man as Male and Female: A Study in Sexual Relationships from a Theological Point of View* (Grand Rapids, MI: Eerdmans, 1975, 142-47). Ronald and Beverly Allen similarly call Gal 3:28 the feminist *credo* of equality, in *Liberated Traditionalism: Men and Women in Balance* (Portland, OR: Multnomah, 1985), 134.

justification, access to grace, initiation through baptism, union in Christ, or one's eschatological destiny), but insist that it does not call for an elimination or change of gender roles or function in the home, church, or society.[4] In the previous edition of *Discovering Biblical Equality*, Gordon Fee supported the egalitarian reading of Galatians 3:28 primarily by showing how it was consistent with new-creation theology in the New Testament.[5] However, interpreters who believe that the Bible teaches that God ordains hierarchical relationships between men and women insist that their reading is consistent with their own biblical theology of salvation, authority, and gender. Other than simply choosing sides because of our theological presuppositions, how does one adjudicate between the two claims? What does the phrase "there is neither male nor female" mean? Are the categories male and female now *totally* irrelevant in Christ? How do the three pairs relate?[6]

This chapter primarily focuses on the text in its own context—which includes the context of the Greek language, the context of the immediate passage, the context of the entire letter, and the context of the situation and culture, though it also draws on some parallel Pauline passages that expand on the meaning of the text. I particularly focus on how the verse and the wording are understood and interpreted in the context of Paul's argument and the information given in Galatians. The first thing to clarify is that Paul is addressing the Galatian church, not the Greco-Roman culture—the social and political structures outside the church were not directly targeted by Paul's teachings in the first century.[7] So the

---

[4]For instance, Richard W. Hove argues that Gal 3:26-29 is about "the universal nature of the benefits brought about by the advent of Christ" and the three couplets of "polar opposites" is a "merism to refer universally to all people" in *Equality in Christ: Galatians 3:28 and the Gender Dispute* (Wheaton, IL: Crossway, 1999), 81, 86.

   Though Moo contends the "erasure of difference," he criticizes such a "severe delimitation in applying the principle that Paul announces here. . . . This would go too far in the other direction" in Douglas J. Moo, *Galatians*, BECNT (Grand Rapids, MI: Baker Academic, 2013), 255.

[5]Gordon D. Fee, "Male and Female in the New Creation: Galatians 3:26-29," in *Discovering Biblical Equality: Complementarity Without Hierarchy*, 2nd ed., ed. Ronald W. Pierce, Rebecca Merrill Groothuis, and Gordon D. Fee (Downers Grove, IL: InterVarsity Press, 2005), 172-85.

[6]Hove, *Equality in Christ*, 145-46, raised these excellent questions as a challenge to David Scholer's claim that Gal 3:28 is one of four compelling reasons for "*the fundamental Pauline theological basis for the inclusion of women and men as equal and mutual partners in all the ministries of the church*" (Scholer, "Galatians 3:28," 20). Hove's primary question is, "How does one get 'equality' from a verse that only mentions being 'one in Christ'?" (*Equality in Christ*, 146).

[7]Hans Dieter Betz, for example, stresses the "social and political implications of even a revolutionary dimension" in *Galatians* (Philadelphia: Fortress, 1979), 190.

question of the scope of "there is no male and female" in the church depends on the scope of Paul's declaration that "there is no Jew or Gentile," which is the dominant argument of Galatians. It means that in Christian circles we do not make distinctions or discriminate on the basis of race, socioeconomic categories, or gender.

THE CONTEXT OF THE PASSAGE: MEMBERSHIP AND IDENTITY

In Galatians 3:26-29, Paul states,

> So, you are all God's children who have the status of sons[8] in Christ through faith. Those of you who are baptized in Christ, have clothed yourselves with Christ. There is no Jew nor Greek within him, there is no slave nor free within him, there is no male and[9] female within him. But rather, if you belong to Christ, then you are the offspring of Abraham, heirs according to the promise. (author's translation)

The passage in which Galatians 3:28 occurs restates the concept of justification with one of Paul's favorite metaphors: all believers are now clothed with Christ (Rom 13:12-14; 1 Cor 15:51-54; 2 Cor 5:1-4; Gal 3:25-27; Col 3:9-10, 12; Eph 4:20-24; 6:10).[10] This passage particularly addresses identity and membership in the church. This is a summary statement in Paul's argument in Galatians, which is directed at the relationship between Jews and Gentiles. He states emphatically that the gospel that he preaches forms one people of God through Christ Jesus. We often say that Jew/ Gentile represents a category of race, but the distinction between Jew and Gentile in first-century Judaism not only included family or nation of origin, but the spiritual status of membership in Israel, which was historically the people of God. Gentiles could voluntarily become members of Israel

---

[8]Most translations gloss *huioi* as "children." However, some gloss *huioi* as "sons"—it is sometimes an attempt to bring out the masculine language, but some are attempting to retain the semantics of sons as equal heirs and trust that the clear application to women will prevent gender-exclusive applications.

[9]Many scholars point out the variation in wording in the conjunctions in Paul's description of the three groups: Jew nor (*oude*) Greek, slave nor (*oude*) free, male and (*kai*) female. This will be discussed below.

[10]See Constantine R. Campbell's discussion of the Pauline metaphor of new clothes in *Paul and Union with Christ: An Exegetical and Theological Study* (Grand Rapids, MI: Zondervan, 2012), 310-20.

(proselytes) through obedience to the law, but for men, that meant that they had to be circumcised to belong to the people of God.[11] Gentile men (or women) who practiced Judaism to some extent, and/or supported the synagogue but chose not to be proselytes, are called God-fearers by some scholars.[12] While they may have attended the synagogue and were sympathetic to Judaism, uncircumcised men who were sympathetic to Judaism would never be allowed to enter the part of the temple that was restricted to male Israelites and would be considered impure by some Jewish sects. Paul's gospel states that in Christ salvation and justification were by faith alone. In Galatians, Paul works through and fights for the implications of that simple statement. An uncircumcised Gentile (such as a Greek) could be a full member of the people of God, and Paul relentlessly shows that this is a radical change for the church with practical implications.[13]

Studies on social identity and how membership functions in groups provide some helpful perspectives with which we can understand this passage—sociologists study groups and discover insights through the study of human behavior that corresponds to what we see in Scripture.[14] In the first century as now, people belonged to certain groups because of their inherent characteristics (race/nationality, birth status, gender). But membership in other groups was voluntary, such as membership in the Galatian church through baptism (as in Gal 3:26-29). In general, one joins a group voluntarily because of the benefits one receives. By definition, the identity of a group entails an in-group, which is composed of its members, and an

---

[11]For a good discussion of proselytes, see Eckhard J. Schnabel, *Early Christian Mission: Jesus and the Twelve* (Downers Grove, IL: InterVarsity Press, 2004), 124-29. Schnabel notes that pagan women found the Jewish faith more attractive than men (125), which is not surprising given the requirement of circumcision for men.

[12]*God-fearers* or *devout Greeks* are terms used by Luke in Acts (Acts 10:2, 22, 35; 13:16, 26, 43, 50; 16:14; 17:4, 17; 18:7). Some scholars understand *God-fearer* to be a technical term. See the discussion in Schnabel, *Early Christian Mission*, 129-35.

[13]See the discussion on circumcision and what it changed for males in Christianity in Cynthia Long Westfall, *Paul and Gender: Reclaiming the Apostle's Vision for Men and Women in Christ* (Grand Rapids, MI: Baker Academic, 2016), 181-85.

[14]Social identity theory is the study of group membership and how it contributes to a sense of who people are. Social identity is that part of an individual's self-concept that derives from their knowledge of membership to a social group (or groups) together with the emotional significance of that membership. We will not be dealing with complicated concepts or theories but the simple presuppositions that we possess multiple identities and we (re)organize them in different situations, particularly in groups of which we are members.

out-group, which refers to all others outside the group. The behavior of people in the in-group toward the out-group can typically include favoritism toward members of the group and discrimination and prejudice against those in the out-group. This dynamic is a relevant part of the problem in Galatians in Paul's story about how he confronted Peter for discrimination by eating separately from the Gentiles (Gal 2:11-14).

Galatians 3:26-29 indicates some of the positive benefits for those who have previously been members of outgroups spiritually. The surrounding context gives specific examples of what changes must occur as a result of Gentiles/Greeks being baptized into the body of Christ. Paul claims that both Jews and Gentiles/Greeks are Abraham's offspring and heirs, and argues that this change in status has consequences for the practice and behavior of the Galatian church. In Galatians 3:28, Paul includes other types of identities by which humanity is categorized (social/economic status and gender) and grants them the same status.[15] Every person has a number of identities and organizes their multiple identities in order of importance. Furthermore, different situations or groups bring different identities into play, so that one identity will be more important than the others in a certain group, which most often is directly related to the function and role(s) that one has in that group.[16] In Galatians 3:26-29, the identity of being baptized and placed "within Christ" is the primary or *salient* identity all members share regardless of race/nationality, social status, or gender.[17] But Paul also protects diversity within the fellowship of

---

[15]Recognizing that gender is an identity allows us to move the discussion to a better understanding of the differences that are associated with groups, moving beyond the assumption that difference consists of stereotypical roles that are mutually exclusive. Johnson consistently refers to male and female in terms of assumed role distinctions and treats them as if they were a given or already an established practice in the Pauline churches. See S. Lewis Johnson Jr., "Role Distinctions in the Church: Galatians 3:28," in *RBMW*, 199-213. However, at the time that Galatians was written, Paul was in the process of founding the Gentile churches in homes during his missionary journeys, and assuming that there were established gender roles in place in that context begs the question.

[16]The relative importance of a person's identity is called a salience hierarchy, which is an individual's organization of identities according to priorities. See, e.g., Sheldon Stryker and Richard T. Serpe, "Commitment, Identity Salience and Role Behavior: Theory and Research Example," in *Personality, Roles, and Social Behavior*, ed. William Ickes and E. S. Knowles, Springer Series in Social Psychology (New York: Springer-Verlag, 1982), 199-218.

[17]*Salient* is the technical term in social identity theory for a person's primary or most important identity in a group, so I will be using this word often as a technical term.

faith. Christianity is supposed to be a "come as you are" religion in terms of race, social status, and gender. One of Paul's main points in Galatians is that male Gentile believers should not become Jews by being circumcised. One no longer has to change one's race or nationality to join the people of God.

GOD'S CHILDREN IN CHRIST

In the translation above, the phrase "children who have the status of sons" renders the meaning of the Greek word *huioi*, which attempts to take into account the complexity of the word's meaning in the context of the passage. It is a masculine plural noun that means "offspring." The masculine plural grammatically includes both genders unless the context specifies that the referents are exclusively male, in which case it would be rendered "sons" in English. Therefore, *huioi* should be rendered "children."[18] In Galatians 3:26-29, Paul specifically includes women who have faith in Christ as *huioi* when he says, "you are *all* God's *huioi*," and Paul then spells out the inclusion of women in Galatians 3:28, where he says, "there is no male and female within Christ." Therefore, a good translation would avoid using terminology that would be understood as excluding females as offspring and heirs, or that would create interpretive dissonance, contradictions, or confusion that is not present in the Greek. What must be stressed here is that the household metaphor that defines relationships in the church is notably *not* the Greco-Roman authority relationship of a husband and wife but that of siblings (*huioi*) with equal status. In other words, in Paul's argument, gender does not dictate the status of the siblings.

In the surrounding context, Paul defines God's offspring in terms that would be understood as the status of a free adult male who is an heir of property (an estate), so that *huioi* is functioning as a metaphor in the passage, which can be missed if we simply translate it as "children." In the previous context (Gal 3:23-25), Paul is arguing against the demand of certain Jewish Christians (Judaizers) for Gentile Christians to live under the Mosaic law. He describes the law as a guardian who held the children in

---

[18]However, it should be noted that *huioi* refers to adult children who have reached their majority (the state or time of reaching full maturity or adulthood as recognized by the culture or as codified in law) and are no longer under supervision (Gal 3:25).

custody and kept them locked up (Gal 3:23). Paul equates the condition of being under the law with slavery (Gal 3:4:1-3). He states that now that faith has come, the children are no longer under a guardian (Gal 3:25), and then concludes that the Galatians "are all children of God through faith in Christ" (Gal 3:26) and are no longer slaves (Gal 4:7). As S. Lewis Johnson states, "The children have attained their majority and are sons, freemen of God, through a faith that has brought them into union with Christ."[19]

However, this description is a metaphor whose image depicts free males and would have excluded slaves or females in Greco-Roman culture.[20] Women and slaves were never typically free of a guardian or master; rather, both groups were under what Paul describes as virtual slavery in Galatians 4:1: slaves were perpetually subject to masters as long as they were slaves, and though women were not slaves, they were typically under a type of guardian—they were legally subject to their designated guardians, whether father or husband.[21] The meaning of the word *huioi* in Galatians 3:26 is further constrained in Galatians 3:29 as "heirs according to the promise." A more detailed description of what Paul means by "heirs" is given in Galatians 4:1-7. Among other things, *heir* refers to the one who "owns the whole estate" (Gal 4:1 NIV), which indicates the status of a firstborn son in many ancient cultures. This is an unambiguous example of a male metaphor that is applied to all believers.[22] According to this passage, men cannot have any sort of primogeniture status over women in the church or the people of God because of the order of creation.[23] Everyone who is wrapped

---

[19]Johnson, "Role Distinctions in the Church," 353. Johnson qualifies it as "spiritual status," but in the context in Galatians, its pragmatic application to Jews and Greeks/Gentiles is not consistent with an abstract understanding.

[20]As Craig Keener says, "Under ancient law, sons were heirs, destined to inherit what belonged to their fathers; in contrast, slaves were part of the inherited property." See Keener, *The IVP Bible Background Commentary: New Testament*, 2nd ed. (Downers Grove, IL: InterVarsity Press, 2014), 532.

[21]Consequently, I suggest that the prevalent idea of headship as the necessity of all women having a covering loosely based on presuppositions and inferences drawn from 1 Cor 11:10 is not biblical but rather an extension of the pagan Greco-Roman concept of women requiring a guardian. Paul states explicitly that all believers were like "freedmen" in this metaphor (i.e., "So you are no longer a slave" in Gal 4:7). In Roman culture, when someone was no longer a slave they became a freedman, and this is the clearer passage.

[22]For a discussion of male stereotypes that are applied to all Christians, see Westfall, *Paul and Gender*, 45-51.

[23]A claim to primogeniture status for men is based on an inference from the order of creation in the Genesis narrative and 1 Tim 2:13, in which a causal relationship is inferred between

in Christ shares his status. Just as in the case of Gentiles, this necessitates appropriate change in the customs within the church that communicate out-group status for women.

Paul then states that we are God's children by means of or through faith in Christ (Gal 3:26). The primary point of Paul's message in Galatians 3:1-25 is that sonship happens as a result of justification through faith. Now Paul turns his focus on the nature of that identity, which is our location "in Christ." We have the status of God's children (sons and heirs) only because Jesus is the Son of God.[24] As David deSilva says, the subsequent verse (Gal 3:27) makes the sense of location in Christ explicit, "as Paul will speak of the believers entering 'into' Christ and wrapping Christ around them in the rite of baptism."[25] All believers, including slaves and females, have the same status of sonship as men within church membership because they are all in Christ, who is the firstborn of the family of God and all creation (Rom 8:29; Col 1:15, 18). Everyone who is wrapped in Christ shares his status, which can be described as primogeniture. In Galatians, Paul specifies a number of important things that have to change in the understanding of how membership affects social practices in the church.

BAPTIZED AND CLOTHED WITH CHRIST

Paul uses a clothing metaphor to describe a benefit of baptism and justification: all who have been baptized in Christ have "clothed yourselves with Christ" (Gal 3:27). *Baptism* is a reference to the Christian initiation

---

Paul's practice in 1 Tim 2:12 and the order of creation of male and female, which (it is assumed) gives men priority and authority over women in society, the church, and the home. However, the clear declarative statement in Gal 3:26 in its context should rule out inferences that are primarily based on scarce evidence. See Thomas Schreiner, "An Interpretation of 1 Timothy 2:9-15," in *Women and the Church: An Analysis and Application of 1 Timothy 2:9-15*, ed. Andreas J. Köstenberger and Thomas Schreiner (Grand Rapids, MI: Baker Academic, 2005), 105-7. Primogeniture status is relevant among siblings, as in brothers and sisters in the community of faith. The Genesis account and New Testament interpretations of the creation of man and woman do not use the familial register of siblings for the relationship of man and woman or husband and wife.

[24]As Larry W. Hurtado states, "Paul consistently refers to the sonship of Christians as derived sonship, given through and after the pattern of Jesus, whereas Jesus is the original prototype whose sonship is not derived from another." See Hurtado, "Son of God," in *Dictionary of Paul and His Letters*, ed. Gerald F. Hawthorne and Ralph P. Martin (Downers Grove, IL: InterVarsity Press, 1993), 906.

[25]David deSilva, *Galatians: A Handbook on the Greek Text*, Baylor Handbook on the Greek New Testament (Waco, TX: Baylor University Press, 2014), 76.

ceremony, but Paul treats it as far more than granting theological or abstract spiritual status to identities that were treated as opposites in the culture (Jew or Gentile, slave or free).[26] Being justified and "putting on Christ" at baptism entails all the benefits of membership in the context of Galatians. Paul specifies the pragmatic impact that this membership has on Gentiles, particularly Gentile males. The full inclusion of uncircumcised male Gentiles changed their status in the church's culture, social practices, and authority structure, as will be shown below. They no longer have to be circumcised to be part of the in-group. All those who are in Christ share Christ's identity and status in their relationships and functions within the group, including Gentiles, who had been members of the out-group as far as the identity of the people of God. The point of the metaphor is to say that believers' location in Christ can be viewed like an enveloping garment in which all differences are subsumed under the identity of being in Christ. It has the same effect of the members of a choir wearing a choir robe so that the audience is not distracted by the differences or individuality among the people in the choir—the primary identity of a choir member in that context is that each one is part of the choir, and the function of every member of the choir is singing. The most important point here is that Paul is claiming grace and justification are realized when the believer is baptized and puts on Christ. Therefore, when we talk about the scope of what might change as a result of being in Christ, the evidence lies in what changes as a result of a number of things that Paul has connected, including his gospel, his mission to the Gentiles, justification, grace, and baptism.

NO COMPETING IDENTITIES

Paul becomes more specific and emphatic about how being in Christ should affect the competing identities that could threaten to violate our status in Christ:

---

[26]Hans Dieter Betz, for example, argues that Gal 3:27-28 were part of an early Christian baptismal confession, but he says, "In the liturgy, the saying would communicate information to the newly initiated, telling them of their eschatological status before God in anticipation of the Last Judgment and also informing them how this status affects, in fact changes their social, cultural and religious self-understanding as well as their responsibilities in the here-and-now." See Betz, *Galatians: A Commentary on Paul's Letter to the Churches in Galatia*, Hermeneia (Philadelphia: Fortress, 1979), 184.

There is no Jew nor Greek[27] within him,
There is no slave nor free within him,
There is no male and female within him.[28]

The identity of being in Christ is the salient identity of everyone in the church. Gentiles have been the outgroup that Paul is concerned about throughout the entire letter, but Paul now includes the membership of slaves and women as parallel cases to the membership of Gentiles. The identification of the scope of what changes for Greeks/Gentiles determines the scope of what changes for slaves and women. The implications of justification for Gentiles is one of the main thrusts of Paul's argument in Galatians. *We may confidently conclude that the ways and contexts in which "there is no male and female inside him" will correspond to the ways and contexts that Paul is talking about in Galatians in which "there is no Jew or Greek inside him."* There is a great deal of information in the context of Galatians on which to build that correspondence, which I will explore below.

---

[27]Paul has been using the term *Gentile* in contrast to *Jew* throughout Galatians (see Gal 1:16; 2:2, 8-9 12, 14-15; 3:8, 14). *Gentile* is the term Jews use for the out-group: it is everyone who is not a Jew. *Greek* is used as a subcategory of Gentile in Gal 2:3, where Paul says he was laying his call to evangelize the Gentiles before the Jerusalem leadership (Gal 2:2), and Titus, who is identified as Greek (as opposed to a Gentile), was not required to be circumcised. Greek (or Roman) would be a category that would be used for self-identification that is comparable to Jews.

[28]In the Greek, there is an interesting change in the conjunctions that join the three couplets, namely, a change in the conjunction that joins men and women. Jew/Greek and slave/free are joined with "nor" (*oude*), as in "there is neither Jew nor Greek, there is neither slave nor free," but then there is a different conjunction (*kai*) for the last couplet: "There is not male and female." Some suggest that the grammar reflects the fact that the "antitheses are not parallel, for the distinction between male and female is a distinction arising out of creation" (Johnson, "Role Distinctions in the Church," 206). That would indicate that there is a greater polarity between male/female than there is between Jew/Gentile and slave/free. However, *kai* grammatically signals *similarity*. It occurs "after words implying sameness or likeness," whereas *oude* specifies distinction: "the positive to the negative." See Harry George Liddell, Robert Scott, Henry Stuart Jones, and Roderick McKenzie, *Thesaurus Linguae Graecae Project* (Irvine: University of California, Irvine, 2011), http://www.perseus.tufts.edu/hopper/morph?l=kai%2F&la=greek&can=kai%2F0#lexicon. Grammatically, Paul formalizes a greater distinction between Jew/Greek and slave/free by changing the conjunction in the third couplet. He emphasizes with *kai* that there is continuity. There is more of a unity and similarity between male and female that does not exist between the other two couplets. The creation account (Gen 1–2) stresses a unified purpose of humanity as male and female (Gen 1:27-28) and a common identity and a unity of being "one flesh" (Gen 2:23). Furthermore, Paul specifically addresses and highlights the one-flesh relationship (Eph 5:21). In other words, when Paul evokes the creation account, he stresses the similarity and unity in creation between male and female as an allegory or metaphor for the believer's unity with Christ and in Christ (head and body).

Some ask why Paul would include the additional categories of slave/free and male/female. As Richard Longenecker says, only the categories of Jew/ Greek are "relevant to Paul's argument in Galatians."[29] Longenecker goes on to explain that Paul finds a connection between these categories in other letters that he wrote so that it would appear to be a baptismal formula.[30] The parallel style of poetic repetition and the nature of the statement in the context of the argument may be an emphatic and climactic quotation of a baptismal formula, but one cannot assume that the inclusion of gender was part of a rote baptismal formula, because it is not repeated in other Pauline contexts, which calls attention to the inclusion of gender. In the surrounding context, Paul uses some metaphors and analogies from slave/free and gender to support his argument about the relationship between the Jews and Gentiles/Greeks—if he had not clarified that the same theology applied to the status of slaves and women, several of his other metaphors in Galatians could have been misunderstood, confusing, or misleading. He is specifying that what applies to the relationship between Jews and Gentiles/Greeks also must be applied to the relationship between free and slave as well as men and women, lest his other metaphors be misapplied.[31]

THE SIGNIFICANCE OF BELONGING TO CHRIST

Paul concludes in Galatians 3:29 that if one belongs to Christ through faith and baptism, "you are Abraham's seed and heirs according to the promise." This identity changes everything that makes Gentiles an outgroup in the people of God. When a person is in Christ through faith, faith is the salient feature that identifies a believer as a descendent of Abraham (Gal 3:7-9), even though a Greek is not biologically descended from Abraham by definition. Identity in Christ cuts across competing

---

[29]Richard N. Longenecker, *Galatians*, WBC (Nashville: Nelson, 1990), 154.

[30]Longenecker suggests that there is "a degree of fixity for the same pattern" (1 Cor 12:13; Col 3:11; 1 Cor 7:17-28) in *Galatians*, 154-55.

[31]Paul Grice states that there are four maxims for communication: quantity, quality, relation (relevance), and manner. We are concerned here with quantity and manner: a speaker or writer tries to give as much information as needed and no more, and tries to be brief and clear without obscurity or ambiguity. See Grice, *Studies in the Way of Words* (Cambridge, MA: Harvard University Press, 1989), 22-40.

identities of heritage, race, genetics, or one's genitals.[32] This was revolutionary for Jewish believers, since it was inconceivable that an uncircumcised male could be a full participant in spiritual functions in the people of God—and if representation of Jesus were dependent on one's body being like the body of Jesus, a Jew would never agree that an uncircumcised man's body could represent Jesus' circumcised body. But Paul's teaching that a Gentile male is now wrapped up in Christ like a garment means that he is fully identified with Christ, and circumcision is now a circumcision of the heart rather than the physical body (Rom 2:29). Consequently, a Gentile male can represent Christ in any function because of the condition of his heart, even though in Judaism, his body (genitals) would disqualify him from full participation. The implications for women are that they are also fully identified with Christ in the same way, so the fact that one's genitals are not like Jesus' similarly does not disqualify women from representing Christ in any function.

The identity of the heirs of the promise given to Abraham (Gal 3:29; cf. Gal 3:15-18) cuts across the other social identities of both slave/free and male/female. Believers' status and function in the church overrides whatever has been understood about their other identities within the contexts of the surrounding culture. However, a problem arises when considering slavery. Paul declares that the Galatians "were called to freedom" (Gal 5:13) and urges, "For freedom Christ has set us free. Stand firm, therefore, and do not submit again to a yoke of slavery" (Gal 5:1). Yet he could not set slaves free from their masters. He could only set them free in the context of the church, so the question is, How could this work? It is clear from the case of Jews and Gentiles that identity in Christ cannot be merely an abstract spiritual or eschatological freedom for a slave. Rather, what Paul means is that they are free when they enter the door of the church and should never *voluntarily* enslave themselves there, or compromise in ways and practices that nullify their status and calling in how they relate to God

---

[32] As Keener states, "Israel was called God's 'children' in the Old Testament and often in Judaism. In contrast to standard Jewish teaching, Paul says here that one becomes a spiritual descendent of Abraham (3:29) and child of God through faith, not through ethnic participation in the covenant" (*IVP Bible Background Commentary*, 532).

or one another. Paul thinks that the Gentile Galatians have done just that, which is why he is writing about what has to change in their behavior.[33]

WHAT CHANGED BETWEEN JEWS AND GENTILES?

What specific examples does the context of Galatians provide for what changes must occur as a result of being baptized into the body of Christ? We can trace the impact of Paul's gospel of grace and justification on the status of the Gentiles throughout the letter. The relationship between Jews and Gentiles in the churches, and how it is linked to the relationship between the law and the gospel, is central to Paul's message in Galatians 1:6–5:26. According to Paul, a full understanding of justification creates radical changes in the way that Jews and Gentiles are to relate to each other within the church. It deconstructs the spiritual and religious privilege and control assumed by Jews in the Christian community without eliminating the ethnicity of either group. Regardless of whether one identifies the main theme of Galatians as justification or new creation, the purpose of the letter was to deal with "cultural conflicts, the dynamics of power, and the tension between Law and liberty."[34] Throughout the letter, Paul demonstrates how both justification and new creation change the entry requirement of circumcision for males (Gal 5:2-12; 6:11-16), social practices (including food laws; Gal 2:11-14) and religious calendars and Jewish forms

---

[33]Paul wrote the Christian household codes (Col 3:18–4:4; Eph 5:22–6:10) to help navigate this difficult situation of how believers who are equal relate in the culture's authority relationships in the Greco-Roman household. For example, he was addressing slaves with masters who were not Christians, he had masters with slaves who were not Christians, and he had slaves and masters who were both Christians.

[34]According to Argentine Néstor Oscar Mígues, these three areas in Galatians characterize the conflicts that happen "between factions that emerge from the doubts, questions, and issues that develop when people of different ethnic and religious origins coexist . . . and they carry with them old habits and behaviors from their former socialization." See Migues, "Galatians," in *Global Bible Commentary*, ed. Daniel Patte (Nashville: Abingdon, 2004), 464-65.

Robert Saucy reduces the two topics of new creation and justification to the two theological categories of ecclesiological and soteriological. He then argues for a soteriological topic (because of vocabulary such as *justification, faith, grace,* and "works of the law") so that Galatians is reduced to a description of the gospel that is abstract, individualized, doctrinal, and confessional: "How does a sinner become rightly related to God?" See Saucy, "'Male and Female in the New Creation: Galatians 3:26-29' (Ch 10) by Gordon Fee," *JBMW* 10, no. 1 (Spring 2005): 29-37. Because of abstract categorization and the theological definition of justification (the application of a theological frame on the passage), the primary problem of how the social, cultural, and religious relationships in Galatians nullified Paul's gospel/justification and the line of Paul's argument is lost in Saucy's analysis.

of worship (Gal 4:8-11), and the structure of authority in the local and global church (Gal 1:6–2:19).[35]

The Jerusalem Council officially eliminated the requirements for Gentiles to keep the law and publicly demonstrated apostolic support for Paul's ministry to the Gentiles (Acts 15:22-35).[36] However, we can see in Galatians that Paul was adamant and unrelenting in continuing to work out further implications of the elimination of circumcision as an entry requirement for Gentile men. It meant that Gentile converts were not required to become Jews socially or culturally. They were not expected to keep other aspects of the law or to worship in a Jewish context (including relating to the temple in Jerusalem, the local synagogues, or the practices of Jewish piety in the home). Nevertheless, the status of Gentiles in the church was to be the same as the status of Jews. Consider the pragmatic social, cultural, and religious practices and details that changed in the culture and worship in the church of God, particularly the major adjustments Paul expected Jewish believers to make as the church transitioned from being homogeneous to heterogeneous in its membership and functions. It was a transition from racial segregation to integration, and we understand that ending racial segregation is a complex social issue from the histories of the American South and South African apartheid.

After defending his gospel and authority (Gal 1:1–2:10), Paul tells a story in Galatians 2:11-14 about how, in Antioch, Jewish believers were discriminating against Gentile believers (treating them as an out-group) when they refused to eat with them. Paul opposes and condemns this social practice because "they were not acting consistently with the truth of the gospel" (Gal 2:14). Paul then explicitly explains that the benefits of justification and the grace of God radically changed certain customs that Jews typically practiced as a culture (Gal 2:15-21). The Jews could no longer treat the Gentiles as if they were an outgroup in the people of God, and called on the church to abandon any communal, social, cultural, and religious

---

[35]Porter specifies these changes except for the change in the structure of authority in Stanley E. Porter, *The Apostle Paul: His Life, Thought and Letters* (Grand Rapids, MI: Eerdmans, 2016), 4-5.

[36]As Keener says, "Although many Jews believed that non-idolatrous Gentiles would be saved, almost no one believed that they were adopted into the covenant on equal terms with Jewish people until they were circumcised. That some Jewish believers wanted to force circumcision on Titus is thus not surprising (cf. Acts 15:5)" (*IVP Bible Background Commentary*, 527).

practices that privileged Jews and Jewish culture and communicated an out-group status of Gentiles within the context of the church.

Paul indicates that the Gentile church should not be oriented to the Jewish calendar or any other cultural/religious calendar (Gal 4:11).[37] Much more changed in the church's daily, weekly, monthly, and yearly calendar than simply changing the day of worship from the Sabbath to Sunday— this affected religious festivals and the entire culture of celebration (think of Christmas with all the connected traditions). The calendar may be categorized as "religious," but the corresponding activities of celebration were social in practice. Any cultural practice that treated other members as an out-group had to be rejected. Paul characterizes the pressure on the Galatians to implement Jewish social practices and circumcision as persecution (Gal 4:29). Both Jews and Gentiles had to make significant cultural adjustments in order to fellowship together in a way that appropriately honored the gospel and each other as equal heirs in Christ.[38] The church became a place in which cultural diversity was legitimate and embraced instead of a place in which Jews discriminated against Gentiles, supposedly as an expression of piety and purity. This alone had an enormous impact on the culture of the church.

The text of Galatians reveals how the church's structure of authority shifted because of Paul's call to the Gentiles and his gospel. This hits the heart of the purpose of the letter. People, possibly sent from James, the brother of Jesus, in Jerusalem (Gal 2:12) challenged Paul's gospel concerning the Gentiles, as well as his authority and apostleship (Gal 1:9-11).[39] For Paul, his authority was not a matter of human commission of traditional lineage, succession appointment, or official recognition from Jerusalem (Gal 1:1). Rather it came directly from his encounters with God (Gal 1:11-12). Paul was not one of the twelve apostles appointed, commissioned, and trained by Jesus, nor was he appointed by the Jerusalem apostles; rather,

---

[37]Following either the Jewish or Gentile traditions and customs linked to the calendar is equated to being enslaved. Keener suggests that Paul is targeting pagan calendars. "Paul is saying that by returning to a ceremonial, calendrical religion, the Galatians return to pagan bondage under these spirits in the heavens (4:3, 9)" (*IVP Bible Background Commentary*, 533).

[38]It has been common to suggest or assume that Paul eliminated Jewish culture in the church and required the Jews to reject their Jewish identity and to become Gentiles. However, that goes against a large amount of evidence in the New Testament (e.g., Acts 21:17-26) and historical evidence.

[39]See Porter, *Apostle Paul*, 196-200.

he received his commission and gospel about the salvation of the Gentiles through his experiences (Gal 1:11-24; cf. Acts 9:1-31). In Galatians he is unimpressed if not dismissive of the "pillars" who were the apostolic leadership in Jerusalem (Gal 2:6, 9), and he even confronted Peter in public for not acting consistently with the gospel that he himself preached to the Gentiles (Gal 2:11-14). The authority structure of the early church changed because of Paul's mission to the Gentiles. Paul even claims to be equal in status with Peter (Gal 2:7-8). Some have claimed that the leadership of the churches even shifted from Jerusalem to Antioch before the destruction of Jerusalem because of Antioch's missions and Paul's apostolic leadership.[40] But for a Greek male, an even greater change occurred because of Paul's influence: an uncircumcised Greek who would not have even been allowed to participate in Jewish ceremonies in temple worship was qualified to fill any office or function in the church, and could even be appointed to leadership over Jews. This trajectory eventually culminated in the leadership of the church being dominated by Gentile leadership, which resulted in a major shift in the culture of the church from its foundation.

Paul's mission deconstructed the early church's customs and hierarchy in a way that was consistent with his teaching of how God worked in the church, of its leadership, and of its relationships among members. The "grafting" of the Gentiles into the root (Rom 11:17) completely changed the culture of the people of God because it could no longer be exclusively Jewish. Some of it happened organically (or in the sweep of history), but in Galatians, Paul makes it clear that certain cultural/social and religious practices had to intentionally change as a result of the new status of Gentiles as a result of justification: Gentiles are now "the seed of Abraham" who are equal heirs because they are wrapped in Christ. There are no privileges or authority in the church based on the ontology of race.[41]

---

[40]This is a fallacy based on the belief that the focus of Acts (which places Paul's story in the context of the early church) was the historical focus of the entire church. Acts focuses on Antioch as the hub of Paul's mission, but Jerusalem was the apostolic hub of the active apostolic mission to the Jews, which was evangelizing other areas as well as overlapping with the areas reached by Paul, such as Ephesus (Rom 15:3).

[41]Ontology is the philosophical study of how people or other entities are grouped, subdivided, and related in hierarchies because of the ways that they are the same and the ways that they are different. See, e.g., Brian Epstein, "Social Ontology," Stanford Encyclopedia of Philosophy, March 21, 2018, https://plato.stanford.edu/entries/social-ontology/.

Galatians 3:28 obligates church members to grant equal status in the church to both the traditional and cultural out-groups, and it also removes excuses for any individual failing to be holy as God is holy, rejecting God's call, not exercising one's spiritual gifts, or failing to prioritize Jesus and follow him because of one's identity or disadvantages.

In the context of Galatians, when Paul makes "there is no slave nor free, there is no male and female" parallel to "there is no Jew or Greek," right in the middle of his argument, he is indicating that a similar scope of change in the culture, social practices, and authority structure of the church needs to be implemented to abolish entitlement and discrimination in the church in these other core social relationships.

WHAT HAPPENS TO DISTINCTIVE IDENTITIES?

Diversity and distinctive identities within the fellowship of the people of God are relativized in importance, but they are also mandated, protected, and respected by Paul's teaching. He says, "For in Christ Jesus neither circumcision nor uncircumcision counts for anything; the only thing that counts is faith working through love" (Gal 5:6). In practice this meant that Gentiles should not be required to change their identity. This verse has a clear intertextual tie with another well-known Pauline passage, 2 Corinthians 5:16-17: "From now on, therefore, we regard no one from a human point of view; even though we once knew Christ from a human point of view, we know him no longer in that way. So, if anyone is in Christ, there is a new creation: everything old has passed away; see, everything has become new!"

Paul is saying that the identities of Jew and Gentile/Greek are human categories that are not primary (salient) given our identity in Christ. His conclusion is that "everything has become new!" In other words, in the church, these distinctive identities were not to have the importance that was assigned to them in either Greco-Roman culture or in Judaism.[42]

---

[42]As Moo says, "The saying in [Gal 3:28] is rightly prized as a far-reaching and fundamental claim about the way in which the distinctions that 'matter' in the world we live in are to be left at the door of the church" (*Galatians*, 255). But Moo also rejects teaching that argues an "erasure of difference." The problem is, he seems to assume that if women and men do not maintain distinctive gender roles in the church, it erases the difference. This is a fallacy. If a woman collects the offering, passes out the communion elements, makes an announcement, prays a pastoral prayer,

Identities and relationships between groups are to be reinterpreted and altered by Paul's inclusive commands to the church, which indicate that the believer's salient identity is in Christ. In the Pauline corpus, the unity believers have in Christ is more important than any distinctive identity. Christ forms one humanity out of polarized identities, such as the three pairs in Galatians 3:28, and destroys the hostility between them (Eph 2:14-22; 4:3-4). If a benefit, function, goal, or obligation is characteristic of all members (those who are justified believers in Christ and baptized into one body), then it cuts across any limitations or hierarchies that tradition or culture places on various identities, because Scripture claims that when a person has faith in Jesus Christ, certain things change. Paul teaches that every believer has certain benefits, certain obligations, and incredible potential based on the status of being in Christ and the effects and manifestations of the Spirit. Being in Christ is the salient identity, and when the church is gathered as a group, the benefits and obligations of membership override what culture or tradition or hierarchy in the world may dictate.[43]

This does not override any identity of male and female that may be legitimately drawn from the creation account, but it overrides certain theological constructs about the significance of what is differentiated in creation, and negates the assumed correlation between the various functions in the church and gender roles. This will cause drastic change and discomfort for in-groups that have status in the culture.[44] But it also places

---

gives a teaching, or preaches a sermon, her identity as a female remains intact and is integrated into the function—she is not masculinized in any way by these functions, so the creational differences between men and women are not erased in any way.

[43]The complexity of what culture or tradition or hierarchy in the world dictated in the Greco-Roman world provides an interesting background to Paul's work. In Pauline studies, we see Jews and Judaism as oppressors of Paul and the churches, because the dominant culture and leadership of the early church that Paul challenged was Jewish. However, in the Greco-Roman world, the Jews were oppressed, brutalized by the Roman army, and discriminated against in Palestine and in many contexts in the Diaspora—the Roman army perpetrated a genocide against Palestine in a few short years after Paul's death, in which Jerusalem and the center of Christianity was destroyed. Therefore, Paul's position in this realignment of power and authority is ironic, but this illustrates that Paul believed that all who were won to Christ had a primary citizenship in heaven.

[44]People often feel entitled, humiliated, shamed, and victimized when they do not get what is expected in terms of treatment, status, or special roles and functions, which motivates discrimination and violence against individuals or groups with less power or status. This dynamic has been a major topic of discussion due to events such as mass shootings by "angry White men" and the emergence of the far right because of what masculinities specialist and sociologist Michael

great responsibilities on those who function as out-group(s) in the culture and society. For example, 1 Corinthians 14:33-35 indicates that many women in Corinth had to become better educated and socialized to not disrupt the service by speaking out of turn. By doing so they could participate appropriately as equal members in the worship service.[45]

In the rest of the Pauline corpus, Paul is interested in people being identified in the church according to their spiritual gifts. These are salient identities in the church that cross the lines of race, class, and gender (Rom 12:3-8; 1 Cor 12; Eph 5:1-15).[46] However, the ways that Gentiles, slaves, or women function in any calling or ministry will be different from how a Jew, freedperson, or man would function in the same calling or ministry in things such as manner, style, focus, content, and availability. But whatever the difference, it should have nothing to do with inherent disqualifications from any function in the church. Diversity of identities may nuance the manifestations of the Spirit in a variety of ways, but one will still have the same gift from the same Spirit as individuals in other groups—so that same gifting is a subidentity in the church by which members may be grouped. However, there will still be diversity in such a grouping because of less salient identities. Back to the analogy of the choir, everyone sings in the choir, but the limitations of a person's singing range are typically categorized by gender: bass, tenor, alto, and soprano. However, there is no reason to make a rule against a countertenor male singing soprano (such as Mitch Grassi in Pentatonix) or a woman contralto singing bass. One's capabilities, life experience, and pragmatic advantages, as well as the limitations of one's identity, will often indicate the specifics of God's call as well as directly contribute to our formation as interpreters and theologians.[47] This kind of diversity is a very good thing. A person's call and the detection of one's spiritual gifts are primarily an individual's responsibility (Rom 12:3-8).

Kimmel calls "aggrieved entitlement." See Kimmel, *Angry White Men: American Masculinity at the End of an Era* (New York: Nation Books, 2015), 31-68.

[45]For a fuller discussion of 1 Cor 14:33-35, see Westfall, *Paul and Gender*, 234-41. See also Craig Keener's chapter in this volume.

[46]We should not necessarily require the Spirit to give us a fifty-fifty ratio or have quotas, but we need to be sensitive and alert to imbalances that could be symptomatic of discrimination.

[47]See Elouise Renich Fraser's excellent discussion of how the basic pieces of our identity are "the ties that bind" us as theologians in *Confessions of a Beginning Theologian* (Downers Grove, IL: InterVarsity Press, 1998), 20-32.

However, it is the church's responsibility to utilize the gifts of every member without discrimination (1 Cor 12:21-26). Furthermore, Paul specifically cautions against a person or a group assuming entitlement or privilege in their function in the church:

> For by the grace given to me I say to everyone among you not to think of yourself more highly than you ought to think, but to think with sober judgment, each according to the measure of faith that God has assigned. For as in one body we have many members, and not all the members have the same function, so we, who are many, are one body in Christ, and individually we are members one of another. We have gifts that differ according to the grace given to us. (Rom 12:3-6)

Paul is speaking against individuals or groups preventing other people from functioning in the church because they have too high an opinion of themselves, which is a caution that particularly applies to groups that have more apparent qualifications, status, and/or power according to human standards and traditions, such as Jews, masters, and men. Consequently, those who have authority or influence in the church should never restrict anyone with a priori rules that discriminate against another group because of their identity, however low in the eyes of the world or one's tradition.[48]

WHAT ABOUT AUTHORITY RELATIONSHIPS?

What about the problem of hierarchical relationships that exist outside the church in the household and society, such as employer and employee, teacher and student, child and parent, slave and master, and husband and wife? Paul's teaching on the relationship between master and slave provides a good model. Both the master and slave need to make adjustments in church and outside church. Paul makes it clear in Colossians 3:1-17 that in the church slaves have the same obligation as everyone else to teach and admonish others, which Paul specifies will include people who are free and masters (Col 3:11, 15; 4:1-4). A household code immediately

---

[48]See, e.g., Wayne Grudem's list of 83 ministries in the church and parachurch ranked on greater governing authority to lesser governing authority, encouraging churches to use the list and the Danvers Statement as a guide on where to draw the line on what women can and cannot do, based on whether it involves teaching and authority or power over men. See Grudem, "But What Should Women Do in the Church?," *CBMW News* (November 1995), 1-7.

follows (Col 3:18–4:4) that explains how these roles should work pragmatically, and it is evident Paul does not see a slave's obedience to a master and the benefits and obligations as members as being mutually exclusive. A slave's demonstration of authority in the church in the exercise of the verbal gifts of prophecy or teaching would have violated the Greco-Roman culture's view of a slave's proper role and the master's privileges, but Paul does not consider it to be in violation of a biblical understanding of a slave's obedience in the household (Col 3:15, 22-24). For this to work, Christian masters would have had to voluntarily lay down power and control at the door of the church and refrain from giving their slaves commands that would violate the slave's benefits and obligations of membership in the context of fellowship. A master would have similar limitations as an employer outside the context of the workplace. Paul never disqualifies slaves or former slaves from being leaders or from any other function in the church because of conflicts in status in the household. He never disqualifies children who have parents in the church from being leaders or any other function in the church because of conflicts of status in the household.[49] This same understanding should be applied to the interpretation of the so-called prohibitions in 1 Timothy 2:12, which more plausibly apply to the relationship between a husband and wife in the household rather than a public worship service.[50] There should be a strong commitment on the part of evangelical interpreters to understand this passage in

---

[49]In the Greco-Roman household, the authority relationship between parents and children continued through adulthood until the parents' death. See Westfall, *Paul and Gender*, 248-50.

[50]A major problem with this assumption (often included in Bible subtitles) is that Pauline churches gathered in the domestic context of the home, not in a public context. To see how the assumption that the context of a public worship service contributes to incoherence and a lack of cohesion in the interpretation of 1 Tim 2:11-15, see Westfall, *Paul and Gender*, 286-90. For a fuller explanation of this interpretation of 1 Tim. 2:11-15, see 279-312.

The grammar in 1 Tim 2:12 is not a true prohibition, because Paul is literally reporting his own custom or current practice: that he himself is not permitting a wife to teach or boss around her husband. This sounds more like a correction of the effects of his teaching in Eph 5:21-23, in which the gender reversal that he teaches between husband and wife may have resulted in women in Ephesus taking on the stereotypical dominant behavior of a man, which is the behavior that Paul is trying to eliminate. For gender reversal in Eph 5:21-23 and a discussion of Greco-Roman stereotypical gender behavior, see Westfall, *Paul and Gender*, 16-24, 45-59. For a more technical discussion of these features, see Cynthia Long Westfall, "'This Is a Great Metaphor!': Reciprocity in the Ephesians Household Code," in *Christian Origins and Greco-Roman Culture: Social and Literary Context for the New Testament*, ed. Stanley E. Porter and Andrew Pitts, Early Christianity in Its Hellenistic Context 1 (Leiden: Brill, 2013), 561-98.

a way that does not contradict the overwhelming Pauline teaching on every member's function in the church in the rest of the Pauline corpus, not the least of which is Galatians.

Paul indeed makes a parallel between the roles of males and females in the church with roles in the household, but it is the role of *male siblings who are equal heirs*, as we established from Galatians 3:26. Greco-Roman gender roles and the authority relationship between husband and wife are *not* Paul's model for the functions among members in the church, though he uses the marital relationship in the home as a metaphor for Christ and the church and vice versa.[51] Paul's use of the household metaphor of equal siblings strips away any claims of role distinctions in the church based on gender. The assumption that distinction or difference in identity is equivalent to and necessitates role distinctions and hierarchy in the body of Christ is an interpretive fallacy applied to Galatians 3:28; it is inconsistent with Paul's theology of authority and a failure to understand how multiple identities work in group dynamics.

Therefore, regardless of what the Galatian readers believed was the proper relationship between a husband and wife in the Greco-Roman household or a woman's role in Greco-Roman society, Paul is teaching that the salient identity of all individuals in the church is that they are equal heirs with the same status, benefits, and obligations of membership. Those who restrict the meaning of Galatians 3:28 to an abstract or eschatological meaning tend to assume that gender is the salient identity in the church, rather than our identity in Christ, which goes against Paul's teaching on

---

[51]See Westfall, *Paul and Gender*, 79-84, for how Paul applies the metaphor of Christ as head to the men. Christ is not the equivalent to all men in the church in the metaphor. We should not collapse the Pauline teaching on the household into the teaching on the church. See Campbell's discussion of how Paul uses the metaphor of husband and wife to describe the relationship between Christ and the church, and how he uses the metaphor of Christ and the church to describe the relationship between husband and wife in *Paul and Union with Christ*, 298-310. Other than the equal relationships between siblings, the power dynamics of household relationships are not salient identities in Christ. I offer a biblical and coherent description of the Pauline theology of gender that attempts to sort out these metaphors, among other things, in *Paul and Gender*. The book looks at gender (male and female) in the Pauline Epistles through the lenses of culture, stereotypes, creation, the fall, eschatology, the body, calling, and authority, and concludes with an exegesis of 1 Tim 2:11-15: Paul was not restricting women from roles or functions in the church service but was correcting false teaching by addressing a lacuna in women's discipleship and speaking to their very real concerns about the consequences of the fall with a promise of healing with a solution.

several counts.[52] Johnson argues, "*The antitheses are not parallel*, for the distinction between male and female is a distinction arising out of creation, a distinction still maintained in family and church life."[53] However, this is a contradiction of Scripture, because Paul clearly makes the three opposing relationships in Galatians 3:28 parallel.[54] Johnson qualifies Paul's statement so as to argue against it, because he assumes that differences in identity in the creation of male and female mandate discrete roles and hierarchy in all contexts.[55] This understanding of Scripture is traditional because it characterized the Western Christian worldview during the European colonial period, which presupposed discrete roles, hierarchy, and enslavement on the basis of differences of identity in race, cultures, and social status, based on similar theology, narratives, and arguments.[56] Paul teaches that difference does not correspond to dominance in the church.

---

[52]As I argue elsewhere, the claim that gender overrides our position in Christ has serious implications. If Christ's atonement and justification does not have the same effect on women as it does on men because of the ontology of creation, then women have a different soteriology and eschatology from men, regardless of assurances. As Gregory of Nazianzus said in arguing Jesus' full humanity, "What is not assumed is not healed" (*Epistle* 101, 32). Furthermore, we cannot become what we were not created to be.

[53]Johnson, "Role Distinctions in the Church," 206, emphasis added. Next, he inaccurately claims "that in this context Paul is not speaking of relationships in the family or church, but of standing before God in righteousness by faith" (206). On the contrary, Paul is addressing membership in the church and the entry into membership in this very passage, and he is arguing about the nature of relationships and membership in the church throughout Galatians. Johnson is able to make this argument by reducing Paul's topic to an abstract spiritual principle (justification) and thereby ignoring the details and points of Paul's argument, including the commands. Furthermore, Johnson conflates the cultural roles and stereotypes in the home with the function of member in Christ in the church without justification, and so imposes his understanding of the husband-wife roles of the home on the church, even though Paul's chosen paradigm for men and women is that they are equal siblings.

[54]Paul understands the relevance of gender identity and utilizes Gen 1–3 to help believers navigate their multiple identities in church, home, and society when he discusses other topics (1 Cor 11:2-16; Eph 5:31); see also 1 Tim 2:13-15.

[55]We are distinguishing the relationship between husband and wife from a member's function in the church. However, in Gen 1:27-28 male and female are given the same roles and responsibilities, and roles and hierarchy are not specified in Gen 2 (they are, rather, inferred from the order of creation and an inaccurate understanding of "help").

There are not technically discrete gender roles suggested for the church in which responsibilities and benefits are divided between the two groups—a man can potentially fill any position or exercise any spiritual gift in the church, so that a woman's gender role really refers to what women are not permitted to do (in fact, there is some confusion in the discussion as to what women are permitted to do). Therefore, the term "gender roles" really refers to the commitment to the restriction of women in areas of power (authority), not special areas of calling and function.

[56]The theology and rhetoric of gender roles may be the last stand of the Christian colonial worldview and reflect the mentality of racism and the exclusion laws against minorities such as the

CONCLUSION

In conclusion, in Galatians 3:28, Paul sets an agenda for sweeping changes in racial, social, and gender relationships in the church when this verse is read in the context of what had to change as a result of there being no Jew or Greek because of justification, baptism, and location in Christ. However, these changes must be interpreted within a theological framework of authority that is based on servanthood rather than hierarchy and ontology.[57] Egalitarian theology is best understood as being "equal to serve."[58] That is, all women as well as men are called to sacrificially follow Paul and Jesus, and are qualified to lead by making themselves slaves to all. As Paul says, "You were called to freedom, brothers and sisters; only do not use your freedom as an opportunity for self-indulgence, but through love become slaves to one another" (Gal 5:13). All who are called to true leadership in the church are slaves at the foot of the cross, and every woman is qualified to be a slave.

Nevertheless, Paul lays boundaries for one's personal willingness to lay down position and status and to pay the cost of discipleship in service. In Colossians 2:16-23 (cf. Gal 4:8-11), Paul commands believers to refuse to

---

Jim Crow laws, the new Jim Crow laws, and the exclusion laws against minorities such as Chinese immigrants in the past. In the current position, other differences in identity (such as slavery) may be considered manmade; however, gender identity is often understood as an act of God in creation, so that role distinctions and hierarchy in the case of gender are allegedly ontological. However, this fails to recognize that any specific role distinctions and hierarchy are also manmade and culturally bound. In short, the message in the creation narrative emphatically teaches unity of purpose, partnership, and identity (Gen 1:27-28; 2:18, 23-24). Role distinctions and hierarchy are projected on the creation narrative because of circular presuppositions. Role and hierarchy are the result of the fall, in which the woman becomes the representative of the "other," including all other outgroups (racial, cultural, social, etc.) that are the target of discrimination and oppression because of sin. The horrible consequences of being dominated by another in Gen 3:16 is the only explanation given in the fall for the earliest manifestations of the sins of man against man: hostility, murder, and oppression.

[57]Many theologies of gender that cite Pauline passages contain an embedded theology of authority and power that is not Pauline. They seem to miss that Paul's mission to the Gentiles and the position of apostle was never a road to power and authority with the prestige and salary of a twenty-first-century pastor in a megachurch, or even the power of a priest in a fourth-century basilica. Paul's function as an apostle led to beatings, prison, and death while he had to go without (Phil 4:12) and argue for equal treatment (1 Cor 9:2-6). In the end, he is pictured as having a hard time keeping the loyalty of either his team or the house churches that he planted (2 Tim 1:15; 4:10-16).

[58]This is the premise of one of the earliest egalitarian books that defined the position: Gretchen Gaebelein Hull, *Equal to Serve: Men and Women Working Together Revealing the Gospel* (Grand Rapids, MI: Baker, 1998).

be enslaved by false rules and regulations or disqualified by each other through theology or philosophy based on "simply human commands and teachings" (Col 2:22). Teaching that unilaterally subjugates women and restricts their function in the church because of gender roles is based on human commands and teaching that override or marginalize the lordship of Christ, the will of the Holy Spirit, and clear commands in Scripture. So, we are called to biblical resistance, but the Bible does not call for all women to engage in power struggles or lawsuits in the church for positions in a hierarchy, salary, or other personal benefits in order to serve in ministry. Above all else, we want to ensure that we walk by the Spirit and manifest the fruit of the Spirit in the manner in which we pursue our ministries (Gal 5:22-23), but engaging in angry disputes can all too often manifest the fruit of selfishness, arrogance, and entitlement (Gal 5:19-21).

On the other hand, neither Paul nor Jesus waited for permission, approval, appointment, or a salary to do what they were called to do, and they did not back down from confrontations. Therefore, in a podcast, I tell women, "Go ahead and do what you are called to do. . . . Be committed to doing what God created you to do. If you get beat up, rejected, or frowned upon, well, suck it up. . . . If you follow Christ you will follow him in tough places."[59] That is how I understand the impact of egalitarian theology on women, and it should be transferable across cultures and contexts, though never without risk. Paul believed that a believer's identity in Christ and one's calling in him was every individual's primary (salient) identity (see Col 3:3), so that any identity or role in the home or society became missional rather than ontological. That alone was incredibly subversive to Roman imperial theology.[60] Furthermore, every believer is called to righteousness on behalf of others, including addressing systemic injustices done to the neighbor beyond the doors of the church. The call to righteousness touches on the functions of teachers, prophets, pastors, and other leaders in the church. We are responsible to understand the times and to be biblical in our theology and practice in the light of changing

---

[59]Cynthia Long Westfall, interview with Erin Heim, *Paul and Gender*, OnScript, podcast audio, April 17, 2018, https://onscript.study/podcast/cynthia-long-westfall-paul-and-gender/.

[60]For a brief description of imperial theology, see Cynthia Long Westfall, "Roman Religions and the Imperial Cult," in *Lexham Bible Dictionary*, ed. John Barry (Bellingham, WA: Lexham, 2015).

contexts. This should entail a call for accountability in our influence in society and the use of our resources to address global issues. When we pray, "Thy kingdom come, thy will be done, on earth as it is in heaven," we must consider how what Paul said to the Galatians in the first century now speaks to extending our kingdom relationships in the church to our mission on earth in balanced gender relationships, resisting discrimination and ending oppression.

10

LOVING AND SUBMITTING TO ONE ANOTHER IN MARRIAGE

EPHESIANS 5:21-33 AND COLOSSIANS 3:18-19

Lynn H. Cohick

• • • • •

INTRODUCTION

The Bible is God's word to his people and the world. It is also a set of books, letters, and stories addressed to specific people at particular moments in history. We need to hold these two realities together as we read Paul's letters to the Ephesian and Colossian believers, in order to understand rightly Paul's purposes and expectations. The social and cultural backgrounds of these churches at times mirror our own, and in other cases are remarkably different from our twenty-first-century environment. We will first explore Paul's world, before drawing connections to our modern context.

THE HISTORICAL AND SOCIAL CONTEXTS OF EPHESIANS AND COLOSSIANS

Nympha of Colossae and the church in her house. Sometimes it is better to start at the end of a story, rather than the beginning. As we look at Ephesians and Colossians with our questions about biblical equality, I suggest we start with Nympha, the woman whom Paul greets in his letter to the Colossians (Col 4:15). My reason for doing so is based on the conviction that Paul is consistent in what he says and what he does. When we examine his actions and those of his coworkers, we gain a better sense of what he intends in his injunctions and directions for his congregations. In this case, Paul speaks of a woman leading a house church that meets in her home. There is little doubt that she is an important person, for Paul singles her out for special acknowledgment. Yet the modern questions raised by his greetings can set up our discussion about the experience of women in these churches, and about the expectations for social and familial roles in the church. What we discover is that Paul works within his cultural constraints to present the gospel message, and thereby challenges social assumptions and argues for countercultural behaviors consistent with being "in Christ."

Paul asks that his greetings be given to Nympha and the church in her house. In Greek, the name "Nympha" is written in the accusative case, and we cannot be certain whether it refers to a man or a woman. When we turn to the pronoun describing the church, we find "his" in later manuscripts, but the feminine "her" in earlier manuscripts. From a text-critical vantage point, the feminine is judged to be the harder reading, for we could imagine much more easily a scribe changing a pronoun to the masculine from the existing feminine. Most modern English editions rightly translate the name as Nympha and use the feminine pronoun.

Because the church met in her house, most commentators correctly conclude that she held some sort of leadership role within the church.[1] The precise nature of Nympha's leadership responsibilities eludes us, even as it does for men who had churches meet in their homes. Nevertheless, we can safely assume a bit more about Nympha that would affect our study of biblical equality in Ephesians and Colossians. She would have had enough wealth to live in a house that could accommodate a group of people. With wealth came responsibility to act on behalf of others, and so she functioned within the patronage system that greased the wheels of ancient

---

[1]Margaret Y. MacDonald concludes that Nympha "no doubt played a key leadership role in the churches of the Lycus Valley." See MacDonald, *Colossians and Ephesians*, Sacra Pagina 17 (Collegeville, MN: Liturgical Press, 2000), 188. She adds that this is the "only unambiguous reference in the Pauline correspondence to the leadership of a house church by a woman." See also Carolyn Osiek and Margaret Y. MacDonald, *A Woman's Place: House Churches in Earliest Christianity* (Minneapolis: Fortress, 2006), 162-63.

society. In this she would be similar to Phoebe, who was Paul's benefactor and who carried the letter to the Romans to the churches in Rome.

A pair of women in Philippi, Euodia and Syntyche, are identified by Paul as his fellow workers and could have held similar responsibilities to Nympha.[2] Paul uses a comparable expression when he speaks of Tryphaena and Tryphosa, two women who "worked" with him (Rom 16:12), indicating activities similar to his own apostolic ministry (see also 1 Cor 3:9; 4:12; 15:10; Gal 4:11; 1 Thess 5:12).[3] Another parallel is the couple Priscilla and Aquila, who had churches meet in their homes in both Ephesus and Rome (Rom 16:3-5; 1 Cor 9:5). Luke mentions Priscilla's name first when describing the couple's instruction of Apollos (a learned evangelist; 1 Cor 3:4-6), which could indicate that she had superior teaching abilities (Acts 18:26). It may also denote higher social status, for the Greco-Roman world was highly stratified, and those with greater status were typically listed first in a group (see also Acts 18:18; Rom 16:3; 2 Tim 4:19). Paul indicates that other couples traveled together as they preached the gospel (1 Cor 9:5), including Andronicus and Junia (Rom 16:7). Priscilla and Aquila worked as tentmakers, an occupation shared by the apostle Paul (Acts 18:3). It is unusual to have a woman's occupation identified in a text, and Luke's note reminds us that women were active in commerce and shopkeeping in the ancient cities.[4]

While commentators conclude that Nympha was a leader within the church, they often go on to argue or lament the inconsistency of her leadership position with the marriage verses in the previous chapter of Colossians (Col 3:18-19). That is, interpreters assume that the description of marriage, including the posture of the wife to her husband, promotes a patriarchal worldview that would be at odds with women leadership. Most are content to observe the perceived inconsistency and leave it at that. However, new approaches to understanding personal agency and cultural

---

[2]For an extensive discussion, see Lynn H. Cohick, *Philippians*, Story of God Bible Commentary (Grand Rapids, MI: Zondervan, 2013), 207-13.

[3]Beverly Roberts Gaventa, *When in Romans: An Invitation to Linger with the Gospel According to Paul* (Grand Rapids, MI: Baker Academic, 2016), 6-14.

[4]Lynn H. Cohick, *Women in the World of the Earliest Christians: Illuminating Ancient Ways of Life* (Grand Rapids, MI: Baker Academic, 2009), 233-41. For an in-depth examination of an ancient woman's financial and legal situation, see Philip F. Esler, *Babatha's Orchard: The Yadin Papyri and an Ancient Jewish Family Tale Retold* (Oxford: Oxford University Press, 2017).

construction and maintenance suggest that we do not have inconsistency, but rather the complex interaction of several virtues and social norms that women (and men) regularly negotiate as they preserve and adapt their social worlds.

Women in the early Roman imperial period. A close reading of the early Roman imperial period shows that women were active agents in their social world.[5] Women could be active and modest; they could demonstrate piety toward their family both by keeping house and by defeating enemies of the city. They could, without contradiction, keep quiet in certain public settings and speak on behalf of the gods at a public religious festival. One ramification of this argument is that it calls into question the assumption that any assertion by women of leadership must be toward a countercultural end. It has been argued that women who acted in line with the values of the ancient culture must have been passively accepting the status quo. Now scholars recognize that women could choose conservative cultural values such as modesty in active ways that expressed their convictions. This realization is critical in understanding female leadership within the New Testament, for often biblical values are conservative, such as modesty, humility, compassion. Women who act modestly need not be judged as passive or as lacking leadership; rather, they can be viewed as asserting their convictions.

In sum, women could take an active role in society, including leadership, without contradicting social norms, if they based their actions on underlying virtues. Romans elevated modesty, industry, and loyalty as the three key virtues necessary for women. These virtues, it must be said, could also apply to men, but the activities that demonstrated the virtues were different. For example, both men and women were to be modest, for this virtue demonstrated self-control. Women were to avoid lavish dress, jewelry, and hairstyles that flaunted wealth, even as men were to avoid excessive passion. Understanding that Nympha's leadership in a house church is not at odds with typical expressions of female virtue and agency, we conclude that within the church, women were given the opportunities to lead other women and men without compromising their social decorum.

---

[5]Susan E. Hylen, *A Modest Apostle: Thecla and the History of Women in the Early Church* (Oxford: Oxford University Press, 2015), 7-17.

Paul and the Roman social codes. We should not think, however, that Paul or the early church endorsed all of his culture's social codes. For example, Paul urges both men and women to exhibit the virtue of endurance (Col 1:11). Ancient Romans connected this virtue with women, but not with men. The reason for this was that endurance implied a lack of agency or choice. The virtue was best exemplified by a woman giving birth who is overcome by labor pangs over which she has no control. A man might choose to endure suffering if it was for a greater good, such as an athlete suffering through difficult training so as to win the competition.[6] First-century Stoic Seneca said that a soldier tortured by the enemy should endure in a brave way. Seneca's argument transformed endurance into a masculine virtue.[7] Seneca advocated for men a noble suicide rather than submit to torture or other situations that required endurance, because suicide demonstrated free choice, which was a foundational masculine characteristic.[8]

However, Christians elevated endurance to a first-order virtue for men and women, and the supreme example of endurance was one who suffered, even died, for their faith. Paul explains that those who endure will be raised (Rom 8:25), and he urges the Colossians (both men and women) to practice great patience and endurance (Rom 1:11). By pointing to this virtue, Paul elevates the so-called feminine virtue to apply to Christian men as well and makes a strongly countercultural request to believers. Paul does so because the path to bodily resurrection is paved with endurance, and the virtue characterizes Christ's own obedient walk. Endurance represents humility before God, surrender to his plan, and a sort of passivity toward events that testify to the greater conviction that believers are co-heirs with Christ (Eph 2:5-6).[9]

---

[6]Seneca, *Epistle* 66.

[7]Seneca explains, "if bravery is desirable, so is patient endurance of torture; for this is a part of bravery. . . . For it is not mere endurance of torture, but brave endurance, that is desirable" (*Epistle* 67.6).

[8]Seneca did so in his celebrated *mors voluntaria*, as described by Tacitus (*Annals* 15.61-62). His attempts to die by cutting his veins, taking hemlock, and soaking in a bath all failed to bring a quick end. Yet the prolonged dying gave opportunity for Seneca to opine about the choice to die, that it is in choosing the good, the right, that one's honor is secured and virtue rewarded. See also Seneca, *Epistle* 77.7.

[9]Harry O. Maier focuses on house churches becoming "counter-sites where the usual representational practices of space are reconceptualized and in some cases inverted." See Maier, *Picturing*

As Paul elevates endurance, he reshapes the definition of courage by making it a requirement, not just for men but for women as well (1 Cor 16:13).[10] The Greek verb "be courageous" is built on the root "man" (*anēr*), but interpreters commit an etymological fallacy when they assume that the translation "act the man" excludes women from demonstrating bravery.[11] Paul is not making a claim about masculinity when he uses the common Greek verb for showing courage; quite the opposite, for he challenges the construction of masculinity rooted in Aristotle's views of male and female. While the ancient Greek philosopher presented male and female as opposites, and the female as inferior in all things to the male, Paul drew on the creation narrative in Genesis that emphasizes male and female as being of the same nature, and both fully representing the image of God. Paul applies that to believers who are now in Christ, the one who is God enfleshed (Col 1:15-22). In part based on his conviction about bodily resurrection and the importance of endurance, Paul rejects his wider culture's construction of masculinity.[12]

Unlike Greco-Roman culture, which charted virtues on a gendered, hierarchical platform, Paul's description of discipleship in Ephesians and Colossians does not come in pink and blue options; that is, there are not specific activities that only women or only men are to do in their pursuit of godly living. Instead, each believer is to put off the old self and put on the new self. Each believer is to watch their tongue, show kindness, resist sexual immorality and greed, and live by the Spirit. Most importantly, each

---

Paul in Empire: Imperial Image, Text and Persuasion in Colossians, Ephesians and the Pastoral Epistles (London: Bloomsbury T&T Clark, 2013), 141. He continues that wives submit to their husbands and husbands love their wives, "not in order to assure the right functioning of the city, but because of the church's subjection to Christ." Moreover, "slaves . . . are also citizens; women are soldiers; masters are beloved children."

[10]Lynn H. Cohick, "Mothers, Martyrs, and Manly Courage: The Female Martyr in 2 Maccabees, 4 Maccabees, and the Acts of Paul and Thecla," in *A Most Reliable Witness: Essays in Honor of Ross Shepard Kraemer*, ed. N. DesRosiers and Shira L. Lander (Providence, RI: Brown University Press, 2015), 124-27.

[11]Roy E. Ciampa and Brian S. Rosner, *The First Letter to the Corinthians*, Pillar New Testament Commentary (Grand Rapids, MI: Eerdmans, 2010), 855n45. For a discussion about etymological fallacy, see Darrell L. Bock and Buist M. Fanning, eds., *Interpreting the New Testament Text: Introduction to the Art and Science of Exegesis* (Wheaton, IL: Crossway Books, 2006), 150. See also Moisés Silva, *Biblical Words and Their Meaning: An Introduction to Lexical Semantics*, rev. ed. (Grand Rapids, MI: Zondervan Academic, 1995).

[12]Paul shared his conviction about the value of martyrdom and resurrection of the body with many Jews in his day. See 2 Macc 7.

believer is to extend to others a Christlike love that is self-sacrificial. I want to underline this point, because when we turn to the discussion of marriage, Paul will emphasize that husbands are to love their wives as Christ loves the church, and that wives are to submit to their husbands. We might wrongly imagine that such love is a unique quality of men and submission a singular characteristic of women. But Paul insists that believers, men and women, love each other with a self-giving love, out of reverence for Christ.

Having looked at Nympha's role and status as a leader in the Colossian church, we turn to questions about her family or household. The Greco-Roman world constructed the family as made up of three pairs: husband-wife, parent-child, owner-slave. The superordinate of the pair (husband, parent, owner) was due honor and obedience by the subordinate. Within this structure, wealth and social class could trump gender. It could be that a woman owned a male slave and that a mother instructed her adult son.[13] The household might also include cousins and grandparents, plus freedmen and -women. Within the structure, slave and free children were raised together for their early years, and freed slaves would remain connected to the family in a role similar to clients, with owners now taking a role similar to a patron. The ancient family was a microcosm of the complexity of the Roman hierarchical society, which promoted patriarchy and valued wealth, social prestige, family lineage, and other markers of social worth. We must take that same complexity to bear in our discussion of marriage in Ephesians and Colossians.

Nympha's marital status is not mentioned by Paul. Most scholars agree that she was likely a widow, because it would be natural for Paul to mention her husband if he were a believer. It is possible that her husband was not a Christ-follower and that he did not prevent her from practicing Christianity; however, because Christianity was seen as a foreign cult, most husbands would have been against their wives participating in a local congregation. It is possible that Nympha never married, but such was atypical.[14] If we assume she was a widow, her status highlights an

---

[13]Cohick cites the example of Terentia, the divorced wife of Cicero, and their son, Marcus (*Women in the World*, 43). Part of Terentia's dowry was set aside for Marcus's allowance after the divorce.

[14]Lynn H. Cohick and Amy Brown Hughes discuss the rise of celibacy within the church that grew as an expression of the anticipation of the resurrection life to come. See Cohick and Hughes, *Christian Women in the Patristic World: Their Influence, Authority, and Legacy in the Second*

important point we must keep in mind as we read the biblical passages on marriage, namely, that not every adult was married. Many of these earliest believers were widows or widowers, or were slaves or children of slaves. It was not unusual for a man or woman to be married two or three times, and be widowed or divorced once or twice. This reality of blended families made up of divorced and widowed parents, or single parents raising children, shares much in common with current Western society.

READING EPHESIANS 5:21-33 AND COLOSSIANS 3:18-19 IN CONTEXT

The passages on marriage are found within a discussion of two other groups that make up the ancient household: parent-child and owner-slave. This historical reality must play a significant role in our interpretative process. We must analyze Paul's discussion of the three pairs together and use a consistent hermeneutic throughout. This focus reminds us that the major goal of the household codes is to explain how Christ-followers could reshape their actions and thoughts toward godly living, given the cultural realities they faced in these pagan cities. These realities included patriarchy, slavery, paganism, and a heightened imperial propaganda. Paul pushes against these manifestations of domination and idolatry, and shows special concern for the subordinate member of the pairs: wife, child, and slave. The Greco-Roman world tended to follow Aristotle's ontological rendering of society, which held that females were by nature inferior to males. His views on slavery were similar, as he believed that some men and women were simply born to be enslaved. This view was modified by Stoics: nevertheless; a strong prejudice against slaves continued, and they were deemed inferior based on their enslavement. Paul's conviction that the cross brought together Jew and Gentile into one new humanity countered the prevailing imperial ideology that put Rome and her emperors as the saviors of the world.

Paul and his congregations were immersed in the Greco-Roman world; however, Paul's worldview was shaped predominantly by Judaism, with its

---

Through Fifth Centuries (Grand Rapids, MI: Baker Academic, 2017), xxii-xxiv, 10-15, 99-108, 216-18. It was rare within Gentile and Jewish circles for women to remain unmarried, but a tradition of prophetic singleness for men existed within Judaism, as expressed by John the Baptist, Paul, and Jesus himself.

sacred texts, festivals, synagogue fellowship, and proclamation of the one true God. Paul's letters are saturated with quotations, allusions, and echoes from the Old Testament. Twice in the Ephesians' household codes, Paul cites the Bible, and in both cases men and women are the focus. Paul quotes Genesis 1:28 that a husband and wife become one flesh (body) at marriage (Eph 5:30) and the commandment that children obey their mother and father (Eph 6:1-4). Paul reads Scripture through the lens of Christ's work of redemption, which has created a new, unified people as his body, the church. Unity is a key outcome of the salvation story, and Paul sees marriage as one example of the unity that binds together Christ and his church. In Colossians Paul offers the exalted poem of Christ and continues to insist on his full deity (Col 2:9). This conviction shapes the community, as they are admonished to love each other, and thus be bound in unity (Col 3:14-15). Love and unity are the bedrock for believers, and it is from this foundation that everyday relationships and tasks draw their meaning.

Therefore, it is inadequate to argue, as some do, that the household codes are a mere add-on to Paul's thought or an affirming nod to traditional cultural values that domesticate the gospel.[15] Instead, these teachings are meant to demonstrate the power of Christ's work at the basic level of everyday life.[16] And they challenge the prevailing social hierarchy. For example, these codes address the subordinate member of the pair, which is almost unheard of in other examples outside the New Testament. By so doing, they grant honor and agency to the subordinate and offer a public caution to the superordinate to use their social privilege for the betterment of others. Such demonstrations of love disregard the wider society's evaluations of people based on social privilege and power.[17] Paul could not be

---

[15]David M. Hay, *Colossians*, Abingdon New Testament Commentaries (Nashville: Abingdon, 2000), 137-38.

[16]N. T. Wright observes that Paul "sees the home life of the new people to be a vital context within which the practice of following and imitating the Messiah is to be inculcated and sustained." See Wright, *Paul and the Faithfulness of God* (Minneapolis: Fortress, 2013), 1109. Scot McKnight writes, "The lack of substantive parallels between the various traditions and the uniqueness of the teaching in the Pauline letters, with their emphasis on the Lord (especially in our text) and overtly expressing preference for those with lesser status and power, suggests that Paul's codes are a Christian innovation mixture of traditions on the basis of the normal life in an *oikos*." See McKnight, *Colossians*, NICNT (Grand Rapids, MI: Eerdmans, 2018), 340.

[17]Cynthia Long Westfall points to the common theme of reciprocity that permeates Ephesians and argues that Paul "interprets it in such a way that it is consistent with Pauline teaching and

more direct in his challenge to the wider culture's inequality than his statement to the Colossians, "Here there is no Gentile or Jew, circumcised or
uncircumcised, barbarian, Scythian, slave or free" (Col 3:11 NIV). Paul
pulls down barriers erected by society and replaces them with the proclamation, "but Christ is all, and is in all" (Col 3:11 NIV). The message is
oneness in Christ, and this charge should guide our reading of the household codes, the social reality into which believers live out their gospel
testimony.[18] We must read Paul's message about marriage in proper context within the letters themselves, as well as within the historical contexts
of first-century Judaism and the Greco-Roman world.

Colossians 3:18-19. This text offers only a brief comment on marriage
and focuses much more on the slave-master pair. Male and female slaves
made up perhaps 20 percent of the church. As we think about biblical
equality, we should mention here that female slaves were at the lowest rung
of the social ladder. They suffered the sexual advances of their male owners
and the cruel whims of their female owners. As slave, they could not technically enter into marriage. Owners might allow informal coupling
between two slaves and use their love for each other as leverage for obedient behavior. The owner could threaten to move or sell the slave's beloved
if they did not work hard enough. Their children might be sold from the
household. Against this reality Paul promises that slaves receive an inheritance in the Lord. Additionally, their work is honored by the Lord, and
they are promised that wrongs will be judged fairly. For a woman who had
no legal recourse and no social worth, the gospel spoke hope of a glorious
future and present respectability among believers. And to those women
who owned slaves, Paul charges them with living out the reality that their
slaves are one in the Lord with them. Paul places high, countercultural

---

theology on servanthood and so effectively undermines the assumed privileges of the patron in
the patronage system without denying social realities of power and dependency." See Westfall,
"'This Is a Great Metaphor!' Reciprocity in the Ephesians Household Code," in *Christian Origins
and Greco-Roman Culture: Social and Literary Contexts for the New Testament*, ed. Stanley E.
Porter and Andrew W. Pitts (Leiden: Brill, 2013), 561. David Balch argues that missional and
apologetic themes run throughout 1 Peter, including in the charges to wives to win over their
husbands through their moral behavior. See Balch, *Let Wives Be Submissive: The Domestic Code
in 1 Peter*, Society of Biblical Literature Monograph Series 26 (Chico, CA: Scholars Press, 1981),
81, 97-105.

[18]McKnight, *Colossians*, 338.

expectations on these female (and male) owners, challenging them to godliness toward others and not domination. The institution of slavery was upheld by the threat of violence, and that threat was often carried out. The slave had no voice, no history, no future.

Into this bleak world, Paul preached the gospel of eternal life. Believing slaves now had an inheritance, a family, and a history that included prior generations of faithful followers of God. Biblical equality for Paul in this case meant that owners could not claim special privilege before God, for God shows no favoritism (Eph 6:9). Paul would not tolerate a male owner sexually using his male or female slave, even though his Gentile culture would permit it. Slaves' work was deemed accepted to Christ, and thus dignified. And owners were forbidden from threatening their slaves. This last command cut to the root of slavery's power, for without the threat of punishment, owners had little they could do to control slaves. I suspect that was Paul's intention.

The household as constructed in ancient thought included not only the master-slave pair but married couples and their children. It is not surprising, then, that Paul addresses these groups in his discussion of the family unit. Paul's succinct command in Colossians to wives is that they choose to submit to their husbands, and the verb is in the middle-passive voice (Col 3:18). He qualifies his charge by saying that such submission should be done as fitting in the Lord. This call echoes the previous verse's appeal to do everything in the name of the Lord Jesus. Indeed, this section of Colossians contains seven references to Christ as Lord, which is half of the total number within the letter.[19] There is no talk about the husband's authority or a female's inferior ontological status. Instead, Paul points to Christ, whose word is to dwell deeply within each believer's thankful heart. Paul commands that the husband love his wife (Col 3:19), using the verb *agapeō*, a verb found repeatedly in his charge to husbands in Ephesians. The opposite of such love is harshness, which carries the sense of bitterness. Paul warns against husbands using the domination and power given them by their patriarchal culture such that they despise their wife.[20]

---

[19]Hay writes, "Despite all its reference to human 'superiors,' this brief passage also contains exactly half (seven) of all the references to Christ as Lord in the entire letter" (*Colossians*, 142).
[20]McKnight, *Colossians*, 352.

Submission and the head/body metaphor in Ephesians 5:21-33. While most English readers of Scripture would begin their study of marriage with Ephesians 5:22, that is not where Paul launches the discussion. Back in Ephesians 5:18, Paul commands that believers be filled with the Holy Spirit, and then offers five evidences of that filling, including singing songs and psalms to each other, being thankful, and submitting to each other. Paul draws a picture of their house-church meetings, where praise and thanksgiving are offered to God in Christ's name. Paul emphasizes Christ and his redemption throughout the household codes, consistent with the larger aims of the epistle. As in Colossians, we find repeated the phrase "in the Lord," summarizing the context for all believers' actions.

The last participle, "submitting to" in Ephesians 5:21, encourages believers to submit to each other out of reverence for Christ. The participle is assumed in Ephesians 5:22, which reads in the Greek, "wives to your own husbands as to the Lord." At the level of grammar and syntax, Paul links his discussion of household with the house church.[21] A key question is whether Paul intends to exclude husbands from submitting to their wives as part of the church, or whether Paul seeks to explain how submitting can function within the household. I suggest the latter, for several reasons that will become clear as we march through the verses.

Paul asks that each believer submit to others, and he offers a reason, namely, out of fear or honor of Christ.[22] Submission is linked to the honor-shame culture that governed the hierarchical Roman society. Everyone, male and female, submitted to someone else, and even the emperor submitted to the gods. Submission, therefore, was a proper virtue for both men and women. A male slave submitted to his female owner, an adult son submitted to his father or uncle, and devotees would submit to female priestesses as those who could interpret the gods. Paul states that the spirit of the prophets is in submission to the prophets (1 Cor 14:32). We learn from the gospels that the demons submit to the name of Christ (Lk 10:17). In Ephesians 1:22, Paul uses Psalm 8:6 to explain that God has submitted all things under Christ's feet. Thus, submission in and of itself is not a

---

[21]In Colossians, Paul begins his discussion on the household codes abruptly, with no transitional term.

[22]This phrase is found only in Eph 5:21, but Col 3:22 ("fear of the Lord") repeats Paul's use of the Greek term translated as "reverence."

negative posture in the ancient world; today, Western cultures devalue it while they promote individualism and independence.

Therefore, to ask wives to submit to their husbands is not a culturally negative request. And we must note that Paul does not *command* wives to submit.[23] There is no verb in Ephesians 5:22; the participle requesting every believer to submit to others is (1) what is asked of wives to their husbands, and (2) what defines the command to be filled with the Spirit (Eph 5:18). Moreover, in both Ephesians 5:21 and Ephesians 5:22, Paul insists that submission happens as they honor Christ. What would this look like in church? Would a slave owner serve the Communion cup to her male slave? Would a free woman offer the bread to her slave sister-in-Christ? Such was likely in Paul's mind (see also 1 Cor 11:17-34). This call to submit to each other was radical, countercultural, and in line with the gospel truth that God shows no favoritism (Eph 6:9; see also Acts 10:34). It also aligns with Christ's demonstration of love as selfless and life-giving. Paul underscores the title "Christ" here in Ephesians and uses "the Lord" extensively in Colossians as he develops his picture of discipleship.

Yet Paul does not say specifically that husbands should submit to their wives, so can we find the principle of reciprocity within marriage as we do within the life of the church? My answer has two parts. First, we must remember that Paul expected his congregations to actually put into action what he called them to do. Paul's wider culture was steeped in patriarchy, so it would have sounded nonsensical for a husband to submit to his wife. It would be like an army colonel being told to submit to his lieutenants. Yet we know that a colonel can show such love to the troops that they would "take the hill" if asked. In a similar way, in Paul's culture, the husband had more authority, legally and socially, than his wife. Therefore, Paul does not ask that he submit, but rather Paul *commands* that he love his wife, as Christ loved the church (Eph 5:25). Such love is self-denying and publicly humiliating, even as Christ's death was humiliating. The husband's Christlike love is the opposite of Paul's culture's insistence on honoring the superordinate of the pair.

Second, Paul circumscribes the wife's submission as that which is "as to the Lord." Here Paul makes a distinction from the wider culture by

---

[23]Paul repeats the verb "to submit" in Eph 5:24, using the present indicative active, not the imperative.

explaining that such submission is that which God requires of all followers. Paul does not state that a husband is lord of his wife. Nor does he claim that a wife's submission to her husband is a substitute for her submission to Christ. In Ephesians 5:24 Paul indicates that wives should submit to their husbands "in everything." Paul speaks similarly to slaves and children in Colossians 3:20-22. However, Paul hardly intends any behavior that would override Christ's injunctions to love others and practice godliness. The emphasis here is to elevate domestic tasks done by wives, slaves, and children as worthy demonstrations of discipleship. As we will see below, Christ's redemptive acts include washing and ironing, removing stains— domestic tasks that affirm the quotidian acts representing the bulk of humanity's labor (Eph 5:26-27).[24]

Paul does not ask that wives obey their husbands, which was a typical injunction for his time.[25] Plutarch speaks about the wife obeying and the husband ruling. Only once does he speak of the wife submitting to her husband, and that is in contrast to the wife trying to control her husband.[26] Philo, a first-century Jew from Alexandria, stresses that wives should obey and serve their husbands, using language that Paul does when asking slaves to serve wholeheartedly.[27] Josephus, a Jewish historian who lived in

---

[24]Cynthia Long Westfall, *Paul and Gender: Reclaiming the Apostle's Vision for Men and Women in Christ* (Grand Rapids, MI: Baker Academic, 2016), 23. Westfall also observes that the husband is a "bride" in this section, inasmuch as every believer is part of the church, the bride of Christ (93-94).

[25]McKnight discounts claims that *submit* here could mean "obey," for "the grounding here is neither the husband's authority nor some supposed creation order nor his role as leader"; rather, the grounding is "in the Lord" (*Colossians*, 347).

[26]Plutarch uses terms such as *hēgemonia* and *proairesis* (passage 11) and *kratein* (passage 33) in this treatise (*Coniugalia Praecepta*). The only other extant example of using the verb "submit" is found in the circa 100 BCE author Pseudo-Callisthenes, *A Narrative, Remarkable and Really Marvelous, of the Lord of the World, Alexander the King* 1.22.19-20. Pseudo-Callisthenes writes about Alexander the Great, who speaks to his mother after she has been wronged by his father, Philip, "It is proper for the wife to be submissive to her own husband" (translation in Balch, *Let Wives Be Submissive*, 98).

[27]Philo writes *douleuein* in the phrase, "Other rules again there are of various kinds: wives must be in servitude to their husbands, a servitude not imposed by violent ill-treatment but promoting obedience in all things" (*Hypothetica* 7.3). Translation in James P. Hering, *The Colossian and Ephesian Haustafeln in Theological Contexts: An Analysis of Their Origins, Relationships, and Message* (New York: Peter Lang, 2007), 234-35. See also Philo: "Organized communities are of two sorts, the greater which we call cities and the smaller which we call households. . . . The government of the greater is assigned to men, under the name of statesmanship, that of the lesser, known as household management, to women" (*Special Laws* 3.169-171).

the latter half of the first century, declares that a wife is inferior to her husband in all things and supports his claim with the broad assertion "as the law says."[28] He describes the husband's superiority as analogous to the soul's superiority over the body. Nevertheless, he also insists that the husband have sexual relations only with his wife and that they raise any child born to them. In this, Josephus challenges two key aspects of a Gentile husband's prerogative, namely, the right to have sex outside marriage (with unmarried women) and to practice infanticide. The early church embraced these two Jewish practices, which affirmed the intrinsic value of the wife (and women), and any daughters (and sons) of the union.

Along with the participle "submit to," Paul's declaration that the husband is the head of the wife has generated much heat, and often little light, in the gender wars of the last few decades. Part of the problem is a failure to appreciate the role of metaphor in Paul, and specifically the metaphor of head and body as it functions throughout Ephesians. A metaphor is a figure of speech that brings together two ideas to create a new idea or new insight. In the Hellenistic world, soul and body were understood in an ontological hierarchy, and then applied to social hierarchies such as master-slave. Paul turns the accepted hierarchies upside down. Christ is head of his church, and this is demonstrated by his saving act, his humiliating death on a Roman cross. The head gave himself for the body, forgoing any social honor. Jesus readily took up the shame associated with the cross, so as to destroy it.

We must remember that a metaphor places together two ideas to achieve a new thought, in this case head and body. We do Paul a grave injustice if we focus on a literal meaning of *head* as though it were separate from *body* in this metaphor, for at least two reasons. First, it ignores Paul's argument, which relies on metaphor to create a new meaning. Second, it allows us to import notions of head (or even worse, headship) into the conversation. Paul's focus in the metaphor is to help believers better understand Christ as Savior, and it is the description of savior that should guide our thinking.

The Greek term used for head is *kephalē*, which typically refers to the physical head resting on the neck. In Hebrew, Latin, and English, *head* can be used metaphorically to indicate "leader." It is difficult to make the case

---

[28]Josephus, *Contra Apion* 2.25. He does not identify his source, and scholars today cannot find any place in the biblical text that matches Josephus's claim.

that it refers to "leader" in Greek, for we have almost no evidence of this.[29] Lexicons in the nineteenth and twentieth centuries suggested "source" as a possible metaphorical meaning, but not "leader."[30] Fourth-century church father Cyril of Alexandria speaks of Christ as the second Adam:

> Yet he, though God by nature, has himself a generating head, the heavenly Father, and he himself, though God according to his nature, yet being the Word, was begotten of him. Because head means source, he establishes the truth for those who are wavering in their mind that man is the head of woman, for she was taken out of him. Therefore as God according to his nature, the one Christ and Son and Lord has as his head the heavenly Father, having himself become our head because he is of the same stock according to the flesh.[31]

Chrysostom likewise rejects the meaning "leader" for *kephalē* in his explanation of 1 Corinthians 11:3. He defends the church's teaching that Christ is the same substance as the Father and clarifies that if Paul wanted to stress Father as ruler, he would not have chosen the male-female pair but the owner-slave pair.[32]

Modern authors promote as the metaphorical meaning "source" or "honored part," or "prominent."[33] Cynthia Westfall builds on this evidence,

---

[29]Wayne Grudem argued for the definition "leader." See Grudem, "Does *kephalē* ('Head') Mean 'Source' or 'Authority Over' in Greek Literature? A Survey of 2,336 Examples," *Trinity Journal* 6 (1985): 38-59; Grudem, "The Meaning of *kephalē* ('Head'): An Evaluation of New Evidence, Real and Alleged," *JETS* 44 (2001): 25-65. He examined over two thousand examples of the term *kephalē* in the ancient world and concluded that 2.1 percent of the time, it should be translated with the sense of "leader" or "having authority over," including in the biblical text's examples. Within the Greek translation of the Hebrew Bible (LXX), there are six instances out of 171 occurrences of *kephalē* that might be understood as "authority" (Judg 11:11, 2 Sam 22:44; Ps 18:43 [17:44 LXX]; Is 7:8-9 [twice]; Lam 1:5). Richard Cervin notes that Judg 11:11 includes the gloss "they set him over them as a head, as a leader" using either *hēgoumenon* or *archēgon* to clarify the Hebrew metaphor for the Greek reader. See Cervin, "Does *kephalē* Mean 'Source' or 'Authority Over' in Greek Literature? A Rebuttal," *Trinity Journal* 10 (1989): 10.

[30]The 1843 edition of the Liddell and Scott lexicon included over twenty-five entries under *kephalē*, including the metaphorical meaning "source," but no entry referring to "leader" or "authority over." The ninth edition, published in 1996, likewise does not include "leader" or "authority over" as possible meanings for *kephalē*. Additionally, ancient lexicons do not define *kephalē* as authority or leader; see Cervin, "Does *kephalē* Mean 'Source,'" 85-112.

[31]Cyril of Alexandria, *De recta fide ad Arcadiam et Marinam* 5.6, translation in Westfall, *Paul and Gender*, 86n69.

[32]Chrysostom, *Homilies on First Corinthians*, Homily 26.3.

[33]Gordon D. Fee, *The First Epistle to the Corinthians*, NICNT (Grand Rapids, MI: Eerdmans, 1987), 502-3; Anthony C. Thiselton, *The First Epistle to the Corinthians: A Commentary of the Greek Text*,

incorporating the categories of reciprocity and family. She argues that in the ancient context, the progenitor of the family was its source, and thus was also the prominent member of the family's public face. We find similar emphases earlier in Ephesians, as Paul stresses Christ the head who sustains and causes his body (the church) to grow (Eph 4:15-16; see also Col 2:19). Michelle Lee-Barnewall observes that the head-body metaphor was used to describe the military unit, with the general (or emperor) as head and the troops as his body. The body was expected to give itself to protect the head. Lee-Barnewall rightly points out that Christ reverses this assumption by dying for his body.[34] Christ as head and Savior echoes throughout Ephesians as God has placed Christ's enemies under his feet (Eph 1:20) and has raised him triumphant to God's right hand (Eph 2:5).

Most discussions about Paul's views of marriage focus on his use of the verb "submit to" and the meaning of the noun "head." However, in Ephesians, Paul himself spends twice as much time focusing on the husband's requirement to love his wife. Paul takes special care to define this love as that exhibited by Christ, to offset the wider culture's description of marital harmony and love. Paul's understanding of love goes beyond the culture's encouragement of familial concord.[35] We have several examples of philosophers promoting marital concord and kindness. In these cases, the concord is achieved as the wife learns to accommodate to her husband's wishes. For example, Gaius Musonius Rufus underscores the importance of a wife receiving philosophical training. He argues for a husband to demonstrate self-control as the one who has superior judgment and character. Buttressing his argument is a structure of power that gives full agency to the husband and partial agency to the wife.[36] In a second example, Plutarch

---

NIGTC (Grand Rapids, MI: Eerdmans, 2000), 821. See also Cervin, "Does *kephalē* Mean 'Source,'" 85-112.

[34] Michelle Lee-Barnewall, "Turning ΚΕΦΑΛΗ on Its Head: The Rhetoric of Reversal in Ephesians 5:21-33," in Porter and Pitts, *Christian Origins and Greco-Roman Culture*, 602-9.

[35] It is also the case that Paul writes more to the slaves than to owners, which may be due to the fewer number of slave owners in the churches but is more likely related to his argument that with a single blow cuts to the root of slavery's power. That is, Paul declares that God shows no favoritism, and as such the owner is to forgo the threat of harsh treatment. Without such threat, slavery as an institution is emasculated.

[36] Martha C. Nussbaum, "The Incomplete Feminism of Musonius Rufus, Platonist, Stoic, and Roman," in *The Sleep of Reason: Erotic Experience and Sexual Ethics in Ancient Greece*, ed. Martha C. Nussbaum and Juha Sihvola (Chicago: University of Chicago Press, 2002), 300-313.

urges wives to learn philosophy, not to be better individuals per se, but to be more chaste and interesting companions for their husbands. He explains, "In a well-managed household everything is done by mutual consent, but the husband's supremacy is exhibited, and his wishes are consulted."[37] A third example comes from an inscription, a funerary eulogy to a beloved wife, Turia.[38] It reveals a grieving husband who lauds his wife as having excellent character, including that she is loyal, obedient, industrious (in wool working), modest in appearance, and not superstitious (lines 30-31).[39] In all these cases, marital harmony is created as wives mold themselves to their husbands' wishes and circumstances.

In a strongly countercultural move, Paul commands that the husband love his wife, and he further explains this love by pointing to Christ's self-giving love. The verb used for "to love," *agapeō*, is never used elsewhere in Greco-Roman household codes, probably because the nature of this love upends the patriarchal construct of marriage. With this command to love his wife, Paul insists that husbands relinquish, even reject, the power and authority granted to them by the wider culture. It mandates that husbands accept the social shame that would come with a reversal of masculinity as understood in the ancient world. Instead of having his wife "die" for his honor, now the husband "dies" or lives self-sacrificially on behalf of his wife. This challenge to husbands is that laid before every believer, who is to love the other as Christ loved the church (Eph 5:2). Here we see a similarity with the call for wives to submit in Ephesians 5:22, namely that submission to others is the call for every believer (Eph 5:21).

Paul repeats the command for husbands to love their wives in Ephesians 5:28, adding that the content of such love is bound in the unity of the couple.[40] The head-body metaphor gives way to the one-body or one-flesh image of marriage portrayed in Genesis 1:28. Paul invites the husband to think differently about himself, for his body includes his wife. By implication, his wife can say about her body that it includes her husband. Paul makes this clear to the Corinthians when he states that the husband does

---

[37]Plutarch, *Coniugalia Praecepta* 11.
[38]H. Dessau, ed., *Inscriptiones Latinae Selectae* (Berlin, 1892–1916), 8393.
[39]For a translation and discussion, see Josiah Osgood, *Turia: A Roman Woman's Civil War* (Oxford: Oxford University Press, 2014), 155-69.
[40]Paul writes that the husband "ought" (present active indicative) "to love" (infinitive).

not have authority over his own body, but his wife does (1 Cor 7:4). This radical statement cuts to the heart of patriarchy, for it denies the husband's sexual prerogative. Paul drives home the unity of the couple, because he sees in the marriage union a model of Christ's union with the church. Paul summarizes his thoughts by noting that this union, the union of Christ and the church, is a mystery of great magnitude. Once again, we find Paul stretching our imaginations to think differently about the believer's hope in Christ and the church's relationship to Christ. Earlier, Paul stresses the unity of Jew and Gentile (Eph 2:14-15), as well as a baptismal unity of all believers (Eph 4:4-6). The church, created through Christ's death and resurrection, is characterized by unity.

One final time, Paul commands husbands to love their wives as he closes his passage on marriage (Eph 5:33). The love demonstrated by the husband is that with which he loves himself—which makes sense because his wife is his own body. The wife is asked (not commanded) to respect her husband, using the same noun found in Ephesians 5:21, reverence or respect given to Christ. Overall, this description of marriage speaks not at all of roles for women and men, even less about headship or leadership. Instead, it presents a reversal of common patriarchal assumptions by focusing on self-sacrificial love by the husband to the wife, and submission expressed as honor and respect by the wife to her husband. Both actions are characteristics incumbent on believers, to love each other as Christ loved the church and to submit to each other out of reverence for Christ.

The household codes continue with injunctions to parents and children, and to slaves and owners. Here too, Paul's call for biblical equality permeates his message. In his call to children, he speaks of obeying both father and mother. Paul expects both boys and girls to be educated in the church as to the gospel truth. If Nympha had children, she would have been expected to have them learn the ways of God, much as did Timothy's mother and grandmother (2 Tim 1:5; 3:15). Nympha's children would have shown their respect by obeying her. Paul's charge to fathers to cease exasperating their children highlights the social context wherein the father had more legal and cultural control over his children. Notice that Paul does not identify the human father with the heavenly Father, and he does not suggest that a human father's care is modeled after God the Father's care. This is likely due to the fact that all believers are to express Christ's love (Eph 5:2) and that the biblical commandment is for children to obey father *and mother*. Furthermore, we must recognize that not all children attending house churches had living parents, and the slave children would have had owners, not parents, who oversaw their upbringing. Adult women and men in the church might informally take up the role of parent for younger believers.[41]

CONCLUSION

Paul's call for biblical equality requires the church to see differences in sex, ethnicity, class, education, and the like not on a hierarchical scale, as did his culture, but as a body with equally valuable parts that should function together as they all grow up in Christ (Eph 4:14-16). The unity of the church, based on the work of Christ and the power of the Holy Spirit, testifies to the wisdom of God before a watching world. Paul's gospel encouraged women to be active agents and offer public leadership in service to the church. Women are called alongside men to show courage in the face of suffering and endurance with the sure hope of resurrection.

---

[41]For an excellent discussion of children in Ephesians and Colossians, see Margaret Y. MacDonald, *The Power of Children: The Construction of Families in the Greco-Roman World* (Waco, TX: Baylor University Press, 2014).

11

TEACHING AND USURPING AUTHORITY

1 TIMOTHY 2:11-15

Linda L. Belleville

• • • • •

THE BATTLE OVER WOMEN LEADERS in the church continues to rage unabated in evangelical circles. At the center of the tempest sits 1 Timothy 2:11-15. Despite a broad spectrum of biblical and extrabiblical texts that highlight female leaders, this text continues to be perceived and treated as the great divide in the debate. Indeed, a hierarchical interpretation of this passage has become for some a litmus test for the label *evangelical* and even a necessity for the salvation of nonbelievers.[1]

The complexities of 1 Timothy 2:11-15 are many. There is barely a word or phrase that has not been keenly scrutinized. The focus here will be on the key interpretive issues (context, translation, the Greek infinitive *authentein*, grammar, and cultural background) and on common concerns regarding what this text says about men and women in positions of leadership and authority. This analysis will make use of a wide array of recently available tools and databases that can shed light on what all concede to be hotly disputed aspects of the passage.

---

[1]A case in point is Andreas Köstenberger's rationale in *Women in the Church: A Fresh Analysis of 1 Timothy 2:9-15*, ed. A. Köstenberger, T. Schreiner, and H. S. Baldwin (Grand Rapids, MI: Baker, 1995), 11-12. He argues that a hierarchical view of men and women is necessary for "a world estranged from God" to "believe that God was in Christ reconciling the world to himself" (11-12). *green!*

CONTEXT

Historical context. In getting a handle on 1 Timothy 2:11-15, it is important to be clear about where these verses sit in the letter as a whole. Paul begins by instructing his stand-in, Timothy, to stay put in Ephesus so that he can command certain persons "not to teach false doctrines any longer" (1 Tim 1:3 NIV). That false teaching is Paul's overriding concern can be seen from the fact that he bypasses normal letter-writing conventions (such as a thanksgiving section and closing greetings) and gets right down to business. It is also clear from the fact that the majority of the letter's content is devoted to the topic of false teaching. The posture throughout is corrective. While there is much that is said about church leadership, we learn very little about the leadership roles of the day.[2] Instead, there are details about how not to choose church leaders (1 Tim 5:21-22) and what to do with those who stumble (1 Tim 5:19-20). There is also little interest in the professional qualifications of church leaders. Alternatively, we find a concern for character, family life, and a commitment to sound teaching (1 Tim 3:1-13)—all perfectly understandable against a backdrop of false teaching. Then there are the explicit statements. Two church leaders have been expelled (1 Tim 1:20), and some elders need to be publicly rebuked due to continuing sin "so that the others may take warning" (1 Tim 5:20 NIV).[3] The impact on the church is also plain. There is slander, base suspicions, and wrangling (1 Tim 6:4-5). Some are even said to have missed the mark and wandered from the faith (1 Tim 6:20-21).[4]

Were women specifically involved? They certainly receive a great deal of attention in 1 Timothy. Indeed, there is no other New Testament letter in which they figure so prominently. Concerns include behavior befitting women in worship (1 Tim 2:10-15), qualifications for women deacons (1 Tim 3:11), appropriate pastoral behavior toward older and younger

---

[2]Character qualifications for leaders are outlined in 1 Tim 3:1-13; 5:9-10, but there is no instruction regarding credentials or the specifics of the job.

[3]Since the tense and mood is present indicative, Paul is dealing with a current reality and not a hypothetical possibility. See, e.g., "But those elders who *are sinning* you are to reprove before everyone, so that the others may take warning" (NIV).

[4]For further discussion, see, e.g., Gordon D. Fee, *1 and 2 Timothy, Titus*, NIBC (Peabody, MA: Hendrickson, 1988), 20-23, and Linda Belleville, *1 Timothy*, Cornerstone Theological Commentary Series (Carol Stream, IL: Tyndale House, 2009), 9-10, 20-21.

women (1 Tim 5:2), support of widows in service of the church (1 Tim 5:9-10), correction of younger widows (1 Tim 5:11-15), and familial responsibilities toward destitute widows (1 Tim 5:3-8, 16). Moreover, mention is made of widows who "have in fact already turned away to follow Satan" (1 Tim 5:15 NIV).

Some are quick to point out that there are no explicit examples of female false teachers in 1 Timothy, and they are correct. No women (teachers or otherwise) are specifically named. Yet this overlooks the fact that attention to false teaching and women occupies about 60 percent of the letter. It would therefore be foolish—not to mention misleading—to neglect considering 1 Timothy 2 against this backdrop. That the false teachers "forbid people to marry" (1 Tim 4:3 NIV) explains Paul's stress that "women will be saved [or 'preserved'; NASB] through the birth of the child" (1 Tim 2:15 GOD'S WORD Translation), as well as his command in 1 Timothy 5:14 that younger widows marry and raise a family, which is different from his teaching elsewhere about the value of not marrying (e.g., 1 Cor 7:8-9, 39-40).[5] Also, the language of deception is used of both the Ephesian women and the false teachers. The false teachers deceive others and themselves (2 Tim 3:13), while the Ephesian women are reminded that it was Eve who "was deceived and became a sinner" (1 Tim 2:14 NIV). Further, the parallel language between the itinerant women at Ephesus ("going about from house to house . . . saying things they ought not to"; 1 Tim 5:13 NIV) and the false teachers at Crete ("disrupting whole households by teaching things they ought not to teach"; Titus 1:11 NIV) is striking.

Grammatical and lexical context. The grammar and language of 1 Timothy 2 also dictate such a backdrop. The opening "Therefore I exhort first of all" (*parakalō oun*; 1 Tim 2:1 NKJV) ties what follows in 1 Timothy 2 with the false teaching of the previous chapter and its divisive influence (1 Tim 1:3-7, 18-20). The subsequent "Therefore I want the men" (*boulomai oun tous andras*) eight verses later does the same (1 Tim 2:8 NIV).

---

[5]1 Tim 2:15 has been translated (1) "women [who marry and become pregnant] will be kept safe through the childbearing process" or (2) "women will be saved through the childbearing" (i.e., Christ versus the goddess Artemis). The article and the singular hapax *dia tēs teknogonias* rules out the common translation "women will be saved through bearing children. "Women" is plural, but the rest is singular, "through the [article] Childbirth [versus the common word for bearing children]." See "The Rationale for 1 Timothy 2:13-15" below.

Congregational contention is the keynote of 1 Timothy 2. A command for peace (instead of disputing) is found four times in the space of fifteen verses. Prayers for governing authorities are urged "that we may lead peaceful and quiet lives" (1 Tim 2:2 NIV). The men of the church are commanded to lift up hands that are "without anger or disputing" (1 Tim 2:8 NIV). The women are told to show sound judgment (1 Tim 2:9, 15, *sōphrosynēs*), to learn in a peaceful (not quarrelsome) fashion (1 Tim 2:11; see below), and not to fall prey to Eve's example of deception and transgression (1 Tim 2:13-14). The language of deception, in particular, calls to mind the activities of the false teachers. A similar warning is given to the Corinthian congregation. "I am afraid," Paul says, "that just as Eve was deceived by the serpent's cunning, your minds may somehow be led astray from your sincere and pure devotion to Christ" (2 Cor 11:3 NIV).

Paul's command that women learn quietly (1 Tim 2:11) and behave quietly (1 Tim 2:12) points to some sort of disruption. Some translate the Greek phrase *en hēsychia* as "in silence" and understand Paul to be setting forth public protocols for women in public worship. However, the semantic range for *hēsychia* does not include "silence."[6] The term pertains to a gentle and peaceful disposition and is synonymous with *eirēnikos*, "peaceable."[7] When absence of speech is in view, the Greek term *sigē*, "silence" (and its cognates), is typically found.[8] Paul does not use the Greek term *hēsychion* this way nine verses earlier: "I urge . . . that petitions be made . . . for kings and all those in authority, that we may live peaceful and quiet [*hēsychion*] lives" (1 Tim 2:1-2 NIV).

What is also overlooked is the preposition *en* with *hēsychia*: "Let a woman learn *en hēsychia*" (1 Tim 2:11) and "let a woman behave *en hēsychia*" (1 Tim 2:12). Both prepositional phrases are adverbial, and hence are descriptive of how a woman is to learn and conduct herself,

---

[6]See BDAG; cf. *LSJ* s.v.

[7]Elsewhere *hēsychia* has the sense of a restful attitude (Lk 23:56; Acts 11:18; 21:14; 1 Thess 4:11; 2 Thess 3:12; 1 Pet 3:4) or a quiet demeanor (1 Thess 4:11; 2 Thess 3:12; 1 Tim 2:2).

[8]Nor does Paul use the term *hēsychia* to mean "silence" elsewhere. When he has absence of speech in mind, he uses *sigaō* (Rom 16:25; 1 Cor 14:28, 30, 34). When he has calmness in view, he uses *hēsychia* and its cognate forms. This is also the case for the other New Testament authors. See *sigaō* in Lk 9:36; 18:39; 20:26; Acts 12:17; 15:12-13; and *sigē* in Acts 21:40; Rev 8:1. For *hēsychia* (and related forms) meaning "calm" or "restful," see Lk 23:56; Acts 11:18; 21:14; 1 Thess 4:11; 2 Thess 3:12; 1 Pet 3:4. Some argue for "silence" in Lk 14:4 and, perhaps, Acts 22:2.

namely, "calmly." It is not the equivalent of the adjective *silent* and modifying the noun *woman* but, rather, modifying the infinitive *einai* (to "be" or "behave" calmly).

The other *en* prepositional phrase in these verses is also adverbial, and hence is descriptive of *how a woman is to learn*, namely, "submissively" (*en pasē hypotagē*; 1 Tim 2:11). It is not adjectival and therefore does not refer to submissive women in public worship. It is a common assumption that women are being prohibited from speaking or teaching in a congregational setting as a sign of full submission to their husbands or to church male leadership. However, the phrase "Let a woman learn" (1 Tim 2:11) does not support such an interpretation. Plus, the imperative "let a woman learn" comes first, while the how ("submissively") comes second. In a learning context, it is logical to think in terms of a teacher-student relationship. To learn submissively from a teacher indicates a student's willingness to take direction.[9] The term *hypotagē* supports this. The Greek word is not equivalent to *hypakoē*, "obedience." Rather, it denotes the voluntary waiving of one's rights for the sake of another (see 2 Cor 9:13; Gal 2:5; 3:4).[10] A woman's prerogative to learn was not an issue as long as she did it calmly and with self-restraint—a prerequisite for any learning environment.

Some suggest translating *gynē* in 1 Timothy 2:11, 12-15 as "let a *wife* learn" and "I am not permitting a *wife* to teach or *authentein* a *husband*." Lexically, this is certainly possible. *Gynē* can mean either "woman" or "wife."[11] Yet, "I want the men to pray" (1 Tim 2:8) and "likewise the women" (1 Tim 2:9-10) cannot readily be limited to those who are married. Nor can the verses that follow be read in this way. There is reference to Adam and Eve in 1 Timothy 2:13-14, but it is to Adam and Eve as the prototypical male and female and not as a married couple. The concern for peaceable and submissive behavior suggests that women were disrupting worship. The men were too. They were praying in an angry and contentious way (1 Tim 2:8). A battle of the sexes better fits the overall context.

---

[9]Another option for *en pasē hypotagē* is "with self-restraint" or "self-control." This sense appears in 1 Cor 14:32, where Paul states that those "who prophesy are in control of their spirit and can take turns" (*hai pneumata prophētōn prophētais hypotassetai*).

[10]See BDAG, "ὑποταγή," s.v.

[11]See BDAG, "γυνὴ," s.v.

plus assumption that "authority" is a bad thing to have and someone "have it"?

TRANSLATION CONCERNS

Without a doubt, the most difficult part of 1 Timothy 2:11-15 to unpack is *didaskein de gynaiki ouk epitrepō oude authentein andros*—although the average person in the pew would not know it. English translations stemming from the 1940s to the present tend to gloss over the difficulties. A hierarchical, noninclusive understanding of leadership is partly to blame. Women are not supposed to be leaders, so the language of leadership, where women are involved, tends to be manipulated.

One of the primary places where this sort of bias surfaces is 1 Timothy 2:12. Post–World War II translations routinely render the clause as "I do not permit a woman to teach or to have [or exercise] authority over a man." However, earlier versions and translations were not so quick to do so. This was largely owing to dependence on ancient Greek lexicographers who defined the term as negative "domineer" (or equivalent). In fact, there is a notable translation history beginning with the oldest versions that translates *authentein* negatively as "to domineer," "usurp," "lord over," or "dictate."

Early translations (second–fifth centuries).

- Old Latin (AD second–fourth century): "neither to dominate a man" (*neque dominari viro*)[12]

- Vulgate (AD fourth–fifth century): "neither to domineer over a man" (*neque dominari in virum*)[13]

- Coptic Sahidic (AD third century): "nor to be lord of him" (*oude erjoeis epesha*)[14]

---

[12]See P. G. W. Glare, *Oxford Latin Dictionary* (Oxford: Oxford University Press, 1983): "dŏmĭnor, ātus (ante-class). I. *inf* dominarier *v. dep. n.* [dominus], *to be lord and master, to have dominion, bear rule, domineer.*" While *dominor* could be translated "lord over," "dominate over," or "bear rule over," the more usual Latin term for exercising authority is *auctoritas*, which indeed is the origin of our English word *authority*. Al Wolters claims that fourth- to fifth-century Codex Bobiensis (K) has *non permitto neque praepositam essa viro*, thereby confirming an early understanding of *authentein* as "exercise authority over." See Wolters, "A Semantic Study of αὐθέντης and Its Derivatives," *Journal for Biblical Manhood and Womanhood* 11 (2006): 51. However, this codex only contains fragments from Matthew and Mark. See Codex Bobiensis (Turin, Biblioteca Nazionale Universitaria, 1163; G.VII.15).

[13]*Dominor* with *en* plus the accusative or ablative means "to lord it over," "tyrannize." See Charlton T. Lewis and Charles Short, *A Latin Dictionary* (Oxford: Clarendon, 1879) s.v.

[14]George Horner, *Sahidic Coptic New Testament in English* (Oxford: Clarendon, 1924); W. E. Crum, *A Coptic Dictionary* (Oxford: Clarendon, 1939).

- Gothic (AD fourth century): "nor to usurp authority over the man" (*nih fraujinon faura waira*)[15]

- Syriac Peshitta (AD fifth century): "nor to be assuming over the man" (Murdock); "or to be presumptuous over a husband" (*nā wəlā ləmamrāhū 'al gabrā*)[16]

English translations (sixteenth–early twentieth centuries).

- Erasmus (1519): "nor to usurp authority over a man" (*neque autoritatė ufurpare in viros*)

- Complutensian Polyglot Bible (1520): "neither to dominate a man" (*neque dominari in virum*)

- Bishops (1595): "neither to vsurpe authoritie ouer ye man"

- Geneva (1599): "neither to vfurpe authoritie ouer the man"

- KJV (1611): "nor to vsurpe authoritie ouer the man"

- Websters (1833): "to usurp authority over the man"

- Fenton (1917): "or to dominate a man"

- Goodspeed (1923): "or to domineer over men"

Contemporary translations (late twentieth–early twenty-first centuries).

- Spanish UBS (1966): "nor to dominate the man" (*ni tampoco dominar al hombre*)

- New Berkley Version in Modern English (1969): "neither to domineer over a man"

- NEB (1970): "nor must woman domineer over man"

- Jerusalem Bible in French (*JBCerf* 1974): "neither to *lay down the law for* the man" (*ni de faire la loi*)

- *Nova Vulgata* (1986): "nor to dominate/over a man" (*neque dominari in virum*)

---

[15]*Project Wulfila* (Belgium: University of Antwerp, 2004). Compare Gerhard Köbler, *Gotisches Wörterbuch* (Leiden: Brill, 1989), 166-67. See also Gerhard Balg, *A Comparative Glossary of the Gothic Language with Especial Reference to English and German* (Westermann, 1889), 105: "*Frau-jinon faura* with the dative 'lord it over,' 'rule over.'"

[16]Based on the Philoxeniana, Harklensis, and Palestinian Syriac versions. See James Murdock, *A Literal Translation from the Syriac Peshito Version* (New York: Stanford, 1852); Janet Magiera, *Aramaic Peshitta New Testament Translation* (Erwin: Light of the Word, 2006).

- *French Traduction Oecumenique* (1988): "neither to domineer over the man" (*ni de domineer sur l'homme*)
- New Translation (1990): "or dominate men"
- 21st Century KJV (1994): "nor to usurp authority over the man"
- Websters Revised (1995): "nor to usurp authority over the man"
- *NVB San Paolo Edizione* (1995): "nor to dominate on man" (*né di dominare sull' uomo*)
- CEV (1995): "or to tell men what to do"
- *The Message* (2002): "I don't let women take over and tell the men what to do"
- TNIV (2005 footnote): "I do not permit a woman to teach a man in a domineering way"
- *La Bible. Traduction oecuménique* (2010): "nor to dominate the man" (*ni do dominer l'homme*)
- Modern English Version (2014): "or to usurp authority over a man"
- International Standard Version (2014): "I am not allowing a woman to instigate conflict toward a man"

There are good reasons for the lengthy history of translating *authentein* in a negative way. It cannot be stressed enough that Paul picked a term that occurs <u>only here in the New Testament and once in LXX</u>. In the Wisdom of Solomon 12:6 it is the adjectival form *authentēs* ("<u>murdering</u>") that is used with reference to the indigenous peoples' practice of child sacrifice: "Those [the Canaanites] . . . you hated for their detestable practices . . . these murdering [*authentas*] parents of helpless lives."[17]

This *hapax* LXX occurrence should give us pause in opting for a translation such as "to have [or exercise] authority over." If Paul had wanted to speak of an ordinary exercise of authority, he could have picked any number of words. Within the semantic domain of "exercise authority," biblical

---

[17]Some cite *authentia* in 3 Maccabees 2:28-29 as a second *authentein* reference. However, *authentia* and the more commonly found Hellenistic *authentikos* are formed from the root *authenti-* and mean "original," "authentic." The root of *authentēs* and *authenteō* is *authent-*. Third Maccabees 2 recounts the hostile measures taken by the Ptolemies against Alexandrian Jews toward the end of the third century BC. This included the mandate that Jews register, be branded with the ivy-leaf symbol of the deity Dionysus, and be reduced "to their former status of origin" (*eis tēn prosynestalmenēn authentian*) as Egyptian slaves.

lexicographers Johannes Louw and Eugene Nida have thirteen entries under "Exercise Authority" and forty-eight under of "Rule, Govern."[18] Yet *authentein* is absent from both domains. Why so? The most compelling reason is that *authentein* carried a nuance that was particularly suited to the Ephesian situation. Instead, Louw and Nida put *authentein* under "control" and translate it "control in a domineering manner."

PRIMARY MATERIALS AND SOURCES

Evidence from classical literature. During the sixth to second centuries BC, Greek tragedies used the noun and adjective *authentēs* and the verb *authenteō* exclusively of murdering another person(s) or oneself. Euripides says, "For when I was taken captive, Achilles' son would have me as his wife and I must serve in the houses *of murderers [authentōn]*."[19] Rhetoricians and orators also used the *authent-* word group of murder. Antiphon states, "He complains bitterly, because, according to him, it is a slur upon his son's memory that he should have been proved a murderer [*authentēs*] when he neither threw the javelin nor had any intention of doing so."[20] In the historians and epic writers of the period the *authent-* word group refers to murder as well. Herodotus writes, "O King when I took the boy, I thought and considered how to do what you wanted and not be held a murderer [*authentēs*] by your daughter or by you."[21]

Euripides's *Suppliant Women* 442 is sometimes cited as establishing a fifth-century BC meaning of *authentēs* as "master" or "ruler" (citing George Knight's 1984 article).[22] However, to do so is to overlook the fact that critical editions uniformly consider *authentēs* to be an error in

---

[18]L&N, §37.21.

[19]Compare Euripides, *Trojan Women* 659–660; *Andromache* 172, 614-615; *Fragment* 645; *Madness of Hercules* 839; *Iphigenia at Aulis* 1190; *Rhesus* 873; *Troades* 660; Aeschylus *Agamemnon* 1573; *Eumenides* 42, 212.

[20]Antiphon, *Tetralogies* 2.4.4.3. Compare Antiphon, *Tetrologies* 2.3.11; 2.9.7; 2.10.1; *On the Murder of Herodes* 5.11; Lysias, *Fragments* 348.13.

[21]Herodotus, *Historia* 1.117.12. Compare Thucydides, *History of the Peloponnesian War* 3.58.5.4; Apollonius, *Argonautica* 2.754; 4.479.

[22]George Knight, "ΑΥΘΕΝΤΕΩ In Reference to Women in 1 Timothy 2.12," *NTS* 30 (1984): 143-57. For example, Carroll Osburn erroneously cites this text as "establishing a fifth century BC usage of the term *authentēs* to mean 'exercise authority'" and mistakenly faults Catherine Clark Kroeger for not dealing with it. See Osburn, "ΑΥΘΕΝΤΕΩ" [I Timothy 2:12]—Word Study," *Restoration Quarterly* 25 (1982): 2n5.

transcription, and with good reason. All additional classical literary uses of the noun, adjective, and verb refer to murder, including the other eight instances in Euripides.[23] If so, then the text would result in the nonsensical statement: "Where the people are the *authentēs* ['murderers'] of the land, they rejoice in having a reserve of youthful citizens, while a king counts this a hostile element." The lack of contextual fit led the Loeb editors to emend the text to read *euthyntēs*: "where the people *pilot* the land."[24]

Evidence from Hellenistic literature. The primary literary meaning of the *authent-* word group in the Hellenistic period continued to be "commit murder." This is the case in both biblical and extrabiblical materials. Wisdom 12:6 (cited earlier) speaks of "murdering parents [*authentas goneis*]." In the fifth- to first-century BC Vetera Scholia on Aeschylus's *Eumenides*, the noun *authentēs* is used twice and the perfect participle *ēuthentēkota* once of murder. *Eumenides* 42 recounts the action of Orestes in avenging his father's death by killing his mother: "His [Orestes's] hands were dripping with blood; he held a sword just drawn." The scholium comments: "'were dripping' for apparently there stands he who has just committed murder (*ēuthentēkota*)." Knight finds this usage of *ēuthentēkota* a puzzling exception, while Wolters speaks of an exceptional Attic use at a time when the meaning "committed murder" was no longer part of the living language.[25] Yet on closer inspection, the meaning "murder" is equally numerous in Hellenistic literary authors. Philo (first century AD) is a case in point: "You [Cain] have become a murderer" (*authentēs*). Appian in his *Civil Wars* recounts how the magistrates of Minturnæ did not want to become "murderers" (*authentai*) of Marius. Perpenna is identified as the "murderer" (*authentēn*) of Sertorius, and Brutus is named a "slayer" (*authentēn*) of Julius Caesar.[26]

---

[23]*Andromache* 172, 614-615; *Fragment* 645; *Madness of Hercules* 839; *Iphigenia at Aulis* 1190; *Rhesus* 873; *Troades* 660.

[24]Arthur Way, *Euripides, Suppliants* (Cambridge, MA: Harvard University Press, 1971). See also *LSJ*, s.v. *euthyntēs*. David Kovacs, editor and translator of the 1998 Loeb revised edition, deletes lines 442-55 altogether as not original. Neither "master" nor "ruler" is considered a possibility. See Kovacs, *Euripides, Suppliant Women, Electra, Heracles* (Cambridge, MA: Harvard University Press, 1998).

[25]Knight, "ΑΥΘΕΝΤΕΩ," 144; Albert Wolters, "A Semantic Study of αὐθέντης and Its Derivatives," *Greco-Roman Christianity and Judaism* 1 (2000): 168-69.

[26]Philo, *Det.* 78.7; Appian, *Civil Wars* 1.7.61; 1.13.115; 3.2.16.

There was semantic development during the Hellenistic period, when the range of both the noun and the verb referred not to just the person who committed the murder but also to the one who implemented the deed through others—the "architect," "mastermind," "sponsor," "perpetrator," "author." In Greco-Roman thinking, the one who planned a murder (or other act of violence) was considered as much a killer as the one(s) who actually committed the deed. Ancient lexicographers confirm this. Harpocration defines *authentēs* as "Those who commit murder [*tois phonous*] through others. For the perpetrator [*ho authentēs*] always makes evident the one whose hand committed the deed."[27] The context in each case is negative. For example, regarding the massacre by Thracian soldiers of the people of Maronea, Polybius recounts: "The king [Philip V of Macedon] said he would send Cassander 'the mastermind' [or 'architect'; *ton authentēn*] of the deed so that the [Roman] Senate might learn the truth from him."[28]

It has been recently argued that such Hellenistic texts support the meaning "doer" rather than "author" or "mastermind."[29] However, in each case the context carefully distinguishes between the author (*authentēs*) and the doer(s) of the deed. For example, Josephus states, "But now the punishment was transferred to *the actual author* [*ton authentēn*], Antipater, and took its rise from the death of Pheroras who had been destroyed by poison [administered by Antipater's uncle Theudio]."[30]

Evidence from Koine Greek, nonliterary materials. In Hellenistic materials of a nonliterary nature, the literary "murderer" and "commit murder" in everyday speech became "domineer," "hold sway over," "dictate," and the literary "author" or "architect of a murder" became simply "author," "architect." This mundane sense (though rare) is found in a breadth of materials from the first century BC forward.

Regarding the meaning "author" or "architect," first-century grammarian Aristonicus identifies lines of the *Iliad* that he thinks are either misplaced or misattributed. Line 404 has, "Odysseus spoke and King

---

[27]Harpocration, *Lexicon* 66.7.
[28]Polybius, *History* 22.14.2. Compare Livy, *History* 39.34. Posidonius states, "For he [Gracchus] . . . had in these men not merely supporters but also *sponsors* [*authentas*] of his own murderous exploits" (*Fragment* 1.165.7) and Diodorus Siculus, *Bibliotheca Historica* 16.61.1.
[29]Wolters, "Semantic Study of αὐθέντης," 147-50.
[30]Josephus, *Jewish Wars* 1.582-592; cf. 2.240.

Agamemnon and his people became hushed in silence, marveling at his words." Aristonicus states that line 404 is mistakenly attributed to Odysseus and instead should be ascribed to the earlier speech of Achilles and attributed to him as *ho authentōn tou logou*, "the author" or "architect" of what was spoken.[31] The same vernacular use would also account for the meaning "architect" in second-century AD Shepherd of Hermas 9.5.6.[32] A tower is being built according to the plan of "the *authentēs* who will come" and test the building to see whether there are any defective stones that need to be replaced. Although *ho authentēs tou pyrgou* is sometimes translated "the master of the tower," the context supports "the architect." The architect is the logical one to determine which stones are "defective" and need replacing (the architect in this case being God).

Regarding the meaning "domineer" or "hold sway over," three sources are pertinent: the astrological texts, the papyri, and the polemical texts.

The astrological texts. *Authentēs* with the commonplace meaning "domineer" likely occurs in first-century AD astrologer Dorotheus of Sidon: "If Jupiter aspects the moon from trine . . . it makes them governors or judges of people or soldiers, especially if the moon is increasing; but if the moon is decreasing, it does not make them dominant [*authentas*] but subordinate" (*hyperetoumenous*).[33] While the Dorotheus text might be disputed due to its brevity, the context in Ptolemy's second-century work *Tetrabiblos* 3.13 is clear. The verbal adjective *authentēsas* with the sense "domineer" parallels "dictatorial" (*epitaktikous*). The extended context makes plain that Saturn's domination results in abusive, not beneficent, consequences. Ancient astronomers considered Mars and Saturn to be bad planets, creating the disposition toward a criminal (versus beneficent) career:[34] "If

---

[31]Aristonicus, *De signis Iliadis* 9.694.1-5. The Greek is erroneously translated "authoritative" by Scott Baldwin and replicated by Phil Payne. See Baldwin, "Appendix 2. Αὐθεντεῖν in Ancient Greek Literature," in Köstenberger, Schreiner, and Baldwin, *Women in the Church*, 275; Payne, *Man and Woman, One in Christ: An Exegetical and Theological Study of Paul's Letters* (Grand Rapids, MI: Zondervan, 2009), 360-61.

[32]Parable 9 is thought to be an interpolation, added in the final editing. The Muratorian Canon identfies the shepherd Hermas as the brother of Pius, bishop of Rome (ca. AD 140–154). Irenaeus (ca. 175) is familiar with it, providing a date for the work as circa AD 150–175. See Michael Holmes, *Apostolic Fathers*, 2nd ed. (Grand Rapids: Baker, 1992), 330-31.

[33]Dorotheus of Sidon, *Astrologicum* 346.

[34]As second-century astronomer Vettius Valens notes: "Planetary effects go in many directions, depending on the changes of the zodiac and the interactions of the stars, and yields quite varied

look at not yet the word but its effects

Saturn alone takes planetary control [*tēn oikodespotian*] of the soul and domineers over [*authentēsas*] Mercury and the moon," humanity is negatively affected, "making [them] lovers of the body, obstinate, harsh, opinionated, troublemakers, dictatorial [*epitaktikous*], ready to punish."[35]

Albert Wolters has recently argued that Codices Parisini 1.8.1-7 preserves a text roughly contemporaneous with the New Testament and contains syntax similar to 1 Timothy 2:12 (the verb *authenteō* plus the genitive): "If Mercury aspects Mars, it signifies one who works with fire or iron. But if Mercury aspects Saturn, it signifies one who is skilled in stealing or craftiness. And if Mercury appears in a triangular relationship with Mars and Saturn, it produces *ton pantōn authentounta en tē technē* but gains nothing." Wolters translates the substantival participle as "*he who exercises authority over* everything in an art."[36] Yet, "he who fully dominates" or "gains complete mastery of a skill" equally fit. However, the context is too brief and the point is moot, since scholarly dating of this text is third century AD at its earliest. This is based on lines 169-195, which are excerpts from Ptolemy's second-century *Syntaxis Mathematica*. The claim of a first-century astrological use of *authent-* words to mean "exercise authority over" is thus without foundation.[37]

The papyri. The verbal adjective *authentēkotos* appears in a 27/26 BC letter in which [Tryphō]n updates his brother Asklepiades about the resolution of a dispute regarding the amount for shipping a load of livestock and produce: "I took a firm stand with him [*authentēkotos pros auton*] and he agreed to provide Calatytis the boatman with the full payment within the hour."[38] This fits with Preisigke's *Wörterbuch der griechischen*

---

[35] results" (*Anthology* 9.4.26). See also Tebtunis Papyri 2.276.28. The reconstructed text and translation by J. Gilbert Smyly is as follows: "If Mars appears in triangular relation to Jupiter and Saturn, this causes great prosperity and a person will make acquisitions and *will dominate* [καὶ [α] ὑθεντή[σει]. . . . If, while Jupiter and Saturn are in this position, Mars comes into conjunction with either . . . , after obtaining [wealth] and collecting a fortune that person will spend and lose it." Smyly's "will dominate" fits with Mars's negative influence on human behavior. See Bernard P. Grenfell, Arthur S. Hunt, and J. Gilbert Smyly, *The Tebtunis Papyri: Part III* (London: Humphrey Milford, 1907), 3:30.

[35] F. E. Robbins, *Ptolemy, Tetrabiblos*, LCL (Cambridge, MA: Harvard University Press, 1948), 339n1.

[36] Albert Wolters, "An Early Parallel of Αὐθέντεῖν in 2:12," *JETS* 54 (2011): 673-84.

[37] See Georg Luck, *Arcana Mundi: Magic and the Occult in the Greek and Roman Worlds; A Collection of Ancient Texts*, 2nd ed. (Baltimore: Johns Hopkins University Press, 2006), 148.

[38] Aegyptische Urkunden aus den Königlichen (Staatlichen) Museen zu Berlin 4.1208.

Papyrusurkunden and Mayser's *Grammatik Der Grieschischen Papyri aus Der Ptolemäerzeit*, which render *authentein pros* as *fest auftreten*, that is "to take a firm stand with," "put one's foot down."[39]

Vernacular usage also fits what we know of the Asklepiades archive. As John White notes, this part of the archive (BGU 4.1203-9) is a series of seven letters stuck together on a single roll and consisting of correspondence between family members regarding everyday matters about the family business.[40] There is therefore nothing in the correspondence that warrants a translation such as "exercise authority over him."[41]

Evangelical scholarship has been largely dependent for this translation on Knight's 1984 study and his translation of *authentēkotos pros auton* as "I exercised authority over him."[42] Yet this hardly fits the mundane details of the text—payment of a boat fare. Nor can *pros auton* be understood as "*over* him." The preposition plus the accusative does not bear this sense in Greek. "To/toward," "against," and "with" (and less frequently "at," "for," "with reference to," "on," and "on account of") are the range of possible meanings.[43] Here it likely means something such as "I took a firm stand *with* him."

More recently, Philip Payne proposed, based on the scholarly reconstructed name Tryphōn, that the sender was a slave who was granted the power to "exercise authority" on behalf of the Asklepiades family.[44] Payne thereby sought to establish the singular use of a positive meaning for *authentein*. However, while the sender's name requires reconstruction (due to missing letters), the familial status of the sender is clear.[45] The letter's opening greeting is "[Tryphō]n to his brother, Greetings," and the letter is labeled "A Letter of Tryphon to His Brother Asklepiades" by

---

[39]Friedrich Preisigke, *Wörterbuch der griechischen Papyrusurkunden* (Berlin: Papyrusurkunden Berlin, 1925), s.v. *authentein*; Edwin Mayser, "Abgeletete Verbs," in *Grammatik Der Grieschischen Papyri aus Der Ptolemäerzeit* (Berlin: de Gruyter, 1933–1936), §86.2.

[40]John White, *Light from Ancient Letters* (Philadelphia: Fortress, 1986), 103-6.

[41]See also Ben Witherington, *Letters and Homilies for Hellenized Christians: A Socio-rhetorical Commentary on Titus, 1-2 Timothy and 1-3 John* (Downers Grove, IL: InterVarsity Press, 2010), 227-28.

[42]Knight, "ΑΥΘΕΝΤΕΩ," 145.

[43]See *LSJ*, 1497 C. *with the accusative.*

[44]Payne, *Man and Woman, One in Christ*, 349n1.

[45]See Wilhelm Schubart, ed., *Berliner griechische Urkunden papyri* (Berlin: Staatliche Museen, 1912), 349-51. He situates this letter among the Asklepiades family archive of seven letters. Only six blanks and the final *n* of the sender's name are clear. Schubart filled in the blanks with a common Greek name ending in *n* versus the name of a slave.

editorial scholar Wilhelm Schubart. "I took a firm stand with him" best fits the context of a brother reporting back to his family.

The polemical texts. Authent[ou]sin occurs in first-century BC Philodemus's polemic against rhetors. Rhetors were the villains; philosophers such as Philodemus were the heroes of the Roman Republic. The text reads:

> Rhetors greatly harm a great number of people—"those shot through with powerful desires" [Euripides?]; they [rhetors] fight every chance they get with prominent people even "with powerful [or perhaps *dominant*] lords" [*syn authent[ou]sin anaxin*]. . . . Philosophers, on the other hand, by removing them from harm gain the favor of public figures not making them enemies but friends. (*Rhetorica* 5, fragment 4, line 14)

Knight translates the Greek quotation *syn authent[ou]sin anaxin* as "those in authority," claiming as his source a paraphrase by Yale classicist Harry Hubbell.[46] However, Hubbell actually renders *authent[ou]sin* as it rightly is—an adjective meaning "powerful" modifying the noun "rulers" or "lords" (*anaxin*).[47] While some have noted and corrected Knight's mistake, most have not and continue to perpetuate the error, including *A Greek-English Lexicon of the New Testament and Other Early Christian Literature* (2000), citing Knight as the source.[48]

ETYMOLOGY AND DEVELOPMENT:
GREEK GRAMMARIANS AND LEXICOGRAPHERS

Although recently challenged, general consensus locates the provenance of *authentēs* (and cognate forms) in the Attic *auto + hentēs*, "one who does a thing with his own hand."[49] This is because the Attic *auto + hentēs* continues to best explain both the literary meaning of "murderer" or "perpetrator of a murder" and the Koine nonliterary meaning of *authentein*, "to domineer over," "have one's way with," and *authentēs* "author," "architect."

---

[46]Knight, "ΑΥΘΕΝΤΕΩ," 145. Knight also overlooks the fact that *syn authent[ou]sin an[axin]* is actually a quote from an unknown source, not Philodemus's own words.

[47]Harry Hubbell, *The Rhetorica of Philodemus*, Connecticut Academy of Arts and Sciences 23 (New Haven, CT: Yale University Press, 1920), 306.

[48]Replicated by Wolters, "Semantic Study of αὐθέντης," 156; Baldwin, "Appendix 2," 275.

[49]L&N, §37.35-95; *LSJ*; James Moulton and George Milligan, *The Vocabulary of the Greek Testament, Illustrated from the Papyri and Other Non-literary Sources* (Grand Rapids, MI: Eerdmans, 1929). J. H. Thayer, *A Greek-English Lexicon of the New Testament* (Edinburgh: T&T Clark, 1889).

That *authentēs* and *autohentēs* were used synonymously supports this provenance. Their interchangeability is readily seen in the classical period. "When I see Aegisthus sitting on my father's throne; when I look on him wearing the very robes which my father wore and pouring libations at the hearth where he killed him; and when I see the chief outrage of them all, the murderer [*ton authentēn*] in my father's bed at my wretched mother's side . . ." Then compare, "He was slain, and the god now bids us to take vengeance on his murderers [*tous autohentas*]."[50]

The same interchangeability occurs in the Hellenistic period. First-century AD Roman historian Cassius Dio recounts that Tiberius invited those against whom charges were brought to become their own murderers (*autohentēs*) so that he might avoid the reputation of having killed them. Then compare contemporary Appian, who speaks of Perpenna "as the murderer of Sertorius" (*authentēn*).[51]

The development of a first-century vernacular usage "to dominate, hold sway over" is supported by ancient grammarians and lexicographers. First- to second-century AD lexicographer Harpocration defines the literary *authent-* word group as "he who murders with his own hand" (*autohentēs*) and not to be confused with the vernacular "dictator, one who domineers." Second-century grammarian Phrynichus defines the literary use of the *authent-* word group as "one who commits murder with his own hand" in contrast with the Koine meaning of "one who domineers." Second-century lexicographer Moeris states that *authentēs* has become commonplace for "dictator" and is no longer fit for the literary use of "murderer." As late as the thirteenth century, lexicographer Thomas Magister tells his students that *authentein* is "common" (*koinoteron*) for "to domineer" and thus to be avoided as an Attic literary choice.[52]

Modern lexicographers agree. Theodor Nageli proposes that *authentein* originated in first-century popular Greek as a synonym for *kratein tinos*, "to dominate someone." James Moulton and George Milligan state that the

---

[50]Sophocles, *Electra* 272; *Oedipus Tyrannus* 107.
[51]Cassius Dio, *Roman History* 58.15; cf. 9.38; Appian, *Civil Wars* 1.13.115.
[52]Valerius Harpocration, *Lexicon on Ten Orators*, ed. Gregory Zorzas (Kallithea, Greece, 2009); Arabius Phrynichus, *Eklogē* (London: W. G. Rutherford, 1881), §96; Aelius Atticista Moeris, *Attic Lexicon*, ed. J. Pierson (Leiden: P. van der Eyk and de Pecker, 1759), 58; Thomas Magister, *Attic Lexicon* (Hildesheim: Georg Olms, 1970).

authent- word group is very well established in the popular vocabulary of "despot," "autocrat." Louw and Nida put *authentein* into the semantic domain "to control," "domineer" and translate 1 Timothy 2:12 as, "I do not allow women . . . to dominate men." United Bible Society translators Daniel Arichea and Howard Hatton translate *authentein* in 1 Timothy 2:12 as "to control in a domineering manner."[53]

1 TIMOTHY 2:12-15

The grammar of 1 Timothy 2:12. So how did "to exercise authority over" find its way into so many modern translations of 1 Timothy 2:12? Andreas Köstenberger claims that it is the correlative ("to teach") that forces translators in this direction. He argues that the Greek correlative pairs synonyms or parallel words and not antonyms. Since "to teach" is positive, *authentein* must also be positive. To demonstrate his point, Köstenberger analyzes "neither" + verb 1 + "nor" + verb 2 constructions in biblical and extrabiblical literature.[54]

Yet there is a grammatical flaw intrinsic to this approach. It is limited to *formally* equivalent constructions, excluding *functionally* equivalent ones. Thus, it overlooks the fact that the infinitives ("to teach," *authentein*) are functioning grammatically not as verbs but as verbal *nouns* in the sentence structure. The Greek infinitive may have tense and voice like a verb, but it functions predominantly as a noun or adjective.[55] The verb in 1 Timothy 2:12 is actually "I permit." "Neither to teach nor *authentein*" modifies the noun "a woman," which makes the *authentein* clause the second of two direct objects.[56] Use of the infinitive as a direct object after a verb that already has a direct object has been amply demonstrated by biblical and

---

[53]Theodor Nageli, *Der Wörtschatz des Apostels Paulus* (Göttingen: Vandenhoeck and Ruprecht, 1905); Moulton and Milligan, *Vocabulary of the Greek Testament*; L&N, §37.35-47; 37.48-95; Daniel Arichea and Howard Hatton, *A Translator's Handbook on Paul's Letters to Timothy and to Titus* (New York: UBS, 1995), 58.

[54]Andreas Köstenberger, "A Complex Sentence Structure in 1 Timothy 2:12," in Köstenberger, Schreiner, and Baldwin, *Women in the Church*, 81-103.

[55]See, e.g., Nigel Turner, who classifies infinitives as "noun forms." See Turner, ed., *Syntax*, vol. 3 of *Grammar of New Testament Greek* (Edinburgh: T&T Clark, 1963), 134.

[56]See, e.g., James A. Brooks and Carlton L. Winbery, *Syntax of New Testament Greek* (Lanham, MD: University Press of America, 1979), especially "The Infinitive as a Modifier of Substantives," 141-42.

extrabiblical grammarians.[57] In such cases the infinitive restricts the already-present object. Following this paradigm, the 1 Timothy 2:12 correlative "neither to teach nor *authentein*" functions as a noun that restricts the direct object "a woman" (*gynaiki*).

It behooves us, therefore, to correlate nouns and noun substitutes in addition to verbs. This greatly expands the possibilities. "Neither-nor" constructions in the New Testament are then found to pair *synonyms* (e.g., Gal 4:14), *closely related ideas* (e.g., "neither of the night nor of the dark"; 1 Thess 5:5 NASB) and *antonyms* (e.g., Gal 3:28). They also function to move *from the general to the particular* (e.g., "wisdom neither of this age nor of the rulers of this age"; 1 Cor 2:6 NASB), to define *a natural progression of related ideas* (e.g., "they neither sow nor reap nor gather into barns"; Mt 6:26 NKJV), and to define *a related purpose or a goal* (e.g., "where thieves neither break in nor [then] steal"; Mt 6:20 NASB).[58]

Of the options listed above, it is clear that *teach* and *dominate* are not synonyms, closely related ideas, or antonyms. If *authentein* did mean "to exercise authority," we might have a movement from general to particular. However, we would expect the word order to be the reverse of what we have in 1 Timothy 2:12 ("neither to exercise authority [general] nor to teach

---

[57]F. Blass, A. Debrunner, and R. W. Funk, *A Greek Grammar of the New Testament and Other Early Christian Literature* (Chicago: University of Chicago Press, 1961), §392; Ernest Dewitt Burton, *Syntax of the Moods and Tenses in New Testament Greek* (Chicago: University of Chicago Press, 1900), §378, 387; Turner, *Syntax*, 137-38. This conflicts with Daniel Wallace, who identifies *authentein* as a verb complement ("I do not *permit* to teach") instead of the direct-object complement that it is. See Wallace, *Greek Grammar Beyond the Basics* (Grand Rapids, MI: Zondervan, 1996), 182-89. It is not that Paul does not *permit to teach* a woman but that he does not permit *a woman* to teach. See Rom 3:28; 6:11; 14:14; 1 Cor 11:23; 12:23; 2 Cor 11:5; Phil 3:8.

[58]Other examples (translations in this footnote are from the NASB otherwise noted) include (1) *synonyms*: "neither labors nor spins" (Mt 6:28), "neither quarreled nor cried out" (Mt 12:19), "neither abandoned nor given up" (Acts 2:27), "neither leave nor forsake" (Heb 13:5), "neither run in vain nor labor in vain" (Phil 2:16); (2) *closely related ideas*: "neither the desire nor the effort" (Rom 9:16), "neither the sun nor the moon" (Rev 21:23); (3) *antonyms*: "neither a good tree . . . nor a bad tree" (Mt 7:18), "neither the one who did harm nor the one who was harmed" (2 Cor 7:12); (4) *general to particular*: "you know neither the day nor the hour" (Mt 25:13 NRSV), "I neither consulted with flesh and blood nor went up to Jerusalem" (Gal 1:16-17); (5) *a natural progression of closely related ideas*: "born neither of blood, nor of the human will, nor of the will of man" (Jn 1:13), "neither the Christ, nor Elijah, nor the Prophet" (Jn 1:25), "neither from man nor through man" (Gal 1:1); (6) *goal or purpose*: "neither hears nor understands" (i.e., hearing with the intent to understand; Mt 13:13), "neither dwells in temples made with human hands nor is served by human hands" (i.e., dwells with a view to being served; Acts 17:24-25). See Linda L. Belleville, *Women Leaders and the Church* (Grand Rapids, MI: Baker, 2000), 176-77.

[particular])." On the other hand, to define a purpose or goal actually provides a reasonably good fit and fits the contrast with the second part of the verse: "I do not permit a woman to teach so as to gain mastery over a man," or "I do not permit a woman to teach with a view to dominating a man *but* to have a quiet demeanor [literally, 'to be in calmness']."[59]

Biblical examples of the second member of the correlative defining the goal or purpose of the first member are readily found (Apocrypha included):

- Wisdom 4:3: "Their illegitimate seedlings will neither strike a deep root nor take a firm hold" (i.e., deepen the root with a view to getting a firm hold).

- Matthew 13:13: "They neither hear nor understand" (my translation; i.e., hearing with the intent to understand).

- Acts 17:24-25: "[God] neither dwells in temples made with human hands nor is served by human hands" (my translation; i.e., dwells in a temple with a view to being served like Greco-Roman deities).

The standard grammars allow for the second element of conjoined and correlated constructions to define the meaning of the first.[60] As Nigel Turner states, "the infinitive as a direct object with *verba putandi* (e.g., 'permit,' 'allow' and 'want') restricts the already present object. The second term would then clarify what kind of teaching is being prohibited— teaching that seeks to gain the upper hand."[61]

Köstenberger has recently argued that positive and negative pairings (of either nouns or verbs) cannot be found.[62] However, such pairings do in fact exist. Revelation 2:20 is a key example: "I have this against you [Thyatira] that you tolerate the woman Jezebel, who calls herself a prophetess *and teaches and deceives* my servants" (HCSB; *kai didaskei kai plana tous emous doulous*). That Revelation 2:20 contains an instance where the term *didaskei* is further clarified by the negative activity *plana* ("teaching with a view to deceiving") shows that the same can be true of *didaskein* and *authentein* in

---

[59]See Philip B. Payne, "2.12 and the Use of οὐδέ to Combine Two Elements to Express a Single Idea," *NTS* 54 (2008): 235-53.

[60]See Burton, *Syntax of the Moods*, §378, 387.

[61]Turner, *Syntax*, 137-38.

[62]Andreas Köstenberger, "A Complex Sentence: The Syntax of 1 Timothy 2.12," in *Women in the Church: An Analysis and Application of 1 Timothy 2:9-15*, 2nd ed., ed. A. Köstenberger, T. Schreiner, and H. Scott Baldwin (Grand Rapids, MI: Baker, 2005), 81-103.

1 Timothy 2:12: "teaching with a view to dominating a man." The Revelation 2:20 *kai . . . kai* correlation is a close parallel with the 1 Timothy 2:12 *ouk . . . oude* correlative. Indeed, the syntax is strikingly similar:

> *ouk didaskein oude authentein andros*
> *kai didaskei kai plana tous emous doulous*

First Maccabees 2:36 provides a second example: *kai ouk apekrithēsan autois oude lithon enetinaxan autois.* The first member of the correlative is positive ("neither answered"), while the second is negative ("nor hurled a stone at them").

The rationale for 1 Timothy 2:13-15. Why would the Ephesian men be angry and quarreling (1 Tim 2:8) and women teaching in a domineering fashion (1 Tim 2:12)? A probable explanation is that the women were influenced by the cult of Artemis, in which the female was exalted and considered superior to the male. Its importance to the citizens of Ephesus in Paul's day is evident from the two-hour long chant, "Great is Artemis of the Ephesians" (Acts 19:28). It was believed that Artemis was the child of Zeus and Leto. Instead of seeking fellowship among her own kind, Artemis spurned the attentions of the male gods and sought instead the company of a human male consort named Leimon. This made Artemis and all her female adherents superior to men—a belief that was played out at the feast of the Lord of Streets, when the priestess of Artemis pursued a man.[63]

An Artemis influence would help explain Paul's correctives in 1 Timothy 2:13-15. It was believed that Artemis appeared first and then her male consort. However, the biblical story is just the opposite. Adam was formed first and then Eve (1 Tim 2:13). Then too, it was Eve who was deceived (1 Tim 2:14)—hardly a basis to claim superiority. The Artemis cult would also shed light on Paul's statement in 1 Timothy 2:15 that Christian "women will be kept safe [some: 'saved'] through childbirth." Artemis was viewed as the protector of women. Maidens turned to her as the guardian of their virginity, barren women sought her aid, and women in labor turned to her

---

[63]Pausanias, *Description of Greece*, LCL (Cambridge, MA: Harvard University Press, 1918), 8.53.3. For further details, see Sharon Gritz, *Paul, Women Teachers and the Mother Goddess at Ephesus: A Study of 1 Timothy 2:9-15 in Light of the Religious and Cultural Milieu of the First Century* (Lanham, MD: University Press of America, 1991), 31-41; "Artemis," in *Encyclopedia Britannica*, 11th ed. (Cambridge: Cambridge University Press, 1911).

for help: "The cities of men I [Artemis] will visit only when women vexed by the sharp pang of childbirth call me to their aid. Even in the hour when I was born, the *Moirai* [Fates] ordained that I should be their helper."[64] Paul's corrective is that the Ephesian women no longer place their trust in Artemis but in Christ—their true Savior (1 Tim 2:15).

The impact of the cults on the female population of Ephesus and its environs has been recently challenged by S. M. Baugh, who contends that the lack of any first-century Ephesian high priestess runs counter to an Artemis impact on the church.[65] Although Baugh is correct in saying that *urban* Ephesus lacked a high priestess during Paul's day, he overlooks that *suburban* Ephesus did not. While Paul was planting the Ephesian church, Iuliane served as the high priestess of the imperial cult in Magnesia, a city fifteen miles southeast of Ephesus. Inscriptions dating from the first century until the mid-third century place women as high priestesses in Ephesus, Cyzicus, Thyatira, Aphrodisias, Magnesia, and elsewhere.[66] Artemis is explicitly honored in mid-first-century decrees.[67]

Baugh also claims that the female high priestesses of the day did not serve in and of their own right. They were simply riding on the coattails

---

[64]See Susan A. Stephens, *Callimachus, The Hymn to Artemis* (Oxford: Oxford University Press, 2017). See also Moyer Hubbard, "Kept Safe Through Childbearing: Maternal Mortality, Justification by Faith, and the Social Setting of 1 Timothy 2.15," *JETS* 55 (2012). 743-62. More recently, Sandra Glahn argues that Artemis's virginity brings into question the claim that Artemis was a fertility goddess, mother goddess, and nurturer. See Glahn, "The First-Century Ephesian Artemis: Ramifications of Her Identity," *BSac* 172 (2015): 450-69. However, the primary sources say otherwise. Homer, Apollodorus, Pausanius, and Herodotus all mention her. See "Artemis," 157.

Despite her virginity, both ancient and modern writers have linked Artemis to the archetype of the mother goddess. Artemis was traditionally linked to fertility and was petitioned to assist women with childbirth. Callimachus's *The Hymn to Artemis*, for example, clearly credits her with being the guardian of a maiden's virginity, providing aid for barren women, and helping women in labor. Also, what were originally claimed to be multiple breasts has been rejected in favor of the scrotal sacs of sacrificed bulls used in fertility rites. See Robert Fleischer, *Artemis von Ephesos und der erwandte Kultstatue von Anatolien und Syrien* (Leiden: Brill, 1973); Walter Burkert, *Greek Religion* (Cambridge, MA: Harvard University Press, 1985); Robert Graves, *The Greek Myths* (New York: Penguin, 1960); Seppo Telenius, *Athena-Artemis* (Helsinki: Kirja kerrallaan, 2005–2006); Guy M. Rogers, *The Mysteries of Artemis of Ephesos Cult, Polis, and Change in the Greco-Roman World* (New Haven, CT: Yale University Press, 2012).

[65]Stephen Baugh, "A Foreign World: Ephesus in the First Century," in *Women in the Church: An Interpretation and Application of 1 Timothy 2:9-15*, 3rd ed., ed. A. Köstenberger and T. Schreiner (Wheaton, IL: Crossway, 2016), 25-64.

[66]See R. A. Kearsley, "Asiarchs, Archiereis and the Archiereiai of Asia," *Greek, Roman and Byzantine Studies* 27 (1986): 183-92.

[67]See Otto Kern, *Die Inschriften von Magnesia am Maeander* (Berlin: W. Spemann, 1900), 158.

of a husband, male relative, or wealthy male patron, or their role was purely nominal versus actual.[68] This simply is not true. Many inscriptions naming a woman as high priestess do not name a husband, father, or male patron. In the case of those that do, prestige was attached to being a relative of a high priestess and not vice versa. Iuliane, for example, held her position long before her husband held his. Nor was her position nominal. Priests and priestesses were responsible for the sanctuary's maintenance, its rituals and ceremonies, and the protection of its treasures and gifts. Liturgical functions included ritual sacrifice, pronouncing the invocation, and presiding at the festivals of the deity.[69]

There is Baugh's further claim that in Asia the title of high priestess was given to young daughters and wives of the municipal elite.[70] This too runs counter to Greco-Roman evidence. The majority of women who served as high priestesses were hardly young girls.[71] Vestal virgins were the exception. Delphic priestesses, on the other hand, were required to be at least fifty years old, came from all social classes, and served a male god and his adherents.

All this overlooks the fact that Roman religion and government were inseparable. To lead in one arena was often to lead in the other. Mendora, for example, served at one time or another during Paul's tenure as magistrate, priestess, and chief financial officer of Sillyon, a town in Pisidia, Asia.[72]

CONCLUSION

A reasonable reconstruction of 1 Timothy 2:11-15 would read as follows: The women at Ephesus (perhaps encouraged by the false teachers) were trying to gain an advantage over the men in the congregation by teaching in a domineering fashion. The men in response became angry and disputed what the women were doing.

---

[68]Baugh, "Foreign World," 43-44.

[69]Kearsley, "Asiarchs, Archiereis"; Belleville, *Women Leaders*, 31-36. Baugh overlooks an inscription from Amorium in Phrygia that shows that high priestesses of Asia held office in their own right. See R. M. Harrison, *Amorium Excavations 1989: The Second Preliminary Report* (British Institute of Archaeology at Ankara, 1990).

[70]Baugh, "Foreign World," 43.

[71]See Riet van Bremen, "Women and Wealth," in *Images of Women in Antiquity*, ed. Averil Cameron and Amélie Kuhrt (Detroit: Wayne State University Press, 1987), 231-41.

[72]Inscriptiones Graecae ad res Romanas pertinentes 3.800-902.

This interpretation fits the broader context of 1 Timothy 2:8-15, where Paul aims to correct inappropriate behavior on the part of both men and women (1 Tim 2:8, 11). It also fits the grammatical flow of 1 Timothy 2:11-12: "Let a woman learn in a quiet and submissive fashion. I do not, however, permit her to teach with the intent to dominate a man. She must be gentle in her demeanor." Paul would then be prohibiting teaching that tries to get the upper hand—not teaching per se.

what about 'to teach?

12

A SILENT WITNESS IN MARRIAGE

1 PETER 3:1-7

Peter H. Davids

• • • • •

FIRST PETER 3:1-7 has often been read as a text instructing Christian wives in subordination. Thus Wayne Grudem writes that 1 Peter 3:1 "means willingly to submit to your husband's authority or leadership in marriage," including submission "to good or harsh . . . husbands."[1] Though he makes an exception in cases of "spousal abuse" or a "*morally objectionable* behavior pattern," some evangelicals, such as James Hurley, do not.[2] While other evangelical groups, such as some Mennonites, argue on the basis of 1 Peter 3:3 that this text prohibits women from wearing jewelry and anything other than plain clothing (as defined by the reference group), many evangelical scholars see this verse as culturally relative but still argue that the text as a whole focuses its instruction on female subordination in marriage.

---

[1]Wayne Grudem, *1 Peter*, Tyndale New Testament Commentaries (Grand Rapids, MI: Eerdmans, 1988), 135; Grudem, "Wives like Sarah and the Husbands Who Honor Them: 1 Peter 3:1-7," in *RBMW*, 262, 608n13.

[2]Grudem, "Wives like Sarah," 265, emphasis original. James B. Hurley asserts, "She is to continue to live a godly life even with an abusive pagan husband who can in no way be considered to demonstrate Christ's love for the church. . . . Her willing suffering love for her husband . . . shows the willing suffering and love of Christ." See Hurley, *Man and Woman in Biblical Perspective* (Grand Rapids, MI: Zondervan, 1981), 154. For examination of this issue in the context of both pastoral care and this passage, see Maxine O'Dell Gernert, "Pentecost Confronts Abuse," *Journal of Pentecostal Theology* 17 (2000): 117-30.

Evangelicals who emphasize gender equality take a different approach. Rebecca Merrill Groothuis states that 1 Peter 3 is directed to women with nonbelieving husbands, arguing that it should be read within its cultural context, thus entailing quite different behavior today.[3] Craig Keener sees here a strategy for life within the Greco-Roman world, aimed at witness and reducing grounds for the charge that Christianity was subversive.[4] Either of these is quite a different focus for the passage. Are the egalitarian interpretations or the more hierarchical interpretations correct?

CHRISTIAN WIVES WITH NON-CHRISTIAN HUSBANDS (1 PET 3:1-6)

Wives within the Greco-Roman world. Language is an expression of a given culture existing in space and time. It takes its meaning from the definitions that culture gives to certain sounds and their associated graphic symbols. Furthermore, words in all languages change their meanings over time. In 1 Peter we have language (Greek) from a particular part of the first-century Mediterranean world. In interpreting it we are trying to understand what it meant as an expression of a given historical culture or social world. With this in mind, it is important that we see how the wives addressed in 1 Peter might have heard this instruction within their own social context.[5]

First, it is clear that 1 Peter is addressed to a largely Gentile Christian audience. In fact, several expressions (1 Pet 1:14, 18; 2:9-10, 25; 4:3-4) indicate they were largely converts from paganism.[6] Their earlier state was "ignorance," and they had "futile ways inherited from [their] ancestors."[7] They were once "not a people" and had "already spent enough time in doing what the Gentiles like to do." These descriptions would not have fit

---

[3]Rebecca Merrill Groothuis, *Good News for Women: A Biblical Picture of Gender Equality* (Grand Rapids, MI: Baker, 1997), 172-76.

[4]Craig S. Keener, *The IVP Bible Background Commentary: New Testament* (Downers Grove, IL: InterVarsity Press, 1993), 715.

[5]For a valuable discussion of the hermeneutics of this passage and others dealing with marriage and family, see Stephen C. Barton, *Life Together: Family, Sexuality, and Community in the New Testament and Today* (Edinburgh: T&T Clark, 2001), 3-55. In Barton's terms, what I am attempting to achieve in this chapter is to lay the exegetical framework for a more rounded theological approach to our topic.

[6]Peter H. Davids, *The First Epistle of Peter*, NICNT (Grand Rapids, MI: Eerdmans, 1990), 8-9.

[7]Translations of 1 Peter are my own unless otherwise noted.

Christian Jews. Thus, 1 Peter is addressed to Christians with a pagan or Gentile past. This helps us understand both the background of the wives and the nature of their husbands.

Second, while it is clear that the wives in 1 Peter 3:1-6 are Christians, this is not evident regarding their husbands, who appear to be a separate group from the believing husbands addressed in 1 Peter 3:7. We can be certain that at least some of the husbands in 1 Peter 3:1-6 are not Christians, since 1 Peter 3:1 reads "although some of them do not obey the word," where the grammar implies a condition of fact.[8] The primary reason for advocating wives' appropriate domestic behavior is "so that . . . [nonbelieving husbands] may be won over without a word by their wives' conduct." Therefore, the *focus* of the passage (1 Pet 3:1-6) is on women living with non-Christian husbands in the area of the Greco-Roman world to which the letter is addressed.[9] Even if women with Christian husbands were included, their behavior would likewise be conditioned by the evangelistic motive of this text.

Although we do not have an abundance of information about the specific social world of the women to whom this passage is addressed—those living in the northwestern quadrant of modern-day Turkey—we do know that at that time certain moral literature circulated throughout the entire Greco-Roman world.[10] First Peter appears to reflect this literature—or perhaps it is drawing from the Roman situation where the letter originated.[11] One thing we can be most certain about the Greco-Roman

---

[8]The NRSV "even if" may be read as implying doubt, yet this is a real condition, not one implying doubt, thus my translation "although." See Linda L. Belleville, *Women Leaders and the Church* (Grand Rapids, MI: Baker, 2000), 119.

[9]Since the evangelistic strategy is the expressed purpose, it is quite possible that the "some" indicates the situation of most of the women. This fits with the general theme of this section: minimizing conflict with the non-Christian culture. See further Paul J. Achtemeier, *1 Peter*, Hermeneia (Minneapolis: Fortress, 1996), 208, and the next section of this chapter.

[10]Plutarch's Moralia (ca. AD 100) is a bit later than even the typical later dating of 1 Peter (AD 90) but shows the typical ideas that were circulating long before Plutarch wrote. Aristotle's *Nichomachean Ethics* was more than three centuries earlier than any dating of 1 Peter and was in wide circulation over those centuries. In between come other authors, some of whom did not write directly on ethics, but for whom the family, the raising of children, and who should be educated were still of great import (e.g., Quintilian, *Institutio Oratoria*). With such authors we should include a Stoic known for his rhetorical work, Cicero, but who also wrote the ethical *De finibus bonorum et malorum*. And one must include Jewish authors such as Philo and Josephus as well, who are cited later in this chapter.

[11]See Davids, *First Epistle of Peter*, 5-7.

world in general is that a woman was expected to follow the religious choices of her father and, after marriage, her husband. Plutarch, a Roman moralist of the era, held that a wife ought not to make friends of her own but to enjoy her husband's friends in common with him. Furthermore, "The gods are the first and most important friends. Wherefore it is becoming for a wife to worship and to know only the gods that her husband believes in, and to shut the front door right upon all queer rituals and outlandish superstitions."[12]

To the Roman mind, all beliefs other than traditional Roman religions were "outlandish superstitions." This included Judaism and, along with Judaism, Christianity. When a woman became a Christian independent of her husband's decision, she was immediately suspect as a rebel against the social order.

Related to this was the normal expectation that the husband should rule the wife. This was true for Plato, Aristotle, and their followers.[13] While David Balch has shown that household management was a common topic of discussion in the ancient world, his evidence also indicates a virtually universal perception that women were to be ruled by men, usually with the assumption that they were inferior to men.[14] In this context, "wives, . . . submit to your own husbands" would sound quite normal to the women being addressed.[15] It was what their pagan society had always taught. The unusual part of our passage is the assumption that there is a reason for this behavior that goes beyond its fitting "women's nature."

A strategy for a Christian wife's witness in first-century Rome. This passage is part of a letter. The letter form was well known in antiquity, for

---

[12]Plutarch, *Advice to Bride and Groom* 19; *Moralia* 140D, LCL (Cambridge, MA: Harvard University Press, 1936). Plutarch, it should be noted, was among the most egalitarian writers of his time. See Achtemeier, *1 Peter*, 207.

[13]E.g., Plato, *Republic* 4.431; Aristotle, *Politics* 3.1260a; *Nicomachean Ethics* 8.1160b-61a.

[14]David L. Balch, *Let Wives Be Submissive: The Domestic Code in 1 Peter*, Society of Biblical Literature Monograph Series 26 (Chico, CA: Scholars Press, 1981), 27-29, 44-45. E.g., the Stoic Epictetus makes no positive references to women; his teaching is addressed entirely to men. Women are often described by him as "silly." See further Peter Lampe and Ulrich Luz, "Nachpaulinisches Christentum und pagane Gesellschaft," in *Die Anfänge des Christentums: Alte Welt und neue Hoffnung*, ed. Jürgen Becker et al. (Stuttgart: W. Kohlhammer, 1987), 185-216.

[15]Literal translation. Although the NRSV's "accept the authority of" correctly assumes the expectations of a first-century Roman household, it implies stronger terminology than does the Greek text.

letter writing was an art as well as a means of communication. A letter may be of two types. It may be a *published* document, more a piece of literature than a missive sent to an actual recipient (or recipients). Or it may be an *occasional* document, intended to communicate in a specific way to a particular person or group. First Peter fits into this second category. As a result, we have only half of a two-way communication. That is, Peter has somehow received information about a group of churches in northwest Asia Minor, which stimulated him to write this letter. The topics he chooses and how he selects them are an expression of both his own cultural background and his perception of the situation of the recipients. The interpretation of any such letter involves at least a partial reconstruction of this dialogue.

Our text occurs in the second main section of the letter, the "table of household duties" (1 Pet 2:11–3:22), and must be read as part of this wider context.[16] First Peter 3:1 begins with "submit to your husbands," language that has already been used in 1 Peter 2:13, 18. This is an attitude that Christian subjects are to show to rulers and Christian slaves to masters. But in each case it is a qualified submission, since believers in Christ know themselves in reality to be "immigrants" or "resident aliens" (1 Pet 2:11); thus, they are not really part of the structures of the present age, whether governmental or familial, which are "human creations" (1 Pet 2:13).[17] They are "free" (1 Pet 2:16) and submit to others because God is their true Master and this is God's desire. They behave as they do not because of the intrinsic authority of the other human being but to silence the criticism of nonbelievers through doing what is right (1 Pet 2:15).

Having addressed the issue of submission to "governing structures" in general (1 Pet 2:13-17), Peter turns to two special cases, both addressed by

---

[16]This section is marked out by the *inclusio* (framing device) created by two forms of *hypotassō* = "be in submission" in 1 Pet 2:13; 3:22. Dorothy I. Sly notes the *inclusio*. See Sly, "1 Peter 3:6b in the Light of Philo and Josephus," *Journal of Biblical Literature* 110 (1991): 126. The rhetorical analysis of Barth L. Campbell ends the section in 1 Pet 3:12. See Campbell, *Honor, Shame and the Rhetoric of 1 Peter*, Society of Biblical Literature Dissertation Series 160 (Atlanta: Scholars Press, 1998), 99-171. Certainly at least a subunit ends in 1 Pet 3:12, for by then the book has come to a basic resolution of the issue of suffering for doing good. For our purposes it is the beginning of the section rather than the end that is more critical.

[17]The Greek (*anthrōpinē ktisei*) puts the emphasis not on "human authority" (NIV 2011) but on its being an "institution" (see NRSV) created either by or for human beings. Since this is a heading sentence for the whole section, it may rightly be assumed to cover both government (1 Pet 2:13-17) and the household (1 Pet 2:18–3:7).

pagan moralists.[18] In the first (1 Pet 2:18-25), believing slaves are to submit to their (pagan) masters in imitation of the suffering of Christ. In one sense they could do nothing else, for should they rebel they would receive a beating or worse. As in the case of wives, the general Greco-Roman position was that slaves were by nature created to be ruled by masters, and therefore no choice was given to them in this matter.[19] Where Peter acknowledges slaves could exercise the power of choice is in their acceptance of unjust suffering based on their identification with Christ.[20] There is no admission that their master is just or is exercising his rights. The point is that Christ did indeed die unjustly (1 Pet 2:22). Because of this, one who is suffering unjustly need not resist verbally or physically but can choose to identify with Christ and his silent acceptance of injustice. This is not a slave's legitimizing the rights of their earthly master but a slave's identifying with their true master—the one who died for the sins of others—and thus seeing value in unjust suffering and recognizing that God eventually establishes justice.

The second special situation is that of a believing woman married to a pagan householder. Although, in contrast to slavery, the Bible clearly sanctions marriage, it is nonetheless also a temporal, human institution—that is, it belongs to this age, not the age to come.[21] Thus it is introduced here with "likewise" or "in the same way," as an intentional parallel with slavery. Also parallel with slavery is the way the authority of the "master" is undermined even as it is affirmed. To be sure, the woman accepts her husband's authority, but not because she recognizes it as intrinsic (as Plato and Aristotle would have it) or as a universal divine structure (as some pagan moralists and the Hellenized Jews Josephus and Philo taught). Rather, she does

---

[18]See, e.g., Balch, *Let Wives Be Submissive*, 43. It should be noted that the chapter break at 1 Pet 3:1 is especially unfortunate, since it may cause the ordinary reader to miss Peter's clear connections.

[19]Indeed, it was as much part of household management to rule slaves as it was to rule one's wife. Hence Plato and Aristotle and those coming after them discuss the management of slaves in the same places as the management of wives and children.

[20]In 1 Pet 4:16 the text speaks of suffering "as a Christian," while our section is silent on the cause of suffering, perhaps for apologetic reasons; one reason for unjust suffering was surely a slave's stubborn insistence on remaining a practicing Christian.

[21]Peter does not cite Mt 22:30, although there is evidence that he knew the Matthean tradition, but like Jesus in Matthew and Paul in 1 Cor 7, he views marriage as part of this age and not the age to come. See Rainer Metzner, *Die Rezeption des Matthäusevangeliums im 1. Petrusbrief*, Wissenschaftliche Untersuchungen zum Neuen Testament 2/74 (Tübingen: Mohr, 1995).

so in order to evangelize him and to keep Christian teaching in good repute (1 Pet 2:16). Her husband had sole authority to decide whether her babies lived, whether she would remain his wife, and how she would be treated physically. Here Peter gives her a way of reframing a situation that she cannot avoid so that it has a strategic purpose within God's inbreaking rule in the world.

Yet what she is to do is also, in a sense, subversive. There is no hint that she should reject the worship of her Lord to worship her husband's gods. Indeed, she is expected to willfully hold on to her "superstition" despite the disapproval of her culture and her husband. However, in other culturally defined areas she is to show appropriate "female virtue," for like the slave's quiet acceptance of unjust treatment, these both express Christian values and undermine criticism of Christianity.

Such virtue is described as "purity in fear" (1 Pet 3:2). "Fear" here, as elsewhere in this letter (1 Pet 1:17; 2:18; cf. 1 Pet 3:16 and the related verb in 1 Pet 2:17), most likely means "reverent fear [of God]" (see TNIV, NLT, NABRE, or NIV of 1 Pet 1:17; 2:18) or simply "reverence," as in the CEB. Indeed, Peter specifically *rejects* fearing/reverencing human beings or what they normally fear (1 Pet 3:6, 14). Thus, the address to women begins with encouraging the fear of God and ends with rejecting the fear of human beings (including husbands).

"Purity" includes, as well as transcends, sexual purity, as seen elsewhere in the New Testament (Phil 4:8; 1 Tim 5:22; Jas 3:17; 1 Jn 3:3).[22] Sexual purity can be seen in the instruction to reject the use of outward adornment. Epictetus said, "When [women after puberty] see that they have nothing else but only to be the bedfellows of men, they begin to beautify themselves, and put all their hopes in that." And pagan (especially Stoic) moralists frequently described outward adornment as an indication of sexual seductiveness.[23] This is understandable, since, as Epictetus notes,

---

[22]Friedrich Hauck, "*Hagnos*," in *TDNT* 1:122; Heinrich Baltensweiler, "Pure, Clean," in *New International Dictionary of New Testament Theology*, ed. Colin Brown (Grand Rapids, MI: Zondervan, 1975–1978), 3:100-112.

[23]Epictetus, *Encheiridion* 40. He goes on to instruct, "It is worth while for us to take pains, therefore, to make them understand that they are honored for nothing else but only for appearing modest and self-respecting" (trans. W. A. Oldfather, LCL [Cambridge, MA: Harvard University Press, 1966], 525-26). See Plutarch, *Moralia* 1, 141; Seneca, *De beneficiis* 7.9; Perictione, *On the*

sexual attractiveness was the one power women were able to exert within their society. Moreover, such dress was also a mark of many cults, which were viewed as making women lascivious.[24] Thus Christian women are being exhorted to avoid appearing morally improper by the standards of their culture.[25]

In contrast to women displaying their sexuality, "a gentle and quiet [peaceful] spirit" characterized the pure way of life. The virtue of gentleness is not limited to women, since Jesus uses the word to describe himself (Mt 11:29). And Paul speaks of himself as coming "in a spirit of gentleness" (1 Cor 4:21) and includes "gentleness" as a "fruit of the Spirit" (Gal 5:22; cf. Col 3:12), which is to be exercised when restoring a sinning brother or sister (Gal 6:1). Likewise, the virtue of quietness or peacefulness (not primarily silence but remaining quiet rather than protesting) is applied to both men and women (1 Thess 4:11; 2 Thess 3:12; 1 Tim 2:2), and only in one other passage specifically to women (1 Tim 2:11-12).[26] While these were considered virtues for both men and women in the Greek world, they were viewed as particularly important for women.[27]

Clearly, Christianity had subverted the authority of the Greek husband to determine the religion of his family. But far from disturbing the peace of the household further, Christian wives were to show that they were not sexually provocative (avoiding the charge that Christianity produced loose sexuality) and to contribute to the general peace of the household (rather than being harsh or rebellious). Since these behaviors were Christian

---

Harmony of a Woman 143. Among Jewish writers, see Testament of Reuben 5.5; Philo, De virtibus 39; Vita Mosis 2.243.

[24]See Balch, Let Wives Be Submissive, 101.

[25]It is not clear whether Peter is trying to curtail the actual behavior of some Christian women, since the language is so traditional. If this is a literal reference, it would be addressed to middle- or upper-class women, for female slaves and peasant women would have had only one or two sets of everyday clothing. More likely this is a traditional denunciation of dress as a symbol of sexual seductiveness, thus especially to be avoided by Christian wives.

[26]Seen clearly in Philo, De Abrahamo 27: "The opposite quality to rest is unnatural agitation, the cause of confusion, and tumults, and seditions, and wars, which the wicked pursue; while those who pay due honor to excellence cultivate a tranquil, and quiet, and stable, and peaceful life." See Gerhard Delling, "tassō ktl.," in TDNT 8:47-48.

[27]The two terms are also paired in 1 Clement 13.4 and Epistle of Barnabas 19.4. See Friedrich Hauck and Siegfried Schulz, "Praus, prautēs," in TDNT 6:646: "It is one of the chief virtues in a woman." See Plutarch, Coniugalia praecepta 45; Consolatio ad uxorem 2. Hauck and Schulz add, "One finds it in feminine deities," including Artemis (Anthologia Palatina 6, 271; see also 9, 525, 17) and Leto (Plato, Cratylus 406a).

virtues valued in both men and women, the women were not being asked to act in any way other than a fully Christian manner, a manner that is as appropriate today as then.[28] Since these were also Greco-Roman virtues especially admired in women, they showed that Christianity did not totally undermine the order of the family.

Peter goes on to attribute these virtues to unnamed "holy women who hoped in God" and who "clothed themselves" with these virtues in submission to their husbands. This is a generalizing statement, just as Luke 1:70; Acts 3:21; and 2 Peter 3:2 refer in general to the "holy prophets." That they "hoped in God" means they expected to receive their vindication at the consummation of the age, rather than in the present world order.[29]

At this point Sarah is used as a specific example of the "holy women" who "hoped in God." The terminology changes from "submitting" (*hypotassō*) to "obeying" (*hypakouō*), and it is specifically said that she called Abraham "lord" (Hebrew *'adonai*; Greek *kyrios* = "lord/master," "husband," or "sir"). Only once in canonical Scripture does Sarah use this term regarding Abraham: "So Sarah laughed to herself, saying, 'After I have grown old, and *my husband* is old, shall I have pleasure?'"

---

[28]The virtues are those of "a gentle and quiet spirit" and, earlier, "reverent and chaste behavior," that is, the virtues of reverence (the probable meaning of *phobos*, the motivation of chastity or purity), chastity/purity (*hagnēn anastrophēn*), and gentleness/humbleness/meekness (*praus*) and quietness/well-ordered/tranquility (*hēsychios*) with respect to their spirit. On gentleness or humility, see Mt 5:5; 11:29; 21:5 (the last two applied to Jesus); on tranquility or quietness or peacefulness, see 1 Tim 2:2, 11-12, and the silence that of Acts 22:2 (building on Acts 21:40), which contrasts with concepts such as uproar or (in Latin) *stasis*, which was what Romans feared (likewise, look at passages in which elders are supposed to be "grave" or "serious"—as in Phil 4:8—and others in which "much speaking" is connected with "sin"). Purity or chastity is lauded in 2 Cor 7:11; 11:2; Phil 4:8 (a virtue list); 1 Tim 5:22; Titus 2:5; Jas 3:17 (another virtue list); and 1 Jn 3:3. A glance at BDAG will reveal that many of these virtues were valued in classical Greco-Roman society and are strongly emphasized in the apostolic fathers. From there they continue in the Christian spiritual tradition, showing up in the sayings of the desert fathers and mothers, the Rule of St Benedict (see especially chap. 7 on the twelve stages of humility), and the like. Benedict, of course, is making his rule for men alone, so one will find nothing exclusively feminine about the virtues extolled there. Ours is a loud, verbal, and assertive age, which is far from what has been valued in the Christian tradition from the Wisdom literature down the ages to the present.

[29]Hebrews 11:13-16 also expresses this attitude well, using some of the language found in 1 Peter: "All these people were still living by faith when they died. They did not receive the things promised; they only saw them and welcomed them from a distance, admitting that they were foreigners and strangers on earth. People who say such things show that they are looking for a country of their own. . . . Therefore God is not ashamed to be called their God, for he has prepared a city for them" (NIV). See also the virtues of patient endurance expressed in Jas 5:7-8.

(Gen 18:12).[30] This statement is a disbelieving response to God and indicates no particular submission to Abraham.[31] While Sarah agrees to several requests from Abraham outside Genesis 18:12 (see Gen 12:13; 20:5, 13), she does not use the term *lord* on these occasions, nor is her *obedience* to Abraham mentioned anywhere in the Genesis narrative.[32] On the other hand, Abraham is explicitly said to agree to Sarah's requests in Genesis 16:2; 21:10-12, in the latter at God's direction to do so.[33] In the end, therefore, the information in Genesis, both Hebrew and Greek, does not appear to support the behavior Peter is commending in Sarah, making it unlikely that he is referring directly to Genesis 18:12.

But we do find Sarah frequently using *kyrios* when referring to, or addressing, Abraham in extracanonical Jewish works such as the Testament of Abraham (roughly contemporary with 1 Peter).[34] In this work

---

[30]Bible translations divide over whether to translate this term according to its use in 1 Peter or within the context of Genesis. In Gen 18:12 the NRSV and NAB translate the term contextually as "my husband." The NKJV follows the traditional AV rendering of "my lord." The NIV 1984 has "my master" with the alternative "husband" in a note, but the NIV 2011 has simply "my lord." The NLT compromises with "my master—my husband." Most translations use either "lord" or "master" in 1 Pet 3:6.

[31]This fact leads Mark Kiley to argue that the reference is to her *implicit* obedience in Gen 12; 20. See Kiley, "Like Sara: The Tale of Terror Behind 1 Peter 3:6," *Journal of Biblical Literature* 106 (1987): 689-92, as well as Grudem, *1 Peter*, 141-42. If this is the referent, then Kiley is correct when he states that it refers to what we would call an abusive situation. That is, to require one's wife to make herself available for marriage to someone else in a foreign land away from all support and protection, and to do so to preserve one's own life, without there being an explicit threat to it, can in our present understanding only be read as abusive. However, Achtemeier points out that a "lack of evidence" of other references makes even Kiley agree that Gen 18:12 is the focal passage (*1 Peter*, 215-16, especially n141).

[32]In fact, while the narrative often refers to her as Abraham's wife, it only once refers to him as her husband (Gen 20:3), using the word *ba'al* rather than the more generic *'adonai* used in Gen 18:12. The latter is used in addressing God and men of equal or superior status to the speaker, but is not otherwise used in speaking about another individual in the way it appears in Gen 18:12.

[33]The word translated "obey" (*hypakouō*) in 1 Pet 3:6 is actually used in the LXX in Gen 18:6 to refer to Abraham's "listening to, heeding" Sarah. So, while the Greek Bible used by Peter and these churches never speaks of Sarah's "obeying" Abraham, it does refer to his "obeying" her.

In Gen 16:2, Abraham's agreement to Sarah's request fit his cultural values and thus gave him permission to do what he would have felt was right. In Gen 21:10-12, his agreement violated his cultural values, but divine intervention informed him that his wife was right, so he obeyed. The only other recorded interaction between Sarah and Abraham is his rushed but normal request in Gen 18:6, making a total of only five interactions between them in the Old Testament.

[34]In a summary of the evidence, James R. Mueller states, "Most scholars regard the 1st century B.C.E. or 1st century C.E. as the most likely [date for the work]." See Mueller, "Abraham, Testament of," in *Anchor Bible Dictionary*, ed. David Noel Freedman (New York: Doubleday, 1992). Though the Testament of Abraham may be as late as the late first century, as argued by Troy W.

especially, *kyrios* is used by Sarah to address Abraham (usually "my *kyrios* Abraham"), although only in casual or solemn discourse, not in contexts of "obedience."[35] This reinterpretation of Genesis accords with other Hellenistic Jewish literature from this period. For instance, Philo "indicates that Sarah's obedience to Abraham (or vice versa) was a matter of some discussion among biblical commentators in the first century."[36] Philo looks on instances where men listened to their wives as bringing a curse, using Genesis 3:7 as his prototype. Josephus argues in one place, "A woman is inferior to her husband in all things. Let her, therefore, be obedient to him; not so that he should abuse her, but that she may acknowledge her duty to her husband; for God has given the authority to the husband."[37] Influenced by their culture, these authors developed creative ways of dealing with texts in which women (Sarah in particular) gave instructions that their husbands heeded. They might allegorize the woman so that the man would be heeding virtue rather than a woman, or minimize the woman's (Sarah's) role altogether, or alter the passage by inserting elements on which the text is silent.[38]

Martin, even that could make it in a sense contemporary with 1 Peter, for surely the legends contained in it were recited long before the book was composed. See Martin, "The TestAbr and the Background of 1 Pet 3:6," *Zeitschrift für die neutestamentliche Wissenschaft und die Kunde der älteren Kirche* 90 (1999): 139-46. But the verbal overlap is significant enough that there could be actual dependence.

[35]This work, which probably originated in Egypt sometime in the first Christian century, was likely composed originally in Greek. It comes to us in two distinct but related recensions, recension A being about twice as long as B. In recension A Sarah addresses Abraham this way seven times (5.13 [2×]; 6.2, 4, 5, 8; 15.4), in B two times (4.1; 6.5), while Isaac addresses his father once this way as well (7.2). But it should also be noted that Isaac addresses his mother with this expression (A 3.5, my *kyria* mother), and on one occasion the archangel Michael addresses Abraham this way (A 2.10).

[36]Sly, "1 Peter 3:6b," 126; cf. 127-29.

[37]Philo, *Legum allegoriae* 3.222; Josephus, *Against Apion* 2.25.

[38]For allegorizing the woman so that the man would be heeding virtue rather than a woman, see Philo, *De congressu eruditionis gratia* 63-68. Cf. *De cherubim* 9: "The name of the woman was still Sarai; the symbol of my authority, for she is called my authority . . . [being] classed among things particular and things in species . . . such as the prudence which is in me, the temperance which is in me, the courage, the justice, and so in the same manner." This builds on the picture in *De congressu eruditionis gratia* 2: "The name Sarah, being interpreted, means 'my princedom.' And the wisdom which is in me, and the temperance which is in me, and the particular justice, and each of the other virtues which belong to me alone, are the princedom of me alone."

For minimizing the woman's (Sarah's) role altogether, see Sly, "1 Peter 3:6b," 128: "Philo . . . devotes the treatise *On the Migration of Abraham* to commentary on the first six verses of Genesis 12 but skips over v. 5, which deals with Sarah. In the treatise he mentions Sarah in only three sections (126, 140, 142). In his other treatise on Abraham, he again disregards Gen 12:5, turning

In light of these contemporary ways of presenting the Genesis texts, and given that what Peter does say does not fit the Genesis narrative well, it seems most likely that, in his reference to Sarah he is using material known to his readers from these contemporary Jewish sources.[39] Here Sarah is depicted in terms of an ideal Hellenistic wife, an illustration that serves Peter's purpose. Christian wives will be Sarah's "daughters" (i.e., among the holy women) if they are also good Hellenistic wives and emulate her (Greco-Roman) virtue (that is, do good and refuse to fear).[40] The refusal to fear would apply specifically to the displeasure—and the consequences it would bring—of their non-Christian husbands and Greek society regarding their involvement in the Christian faith.

Contemporary application. One of Peter's strategies is to minimize the tension between Christians and the surrounding society. He wants to make allegiance to Jesus the issue, not unnecessarily divisive behaviors. In particular, he seeks to defend Christians against the charge that they are subverting the social order in a rebellious manner, although at the very core of things (their devotion to Jesus as Lord) believers are very much subverting it at a core level—at the level of ultimate allegiance and worldview. This leads to his general statements in 1 Peter 2:12-13, 15 and to more specific discussions of the behavior of slaves and wives in 1 Peter 2:18-25; 3:1-6 respectively.

Abraham from a family man into a solitary traveler: 'But Abraham, the moment he was bidden, departed with a few or even alone' (*Abr.* 66). When he finally does bring Sarah to the fore (245-46), he changes her into a proper Hellenistic wife, an uncomplaining partner in life's wanderings, privations, and mishaps, whose distinguishing feature is wifely love (*philandria*)." See *De Abrahamo* 245-46, 253.

For altering the passage, see, e.g., Josephus, who writes, "Now Abram . . . being uneasy at his wife's barrenness, . . . entreated God to grant that he might have male issue; and God required of him to be of good courage, and said that he would add to all the rest of the benefits that he had bestowed upon him . . . the gift of children. Accordingly, Sarai, at God's command, brought to his bed one of her handmaidens, a woman of Egyptian descent, in order to obtain children by her" (*Antiquities of the Jews* 1.10.4).

[39]I have not discussed rabbinic developments of traditions about Sarah. There is a parallel to the Hellenistic enlargements on the Sarah tradition in Tanhuma. See Giuseppe Ghiberti, "Le 'sante donne' di una volta (1 Pt 3:5)," *Rivista Biblica* 36 (1988): 287-97. However, Tanhuma is from the fourth century BC (Tanhuma bar Abba) or later. Furthermore, 1 Peter does not demonstrate significant contact with rabbinic traditions. Interestingly, Genesis Rabbah, when commenting on Gen 18, does not mention Sarah's obedience or her calling Abraham "lord," obviating the issue.

[40]Exactly how "doing good" and "refusing to fear" (participles) fit with being a daughter of Sarah is debated. I have chosen to understand them as circumstantial. For a fuller discussion see Martin, "TestAbr and the Background," 143-44.

In the latter two cases, the attempt to present Christianity as nonsubversive is complicated by the fact that Peter will not compromise on a central point: both slaves and wives must be free to commit themselves to the Christian faith regardless of the wishes of their masters or husbands. While not every slave would have a non-Christian master, or every wife a non-Christian husband, the tendency of the passage in each case is to assume that they do. This makes the best sense of the apologetic tone. In the case of the wives, the apologetic defense was particularly important, for their refusal of the family religion determined by their husband would be more public, as well as more intimate, and more influential in that typically wives were responsible for raising children for the first period of the children's lives.[41]

Peter's strategy was to advise wives not to talk about their religion but to model culturally appropriate behavior that was also universal Christian virtue. This dictated that they not be sexually provocative outside the home, that their words be few, that they show gentleness, and that they not foment revolution within the household.[42]

Two encouragements are given to support such behavior. First, this kind of behavior can lead to the conversion of a nonbelieving husband. Second, it puts the wife in a class with the "holy women" of Judaism whose behavior brought divine approval. Peter's example is Sarah, especially as portrayed in the Testament of Abraham. If Christian wives follow this model, they will likewise be considered holy women, approved by God, for they will fit the virtues of their culture insofar as those virtues are consistent with Christian virtues.

However, unless we assume that first-century Greco-Roman society is the only form of society upholding virtues approved by God, we may find

---

[41]Slaves might indeed be intimate with the master in that many masters used both male and female slaves sexually, but their intimacy was less official. Furthermore, slaves had quarters to withdraw to, so their devotional practice was less public. Also, they were not as involved in the family religious practices as were the wives.

[42]In the case of at least upper-class wives in some parts of the Roman Empire, wives would also not be sexually provocative within the home. The ideal wife was sexual enough to get pregnant and bear three or so children but would give up sexual relations altogether by her mid-twenties and even before that would expect her husband to get his main sexual needs met elsewhere. See Aline Rousselle, "Body Politics in Ancient Rome," in *A History of Women*, ed. Pauline Schmitt Pantel (Cambridge, MA: Harvard University Press, 1992), 313-24. Cf. Reay Tannahill, *Sex in History* (New York: Stein and Day, 1982), 132-35.

that a unilateral application of Peter's teaching in modern and postmodern societies would subvert his original intentions. Language and behavior have particular meaning within a cultural context. This has generally been recognized when it comes to the application of the passage about slaves, women's dress in church (1 Cor 11), braided hair, gold ornaments, or fine clothing (1 Pet 3:3).[43] Today hairstyle is—within limits—generally viewed indifferently with respect to Christian virtue. Braiding is often regarded as a conservative hairstyle rather than being sexually provocative. Women in most churches can be seen wearing gold jewelry, and the use of decorative clothing (rather than purely functional clothing) is often characteristic of "going to church." This is because in Western culture the wearing of decorative clothing and gold jewelry is not considered seductive or dishonorable. Indeed, in some cases it might be viewed as dishonoring (to oneself, one's role, or to one's husband) if a woman dressed in an unstylish or plain manner. Groups that insist on a literal application of this text—forbidding all decorative clothing and jewelry (although not normally braided hair)—are often viewed by the culture as making Christianity less attractive rather than as upholding and supporting the social order. This would be contrary to Peter's strategy.

So how should we apply the silent witness of 1 Peter 3? Unlike Greco-Roman society, modern societies generally do not give exclusive authority to husbands. Nor would it be regarded favorably for a wife to call her husband "my lord" (though women in the Victorian era did). This is because, unlike Greco-Roman society, our society expects marriage to be a partnership with a significant degree of intimacy. The removal of the husband's unilateral authority—a concept illustrated but not prescribed in Scripture—has greatly increased such intimacy. At the same time, marital intimacy is not enhanced by a barrage of criticism or a constant harping on the theme of religious beliefs. While wives are expected to be sexual within the boundaries of the marital relationship, faithfulness and a lack of seductiveness outside that relationship are appropriate Christian

---

[43]The adjective *kosmos*, translated "fine" in the NRSV, in this context carries the meaning "to beautify or adorn." Thus the accurate translation "You should not use outward adornment to make yourselves beautiful as in the way you fix your hair or in the jewelry you put on or in the dresses you wear," in L&N, no. 6.188; cf. 79.12.

virtues and would certainly constitute appropriate purity today for both men and women.

Women are expected to be assertive in contemporary Western culture, but there is a difference between harshness and gentle assertiveness. The latter is entirely in keeping with Christian virtue for both men and women. The idea of "being at peace" entails not trying to rebel against or overthrow societal structures. Within the context of marriage this would at least include a commitment to the marital relationship.

Ironically, interpretations that focus on the unilateral obedience or submission of wives to husbands, regardless of cultural context, achieve the opposite of Peter's intention. Rather than promoting harmony with culture, they heighten the tension, and Christianity is perceived as undermining culture in a retrogressive way. First Peter might agree that this tension should exist, but only if the virtues are present in both men and women.

Thus, if we want to preserve 1 Peter's strategy and intention within Western culture, we might appropriately paraphrase its teachings this way:

> Wives, embrace your marital relationship, so that even if your husband is not a believer he may be won without a word by your behavior when he observes that your sexuality is for the marriage alone and your piety is genuine. So don't be sexually provocative in your dress outside the home. Instead let your "dress" be a gentleness arising from an inward peace and a commitment to the marital relationship, which are precious in God's sight. That's how the holy women of long ago lived. They were committed to their marriages. Sarah was committed to Abraham and expressed this accordingly within her culture. You are her daughters if you do what is good and do not let threats from your husband turn you from your faith.

CHRISTIAN HUSBANDS WITH CHRISTIAN WIVES
(1 PETER 3:7)

A Christian husband's treatment of his wife in first-century Rome. The address to the believing husbands completes the section on wives and husbands. A brief treatment is appropriate in view of the brevity of the instruction.[44]

---

[44]For a more extensive treatment, see Davids, *First Epistle of Peter*, 122-23.

First, although the behavior of wives is not explicitly described in this verse, most scholars have argued that the husbands in question are married to Christian wives. This is certainly true if the women are "fellow heirs of the grace of life," which is the most natural reading of the sentence.[45] Thus we are dealing with women who have come to faith, either on their own or following their husbands (as would be natural in a Greco-Roman setting).

Second, there is no main verb in this sentence. The husbands are "likewise" to do something (parallel to 1 Pet 3:1, which picks up on 1 Pet 2:13, 18) by means of the two following participial clauses (i.e., showing consideration for and paying honor to their wives). Is the implied verb "be submissive to" (see 1 Pet 3:1; 2:18, 13)? Likely so, in which case the reference is to 1 Peter 2:13—the authority of human institutions, in this case marriage. Nor is this surprising in that Christ himself served human beings, taking a subordinate position (e.g., Mk 10:45; Phil 2:1-11). Whatever the exact referent, the implication is that the husband is experiencing a limitation on his freedom parallel to that which the wife and slave have previously experienced.

Third, the husband needs to live with his wife recognizing that she is "weaker."[46] How she is weaker is not specified. Evidence from the Greco-Roman worldview could support an assumption of physical weakness, social weakness, intellectual weakness, or moral weakness.[47] The point is that the husband is in some respect stronger and needs to recognize this fact in his life with his wife, so that he does not exploit this disparity in strength, consciously or unconsciously. Rather, he is to treat her as an equal, a "fellow heir of the grace of life"—a complementary equality.[48] His

---

[45]For a contrary opinion based on the fact that the "weaker vessel" of 1 Pet 3:7 is singular and the "fellow heirs" is plural, see Carl D. Gross, "Are the Wives of 1 Peter 3:7 Christians?," *Journal for the Study of the New Testament* 35 (1989): 89-96. He translates the phrase "giving her honor as you also do to your fellow heirs of the grace of life," i.e., treat her as honorably as you do your Christian brothers and sisters. This is, however, a minority position and overlooks (1) that this verse seems almost an afterthought rather than part of the larger structure and (2) the verse's beginning with "husbands" (plural) would make the shift from singular to plural for the wives quite natural.

[46]Weakness is also attributed to Jesus in 2 Cor 13:4, so being weak does not necessarily describe an inferior person but may be the means by which one overcomes evil, i.e., suffering service rather than active resistance.

[47]Gross, "Are the Wives," 123.

[48]Complementary equality means an equality as "an heir of the grace of life" that the husband recognizes as his complement. There is no question that the husband has the social position

words and actions are to accord her this status, *honor* being a key status term in Greco-Roman culture.

Fourth, the reason for the husband's need to do this is so that "your" prayers may not be hindered (either those of the husband—which is more likely since he is being addressed—or those of the couple). In other words, a failure to treat his wife as an equal will, by implication, result in divine displeasure and a damaged relationship in which prayers are not answered.

Here Peter follows the general New Testament strategy of requesting that those with power give up their power as Christ did. When addressing those without power (slaves and wives), he does not call for revolution but upholds the values of the culture insofar as they do not conflict with a commitment to Christ. He then reframes their behavior by removing it from the realm of necessity and giving it a dignity, either that of identification with Christ or of identification with the "holy women" of Jewish antiquity. When speaking to the ones with power, however, he asks them not to use their power but to treat those they could dominate as their equals—for in fact they are. In this he is acting analogously to Paul's strategy in Philemon concerning slavery.

Contemporary application. The question for today is, Will men/husbands insist on an authority over their wives that once was given them by the surrounding culture but now for the most part they no longer have?[49] Or will they follow Christ and the way of the cross and drop power, treating their wives as equals, reaping not only a more intimate marriage relationship but also divine pleasure as they develop the virtue of humility extolled in spiritual literature down the centuries?

---

either to recognize it or not. The call is that he recognizes that it is a complementary *equality* and not a complementary *inequality*.

[49]Naturally, the average man is in some respects physically stronger than the average woman. Also, women are economically and socially disadvantaged even in Western culture. However, Western culture, which is the context of this study, no longer sanctions such differences, nor does it sanction the use of male physical strength against women, even if everyday life has not caught up with moral theory. For more on the data within the social sciences regarding differences between men and women (and the lack thereof), see M. Elizabeth Lewis Hall's chapter in this volume.

PART II

THINKING IT THROUGH

Theological and Logical Perspectives

13

THE PRIORITY OF
SPIRIT GIFTING FOR
CHURCH MINISTRY

Gordon D. Fee

• • • • •

THIS CHAPTER WILL EXPLORE how the gifting of the Spirit affects
our understanding of people's ministries and areas of service in the church.
I begin with a disclaimer about the concept of equality. What is at stake is
not whether all people are equally gifted; they are not. What is at stake is
whether God the Holy Spirit, in his gifting the people of God, ever makes
gender a prior requirement for certain kinds of gifting. I will argue that
what biblical data we do have seem clear: the Spirit does not.

But in order to get there, we need to cover some much-covered ground
yet again, regarding (1) the nature of biblical revelation and authority,
including the hermeneutics of ad hoc documents that do not speak to a
given concern as a matter of advocacy, and (2) the complex nature of early
church structures that are reflected in our documents, which do not
address those structures as a primary concern. At issue in the use of such
texts is the question, What does the Bible teach—and what does one mean
by *teach*, when the teaching is not explicit? Then there is our constant use
of *biblical* in our rhetoric: What do we mean by this term—that something is biblical only when it is prescriptive? And if we include what is
otherwise merely descriptive, on what grounds do we move from description to prescription?

So, what I hope to do in this chapter is threefold: (1) to point out the ambiguity of the biblical texts with regard to church structures and ministries, and thus (2) to define a hermeneutical starting point from which our quest might legitimately be carried forward, and (3) to look at a variety of texts that state or imply that Spirit gifting precedes all questions of structures and gender.

THE BIBLE'S AMBIGUITY REGARDING CHURCH STRUCTURE AND MINISTRIES

One thing that should perhaps strike the serious reader of Scripture is the general lack of concern in the New Testament about the way the church ordered its corporate life, whether in its structures (offices, etc.) or its gatherings for worship.[1] So much is this so that every present form of church government appeals to New Testament texts in support of its particular organizational flow chart.[2] This is true from the ultimate hierarchical understanding of church in Roman Catholicism to the much more subtle hierarchy of the Plymouth Brethren, not to mention Baptists and Presbyterians in between. The New Testament documents simply show no interest in defining these matters; their ecclesiological interest rather is on the who and how of the composition of the people of God under the new covenant effected through Christ and evidenced by the Spirit.[3]

It is precisely the opposite, however, with regard to the former covenant ratified at Sinai between Yahweh and Israel. Here there are specific, intentional instructions about how Israel will function both as a people and in its worship of Yahweh. Although women such as Deborah functioned as both prophet and judge/leader (Judg 4), and Huldah as a prophet (2 Kings 22:14), there was no place for women in the priesthood, whose

---

[1]Take the long-standing difficulty of determining the relationship between the meal and the Lord's Table that arises in Paul's heated response in 1 Cor 11:17-34 and how this is further related to the spontaneous Spirit utterances in 1 Cor 14:26-33.

[2]See Gordon D. Fee, "Reflections on Church Order in the Pastoral Epistles, with Further Reflection on the Hermeneutics of Ad Hoc Documents," *JETS* 28 (1985): 141-51.

[3]The "how" of course is by faith in Christ and the gift of the Spirit; the "who" is Jew and Gentile, slave and free, male and female (Gal 3:28; cf. 1 Cor 12:13; Col 3:10); see chapter nine in this book. So much is this so that I have considerable difficulty with the theological rubric *ecclesiology*, which should refer to discussion about the people of God but has been generally co-opted to refer to structures, ministry, and function. Perhaps we need a word such as *laiology* in order to talk about the real issues: what it means for the church to be the people of God.

rules were very explicitly laid out in terms of men only. Such instruction is completely missing from the New Testament, where the Old Testament priesthood has been made obsolete through the crucifixion of Christ and the subsequent new-covenant gifting of the Holy Spirit (in fulfillment of Joel 2:28-29)—a gifting that comes upon men and women, old and young, slave and free alike.

The net result is that we know very little about the organization of the early church, either as a whole or in its local expressions. What we do learn, we gather from gleanings of texts, not from intentional instruction. The closest thing to the latter appears in 1 Timothy 3:1-13 and Titus 1:5-9; but here, to our dismay, we learn only about the qualifications for certain positions of leadership; we learn next to nothing about who they were or what role they played. And the concept of office, in the sense that there were offices in the church that needed to be filled with persons, is just barely a possibility in 1 Timothy 3:1 and appears nowhere else in the New Testament. Rather, there were persons who *functioned* in certain capacities, whose function eventually was expressed in a more titular way. That is, before there were prophets, individuals prophesied, and they were sometimes called prophets; and elders (a term with roots in the synagogue) gave oversight to the community and eventually came to be called *episkopoi* (overseers), a term derived from the Greco-Roman world.

Even here we get just enough information to whet our appetites for more, but nothing bordering on certainty. Thus, when one asks, on the basis of Paul's use of *elders* and *overseers* in 1 Timothy 3; 5 and Titus 1, how these people might be distinguished from one another, we get an amazing spread of answers, precisely because of the *ambiguity of our texts*. For example, I have argued that the best solution is to see *elder* as the broad term that included both overseers and deacons, but I also recognize how foolish it would be to press that or to make church order based on it because such an opinion is the result of exegetical decision making, not of clear intentional revelation from the Holy Spirit.[4]

Thus, what is totally lacking in our documents is any instruction intentionally stipulating who, what, how many, and the duties of these various

---

[4]See Gordon D. Fee, *1 and 2 Timothy, Titus*, NIBC (Peabody, MA: Hendrickson, 1988), 78.

people. At the church universal level we get tantalizing glimpses, but scarcely anything on which all can agree. The role of the Twelve is especially ambiguous. What seems certain from the data is the significance of the number twelve, precisely because Jesus was deliberately offering himself as the new expression of Israel in the coming rule of God. This seems to be made certain by Luke's narrative in Acts 1 about the filling out of that number. But when one gets into the rest of the narrative of Acts, the role of the Twelve becomes more and more ambiguous: they never appear again as a group, and when the church gathers in a semiofficial way in Acts 15, it is James, not one of the Twelve, who leads the deliberations.[5]

This is likewise the case with Paul. A comparison of a passage such as Acts 15 with a variety of passages in Paul's letters leaves us with several impressions but with nothing in sharp focus. It seems, for example, that Paul did not think of apostleship as an office in the church charged with oversight of the whole; in fact, it is quite the opposite. He mentions "the Twelve" (even when they were only eleven!) only in their historic role as eyewitnesses to the resurrection of Jesus (1 Cor 15:5). But there is no sense in which he defers to them. Rather, when he refers to James and two of the Twelve in Galatians 2:1-10, he speaks in terms of their being esteemed as leaders, not in terms of their official, God-given authority.

Similarly, Paul's own authority as an apostle had to do with the churches he had founded, not with the church universal.[6] Thus, he is as prepared to resist any form of outside interference with "his" churches (see Galatians and 2 Cor 10–12) as he is deferential when writing to a church that he did not found (see Rom 1:8-15).

When we look at the church at the local level, it is even more the case that we do not know enough to be certain about very much—even at the purely descriptive level, let alone at any prescriptive level. We can make an educated guess, if the majority opinion is correct about the letter of James, that the local communities in Palestine were patterned after the Jewish

---

[5]In fact, one of the mysteries of early church history is how and when this happened, not to mention the mystery of whatever happened to the Twelve.

[6]Founded on the basis that he had seen, and had been commissioned by, the risen Lord (1 Cor 9:1; cf. 1 Cor 15:7-11). See Gordon D. Fee, *The First Epistle to the Corinthians*, NICNT (Grand Rapids, MI: Eerdmans, 1987), 395n16.

synagogue (see Jas 2:2, where that language occurs).[7] Likewise, even though we can be sure that the communities founded by Paul in the Greco-Roman world took the form of house churches, what we cannot be sure of is whether they were also patterned after the Greco-Roman household. Many of us think so, especially since Paul uses this very language at times as an image for the church (see "God's household" in 1 Tim 3:15). But others would argue that the synagogue still functioned as the pattern for the household church. And even though I think that is most highly unlikely, in the end I too must admit that the reason one can so argue is that the evidence itself is not clear.[8]

Moreover, if I am right about the structure of the house(hold) church, then it would follow naturally (or so it could be argued) that the householder functioned in the same way in the household church as in the household as such. If so, then women such as Lydia (Acts 16:13-15) and Nympha (Col 4:15) would have ordinarily functioned that way in their households. But many think otherwise, precisely because the texts are ambiguous, and in such cases we tend to bring some prior hermeneutical or religious commitments to our reading of them.

Ordinarily, having come this far in such an argument, one would go on and try to ferret out from our various snippets of data what we *can* have a degree of certainty about—for example, that the churches did have leadership and that leadership was important, even if we do not know what it looked like. But my concern here is simply to point out the high degree of uncertainty all of us face when asking questions about this dimension of church on the basis of the New Testament evidence. We have enough information to offer descriptive guesses with varying degrees of certainty. But what we lack is the one essential thing: intentional instruction about the church—its structures, the nature of its leadership, both local and beyond; and its worship—the various aspects of it, who led it, and its order.

---

[7]This may also be true of Heb 13; in any case, the difference between Heb 13:17 ("have confidence in your leaders and submit to their authority"; NIV) and 1 Thess 5:12 ("acknowledge those who work hard among you, who care for you in the Lord and who admonish you"; NIV) is considerable and probably reflects two different kinds of church.

[8]Where in the synagogue, for example, would there be a place for something like the Lord's Table, which fits the household extremely well, or for spontaneous utterances from the Spirit as envisioned in 1 Cor 14:26-33, which fits better the *symposium* of the Jewish mystical group described by Philo (*On the Contemplative Life* 64-90) in the context of a meal?

And that leads to my second concern: What degree of hermeneutical certainty should we impose on texts that are not intentional in their instruction, and from which we learn only by bringing our questions to the text and ferreting out the evidence?

A HERMENEUTICAL STARTING POINT

One of the greatest difficulties that "biblical Christians" have is to come to terms with the term *biblical* in that formula. At issue here is how prescriptive we make biblical texts that only narrate what is and do not say explicitly that this is also the way things *must be*. Do analogies and examples carry the same freight "for all times in all places" as explicit instruction? And if so, how so? What is the guiding hermeneutic that makes some merely descriptive matters such as church order and the relationship of gender to ministry and gifts become *prescriptive*, while at the same time among many who hold such a view, a very prescriptive word by Paul, "Be eager to prophesy, and do not forbid speaking in tongues" (1 Cor 14:39 NIV), is consistently, sometimes cavalierly, disobeyed? The answer, of course, is a hermeneutic that is culturally conditioned and unrelated to the biblical data! And since the texts themselves do not prescribe, on what grounds do some believers develop a hierarchy of hermeneutics that argues for the eternal validity of 1 Timothy 3:1-11 (and includes the *duties* of overseers, even though the texts do not speak to this question), while instruction about the care for and remarriage of widows in 1 Timothy 5:1-16 carries no weight at all?

Some years ago, in searching for some hermeneutical solid ground regarding our use of biblical narratives for what is normative in the church, I argued that normativity must finally lie with authorial intentionality.[9] In that piece I pointed out that doctrinal statements tend to be of three kinds: Christian theology (what Christians believe), Christian ethics (how Christians ought to live in relation to others), and Christian praxis (what

---

[9]See Gordon D. Fee, "Hermeneutics and Historical Precedent: A Major Problem in Pentecostal Hermeneutics," in *Perspectives on the New Pentecostalism*, ed. Russell P. Spittler (Grand Rapids, MI: Baker, 1976), 118-32. This material was then recast for a larger Christian audience in chap. 6 of Gordon D. Fee and Douglas Stuart, *How to Read the Bible for All Its Worth* (Grand Rapids, MI: Zondervan, 1982), 94-112. These two pieces set off a flurry of activity over my use of the word *normative*, which I took—and still take—to mean "that which is required practice for the church in all times and all places, so that not to do so is to disobey." In any case some clarification was needed, which was incorporated into the second edition of the book (Zondervan, 1993), 105-12.

Christians do as religious people). Moreover, within these three kinds of statements there are some that are primary and nonnegotiable (e.g., the deity of Christ), while others are secondary (e.g., the two natures and how they cohere). The difference between these two is that the first are always explicitly taught in Scripture; the second are derivative from what is explicit. It seems to be a plain fact of church history that most of the differences between Christians lie in two places: (1) with the secondary-level statements in the first two categories (theology and ethics) and (2) with both levels of statements in the third category (praxis).[10]

For example, now picking up only on the third category of Christian praxis, most Christian communions believe that the celebration of the Lord's Table is explicitly taught in Scripture, but the church is unfortunately deeply divided over almost everything else about the Table: the meaning of the bread and wine, the frequency of participation, who are the legitimate participants, who can administer, and so forth.[11] And it will take very little by way of observation to note that all these differences are predicated on *different readings of texts that give no explicit instruction*; everything is implied.

This is precisely what lies behind our differences pointed to above in the area of church order and ministry as well. *That* the church has some form of recognizable organization, we may well assume on the basis of our many scattered data; but *what form* that structure took can be derived only from the reading of texts by implication, not from gathering explicit statements intended to guide us in these matters.

And the same is especially true with regard to the matter of gender as it relates to structures and ministry. The texts simply do not have explicit teaching on these matters.[12] Therefore advocates on both sides are left with

---

[10]That is, all would agree that the sovereignty of God is taught throughout Scripture, both explicitly and implicitly, but churches are deeply divided over the implications of this reality of the matter of the freedom of the will—a matter, I am quick to point out, that is less certainly addressed in the biblical texts. And so also with Christian ethics; consider the command "keep yourselves pure" and how that is worked out in many different Christian communions, often in very divisive ways.

[11]The celebration of the Lord's Table is commanded by our Lord himself, "Do this in remembrance of me" (Lk 22:19; 1 Cor 11:24-25).

[12]Many will demur on this point, pointing to 1 Tim 2:11-12, but here the issue is, explicit about what? It is extremely tenuous to derive church office from this text. Those who do so bring a carload of presuppositional baggage to their reading of the text. The immediate context has to

sharply contrasting readings of the biblical texts, precisely because the biblical texts themselves do not have an agenda on this question. Rather, they speak into a wide variety of ad hoc situations that reflect a wide variety of scenarios, which, when they are all put side by side, seem to show evidence of a wide variety of practices.

But what they do *not* do in an intentionally instructive way is to speak to the question whether women may or may not be in leadership; and except for 1 Timothy 2:11-12, they do not otherwise speak to the issue of women's participation in some, but not other, activities of ministry. The obvious difficulty with the 1 Timothy passage is that it stands in unrelieved tension with passages that either narrate (Acts 18:26) or imply (1 Cor 14:26, 29-31) that women were involved in some form of teaching. It will simply do no good here to go through a series of circuitous exegetical hoops to argue that "teaching" implies the office of "teacher," and therefore there are different kinds and levels of teaching, some of which women can be excluded from. What is derived only from a series of exegetical jumps can scarcely be regarded as either the plain teaching of Scripture or a norm for the contemporary church.

Finally, it should be noted that our hermeneutical difficulties here are exacerbated by the fact that our only experience of church, even for those who have broad intercommunion experience, is of a later development of church that looks almost nothing like the house churches of the first-century Greco-Roman world. This is not a criticism of us; it is simply a statement of reality. But our hermeneutical difficulty here is seldom addressed, and that is, how do these first-century texts apply when we cannot be sure how our own reality is related to theirs? For example, Paul regularly puts the activities of apostles and prophets together in the church (1 Cor 12:28; Eph 2:20; 3:5; 4:11), but for a variety of reasons, historical and otherwise, very few contemporary expressions of the church are comfortable with

---

do with "prayers for all people" because God wants all people to be saved (1 Tim 2:1-7) and proper *demeanor* in prayer, with instruction/correction first to the men (1 Tim 2:8) and then to the women (1 Tim 2:9-15). To argue that 1 Tim 2:13 has to do with church order is to throw a red herring about structures into an otherwise clearly corrective admonition—most likely based on the ad hoc situation of this letter. After all, the final resolution in 1 Tim 2:15 sounds like 1 Tim 5:14: the fact that some younger widows have "already turned away to follow Satan" (1 Tim 5:15 NIV) is what lies behind the correction given in 1 Tim 5:14.

these designations for church offices of any kind. On the other hand, Paul in one place (Eph 4:11) and Peter in another (1 Pet 5:1) refer to some who are called shepherds (often brought into English as "pastors"). The single article controlling the two final nouns in the Ephesians passage indicates that the "shepherds" were also "teachers." Together these passages could be understood to refer to the "elders" who gave leadership to a local assembly.[13] But what is not clear at all is that there is a true correspondence between this biblical designation and the contemporary Protestant use of the term *pastor* to refer to the chief administrative officer and preacher of a local congregation!

In light of the ambiguities and consequent difficulties, therefore, a proper hermeneutic for such matters would be similar to the one I suggested for biblical precedent regarding the narratives of Scripture.[14] In matters of Christian practice, a biblical precedent that comes to us by way of narration or implication alone may often be regarded as a repeatable pattern for the later church; but nothing that is merely narrated or described, even if narrated more than once, should be understood to be normative for the church in all places at all times. I use *normative* here in the sense that we are disobedient if we do not follow the norm.

Thus, regarding church order, the ambiguity between the synagogue model and the household model should probably leave plenty of room for variety within the ongoing life of the church. And since the New Testament does *not* teach explicitly that only men may lead or serve in certain ways, and in fact seems to leave the door open on this matter (in the case of women as householders), the issue should more likely be giftedness, not gender. Indeed, I for one have as much resistance to the notion that women *ought to be* in leadership along with men as to the notion that *only* males are gifted to lead. The former notion also assumes a gender-based, not gift-based, model for leadership, and both Scripture and common experience give the lie to the second notion.

---

[13]This is rather explicit in 1 Pet 5:1; one gets there in Paul by noting his use of "apostle and prophet" elsewhere in Ephesians to refer to those who founded churches, thus perhaps reflecting itinerant ministries, while the shepherd-teachers would be the local elders. But this is only a (reasoned) exegetical guess.

[14]See note 9 above.

On the other hand, those who have been recognized by the community as a whole to be gifted for ministry and leadership should receive the laying on of hands on that basis alone, whether male or female. And that leads to my final point. Does this view hold up under the scrutiny of the biblical evidence?

VERBAL MINISTRIES IN THE NEW TESTAMENT CHURCH

When we come to questions about gift-based ministry, there are two kinds of issues that need to be looked at. (1) What does *ministry* mean? Can one make a legitimate distinction between ministry as office in the church and ministry as serving the church in other capacities? (2) What is the evidence that women were involved in ministry that included teaching, especially instructing others in Scripture? The place to begin is with the biblical evidence for the latter concern: gift-based ministry on the part of women.

1 Corinthians 11:4-5. Although some have denied it, there can be little question that this passage implies that women prayed and prophesied in the gathered community.[15] At issue here is whether a woman should do so "uncovered as to her head." Because of the somewhat (apparently, at least) offhand way this is said, it is very likely that these two words represent all such activity in the assembly. Prayer is the primary form of speech directed toward God in such settings, and thus it probably stands for all speech directed to God (and would therefore also include speaking in tongues; 1 Cor 14:2, 28). Likewise, prophecy is Paul's preferred form of speech addressed to the rest of the community and as such probably stands for all such forms of speech (teaching, revelation, word of knowledge, word of wisdom, etc.; see 1 Cor 14:6). The point is that prophecy at least is Spirit-inspired speech, and the clear implication of this text is that it was practiced by women and men alike.

1 Corinthians 14:23-33. This passage should be read in light of the preceding one. Here Paul says twice, "All prophesy" (1 Cor 14:24, 31). Even though the first of these is stated with hypothetical all-inclusiveness, that very fact indicates that prophecy in the gathered community *potentially* included everyone, male and female alike. This is even more the case in

---

[15]For such denial, see Fee, *First Epistle to the Corinthians*, 497n22.

1 Corinthians 14:31, where he gives explicit instruction: "You can all prophesy in turn" (NIV). What is important about this sentence is that it gives the purpose of such prophesying as "so that everyone may *be instructed* and *encouraged* [or *exhorted*]." These latter two verbs are most often associated, first, with receiving instruction through teaching and, second, with proclamation—which suggests that Paul did not have neat categories for these various verbal expressions prompted by the Spirit.

It should be pointed out further that up to 1 Corinthians 14:29-33 in the argument of 1 Corinthians 14 Paul refers to prophecy and tongues mostly with verbs. His emphasis is clearly on the *activity* of prophesying, not on the content of the speech or the person of the prophet.[16] But at 1 Corinthians 14:29 he begins with the designation *prophets*, about whom he speaks in terms of receiving a revelation, and finally comes back to their activity of prophesying. This seems to indicate that *prophet* is not used to refer to a specific group in the church who are known as prophets but simply to those who engage at times in the activity of prophesying.

It is important to note that 1 Corinthians 14:26 is a *corrective* text; that is, it is Paul's way of resolving the apparent fact that when they gather "everyone speaks in tongues" (1 Cor 14:23 NIV), which most likely included the women as well as the men. In this corrective he explicitly says, "When you come together, each of you has a hymn, or a word of instruction, a revelation, a tongue or an interpretation" (1 Cor 14:26 NIV). Even though this text gives rather explicit directives, most subsequent Christians who look at 1 Corinthians as sacred Scripture see this ad hoc listing not as normative (as what *must* happen in all churches at all times) but as representative of the variety of ways the Spirit can speak through people, again both men and women, so that the whole community might be built up.

Ephesians 5:18-20/Colossians 3:16. These two texts must be looked at together, because they have so much in common and because both assume the context of the household. There are three significant points to make here. First, the worship that is depicted is, as in 1 Corinthians 11:4-5, double-focused; very much like the Psalter, the singing involves praise and

---

[16]Indeed, when he does refer to the speech itself, he mentions both prophecy and revelation in 1 Cor 14:6; but then in 1 Cor 14:30 he seems to merge the two, while in 1 Cor 14:26 *revelation* almost certainly stands in for *prophecy*. Precision in language is obviously not Paul's concern.

thanksgiving to God while at the same time it instructs and admonishes the people (indeed, the verb in Ephesians is "*speak* to one another [through song]"). Second, the singing itself is Spirit-inspired; they are to sing in this praising and instructional way as they are "filled with the Spirit." Third, the focus as they "teach and admonish one another . . . through psalms" is "the message of Christ" (Col 3:16 NIV).

Summary of the biblical data. When we put all of this evidence together, several generalizations can be made. First, one finds a general lack of precision in Paul when it comes to describing verbal ministries within the community of faith. Both prophesying and singing, for example, are addressed at times in the language of teaching or instruction. Second, in no instance in Paul's letters does he mention leader(s) who are to be in charge of what takes place; for him the Spirit is the obvious leader of the community in its worship.[17] Third, there is no distinction of any kind between men and women when it comes to the actual verbal activities involved; indeed, a straightforward reading of all the texts together seems to imply that "all" means both men and women.

If there are not more data than these, that should not surprise us, because for the most part what we do learn is in the context of correcting an abuse of some kind in the church. Worship for these believers was like eating; it is something one did all the time. It would simply never have occurred to any of the early Christians that they should either describe their worship in full or lay down rules for it for a later time.

At the same time, it is this collection of evidence that makes the two well-known and much-debated texts, 1 Corinthians 14:34-35 and 1 Timothy 2:11-12, seem to stand in open contradiction to the rest of the evidence.[18] Despite protests from some, I continue to believe on text-critical grounds

---

[17]The possible exception to this is Phil 4:3, where he addresses a trusted friend and companion to lead the way in bringing reconciliation between Euodia and Syntyche.

[18]Despite a number of ploys used to get around the plain sense of the 1 Corinthians passage, the plain sense must prevail: In an argument based on the law (in Paul, of all things), women are forbidden *absolutely* to speak in the assembly. Even for learning they must ask their husbands at home. To make this refer to speaking in tongues or to the discerning of prophecies (so that they are not judging utterances from their own husbands) is a form of special pleading that does injustice to both the language and the structure of the two sentences and Paul's argument, and exists only because the text stands in such unrelieved contradiction to the rest of Paul's writings. For a different view, see Craig S. Keener, "Learning in the Assemblies: 1 Corinthians 14:34-35," in the present volume.

that the first of these is not a part of Paul's inspired letter.[19] Those who take issue with me on this score have yet to offer an adequately historical answer to the *textual* question that drove me to this view many years ago. If it is original with Paul, then how does one explain that in one whole sector of the church it is known only at another place in the text? There is simply no comparable instance of such a radical displacement of an argument in Paul's letters on the part of copyists, and I do not find "for reasons unknown to us" to be a satisfactory answer when a well-attested *historical* explanation lies at hand: a marginal gloss that was placed into the text at two different places.

Similarly, within a deluge of literature that has appeared on 1 Timothy 2:11-12 since my commentary on these letters, I have yet to find one that has given convincing arguments (for me, at least) demonstrating that this is *not* an ad hoc word to a very case-specific issue in the churches of Ephesus.[20] In any case, there is still more that we do not know than that we do about this one text that stands in tension with the rest of the New Testament evidence. Whatever else, it does not seem to be dealing with offices in the church; at least that certainly cannot be demonstrated, even if one were to wish desperately for it to be so.

IMPLICATIONS FOR WOMEN IN CHURCH OFFICES: GIVING THE SPIRIT PRIORITY

It is one thing to allow, as many do, the priority of Spirit gifting for the verbal ministries as outlined here. It is quite another, they would argue, for women to hold offices in the church. So, some final words need to be added about this matter. Our problems here are especially complicated by the ambiguities outlined in the first section of this essay. It must be said again with all candor that the biblical record simply does not express

---

[19]See my response to some critiques in the excursus on these verses in Gordon D. Fee, *God's Empowering Presence* (Peabody, MA: Hendrickson, 1994), 273-81.

[20]The appeal to the order of creation in 1 Tim 2:13 as a theological statement is surely in the eye of the beholder, since Paul's concern in 1 Tim 2:9-15 is *not* with the men but with the women; and he immediately follows 1 Tim 2:13 with the analogy that he is really after: the man was created first, but the woman was first to be deceived and thus to fall into transgression. There is not a hint in the Genesis narrative that the sequence of their creation has theological meaning, nor that the woman fell because she did not follow the lead of her husband, nor of countless other imaginative ways of trying to make a point that Paul is not making at all.

the same level of urgency about this matter that one can find in many quarters in the contemporary church—not to mention the history of the church in general.

Since the biblical data are either nonexistent or ambiguous at best, there are generally three ways to go on this matter: try to muster the evidence in such a way as to negate women in leadership offices; or try the opposite of mustering the evidence so as to support them; or admit that the New Testament simply does not explicitly teach on this matter and let Spirit gifting have the priority. I obviously opt for the last. In support of this view I would make a few observations.

First, the very fact that the biblical revelation does not show concern about the nature and structures of church order should catch our attention. This does not mean that there is not some evidence for certain kinds of structures, although the concept of offices per se is surely a debatable one. Nor does it deny that the leadership that does emerge in the New Testament documents was primarily male; it was indeed. But it does mean, to repeat, that its writers did not show sufficient interest in these matters as to offer explicit, intentional instruction on them.

In this regard, there is an often overlooked bit of evidence from Paul's writings that should strike us but apparently rarely does: Paul never addresses the leaders of the churches when he writes to them, either to take charge of a situation that has gone awry or to commend them for work well done.[21] Even in the Pastoral Epistles (1–2 Timothy and Titus), Paul writes to the churches of Ephesus and Crete through Timothy and Titus because these younger colleagues were there in *his* place, not because they were the permanent leaders. In both cases, the letters make it clear that he wants them to leave in due time (2 Tim 4:9; Titus 3:12), and in neither case is there any instruction for them to hand over to local leaders the task of correction.

The reason for this seems ready enough at hand; most of Paul's letters were addressed to his own churches, where he understood himself to have

---

[21]The puzzling apparent exception in Phil 1:1 is actually a case in point. He addresses the whole church "together with the overseers" (NIV), perhaps in this case because two of them were women who were not seeing eye to eye on things, and when he does address someone in the second person singular to oversee this matter (Phil 4:3), he is most likely speaking to one of his trusted itinerant companions, perhaps Luke. See Gordon D. Fee, *Paul's Letter to the Philippians*, NICNT (Grand Rapids, MI: Eerdmans, 1995), 66-69, 393-95.

the primary role of leadership. But even so, it is remarkable indeed that he never speaks to the leaders, or addresses his letters to the leaders, as those responsible for carrying out the directives. He does at times tell the community to "recognize" its leaders, but the language is in the form of verbs describing their activities rather than nouns that indicate their offices (see 1 Thess 5:12-13). Moreover, this is still the case in the one certain letter to a church (Romans) that he did *not* found and over which he apparently felt no sense of jurisdiction.

My point is a simple one. Concern over these matters seems to arise at a later time in the church (see, e.g., 3 John) and can be found in full bloom in the letters of Ignatius from the second decade of the second Christian century. But they are not part of Paul's writings. How is it, one wonders, that the later church can exercise so much energy in getting it right with regard to leadership, when the New Testament itself shows so little interest in this?

The reason finally for urging Spirit gifting as the key both to ministry and to leadership is that it recognizes the priority of gifting over gender; and that is certainly one biblical way of looking at things. It is not that Spirit gifting does not need to be discerned; indeed, it does. That, after all, is said in a very prescriptive way in 1 Thessalonians 5:19-22. But in the end there are three advantages to going this way biblically, rather than going the route of gathering a load of implicit information and making it normative for all times and places.

First, it is less authority driven and more ministry driven. The priority of Spirit gifting does not usually lead to asking, "Who's in charge around here?" Rather, it sets the whole community free to discern and encourage the giftings within the body, so that all may grow and be built up. Perhaps such a priority might lead to a more important question: Are we all ministering and being ministered to in love by the Spirit of Christ (Rom 12; 1 Cor 12–14)?

Second, it alleviates an age-old problem that often emerges in seminaries, where many male students assume they are gifted for ministry precisely because they meet the assumed first requirement: being male. To begin with gender rather than gifts and calling simply puts the emphasis at the wrong place, especially for the new-covenant people of God, where

there is no longer any priesthood (at least not as part of biblical revelation!). Further, God explicitly announced that he would pour out his Spirit
on *all* people for prophetic ministry (Joel 2:28-29), where *all* is explicitly
defined in categories of men/women, slave/free, and young/old.

Third, and most important, it opens the door to the possibility that
ministry is a two-way street. It seems a sad commentary on the church
and on its understanding of the Holy Spirit that "official" leadership and
ministry is allowed to come from only one half of the community of faith.
The New Testament evidence is that the Holy Spirit is gender inclusive,
gifting both men and women, and thus potentially setting the whole body
free for all the many parts to minister and in various ways to give leadership to the others.

Thus, my issue in the end is not a feminist agenda—an advocacy of
women in ministry. Rather, it is a Spirit agenda, a plea for the releasing of
the Spirit from our strictures and structures so that the church might minister to itself and to the world more effectively.

14

THE NATURE OF AUTHORITY IN THE NEW TESTAMENT

Walter L. Liefeld

● ● ● ● ●

AN UNDERSTANDING OF AUTHORITY in the New Testament is crucial to decisions regarding the ministry of women in the contemporary church. It is important to consider not only what kinds of authority existed in the New Testament churches but also the varieties of church government, styles of ministry, and forms of authority in contemporary churches so we can correctly apply the relevant Scriptures. Therefore, after a few brief observations on the present situation, I will deal with the biblical evidence and then return to the contemporary scene for proposed application.

INITIAL OBSERVATIONS ON THE ISSUES

Many Christians today seem overly concerned with the question, Who's in charge here? Others, more concerned with the involvement of all believers in ministry, easily overlook the importance of order. The rapid growth of independent churches today makes the problem more difficult to solve, because lines of authority are even less uniform from church to church. Also, the variety of books, articles, and seminars on leadership over the past several decades has resulted in a diversity of terms and goals.

We may distinguish authority from leadership on the one hand and from raw power on the other.[1] *Leadership* is used here as a general term to

---

[1]This is not an attempt to deal with the more precise vocabulary sociologists employ. A frequently quoted and useful treatment of such matters is Bengt Holmberg, *Paul and Power: The Structure of* ❧ *Authority in the Primitive Church as Reflected in the Pauline Epistles* (Philadelphia: Fortress, 1978).

describe personal influence that generates a positive response among followers. It is earned, it may be invited, and it is voluntarily accepted. *Authority*, in the sense under consideration, is a narrower term used to describe the right to command others and to enforce obedience. It is usually conferred, through appointment or election, on someone having a position in an organizational setting. *Power* is usually thought of as influence and authority that are seized rather than earned or voluntarily conferred. Often what begins as welcomed leadership or acknowledged authority is later transformed by an ambitious person into power or even tyranny.

Such power can be identified as existing in one or another form in some churches today, and Scripture condemns it.[2] The difference between leadership and authority is more difficult to assess. For example, a church might debate inviting a woman to teach an adult class of men and women under the assumption that 1 Timothy 2:12 forbids "teaching authority." But what they need to decide is whether a person who does that kind of teaching is thereby assuming a position of authority or simply exercising a spiritual ministry of leadership. Such an example, of course, could be multiplied, but it serves to indicate something of the gray area between these two words.

INSTANCES OF AUTHORITY IN THE NEW TESTAMENT

Examples of authority in the New Testament are numerous. The following are chosen because they involve authority language, background, principles, or instructions important for decisions in contemporary circumstances, especially where the authority of women is in question.

The authority of Jesus. Jesus taught, healed, and cast out demons with unique authority (Mt 7:29; Mk 1:22, 27; Lk 4:32, 36). Unlike the rabbis, Jesus did not cite the teachings of his predecessors for support. The Sermon on the Mount shows that Jesus interpreted the Old Testament Scriptures on his *own* authority. His authority to teach was backed up by his power to cast out demons and to heal people.[3] Jesus also had authority to forgive sins. Indeed, when his authority to do so for a paralyzed man is

---

[2]Third John 9 criticizes Diotrephes, "who loves to be first" and would "have nothing to do" with John.
[3]This is especially striking in Lk 4:32, 36. It is noteworthy that of over twenty occurrences of the term *authority* in Luke–Acts, this is the only one that is connected with teaching. See R. H. Stein, *Luke*, NAC (Nashville: Broadman, 1992), 162-63.

called into question, Jesus responds by healing the man (Mt 9:2-8; Mk 2:3-12; Lk 5:18-26).

The leaders in Jerusalem challenge Jesus' authority during the week preceding his crucifixion, and he refuses to answer them on their terms but tests their response to the authority of John the Baptist (Mt 21:23-27; Mk 11:27-33; Lk 20:1-8). Prior to his ascension Jesus issues the Great Commission, based on the fact that "all authority in heaven and on earth" has been given to him (Mt 28:18). At issue for us is what dimension of his unique authority, if any, was passed on to his followers.

The authority of the Twelve. It is common, when considering apostolic authority, to think of preaching and teaching. Yet in the instructions of the Lord Jesus to the Twelve, the only mention of *exousia* ("authority") relates to authority over demons. This is clear in the word order: "He appointed twelve that they might be with him and that he might send them out to preach and to have *authority to drive out demons*" (Mk 3:14-15 NIV). Clearly the authority was not connected with preaching but with exorcism.

Similarly, in the sending of the Twelve in Matthew's account (Mt 10:1), Jesus gave them "*authority to drive out evil spirits* and to heal every disease and sickness" (NIV). Instructions about preaching do not occur until Matthew 10:7, and authority is not mentioned in that verse. The same connections and emphases occur also in Luke 9:1-2 and Mark 6:7. In all these narratives the evidence is uniform that authority applies not to preaching but to exorcism and healing, and one rarely hears arguments about whether women should perform the latter.[4]

True, Peter was given the "keys" of the kingdom so as to "bind" or "loose" (Mt 16:19; 18:18); and there is implied authority here, even though the actual word is not used.[5] But in neither case is there a reference to teaching and preaching. The context of its use in Matthew 18 is church discipline, which has led to a wide variety of interpretations. Evangelicals tend to see the keys as opening the way to forgiveness and the kingdom by the

---

[4]The significance of this should not be overlooked. Along with our insistence on the Reformation elevation of the authority of Scripture, we have tended also to elevate the authority of *the preacher*. But the preacher, whose responsibility is to interpret the Word correctly, stands *under* the authority of that Word as it is being preached, along with those who hear.

[5]It should be noted that terminology of "binding and loosing" was used in rabbinic circles, though it was not until a later time that teaching authority was connected with it.

proclamation of the gospel (see also Jn 20:22-23, regarding Jesus' bestowal of the Holy Spirit in connection with forgiving sins).[6]

Important for the current discussion is that near the conclusion of his ministry Jesus specifically prohibited his disciples from adopting the authoritarian, domineering attitudes of Gentile rulers (Mt 20:25-28; Mk 10:42-45; Lk 22:25-26). The two verbs used to describe the forbidden attitude are *katexousiazō* ("have the right of control"; a verbal form of *exousia*) and *katakyrieuō* ("bring into subjection," "have mastery"). The authority given to the Twelve was over evil powers, not over the Lord's people.

We have seen thus far that there *are* aspects of Jesus' authority that were given to the Twelve, notably authority over demons, authority to heal diseases, and authority to proclaim forgiveness of sins (though not the same as Jesus' divine authority actually to forgive sins). By contrast, it is noteworthy that the Gospels do *not* say that Jesus' teaching authority was transferred to the Twelve.

Paul's apostolic authority. Paul's paternal authority over the churches he founded shows itself throughout his epistles and hardly needs illustration. But several things deserve special notice. First, he exercised authority over his coworkers (e.g., 2 Cor 8:16-24; Phil 2:19-30) and churches he himself had founded.[7] Second, he primarily uses *exousia* ("authority") language in a struggle with the Corinthians over "rights" (1 Cor 8:9; 9:1-18).[8] Third, with the exception of urgent and emotional cases, he was usually gentle in his authority, "urging" rather than commanding Timothy and Titus (1 Tim 1:3; 2 Cor 8:6) and not issuing a "command" to the Corinthians (2 Cor 8:8).[9] I will mention below the extension of his apostolic

---

[6]Another ongoing issue is whether this authority given to the disciples in these passages (especially regarding forgiveness) is now the province of clergy only or whether it is extended to all believers who proclaim the gospel of forgiveness. While an important question in its own right, it is not a part of contemporary discussion among evangelicals about the role of women, and therefore it is not pursued here. For a useful introduction, see D. A. Carson, "Matthew," in *The Expositor's Bible Commentary* (Grand Rapids, MI: Zondervan, 1984), 8:370-74.

[7]See his more deferential attitude toward Roman believers (Rom 1:8-13; 15:14-16). In terms of exercising authority over coworkers, at least those who were his traveling companions; he obviously did not have authority over a coworker such as Apollos (1 Cor 16:12).

[8]He also uses it of his apostolic authority in 2 Thess 3:9 and 2 Cor 10:8; 13:10.

[9]Of course, the volatility of Paul's emotions in his relations with the Corinthians and Galatians is well known. But in fact, his mood fluctuates dramatically in these letters between such volatility and tender appeal.

authority to Timothy and Titus in the Pastoral Epistles. Apart from that extension it is questionable whether a pastor can rightly assume such individual authority today.

The question of authority and church government. While there is clear evidence for the fact of early church governance, there is no express teaching on the subject in the New Testament. Nonetheless, several important passages need to be studied. One is Hebrews 13:17, "Obey your leaders and submit to them." Here the Greek word rendered "obey" (*peithō*) is quite fluid in meaning. In the active voice it carries the sense of "persuasion" and relation connotations, but in the middle and passive voices the meanings flow from "being persuaded" to "believing" and "trusting," and finally to the less common sense of "being won over as the result of persuasion" (BDAG), hence "obeying."

This last meaning is the one most translations choose for this verse, but it has been called into question. The reason is that there are very few texts where it appears to have that meaning. The rest of the New Testament evidence for the sense of "obey" for this verb is problematic, and there are only a few classical texts where the verb can be translated "obey."[10] The most we can say is that "obey" is only an *available* meaning *if* the context requires or strongly suggests it. For these reasons the NIV has rendered the imperative "Have confidence in your leaders and submit to their authority."

But attention must also be given to the *object* of this verb, "your leaders" (literally "those who lead"). In Matthew 2:6 the corresponding noun form clearly means "ruler" ("out of you will come a ruler," NIV), as it does in Acts 7:10, where it refers to Joseph as a ruler of Egypt. In nineteen occurrences of the noun form it can be rendered "governor."

All of this means that Hebrews 13:17 can certainly be offered as evidence of governing authority in the early church, bringing into question any idea that there is no authority in the church. However, it would also be improper

---

[10]The most probable instance where "obey" is a proper rendering of *peithesthai* is Jas 3:3 ("we put bits into the mouths of horses to make them obey us," NIV). Less certain is Gal 5:7 ("who cut in on you to keep you from obeying the truth?" NIV), where the NLT has "following the truth," since the plain sense of the question has to do with no longer *being persuaded by* the truth. So also in Rom 2:8, where the NRSV has "obey not the truth," the NIV has "reject the truth and follow evil." This is in contrast to the use of the verb *hypakouō* used, e.g., of the required obedience of children and slaves (but not wives) in Eph 6:1, 5 (cf. Col 3:20, 22). On classical texts, see *LSJ*, 1354.

to ignore its very moderate tone, with words that are clearly temperate in comparison to stronger terms in the same semantic domain. One needs only to consider the stronger terms for the authoritarian ways of worldly rulers used in Matthew 20:25 and Luke 22:25 to see the contrast between their kind of rule and the temperate authority of Christian leaders. This is consistent with the quality of gentleness required of overseers in 1 Timothy 3:4 (cf. Titus 1:7-8).

This discussion must also take into consideration Paul's use of *proistēmi*, a verb whose eight New Testament occurrences are all in his letters, six of them in the Pastoral Epistles. By the Hellenistic period this verb was used in two distinct ways: "to show concern/care for/devote oneself to" and "to be at the head of" (thus to exercise leadership). Its use in Titus 3:8, 14 unambiguously carries the former meaning. But its usage elsewhere is more ambiguous.[11]

Its two appearances outside the Pastoral Epistles (Rom 12:8; 1 Thess 5:12) occur in settings describing people who minister in some way. In 1 Thessalonians it sits between "those who work hard among you" and "who admonish you." Together the three phrases clearly refer to people in leadership roles. While most translations have something like "who are over you in the Lord" (NIV), the NIV has opted for "who care for you in the Lord" (Louw and Nida, "who guide you"). In any case, the verb lacks any connotation of authority in this passage.

In Romans 12:8 it occurs sixth in an ad hoc list of seven *charismata* ("spiritual gifts"). Even though it is often translated as having to do with "leadership" as such (NIV, NRSV, etc.), two factors suggest that here it also carries the sense of "providing care for": (1) it occurs sixth in a list whose first four items are prophesying, serving, teaching, and exhorting/encouraging, and (2) it rests at the end of the list between "giving generously" and "showing mercy." Hence the NIV is probably the correct one: "if it is to lead, do it diligently."

---

[11]It is of some importance to note here that in L&N, this verb appears under three domains ("guide," "be active in helping," "strive to") but not at all under "exercise authority," "rule," or "govern." For the clear distinctions between this verb and a verb of ruling, see Josephus, *Antiquities of the Jews* 14.196 (citing a letter from Julius Caesar regarding Hyrcanus): "That his children shall rule over [*archē*] the Jewish nation . . . and that the high priest, being also an ethnarch, shall be the protector [*proistetai*] of those Jews who are unjustly treated."

Authority in the Pastoral Epistles. That leads, then, to the four other occurrences of *proistēmi* in the Pastoral Epistles. Three of these (1 Tim 3:4-5, 12) relate to an elder's or deacon's relationship to his family: he must "manage [or 'guide' or 'care for'] his own family and see that his children obey him, and he must do so in a manner worthy of full respect" (1 Tim 3:4). When this idea is elaborated in 1 Timothy 3:5, Paul repeats the verb in the first clause, having to do with the family ("if anyone does not know how [to] *prostēnai* his own family"). But in the second clause, where it is applied to the church, Paul switches to a verb whose only meaning is "to care for" (how can he take care of [*epimelēsetai*] God's church?).[12] This suggests that this is also the nuance of the verb *proistēmi* in these verses.

The final instance of *proistēmi* is in 1 Timothy 5:17, which does have a stronger image of elders as leaders in the church. But it is especially problematic whether one can rightly translate this verb "rule" (as do NRSV, ESV, following the KJV), since that strong nuance would be exceptional given the verb's normal semantic domain.[13] The NIV moves in the direction of "guide" ("direct the affairs of the church"), which better fits both the established meaning of the verb and its other uses in 1 Timothy.

Such leaders are also "worthy of double honor" (NIV), especially those whose ministry is preaching and teaching.[14] What was noted above as to the meaning of *proistēmi* applies here as well. These persons brought the authoritative *Scriptures* to bear on the life of the church, and in that sense their words carried authority. As with 1 Thessalonians 5:12, this description shows evidence of a plurality of leadership, a group who are to be respected, esteemed, loved, and honored (probably with financial support).

The result of our biblical inquiry so far, therefore, is to discover that church leadership is described more in terms of guidance and caring for

---

[12]This verb occurs only two other times in the New Testament, both in the parable of the good Samaritan (Lk 10:34-35), where the Samaritan "took care of" the victim and then paid the innkeeper to "take care of" him.

[13]BDAG, which includes the usage in this verse under the general heading "to exercise a position of leadership, *rule, direct, be at the head (of),*" does not distinguish readily between leadership and ruling, a distinction Louw and Nida think is necessary (L&N 1:466, par. 36.1).

[14]The word translated "especially" in 1 Tim 5:17 can also be translated "I mean," in which case it indicates that all the leaders in mind preached and taught, not only a select group who are chosen to receive the benefit indicated.

than of exercising authority, an important point when considering whether women should or should not be church leaders.

It should also be noted, however, that in other places in the Pastoral Epistles the tone is somewhat different. In 1 Timothy 1:3 Paul tells Timothy to *command* (not just urge) certain people to stop teaching false doctrines. But it is equally clear that Timothy is *not* functioning as an elder or local pastor but as Paul's own apostolic representative, carrying Paul's full authority in the church. The verb Paul uses for "command," *parangellō*, occurs thirty-two times in the New Testament (mainly in the Gospels and Acts), five of which are in 1 Timothy. This letter also has two out of five New Testament occurrences of the noun form of that verb. And while the verbal form of another word that means "command" (*epitassō*) is not used at all in the Pastoral Letters, three of seven occurrences of the *noun* form (*epitagō*) do occur in these epistles. The first occurrence is in 1 Timothy 1:1, where it refers to Paul's apostleship as being "by the command of God." This indicates how important the idea of authority is in the Pastoral Letters; but the authority to command is vested in the apostle Paul, not in the local leaders.

Thus, Timothy and Titus were responsible to transmit Paul's authoritative commands to those churches. But nowhere are they told to transfer or transmit the "commanding" to others in the church. Indeed, the idea of transmission occurs only in 2 Timothy 2:2, and here Timothy is told to "entrust" the *content* of what Paul has taught to persons "who will be able to teach others as well." Today the appropriate equivalent of these younger delegates representing the apostle Paul in the churches is not a local pastor but the canonical New Testament containing Paul's own words.

Specifically gender-related passages. There are two passages regarding the relationship between men and women in the New Testament that contain a word in the *exousia* ("authority") word group. One is 1 Corinthians 7:1-5, which deals with the sexual relationship between husband and wife. This is a significant passage for those advocating exclusively male leadership, given that they argue the male-female relationship *in marriage* is basic to the proper role relationship of men and women *in the church*. First Corinthians 7:4 begins, "The wife does not have authority over [*exousiazei*] her own body but yields it to her husband" (NIV). Then it continues,

"In the same way, the husband does not have authority [same verb] over his own body but yields it to his wife" (NIV). Thus, in the most intimate aspect of marriage the authority of husband and wife is equal.

The other gender-related passage containing the word *exousia* is 1 Corinthians 11:11-12. In this passage about women's head coverings, scholars disagree about the exegesis and the nature of authority in view. Does the woman have authority (the right) to pray and prophesy, or authority (control) over her head? One thing is less debatable; the use of a head covering is *not* a "sign" that the woman is *under* authority.[15] For our present purposes it is sufficient to note that however the head-covering issue may be decided, this passage assumes not silence but vocal participation of women in prayer and prophesying in public worship.

On the much-discussed 1 Timothy 2:12, see chapter eleven in this book. Here I simply note the following. This sentence does not contain *exousia* or *exousiazō* but rather *authenteō*, a word that occurs only here in the New Testament. In *A Greek-English Lexicon of the New Testament and Other Early Christian Literature* this verb is defined as "to assume a stance of independent authority, give orders to, dictate to." Research on this word continues. Church decisions concerning the extent of authority to be granted women are often made on the assumption that 1 Timothy 2:12 forbids women from ever having *any* authority. But the *Greek-English Lexicon of the New Testament and Other Early Christian Literature* definition of the verb, in addition to sound exegetical reasons, warns us to question that assumption. These considerations, to say nothing of the whole context of 1 Timothy, including 1 Timothy 2, are so complex that a broad application of that term to forbid any kind of authority is highly questionable. As many have rightly concluded, Paul's instructions (or his *practice* at that time, since no command is given) most likely had a specific and limited objective in the circumstances existing at that time.

Our task, then, is to determine what, if any, circumstances today correspond sufficiently to those in Ephesus at the time 1 Timothy was written

---

[15]Among useful recent discussions of this are Linda L. Belleville, "Women in Ministry," in *Two Views on Women in Ministry*, ed. James R. Beck and Craig L. Blomberg (Grand Rapids, MI: Zondervan, 2001), 105n54; and Craig Blomberg, *1 Corinthians*, NIVAC (Grand Rapids, MI: Zondervan, 1994), 212. See also Gordon D. Fee, "Praying and Prophesying in the Assemblies: 1 Corinthians 11:2-16," in the present volume.

to justify forbidding authority to women now. Although quests for a background to 1 Timothy 2:12 have yielded different results, a consideration of the doctrinal concerns of the Pastorals, as well as of Paul's teachings and missionary concerns expressed elsewhere, shows us that *our* ecclesiastical practices ought not stand against the ministry of all believers, including the leadership of women.

ORDER AND STRUCTURE IN NEW TESTAMENT CHURCHES

Discussion about authority in today's church can easily move in the wrong direction. It often starts with one's own church structure and with assumptions that are more characteristic of our times than of the first century. It then moves back to the New Testament, seeking to fit its teachings into our contemporary structures. However, the proper direction is the reverse, to start with the nature of churches and ministry and the instructions to churches in the New Testament, as far as that can be determined. Then we should submit our contemporary styles of worship and ministry to the New Testament for possible correction and reforming.

Organization, ministry, and leadership. Churches in New Testament times met in homes, often with several congregations in a city. The homes were usually small, though not necessarily tiny, since rooms in larger homes could accommodate more people than the average living or family room today. Church organization probably differed somewhat from place to place, but as noted above, churches founded by Paul, at least, had plural leadership by elders. The early church had no equivalent to the Old Testament priesthood, nor is there evidence in the New Testament that one person with special authorization presided at the Lord's Supper.[16]

Leadership roles were quite different from those of today. Apostles, prophets, and teachers are given pride of place (NIV "first of all") in 1 Corinthians 12:28. But that is very likely primarily a temporal ordering, not structural, and there is no firm dividing line between them and the workers of miracles, those with gifts of healing, and so on.[17] Interestingly, those

---

[16]Both 1 Pet 2:5, 9 and Rev 1:6; 5:10 echo Ex 19:5-6, where Israel (and now the church) is to function as God's priesthood for the nations.

[17]That is, this is the chronological order of the church's founding and its subsequent growth. See Gordon D. Fee, *The First Epistle to the Corinthians*, NICNT (Grand Rapids, MI: Eerdmans, 1987), 619-20; cf. Blomberg, *1 Corinthians*, 247. This also best explains why, in using building

with gifts "of guidance" (NIV) are not at the top.[18] The point of the whole chapter, after all, is that each needs the other. Apostles unquestionably were acknowledged as the leading figures in the church; but no provision is made in the New Testament for their succession. People designated as pastors (Eph 4:11) functioned *within* congregations, not above them. The upshot is that we are given ministry designations, which have been carefully scrutinized (especially in Eph 4:11), but no certain definitions of their role or rank.

With the exception of the Pastoral Epistles, addressed to Paul's apostolic delegates, Paul's letters are addressed to the churches themselves. None is addressed to a single leader, nor is one person ever spoken to as being in charge of the church. At Philippi the overseers and deacons (both plural) are also addressed, but not first (Phil 1:1). Eventually there was more than one congregation (house church) in a city, and it is not possible in such cases to know with certainty from the biblical references whether every congregation had more than one elder.

This is also the picture presented in Acts. Although Peter is the early spokesman for the church in Jerusalem, he is clearly presented as one among equals (Acts 2:14; 3:3-4; 4:13). The first group decision (Acts 6:1-6) is by the Twelve, with the specifics left to others. Similarly, in Acts 15, James "leads" the council toward a decision, but the decision itself is by "the apostles and elders, with the whole church" (Acts 15:25), and the letter that was circulated adds that the Holy Spirit was in accord with the decision. At the local level we are told (Acts 14:23) that Paul and Barnabas appointed elders (plural) in *each* church (*kat' ekklēsian*).

The letters to the seven churches in Revelation 2–3 are a special case, and the significance of the angels of the churches is debated, some thinking they are pastors—but the evidence for this is especially slender. Some think the "lady" addressed in 2 John was the host and therefore the leader of the church in her home, but her position is unclear. Third John is

---

imagery (household/temple) for the church in Eph 2:19-22, Paul speaks of apostles and prophets as the foundation.

[18]The NIV's use (prior to 2011) of *administration* seems to be an anachronism. See Fee, *First Epistle to the Corinthians*, 622; cf. Ben Witherington, *Conflict and Community in Corinth* (Grand Rapids, MI: Eerdmans, 1995), 261.

addressed to Gaius precisely because Diotrephes wanted to be prominent, but Gaius's own role is not described.

The role of teachers. Because the modern term *teaching authority* is prevalent in discussions of women's role in the church, we need to look briefly at teaching in the New Testament church. Most relevant to the issue of authority is the mention of teachers as recognized church leaders in Romans 12:7; 1 Corinthians 12:28; and Ephesians 4:11; but in each list they appear no higher than third. Furthermore, there is no verbal connection in the New Testament between the word *teacher* and the vocabulary of *authority*. Hence the very term *teaching authority*, as though authority were vested in the teacher rather than in what is taught, is an anachronism when we are discussing teaching/teachers in the New Testament.

What is often overlooked in these discussions is that women traditionally were not welcomed as teachers in either Greek or Jewish society.[19] To restrict the ministry of teaching to men would not have been surprising in the world of the New Testament. If missionaries, like Paul, were to be all things to all people to win them to Christ (1 Cor 9:22), public proclamation of Christian teachings would ideally be done by men.

The case of Priscilla is debated, but it seems specious and unreasonable to argue that hers was not legitimate teaching because she instructed Apollos in her home and not in a church service or because she is said to have "explained" the "Way of God" rather than to have taught the Scriptures (Acts 18:26). After all, the church *met* in her home (Rom 16:3-5), and in any case, how does one explain something without teaching? "The Way of God" was a recognizable phrase for God's truth and the gospel in those early days when the New Testament Scriptures were not yet completed.

The limitations on a woman's teaching and promoting Christianity in New Testament times can be understood better when we notice that although the Gospels show that women were the first at the empty tomb, Paul does not cite them as witnesses to the resurrection. This reflects the historical situation in which a woman's testimony was not considered reliable.

---

[19]James G. Sigountos and Myron Shank, "Public Roles for Women in the Pauline Church: A Reappraisal of the Evidence," *JETS* 26 (1983): 283-95. Of course, the Romans were not as uniform and restrictive regarding women, and actually the aggressive enterprise of some women became a threat to the men. However, I believe the evidence of restriction in the ancient world is broad and strong enough to be factored into our hermeneutics.

In summary, teaching was a widespread ministry in the early church, often carried on mutually but with a clearly distinguished group of leaders at the forefront. The Word was their authority, but in the earliest days before that Word was available, it was the word of the witnesses and teachers that had to be relied on as authoritative. This is probably relevant to 1 Timothy 2:12.[20]

The role of elders. Although Acts 14:23 tells us that at the beginning Paul and Barnabas appointed elders in each church, this language does not emerge in Paul's letters until the very end (1 Tim 4:14; 5:17; Titus 1:5). That they were appointed (Titus 1:5) shows that they were a clearly delineated group. In a context such as this, the verb "appointed" (*kathistēmi*) can indicate the conferring of a position, status, or responsibility (see Mt 24:45, 47; 25:21, 23; Lk 12:14, 42, 44; Acts 6:3; 7:10, 27, 35; Heb 5:1; 7:28; 8:3).

It thus seems clear that eldership was a position with a degree of authority exceeding that of just leadership, but with two caveats. First, there is no evidence of an individual elder who acted with autonomous authority. Eldership was plural, whether in a church or in a town. This should be a pertinent consideration for those who believe the Bible prohibits a woman from having authority in the church. For if elders act in concert on administrative matters, the presence of a woman among the elders would not grant her individual authority any more than it would a man. Second, elders were shepherds, not a board of directors.[21]

---

[20]It may be noted in connection with the topic of teaching that the Catholic Church has a clear position on teaching authority. Their theologians deal with the theological contours of the faith, but it is the pastoral wing of the church (bishops and the pope) that declares what must be believed. It is in this connection that Catholics employ such terms as "teaching authority" or "magisterium." Thus, for example, although Sister Agnes Cunningham holds the honor of having been the first female president of the Catholic Theological Society of America, she could never become a bishop or priest and thereby have authority to declare what the church must believe. This comparison, made respectfully, illustrates the importance of teaching authority in the Catholic Church. Protestant pastors who claim an office and a teaching authority that others do not have are conforming in part to the Catholic position.

[21]Historically (as well as biblically) elders and bishops have correctly been designated as shepherds (Greek *poimēn*, Latin *pastor*). According to Paul's charge to the Ephesian elders, that is their commission ("keep watch over yourselves and over all the flock, of which the Holy Spirit has made you overseers," Acts 20:28). Cf. 1 Pet 5:2-3: "Be shepherds of God's flock that is under your care, watching over them—not because you must, but because you are willing, as God wants you to be; not pursuing dishonest gain, but eager to serve; not lording it over those entrusted to you, but being examples to the flock" (NIV). Being a shepherd certainly implies the feeding of the sheep with the authoritative Word of God; equally, it expressly excludes lording it over them.

On the other hand, nowhere does Paul say that individuals or groups possessing an ongoing authority made the decisions. In his earlier letters the local church as a whole was to carry out Paul's instructions (1 Cor 5:4-5). The rhetoric in 1 Corinthians 6:1-6 allows for the possibility of one person acting as judge, but the whole church is being brought to task for failure to handle this problem from within.[22] Apparently whatever role the elders played, it would be to lead the whole church in the decision-making process.

Ordination. It is increasingly recognized that while ordination is significant, it is not found in its usual modern sense in the New Testament or in early Christianity. The practice as we know it developed toward the third Christian century. Although the laying of hands on Timothy (1 Tim 4:14; 2 Tim 1:6) is sometimes cited as an ordination, several facts militate against this: (1) what is conferred on Timothy is a "gift" (*charisma*), not a status; (2) that gift is not an office—the gift is "in" him and can be "fan[ned] into flame" (2 Tim 1:6); (3) it is not a Christian counterpart to rabbinic ordination because, among other reasons, that did not involve the laying on of hands.[23]

Whatever else, the laying on of hands was not an appointment to an office but corporate recognition of a ministry already in progress, which is the point of 1 Timothy 5:22. It is equally so in Acts 13:3 in the case of Barnabas and Paul, who were already engaged in Christian ministry. Theirs was not a lifetime empowerment to an office but a commissioning for a specific missionary trip that was declared completed in Acts 14:26.

That the New Testament church did not practice ordination as commonly understood today is significant, because spiritual authority has long

---

Leadership is commanded; domination is forbidden. This surely accords with Jesus' words, referred to earlier, prohibiting the disciples from dominating other believers in a worldly way.

[22]The NIV et al. suggest that the church is to appoint judges to handle this matter, but it is altogether unlikely that *kathizete* is an imperative here, coming at the end of Paul's sentence as it does. Therefore, its more likely sense is "to seek for a ruling" from someone (as in Josephus, *Antiquities of the Jews* 13.75). See Fee, *First Epistle to the Corinthians*, 236; cf. Blomberg, *1 Corinthians*, 117n3.

[23]There are various instances of the laying on of hands in Scripture. They are connected with the identifications of one's successor (such as Joshua, Num 27:23), the setting apart of the Levites (Num 8:10), the establishment of the group to distribute food to the Grecian widows (Acts 6:6), numerous acts of healing, and other acts that are not liturgical or official.

been connected with ordination.[24] In summary, the issues surrounding ordination are complex, but it is extremely doubtful that a woman's ordination or nonordination should determine the bounds of her ministry and authority.

The use of titles and the term office. The use of titles has always been a means of portraying superiority and authority. Jesus said,

> But you are not to be called "Rabbi," for you have only one Master and you are all brothers. And do not call anyone on earth "father," for you have one Father, and he is in heaven. Nor are you to be called "teacher," for you have one Teacher, the Messiah. The greatest among you will be your servant. For those who exalt themselves will be humbled, and those who humble themselves will be exalted. (Mt 23:8-12)

Along with titles, a perception of authority can be conveyed by the use of the term *office*, as in "pastoral office" or "teaching office." But *office* is not a New Testament church term. The concept of office can be traced to the use of this English word in the KJV, which gave the impression that it is in the Greek text; but in none of the passages in which the KJV has the word *office* (except concerning the Jewish priesthood) does any word meaning "office" occur in the Greek.[25]

Considerable debate has taken place during the past few decades over the difference between office and function. That debate is beyond the focus of this chapter; the point to be made is that our common use of the non-biblical term *office* enhances perceived authority. To be sure, it can be argued that the terms used in the New Testament to describe leadership in the early church together form a mosaic that could be described by the

---

[24]While much of the contemporary discussion over what authority women may or may not have centers on eldership, teaching, preaching, and the pastorate (especially the senior pastorate), historically the issues of authority included such functions as presiding at Communion and performing baptisms. Early in Christian history it was argued by some that women could not be ordained because for a woman to be at a raised altar presiding over the sacrament of Communion during her period was unthinkable.

[25]The KJV "I magnify mine office" (Rom 11:13) represents *diakonia*, "service." "All members have not the same office" (Rom 12:4 KJV) renders *praxis*, "function or work." "Office of a bishop" (1 Tim 3:1 KJV) is *episkopē*, "superintendence." "Use the office of a deacon" (1 Tim 3:10 KJV) renders the verb *diakonei*, "serve" (also in 1 Tim 3:13). Two instances where the word *office* actually *is* appropriate are "priest's office" (Lk 1:8-9 KJV) and "office of the priesthood" (Heb 7:5 KJV), which are renderings of the verb *hierateuō*, meaning to serve as a priest, and *hierateia*, which refers to service, office, or position of a priest.

general term *office*. However, such a term is ours, not the biblical authors', and it can be misleading. Function is more important than office.[26]

CONTEMPORARY EXPRESSIONS OF AUTHORITY

De jure, de facto, and **de senso** *authority.* If decisions regarding authority in the contemporary church are to be considered biblically legitimate (= de jure) for the church, they must derive from biblical principles and precedents such as those discussed above. Yet it would be unrealistic to ignore that often individuals have an actual (de facto) rule over others in a setting where Scripture does not grant them de jure authority. An aura of de facto authority, for example, sometimes marks the founders of the congregation. Their status is such that others would not make major decisions without consulting them even if they do not hold an elected or appointed position at the time. Status in the church is also often granted to people with advanced degrees, community leaders, business leaders, the wealthy, and others with social standing.

Further, the *perception* of authority has changed in recent years. The past half-century has seen the growth of lay-centered and lay-empowered movements. Paradoxically, however, the prominence of today's senior pastor and preacher has tended to increase the perceived (or what we might call *de senso*) authority of the person in the pulpit over those in the congregation. In some cases, the pastor builds on that perceived authority even to the point of exercising veto power over all church board or congregational decisions. One pastor recently asserted that to oppose him was to oppose God. If one views megachurches as "apostolic," it is just a short step to considering the pastor an apostle with authority like that of the New Testament apostles.[27]

It is extremely difficult for many to imagine a woman in such an authoritative role. It must be said, however, that strong leadership is important and necessary in such churches, and it is due to such leadership that those

---

[26]Two of the studies that deserve consideration regarding office are R. Y. K. Fung, "Function or Office? A Survey of the New Testament Evidence," *Evangelical Review of Theology* 8, no. 1 (1984): 16-39; and Holmberg, *Paul and Power*.

[27]See C. Peter Wagner, *The New Apostolic Churches* (Ventura, CA: Gospel Light, 1998). This seems to be jargon in some charismatic circles for those who have founded megachurches, but such usage has its obvious downside.

churches exist. The questionable perception of authority I speak of is not inevitable but depends on the attitude of the pastor.

Further practical issues. I have already noted the different types of authority that can exist in religious contexts. The sociological literature on power would open up even further ways to examine the subject. But there are other issues that confront Christians who think it is necessary to limit the authority of women.

Given the biblical evidence, is there actually any clear locus of authority in the church? Our survey has shown that the answer must be positive. Without clear, wise, and gentle authority there can be no guarding of doctrine, shepherding of the flock, or exercising of discipline.[28] But churches and denominations differ as to where authority resides, and the possible role of women will differ in each structure, if women's authority is deemed limited by those churches.

If authority is in the church itself as a "committee of the whole," do women have a vote? Theoretically, in a church with a majority of women, they could make the difference in hiring or firing a pastor, thereby having ultimate authority over the pastor.

If authority resides in a leadership group such as a church board, the scenario could be the same in voting if women are in the majority on that board (we lack biblical evidence that an individual elder has personal authority; the authority seems to lie in the group as a whole, and the authority is therefore always plural).

It is increasingly common, especially in Baptist and independent churches, for the senior pastor to have ultimate, perhaps absolute, authority, especially if that person is the founding pastor. A woman is rarely found in that position.

Sometimes the circumstances and questions are even more complex. What about the paradox that sometimes exists when a church forbids women to become elders but includes female deacons on a church board

---

[28]The assertion that "it is the church that possesses authority and not particular individuals (or positions, for that matter)" (Belleville, "Women in Ministry," 106n20) is certainly true with regard to the church's authority over external forces of evil, and it is realized with greater or less success in congregational-type churches that practice government by a simple majority of the whole. But government by the whole is hard to imagine as being functional in a church of any size. Some kind of internal authority seems not only biblical but also necessary to prevent chaos.

that has veto power over the elders' proposals? And, concerning the role of a senior pastor, how far does the pastor's de jure leadership actually *enforce* compliance of staff or congregation? Another issue is whether the preaching of a sermon is an authoritative act, because that logically carries the implication that the congregation *must* obey the imperatives *in the sermon*, not just those in the Scripture being quoted. Further, churches may differ as to whether baptism and presiding at the Lord's Supper are acts of authority that should be restricted to ordained clergy. This is de jure in some denominations but undocumented and therefore de facto in some churches.

It is understood, of course, that a church or denomination in a democratic society has the right to decide on its own organizational arrangement, but it also has the responsibility to be open to the question of scriptural precedence. A further complexity exists regarding spiritual authority outside the local church. This can exist in several forms, including within denominational, missionary, and parachurch organizations, but these will not be examined here.

CONCLUDING OBSERVATIONS: FOUR DISTORTIONS

There are four instances of distortion that emerge from the picture of the contemporary church as we compare it with the church in the New Testament. Women are usually excluded from leadership on the basis of these distortions, not on the basis of New Testament teaching itself.

Formalization. The legitimate and functionally efficient roles of leaders prescribed and portrayed in the New Testament, such as those of pastor, teacher, and elder, have been formalized through an overstressing of their authority. Thus, we have developed the artificial and exclusive office of pastor, teaching office, and office of elder. We have also changed the legitimate and necessary recognition of leaders and missionaries, often expressed by the laying on of hands in ordination, into a ceremony that elevates the individual and bestows privileges not envisioned in the New Testament.

Normalization. The distinctive and indeed extraordinary authority of New Testament apostles has sometimes been assumed by pastors as *their* normal right and as the legitimatization of their control over the church. But such a transfer has no biblical basis of any kind.

Generalization. The particular kind of authority described by the word *authenteō* and the kind of teaching that would have been shameful and offensive if done by women in the New Testament world has been generalized in our churches to cover all authoritative roles and all teaching of men by women. They are therefore excluded from ministries in a way Paul would probably not have intended for his churches.

Minimalization. Along with the above distortions is the tendency to view the ministries in which women served in the New Testament as less important than they were. Thus, the teaching of Priscilla and her husband Aquila is reduced in its significance. Likewise minimized are the ministries of Phoebe as a deacon and as Paul's benefactor, and of Junia as an apostle (Rom 16:1, 7).[29]

Finally, we do well to remember that all church authority is under Christ, under the Scriptures, and under the leading of the Holy Spirit. The purpose of authority is to glorify the Lord and to facilitate his mission in the world. Elders and pastors are primarily shepherds, not bosses. Leadership is a form of servanthood. When we become obsessed with the question, Who's in charge? we may obscure the more important question, Who is a servant?

---

[29]On these passages see Linda L. Belleville, "Women Leaders in the Bible," in the present volume.

15

IMAGE OF GOD AND DIVINE PRESENCE

A CRITIQUE OF GENDER ESSENTIALISM

Christa L. McKirland

• • • • •

INTRODUCTION

I have a daughter and a son. Sometimes I dress my daughter in blue and my son in pink. Sometimes, my daughter plays with male superhero dolls, and when my infant son gets a bit older, I will give him some of those same dolls plus Wonder Woman and Rey from Star Wars. More importantly, as they grow up, my husband and I will teach both of them that they can pursue any vocation—president, pastor, police officer, or whatever.[1] We will teach them both to be responsible for their own spiritual lives. We will encourage them both to be leaders or followers depending on the situation. Are any of these actions or practices morally problematic? Some would say yes, especially if they hold to a certain understanding of sex and gender that collapses maleness and femaleness into prescriptive expressions of masculinity and femininity. By contrast, this chapter will suggest a

---

[1] As this volume is an explicit response to *Recovering Biblical Manhood and Womanhood* and subsequent works since then, John Piper will be my main interlocuter, although the implications extend beyond his line of argument. I have specifically chosen these vocations because John Piper has claimed that these are inappropriate jobs for a woman to have. See John Piper, "Should Women Be Police Officers?," Desiring God, August 13, 2015, www.desiringgod.org/interviews /should-women-be-police-officers; "Why a Woman Shouldn't Run for Vice President, but Wise People May Still Vote for Her," Desiring God, November 2, 2008, www.desiringgod.org/articles /why-a-woman-shouldnt-run-for-vice-president-but-wise-people-may-still-vote-for-her.

scriptural account of the significance of maleness and femaleness that rejects rigid characterizations of masculinity and femininity.[2]

In order to situate the significance of maleness and femaleness, this chapter will proceed in three parts: first, to propose a Christocentric theological anthropology based on a particular understanding of the *imago Dei*; second, to articulate the logical flaws of gender essentialism that undermine this Christocentric interpretation; and third, to conclude with thoughts on the significance of maleness and femaleness in light of this Christocentricity and apart from a gender-essentialist interpretation.[3] Ultimately, I urge readers to see that a christologically grounded conception of the *imago Dei* reveals that the divine intention for men and women is the same: to be intimately united to God (through the indwelling Holy Spirit) as they become more like the true image, Jesus Christ. In light of this eschatological telos, they are also meant to have the ongoing human function of royal priests. Due to this inclusive priesthood, humanity's glory-giving capacities are far less about following a prescribed, created list and far more about following the exalted, uncreated Lord.[4] Therefore, this chapter seeks to elucidate the priorities of Scripture regarding humanity's initial and eschatological purpose in order to more accurately situate the significance of maleness and femaleness. Before moving into the three major sections of the chapter, a brief overview of gender essentialism and what is at stake is necessary.

OVERVIEW OF GENDER ESSENTIALISM

In some influential strands of Christian theology, the deeply flawed concept of hierarchical gender essentialism has developed. Gender essentialism is here understood as "the belief that males and females are born with distinctively different natures, determined biologically rather than

---

[2]Further, alongside the contributors to this volume, I recognize the Bible (Hebrew Bible and New Testament) to be the authoritative norm for my argument and will be focusing especially on Gen 1–2 and briefly on Eph 5 due to space constraints.

[3]This Christocentric theological anthropology will necessarily be brief for such a short chapter; however, a longer defense of this anthropology will be forthcoming in my future work with Baker Academic Press.

[4]For an example of a painstakingly detailed list of what women can and cannot do, see Wayne Grudem, "But What Should Women Do in the Church?," *CBMW News* 1, no. 2 (November 1995): 1-17.

culturally. This involves an equation of gender and sex."[5] In other words, men and women are *essentially* different on the basis of being a man or a woman.[6] By equating gender and sex, there are male persons who are meant to act like men (masculinity), and there are female persons who are meant to act like women (femininity). This would typically be discussed in terms of sex (biological givenness) and gender (cultural convention for how to express biological givenness).[7] Instead of recognizing that biological sex and gender expression can be separated, for gender essentialism, male or female "natures" determine the proper masculine or feminine role a person is supposed to perform. When gender essentialism is operating, especially in a Christian context, the result is that being male morally requires acting in a masculine way and that being female morally requires acting in a feminine way.[8] Specifically, men (because they are male) should act as leaders, initiators, and providers, while women (because they are female) should be followers, nurturers, and provided for—and to do anything less not only violates what it means to be male or female, but violates the very will of God. Since sex and gender are conflated, so are natures and roles.[9]

Wayne Grudem and John Piper explicitly connect roles and natures: "We are concerned not merely with the behavioral roles of men and women

---

[5]"Gender essentialism," in *Oxford Reference*, accessed June 22, 2019, www.oxfordreference.com /view/10.1093/oi/authority.20110803095846595.

[6]There can also be strong and weak forms of gender essentialism. For instance, a weak form may be defined in terms of a set of propensities (e.g., the property of being strongly inclined to exhibit stereotypically masculine behavior) while allowing that actualizing these essential propensities is not required for flourishing *as* a man or *as* woman. The weaker the form, the less prone to the concerns listed below—although determining what is masculine or feminine still raises questions about the consistency of this view. It should be noted that egalitarians can also hold to gender essentialism as part of an effort to recognize the unique contributions and value that women bring to the church and home; however, in its strong form especially, it too comes at a high cost. The focus of this chapter will be on critiquing strong forms of gender essentialism, especially those of a hierarchical sort. Strong hierarchical gender essentialism sees maleness and femaleness as fixed, and thus the hierarchical roles men and women are allowed to perform are also fixed. When "gender essentialism" is used, therefore, this is the specific version under critique.

[7]In most current academic discourse, sex is also understood as constructed, and this chapter pushes against that understanding.

[8]For more specifics on the "morally defined sex roles," see George Alan Rekers, "Psychological Foundations for Rearing Masculine Boys and Feminine Girls," in *RBMW*, 2nd ed., 310.

[9]Rebecca Merrill Groothuis addresses this conflation in "Equal in Being, Unequal in Role: Challenging the Logic of Woman's Subordination" in the present volume.

but also with the underlying natures of manhood and womanhood themselves."[10] When asked whether gender roles will persist in heaven, Piper responds, "I think that our personhood is so wrapped up in our gender, or you could say our gender is wrapped around our personhood, that if we were stripped of our maleness or femaleness, we would be unrecognizable."[11] Consequently, instead of competency, maturity, and gifting determining roles, "*deeper realities* rooted in how we differ as men and women" should be determinative for human function.[12] Since these roles are understood as fixed (essence based), so are these functions, and for those in this school of thought, nothing less than God's eternal glory is at stake, should these distinctions become blurred.

However, the stakes increase for those who see maleness and femaleness as central to the grand narrative of God's redemption of humanity. The primary scriptural rationale for this form of gender essentialism comes from Genesis 1–2 and Ephesians 5. The interpretation of the Genesis text equates the *imago Dei* (image of God) with maleness and femaleness. Since the *imago* is used to ground the meaning of personhood, personhood is thereby understood as male or female. Maleness and femaleness become the two ways of being human, and thus the meaning of masculinity and femininity is then imported into the interpretation to make sense of this gendered *imago Dei*. Piper and Grudem claim, "Male and female

---

[10]John Piper and Wayne Grudem, "50 Crucial Questions: Gender, Culture, and Hermeneutics," CBMW, February 28, 2014, https://cbmw.org/2014/02/28/50-crucial-questions-gender-culture -and-hermeneutics/. "One of the theses of this book is that the natural fitness of man and woman for each other in marriage is rooted in something more than anatomy" (*RBMW*, 107). Such thinking is consistent among other theological gender essentialists as well. See Michelle A. Gonzalez, "Hans Urs von Balthasar and Contemporary Feminist Theology," *Theological Studies* 65, no. 3 (September 2004); John Piper, "For Single Men and Women (and the Rest of Us)," in *RBMW*, 29-30; Piper, "A Vision of Biblical Complementarity: Manhood and Womanhood Defined According to the Bible," in *RBMW*.

[11]John Piper, "Biblical Womanhood in 5 Minutes," Desiring God, March 7, 2013, www.desiring god.org/interviews/biblical-womanhood-in-five-minutes#full-audio. This also builds on theologian Emil Brunner's thoughts that "Our sexuality penetrates to the deepest metaphysical ground of our personality. As a result, the physical differences between the man and the woman are a parable of psychical and spiritual differences of a more ultimate nature." See Emil Brunner, *Das Gebot und die Ordnungen: Entwurf einer protestantisch-theologischen ethik* (Tübingen: Mohr Siebeck, 1933), 358. Cited in Paul K. Jewett, *Man as Male and Female* (Grand Rapids, MI: Eerdmans, 1975), 173.

[12]John Piper, "Do Men Owe Women a Special Kind of Care?," Desiring God, November 6, 2017, www.desiringgod.org/articles/do-men-owe-women-a-special-kind-of-care, emphasis added.

personhood, with some corresponding role distinctions, is rooted in God's act of creation (Genesis 1 and 2) before the sinful distortions of the *status quo* were established (Genesis 3)."[13] Consequently, men and women are seen to have beneficial differences, though the woman is specifically a "complement to her husband and a necessary completing part of his being."[14]

Beyond the importance of men and women's complementary differences, maleness and femaleness are seen as creaturely indicators of a theological reality. Piper and Grudem are not alone in seeing the male-female distinction as symbolizing a greater cosmic reality and intention. Thinkers such as Karl Barth, Hans Urs von Balthasar, and John Paul II all maintain the equal dignity of man and woman while seeing their difference as critical to understanding the divine life and human purpose.[15] For all five of these men, the Ephesians 5 text regarding Christ and the church is critical to their understanding of the significance of maleness and femaleness.[16] Piper makes this explicit:

> The ultimate meaning of true womanhood is this: it is a distinctive calling of God to display the glory of his Son in ways that would not be displayed if there were no womanhood. If there were only generic persons and not male and female, the glory of Christ would be diminished in the world. When God described the glorious work of his Son as the sacrifice of a husband for his bride, he was telling us *why* he made us male and female. He made us this way so that our maleness and femaleness would display more fully the glory of his Son in relation to his blood-bought bride.[17]

For Piper, there is male and a right way to be male (manhood/masculinity), and there is female and a right way to be female (womanhood/femininity).

Piper and Grudem's language of male and female natures and personhood sufficiently demonstrates the centrality of maleness and femaleness

---

[13]Piper and Grudem, "50 Crucial Questions."

[14]Dorothy Patterson, in *RBMW*, 2nd ed., 374.

[15]Agneta Sutton, "The Complementarity and Symbolism of the Two Sexes: Karl Barth, Hans Urs von Balthasar and John Paul II," *New Blackfriars* 87, no. 1010 (July 2006): 418-33. As Catholics, Balthasar and John Paul II recognize Mary to be the ideal expression of womanhood, whereas Barth and Piper do not appeal to Mary in this way.

[16]Sutton, "Complementarity and Symbolism," 427.

[17]John Piper, "The Ultimate Meaning of True Womanhood," Desiring God, October 9, 2008, www .desiringgod.org/messages/the-ultimate-meaning-of-true-womanhood, emphasis added.

for their understanding of what it means to be human. However, as this chapter will argue, the Scriptures do not make maleness and femaleness central to being human, nor can particular understandings of masculinity and femininity be rigidly prescribed, since these are culturally conditioned. Scripture makes Jesus Christ central to what it means to be human, and becoming more like Christ, through the empowerment of the Spirit, is the intended telos of all human persons.

A CHRISTOCENTRIC CONSTITUTION OF THE *IMAGO DEI*

As we will see below, the opening chapters of Genesis are powerfully dignifying for establishing the value and intended function of men and women. However, these are just the beginning of the story. Creation and eschatology have always been bound together in the true image, Jesus Christ.[18] If we begin with Jesus for understanding what it means to be fully human, we find that the image of God is Jesus Christ, to whom all of humanity is meant to be conformed.[19] As the perfect king and priest, Jesus inaugurates a new priesthood, one open to all who participate in his life.[20] Consequently, the primary way of understanding what it means to be human is typified in the person of Jesus Christ, the one who embodies the divine presence and who gives humankind access to this presence. This does not negate embodied differences (whether sexual or otherwise) but subordinates these differences to the Spirit-given identity of being God's royal priests.

Jesus Christ has always been plan A as the ultimate end for humanity, and the New Testament affirms this precreational intent: "For those whom he foreknew he also predestined to be conformed to the image of his Son" (Rom 8:29); "who saved us and called us to a holy calling, not because of

---

[18]Space constrains a full defense of this view; however, many theologians hold to this understanding. For an excellent overview, see Marc Cortez, *Christological Anthropology in Historical Perspective: Ancient and Contemporary Approaches to Theological Anthropology* (Grand Rapids, MI: Zondervan, 2016). For a brief treatment, see Christa L. McKirland, "What's So Unique About Being Human?," Logos Questions Series, http://logos.wp.st-andrews.ac.uk/files/2019/07/Logos -Institute-booklet-6-web.pdf.

[19]Colin E. Gunton, *The Triune Creator: A Historical and Systematic Study* (Grand Rapids, MI: Eerdmans, 1998), 196; Gunton, *Father, Son and Holy Spirit: Toward a Fully Trinitarian Theology* (London: Continuum, 2003), 80-81; Gunton, *The Christian Faith: An Introduction to Christian Doctrine* (Oxford: Blackwell, 2002), 14.

[20]See Stanley J. Grenz, "Biblical Priesthood and Women in Ministry," in the present volume.

our works but because of his own purpose and grace, which he gave us in Christ Jesus *before the ages began*" (2 Tim 1:9); "But we impart a secret and hidden wisdom of God, which God decreed *before the ages* for our glory" (1 Cor 2:7 ESV); "He was foreknown *before the foundation of the world* but was made manifest in the last times for the sake of you" (1 Pet 1:20 ESV). All of these passages support the second Adam preceding the first in the mind and intentions of an all-knowing God. God has always intended humanity's conformity into the image of Christ, as this *is* the image of God.

The identity of the image of God with Jesus runs consistently throughout the New Testament: "In their case the god of this world has blinded the minds of the unbelievers, to keep them from seeing the light of the gospel of the glory of Christ, *who is the image of God*" (2 Cor 4:4 ESV); "*He is the image* of the invisible God, the firstborn of all creation" (Col 1:15 ESV). In contrast to what we will see below, the prepositions that separate human beings from being equated with the image are not in place when referring to Jesus *as* the image. Thus, an understanding of Christ's humanity is central to understanding human destiny. What we see in the incarnation is the collision of heaven and earth through the life of the God-man. This perfect image bearer had perfect connection with God and was the perfect reflection of God. Jesus is the perfect high priest and the royal Son, whose whole ministry consisted of expanding the kingdom of God into all the earth, an expansion in which we too are invited to participate.

At the same time, such an invitation would not have been entirely foreign to the first-century Jewish audience. The Pentateuch was already known to have established the royal-priestly function of humankind, even if its fullness was not yet known until the entrance of Jesus Christ. To understand this backdrop, as well as the significance of maleness and femaleness for understanding the human vocation as originally articulated and as typified in Christ, I turn to Genesis 1–2.

Maleness, femaleness,* imago Dei, *and priesthood. While the opening chapters of Genesis do not provide the explicit content of the image of God, they do provide helpful minimums to exegetically frame the boundaries of this concept.[21] Specifically, these boundaries (which will be discussed in

---

[21]Given how much has been overread into these texts, especially on the meaning of the image of God, a minimalistic approach will be employed in this chapter.

more detail below) indicate that (1) humanity's special status of being uniquely related to God is not contingent on a specific function or sexed embodiment, and (2) a primary consequence, though not the content, of being in the image of God for the human beings includes dominion. A third boundary can be drawn when looking at how the Garden is functioning in Israel's cosmology, leading to (3) this dominion's being bound to the male and female having a royal-priestly identity, which is inseparable from relation to and expansion of the divine presence. Therefore, the opening chapters of Genesis do not provide warrant for a gender-essentialist reading but instead put emphasis on God's relation to humanity as well as their shared purpose as creatures uniquely created in God's image.

Boundary 1: Special status. The Genesis texts do not state what the image of God is. Instead, they provide what the resultant function is intended to be for creatures who have this unique relationship with God. The way the Hebrew grammar works, "in our image" signifies in whose image humankind is to be created. Such consistency of these prepositions, glossed as "in," "after," and "according to," likely communicate something of a derivative nature.[22] While derivative, the relationship of the human person to God remains unique, even while the precise content of the image remains underdetermined. Since Mary L. Conway's chapter, "Gender in Creation and Fall: Genesis 1–3," in the present volume has already given a detailed treatment of the first boundary, the second and third will be the focus here.

Boundary 2: Special function. The second minimal boundary for understanding the image-likeness concept is that a primary consequence, though not the content, of being in the image of God for both the male and the female includes dominion.[23] In other words, whether or not a person exercises dominion, they are made in God's image. Whether they are male or female, they are made in God's image. The status of being in

---

[22]Grant Macaskill, *Union with Christ in the New Testament* (Oxford: Oxford University Press, 2018), 197.

[23]*Dominion* is closely associated with representation of God, since the charge to rule is as an extension of God's rule and arguably the means by which God's presence expands into all the earth. In this sense, humans are vice-regents, faithfully extending God's loving care throughout the entire creation. Again, as this is a consequence of the unimpeachable status of being made in God's image, regardless of whether people enact this divinely given vocation, they are still created in God's image.

God's image does not rely on having a particular human body or exercising a particular function. Instead, an intentional consequence of this status is having dominion, which sets the human creature apart as unique from the rest of creation. Grammatically, the interpretation of dominion as the consequence of being in the image of God is strong, since the "cohortative followed by imperfect marks purpose or result," thereby producing the reading: "let us make humankind [*'adam*] . . . *so that* they may rule."[24] Notably, the charge of having dominion connects to the divine presence, as will be seen in the third boundary articulated below. The kind of dominion the human beings are meant to exercise is not due to an intrinsic authority that they possess, but is a dignifying function granted to them by the Creator to exercise on the Creator's behalf.

Like dominion, being sexually differentiated is not the content of being in the image of God either.[25] Furthermore, in contrast to the role of dominion, sexual difference may not even be understood as the consequence of being in the image, since maleness and femaleness are held in common with other nonhuman creatures. The command to "be fruitful and multiply" is given to other creatures not explicitly made in God's image (to birds and fish in Gen 1:22). Thus, while maleness and femaleness are significant, adjoining the content of the image with sexual differentiation presses the text too far. Instead, being male and female is the means by which humans might multiply via sexual reproduction, whereby more humans in God's

---

[24]Peter J. Gentry and Stephen J. Wellum, *Kingdom Through Covenant: A Biblical-Theological Understanding of the Covenants* (Wheaton, IL: Crossway, 2012), 188. For support for this grammatical argument, see Paul Joüon, *Grammaire de l'hébreu biblique* (Rome: Biblical Institute Press, 1923), 116; Thomas O. Lambdin, *Introduction to Biblical Hebrew* (New York: Charles Scribner's Sons, 1971), 107; W. Randall Garr, *In His Own Image and Likeness: Humanity, Divinity, and Monotheism*, Culture and History of the Ancient Near East 15 (Boston: Brill, 2003). Others who distinguish between the constitution and consequence of the image include Karl Barth, *Church Dogmatics*, vol. III/1, *The Doctrine of Creation* (Edinburgh: T&T Clark, 1958), 187; Gerhard von Rad, *Genesis: A Commentary*, 2nd ed. (London: SCM Press, 1963), 57; F. Horst, "Face to Face: The Biblical Doctrine of the Image of God," *Interpretation* 4 (1950): 259-70; Francis Watson, *Text and Truth: Redefining Biblical Theology* (New York: T&T Clark, 1997), 293; N. W. Porteous, "Image of God," in *The Interpreter's Dictionary of the Bible*, vol. 2, *E-J*, ed. Keith R. Crim (Nashville: Abingdon, 1993), 684.

[25]Catherine L. McDowell, *The Image of God in the Garden of Eden: The Creation of Humankind in Genesis 2:5–3:24 in Light of the Mīs Pî Pit Pî and Wpt-r Rituals of Mesopotamia and Ancient Egypt*, Siphrut: Literature and Theology of the Hebrew Scriptures (Winona Lake, IN: Eisenbrauns, 2015), 18.

image might continue to fill the earth.[26] Maleness and femaleness are therefore not the content of the image, since being in God's image is a status unique to human creatures, and maleness and femaleness does not fit this criterion of uniqueness.

Peter Gentry and Stephen Wellum make a compelling syntactical argument that supports the strength of dominion as a consequence of being in the image of God while also contrasting this with the textual significance of maleness and femaleness. Their argument comes from recognizing the chiasm within the text, "which emphasizes maleness and femaleness associated with being fruitful and multiplying whereas having dominion is directly correlated with the image itself."[27] This structure is as follows:

A: in the image of God he created him[28]

B: male and female he created them

B': be fruitful and increase in number and fill the earth

A': and subdue it and rule over the fish/birds/animals

Such a structure (note A and A') supports the idea that having dominion is a consequence of being in the image of God. The declaration of intent "*so that* they may have dominion" is then reinforced by the execution of this intention. In contrast, maleness and femaleness moves my thought forward regarding how this population will increase.[29] This does not make sexed embodiment inconsequential, but it does position it as secondary (at best) to being made in the image of God and being tasked with

---

[26]J. Richard Middleton elaborates on the biological continuity of humans with animal kinds, saying, "Not only, then, does the phrase *male and female* in 1:27 not define the content of the image in social-relational terms at all, but its role is anticipatory, looking ahead and preparing us for 1:28, where human beings (having been created biologically male and female in 1:27) are blessed with fertility and commissioned by God to reproduce, in order that they might fill the earth and subdue it." See Middleton, *The Liberating Image: The Imago Dei in Genesis 1* (Grand Rapids, MI: Brazos, 2005), 50.

[27]Gentry and Wellum, *Kingdom Through Covenant*, 189.

[28]The singular direct object should not be read as delimiting the status of being in the image to an individual. The Hebrew grammar includes humankind in general, even though it is singular. See Gordon J. Wenham, *Genesis 1–15*, WBC (Waco, TX: Thomas Nelson, 1987), 32-33.

[29]Middleton elaborates on this, saying, "it is clear that the third line in three-line Hebrew poetic units typically do not repeat a previous idea, but more usually serves a progressive function, introducing a new thought. It is thus doubtful, on syntactical grounds, that 'male and female' specifies in any way the nature of the image" (*Liberating Image*, 49-50). He cites Robert Alter, *The World of Biblical Literature* (San Francisco: Basic Books, 1992), in support of this syntactical reading.

dominion. All humankind is given the commission to have dominion over the rest of the creation. Additionally, dominion is closely associated with representation of God, since the charge to rule is an extension of God's rule and arguably the means by which God's presence expands into all the earth.

So, it seems that being in the image of God is first a unique status of humanity, whereby a unique function results: dominion. Both status and function link to the divine presence, reinforcing the special relationship that humanity has with the Creator God.[30] Such an interpretation finds further support as we move into the third boundary.

Boundary 3: Dominion and divine presence. The third boundary becomes clearer in light of biblical scholarship on Jewish cosmologies as well as the surrounding ancient Near Eastern cultures. This boundary indicates that dominion is tied to the human beings having a royal-priestly function, which is inseparable from the divine presence. Given the overlap of sacred task with sacred space, the role of a priest becomes important here. A basic definition of a priest is "a person who enjoyed direct access into God's presence. A priest had a two-way function, as a representative of others who offered sacrifices and prayers to God, and as a mediator of God's will to those he represented."[31] Since sin was not yet a part of the story, the two-way function would not have been necessary in terms of representing humanity to God. However, the enjoyment of direct access to God's presence seems to be exactly what the man and the woman experienced in the Garden, alongside representing God's benevolent care for the created world. The reason this is understood as priestly, however, is due to receiving the creation stories after human sinfulness. Had sin not occurred in human history, it seems not only reasonable but highly probable that the word *priest* would have been meaningless, since direct access to God would have been true for all people.[32]

---

[30]L. Michael Morales, *Who Shall Ascend the Mountain of the Lord?: A Biblical Theology of the Book of Leviticus* (Downers Grove, IL: IVP Academic, 2015), 46-47.

[31]Martin J. Selman, Martin H. Manser, and Stephen Travis, "Priest," in *Macmillan Dictionary of the Bible* (Macmillan, 2002). According to T. Desmond Alexander, "because they met God face to face in a holy place, we may assume that Adam and Eve had a holy or priestly status. Only priests were permitted to serve within a sanctuary or temple." See *From Paradise to the Promised Land: An Introduction to the Pentateuch*, 3rd ed. (Grand Rapids, MI: Baker Academic, 2012), 125.

[32]In the same way that *temple* would be meaningless since all space would be temple/sacred.

Unfortunately, sin does enter the human story, but God's intentions for humankind's communion with Godself continue. Thus, while Eden features explicitly in only a few texts, this Garden echoes throughout the biblical witness, continually pointing the reader to the original intentions of the Creator. The purpose for this Edenic space was to provide a temple context for God to dwell with humanity and the rest of the created world, as well as a space for humanity (and the rest of creation) to respond in worship to their Creator. Part of this worship included the expansion of God's presence into the rest of the world, as evidenced by the linguistic overlap of temple-specific language. For instance, the verb for "walking" (*halak*) that God is doing in the Garden is the same verb used for the presence of God walking in the tabernacle in Leviticus 26:12; Deuteronomy 23:14; and 2 Samuel 7:6-7.[33] Additionally, when turning to the second creation account in Genesis 2, humans are collectively given duties to curate this space for God's manifest presence. The duties given in Genesis 2:15 are the same duties given to the Levites as ministers and priests in the sanctuary "to work" and "to keep/guard." Genesis 2 is the only other place in the Pentateuch where these verbs appear together.[34] All of these points indicate that the Garden is where God could be directly with the man and the woman, which can be understood retrospectively as entailing their priestly status.

However, some might argue that these functions only applied to the man, since the woman was not yet created in this account of the creation sequence (Gen 2:15). Although the woman does not receive specific address (at least, not recorded in the text), this does not mean she is not included in this charge, especially given the creation account of Genesis 1, where she is explicitly included. Furthermore, following the line of

---

[33]For a lengthier treatment of the priestly function of the human pair, see Alexander, *From Paradise to the Promised Land*, 123; cf. Gentry and Wellum, *Kingdom Through Covenant*, 212-13. Dumbrell concurs with Wenham's verbal highlighting of cultivate/work, serve, and guard with priestly service in the tabernacle (Num 3:7-8; 8:25-26; 18:5-6; 1 Chron 23:32; Ezek 44:14; see also Is 56:6). See William J. Dumbrell, *Covenant and Creation: An Old Testament Covenant Theology*, 2nd ed. (Milton Keynes, UK: Paternoster, 2013), 59.

[34]Gentry and Wellum, *Kingdom Through Covenant*, 212-13; Alexander, *From Paradise to the Promised Land*, 123; Scott Hahn, "Canon, Cult and Covenant: The Promise of Liturgical Hermeneutics," in *Canon and Biblical Interpretation*, ed. Craig Bartholomew et al. (Grand Rapids, MI: Zondervan Academic, 2010), 213.

reasoning that this priestly language is gender exclusive, one would also have to conclude that the command not to eat from the tree of good and evil was only required of the man, since the woman was not given this prohibition directly. This is expressly not the case given the woman's culpability both in God's direct address in Genesis 3 and in later interpretations of the Genesis story (1 Tim 2; 2 Cor 11). Also, given the argument that Eden was a sacred space, the woman should not have been allowed into the domain in which God walked unless she too had a priestly status. This may also be supported by Genesis 3:21, in which God makes garments of skin for the man and the woman, using the same vocabulary as the priestly donning of clothing (Ex 28:41; 29:8; 40:14; Lev 8:13).[35] However, whether the man or woman would have known or used language of "priesthood" does not detract from the most central points of this story. The woman and the man function as priests in that they have access to where God is personally present and are meant to be representatives of this presence, and the covenants established later are to provide continued access to this presence for humanity.[36]

This brings us to a closer examination of the second creation account, in Genesis 2. While Genesis 1 treats man and woman as a unified humanity and specifically uses language of male (*zakar*) and female (*neqevah*), Genesis 2 treats each of their formations separately and uses language of man (*'ish*) and woman (*'ishah*), implicitly introducing "social categories."[37] And yet, the second creation story focuses on the man and woman's similarity, not their difference. Picking up in Genesis 2:18, the problem of the man's

---

[35]See Gordon J. Wenham, "Sanctuary Symbolism in the Garden of Eden Story," in *Cult and Cosmos: Tilting Toward a Temple-Centered Theology*, ed. L. Michael Morales, Biblical Tools and Studies 18 (Leuven: Peeters, 2014), 163-64; Dumbrell, *Covenant and Creation*, 59; McDowell, *Image of God*, 140-41.

[36]For more on Israel's cosmology regarding temple, see Alexander, *From Paradise to the Promised Land*; Gregory K. Beale, *The Temple and the Church's Mission: A Biblical Theology of the Dwelling Place of God* (Downers Grove, IL: InterVarsity Press, 2004); Jon D. Levenson, "The Temple and the World," *Journal of Religion* 64, no. 3 (July 1984): 288; J. Richard Middleton, *The Liberating Image: The Imago Dei in Genesis 1* (Eugene, OR: Wipf & Stock, 2005); Moshe Weinfeld, "Sabbath, Temple and the Enthronement of the Lord: The Problem of the *Sitz im Leben* of Genesis 1:1–2:3," in *Cult and Cosmos: Tilting Toward a Temple-Centered Theology*, Biblical Tools and Studies 18 (Leuven: Peeters, 2014); Stephen Um, *The Theme of Temple Christology in John's Gospel* (New York: Bloomsbury, 2006), 20-31; John H. Walton, *The Lost World of Genesis One* (Downers Grove, IL: InterVarsity Press, 2009).

[37]Middleton, *Liberating Image*, 50.

aloneness is rectified in an odd but intentional manner. It is as if God is walking the man through a teaching illustration in order to ensure that he understands the dignity of the human being he is about to create. God brings all of the animals before the man so that the man might identify them and see whether they are a fit for him. However, after identifying (through the act of naming) all of them, he does not find one who is suitably his counterpart (Gen 2:19-20). Thus, God puts the man in a deep sleep, forms the woman, and wakes the man (Gen 2:21-22). Upon seeing her, he exclaims, "This at last is bone of my bones and flesh of my flesh; she shall be called Woman [*'ishah*], because she was taken out of Man [*'ish*]" (Gen 2:23 ESV). Linguistically, this is the most similar word he could call her. Thus, in light of the woman's similarity to him, the narrator concludes, "Therefore a man shall leave his father and his mother and hold fast to his wife, and they shall become one flesh" (Gen 2:24 ESV). The narrator then closes this account with the comment "And the man and his wife were both naked and were not ashamed" (Gen 2:25 ESV).

This final comment from Genesis 2:25 is significant. Implicitly, throughout the whole second narrative, the man is naked. Consequently, it would seem that he is looking for another creature who is both like him as a human and also sexually compatible with him. Indeed, this is what the earlier chapter set up in anticipation (Gen 1:26-28). Finding no other creature like him, God makes it clear to the man that this woman is like him.[38] Thus, the man and the woman are formed from one flesh, underscoring to the man the extent to which woman is his equal and that they are meant to become one flesh again (Gen 2:24). This bond is unlike the bond of animals, since the animals were not formed from one flesh. Consequently, the social bond of the man and the woman is meant to be lifelong, while also forming a new kinship unit. The second account does not provide prescriptions for how females are supposed to be women, nor how males are meant to be men. We are thus left with a reiteration of the goodness of maleness and femaleness, a strong case for the similarity of man and woman, and the establishment of an intimate bond with each other set within the sacred space where they commune with the living God.

---

[38]For more on *'ezer kenegdo*, a "help(er) corresponding to him" (Gen 1:18, 20), see Mary L. Conway, "Gender in Creation and Fall: Genesis 1–3," in the present volume.

Cast against this temple/sacred-space backdrop, the Genesis story is therefore incredibly dignifying to the man and woman, and the whole cosmos. This cosmic temple is not a stagnant locale but is intended to expand through the stewardship of the male and female human beings, who are in the image of God. Through their relationship to God, they are meant to see God's presence increase throughout the entire earth.[39] By their filling the earth, the reign of God was intended to spread throughout the created world as a vocational consequence of humanity being made in the image of God. This presence-expansion was their act of worship as archetypal rulers and priests. For instance, the prevailing religious practice of ancient Near Eastern cultures was to honor each god with a statue or image and place it in the innermost part of the temple.[40] While the human beings may not have been understood as identical to the presence of God (they are "in" and "according to" the image, not the image itself), they would have been closely associated with God's presence due to their designation as being in the image of God and being charged with having dominion.

To summarize, Israel and the surrounding ancient Near Eastern cultures consistently related temple building and images of god with that god's divine presence in the world—often located in their temples. If Eden functions as a temple, and humanity is representing God by being in the *imago Dei*, then *all* of humanity is intimately bound to the divine presence. We were intended, from the beginning, to be royal priests mediating God's presence in the world. The focus of the texts of Genesis 1–2 is on humanity's unique relationship to God and their function on behalf of God. Genesis 2 goes out of the way to express the similarity of the woman to the man, which is the rationale behind a man leaving his family to become one with his wife. At the same time, while maleness and femaleness do feature in these creation accounts, masculinity and femininity do not. Instead, when male and female are discussed in detail, the point is to show the similarity of the man and the woman. What *is* central to this text is God's presence and that humanity (without any division of roles or natures) is meant to expand this presence into the world since they are made in God's image.

---

[39] Alexander, *From Paradise to the Promised Land*, 25.
[40] Beale, *Temple and the Church's Mission*, 89.

What we find when we look at the life, death, resurrection, ascension, and ongoing ministry of Jesus in the heavenly throne room is the epitome of that vocation's realization.

THE LOGICAL FLAWS OF GENDER ESSENTIALISM

In the same article by John Piper cited in the introduction, he states:

> In Ephesians 5:31, Paul quotes Genesis 2:24, "Therefore a man shall leave his father and mother and hold fast to his wife, and the two shall become one flesh." And then he adds this, "This mystery is profound, and I am saying that it refers to Christ and the church." In other words, from the beginning, manhood and womanhood were designed to display the glory of Christ in his relationship to the church, his bride.[41]

Taken in conjunction with Piper's other claims quoted in this chapter, Piper overly emphasizes the significance of maleness and femaleness. In contrast, the consistent message across the Testaments seems to be human-kind's access to the divine presence and their invitation to expand this presence as creatures made in God's image. Given that the true image is Jesus Christ, the focus of the biblical drama is not on what it means to be a man or what it means to be a woman, but what it means to be conformed to the likeness of the Son—an intended destiny equally true for men and women. Piper's logic, however, seems to be that the relationship of Christ to the church is the original template after which the relationship between man and woman is patterned. Men are therefore meant to imitate Christ and his love for the church, and women are supposed to imitate the church and her submission to Christ. Piper asserts that these are the ultimate expressions of our male or female personhood, which bears witness to Christ and the cross. Some of his logic raises serious concerns. Thus, this section will focus on the exegetical, theological, philosophical, and empirical problems with this view.

Exegetical. The exegetical concerns with Piper's interpretation are (1) overreading the meaning of maleness and femaleness into the content of the relationship between Christ and the church, (2) overreaching with this metaphor as determinative for the meaning of maleness and

---

[41]Piper, "Ultimate Meaning of True Womanhood."

femaleness and the telos of human personhood, and (3) underarticulating what *glory* means and whether this text provides enough warrant for his claims about manhood and womanhood giving glory to Christ.

Recalling from Genesis that maleness and femaleness are shared in common with birds and fish, what is unique to humanity is their one flesh union of fitting partners—their covenant bond—which is why the man will leave his family to become one with his wife (Gen 2:24). Their similarity-based relation is the focus of the Genesis text, not maleness and femaleness per se. Piper conflates the *relationship of union* between the man and the woman with *being* a man and a woman. Consequently, in his view, maleness and femaleness have always found their ultimate meaning in the Christ-church relationship. Yet this understanding of the meaning of maleness and femaleness is patently not the purpose of maleness and femaleness as seen in Genesis 1. Instead, the radical message of Ephesians 5 is that the union between the husband and wife "was originally intended to prefigure and to illustrate the union that Christ now has with the church."[42] Such a relationship is rightly called a mystery given that the God of the universe took on human flesh in order to submit himself to death so that sinful humanity might be reunited to him. Such a loving relationship is beyond comprehension.[43]

The reason the relationship is the focus, and not the maleness or femaleness of the parties, is its intimacy and voluntary nature: "the relation of Christ and church must be as close as that."[44] Unlike the relationship between a parent and a child, the two parties willfully choose to be faithful to each other in a lifelong covenant. Treated in context, the thrust of Ephesians is the unity of Jews and Gentiles due to the death and resurrection of Jesus Christ. Thus, as the rest of the letter builds up to Ephesians 5–6, "the crucified Christ reaches out to embrace Gentiles, formerly at enmity with the people of Israel but now a holy temple built upon the foundation of the

---

[42]Frank Thielman, Robert Yarbrough, and Robert Stein, *Ephesians* (Grand Rapids, MI: Baker Academic, 2010), 389-90. Ephesians commentator Ernest Best also recognizes that "it is probably not the man and wife whom AE [the author of Ephesians] says are the mystery but the union of Christ and the church." See Best, *Ephesians* (Edinburgh: Bloomsbury T&T Clark, 2004), 557.

[43]Thielman, Yarbrough, and Stein go on to say that "this is why God instituted marriage in the first place. On the human level it illustrates the extent of God's great love for his people in Christ" (*Ephesians*, 392).

[44]Best, *Ephesians*, 561.

Jewish apostles and prophets (Eph. 2.11-22). In Christ, the two become one as the enmity is dispelled (2.14)."[45] Jesus does not unite himself only with the chosen people of Israel, but with the Gentiles who now also make up his body. This marital bond is thus the mysterious, awe-inspiring focus of this text. To ground the very meaning of maleness and femaleness in this passage thus overreads Piper's interpretation into this text.

A second exegetical question involves Piper's methodology and why he exclusively uses the metaphor of the marital bond for understanding the meaning of maleness and femaleness. For instance, why does he not engage our adoption "as sons" (Rom 8)? This seems to be a more central metaphor across the Testaments and has a much clearer connection to glory (a chief concern of Piper's), especially in Romans.[46] Erin Heim traces the theme of adoption through the New Testament while recognizing the importance of understanding this concept in the Hebrew Bible: "in the Old Testament, sonship is a model most often employed to express Israel's particular relationship to YHWH" (e.g., Ex 4:22; 2 Sam 7:14; Ps 2:7; Deut 8:5, 14:1; Prov 3:11-12; Is 43:6-7; Jer 31:9; Hos 2:1 [MT]; Mal 3:17).[47] This filial bond is a relationship extended by God's gracious gift, not based on Israel's merit or righteousness. Israel was meant to keep the covenant, as God's children, thereby being people of the presence for their own benefit and for the sake of the nations (Ex 19:6). Thus, sonship, covenant, and presence are intertwined.[48] Israel and the church corporately act as God's adopted son—and yet this is not the metaphor Piper chooses to establish a cosmic rationale for maleness. To do so would press the point of the metaphor beyond what it is intended to express. The point of our relation to God as sons is to tell us something about the unconditional nature of this relationship, not to tell us something about maleness. In the same way, grounding

---

[45]Francis Watson, *Agape, Eros, Gender: Towards a Pauline Sexual Ethic* (New York: Cambridge University Press, 2000), 258.

[46]As Heim argues, "the adoption metaphors in the New Testament point to Christ as the locus of adoption and also present adoption as the *telos* of human experience." See Erin Heim, "In Him and Through Him from the Foundation of the World: Adoption and Christocentric Anthropology," in *Christ and the Created Order*, ed. Andrew Torrance and Thomas McCall (Grand Rapids, MI: Zondervan, 2018), 132.

[47]See Erin Heim, "In Him and Through Him," 132.

[48]In citing the work of Frank Moore Cross, Macaskill brings these concepts together explicitly in relating the "concept of 'adoption' to covenant: chosen by Yahweh, Israel becomes God's son (Ex 4:22-3)" (*Union with Christ*, 104-5).

the meaning and fixity of maleness and femaleness in Ephesians 5 overextends the metaphor's reach.

A third exegetical concern is Piper's linkage of maleness and femaleness to the Son's glory in Ephesians 5. Because Piper is chiefly concerned with God's glory and believes that acting in accordance with rigid categories of manhood and womanhood is necessary for this glory to be maximized, more needs to be said about glory. Unfortunately, in Piper's account, this connection between maleness and femaleness and glory is not argued; it is simply stated. In fact, glory is not part of Paul's argument in Ephesians 5 but must be imported from elsewhere. Additionally, glory is a heavily weighted term in biblical scholarship, and how it is being used from verse to verse is not always equivalent.[49] Recent work on glory in biblical studies suggests that Piper's definition of *glory* as "the radiance of his holiness, the radiance of his manifold, infinitely worthy and valuable perfections" is not the only or primary way to understand glory, especially in relation to how humans glorify God.[50] Finally, Piper fails to distinguish between two separate concepts of glory: the glory of God, and the glory that humans participate in through the Son. These are two different concepts and should not be conflated.[51]

Theological. The theological concerns with Piper's line of reasoning are (1) the exclusive relation of men to Christ and women to the church, (2) the use of glory as his overarching rationale for this reading, and (3) the way Christ, as a man, could redeem all of humanity if being a man or a woman is essential to an individual's very being and personhood.

The first theological concern regards the fixity of men representing Christ and women representing the church. According to Piper, "Men take their cues from Christ as the head, and women take their cues from what

---

[49]For an excellent overview of this debate and a convincing articulation of glory, see Haley Goranson Jacob, *Conformed to the Image of His Son: Reconsidering Paul's Theology of Glory in Romans* (Downers Grove, IL: IVP Academic, 2018). More to the point, she argues specifically that Rom 8:29 "refers to believers' eschatological glory only if *glory* is understood as something *other than* splendor/radiance or the visible, manifest presence of God" (10, emphasis original).

[50]John Piper, "What Is God's Glory?," Desiring God, July 6, 2009, https://www.desiringgod.org /interviews/what-is-gods-glory. For a critique of Piper's broader theology of divine sovereignty, which is derived from his understanding of glory, see Thomas H. McCall, "I Believe in Divine Sovereignty," *Trinity Journal* 29, no. 2 (2008): 205-26.

[51]Goranson Jacob, *Conformed to the Image*, 256.

the church is called to be in her allegiance to Christ. This is described by Paul in terms of headship and submission." He goes on to define headship as "the divine calling of a husband to take primary responsibility for Christ-like, servant leadership, protection, and provision in the home," with submission as "the divine calling of a wife to honor and affirm her husband's leadership and help carry it through according to her gifts."[52] Using Ephesians 5 in this gender-essentialist manner presents significant issues for men and women. Following Piper's logic, if women—as women—are taking their cues from the church and if men—as men—are taking their cues from Christ, then it would seem that being like Christ will violate women's natures and being like the church will violate men's natures. On his view, women seem essentially unable to become like a male savior. Thus, following Piper's logic, men will always have an essentially greater capacity for Christlikeness. However, all of humanity's ultimate purpose is to become like Christ through submission to the Holy Spirit. This raises another concern: How can men participate in being the Bride, which requires receptive submission, since this would seemingly violate their male essence?[53] With such a rigid conception of this metaphor's theological significance for grounding the very meaning of maleness, femaleness, manhood, and womanhood, these implications emerge when carried to their logical conclusion.[54]

A second theological concern returns to Piper's understanding of glory. Looking again at Goranson Jacob's work, she claims that "humanity's glory as caretakers of creation in Psalm 8 is closely associated with humanity's role as image bearers and thus caretakers of creation in Genesis 1:26-28. . . . This echo of humanity's created purpose is at the heart of Paul's anthropology and new-Adam Christology throughout Romans."[55]

---

[52]Piper, "Ultimate Meaning of True Womanhood."

[53]Tina Beattie makes a similar point in her critique of Balthasar (cited in Sutton, "Complementarity and Symbolism," 423).

[54]This is not to say that Piper would disagree with women being intended to become like Christ, or that men should not submit to Christ as members of the church. However, the concern I have is *how* he can agree with these statements given an essentialist understanding of the nonoverlapping difference between men and women. See John Piper, "Glorification: Conformed to Christ for the Supremacy of Christ," Desiring God, August 11, 2002, www.desiringgod.org/messages /glorification-conformed-to-christ-for-the-supremacy-of-christ.

[55]Goranson Jacob, *Conformed to the Image*, 258. Goranson Jacob is not without dissenters, however. See Carey C. Newman, *Paul's Glory-Christology: Tradition and Rhetoric* (Leiden: Brill, 2014).

If we are going to stake everything on God's glory, we need to be exegetically and theologically confident about its meaning, and then we need to have a clear rationale for binding this to maleness and femaleness. If Goranson Jacob is correct, the glory humans can give God is better tied to humanity's royal-priestly function as participants in the identity of the second Adam.[56] As this is equally accessible to men and women and is not a gendered function, one wonders how giving glory to the Son requires masculinity and femininity.

A final theological concern is that if human personhood is essentially male or female, then Jesus would necessarily have had male personhood. If this is true, it is unclear how women and those in the intersex community (more on intersex persons below) would be fully redeemed, since their natures were not fully assumed by the incarnate Christ. While Piper and Grudem are explicit that women share in the same human nature as men, which is "equal to him in godlike personhood," this is incompatible with their multiple claims about the absolute difference between a male and female nature.[57] One cannot have one's ontological cake and eat it too.[58] Further, Jesus would also have had an incomplete humanity, since he would only be the male part of the image of God and not the full image of God. However, Jesus redeemed humanity fully because he became completely human—with human personhood, not male personhood (Jn 3:16; Rom 3:22; 5:18).[59] He is also consistently referred to as the image of God in its fullness (2 Cor 4:4; Col 1:15; cf. Heb 1:3), which is at odds with requiring male and female to constitute the entire image.

---

[56]She cites the work of James Dunn, Robert Jewett, Tom Schreiner, Brendan Byrne, and N. T. Wright as supporting her argument that "when believers are conformed to the image of the Son, they are conformed to his status and function as the Son of God who rules over creation" (Goranson Jacob, *Conformed to the Image*, 10). Given what has been argued above in the first two sections, this seems to comport with the larger messages of Scripture regarding humanity's intended destiny.

[57]John Piper and Wayne Grudem, *50 Crucial Questions: An Overview of Central Concerns About Manhood and Womanhood* (Wheaton, IL: Crossway, 2016), 73.

[58]This has been critically engaged by many scholars including Rosemary Radford Ruether, *To Change the World: Christology and Cultural Criticism* (London: SCM Press, 1981); Elisabeth Schüssler Fiorenza, *Jesus: Miriam's Child, Sophia's Prophet* (London: SCM Press, 1995); Elaine Storkey, "Issues in Christology and Feminist Theology," in *The Gospel and Gender*, ed. Douglas A. Campbell (London: T&T Clark, 2003).

[59]Francis Watson discusses Eph 5 in that "woman and man, wife and husband, is neither eradicated by the new identity nor absolutized. . . . Although the gender difference is important it is not all-important" (*Agape, Eros, Gender*, 227).

Philosophical. The primary philosophical concern relates to the equal personhood of all human beings. While a definition of personhood is contentious, here it is understood theologically as beings who both stand in need of a divine address and are intended to give a certain human response.[60] Since male and female humans stand in need of the same divine address and are responsible for the same kind of response, it is universal personhood that is critical to the realization of our intended telos, not maleness or femaleness. In other words, maleness and femaleness do not constitute personhood, even if how human persons live is deeply affected by their sexed embodiment, which leads us to a final area of concern with gender essentialism.

Empirical. While maleness and femaleness have been the focus of this chapter, a major empirical objection to gender essentialism is that there are some people who do not fit the male or female bodily expectations at birth. Additionally, under gender essentialism, maleness and femaleness are seen as synonymous with manhood and womanhood, which further compounds embodied dissonance for these persons. This group, known as intersex persons, has challenged the model types of male and female, especially their medical and social definitions.[61] Though intersex persons have existed throughout human history, only recently has this group become more visible in the West. The most conservative estimates place intersex occurrence at one in two thousand, but many believe the figure is closer to one in every fifty births.[62]

Causes of intersexuality are typically genetic or hormonal and primarily include a different chromosomal makeup besides XX or XY, such as XXY; a mosaic karyotype; or missing a common gene or an uncommon combination of genes (either passed down from mother or father or by chance).[63] Intersexuality can occur based on hormonal processing, such as androgen

---

[60]Gunton, *Father, Son and Holy Spirit*, 16.

[61]For an overview of the different intersex conditions and a thorough theological engagement with this community, see Megan K. DeFranza, *Sex Difference in Christian Theology: Male, Female, and Intersex in the Image of God* (Grand Rapids, MI: Eerdmans, 2015), 23-67.

[62]Anne Fausto-Sterling, *Sexing the Body: Gender Politics and the Construction of Sexuality*, new ed. (New York: Basic Books, 2000).

[63]Consortium on the Management of Disorders of Sex Development and Intersex Society of North America, *Clinical Guidelines for the Management of Disorders of Sex Development in Children* (2006), 5.

insensitivity syndrome. This is a condition in which someone is born with XY sex chromosomes but is unable to process male hormones and thus appears female, with female external genitalia but internal, undescended testicles.[64] However, if androgen insensitivity syndrome is only partial, and some male hormones can be processed, then the body can fall along an entire spectrum: from a functional penis, to a "small" penis, to an "enlarged" clitoris.[65] Another condition known as 5-alpha reductase deficiency syndrome occurs when someone with XY sex chromosomes appears female at birth but then develops male genitalia and features during puberty.[66] Congenital adrenal hyperplasia is a condition in which XX (genetic female) individuals have androgen levels similar to XY individuals, leading to the labia becoming a scrotum and the clitoris becoming enlarged to the extent of looking like a penis.[67] Congenital adrenal hyperplasia can, at times, be so pronounced that infants are classified as male and raised as boys.[68]

All of this leads to questions regarding what "underlying natures of manhood and womanhood" would capture the nature of an intersex person, especially in these extreme cases. Further, even if it is granted that some expressions of intersexuality are a result of a fallen human reality, this does not change the question of how a person in this context would determine their "true manhood" or "true womanhood."[69] Further, this would call into question how a radically other personhood of a male Jesus could also redeem intersex persons.

---

[64]DeFranza, *Sex Difference in Christian Theology*, 25-45.

[65]Scare quotes are used since the determination of what is normal is largely based on societal expectations.

[66]DeFranza, *Sex Difference in Christian Theology*, 42-43.

[67]DeFranza, *Sex Difference in Christian Theology*, 30-35.

[68]This is the only intersex condition that needs to be recognized and treated at birth since it can cause severe dehydration, leading to death of the newborn (DeFranza, *Sex Difference in Christian Theology*, 31).

[69]Not to mention the importance of engaging transgender persons, for whom the significance of sex and gender is especially felt. Given the complexity of how sexual chromosomes and sexual hormones influence the brain, much is still unknown regarding why some people feel trapped in the wrong body. See Austen Hartke, *Transforming: The Bible and the Lives of Transgender Christians* (Louisville, KY: Westminster John Knox, 2018), 31. More will be said on this below. Furthermore, as is well attested in disability studies, many within the disabled community find claims about what is a result of the fall to be inherently degrading, which is why theologizing of this sort should be done with great caution. For a great resource, see Kevin Timpe, "Disability in Heaven," June 13, 2018, https://kevintimpe.com/disability-in-heaven/.

Having articulated these objections to a gender-essentialist reading of Scripture alongside a Christocentric theological anthropology, we are now better situated to discuss the significance of maleness and femaleness.

THE SIGNIFICANCE OF MALENESS AND FEMALENESS

The overarching aim of this chapter has been to elucidate the priorities of the scriptural texts regarding humanity's initial and eschatological purpose in order to better situate the significance of maleness and femaleness. So, what has the text said? First, the goal of the creation account is not to tease out what it means to be male or female. All of humankind is invited into a royal priesthood, and maleness and femaleness are critical to the expansion of humankind into the created world. Thus, we see the goodness of maleness and femaleness in the creation accounts, but we do not have prescriptions on masculinity and femininity.[70] Second, humanity's special status as beings made in the image of God is directly related to the true image, Jesus Christ. All of humankind is meant to become like Jesus, a first-century Jewish male, who is also the perfect high priest and royal Son. And yet, each of us is called to this telos, by the Spirit, as the particularly embodied creatures that we are. Consequently, the Scriptures have little to say on what it means to be a man or what it means to be a woman.[71] They are concerned with what it means to grow in Christlike maturity.

However, we do follow Jesus as embodied persons, and for this reason our bodies matter. What is accidental (in the philosophical sense, meaning that one would be human regardless of one's sexed embodiment) is not therefore incidental. Thus, a rejection of gender essentialism does not entail a rejection of sex difference or a rejection of the importance of sexed embodiment.[72] Every human person is born with sex

---

[70] As noted in note 74 below, the goodness of maleness and femaleness does not logically entail the badness of other kinds of bodies.

[71] Much of this volume addresses scriptural texts that seem to make unilateral distinctions in actions of men and women—that men are to love and lead women, and women are to respect and submit to men. What other chapters have made clear is that specificity of an exhortation does not entail exclusivity of an exhortation. Men and women are both meant to love, respect, lead, and submit to one another. These are given in a gender-specific way, but they are not gender-constituting, nor gender exclusive. First Corinthians 11:1-16 may seem an exception to this and is addressed in note 74 below.

[72] Textually, I ground this in the creation of the man and the woman in Gen 1 as well as in the intentionality of creating woman in Gen 2.

chromosomes, which (alongside genes) inform each person's biological givenness. Whether these fit into XX (female) or XY (male) combinations, and how this affects sex hormones and gonadal formation, is another matter.[73] This biological variety is compounded by the reality that we do live in a fallen world and thus have difficulty adjudicating the difference between diversity and depravity. For instance, diversity in sex characteristics (such as many expressions of intersexuality) may mirror the diversity we see in the natural world that is not listed in the Genesis accounts.[74] This is where there can be a celebrated diversity. However, on the other hand, in circumstances where intersex persons want to have children but have anatomy that inhibits doing so, or in the case of congenital adrenal hyperplasia, which can cause death when untreated, a person with this condition may recognize that things are not as they are supposed to be.

---

[73]In order to speak in terms of the complexity of sex formation, this is what Cordelia Fine refers to as "genetic-gonadal-genital sex." See Fine, *Testosterone Rex: Myths of Sex, Science, and Society* (New York: W. W. Norton, 2017), 85.

[74]We often read Gen 1 as including all things in between, such that platypuses and amphibians are understood to be a part of God's good creation as well. At the same time, the content in between does not negate the stated pairs. There is still night and day, the sun and moon, etc. This point can also be made implicitly with Jesus' radical statements about eunuchs in Mt 19:12. The existence of eunuchs does not negate there being male and female, but it does speak to those who do not fit the male or female categories—there is space for those in between. Such is emphatically the case not only from the words of Christ, but also with the inclusion of the eunuch in Acts 8:27 and of eunuchs in Is 56:4-5, where Yahweh honors those who are faithful to his covenant above those who are able to have children. Finally, one might object that Scripture does provide prescriptions for masculinity and femininity. For instance, the text of 1 Cor 11 records Paul's requirements for gender distinctions as men and women pray and prophesy together. However, throughout this letter, the Corinthians seem fascinated with angels and may have been taking Jesus' words in Mt 22:30 too far in this life. See Ronald W. Pierce and Elizabeth A. Kay, "Mutuality in Marriage and Singleness: 1 Corinthians 7:1-40," in the present volume, including reference to Gordon Fee's commentary to this effect: Fee, *The First Epistle to the Corinthians*, NICNT (Grand Rapids, MI: Eerdmans, 1987), 12, 269, 290, 330. The Corinthians may have believed they would be like the angels in the here and now and thus were beginning to act like this was a realized reality by shedding all gender distinctions, which would indicate their maleness and femaleness. Paul urges them to maintain the present reality of their male and femaleness—cued by women wearing head coverings—in order to maintain unity in the body of Christ (the focus of this letter), thereby experiencing the living presence of God in their midst and also bearing witness to this presence so that it moved ever outward. Interestingly, we seem to recognize that this is not a morally required gender distinction given that most Christian women do not cover their heads when they go to church today. Instead, the limited focus is on the present goodness of maleness and femaleness, but only insofar as it contributes to the unity of the body of Christ for the sake of expanding God's presence in the world.

This feeling of things not being as they should be is engaged by Austen Hartke, who identifies as a transgender Christian man.[75] For instance, language used by trans persons includes feeling as if they were "born into the wrong body."[76] He suggests that, for some transgender persons, the feeling of dissonance between the body that they were born with and the gender that they believe themselves to be is rooted in "the gendered expectations that other people hold them to that cause a problem."[77] When we have rigid definitions of what it means to be masculine or what it means to be feminine, which are bound to personhood, and a person does not fit into his or her assigned gender category, then there can be a feeling that a person is in the wrong body.[78] Hartke suggests that this transgender experience is an external effect of the fall—when the expectations of others cause personal angst.[79] Given what has been argued thus far in this chapter, this is an angst that could be lessened by a loosening of the definitions, surveillance, and enforcement of masculinity and femininity. Thus, the

---

[75]While questions about transgender persons are also highly complex, the Christian community would benefit from listening more, even when we disagree. Hartke's book does not provide a robust theological treatment of sexual ethics (nor is that its purpose) but raises interesting points while highlighting a minority perspective through the sharing of transgender Christian stories. Given how quick theologians have been to say what is a result of a fallen world (which is especially, and unfortunately, prevalent in discussions on disability), I have chosen to integrate Hartke's perspective on what may be a result of sin. Even if what he proposes is not the case (or even entirely consistent within Hartke's own view; see *Transforming*, 2, 12, 38), my hope is to engage with a trans perspective instead of engaging with someone else's account of a trans perspective.

[76]Whole books have and will be dedicated to that project, which is why this treatment will be insufficient. To name just a few from a diversity of perspectives: James K. Beilby and Paul Rhodes Eddy, eds., *Understanding Transgender Identities: Four Views* (Grand Rapids, MI: Baker Academic, 2019); Michele Moore and Heather Brunskell-Evans, *Transgender Children and Young People*, 2nd ed. (Newcastle upon Tyne, UK: Cambridge Scholars, 2018); Mark A. Yarhouse, *Understanding Gender Dysphoria: Navigating Transgender Issues in a Changing Culture* (Downers Grove, IL: InterVarsity Press, 2017); Hartke, *Transforming*; and for those wanting to hear more from male-to-female trans Christians, see Mark A. Yarhouse and Trista L. Carrs, "MTF Transgender Christians' Experiences: A Qualitative Study," *Journal of LGBT Issues in Counseling* 6, no. 1 (1 January 2012): 18-33.

[77]Hartke, *Transforming*, 38.

[78]In responding to gender essentialism, Yarhouse states, "I am not saying there are no differences in gender identity, but the underlying assumption of a fundamentally dichotomous gender identity difference may not be as helpful and may lead to a kind of rigid stereotyping that could actually exacerbate questions about gender identity" (*Understanding Gender Dysphoria*, 43).

[79]Hartke, *Transforming*, 38. Yarhouse comments, "Too often Christians can fall into more rigid stereotypes about gender that reflect more cultural concerns than biblical concerns, and people can overcorrect toward stereotypes out of concern for the deconstruction of sex/gender norms" (*Understanding Gender Dysphoria*, 159).

compassionate, sensitive, theatrical boy is no longer shamed for being girly, nor is the headstrong, agentic, athletic girl shamed for being boyish. These are simply seen as differing personality traits expressed by two children— one who has a boy's body and one who has a girl's.

However, Hartke goes on to describe another experience that he classifies as an internal effect of the fall.[80] For those for whom the feeling of being in the wrong body "would exist even if you picked them up and set them on a desert island," he comments that, in his view, "this is the only point at which it might possibly be justifiable to think of gender dysphoria as a product of the fall—the point at which the trans person experiences suffering that is neither self-inflicted nor caused by others."[81] In these cases, for whatever reason, trans persons genuinely feel like they should have differently sexed anatomies. Given what has been discussed above in terms of sex chromosomes and sexual development, in utero, to puberty, and throughout life—sexed embodiment is complicated. Consequently, for some people their givenness is not experienced as a gift. For some people, things do not seem as they should be. Where intense controversy remains is in how to address this; Mark Yarhouse's work provides several frameworks from which to think through how these persons might move forward.[82] The implications of this chapter, however, are not to provide a moral prescription for transgender persons, but to (1) show how gender-essentialist logic may actually be contributing to the internal angst of some trans persons, and (2) to emphasize that the priority of the scriptural text is on following Jesus, not being "real men" or "real women." For those who are discerning whether their givenness should be altered, the New Testament rubric for any such choice (which would include all bodily modifications, not just those affecting sexual anatomy) is how such can be done in submission to the Spirit and in order to become more like Christ.[83]

---

[80]I recognize that this is highly controversial and that Hartke's opinion should not be understood as representing all transgender Christian perspectives. However, given the lack of published work from trans Christians, I have decided to engage his voice since he has first-person experience as a trans person and is also interested in thinking theologically about these concerns.

[81]Consequently, Hartke provides two ways of thinking of gender dysphoria—one that is constructed and one that is not (*Transforming*, 38).

[82]Cited in the resource list in note 76 above.

[83]Such decisions are also best done in healthy communities in order to support and discern with that person how best to move forward with such weighty and personal decisions. It should also

In summary, what rejection of gender essentialism does is to challenge the centrality of maleness and femaleness for understanding human personhood. For gender essentialists, this understanding is typically codified in narrow expressions of masculinity and femininity that are then made to be morally binding. The moral emphasis of the Scriptures, however, is to expand the presence of God in all the earth, and this expansion is not bound to adhering to cultural interpretations of what it means to be male and female.

CONCLUSION

The biblical texts are not consumed with the questions of what it means to be a man or what it means to be a woman. The scriptural texts are consumed with questions about the personal divine presence of God and how it might expand into all the earth. The answers to these questions were first provided in the original creation stories with the inclusive royal priesthood of the man and the woman. The answers were then deepened in human history with the entrance of the ultimate high priest and royal Son, and they will continue to deepen still as we move into new heavens and the new earth by the power of the Spirit. For now, as we sit in the tension of the already and the not yet, may we press into our collective priesthood, representing Christ through our particularities as we are united by the Spirit into one body, expanding God's personal divine presence ever outward.[84]

---

be clear that by becoming more like Christ, I am clearly not advocating becoming more like his male body.

[84]While the views expressed in this paper on my own, I am indebted to the critique of the Logos Institute work-in-progress-group at the University of St Andrews, especially Hannah Craven, Jonathan Rutledge, and Joshua Cockayne. Mary Lynn Kirby, Hugh Kirby, Michelle Panchuk, Lisa Igram, Mike Rea, and Matthew McKirland also gave excellent input over multiple drafts.

16

BIBLICAL PRIESTHOOD
AND WOMEN IN MINISTRY

Stanley J. Grenz

• • • • •

SINCE THE 1970s, the propriety of women serving in the pastoral office in the church has been a contentious issue.[1] The controversy has increasingly polarized evangelical participants in the discussion into two basic positions. On the one side stand those who support gender equality, who assert that the Holy Spirit may call both men and women to all leadership roles in the church. Their position is opposed by male-leadership advocates, who aver that certain ecclesiastical positions (or functions) are for men only.

Advocates of male leadership are united in the conviction that some restrictions are to be placed on the service of women in the church. Nevertheless, they do not speak with one voice as to what specific offices are off-limits. Hence some would bar women from any position that places men under their authority, whereas others reserve only the "role of authoritative pastoral leadership" embodied in the office of sole pastor or senior pastor.[2] Whatever the degree of restriction they may advocate, those arguing for male leadership build their theological case for limiting the role of women from the fundamental belief they all share that God has placed within creation itself an ordering of the sexes that delegates to men the

---

[1] This essay is adapted from Stanley J. Grenz and Denise Muir Kjesbo, *Women in the Church: A Biblical Theology of Women in Ministry* (Downers Grove, IL: InterVarsity Press, 1995), 173-230.
[2] J. I. Packer, "Let's Stop Making Women Presbyters," *CT* 35, no. 2 (1991): 20.

prerogative of leading, initiating, and taking responsibility for the well-being of women, and entrusts to women the role of following male leadership, as well as supporting, enabling, and helping men. Because the pastoral office (or function) entails by its very nature authoritative oversight, male-leadership proponents conclude that this role is—as J. I. Packer so tersely put it—"for manly men rather than womanly women."[3]

A corollary to the claim that the pastoral office is authoritative, and hence off-limits to women, is the idea that the pastoral role is priestly in character. Because women could not serve as priests in the Old Testament, the argument runs, the pastoral office (or function) is properly filled by men only. The view that the pastorate is priestly in character is widely assumed among opponents of women's ordination in the more liturgical traditions—the Orthodox, Roman Catholic, and Anglican communions.[4] But it has found its way into the thinking of partisans in free churches as well.[5]

The goal of this essay is to interact with the thesis set forth by those who would restrict pastoral leadership to males regarding the priestly character of the pastoral office. In what follows, I explore the relationship between the concept of priesthood and the propriety of women in the pastorate. More specifically, I tackle the question, Does whatever priestly character that may be predicated of the pastoral office (or function) necessitate an all-male pastorate? To this end, I engage first with the idea of a connection between the Old Testament priesthood and the pastorate and relate this to the New Testament doctrine of the priesthood of all believers. Then I tackle the question of the representational character of the pastorate. Finally, I indicate the implications of the New Testament focus on the priesthood of gifted persons for our understanding of the pastorate. In this manner, I will argue that whereas an all-male pastorate might logically follow from the link between priest and pastor (erroneously) forged by

---

[3]Packer, "Let's Stop," 20. Packer's article provides a succinct articulation of this widely propagated view.
[4]Patrick Henry Reardon, "Women Priests: History and Theology," *Touchstone* 6, no. 1 (1993): 26-27; Michael Novak, "Women, Ordination and Angels," *First Things* 32 (1993): 25-32. See the summary of the position of Canon Geddes MacGregor in Paul K. Jewett, *The Ordination of Women* (Grand Rapids, MI: Eerdmans, 1980), 15-16.
[5]See, e.g., Bernard E. Seton, "Should Our Church Ordain Women? No," *Ministry* 58, no. 3 (1985): 16. Seton is a former associate secretary of the General Council of the Seventh-day Adventists.

theologians in liturgical traditions, the understanding of the church most widely espoused in evangelical circles leads to viewing the pastorate as a gifted leadership serving within a gifted people.

THE LEVITICAL PRIESTHOOD AND THE PASTORATE

Many opponents of women in ministry claim that the pastorate is to be understood in a priestly manner and that this office (or function) is the ecclesiastical instantiation of the general biblical principle of male priesthood. Bernard Seton, for example, offers this sweeping statement: "The Bible establishes an all-male priesthood or ministry, both within and outside the family."[6]

At first glance, the correctness of the contention that God intends that the priestly role be limited to males appears almost self-evident. Male-leadership advocates find what they see as God's intention displayed throughout salvation history. In the Old Testament, priestly functions were performed by men, not women. These functions included representing the people to God, accepting the people's offerings, and presenting the offerings to God in sacrifice. Later, the priestly function was more formally codified when God established Israel as his people and selected the sons of Levi—specifically, Aaron and his male descendants—for this role.

Rather than overturning the Old Testament precedent, male-leadership proponents add, the New Testament reaffirms it. They find the foundation for its continuation in Jesus' selection of twelve male apostles, for in so doing our Lord maintained the older principle of the male priestly ministry, even while he himself superseded the priestly order. Seton explains: "The days of the Levitical priesthood had passed; the apostolic age was about to dawn. But in each age men filled the priestly roles."[7] The church, in turn, followed Jesus' lead by replacing Judas with a male successor and later by ordaining men such as Paul and Timothy to leadership roles and by establishing an all-male presbytery. The presbytery (that is, the pastorate), it is concluded, is the ecclesiastical analogue to the ancient priesthood. Hence Thomas Schreiner, who only cautiously endorses the argument from the all-male priesthood in the Old Testament, remains true to the

---

[6]Seton, "Should Our Church Ordain Women?," 16.
[7]Seton, "Should Our Church Ordain Women?," 16.

basic male-leadership line when he writes, "There is a suggestive pattern in that women functioned as prophets in both the OT and the NT, but they do not serve as priests in the OT nor as elders in the NT."[8]

Several considerations indicate that it is unwarranted to extend the Old Testament priesthood to the New Testament pastorate in a manner that bars women from the latter. Let me mention only one. The male-leadership apologetic builds from the assumption that the priesthood in ancient Israel exemplifies a divinely instituted pattern incumbent on God's people in all ages and that the pastorate parallels, by divine design, this Old Testament structure. The argument runs aground, I maintain, on the great theological principle known as the priesthood of all believers.

Believer priesthood and the leadership of women. The book of Hebrews asserts that the great high priest toward whom Old Testament worship pointed is Jesus himself (Heb 4:14–10:18). Because of Christ's work, all believers may now confidently approach "the throne of grace" and receive mercy (Heb 4:16). All may enter the Most Holy Place (which in the temple had been the prerogative solely of the high priest) and "draw near to God" (Heb 10:19-22 NIV). Indeed, Christ has made all believers priests of God (Rev 1:6; 5:10; 20:6). Consequently, together they constitute "a holy priesthood, to offer spiritual sacrifices acceptable to God through Jesus Christ," including "the mighty acts of him who called you out of darkness into his wonderful light" (1 Pet 2:5, 9; cf. Rom 12:1; Heb 13:5). And all share in the privilege of interceding for one another before God (2 Thess 3:1; 1 Tim 2:1-2; Jas 5:16). With a view toward the new status all believers now share, Jesus repeatedly warned his disciples against adopting the attitude of the Pharisees, who elevated themselves as teachers and masters over the people (Mt 23:8-12; see also Mk 10:42-44; 1 Tim 2:5). In short, the New Testament presents the church as a fellowship of believer priests.

The New Testament portrayal of the church as a priesthood of believers implies that the parallel to the Levitical priesthood is not the ordained office (or leadership function) but the church as a whole. If the people—and not merely church leaders—are God's holy priesthood, then the exclusion of women from the pastorate on the basis of the all-male nature of the

---

[8]Thomas Schreiner, "Review of Stanley J. Grenz and Denise Muir Kjesbo, *Women in the Church,*" *Trinity Journal* 17, no. 1 (1996): 121.

Old Testament priesthood is unwarranted. Moreover, appeals to the priestly character of the pastorate risk losing the glorious truth of the gospel that the prerogative of serving as priests before God and toward one another—a prerogative once reserved for a small, select group among the people of God—has now been given to all through the work of Christ and by the outpouring of the Spirit.

Concern for this was one factor that triggered the Reformation rediscovery of the universal priesthood. Luther's quest for a gracious God led him to the theological issue of access to divine grace. According to the theology of the Middle Ages, the faithful become recipients of this grace through the sacraments of the church. The clergy are crucial in this process, according to medieval theology. Clergy act as priestly mediators between God and the people, serving as God's instruments in dispensing divine grace and forgiveness and acting as representatives of the people in bringing their offerings and prayers to God. Against the medieval understanding, Luther asserted that believers enjoy direct access to God apart from any human mediators (except Christ). They receive God's grace directly through faith, and they have the privilege of coming to God themselves.

Although the principle of the priesthood of all believers has gained nearly universal acknowledgment among evangelicals, those advocating male leadership aver that the principle does not necessarily entail that the pastorate is open to all believers regardless of gender. Denying that the priesthood of all believers opens the door to women in ministry requires, however, that this doctrine be deemed irrelevant to the issue of pastoral leadership.

Susan Foh makes this argument by first rejecting any connection between the Levitical priesthood and the ordained office: "There is no continuity between the office of priest, which ceased when Christ sacrificed himself once for all (Heb 7:11–10:25), and the office of elder or pastor-teacher." According to Foh, the priesthood of all believers involves our offering of ourselves as spiritual sacrifices to God and our access to God through Christ. "Women are priests in these senses just as men," she affirms. Yet "this status does not qualify anyone for any church office."[9]

---

[9]Susan T. Foh, "A Male Leadership View," in *Women in Ministry: Four Views*, ed. Bonnidell Clouse and Robert G. Clouse (Downers Grove, IL: InterVarsity Press, 1989), 93-94.

Foh's approach is a marked departure from the arguments of those male-leadership proponents who appeal to male Levitical priesthood as a model for the church's ordained office. In fact, her disjoining of the Old Testament priest and the New Testament pastor—which when viewed from the perspective of actual mediatory function is technically correct—serves to knock a prop out from under the case for an all-male pastorate. Foh likewise correctly interprets the New Testament priesthood as universal. She acknowledges that as priests all believers enjoy direct access to God and offer spiritual sacrifices to him. Yet at one point she is quite mistaken. Rather than not qualifying anyone for any church office, as she concludes, the status of priest is exactly what forms the basic qualification for all church offices.[10] Because Christ has qualified all believers to stand in God's presence, regardless of race, social status, or gender, we are all ministers within the fellowship. As priests of God—and only because we are priests—we are called by the Spirit to ministries among Christ's people, and some of these ministries include positions of leadership.

Evangelical ecclesiology and the leadership of women. Although the principle of believer priesthood has gained acceptance in nearly all Christian traditions, historically evangelicals have been at the forefront of emphasizing the concept and drawing out its implications. Commitment to the priesthood of all believers is connected with the evangelical understanding of the church as consisting ultimately in the people themselves and not in the ordained clergy. In short, evangelicals view the church as a community of reconciled sinners rather than as a dispenser of divine grace.

Evangelicals have understood believer priesthood to mean as well that the task of the church belongs to the people as a whole. This has provided the impetus among evangelicals for promoting the inclusion of all believers in the life of the church and for elevating the importance of every believer's contribution to the work of the ministry. In other words, the evangelical emphasis on the shared responsibility of all the people of God for the work of the congregation leads quite naturally to an egalitarian view of the pastorate. Evangelicals typically do not see clergy as mediators between God and the people. Pastors are not a special class of Christians

---

[10]This position has enjoyed adherents throughout church history. See Ida Raming, "The Twelve Apostles Were Men," *Theology Digest* 40, no. 1 (1993): 24.

who mediate God's grace to the people. Nor do clergy mediate Christ's authority to the church; they are to assist the people in determining the will of the risen Lord for his church. Simply stated, ordained ministers are persons chosen by God and acknowledged by the church, who have been charged with the responsibility of leading the people as a whole in fulfilling the mandate Christ has given to the entire church.

The centrality of these themes means that the evangelical understanding of the church not only poses no inherent roadblocks to women serving in leadership capacities but demands the full partnership of male and female within church life. A church in which all participate in the mandate they share is one in which women and men work side by side in the varied ministries of the community. They learn from each other, uphold one another, and contribute their personal strengths to the common mission without being prejudiced by gender distinctions. In such a church, how could the partnership suddenly dissolve at the leadership level, with only men being viewed as qualified to serve in teaching and leadership? Why would a church of believer priests that otherwise focuses on the activity of all persons in the common ministry suddenly erect an ordained office (or foster a leadership role) characterized by a hierarchy of male over female?

The extension of the Old Testament structure of male priesthood to the New Testament church fails to understand that the priesthood has been radically transformed by the new covenant, which our Lord inaugurated. No longer do believers look to a special priestly class to whom God has entrusted the central responsibility for carrying out the religious vocation of his covenant people. Rather, all are participants in the one mandate to be ministers of God, and to this end all serve together. The role of the pastorate arises solely out of the ministry of the entire fellowship of believers. The pastoral office (or function) is an extension of the universal ministry of Christ's body, the church. This dimension of the church's ministry, as well as the church's ministry in general, is best fulfilled as women and men work together.[11]

Evangelicals agree that the sovereign Spirit calls different persons to differing functions in the church, including oversight responsibilities. The

---

[11]Paul King Jewett, "Why I Favor the Ordination of Women," *CT* 19, no. 18 (1975): 9.

principle of the universal priesthood implies that the Spirit's call of some to the pastorate arises fundamentally out of his call to all believers to be ministers of Christ. Within this fellowship of believer priests, race, social status, and gender cannot be overriding factors that disqualify a believer priest for selection to leadership among God's people, for service in the pastorate is based on the Spirit's sovereign call and gifting of certain persons for this particular ministry.

Before arguing this point explicitly, however, I must address another supposed priestly dimension of the pastorate that carries implications for the ministry of women: its representative character.

THE REPRESENTATIVE PRIESTHOOD AND THE PASTORATE

In his defense of an all-male pastorate, C. S. Lewis asserts that the central issue that divides him from proponents of women in ministry is the meaning of the word *priest*. Lewis claims that his opponents forget that the basic role of a priest is representational, that a priest "represents us to God and God to us."[12] According to Lewis, the second aspect is the crucial consideration, for in his estimation a woman cannot fully represent God. Patrick Henry Reardon presses the point even further. He asserts that "ordaining the male sex to minister at the Eucharist has to do with the 'correct appearance' ('orthodoxy' in Greek), the proper iconography," and that altering the icon eventually will lead to the worship of "a different god." Consequently, Reardon concludes, ordaining women is "a grave act of disobedience and a first, but firm, step toward apostasy."[13]

The gravity of these charges requires a careful appraisal of a second dimension of the argument put forth by some male-leadership advocates, the representational aspect of the pastorate, especially the supposed role of the pastor in representing Christ. Putting the issue in the form of a question, Are pastors priests who represent Christ? And if so, in what sense?

Eucharistic representation. Those who would bar women from the pastorate on the basis of the representational character of the ordained office

---

[12]C. S. Lewis, *God in the Dock* (Grand Rapids, MI: Eerdmans, 1970), 236.
[13]Reardon, "Women Priests," 27.

claim that pastors are priests who represent or "image" Christ.[14] For example, J. I. Packer declares, "Since the Son of God was incarnate as a male, it will always be easier, other things being equal, to realize and remember that Christ is ministering in person if his human agent and representative is also male."[15] Those who follow this line of reasoning generally find this representational function most readily displayed as ordained ministers represent Christ at the Eucharist.

In the West, the idea of the priest as Christ's representative at the Eucharist developed out of the commonplace designation of the officiator as acting "in the person of Christ" (*in persona Christi*). Although the theological use of this idea may have arisen with Thomas Aquinas, since the Second Vatican Council it has been used widely in Roman Catholic circles to describe the priest as impersonating our Lord. According to official church teaching, in pronouncing the words of consecration at the Eucharist, the priest takes the role of Christ to the point of being his very image. Because those who take Christ's role must have a natural resemblance to him, women cannot be ordained to the priesthood.

Protestants generally reject the Roman Catholic theology of the Mass, of course. Yet the idea of eucharistic representation remains embedded in the widely held perception that the Communion service is a reenactment of the Last Supper, in which the officiating pastor plays the part of Jesus. As a consequence, in the eyes of many Christians, only a man can officiate at the Communion observance.

The officiant at the Lord's Supper does fulfill a certain representational function. But this representation is fundamentally vocal rather than visual.[16] In the eucharistic celebration, the presider announces Christ's words of invitation, thereby serving as the mouthpiece for the risen Lord, who is the true host. Nothing inherent in this representational function would bar someone from officiating at the table on the basis of gender. On

---

[14]This argument is cited in Madeleine Boucher, "Ecumenical Documents: Authority-in-Community," *Midstream* 21, no. 3 (1982): 412.

[15]Packer, "Let's Stop," 20.

[16]Mark C. Chapman, "The Ordination of Women: Evangelical and Catholic," *Dialog* 28 (1989): 135. Cf. Martin Luther, *Book of Concord*, ed. Theodore G. Tappert (Philadelphia: Fortress, 1959), 448. Hull hints at a similar position. See Gretchen Gaebelein Hull, *Equal to Serve* (Old Tappan, NJ: Revell, 1987), 220.

the contrary, the church's eucharistic doctrine might actually be enhanced by women's presiding at the Lord's Table. As theologians of various denominations have concluded, an all-male clergy perpetuates the erroneous ideas that the Eucharist is a mass in which the priest acts as Christ, offering our Lord's body and blood to God, or that it is simply a reenactment of the Last Supper in which the pastor acts the part of Jesus.[17] Evangelical theologians are quick to point out that the Lord's Supper is not a reinstitution of Calvary. And although it is in a sense a reenactment of the upper room events, it is not merely an artistic drama. If limiting the officiators to men tends to perpetuate inaccurate and limited understandings of the Eucharist, then permitting both women and men to officiate could enhance the church's experience of this significant ordinance.[18]

Ontological representation. The representative function of those who officiate at the Eucharist is understood by some traditions to be an *ontological* representation of Christ; that is, the pastor is believed to embody in some symbolic manner the actual nature of our Lord. As the earlier quotation from J. I. Packer indicates, the idea of ontological representation provides a powerful rationale for the exclusion of women from the ordained office. Because the incarnate and exalted Lord is male, and insofar as Jesus' maleness is not inconsequential but is of timeless, cosmic significance, those who represent Christ must likewise be male.[19]

Despite its seemingly unassailable logic, this argument has been questioned by a long list of Protestant and Roman Catholic scholars.[20] Critics do not necessarily reject the representative function of the ordained office. Rather, they aver that clergy represent Christ in his humanness, not in his maleness, a point that finds support in both the biblical documents and the church fathers.[21] The great declarations of the incarnation in the New

---

[17]John Austin Baker, "Eucharistic Presidency and Women's Ordination," *Theology* 88, no. 725 (1985): 357.

[18]This point is argued in Baker, "Eucharistic Presidency."

[19]E.g., Sara Butler, "Forum: Some Second Thoughts on Ordaining Women," *Worship* 63, no. 2 (1989): 165. S. M. Hutchens, for example, sees Jesus' maleness as indicating a cosmic priority of the male. See S. M. Hutchens, "God, Gender and the Pastoral Office," *Touchstone* 5, no. 4 (1992): 16-17.

[20]Constance F. Parvey, "Where Are We Going? The Threefold Ministry and the Ordination of Women," *Word and World* 5, no. 1 (1985): 9.

[21]Stephen C. Barton, "Impatient for Justice: Five Reasons Why the Church of England Should Ordain Women to the Priesthood," *Theology* 92, no. 749 (1989): 404.

Testament emphasize that Christ became human, not that he became male. John announces that "the Word became flesh" (Jn 1:14). And in speaking of Jesus Christ as "being born in human likeness" (Phil 2:7), Paul uses the general Greek word *anthrōpos* ("human") rather than the gender-specific *anēr* ("man"). Following the lead of the New Testament, the Nicene Creed declares that our Lord became a human being (*enanthrōpēsanta*), thereby taking to himself the likeness of all who are included within the scope of his saving work. For the church fathers, the focus on the inclusiveness of Jesus' humanity was a theological necessity based on an important theological principle: what the Son did not assume in the incarnation he could not redeem.[22]

Advocates of gender equality find in Jesus' inclusive humanness important implications for the ordination of women. They argue that to elevate maleness as an essential requirement for ministry is to stand in opposition to the inclusive significance of Christ's saving work. Thus, rather than barring women from ordination, classical Christology demands their inclusion in the ordained office. Madeleine Boucher explains concisely: "It may be argued that a priestly ministry of women and men would better image and represent the universality of Christ and redemption."[23]

But what about the undeniable maleness of Jesus? Certainly we do not wish to discount Jesus' gender any more than his Jewishness or his socioeconomic status. What is at issue is the *soteriological* or saving significance of these aspects of our Lord's earthly existence. Boucher speaks for many when she explains, "We affirm—and affirm properly—that Christ redeems us *as* a man, as a Jew, as a poor person, and so on. The difficulty arises when it is implied that Christ redeems us *by virtue of the fact* that he is a man, as though his maleness were a necessary condition for God's saving

---

[22]This principle dates at least to Irenaeus. See Irenaeus, *Adversus Haereses* 5.14, in *The Ante-Nicene Fathers*, ed. Alexander Roberts and James Donaldson (Grand Rapids, MI: Eerdmans, 1975), 1:541. It formed an important consideration in the christological controversies. Against Apollinarius, for example, Gregory of Nazianzus asserted: "If any one has put his trust in him as a man without a human mind, he is himself devoid of mind and unworthy of salvation. For what he has not assumed he has not healed; it is what is united to his Deity that is saved." See "An Examination of Apollinarianism," in *Documents of the Christian Church*, 2nd ed., ed. Henry Bettenson (London: Oxford University Press, 1963), 45. See also J. N. D. Kelly, *Early Christian Doctrines*, 5th rev. ed. (London: Adam and Charles Black, 1977), 297.

[23]Barton, "Impatient for Justice," 404, 413. See also Untener, "Forum: The Ordination of Women," 57.

work in him."[24] Hence although the incarnation in the form of a male may have been historically and culturally necessary, attaching soteriological necessity to this would undercut Christ's status as representing all humans—male and female—in salvation.[25]

If clergy do represent Christ, then this demands that women and men serve together within the ordained office. Restricting the ordained office to males can cloud the symbolism of Christ's inclusive humanity. Moreover, whatever representative function ordained ministers fulfill is indirect, arising from their role within the church. Pastors function as ontological representatives of our Lord only insofar as they represent the church, which is Christ's body—and hence is, in this sense, the ontological representation of Christ.[26] Because Christ is creating one new human reality (Eph 2:15) in which distinctions of race, class, and gender are overcome (Gal 3:28), the church—and consequently Christ—is best represented by an ordained ministry consisting of persons from various races, from all social classes, and from both genders.

Yet I must voice a slight caveat here. I do not believe that these considerations necessitate denying all soteriological significance to Jesus' maleness. In fact, to do so is to reduce the importance of our sexuality, which is an indispensable dimension of embodied human existence.[27] Because Jesus was a particular historical person, his maleness was integral to the completion of his task. More particularly, being male facilitated Jesus in revealing the radical difference between God's ideal and the social structures of his day. Only a male could have offered an authoritative critique of those power structures.[28] Coming to this earth as a man, Jesus liberated both men and women from their bondage to the social orders that violate God's intention for human life-in-community. Jesus freed males from their slavery to the role of domination that belongs to the fallen world, in order that they can be truly male. On behalf of women Jesus acted as the

---

[24]Boucher, "Ecumenical Documents," 412-13. (Boucher then cites John Macquarrie, *Principles of Christian Theology*, 278.)
[25]Parvey, "Where Are We Going?," 9.
[26]E. J. Kilmartin, "Apostolic Office: Sacrament of Christ," *Theological Studies* 36, no. 2 (1975): 263.
[27]Butler, "Forum: Some Second Thoughts," 165.
[28]Suzanne Heine, *Matriarchs, Goddesses and Images of God*, trans. John Bowden (Minneapolis: Augsburg, 1989), 137-45.

paradigmatic human standing against the patriarchal system, bringing women to participate in the new order where sex distinctions no longer determine rank and worth.

But notice the implication: the church, in turn, best reflects, embodies, and announces the liberating significance of Jesus' incarnation as a male by following the principle of mutuality he pioneered. This mutuality emerges as women and men work together in all dimensions of church life, including the ordained ministry.

THE PRIESTHOOD OF GIFTED PERSONS AND THE PASTORATE

Marianne Meye Thompson offers a helpful appraisal of the current state of the debate over the role of women in the church:

> Both those who favor women in ministry and those who oppose women in ministry can find suitable proof texts and suitable rationalizations to explain those texts. But if our discussion is ever to move beyond proof texting, we must integrate these texts into a theology of ministry. I suggest that the starting point for such a theology of ministry lies in the God who gives gifts for ministry and in the God who is no respecter of persons.[29]

In keeping with this insight, I want now to move to the positive side of my argument: to draw out the implications of the great evangelical acknowledgment that the Spirit's gifting is the basis for church leadership. This focus on the Spirit means that rather than being the New Testament counterpart to the Old Testament priesthood, the pastoral office (or role) is charismatic in character. It is to be filled by persons gifted for the pastorate, whether male or female, serving among the gifted people of God, who as a whole constitute the ecclesiastical counterpart to the Levitical priesthood.

The New Testament presents a gender-inclusive conception of spiritual gifts (or *charismata*). Paul indicates that lying behind all gifts, regardless of who receives them, is a common source—God (1 Cor 12:6, 28). Gifts are given not on the basis of human merit but by the will of the sovereign Holy Spirit (1 Cor 12:7-11) and the risen Christ (Eph 4:7, 11). The Spirit's

---

[29]Marianne Meye Thompson, "Response to Richard Longenecker," in *Women, Authority and the Bible*, ed. Alvera Mickelsen (Downers Grove, IL: InterVarsity Press, 1986), 94.

endowments are bestowed on each believer, not merely a select few. The Lord of the church accords these gifts for the good of the church as a whole (1 Cor 12:7) and the completion of the common task of Christ's people (Eph 4:12). The egalitarian perspective of the New Testament raises two crucial questions for the pastoral office (or role) and the matter of who may serve in it.

First, what is the relationship of spiritual gifts to the pastoral office? Regarding this question, the New Testament witness to the practices of the early church suggests certain guiding principles. First, because pastors are to engage in certain specific activities, including preaching, teaching, and leading, only those entrusted with the *charismata* that facilitate these aspects of ministry are appropriate candidates for the pastorate. Second, because some gifts are intended to be used only intermittently and in specific individual contexts, whereas others are designed for regular, constant use within the ongoing structure of wider community life, only those persons whom the Spirit has gifted for the regular public ministry of the community as a whole are likely to function in the pastorate. Third, insofar as leaders are to be involved in overseeing the ministry of the community, the church is to set in leadership those whom the Spirit has endowed with the appropriate gifts (such as administration) for leading the whole people of God in "works of ministry" (Eph 4:12).

Lying behind these principles is the assumption that spiritual gifts are foundational to office. For this reason, as male-leadership Bible scholar Ronal Fung notes, "the charismata are the wherewithal, the tools, the means of ministry. . . . It is by the endowment of charismata that its ministers are made sufficient."[30] In short, giftedness for the functions of the ordained ministry is the indispensable prerequisite for setting someone apart for such a ministry. The integral relation between gifts and ministry leads to the general principle that the church must give place for the giftedness of all persons, whether male or female. Men and women are to serve together, using whatever gifts the Spirit bestows on them.

This raises a second crucial question: Does the Spirit endow women with the gifts essential for the pastorate? On this matter there seems to be

---

[30]Ronald Y. K. Fung, "Ministry in the New Testament," in *The Church in the Bible and the World*, ed. D. A. Carson (Grand Rapids, MI: Baker, 1987), 178.

little disagreement. Alvera Mickelsen's concise remark summarizes what most scholars would admit: "In Paul's lengthy discussions about spiritual gifts, he never indicates that some gifts are for men and other gifts for women."[31] This conclusion is exactly what we would expect from the observation made previously that the Holy Spirit is ultimately sovereign in endowing God's people with gifts for ministry. Because this task is the prerogative of the Spirit, it is not ours to decide on whom he can and cannot bestow certain gifts. On the contrary, the Old Testament prophets, who lived during the days of the all-male priesthood, anticipated a time when the Spirit would work through both women and men (e.g., Joel 2:28-29). According to Luke, the promised era dawned with Pentecost (Acts 2:14-18). Consequently, the Spirit is now at work freely in the church endowing whomever he chooses—both male and female—with whatever gifts he wills.

This point of agreement has important implications for the ministry of gifted persons—including women—in the church. To accomplish the mandate Christ has entrusted to the community of faith, our Lord has poured out the Spirit, who endows believers with spiritual gifts. These are distributed throughout the community according to the Spirit's will. The New Testament offers no hint that the Spirit restricts to men the gifts that equip a person to function in the ordained office (e.g., teaching, preaching, leadership), while distributing without distinction the gifts necessary for other ministries. Margaret Howe raises the obvious rhetorical question: if gifts equipping for pastoral ministry "are distributed by *God* to women, what higher authority does the church have for denying the women their expression?"[32]

Those who would restrict pastoral leadership to males, however, are quick to respond: important as they are, the *charismata* do not constitute the only factor in determining the role of women in the church. Rather, as Fung declares, "Paul's practice and his teaching with regard to women in ministry also need to be taken into account." He and his colleagues are

---

[31] Alvera Mickelsen, "An Egalitarian View: There Is Neither Male nor Female in Christ," in Clouse and Clouse, *Women in Ministry: Four Views*, 191.

[32] E. Margaret Howe, "The Positive Case for the Ordination of Women," in *Perspectives on Evangelical Theology*, ed. Kenneth S. Kantzer and Stanley N. Gundry (Grand Rapids, MI: Zondervan, 1979), 275.

convinced that in this matter Paul follows the principle of male leadership and female subordination. Hence Fung concludes from his study of the New Testament that "a woman who has received the gift of teaching (or leadership, or any other charisma) may exercise it to the fullest extent possible—in any role which does not involve her in a position of doctrinal or ecclesiastical authority over men."[33]

But notice what Fung is saying. To skirt the ecclesiological implications of the New Testament teaching on spiritual gifts, he must drive a sharp wedge between *charismata* and the ordained office. Fung finds no contradiction between "Paul's teaching concerning the indiscriminate distribution of spiritual gifts to men and women alike" and the restrictions he claims "Paul imposes on women's ministry by reason of woman's subordination to man." But to harmonize these two principles, Fung must declare unequivocally that "*gift* and *role* are to be distinguished."[34] In other words, to salvage their interpretation of Paul's approach to women in ministry, male-leadership proponents impose what appears to be an artificial dichotomy between the Spirit's gifting and the exercise of the ordained office.

This move evidences an even deeper problem with the male-leadership position. The limitation on a woman's use of the gift of teaching to those roles that do not place her in authority over men subsumes ecclesiology (the doctrine of the church) under anthropology (our understanding of what it means to be human). In the end, the case against women in the pastorate rests on a supposed divinely intended hierarchical ordering present within creation. Yet even if God had so ordered the sexes from the beginning (which he did not), this would not necessarily require that the church continue to be governed by structures that perpetuate male leadership and female subordination. Christ established the church not merely to be a mirror of original creation but to be the eschatological new community, living in accordance with the principles of God's new creation and thereby reflecting the mutuality that lies at the heart of the triune God.

---

[33]Fung, "Ministry in the New Testament," 179, 209.
[34]Fung, "Ministry in the New Testament," 209.

CONCLUSION

The controversy over women in ministry hinges on the deeper question of what kind of church Christ came to inaugurate and, in turn, what kind of pastoral office advances our Lord's intention. Male-leadership advocates envision a church in which men lead and women—regardless of their spiritual gifts—follow male leadership. To this end, they view the pastorate as the ecclesiastical instantiation of an all-male priesthood. Egalitarians, in contrast, contend that Christ intends the church to be a fellowship in which all serve as they are gifted and called by the Spirit, which requires that pastoral leadership be open to those whom the Spirit has gifted for this role.

I am convinced that the impulses born in the Reformation and advanced through the evangelical awakenings lead directly to the second of these two visions. I believe that the evangelical model of the church is one in which gifted leaders serve within a gifted people. In this church, pastors—both male and female—serve together as instruments of the Spirit in the glorious task of empowering the people of God for the work of the ministry.

17

GENDER EQUALITY AND THE ANALOGY OF SLAVERY

Stanley E. Porter

• • • • •

INTRODUCTION

The analogy of slavery is usually used in the following way in discussion of gender equality: slavery was seen to be a sanctioned institution within the biblical world, starting in the Old Testament and then continuing into the New Testament. Ancient Israel, followed by the Christian church, was a participant in the support of the institution of slavery. Even if there are some statements in the Bible, especially the New Testament, that show some regard for slaves, there are no explicit statements that instruct Christians to condemn or abolish the institution. As a result, there were many Christians who continued to participate in slavery, although through time enough Christians came to realize the inhumanity of the institution and were instrumental in its abolition, a move long overdue. In the same way, gender inequality was institutionalized within the ancient world of both the Old and New Testaments, with some of the biblical writers, including Paul, participating in the unequal treatment of women. It was only in modern times that some Christians came to embrace fully gender equality, in conjunction with the liberation from oppression of women within Western society.

There have, however, been at least two other ways in which the analogy of slavery has been used in discussion of gender equality. In the trajectory approach, some biblical scholars have seen a trajectory develop from the

Old to the New Testaments and then to the modern world, with regard to both slavery and gender equality. In other words, both of these movements move along a parallel path—as they do above in the first scenario—but with the New Testament comprising a less oppressive position along the path toward liberation for both slaves and women. This position has been argued most fully in recent times by those holding to the redemptive-historical view.[1]

The third view, and the one that I wish to argue for in this paper, is that there is an imperfect analogy between slavery and gender equality in the Bible. Ancient Israel of the Old Testament accommodated slavery within its socioeconomic institutions, but the New Testament, in particular Paul—though living within the Roman empire—took a countercultural view of slavery that called for liberating treatment of slaves within the constrictions of living within the Roman empire. In that sense, the slavery analogy has a trajectory from accommodation to critique of the institution of slavery, at least so far as it was an institution within the Christian church. The analogy with gender equality is similar, in that the New Testament promotes gender equality that, while not seen to the same extent within the Old Testament, is grounded in fundamental scriptural passages.

I will begin this chapter with a short description of whether slavery and gender equality are analogous, and then offer a summary of my view of gender equality and an exposition of the liberating message of the New Testament regarding slavery.

IS SLAVERY AN ANALOGY FOR GENDER EQUALITY?

The first question to ask, before discussing the biblical evidence, is whether slavery and gender equality constitute a legitimate analogy. From the outset, we must recognize that there are few if any true analogies, that is, identical circumstances that allow exact comparison of elements,

---

[1]This position is taken by a small number of scholars, although the larger pattern of rejecting slavery now regardless of how it was treated in the Bible is endorsed by a number of scholars. The redemptive-movement position is found in William J. Webb, *Slaves, Women and Homosexuals: Exploring the Hermeneutics of Cultural Analysis* (Downers Grove, IL: InterVarsity Press, 2001); and Webb, "A Redemptive-Movement Model," in *Four Views on Moving Beyond the Bible to Theology*, ed. Gary T. Meadors (Grand Rapids, MI: Zondervan, 2006), 251-48, along with his responses to other positions presented in the latter volume.

otherwise they would be instances of the same phenomenon. The question is, instead, whether the institution of slavery, and how it was treated in the Bible and then throughout church history, serves as a useful parallel to issues of gender equality in the Bible and then throughout church history. There are several lines of evidence to consider regarding this suitability.

The first concerns how the two are considered within the Bible itself and then society. I will concentrate on the New Testament. In the New Testament, there is evidence that slavery and gender were considered to be commensurable topics for discussion. In the ancient world, three important socioeconomic distinctions were race or ethnicity, social status, and gender. In 1 Corinthians 12:13 and Colossians 3:11, Paul mentions both race and social status, speaking of Jews and Greeks (circumcised and uncircumcised) among others, and slave and free, but asserting that all are baptized into or are one in Christ. In Galatians 3:26-29, Paul treats both race and social status but also introduces gender to form a triad that is again baptized into Christ. That these three topics constituted major pillars of the socioeconomic foundation and structure of ancient society places them on a similar footing for consideration as a suitable analogy. There is further evidence from the way in which both slaves and women have been viewed throughout history that they have both been treated as disenfranchised members of society, with free males constituting those with the dominant hierarchical power. This was true in the ancient Near East, ancient Israel, the Roman Empire, and virtually all Western societies up until fairly recent times (some would say up to the present). Throughout history the free male has been the dominant and oppressive power, and slaves and woman have been viewed in relatively similar terms as subordinate and oppressed to the point of mistreatment.

There are arguments against using the analogy, however. If one considers ethnicity, social status, and gender as three pillars of the ancient sociocultural milieu, one realizes that ethnicity and gender are unlike social status, including that of slavery. Throughout history, there has been provision for some changes in social status, even if such changes were difficult and unlikely. I will review below how both the ancient Near East, including ancient Israel, and the Roman Empire viewed possible changes in social status, including limited provision for manumission. Within the Roman world, manumitted slaves could in exceptional circumstances attain positions of responsibility and possibly wealth and influence. The same cannot be said to be true of race and gender. At least up until the contemporary world (and it is arguable that such is the case), one's sex was fixed at birth, and this established one's gender and hence gender roles, in the same way that one's racial or ethnic status was fixed at birth. Paul himself recognized that, though being in Christ eliminated racial or ethnic boundaries, there was still a role to be played by ethnic Israel in the future at the end of the age. In this sense, the three do not form a perfect analogy.

Nevertheless, despite the possible problems with the analogy, there are enough parallels that it has been used in discussion of gender equality, with the analogy being that slavery forms a suitable analogous instance of liberation and equality within the New Testament.

GENDER EQUALITY IN THE BIBLE

This entire volume is concerned with presenting the evidence for gender equality in the Bible. That is, the position of this volume, if I have understood the task correctly, is not simply to argue that enlightened humans in the contemporary world—despite the evidence within the Bible—have concluded that gender equality is the proper stance for gender relations, but that gender equality is established and firmly grounded within the Bible itself. I am certain that I cannot add anything of significance in regard to the evidence marshaled for this case elsewhere except to offer the following brief summary to set the stage for discussion of slavery.

The basis of gender equality in the Bible is not necessarily found in only a single passage but in an entire complex of teaching that unfolds most clearly in the New Testament. There is a thematic formation regarding gender equality that runs from creation itself to the New Testament. A thematic formation is a semantic notion of formation of thought around a subject, and hence a theme, that was posited, discussed, and formative for discourse within a cultural context. Such thematic formations can be identified in particular texts that activate and encapsulate the thematic formation, and they are intertextually communicated across texts.[2]

---

[2]I am consciously drawing on the notion of intertextual thematic formation from Jay Lemke, although I am using it in a way that, within the wider conceptual sphere of his formulation, is

Genesis 1:27 states that "God created humanity in his own image, in the image of God he created them; male and female he created them" (my translation, based on the TNIV). Genesis 1 makes clear that the creation of humanity is a two-stage act, in which humanity as a whole is described, before humanity is divided into its two component and complementary parts. The passages states first that "God created humanity in his own image" (see Gen 1:26).[3] At this point in the account, there is not a differentiation among humanity, but the human is treated as a whole as a being that is created in God's own image. The important point here is not to determine the exact nature of creation in the divine image but to note that the human being as humankind is the only human creature said to have been so created.[4] The second stage of the process is a distinction made within humanity. The author states: "he created them, male and female he created them." The use of the plural *them* makes clear that the original human was not androgynous, but that humanity was created equally with both male and female.[5] There are many different ways in which humanity could have been differentiated, as many ways as humans still continue to differentiate among themselves. However, the Genesis passages says that God created humans "male and female" without further distinction.

The New Testament draws on the Genesis passage in an intertextual thematic discussion, in particular in Galatians 3:2-29.[6] Richard Longenecker uses it as the basis of his New Testament social ethic, as it directly addresses the major ethical issues that have been important not just in

---

particularly adapted to discussing this biblical theme. See Jay L. Lemke, *Textual Politics: Discourse and Social Dynamics* (London: Taylor and Francis, 1995), supported by a dozen or so other articles. For the most detailed examination and utilization of Lemke's notions, see Xiaxia E. Xue, *Paul's Viewpoint on God, Israel, and the Gentiles in Romans 9–11: An Intertextual Thematic Analysis* (Carlisle, UK: Langham Monographs, 2015), esp. 26-40.

[3]See Gerhard von Rad, *Genesis*, rev. ed., trans. John H. Marks, New Testament Library (London: SCM Press, 1972), 57. This account in Gen 1 is traditionally attributed to the Priestly source, on the basis of a variety of distinctions from the Yahwist. Whether these are pertinent is a debatable point.

[4]For an enduring study of humanity in God's image, see D. J. A. Clines, "The Image of God in Man," *Tyndale Bulletin* 19 (1968): 53-103.

[5]Von Rad, *Genesis*, 60. Cf. C. F. Keil and F. Delitzsch, *Commentary on the Old Testament in Ten Volumes*, vol. 1, *The Pentateuch* (Grand Rapids, MI: Eerdmans, n.d.), 65.

[6]See Stanley E. Porter, "Reframing Social Justice in the Pauline Letters," in *The Bible and Social Justice*, ed. Cynthia Long Westfall and Bryan R. Dyer, McMaster New Testament Studies (Eugene, OR: Wipf & Stock, 2015), 130-35.

Roman times but for humanity from ancient times to the present: race or ethnicity, economic status, and gender, as noted above, within the context of what it means for a human to be baptized into Christ and therefore to be "in Christ Jesus," that is, to be a part of the community of Christ-followers.[7] Of importance to note for this discussion is that the first two of the three pairs of elements ("not Jew nor Greek," "not slave nor free") are doubly negated, while the third, "not male and female," is only singly negated, and its two items link by the conjunction *and* rather than *nor*. Whereas race and economic disparity are descriptive categories of one's condition—one is either Jew or Greek, or slave or free—humankind is constituted as "male and female." The change in the negated clauses should make us aware of the fact that Paul is making this intertextual reference to Genesis 1:27 and its gender-equal creation account.

The rest of the New Testament supports this thematic formation, from the inclusiveness of Jesus' ministry, in which his closest group of followers included women (the "disciples" were the second concentric group of Jesus' students, followed by the group of seventy, etc.), to Paul's ministry, which included women in various leading functions, such as church planters and supporters (Acts 16:14-15, Lydia), deacons (Rom 16:1, Phoebe), and apostles (Rom 16:2, with Junia a woman; see also Priscilla in Rom 16:3 as Paul's coworker, along with other women mentioned in Rom 16:1-16, such as Mary, Tryphena, Tryphosa, Persis, Rufus's mother, Julia, Nereus's sister, and possibly others included within the "saints" and "brothers"). Two sets of passages are sometimes seen as problematic for such an egalitarian position. The first is the household codes (Eph 5:21–6:9; Col 3:18–4:1; 1 Tim 6:1-2; Titus 2:1-10; 1 Pet 2:18-19). However, in many of these codes the relationship between men and women is reciprocal, indicating a relationship of equality rather than hierarchy (see discussion below). The second set of potentially problematic passages is 1 Corinthians 14:33-35 and 1 Timothy 2:11-15. The women's silence in 1 Corinthians 14:34 (arguments for removing the passage are not convincing and smack of special pleading) must be seen in light of both the statements about women praying and prophesying (1 Cor 11:5) that indicate that women in fact were not silent in the

---

[7]Richard N. Longenecker, *New Testament Ethics* (Grand Rapids, MI: Eerdmans, 1984), 30-34, and then structuring his major chapters around the passage.

Corinthian church, and the use of the article with *women*, which specifies a particular group of problematic women who are instructed to learn at home. The statement in 1 Timothy 2:11-15 (I believe written by Paul, not by some later supposedly chauvinistic Pauline interpreter) occurs within a passage concerned with propriety and right behavior, not women keeping silent, with the admonition being for women not to teach inappropriately regarding such standards of behavior or to usurp authority.[8] I realize that both of these interpretations may be controversial in some quarters but believe that they are defensible and consonant with the intertextual thematic formation of the Bible regarding gender equality.[9]

I could say much more about gender equality in the Bible but leave it to others to speak at more length, as my task is to address the analogy of slavery. At this point I wish to discuss the biblical view of slavery as a basis for establishing that the analogy of slavery is in fact an appropriate one for gender equality, but that the Bible, and especially the New Testament, has analogous liberating views of both slavery and gender equality.

SLAVERY IN THE ANCIENT WORLD

In this section, I wish to examine the institution of slavery as it is described in the Bible. I begin with the ancient near east and Old Testament and then proceed to the Roman world.

Ancient Near East and Old Testament. Old Testament slavery must be understood within the wider scope of the ancient Near East.[10] Slavery within the ancient Near East was an accepted socioeconomic reality, apparently little questioned by either the free or slaves. Slavery was also a much broader institution than is thought of today, encompassing varying degrees of servitude due to the ancient subsistence economy. Slavery therefore

---

[8]On Pauline authorship of 1 Tim 2:11-15, see Stanley E. Porter, *The Apostle Paul: His Life, Thought, and Letters* (Grand Rapids, MI: Eerdmans, 2016), 419-31.

[9]Alternative interpretations are usually of two kinds. Mediating views of these passages are probably the least convincing, as they require distinctions regarding various functions not found within the New Testament (limits on women as senior pastors, etc.). The consistent but absolute interpretations (women cannot speak or teach or have authority) must die the deaths of innumerable qualifications within the Bible itself, to say nothing of contemporary life (i.e., silence does not really mean silence, no authority does not really mean no authority). For more on 1 Tim 2, see chapter eleven by Linda L. Belleville in this volume.

[10]See Muhammad A. Dandamayev, "Slavery (ANE)," in *Anchor Bible Dictionary*, ed. David Noel Freedman (New York: Doubleday, 1992), 6:58-62, for a survey of the pertinent evidence.

included those who were deprived of freedom and ownership of their own production, but it also overlapped with those who were beholden and forced to work the land for the benefit of others. Whereas some entered into slavery involuntarily after conquest or similar means of enslavement and were then transported to the conquering country, most of these captives did not become slaves in the narrower sense but became those who worked the land for others. There were also numerous people, including those from within a land, who sold themselves into slavery often to pay off debts. Sometimes there were limits on the terms of their indenturement and other times not, with some restrictions applying to their descendants as well. Despite the language of slavery being regularly used in ancient Near Eastern documents, slavery as an institution was not as prominent as one might imagine, not least because there were not the same institutional structures in place to manage a sizable slave force, as came to be the case during later Roman times.

In many ways, slavery in the Old Testament was very similar to slavery within the wider ancient Near East.[11] It was a broadly defined socioeconomic system that encompassed both those who were completely subject and those of restricted benefit of their labors. The ancient Israelites also at times had put into slavery those whom they conquered, although the terms of such slavery varied as in the ancient Near East, with some becoming enforced slaves and others servants and tribute payers. Ancient Israel also had a system of debt slavery by which debtors would indenture themselves to others, often for a fixed period of time, in order to repay a financial obligation. Whereas some ancient Near Eastern cultures recognized the differences between foreign and domestic slaves, the ancient Israelites seemed to make such a distinction more consistently, with varying standards for treatment. Being an Israelite slave provided, at least according to the Deuteronomic law, for fixed terms of indenture, usually six years, before one's debt was considered repaid or the person freed from service. There were also some considerations in the law for the treatment of slaves, such as whether they were to be required to work on the Sabbath (e.g., the fourth commandment; Ex 20:10; 23:12; Deut 5:14), or

---

[11]See Dandamayev, "Slavery (OT)," 6:62-65, for information and biblical examples.

whether they would be circumcised and hence included within the cultic community (e.g., Gen 17:13, 23, 27; Ex 12:44; Deut 12:12, 18; Lev 22:11), and how they were to be treated by their owners or masters. However, there is serious question whether and how these laws were enforced or obeyed, especially late in Israelite history. As in the surrounding ancient Near East, slaves probably played a lesser role in Israelite society than they did in later Roman society.

Roman world. The Roman world was at least as complex as the ancient Near East and ancient Israel. First-century Roman society was formulated around widespread socioeconomic inequity at virtually all levels, with very little social mobility.[12] The transition from the republic to the principate heightened the disparity, so that more wealth was accumulated by the few. The lower economic strata, such as slaves, servants, and poor (not all differentiable), had increased, while the wealthy had decreased to only about 1 to 3 percent of the population, with the middle and lower strata occupying the other 97 percent.[13] Whereas in ancient Israel slaves were not central to the economy, they were essential to Rome, with the economy depending on a constantly growing slave population. Once the Roman Empire stopped expanding and fewer slaves became available through conquest, the Roman economy began to disintegrate, with fewer new and cheap workers to support the financial system. Many peasants also had been forced to sell their property and become servants or slaves in order to guarantee a sustainable life in the midst of subsistence living for the vast majority of the population. These slaves of various types performed a wide range of tasks, from working in the most desperate conditions, such as in mines, to occupying places of importance within the households of the wealthy, and all of the situations in between. The Roman slavery system also had rules and regulations regarding manumission, a process of becoming citizens, and ascending the socioeconomic scale—but those

---

[12]See Porter, "Reframing Social Justice," 127-30. Cf. S. Scott Bartchy, *First-Century Slavery and 1 Corinthians 7:21* (Atlanta: Scholars Press, 1973); J. Albert Harrill, *The Manumission of Slaves in Early Christianity*, Hermeneutische Untersuchungen zur Theologie 32 (Tübingen: Mohr Siebeck, 1992) 11-67; Harrill, "Paul and Slavery," in *Paul in the Greco-Roman World*, 2nd ed., ed. J. Paul Sampley (London: T&T Clark, 2016), 2:301-45, esp. 301-15; and Murray J. Harris, *Slave of Christ: A New Testament Metaphor for Total Devotion to Christ* (Leicester, UK: Apollos, 1999), 25-45.

[13]For recent discussion of ancient socioeconomics, see Bruce W. Longenecker, *Remember the Poor: Paul, Poverty, and the Greco-Roman World* (Grand Rapids, MI: Eerdmans, 2010), e.g., 146.

who did were relatively rare compared to those who remained at the bottom and in disprivileged position throughout their lives.

THE NEW TESTAMENT ON SLAVERY

Popular perception regarding slavery in the Bible, including the New Testament, is that it not only depicts but endorses slavery. As noted above, in contrast with most of its neighbors, ancient Israel gave greater consideration to the condition of its slaves, although still within institutionalized slavery. The New Testament was written in an environment in which slavery also was institutionalized—though not always willingly accepted, as witnessed to by slave revolts during Roman times, the most famous being led by the slave Spartacus and violently suppressed in AD 71. However, there is abundant evidence that the major New Testament author who wrote on moral issues, the apostle Paul, did not support and endorse the practice of slavery.[14] I will first make a few comments about the Gospels and then deal with the rest of the New Testament.

The Gospels and Acts. Numerous statements about slaves make clear that slavery was an established and unquestioned institution in the Roman world. The Gospels, for example, are full of references to slavery. Murray Harris has pointed out at least two bodies of evidence regarding slaves. The first set is parables of Jesus in which slaves are prominent. He identifies thirteen such parables.[15] These passages illustrate the reality of the socioeconomic situation of first-century Palestine, in which slaves played an important role, especially in agriculture, to which most of the parables are devoted. These parables make no judgment as to the acceptability or

---

[14]Contra Webb, *Slaves, Women and Homosexuals*, 30-55, 74-76, 84, 162-64; Webb, "Redemptive-Movement Model," 221-28, and his response on 64-70. Webb mostly, though not entirely, summarizes the Old Testament view on slavery as representative for the entire Bible and contrasts this position with that of the ancient Near East, as evidence of his redemptive-movement hermeneutics. Where he treats Philemon, he is overly negative in his assessment, possibly to make this book conform to his view that still requires redemption. He equally minimizes other important New Testament passages, such as Gal 3:28; 1 Cor 7:21.

[15]Harris, *Slave of Christ*, 47-48. See the parable of the weeds (Mt 13:24-30), of the unmerciful servant (Mt 18:23-35), of the vineyard workers (Mt 20:1-13), of the wicked tenants (Mt 21:33-44; Mk 12:1-11; Lk 20:9-16), of the wedding banquet (Mt 22:1-14; Lk 14:16-24), of the overseer (Mt 24:45-51; Lk 12:42-48), of the talents (Mt 25:14-30; Lk 19:11-27), of the doorkeeper (Mk 13:32-37), of the waiting slaves (Lk 12:35-38), of the barren fig tree (Lk 13:6-9), of the prodigal son (Lk 15:11-32), of the shrewd manager (Lk 16:1-8), and of the obedient slave (Lk 17:7-10).

condemnation of slavery, but instead simply depict it as a social institution. One might have expected Jesus to have been more proactively seeking human liberation and condemning the institution of slavery. However, he did not.

The second body of evidence is episodes in which slaves take an active part. Harris here identifies six such passages.[16] As with the parables above, these sometimes almost incidental accounts illustrate how the institution of slavery was interwoven within the fabric of Roman society, to the point of slaves appearing in various incidents without arousing any further concern.

The depiction of slaves within the Gospels and Acts perhaps should not surprise us particularly much, when we realize that these narrative accounts are not primarily concerned with providing social commentary while tracing the ministry of Jesus and his early followers.

Paul along with Peter. We must turn instead to exhortative material that has a conscious intention to address social behavior, especially within the church. In such passages we might well be able to identify passages that raise questions about slavery. There is also one major Petrine passage that I treat below, but the majority of passages on slavery are found in the writings of Paul, who, although he too was a product of his ancient Mediterranean upbringing, was much more bold in suggesting a consistent egalitarian ethic within the church that made slavery redundant, as an antiquated practice within Roman society that the church had made obsolete. I divide the discussion into four sections: Galatians 3:26-29; 1 Corinthians 7:21; Philemon; and the household codes, in which I include Ephesians 5:21–6:9; Colossians 3:18–4:1; 1 Timothy 6:1-2; Titus 2:1-10; and 1 Peter 2:18-19.

Galatians 3:26-29. The first passage to discuss is Galatians 3:26-29, already briefly discussed above.[17] In his letter to the Galatians, Paul summarizes the Roman sociocultural situation by explicitly addressing its three major structures. The central focus of my comments is Galatians 3:28 (translated literalistically): "There is not Jew nor Greek, not slave nor free,

---

[16]Harris, *Slave of Christ*, 48-49. See the healing of the centurion's slave (Mt 8:5-13; Lk 7:1-10), the similar incident with the official's son (Jn 4:46-53), Jesus' arrest (Mt 26:50-51; Mk 14:46-47; Lk 22:49-51; Jn 18:10), Peter's denial of Jesus (Mt 26:69-75; Mk 14:66-72; Lk 22:54-62; Jn 18:15-18), Cornelius and Peter (Acts 10:7, 17-23), and Peter's escaping from prison (Acts 12:13).

[17]Porter, "Reframing Social Justice," 130-33; Harrill, "Paul and Slavery," 328-34.

not male and female." The three pairs that Paul identifies—race or ethnicity, socioeconomic status, and gender—are at the center of the socio-hierarchical imbalance of the Roman world. Paul makes strikingly similar statements elsewhere. For example, in Colossians 3:11, he states: "where there is not Greek and Jew, circumcision and uncircumcision, barbarian, Scythian, slave, free, but Christ is all things and in all things" (my translation), in which Paul conflates racial/ethnic distinctions (Greek, Jew, circumcision, uncircumcision, barbarian, Scythian) and socioeconomic (slave, free) distinctions into one list of prohibited identifiers; or in 1 Corinthians 12:13, he says: "For in one spirit we all are baptized into one body, either Jew or Greek, either slave or free, and all drink of one spirit" (my translation), in which Paul again draws on two of the three pairs, here racial/ethnic and socioeconomic. In other words, there are a number of passages in Paul's letters where he addresses the socioeconomic distinctives of his times, but to dispute their having status within the Christian community. In that sense, Paul in several places implies, if he does not outright make, emancipatory statements regarding slavery.

In this passage in Galatians 3, Paul, in addressing the southern or Roman provincial Galatian believers at the heart of the Roman establishment, recognizes that, through faith in Christ Jesus, the Galatians are sons of God, or adopted into God's family. This status is indicated through baptism, which enfolds or engulfs all believers alike, with the result that there is no such thing as a slave or free person (or Jew or Greek, or male and female). The double negation of the first two clauses, including "not slave nor free," makes clear that the entire clause, as well as the elements of the opposition, is negated. I think that the nature of the negation, especially when compared to the negation of the third pair ("not male and female," in which the individual elements are maintained, even if status on their basis is not), makes clear that Paul is saying that such categories as slavery or freedom do not obtain or have status within the Christian community. In the sphere of being in relation to Christ Jesus, the Galatian believers are constituted as one, and all participate together as the inheritors of the promises to Abraham, without regard for socioeconomic status of being slave or free, to the point that the categories themselves are no longer valid.

With such a statement, Paul attacks the fundamental socio-hierarchical distinctions within the Roman world and states that distinctions on the basis of servitude, whether one is a slave or a free person, are not functionally germane to those within the group of followers of Christ. Such a statement, while admittedly limited to the church, the sphere in which Paul had some influence, is a strong declaration of Christian emancipation. Despite such a statement, Paul has nevertheless still been criticized for failing to advocate for a modernist conception of social equality, by this usually meant a contemporary view of freedom and opposition to slavery. Such an expectation is anachronistic. If Paul were in the modern world, he would no doubt be opposed to slavery (which still unfortunately exists worldwide, including in North America, to the point where some estimate more people are now enslaved than during the time of slavery in the United States in the nineteenth century, which should make those who demand modernist statements of Paul to be cautious). However, Paul was also strongly opposed to slavery within his own contemporary context and created the means for its abolition. The Roman economy was built on the backs of slaves, who were vital to the Roman economy, with many owning slaves, from the poorest tenant farmers and sometimes slaves up to the wealthiest, who sometimes owned thousands of them. With thousands of slaves, there was the opportunity of slave revolt, something Romans hated. Paul was wise enough to recognize that a slave revolt, like most forms of social unrest, would have put fear into the Romans, to the point of their probably attempting to crush the nascent Christian movement. Paul's tactics are therefore more nuanced than simply calling for an outright slave revolt. Nevertheless, Paul lays the basis for such human equality without such socioeconomic distinctions when he says that, at least at the outset, within the church (for Paul, a more important institution than Rome) there are to be no such categories and no distinctions to be made on that basis.

1 Corinthians 7:21. First Corinthians 7:17-24 contains an extended discussion of Paul's view of how one is to live one's life in relationship to one's Christian calling and social status. Paul says that each one should live as he or she is called. For those who are circumcised, this means not to undo circumcision, and for one uncircumcised this means not to be circumcised, but for both to remain as they are, because neither one has significance within the Christian community. Here Paul addresses the racial/ethnic distinctions already noted above in Galatians 3:26-29, to dispute their significance. Paul then turns to the one who is a slave. He states (1 Cor 7:21): "Were you called as a slave? Let it not be a concern to you. But if indeed you are able to become free, rather make use of it [i.e., freedom]" (my translation). Paul's reason for taking this step is because "in the Lord," if one is called as a slave, one is a free person of the Lord, as in the same way, one who is called as a free person is a slave of Christ—terminology to which I will return below. Our costly redemption means that we should not become slaves of human beings, even if we overall should remain in the condition in which we were called, because these conditions, so far as Paul is concerned, are of no account. Nevertheless, if these conditions are of no account, Paul is clear that we are not to voluntarily enslave ourselves to other human beings.

In the interpretation of the passage above that I have offered, I have presented what I think is the best interpretation of 1 Corinthians 7:21.[18] However, there has been significant discussion by scholars over the meaning of the clause translated above as "rather make use of it" and the object to be supplied (as I have indicated above by putting it in brackets). There have been two major positions.[19] One argues that Paul is saying, in light of his argument throughout the passage, that one should be content with one's condition of remaining in bondage: make use of one's slavery. The argument is supposedly based on the connective word (translated "rather") as indicating contrast between two items, and so between freedom and slavery, and on the fact that if manumission were offered, one could refuse such manumission and was not required to accept it and hence take freedom. The other position argues that Paul is saying, on the basis of the exception being made in this verse from the rest of the passage, that the slave is to accept the opportunity for freedom: make use of one's freedom. The argument is here based on the connective word contrasting not with freedom but with the notion of remaining in one's condition. In an earlier

---

[18]Harrill, "Paul and Slavery," 319-28.

[19]See Harrill, *Manumission of Slaves*, 80-108, for a detailed survey of scholarship; see now also Harris, *Slave of Christ*, 59-61, where he weighs in for the second position; Harrill, "Paul and Slavery," 316-19.

study, I note that it appears that Greek grammarians tend to opt for the latter, and I think that the better arguments are still in its favor.[20]

The significance of this statement within its context must not be overlooked. Regarding racial/ethnic distinctions, Paul states in 1 Corinthians 7 that one should not necessarily try to transcend one's boundaries, because the distinguishing factors are insignificant. He says the same thing regarding the socioeconomic boundaries of slave and freeman—that one's status in the earthly realm is insignificant in relation to one's relationship to the Lord or Christ. Nevertheless, Paul also says to the slave—but not to the free person—that if an opportunity presents itself for freedom that the slave should take advantage of that freedom. This is a statement of advocacy of manumission—even if it is not a complete denunciation of slavery—that pushes the boundary of the institution.

Letter to Philemon. Whereas in Galatians 3:26-29 and 1 Corinthians 7:21 we find Paul's principles regarding slavery, the book of Philemon contains Paul's clearest exemplification of what it means to challenge the institution of slavery within the Christian community.[21] In this letter, Paul reformulates the relationship between Philemon and Onesimus from one of hierarchy typical of the Roman socio-hierarchical structure to one of fictive kinship and egalitarian relations.[22]

The traditional view is that Philemon was a runaway slave who had absconded with some of his master, Onesimus's, belongings, and had by some means come into contact with Paul and had become a follower of Jesus Christ, whether that encounter occurred in Rome (the traditional location) or elsewhere. In light of this, and Paul being a good Roman citizen, Paul was obligated to return the runaway slave to its rightful owner, which he does by means of sending Onesimus with the letter to Philemon, in which he recognizes the legal situation and offers to pay for any damages incurred by Onesimus. Within the last fifty or so years, there have been a few scholars who have challenged the traditional view of the letter

---

[20]Stanley E. Porter, *Verbal Aspect in the Greek of the New Testament, with Reference to Tense and Mood*, Studies in Biblical Greek 1 (New York: Peter Lang, 1989), 357-58.

[21]See Porter, "Reforming Social Justice," 133-35; Harrill, "Paul and Slavery," 319-28; Harris, *Slave of Christ*, 57-61.

[22]See Norman R. Petersen, *Rediscovering Paul: Philemon and the Sociology of Paul's Narrative World* (Philadelphia: Fortress, 1985).

to Philemon by contending that he was not a runaway slave at all but perhaps a slave sent by Philemon to Paul to serve him for a while and who is now being returned to him.[23] But as some have pointed out, the major alternative proposal has taken up a casual statement by John Knox and made it into an entire reconstruction—one arguably far more tentative than the traditional understanding of the letter.[24]

In any case, whether Onesimus was a scoundrel or not, in the letter he is being sent back to Philemon (or Archippus, according to one alternative reading) with a letter. From the outset of the letter, Paul styles himself as one oppressed. He is a "prisoner of Christ Jesus" (Philem 1). He describes Philemon as a friend and fellow worker, along with the other recipients of the letter, Apphia, as a sister, and Archippus, as a fellow soldier. In the thanksgiving portion of the letter, Paul notes that he remembers Philemon in his prayers, that he has heard about his love and faith, and that his love has given Paul great joy and encouragement because he has refreshed the saints (Philem 4-7). Paul addresses Philemon as his brother (Philem 7). This now leads to Paul's main order of business. Paul could command Philemon to do his duty toward Paul (Philem 8), but instead he appeals out of love (Philem 9). Although Paul is now old and a prisoner, Paul informs Philemon that the once-useless Onesimus—there is a play on Onesimus's name in Greek, indicating that he was useless either because he was a troublesome slave or perhaps because he was not a believer in Christ Jesus—is now being returned to Philemon as a useful person and a son of Paul and a brother of Philemon, that is, as one who is now useful to both of them (Philem 11). Paul has become Onesimus's spiritual father (Philem 10). As a result, Paul would have liked to keep Onesimus with him to help him while he is a prisoner (Philem 12), but he does not want to do anything untoward or illegal (Philem 14). Paul prefers to do what he wishes done with Philemon's endorsement (Philem 14). Now Paul returns Onesimus to Philemon so that he may be returned forever (Philem 15), not as a slave but as more than a slave, as a beloved brother (Philem 16). Paul tells

---

[23]The best discussion of how to adjudicate varying interpretations is Brook W. R. Pearson, *Corresponding Sense: Paul, Dialectic and Gadamer*, Biblical Interpretation Series 58 (Leiden: Brill, 2001), 46-92.

[24]Markus Barth and Helmut Blanke, *The Letter to Philemon*, Eerdmans Critical Commentary (Grand Rapids, MI: Eerdmans, 2000), 227.

Philemon to welcome Onesimus as one would welcome Paul himself (Philem 17). If Onesimus has done anything wrong or owes anything, he himself, Paul says, will pay any debt (Philem 18)—but remember that Philemon owes him his very self (Philem 19). Paul says that he is confident that Philemon will be obedient to his request, to the point of exceeding his request (Philem 21). But just in case there is a lack of clarity, Paul instructs Philemon to prepare a room for him for when he arrives, so he can check on him (Philem 22).[25]

Several important transformative moments occur in Paul's letter to Philemon, especially in relation to slavery. The first is that Paul sets his command within the parameters of the Christian community. He is writing as a Christian leader to a leader of the church in Colossae. The second is that the way that people relate in the Christian community is based on a different set of values from the surrounding culture. That Christian set of values is related not to Roman socio-hierarchical status but to incorporation into God's family. The result is terms of fictive kinship, in which, no matter one's extra-community legal status, within the community one occupies a place of familial relation. In this community, Paul is the father figure, and Philemon and Onesimus, who may have been related by a legal and hierarchical relationship before, are now reconceived as brothers in Christ, in a new egalitarian relationship based in their common faith. Those in Christ are family—one of the most important institutions in the Roman world, in which the *paterfamilias* controlled the lives and destinies of its members—in which Paul is clearly the father, with his now two sons, both brothers in the Lord.

The third important moment is that this new conception of relationships completely vacates the strength of the institution of slavery. Paul requests that Philemon return Onesimus to him so that he can be of greater use to Paul than to Philemon. How can Philemon refuse, when the letter indicates that Philemon owes to Paul a much greater debt than anything Onesimus may have incurred in his thievery—he owes to Paul his very life,

---

[25]For a different reading that preserves Onesimus's slavery, see Webb, "A Response to Walter C. Kaiser Jr.," in Meadors, *Moving Beyond the Bible*, 64-70, but that is questionable at numerous places. For example, he understands Philem 16 as indicating "no longer [purely!] a slave" or "no longer a slave [only!]," rather than, as Paul states, "no longer a slave" but "more than a slave," by implication one whose slave status has been effectively nullified.

that is, his own Christian faith? More importantly, what does slavery now mean in this context, when the slave owner and slave are brothers in Christ, both answering directly to their spiritual father on equal terms, and hence to God in equal terms? F. F. Bruce, along with a few other scholars, notes the significance of this letter for the institution of slavery, at least within the Christian church.[26] Bruce sees the letter to Philemon as a letter of emancipation for him (even if not a general letter of emancipation), effectively marking what should have been the end of slavery as an institution within the Christian church, when master and slave sit down together as brothers.

Household codes. The final set of passages to consider is the New Testament household codes. One might accept the interpretations of the passages above and still have difficulty accepting the statements found in the household codes, which apparently enshrine a traditional socio-hierarchical ethic, revolving around the family.

There are multiple theories on their origins, including Stoic, Jewish, Christian, Roman, and contextual environments.[27] Almost all interpreters believe that the household codes have some relationship to Aristotle's treatment of the family and the state, which included discussion of master and slave, husband and wife, and father and child. Whatever their origins, the household codes reflect the social and theological contexts of the New Testament, even if they reformulate or call into question these social and theological factors. There are four Pauline passages and one Petrine passage to consider. That all of them appear in letters that are often disputed among Paul's letters should not detract us from examining them (especially for those of us who hold to Pauline authorship of the thirteen letters attributed to him) or enable us to easily dismiss them from serious consideration in this discussion.[28]

Ephesians 5:21–6:9. The first major question regarding this household code is its parameters: whether the passage begins with Ephesians 5:21 or Ephesians 5:22. Scholars vary, as indicated in differences in translations

---

[26]F. F. Bruce, *Paul: Apostle of the Heart Set Free* (Grand Rapids, MI: Eerdmans, 1977), 401. Another to take such a position, in fact in stronger terms, is Petersen, *Rediscovering Paul*, 269, 289-90.

[27]Stanley E. Porter, "Paul, Virtues, Vices, and Household Codes," in Sampley, *Paul in the Greco-Roman World*, 369-90, esp. 372-73, 381-84.

[28]See Porter, *Apostle Paul*, 386-93, 356-64, 419-31.

and editions of the Greek New Testament. The statement in Ephesians 5:21, "submitting to each other in fear of Christ," is usually translated as a command ("submit") and seems like an appropriate introduction to the code. This translation, however, masks that it is a participial clause (as in the translation above) that is dependent on the verb "be filled" in Ephesians 5:18, along with participles in Ephesians 5:19-20. More problematic still is that if the unit begins with Ephesians 5:22, "wives to their own husbands as to the Lord" (my translation), there is no finite verb in a main clause until Ephesians 5:24. The best explanation is to consider the household code as part of a larger section on Christian behavior that begins possibly as far back as Ephesians 5:6 and what constitutes behavior in the Spirit. That the code does not contain a strong grammatical break from the main text of the letter to the code itself indicates that Paul, despite appropriating a tradition that others have used going back to the time of Aristotle, took the form with which he was familiar and then adapted it for both content and placement.

The code in Ephesians 5:21–6:9 is divided into three major conceptual sections. Each of these sections is divided into two parts, with reciprocity between the two in each section. The first section concerns wives and husbands. In Roman society, the *paterfamilias* was the head of the Roman household, which consisted of the father and his extended family living together. The *paterfamilias* exercised authority over the entirety of the family, often in cruel and inhumane ways. In Paul's code, wives are to be submissive, and husbands are to love sacrificially and in the same way as they love themselves, a reciprocal relationship with more demanded of the husband than the wife. The second section concerns children and parents. Children are to be obedient, while fathers are not to provoke their children to the point of anger. In the third and final section, slaves are told to obey their earthly masters just as they would obey Christ if he were observing them, as he is in fact their master. Masters are to do the same and for the same reason: they have a master in heaven who does not play favorites. In other words, the context of master-slave relations is transformed into a much larger Christian configuration, where the master is himself now in obedience to Christ, with the result that master and slave are on the same level within the Christian household in obedience to Christ.

Colossians 3:18–4:1. The household code in Colossians 3:18–4:1 resembles the one in Ephesians in many regards, although it is much shorter. The Colossian code is organized around three major sections with each section divided into two parts, with each individual element relatively self-contained but also reciprocal with its paired item. Hence the opening admonition to wives has its own main verb, "submit." The first section addresses wives and husbands, with wives to be submissive to their husbands and husbands to love their wives and not embitter them (again, demanding more of the husband). The second section concerns children and parents, with children to obey their parents and fathers not to provoke their children. The third section concerns slaves and masters, the longest section of the code. Slaves are to obey their earthly masters and do their tasks as if to the Lord, who will ultimately reward them. Masters are to treat their slaves justly and fairly, as they also have a master in heaven. As in the Ephesians code, the household is transformed into a divine household, with master and slave both obedient to God and placed on the same level as servants of God.

1 Timothy 6:1-2. I include 1 Timothy 6:1-2, although it is not a complete household code but only treats slaves and (incidentally) masters, because it does include slaves. This short set of instructions for slaves and masters, if it is a portion of a code, instructs slaves to give honor to their masters so as not to blaspheme God, and those with believing masters are to serve these masters more diligently because their masters are brothers and beloved. Not only is the role of the slave transformed, but so is that of the believing master, with both now being brothers. One must also note that, in 1 Timothy 1:10, Paul lists slave traders (or those who kidnapped others, a form of enslavement) as those who are lawless and acting contrary to sound teaching, a clear proscription of at least an element of the institution of slavery.

Titus 2:1-10. This final Pauline section, if it is a household code, has major differences from the others, especially in Ephesians and Colossians, by its inclusion of a number of virtue and vice lists. This code is not addressed to a family, as are the other two, but concerns the entire family of God. The code has three sections, in which the pairings are interwoven within the sections. The first section concerns both older men and women, with the men to be virtuous in their actions and the women to avoid certain vices, a form of a virtue-and-vice list. The older women are also to encourage the young women in virtuous behavior, while the younger men are also to do good works, both examples of short virtue lists. The third section concerns slaves and their masters. Slaves are instructed to be submissive to their masters and engage in virtuous behavior and avoid bad behavior, so that they can be trusted and exemplify the teaching about God as Savior. This short code does not have the same egalitarian elements as the others, probably because it is not a fully developed list. Not every list has every element.

1 Peter 2:18-21. This Petrine section is not a complete household code but addresses behavior within the Christian community, especially in relation to the surrounding culture. Whereas Paul's admonitions are usually found in sections, with paired elements, Peter in this passage deals in specific terms only with slaves, and by implication masters. Peter instructs slaves to submit to their masters, whether they are good or bad (note that Paul seems to entertain a Christian master, above). They are to be commended still more if their master is not good, punishing them for good behavior, as God commends this. Peter's household code is not reciprocal in the same way that Paul's major ones are.

The first two examples, in Ephesians and Colossians, are fully formed household codes, and the second two examples contain units that address slavery, while including other elements, such as virtue-and-vice lists, and the fifth is at best a fragment addressing slaves of probably non-Christian masters. As a result, it is perhaps not surprising that the third and fourth examples, 1 Timothy 6:1-2 and Titus 2:1-10, include some elements not found in the household codes while excluding others. The examples from Timothy and Titus definitely emphasize the importance of virtuous behavior and the avoidance of bad behavior. However, they do not have the explicit reciprocity of the household codes in Ephesians and Colossians. The overall admonitory force of the third and fourth examples, in Timothy and Titus, is for slaves to honor or submit, but this is seen within the larger scope of the slave having concerns for the master as a fellow believer and as brother, and their being a part of promoting the message of the gospel. The Petrine admonition recognizes the reality of nonbelieving masters. In some ways, such statements may endorse good behavior as civic virtue, but the attention to performing their duties within the Christian community adds a dimension not typically found in other extrabiblical household codes, and in effect places slaves and masters on the same level within the Christian community as to expectations and status. The Ephesians and Colossians codes are full household codes, with clearly stated reciprocal responsibilities between the appropriate pairs.

The statements regarding masters and slaves place the behavior of both within a similar larger Christian context. Their behavior is not just reciprocal with each other but to be seen in light of their both having similar status with each other in that they both answer to a higher master, God himself. Harris summarizes the focus of these passages in seven concluding statements: (1) both slaves and masters receive instruction from apostles and are therefore on the same level of instruction and possibly status so far as God's expectations of behavior are concerned; (2) the fundamental motivation for good behavior is one's being in Christ; (3) God's expectations for all, slave or master, show no favoritism; (4) one's position before God "in Christ" (see 2) is one of equality, whether one is slave or free; (5) both slave and free are equally responsible to the same heavenly master; (6) the Christian community was to welcome all, including slave and freeman, as equal participants; and (7) use of fictive kinship terminology such as *brother* emphasizes the recalibrated nature of relationships within the church.[29] These household codes, while not perhaps as close to being manumission statements as in Philemon, at least promote an egalitarian ethic within the Christian community, in which slaves and masters are both responsible to each other and responsible to God. Slaves realize that they are to be obedient to the same master as are their masters, and masters recognize that their obedience is to be equivalent to that of a slave, both in relation to the God who stands as the *paterfamilias* of the entire Christian community. Richard Hays goes so far as to state that these are new norms "warranted by the gospel."[30]

---

[29]Harris, *Slave of Christ*, 54-57.
[30]Richard B. Hays, *The Moral Vision of the New Testament: Community, Cross, New Creation; A Contemporary Introduction to New Testament Ethics* (Edinburgh: T&T Clark, 1996), 64.

Paul's use of the notion of being a slave of Christ (e.g., Rom 1:1; Phil 1:1; Titus 1:1; and other places) supports this recalibration. Although the language appears at first to support the notion of slavery, it only does so within the larger context of servitude of Christ spelling liberation from and equality with other humans. In distinction from the usual family structure, in which there is a hierarchy of adults to children to slaves, those who are members of God's family, through fictive but theological and salvific kinship, are now all "brothers and sisters" in Christ. Whereas the socio-hierarchical categories may still be in effect in the surrounding culture, within the Christian community these have been abolished in the new relationship that each enjoys with Christ. Even if Paul issues no direct statement of manumission (at least as we would envision it in the twenty-first century), all of the major passages that we have examined point toward a new set of egalitarian relations within the Christian household.

CONCLUSION

In light of this discussion, we must revisit the question of the suitableness of the analogy of slavery for gender equality. I believe that the analogy is a generally appropriate one, if one understands the biblical evidence as I have stated it. In other words, rather than the analogy of slavery indicating a disjunction between the biblical claims and modern sensibilities, I believe that, especially in the New Testament and more specifically in the statements of Paul, there is a Christian emancipation of slavery at least within the Christian community.[31] The letter of Philemon alone should have marked the end of slavery by and among Christians and the ultimate downfall of the institution within the wider culture. This did not happen, much the same way as gender equality has been denied to women in many historical periods and cultures, extending to the present. However, the biblical and especially New Testament evidence for gender equality also indicates that the early church was to be a community of equals because they are equals. Galatians 3:28 provides a powerful egalitarian statement regarding both slavery and gender relations when Paul states

---

[31]In that sense, Webb's redemptive-movement hermeneutic has some bearing, as the New Testament has definite manumitic tendencies, as well as egalitarian beliefs regarding gender relations.

that, in Christ, there is to be no distinction between them for the purposes of membership within the Christian community, grounded in a more fundamental equality. He supports this statement in various other places within the rest of his writings, for both the matter of slavery and of gender relations.

18

THE TRINITY ARGUMENT FOR WOMEN'S SUBORDINATION

THE STORY OF ITS RISE, ASCENDANCY, AND FALL

Kevin Giles

• • • • •

WHEN I WROTE MY CHAPTER on the Trinity for the first edition of *Discovering Biblical Equality*, early in 2003, "complementarians" were united in insisting that the three divine persons that constitute the Trinity are hierarchically ordered and that this ordering is prescriptive for the male-female relationship on earth.[1] I found no dissenting voices. Early in 2016, no one anticipated any split among complementarians on their doctrine of the Trinity. They asserted confidently and with one voice that their doctrine of a hierarchically ordered Trinity is what the Bible teaches, and it is historic orthodoxy. Then the unimagined happened. "Civil war" broke out in the complementarian army.[2] Some complementarians in very stark language began accusing other complementarians of heresy and of departing from the clear teaching of Scripture on the doctrine of the Trinity. In a very short

---

[1]In this chapter, out of courtesy, I use the post-1980s, self-chosen name for those who believe the Bible sets men over women. I do so although, like all evangelical egalitarians, I believe God has created two complementary sexes—they *complete* what it means to be human. I am thus happy to use the term *complementarity* in the dictionary sense of this word.

[2]"Civil war" is the term Caleb Lingren of *Christianity Today* used as the title of his article telling the world of this sharp dispute among complementarians. See "From Proxy War to Civil War," *CT*, June 16, 2016, www.christianitytoday.com/ct/2016/june-web-only/gender-trinity-proxy-war-civil-war-eternal-subordination.html.

period of time the de facto leaders of the complementarian movement, Wayne Grudem and Bruce Ware, found themselves under attack.

In what follows I will outline how the contemporary complementarian argument for a hierarchically ordered doctrine of the Trinity, and the idea that this is the primary basis for the hierarchical ordering of the sexes, was invented, was popularized, and gained ascendancy in the evangelical and Reformed world, and then surprisingly, when it seemed it had triumphed, came under attack by leading self-confessed complementarians who argued it was heresy.[3]

THE RISE OF THE HIERARCHICAL COMPLEMENTARIAN DOCTRINE OF THE TRINITY (1977-2016)

George W. Knight III (1977). Faced with the growing impact of egalitarian ideals in the churches in the mid-1970s, one of the most creative conservative Reformed theologians of the twentieth century, George Knight III, wrote in opposition to this new thinking on the equality of the sexes, which was getting a good hearing among evangelicals. In his highly influential 1977 book, *New Testament Teaching on the Role Relationship of Men and Women,* he rejected the historic way of speaking of men as "superior" and women "inferior" that had reigned until the middle of the twentieth century, arguing instead that men and women are "equal" yet "role differentiated." These differing "roles," he added, were given in creation before the fall. As such they represent the ideal and are transcultural and permanently binding. They are grounded in and illustrated by the doctrine of the Trinity, and he appealed to 1 Corinthians 11:3 as proof. The Father is "head over" the Son just as man is "head over" woman. He was emphatic: Paul is hierarchically ordering the man-woman relationship in general, not just the husband-wife relationship. Knight saw in this text a "chain of command."[4] In parallel with how he speaks of the differences between men and women, Knight speaks of the differences between the three divine persons in terms of differing authority and differing "roles." The Father has the role of commanding and directing, and the Son the role of obeying.

---

[3]I tell this story more fully in my book *The Rise and Fall of the Complementarian Doctrine of the Trinity* (Eugene, OR: Cascade, 2017).

[4]Knight, *New Testament Teaching,* 32-36.

Before Knight wrote, the word *role* had never been used to speak of the essential difference between men and women or of the essential difference between the divine three persons. Now we see the huge significance of his work. This one man produced a way of speaking of the man-woman relationship that preserved what he called the "traditional" understanding of male headship that sounded acceptable to modern ears, and in doing so, redefined the doctrine of the Trinity in the terms he had invented to speak of the primary difference between the sexes. From then on, in ever-growing numbers, evangelicals became convinced that his novel theological construct defining the relationship of the sexes and the divine three persons was "what the Bible teaches."

What is to be carefully noted is that Knight and his followers were arguing that the Son and women *are defined by their subordination*. They do not simply function subordinately, but they *are* subordinated persons, and this can never change. Difference in authority is what primarily and irrevocably differentiates them. In a moment of openness, Knight admitted that the Father-Son and man-woman relationship not only involve "role" subordination and differentiation but also a difference in their "ontological relationship."[5]

Before leaving Knight's creative and novel construct, I highlight its circular nature. First, he reformulated the doctrine of the sexes by differing them on the basis of differing roles, by which he meant differing authority. Then he reformulated and reworded the doctrine of the Trinity exactly in the same way, and then finally he appealed to his newly invented doctrine of the Trinity to substantiate his teaching on the sexes.

The ascendancy of the Trinity argument. Wayne Grudem, Systematic Theology *(1994).* Knight's novel ideas on the role subordination of women and the role subordination of the Son, the former being the basis for the latter, came to fruition in 1994 with the publication of Wayne Grudem's *Systematic Theology.* The impact of this publication on evangelicals, Pentecostals, and charismatics cannot be overestimated. It is the most widely used systematic theology text book in Bible colleges and evangelical and Pentecostal seminaries around the world. Grudem is emphatic; *the eternal subordination of the Son in authority* stands right at the heart of the

---

[5]Knight, *New Testament Teaching*, 56.

orthodox doctrine of the Trinity. What he teaches, he claims repeatedly, the best theologians from the past and the creeds teach. For Grudem, the Father has "the role of commanding, directing, and sending," and the Son has the role of "obeying, going as the Father sends, and revealing God to us."[6] It is differing authority that primarily differentiates the divine persons, as it does the two sexes. He writes, "Authority and submission between the Father and the Son . . . and the Holy Spirit, is the fundamental difference between the persons of the Trinity."[7] And again, "If we did not have such differences in authority in the relationships among the members of the Trinity, then we would not know of any differences at all." For Grudem, nothing is more important than the authority structure both in the Trinity and between men and women. It is, he says, "the most fundamental aspect of interpersonal relationships in the entire universe."[8]

Quoting 1 Corinthians 11:3, Grudem claims the Bible explicitly teaches that the Father is "head over" the Son and *husbands* "head over" their *wives*, despite the fact the text speaks of "every" man and "every" woman (1 Cor 11:3-5), as Knight stresses. Furthermore, Grudem claims this text connects these two things. "Just as God the Father has authority over the Son, though the two are equal in deity, so in marriage, the husband has authority over his wife, though they are equal in personhood. In this case, the man's role is like that of God the Father, and the woman's role is parallel to that of God to the Son."[9]

Grudem's *Systematic Theology* was the first evangelical systematic theology to enunciate the doctrine of the *eternal subordination* of the Son in function/role, and to make this the basis for the *permanent subordination* of women in function/role—meaning in plain English in both cases, subordinate in authority. In his many later books and articles advocating the subordination of women, the Trinity argument is at the fore. Writing in 2004, he says that for twenty-five years he has believed that how the

---

[6]Wayne Grudem, *Systematic Theology: An Introduction to Biblical Doctrine* (Grand Rapids, MI: Zondervan, 1995), 250.

[7]Wayne Grudem, *Biblical Foundations for Manhood and Womanhood* (Wheaton, IL: Crossway, 2002), 31, emphasis added.

[8]Wayne Grudem, *Evangelical Feminism and Biblical Truth* (Eugene, OR: Multnomah, 2004), 433, 429, emphasis added.

[9]Grudem, *Evangelical Feminism*, 459-60.

Trinity is understood "may well turn out to be the *most decisive* factor in finally deciding" the bitter debate between evangelicals about the status and ministry of women.[10] In other words, he is convinced that the case for the permanent subordination of women more than anything else rests on winning the Trinity debate. This, for him, is the most important element in the complementarian case.

Following the publication of Grudem's *Systematic Theology*, complementarians almost universally made the eternal subordination of the Son the primary argument for the permanent subordination of women.

Bruce Ware, Father, Son and Holy Spirit *(2005)*. Possibly the most influential monograph putting forward this position, and doing so starkly, was Bruce Ware's *Father, Son and Holy Spirit*. He says "hierarchical" ordering in the life of the Trinity "marks the *very nature* of *the eternal Being* of the one who is three. In this authority-submission structure, the three Persons understand the rightful place each has. The Father possesses the place of supreme authority . . . the Son submits to the Father."[11] This hierarchical ordering of the Father and the Son, he argues, prescribes hierarchical ordering in the male-female relationship. Quoting 1 Corinthians 11:3, he says this text teaches that

> the Father has authority over the Son. There is a relationship of authority and submission in the *very Godhead* on which other authority and submission relationships of Christ and man, and man and woman depend. The *taxis* [order] of God's headship over his Son accounts for the presence of a *taxis* in man's relationship with Christ and the woman's relationship with man.[12]

Bruce Ware and John Starke (editors), One God in Three Persons *(2015)*. This distinctive complementarian teaching on the Trinity reached its zenith in 2015 with the publication of a collection of essays, *One God in Three Persons: Unity of Essence, Distinction of Persons, Implications for Life*, edited by Bruce Ware and John Starke.[13] The aim of this book was to ground women's subordination once and for all in the eternal life of God

---

[10]Grudem, *Evangelical Feminism*, 411n12, emphasis added.

[11]Bruce A. Ware, *Father, Son and Holy Spirit* (Wheaton, IL: Crossway, 2005), 21, emphasis added to bring attention to the ontological language used.

[12]Knight, *New Testament Teaching*, 77, emphasis added. He says much the same in other words on 72.

[13]Bruce A. Ware and John Starke, eds., *One God in Three Persons* (Wheaton, IL: Crossway, 2015).

and to rout those evangelicals who were arguing that the complementarian doctrine of the Trinity is heretical. The book was widely and enthusiastically endorsed by many of the most prominent evangelical and Reformed leaders. Jared Moore, in his review, written for the Southern Baptist Convention website, says,

> Complementarians believe that God has created men and woman as equal image-bearers of God, yet with differing roles in the church and home. Many, however, balk at this notion arguing that a hierarchy in the church or home necessarily means that one gender is less valuable than the other. But if complementarians can prove that there is a hierarchy in the immanent (ontological) Trinity, *then they win*, for if a hierarchy exists among the Three Persons of God, and these Three Persons are equally God, then surely God can create men and women equal yet with differing roles in the church and home.[14]

The *if* in this paragraph speaks not of a possibility. Moore clearly believes that complementarians have won the battle. The Trinity is hierarchically ordered, and this is proof that the man-woman relationship is hierarchically ordered by God's design. Moore expresses accurately complementarian opinion in early 2015. Complementarians were sure at this point of time that they had triumphed over those dangerous "evangelical feminists" who had been opposing their "biblical" teaching on the Trinity and women. They were united in this conviction.

The **coup de gras** *(2015–2016)*. Following the publication of *One God in Three Persons* in mid-2015, three other books written by evangelical and Reformed theologians appeared in the next twelve months, all arguing for the eternal subordination or submission of the Son and predicating the subordination of women on the hierarchical ordering of the divine persons in heaven.

First came Rodrick K. Durst's book published in November 2015, *Reordering the Trinity: Six Movements of God in the New Testament*.[15] He says

---

[14]Jared Moore, "The Complementarians Win: A Review of *One God in Three Persons*," SBC Voices, May 19, 2015, http://sbcvoices.com/the-complementarians-win-a-review-of-one-god-in-three -persons/.

[15]Rodrick K. Durst, *Reordering the Trinity: Six Movements of God in the New Testament* (Grand Rapids, MI: Kregel, 2015).

many helpful things about the Trinity but is completely dismissive of the creedal and confessional heritage of the church and thus feels free to endorse the idea that the Son is eternally "submissive" to the Father.[16] To be necessarily and eternally submissive means the Son is subordinated God.

The next book published, in April 2016, was Malcolm B. Yarnell's *God the Trinity: Biblical Portraits*. Like Durst, he offers many helpful insights on the Trinity but has virtually no interest in the creeds and confessions of the church. Thus, again like Durst, he feels free to argue that the Son is *eternally* "subordinate" to the Father. To deny this (as he rightly accuses me of doing), he says leads to "the radical equalization of [the divine persons] of the Trinity in [contemporary] evangelicalism." In reply I ask, does not the Athanasian Creed speak of the divine three as "co-equal" persons? For Yarnell, the dispute among evangelicals over the Trinity is entirely between evangelical egalitarians bent on furthering their "radical equalization" agenda and complementarians, who represent historic orthodoxy.[17]

Then last of all in May 2016 appeared Michael J. Ovey's book *Your Will be Done: Exploring Eternal Subordination, Divine Monarchy and Divine Humility*.[18] He was, when he wrote, the Principal of Oak Hill [Anglican] Theological College, London.[19] Before ordination, all prospective Anglican clergy must give assent to the three historic creeds and the Thirty-Nine Articles of the Church of England. His book is from cover to cover a defense of hierarchical ordering in divine life. He appeals in support of his views to a number of creeds that appeared after AD 340 that teach the eternal subordination of the Son.[20] The problem for him is that the most informed patristic scholars conclude these creeds express *homoian* Arianism.[21] If this is the case, then he has proved that the contemporary

---

[16]In these very brief comments on this and the next two books I do not do them justice. I more fully outline what each book says in *Rise and Fall*, 29-34. The books themselves should be read.

[17]Malcolm B. Yarnell, *God the Trinity: Biblical Portraits* (Nashville: B&H Academic, 2016), 147, 171-74.

[18]Michael J. Ovey, *Your Will Be Done: Exploring Eternal Subordination, Divine Monarchy and Divine Humility* (Oxford: Latimer Trust, 2016).

[19]Sadly, he passed away in January 2017.

[20]In support for what follows, see my discussion of Ovey's argument given in in my extended review of Ware and Starke's book, "Extended Review of *One God in Three Persons*," *PriscPap* 30, no. 1 (2016): 21-30; Giles, *Rise and Fall*, 33.

[21]Arius initiated the disputes over the Trinity that engulfed the church for fifty years, but many of his ideas were in fact rejected or significantly modified by those who came after him, whom the

complementarian doctrine of the Trinity reflects in some ways Arianism as it was expressed in the middle of the fourth century, and worse, he has broken his ordination vows. As I will show shortly, the creeds and the Thirty-Nine Articles categorically exclude hierarchical ordering in divine life.

In May 2016 it seemed that complementarians had won the Trinity debate. Through their writings they had inflicted a *coup de gras* on evangelical egalitarians. Women's permanent subordination is predicated on the eternal subordination of the Son. This is what complementarians believed, and there were no dissenting voices in their ranks.

ASSESSING THE ARGUMENT THAT THE FATHER-SON RELATIONSHIP IN ETERNITY PRESCRIBES THE MALE-FEMALE RELATIONSHIP ON EARTH

Before outlining what followed from this point of time, I must digress briefly to clearly explain why the doctrine of a hierarchically ordered Trinity is of such fundamental importance to complementarians and why it is incoherent. It is of fundamental importance for complementarians because, since the publication of Wayne Grudem's *Systematic Theology*, they have believed it is the most telling and compelling argument in support of the permanent subordination of women. It grounds the subordination of women in the eternal life of God. Just as the Son obeys the Father in heaven, so women should obey the men set over them on earth.

This argument that the Father-Son relationship in heaven is prescriptive for the male-female relationship on earth is novel and must be critically examined. It was unheard of before the twentieth century. Theologians have agreed that the Trinity is our distinctive Christian doctrine of God,

---

pro-Nicene fathers lumped together, calling them all Arians. At least four kinds of fourth-century Arianism can be distinguished. The so-called *homoian* Arians rejected the term *homoousios* (one in being) to define the Father-Son relationship, arguing instead that the Son was "like" the Father in being (Greek *homoios*). Distinctively, they affirmed that Jesus Christ is God and thus *like* the Father in divine being, and yet at the same time he is eternally subordinated to the Father in authority. This teaching parallels the complementarian position; the Father and the Son are fully God (ontologically equal), yet the Son is eternally subordinated in authority. On fourth-century Arianism, see R. P. C. Hanson, *The Search for the Christian Doctrine of God: The Arian Controversy 318–81* (Edinburgh: T&T Clark, 1988); L. Ayres, *Nicea and Its Legacy: An Approach to Fourth Century Trinitarian Theology* (Oxford: Oxford University Press, 2004); R. Williams, *Arius: Heresy and Tradition* (London: Darton, Longman & Todd, 2001).

not our social agenda. Furthermore, a compelling answer cannot be given to the question as to how and why the doctrine of the Trinity might inform our doctrine of the sexes. The Trinity is three divine persons, all analogically spoken of in male terms.[22] How can a threefold analogically all "male" relationship in heaven prescribe a twofold male-female relationship on earth? No analogical correlation is possible. The argument just does not make sense. To be consistent, the logic of this argument would be that threesomes or male-male relationships are the God-given ideal.

But there is another insurmountable problem for this argument. The most dangerous element in Grudem and Ware's argument for the eternal subordination of the Son is that it is predicated not primarily on Scripture but on an analogical correlation between human sonship and divine sonship. They argue that, just as all human sons are subordinate to their father and must obey him, so the divine Son is subordinate to his Father and must obey him. On this reasoning they define divine relationships in terms of fallen human relationships and end up with an entirely human understanding of the triune life of God. Grudem puts this argument starkly. He likens the Trinity to a human father and mother and their one child.[23] In doing so he feminizes the Son—the Son becomes an analogue of the woman—and implies that the Son is begotten by sexual union. This family picture of God has nothing to do with the revealed doctrine of the Trinity. It sounds more like Greek mythology. Todd Pruitt, a confessional Reformed gender-complementarian says, "The stubborn insistence of Drs. Ware and Grudem to force a parallel between the Father and the Son to a husband and wife is worse than troubling. . . . These parallels have far more in common with pagan mythology than Biblical theology." In his opinion this paralleling is "blasphemous."[24]

Confessional Reformed gender-complementarian Robert Letham is of the same opinion. He roundly condemns Grudem and Ware for predicating their understanding of the Father-Son relationship on fallen human relationships. He says this is an "Arian argument" that must be

---

[22]Despite the fact that the Hebrew word *ruah*, translated into English as "spirit," is grammatically feminine, and the Greek word *pneuma*, translated into English as "spirit," is grammatically neuter.

[23]Grudem, *Systematic Theology*, 257.

[24]Todd Pruitt, "A Mythological Godhead," Reformation 21, July 9, 2016, www.alliancenet.org /mos/1517/a-mythological-godhead#.wv3sidsgouk.

categorically rejected. He writes, "The Arian argument that human sons are subordinate to their fathers led to their contention that the Son is subordinate to the Father. The church rejected the conclusion as heretical and opposed the premise as mistaken. Rather, [it taught], the Son is equal with the Father in status, power and glory."[25] Evangelicals should never seek to explain God in human terms or relationships. To do so is to fall into idolatry, depicting God as a creature like us. Scripture should be our teacher. What is more, the Bible does not use the title *Son* to speak of the subordination of Jesus Christ. It uses this title, rather, to speak of him as the messianic King who will rule for ever and ever (2 Sam 7:12-14; Lk 1:32-33; Rom 1:4; Rev 11:15). It is an honorific title.

Appeal to 1 Corinthians 11:3 does not save this argument. This is not a trinitarian text; the Spirit is not mentioned, and the Greek word *kephalē* ("head") almost certainly carries the metaphorical meaning of "source" in this context. Woman (Eve) comes from man (Adam; 1 Cor 11:8, 12), and the Son comes "from" the Father in his eternal generation or incarnation. To argue that *kephalē* in this text means "authority" over makes no sense. Why then would Paul immediately go on to speak of men and women *leading* the church in prayer and prophecy (1 Cor 11:4-5)? And why in this one instance would Paul have the Father ruling over the Son, where elsewhere he consistently speaks of Jesus Christ as "Lord," the supreme ruler?

What all this tells us is that if evangelicals want to be correct in their doctrine of the Trinity—the primary and foundational doctrine of the Christian faith—they must completely separate the doctrine of the Trinity from their doctrine of the sexes. They are not connected biblically, and when they are connected theologically, both doctrines are corrupted.

Often complementarians claim that it is egalitarians who seek to ground gender equality in divine life. The truth is, the appeal to the Trinity is characteristically a complementarian phenomenon.[26] CBE International, in its outline of the egalitarian position, make no reference to the Trinity, and not one of the twenty-nine essays in the 2004 and 2005 editions of *Discovering Biblical Equality* grounds the equality of the sexes in the

---

[25]Robert Letham, "Eternal Generation in the Church Fathers," in Ware and Starke, *One God in Three Persons*, 122.

[26]I say more on this in Giles, *Rise and Fall*, 15.

coequality of the divine three persons. I have written extensively in recent years in opposition to making this correlation. I do not think either the equality of the sexes or the subordination of women can be grounded in the life of God in heaven, and the Bible never suggests this.

THE FALL OF A HIERARCHICAL ("COMPLEMENTARIAN") DOCTRINE OF THE TRINITY (2016–2019)

Just when the complementarian doctrine of the Trinity seemed to have been embraced by most evangelicals in America and the rest of the world, it came under attack by complementarians of confessional Reformed convictions. All of a sudden it became clear that the evangelical debate over the Trinity was not between evangelical egalitarians and complementarians but between those who believe that the creeds and confessions of the church spell out the communally agreed and historically tested way to rightly interpret the Bible on the major doctrines—in this case the Trinity—and those who think they are free to formulate doctrines on the basis of their own individualistic interpretation of the Bible.

Liam Goligher. Dramatically and unexpectedly on June 2, 2016, Liam Goligher broke ranks with other complementarians.[27] He is the senior pastor of the Tenth Presbyterian Church in Philadelphia, a confessional Reformed theologian and an unequivocal gender complementarian. He combatively asserted that what his fellow gender complementarians were teaching on the Trinity was heresy and that many of their comments about women were farcical. He began by saying, "I am an unashamed biblical complementarian," but then added that some complementarians today, "like the Pharisees of old are going beyond Scripture and heaping up burdens to place on believers' backs, and their arguments are slowly descending into farce." Worse still, he said,

> They are building their case by reinventing the doctrine of God, and are doing so without telling the Christian public what they are up to. What we have is in fact a departure from biblical Christianity as expressed in our creeds and confessions. . . . This is to move into unorthodoxy. To speculate, suggest, or say, as some do, that there are three minds, three wills, and three

---

[27]See further Giles, *Rise and Fall*, 39-41, where I note that two gender complementarian women, Rachel Miller and Aimee Byrd, spoke up first.

powers within the Godhead is to move beyond orthodoxy (into neo-tritheism) and to verge on idolatry (since it posits a different God). It should certainly exclude such people from holding office in the church of God. On the other hand, to say, suggest, or speculate that God's life in heaven sets a social agenda for humans is to bring God down to our level.[28]

And he concludes: "The teaching is so wrong at so many levels that we must sound a blast against this insinuation of error into the body of Christ's church. Before we jettison the classical, catholic, orthodox and Reformed understanding of God as he is we need to carefully weigh what is at stake—our own and our hearers' eternal destiny."[29]

Carl Trueman. On June 7 of the same year, Carl Trueman, professor of church history at Westminster Seminary, Philadelphia, endorsed what his friend Liam Goligher had written and added,

> Complementarianism as currently constructed would seem to be now in crisis.
>
> But this is a crisis of its own making—the direct result of the incorrect historical and theological arguments upon which the foremost advocates of the movement have chosen to build their case and which cannot actually bear the weight being placed upon them.
>
> All Liam Goligher and I did was pull on a rope. The next thing we knew, the whole ceiling came crashing down around us. If that tells you anything at all, it is surely something about how well the [complementarian] ceiling was constructed in the first place.[30]

Denny Burk. Other well-informed gender complementarians then began speaking up in opposition to a hierarchically ordered Trinity, and in July the president of the Council of Biblical Manhood and Womanhood, Denny Burk, capitulated. He said that, confronted by the pervasive rejection of the complementarian doctrine of the Trinity, he had "done more

---

[28]Aimee Byrd, "Is It Okay to Teach Complementarians Based on Eternal Subordination?," Mortification of Spin, June 3, 2016, www.alliancenet.org/mos/housewife-theologian/is-it-okay-to-teach-a-complementarianism-based-on-eternal-subordination#.wggylfb96ul. Because I have copied and pasted from this blog, readers should read the text in full.

[29]Aimee Byrd, "Reinventing God," Reformation 21, https://www.reformation21.org/mos/housewife-theologian/reinventing-god.

[30]Carl Trueman, "Motivated by Feminism? A Response to Recent Criticism," Reformation 21, June 14, 2016, www.alliancenet.org/mos/postcards-from-palookaville/motivated-by-feminism-a-response-to-a-recent-criticism#.wfumrvb96um.

reading on Nicene Trinitarianism in the last two months than I have ever done previously. It has been good for me, and I am thankful to God for it. . . . The controversy has been unpleasant, but I would not trade the growth that's come from it for anything in the world."[31]

He says, "I now believe in the whole Nicene package," and he openly acknowledges that the complementarian doctrine of the Trinity cannot be reconciled with it. For this reason, he says he does not agree with "the specific formulations of Grudem and Ware," "my friends." Because he is now personally committed to the Nicene doctrine of the Trinity that excludes hierarchical ordering in the Trinity, he says, "I think it is good and right to leave behind the language of 'subordination.'"[32]

This unconditional surrender by the appointed leader of the complementarian movement on behalf of all complementarians is breathtaking. Denny Burk openly admits that to eternally subordinate the Son to the Father is a denial of the Nicene faith, a denial of historic trinitarian orthodoxy. Grudem and Jared Moore highlight the monumental significance of this capitulation. They emphatically said, as we noted above, that more than anything else the complementarian gender agenda stands or falls on who wins the debate about the Trinity—and they lost this.

Robert Letham. Certainly, the most significant gender complementarian theologian to change his mind is Robert Letham. In his 2004 edition of his book *The Holy Trinity in Scripture, History, Theology, and Worship*, which is over five hundred pages, Letham gives a masterful account of the historically developed doctrine of the Trinity, which overall cannot be questioned. But at the same time, he speaks of the eternal "obedience" of the Son, of the eternal "submission" of the Son, and of "a biblical and orthodox subordinationism," all of which complementarians understandably took to be an endorsement of their hierarchically ordered doctrine of the Trinity.[33] He is also critical of my work on the doctrine of the Trinity, accusing me of "some troubling modalistic tendencies" in my quest to

---

[31]Denny Burk, "My Take-Away's from the Trinity Debate," August 10, 2016, www.dennyburk.com /my-take-aways-from-the-trinity-debate/.

[32]Burk, "My Take-Away's."

[33]Robert Letham, *The Holy Trinity in Scripture, History, Theology, and Worship* (Phillipsburg, NJ: P&R, 2004), 251, 392-93, 395, 398, 402, 492-93. The 2019 revised edition of this book is acknowledged and cited below. I discuss this in some detail in Giles, *Rise and Fall*, 21-24, 41-44, 55.

"eliminate all forms of subordinationism."[34] In my 2006 review of his book, I argued it should be retitled "*Two Views on the Trinity*."[35] In the following fifteen years, Dr. Letham and I have had an ongoing debate over the doctrine of the Trinity in print and in personal emails. Surprisingly, in this process we have become good friends. When he told me that he was preparing a second edition of his book on the Trinity I sent him a list of all the passages in his 2004 edition that I found troubling, and I was pleased to note that in the 2019 edition he had changed his wording in every case and deleted any criticisms of my teaching on the Trinity. He unambiguously and emphatically rejects the idea that the Son is eternally submissive and obedient. It is his view now, he says, that, "The evangelicals who have argued for the subordination of the Son have embarked on a dangerous path. . . . In proposing plural wills [in the one triune God they] have wandered toward or even across the line."[36]

Later, in 2019, the last nail in the coffin containing the body of the complementarian hierarchically ordered Trinity was driven home by Michael F. Bird and Scott Harrower in their book *The Trinity Without Hierarchy: Reclaiming Nicene Orthodoxy in Evangelical Theology*.[37] In this symposium, sixteen well-known and able theologians—some egalitarians and some complementarians—with one voice, reject the complementarian doctrine of the Trinity in which the Father rules over the Son for all eternity. They are agreed, this construal of the Trinity runs counter to what the Bible says, and it is a denial of historic trinitarian orthodoxy. The cumulative voice of these theologians cannot be ignored.

THE COMMUNALLY AGREED DOCTRINE OF THE TRINITY

To conclude this chapter, I now outline what the creeds and confessions of the church teach on the Trinity. These documents represent what the church communally has agreed is the teaching of Scripture, a conclusion

---

[34]Letham, *Holy Trinity*, 493-94.

[35]Kevin Giles, review of Robert Letham, *The Holy Trinity in Scripture, History, Theology, and Worship*, *Evangelical Quarterly* 79 (2006): 85-94.

[36]Robert Letham, *The Holy Trinity in Scripture, History, Theology, and Worship*, rev. ed. (Phillipsburg, NJ: P&R, 2019), 485.

[37]Michael F. Bird and Scott Harrower, *The Trinity Without Hierarchy: Reclaiming Nicene Orthodoxy in Evangelical Theology* (Grand Rapids, MI: Kregel Academic, 2019).

that has stood the test of time despite many challenges across the centuries by individuals, almost invariably quoting one or more texts that they thought subordinated the Son to the Father in the immanent Trinity.

The Nicene Creed (381). The Nicene Creed is the definitive summary of the doctrine of the Trinity for more than two billion Christians today, and of countless millions since the late fourth century, when it was first promulgated. It is binding on all Roman Catholic, Eastern Orthodox, Anglican, Lutheran, Presbyterian, and Reformed Christians. They agree that to deny what is taught in the Nicene Creed is to place oneself outside the catholic faith, and for any community of Christians to reject what the Nicene Creed teaches is to become a sect of Christianity. On this basis, Jehovah's Witnesses are not accepted as orthodox Christians because they cannot confess this creed, even though, like evangelicals, they uphold the inerrancy of Scripture.

We should not place this creed or any other creed or confession above or on an equal basis with Scripture. For confessional Christians, this creed expresses what the church has agreed is the teaching of Scripture. In the Nicene Creed we have the most authoritative interpretation of what Scripture teaches on the Father-Son relationship.

This creed first affirms, "We [Christians] believe in one Lord, Jesus Christ." These words reflect exactly 1 Corinthians 8:6. In this verse Paul makes the Jewish Shema (Deut 6:4), which is a confession that God is one, a confession that the one God is God the Father and God the Son. The term "Lord" (*kyrios*) is the name of God in the Greek Old Testament. In this confession, we are therefore saying we believe that Jesus Christ is the "one Lord," Yahweh. In the New Testament Jesus Christ is confessed as "Lord" over six hundred times. The title "Lord" excludes the thought that Jesus Christ is eternally subordinate or submissive to God the Father. If the Father and the Son are both rightly confessed as Lord, the supreme co-rulers over all, then *they are not differentiated in authority*. They are one in dominion, rule, power, and authority.

Second, in this creed we confess, "We believe in one Lord, Jesus Christ, the only [*monogenēs*] Son of God." The word *monogenēs* primarily means "only" in the sense of "unique"; "one of a kind." The Greek church fathers,

as Greek speakers, also knew it primarily carried this meaning.[38] None of
them appealed to this word or the texts in which it is found as the basis for
their doctrine of the eternal generation of the Son.[39] Characteristically they
use this word as an honorific title for the Son.

John uses the word *monogenēs* of Jesus Christ five times (Jn 1:14, 18; 3:16,
18; 1 Jn 4:9). This designation of the Son was deliberately included in the
creed because it explicitly excludes the disastrous error made by all the
fourth-century Arians and all those committed to the complementarian
doctrine of the Trinity, namely, that human sonship defines divine sonship.
The argument then and now is that because Jesus Christ is called "son," he
is like a human son, subordinate to and having to obey his father. What
this clause in the creed is saying is that Jesus' sonship is *not* like human
sonship. There is something about his sonship that is absolutely different
from creaturely sonship. In the New Testament Jesus Christ is called the
Son/Son of God to speak of his kingly status, not his subordination.

Third, we say, "We believe . . . the unique Son of God" is "eternally
begotten [*gennaō*] of the Father." Now we come to what is called the doctrine of the eternal generation of the Son, what I and most other orthodox
theologians believe safeguards the two foundational elements in the doctrine of the Trinity: the immutable self-differentiation of the Father and

---

[38]This is what most contemporary linguists conclude. This conclusion has been recently contested
by Charles Lee Irons, "A Lexical Defense of the Johannine 'Only Begotten,'" in *Retrieving Eternal
Generation*, ed. Fred Sanders and Scott R. Swain (Grand Rapids, MI: Zondervan, 2017), 98-116.
Irons does not claim that *monogenēs* always means "only begotten" and never "only one of its
kind" in the Greek Bible and in the Greek-speaking church fathers. His argument is that it can
mean "only begotten" and in the five uses in John's Gospel this is its meaning, and "thus [it]
provides part of the exegetical basis for the traditional doctrine of the eternal generation of the
Son" (116). With most contemporary exegetes, I am not convinced that in the Johannine writings
monogenēs bears the meaning "only begotten." And I stand by my claims that in the Greek
church fathers in all the examples I found it speaks of the uniqueness of Christ, who is unique
because he alone is eternally begotten of the Father, and that they do not quote the five Johannine texts as the ground for the doctrine of the eternal generation of the Son. In reply to Irons
see in this same volume, Lewis A. Ayres, "At the Origins of Eternal Generation," 149-62, and
D. A. Carson, "John 5:26 *Crux Interpretum* for Eternal Generation," 79-97. Ayres concludes that
"the title *monogenēs* is, for Origen not by itself the source of the doctrine of the Son's eternal
generation" (162; cf. 155). I think this is true of all the Greek-speaking church fathers. Carson,
on his part, critically assesses all of Iron's arguments (88-90) and finds none of them
compelling.

[39]Besides my book *The Eternal Generation of the Son*, where I argue this, see, in relation to Origen,
Ayres, "At the Origins," and Keith E. Johnson's essay in relation to Augustine, "Eternal Generation," in Sanders and Swain, *Retrieving Eternal Generation*, 163-79.

the Son, and their unity in divine being (*homoousios*). The Father is not the Son because he is unbegotten God; the Son is not the Father because he is begotten God; yet they share perfectly the one divine being as a father and a son. This is the only difference between the Father and the Son the Nicene Creed mentions and allows, and this difference is essential to the doctrine of the Trinity. For over twenty years, Grudem and Ware denied the doctrine of the eternal generation of the Son.[40] As of November 2016, they finally accepted this doctrine![41]

Fourth, as a consequence of his eternal begetting we confess that the Son is "God from God, Light from Light, true God from true God." What these words assert is that, on the basis of his eternal generation, the Son is everything the Father is. Derivation does not imply the diminution of the Son in any way, or any division or separation between the Father and the Son. These words make the point emphatic: the Son is "begotten of the Father" and "from" the Father, yet he is no way less than, inferior to, eternally subordinated to, or submissive to the Father.

To argue that the Nicene Creed speaks of the eternal begetting of the Son to teach the eternal subordination of the Son, as Grudem does, is perverse.[42] For the bishops who promulgated this creed and all orthodox theologians across the centuries, the eternal generation of the Son teaches that the Son is "God from God, light from light, True God from True God."

Finally, and climatically, as a consequence of his eternal begetting we affirm that the Son is "one being [*homoousios*] with the Father." This is not a word the Bible uses of the Son. It is an implication drawn from revelation, namely, that the Son is God without any caveats (Jn 1:1). He is "the Lord." Let me explain the force of the Greek word *homoousios*. All of us share *the same* human "being," and the Father and the Son certainly share the same divine being, but the Father and the Son are also united in (divine) being—they are the one God. If the Father and the Son are the one God, this means that they cannot have two wills; they cannot be separated in what

---

[40]Grudem, *Systematic Theology*, 1234; Ware says this "doctrine is highly speculative and not grounded in biblical teaching" (*Father, Son and Holy Spirit*, 162).

[41]They both did so publicly before about five hundred theologians at the 2016 Evangelical Theological Society annual conference in San Antonio. See Giles, *Rise and Fall*, 44-47.

[42]Grudem, *Systematic Theology*, 251-52, 1234; Grudem, *Countering the Claims of Evangelical Feminism* (Colorado Springs, CO: Multnomah, 2006), 239-40; Grudem, *Evangelical Feminism*, 210-13.

they do; their glory is one, and one cannot rule over the other. The word *homoousios* absolutely excludes *any dividing or separating of the divine persons*. This is why all the Arians of the fourth century repudiated this term. Modern-day evangelicals who separate and divide the Father and the Son, setting the Father above the Son, accept the term because they do not understand its force. They think it means simply that the Father and the Son have the same divine being. They miss the fact that it also asserts that the Father and the Son share the one divine being; the three divine persons are the one God.

Sixth, the Nicene Creed says of the Son that "Through him all things were made." These words reflect exactly the words of Scripture (1 Cor 8:6; cf. Jn 1:3; Heb 1:2; Col 1:16). For the Nicene fathers, the most fundamental division in the whole universe is between the Creator and what he creates. These words are thus included in the creed to make the point emphatically that the Son is the omnipotent co-creator, yet as in all things, he and the Father contribute to this work distinctively as the Father and the Son. In this instance, the Father creates *through* or *in* the Son (Col 1:16).

In contrast, Grudem says, the Son in creation is simply "the active agent in carrying out the plans and directions of the Father"—which is exactly what Arius taught. Bruce Ware says the Son "creates under the authority of the Father."[43] There is no support for these assertions in the Nicene Creed or in Scripture. The Bible speaks of the Son as the co-creator.

Seventh, the Nicene Creed says, "For us and our salvation he [the Son] *came down from heaven*, by the power of the Spirit he was incarnate of the Virgin Mary, *and became man.*" In this phrase the creed reflects Philippians 2:4-11. Jesus Christ, God the Son, had "equality with God [the Father]," yet he "emptied himself, taking the form of a servant, being born in human likeness. And being found in human form he humbled himself, and became obedient to the point of death."

What Philippians 2 teaches is *the willing, self-chosen, and temporal subordination and subjection* of the Son for our salvation. On this basis, orthodox theologians with one voice insist that the subordination and

---

[43]Grudem, *Systematic Theology*, 266; Bruce Ware, "Equal in Essence, Distinct Roles: Eternal Functional Authority and Submission Among the Essentially Equal Divine Persons of the Godhead," *JBMW* 13, no. 2 (2008): 49.

obedience of the Son seen in the incarnation should not be read back into the eternal life of God. To do so is to repeat the error all the Arians of the fourth century made. In the incarnate Son we meet in the Gospels, we see *kenotic*-God, self-emptied God: the Son of God who came down from heaven and became a human being.

The Athanasian Creed. In the so-called Athanasian Creed, composed in about AD 500, Augustine's teaching on the Trinity is identified as "the catholic faith." In this creed the unity of the divine Trinity is at the fore, and any suggestion that the Son or Spirit is subordinated in being or authority is unambiguously excluded. Three clauses specifically deny that the Son is less than the Father in authority.

> So likewise, the Father is almighty, the Son almighty, and the Holy Spirit almighty. And yet there are not three almighties but one almighty.
>
> So likewise, the Father is Lord, the Son is Lord and the Holy Spirit is Lord. And yet not three Lords but one Lord.
>
> In this Trinity none is afore or after another: none is greater or less than another . . . all are co-equal.[44]

In these words, all hierarchical ordering is absolutely excluded.

The only difference allowed among the members of the Trinity is that of differing origination, and this does not in any way imply subordination in being, work, or authority. Nothing could be plainer. The Athanasian Creed is emphatic: the Father, Son, and Spirit are "co-eternal" and "co-equal" God, and therefore indivisible in power and authority. Thus, it is asserted, "Such as the Father is, such is the Son, and such is the Holy Spirit." Only in identity—one is Father, one is Son, and one is Spirit—and in origination—one is "unbegotten," one is "begotten," and one "proceeds"—are the divine three differentiated. All Roman Catholics, Anglicans, Lutherans, and many Reformed churches take this creed as definitive of trinitarian orthodoxy.

The confessions. The Reformation and post-Reformation confessions could not more emphatically exclude hierarchical ordering within the

---

[44]These are direct quotes from the creed. For the text see "The Athanasian Creed," Christian Reformed Church, www.crcna.org/welcome/beliefs/creeds/athanasian-creed (accessed March 29, 2016).

eternal Trinity. Characteristically they affirm that the three divine persons are eternal and that they are one in being/essence/substance and one in power/authority.[45]

- The Augsburg Confession of 1530 states, "There are three persons in this one divine essence, equal in power and alike eternal."

- The Thirty-Nine Articles of the Church of England, 1563, article 1, states that "in the unity of this Godhead there be three persons, of one substance, power, and eternity."

- The Belgic Confession of 1561, article 8, says, "The Father was never without the Son, nor without the Holy Spirit, since all these are equal from eternity, in one and the same essence. There is neither a first nor a last, for all three are one in truth and power, in goodness and mercy."

- The Second Helvetic Confession of 1566, chapter 3, says, "The three persons [are] consubstantial, coeternal, and coequal; distinct with respect to hypostases, and with respect to order, the one preceding the other yet without any inequality. For according to the nature or essence they are so joined together that they are one God, and the divine nature is common to the Father, Son and Holy Spirit. . . . We condemn all heresies and heretics who teach that the Son and Holy Spirit . . . [are] subservient, or subordinate to another in the Trinity."

- The Westminster Confession of 1646, article 2, says, "In the unity of the Godhead there be three persons, of one substance, power, and eternity."

- The London Baptist Confession of 1689, chapter 2, paragraph 3, says the divine three persons are "one substance, power, and eternity."

- The Methodist Articles of Religion of 1784 says, "In the unity of the Godhead there are three persons, of one substance, power, and eternity."

In the end, we must agree, the creeds and the confessions on any fair reading exclude any hierarchical ordering in divine life, specifically in being/essence or power/authority.

---

[45]In trinitarian technical terminology, the words *being*, *essence*, and *substance* are synonyms to speak of what is one in God. The words *power* and *authority* are also synonyms. If the three divine persons are all powerful (omnipotent), and they are, then they have all authority without distinction.

POSTSCRIPT

I am not so naive to think that the Trinity argument for the permanent subordination of women will be heard of no more. The stakes are too high for most complementarians to ever concede to their critics on any matter of importance to their case. Thus, this argument for the permanent subordination of women is still being voiced.[46] In reply to those so reluctant to admit they are wrong on the Trinity, I sum up the points I have made in this chapter. (1) The argument that the threefold relationship of the divine Father, Son, and Spirit in heaven, however understood, is prescriptive for the twofold male-female relationship on earth is logically incoherent and has no biblical support. (2) The most telling and strongly worded rejections of the complementarian doctrine of a hierarchically ordered Trinity have come from the most theologically informed complementarians. (3) To teach that the three divine persons are ordered hierarchically explicitly contradicts the creeds and confessions of the church that represent what Christians communally have agreed is the teaching of Scripture. And (4) this means that for those who acknowledge the authority of these documents, the idea that the three divine persons are ordered hierarchically is heretical—heretical in the sense that it is an explicit denial of what the creeds and confessions of the church rule is the teaching of Scripture.

---

[46]See, e.g., Carson, "John 5:26 *Crux Interpretum*," 92-94; Irons, "Lexical Defense," 115-16.

19

BIBLICAL IMAGES OF GOD AS MOTHER AND SPIRITUAL FORMATION

Ronald W. Pierce and Erin M. Heim

• • • • •

A HEBREW POET ONCE PENNED, "I do not concern myself with great matters or things too wonderful for me. But I have calmed and quieted myself, I am like a weaned child with its mother; like a weaned child I am content" (Ps 131:1-2 NIV). In this chapter, we explore and contemplate God's self-revelation through Scripture's metaphors of motherhood as they relate to our personal spiritual formation, that is, asking how these metaphors inform, form, and shape our identity as God's people.[1] Because of the nature of such an inquiry, we as coauthors have chosen to begin our exegetical and theological discussions of the relevant Old Testament and New Testament texts with brief descriptions of our personal experiences with our respective mothers, as well as with our journeys in spiritual

---

[1]Exploring the fatherhood metaphor for God in Scripture is beyond the scope of this essay, in part because such publications are readily available. For example, see Christopher J. H. Wright, *Knowing God the Father Through the Old* Testament (Downers Grove, IL: InterVarsity Press, 2007); Marianne Meye Thompson, *The Promise of the Father: Jesus and God in the New Testament* (Louisville, KY: Westminster John Knox, 2000); Abera M. Mengestu, *God as Father in Paul: Kinship Language and Identity Formation in Early Christianity* (Eugene, OR: Wipf & Stock, 2013).

Spiritual formation is sometimes referred to as soul formation or spiritual transformation. For example, consider the titles used by these similar organizations to represent their spiritual formation ministries: www.soulformation.org and www.transformingcenter.org. Evangelical organizations such as these provide resources for Christian leaders to grow in this dimension of their lives and to minister more effectively to others to this end.

formation. The goal is to understand better and experience more fully the person and work of the triune God, Father, Son, and Spirit, who is also portrayed in terms of motherhood. In addition, we wish to challenge the contemporary church to a deeper level of biblical fidelity in its language of worship and soul formation as this regards divine motherhood metaphors in Scripture.[2] With this in mind, we invite you, the reader, to journey alongside us with an open mind as well as with an open heart toward God.

TWO PERSONAL NOTES

Erin. I am adopted and thus well aware that the biological functions of motherhood do not automatically make someone a mother. Nor does our lack of biological connection make me any less my adoptive mother's child.[3] Her embodied experience of motherhood has a different, but no less valid, narrative. Motherhood metaphors in Scripture draw primarily on biological experiences of motherhood, which in the ancient Near East were inextricably linked to motherhood. Yet biological expressions of motherhood form only the framework of the metaphors drawn from them. To be clear, this does not mean that women who choose not to have children or who cannot have children are in any way deficient in their womanhood. Although we are focused here on biological motherhood in the Old Testament and New Testament, we wish to be clear that these metaphors are revealed in Scripture for the spiritual formation of all of God's people—not just for mothers and not just for women. Further, I acknowledge that my motherly love is a poor and pale reflection of God's relentless and fierce motherly love for Israel throughout the Hebrew Bible. Nonetheless, it reflects that love. Yahweh carries, births, nurses, and nurtures Israel like a mother. Whereas these metaphors do not exhaustively reveal who God is, they do reveal important aspects of who God is. If we profess to be people who submit to God, then we must take into consideration all of the ways in which God is revealed—including those communicated through feminine language and metaphors.

---

[2]We are indebted to Margo G. Houts, "Language, Gender, and God: How Traditionalists and Feminists Play the Inclusive Language Game" (PhD diss., Fuller Theological Seminary, 1993).
[3]Paul's adoption metaphors speak in a powerful way to this point (e.g., Rom 8:15, 23; 9:4; Gal 4:5; Eph 1:5).

Ron. I was born the fifth child of a young Christian mother at the end of World War II. With a mostly absent father, Mom was my principal spiritual influence from my earliest impressions until I left home as a first-generation collegiate pursuing God's calling to ministry. Now, more than fifty years later, rich and enduring memories of her persistent love for me remain, a love that was frequently demonstrated through her warmth, comfort, security, compassion, nurture, care, and sacrifice—aspects of God's motherly love found in Scripture and explored here. To be clear, she was far from perfect, although those shortcomings have not held a lasting place in my heart. As Lois and Eunice were to Timothy (2 Tim 1:5), so Mom was to me. After forty-plus years later as a theologian—especially over the past four years—I have sought to enhance my usual teaching, writing, and mentoring responsibilities with Christian college students by exploring my own spiritual formation as well as training in the ministry of spiritual direction—by which I mean walking alongside others as their lives are being spiritually transformed. In this two-way, life-giving context—even though, as a man, I cannot experience mother-hood physically—I am still able to explore the richness of the biblical metaphors of God as mother that have so deeply affected me as well as those with whom I now journey.

THE TRIUNE GOD AND GENDER

At the outset it is important to be clear: we are not arguing that Yahweh is a goddess, or that "God the Father" is better thought of as "God the Parent" or "God the Mother."[4] Moreover, the metaphor of father does not mean God is a man in contrast to a woman. It is imperative to "avoid projecting creaturely gender into God" through the use of "sensual images taken from our human relations."[5] Motherhood language predicated of Yahweh in the Hebrew Scriptures is true of the whole Trinity, revealing something

---

[4]God is portrayed directly as Father fifteen times in the Old Testament: Deut 32:6; Is 63:16 (twice); 64:8; Jer 3:4, 19; 31:9; Mal 1:6; 2:10; 2 Sam 7:14; 1 Chron 17:13; 22:10; 28:6; Ps 68:5; 89:26. Otherwise, father imagery is seen without the actual term: Ex 4:22-23; Deut 1:31; 8:5; 14:1; Ps 103:13; Jer 3:22; 31:20; Hos 11:1-4; Mal 3:17.

[5]The Nicaean theologies of Athanasius and Gregory of Nazianzus provide examples of this concern. See T. F. Torrance, *The Trinitarian Faith: The Evangelical Theology of the Ancient Catholic Church* (Edinburgh: T&T Clark, 1988, 1995), 69-71.

just as true about God's essential nature as masculine metaphors. This form of speech allows us to gain insight into the inner life of the Trinity, where the Father, Son, and Spirit relate to one another in eternal states of grace and love, each as "an uncreated person, one in essence, equal in power and glory."[6]

Without question, the triune God of the universe transcends gender, yet chooses in love to communicate and enter into relationship with people who are created with human sexuality to be expressed in gendered relationships with others. Therefore, it is no surprise that we find both masculine and feminine metaphors for God in Scripture. Indeed, the presence of such metaphors underscores a qualitative difference between God and humanity. God in his mysterious magnificence is the perfection of men and women—as well as those born intersex—so that we together with all of our rich diversity can better reflect the divine image in the process of the spiritual formation of our souls. Yet, our perception of God should not be limited to Scripture's gendered metaphors, for many nongendered metaphors for God are also found in the Bible.[7] The fullness of God's being cannot be contained by any one of these. Therefore, in our drawing attention to the feminine images of motherhood, we are not implying that God is a gendered being—male or female. To borrow from the words of Jesus to a Samaritan women, "God is spirit, and his worshipers must worship in the Spirit and in truth" (Jn 4:24 NIV).

Across church history motherhood language for God has often been downplayed to the detriment of a robust theology that seeks to understand God's person and discern God's work in the lives of believers.[8] However, many notable exceptions can be found, such as Julian of Norwich, who boldly asserted,

> God is our mother as truly as he is our father; and he showed this in everything, and especially in the sweet words where he says, "It is I," that is to say, "It is I: the power and goodness of fatherhood. It is I: the wisdom of

---

[6]See the doctrinal basis of the Evangelical Theological Society: "About the ETS," Evangelical Theological Society, www.etsjets.org/about (accessed May 31, 2019).

[7]For example, Rock (Gen 49:24), Strong Tower (Ps 61:3), Living Water (Jn 4:10-11), Bread of Life (Jn 6:35, 48), etc.

[8]For example, in the fourth century AD, Ambrose spoke of Christ as begotten from the "womb of the Father" (*De fide* 1.19.126).

motherhood. It is I: the unity. I am the sovereign goodness of all manner of things. It is I that make you love. It is I that make you long. It is I: the eternal fulfilment of all true desires."[9]

METAPHOR IN SCRIPTURE AND THEOLOGY

Metaphorical language, simply put, speaks of one thing in terms of another.[10] Moreover, speaking of God though gendered metaphors does not communicate truth of a lesser order than so-called literal speech. In fact, the majority of the language used of God in Scripture is metaphorical, communicating to us the nature of God's essential being and how God chooses to work with humanity. With that in mind, feminine language about God in Scripture speaks of God as a birthing mother (Is 42:13-15), nursing mother (Is 49:14-15), comforting mother (Is 66:12-13), a mother bear (Hos 13:8) or eagle (Dt 32:11-12), or even mother hen (Mt 23:37; Lk 13:34).[11] All of these metaphors reveal something of the nature, character, and personhood of God, yet none exhaustively reveals the fullness of God's person.

Much of my (Erin's) research has focused on how metaphors work to shape and form the identity of the communities that use them.[12] Therein, I have concluded that cognitive linguistics and sociolinguistics show definitively that metaphors have the ability to change perceptions.[13] They are

[9]Julian of Norwich, *Revelations of Divine Love, Short Text and Long Text*, trans. Elizabeth Spearing (London: Penguin Books, 1998), section 59, 139. See similar statements in her *Long Text*, section 52, 125-27; sections 58-63, 137-47; section 74, 162-64; section 83, 176-77. Other examples include John Chrysostom (fourth century); Bede (seventh to eighth century); Bernard of Clairvaux, Alfred of Rievaulx, and Anselm of Canterbury (twelfth century); Thomas Aquinas, Angela of Foligno, and Catherine of Siena (thirteenth to fourteenth century); Margery Kempe (fourteenth to fifteenth century); and the list continues. See Virginia Ramey Mollenkott, *The Divine Feminine: The Biblical Imagery of God as Female* (New York: Crossroad, 1983), 9-10.

[10]See Janet Martin Soskice, *Metaphor and Religious Language* (Oxford: Clarendon, 1987).

[11]This is aside from the images drawn from women's cultural activity in the ancient world, such as seamstress (Neh 9:21), midwife (Ps 22:9-10; 71:6; Is 66:9), cooking (Lk 13:18-21), and seeking a lost coin (Lk 15:8-10).

[12]See Erin M. Heim, *Adoption in Galatians and Romans* (Leiden: Brill, 2017); Heim, "Paths Beyond Tracing Out: The Hermeneutics of Metaphor and Theological Method," in *The Voice of God in the Text of Scripture*, ed. Oliver Crisp and Fred Sanders (Grand Rapids, MI: Zondervan, 2016), 112-26.

[13]See especially George Lakoff and Mark Johnson, *Metaphors We Live By* (Chicago: University of Chicago Press, 2003); Mark Turner, *Death Is the Mother of Beauty: Mind, Metaphor, Criticism* (Chicago: University of Chicago Press, 1987); Gerard Steen and Raymond Gibbs, eds., *Metaphor*

powerful tools of communication, and their role in shaping individual and corporate identity must be taken seriously. Our brains process metaphors as sensate experiences. Reading or hearing about doing something is not significantly different from actually doing something, although this becomes more complicated when reading about things that we are incapable of doing.[14] For example, a woman does not experience passages about circumcision in the same way a man does, nor can a man truly understand what it is like to be pregnant, give birth, or breastfeed. Nevertheless, we are at least capable of imagining what it would be like to experience those things, and in such imagining we are shaped and formed not only by the cognitive content of the metaphor but also by experiencing the metaphor holistically with all of our senses.

SPIRITUAL FORMATION

Among the wide-ranging definitions of spiritual formation, we speak here of "a process of being conformed to the image of Christ for the sake of others."[15] In this process, we can learn how to inhabit Scripture's metaphors of God as mother—how to put them on and wear them around as we go about our lives. We need to experience our relationships to God and one another through and from within these metaphors. Scripture's metaphors, including feminine metaphors if we are willing to submit to them, should mold and form us into the image of Christ. It is not enough for the people of God to hold these metaphors at arm's length, to understand what they communicate, yet to refuse to be challenged and transformed by them. We must learn to live by them. Therefore, the tasks of this chapter are twofold: first, to show that the feminine language for God in Scripture is essential to our understanding of who God is; and second, to use Paul's ministerial motherhood metaphors to show how the people of God might

---

in Cognitive Linguistics (Philadelphia: J. Benjamins, 2001); Raymond W. Gibbs Jr. and Teenie Matlock, "Metaphor, Imagination, and Simulation: Psycholinguistic Evidence," in *The Cambridge Handbook of Metaphor and Thought*, ed. Raymond W. Gibbs Jr. (Cambridge: Cambridge University Press, 2008), 161-76.

[14]See Benjamin Bergen, *Louder Than Words: The New Science of How the Mind Makes Meaning* (New York: Basic Books, 2010), for a summary of this research.

[15]M. Robert Mulholland Jr., *Invitation to a Journey: A Road Map for Spiritual Formation* (Downers Grove, IL: InterVarsity Press, 1993), 15-44.

be changed and transformed into the image of Christ by learning to put on this imagery.

Motherhood imagery reveals the nature and character of God's love, for love is not merely something God does, but it is part of who God *is* in the divine essence: "Whoever does not love does not know God, because God is love" (1 Jn 4:8 NIV). Metaphors of God's motherly love go beyond divine activity to give humanity a glimpse into the quality of love eternally existing in the Trinity. Yet, this may differ between genders. For example, although God's love is beyond our comprehension, we can lean against God as a three-year-old child often leans against his or her mother. A son may say, "Mom, I wuv you so much," and mean it with every fiber of his three-year-old being. And the mother may reply, "And I love you so much," and mean it with every fiber of her thirty-three-year-old being. They both are saying the same thing, but the mother's love for her son is not precisely of the same quality as the son's love for his mother. Similarly, the love of a mother and a father for a son each reveals its own unique character. In this simple illustration we can find a beautifully diverse image of human complementarity as God intended it.[16] The embodied experiences of this love as mother and father are different. In this case, a mother's love for her son begins as he grows inside her, as she brings him forth in labor and delivery, and as her body continues to nourish her growing child until he is weaned. Her feelings of love for him become deeply rooted in these physical, emotional, and spiritual experiences. For her, motherhood brings about a fierceness in love that she did not know prior to becoming a mother. It comes from the depths of her being—indeed, from the womb.

Images of motherhood in the Bible are intended to evoke sensate and visceral reactions because motherhood is physically, emotionally, and spiritually demanding. And, like all human love, motherly love is embodied. Mothers have physical connections to their children and bear physical burdens in caring for them. They carry their children in their wombs, nurse them at their breasts, hold them in their arms, and comfort them with their bodies when they cry. Yet such feminine metaphors for God

---

[16]It is necessary in a volume like this to clarify that *complementarity* is being use here to mean "beneficial differences." We are *not* associating it with the so-called complementarian movement that advocates for male leadership (see introduction to this book).

also draw on these same embodied experiences of motherhood to communicate the fierceness, tenderness, compassion, and provision of God's love. Perhaps it should also not surprise us that in the Old Testament the language of labor and travail is used in the context of battle when warriors fight "like a woman in labor" (Is 13:8). Words cannot fully capture the whatness of such motherhood metaphors, yet these are clearly used to communicate emotions and bonds that come from the very depths of one's being. Compassion and life spring forth from the womb of Yahweh (Is 46:3; Jer 31:20). Yahweh's breasts nourish and feed Israel (Ps 22:9). Yahweh, the Spirit, and even the apostle Paul labor and travail for God's people (Gal 4:19).

YAHWEH THE COVENANT GOD OF ISRAEL AS MOTHER

Four distinct phases of human motherhood appear in Old Testament metaphors for Yahweh: (1) a mother carrying her unborn child, (2) a mother birthing her child, (3) a mother nursing her child, and (4) a mother nurturing her weaned child. Each of these is considered here in turn.

A mother carrying her unborn child. The initial stage of motherhood, that of pregnancy, shows God's firm but loving care for Israel. For example, Isaiah confronts Israel on behalf of Yahweh, saying, "Listen to me, you descendants of Jacob, all the remnant of the people of Israel, you were the load from my belly [Hebrew *ha'amusim minni-beten*], and I have carried you from the womb [Hebrew *Rachem*]" (Is 46:3, our translation). Although this rendering may not seem eloquent, it captures in a powerful way the feeling of a mother's long months of pregnancy sustained far after childbirth. God's love for us is so great that we are carried within the divine womb in our earliest stages of spiritual formation.[17]

Similarly, Yahweh's yearning and compassion is expressed in the rhetorical question, "'Is not Ephraim my dear son, the child in whom I delight? Though I often speak against him, I still remember him. Therefore my [womb; Hebrew *me'ay*] yearns for him; I have [motherly womb-love;

---

[17]See John N. Oswalt, *The Book of Isaiah 40–66*, NICOT (Grand Rapids, MI: Eerdmans, 1998), 230n18. There he rightly notes that texts such as this in the Old Testament are carefully worded "to distance God from the fertility rites of pagan religion with their sexualizing of deity." However, Oswalt goes much too far by claiming "the picture of a mother carrying her children in her arms . . . is not part of the OT imagery."

Hebrew *raham a'rachamennu*] for him,' declares the LORD" (Jer 31:20 NIV).[18] The image of divine love draws its meaning from a mother's love, grace, and compassion for the child she once carried but who is now lost in exile. Jeremiah reveals the broken heart of Rachel as God weeps with her like a mother "trembling with powerful emotion."[19] He speaks with pathos, comfort, and assurance, for as "Mother-Rachel has had unrequited pathos, so the God of Israel is moved by deep pathos."[20]

A mother birthing her child. In Isaiah 13:6-9, when the day of Yahweh draws near, "terror" seizes the warriors, and "pain and anguish" grip them so that they "writhe like a woman in labor" (NIV). Also, in response to Babylon's destruction, the prophet himself cries out, "'At this my body is racked with pain, pangs seize me, like those of a woman in labor . . . '" (Isa 21:3), Isaiah's 'emotional reaction with deepest anguish.'"[21] Later, in Isaiah 42:13-15, Isaiah describes Yahweh as one who marches out "like a warrior," yet exclaims, "like a woman in childbirth, I cry out, I gasp and pant" (NIV). But Yahweh is not terrified at a coming catastrophe, nor cast down in its face. Moreover, these images of warriors and women are not contradictory but underscore the power of Yahweh in the impending judgment with vocalizations reminiscent of both warriors and women in labor.[22]

R. N. Whybray comments on Isaiah 42:13-15, "The simile of the woman in travail, which is reinforced in the Hebrew by a breathless and convulsive style which seems ugly to modern western taste, is intended to convey not only a sudden burst of noise and commotion, but also the idea that something new is about to be born."[23] Although he rightly notes the end goal of this passage, he fails to appreciate its use of this dual metaphor related to motherhood that is clearly indicated in the metaphor. These pants and

---

[18]On "motherly womb-love," see Paul R. Smith, *Is It Okay to Call God "Mother"?: Considering the Feminine Face of God* (Peabody, MA: Hendrickson, 1993), 56-57.

[19]Christopher J. H. Wright, *The Message of Jeremiah: Against Wind and Tide* (Downers Grove, IL: InterVarsity Press, 2014), 320; Tremper Longman III, *Jeremiah, Lamentations* (Grand Rapids, MI: Baker, 2008), 207-8.

[20]Walter Brueggemann, *A Commentary on Jeremiah: Exile and Homecoming* (Grand Rapids, MI: Eerdmans, 1998), 287.

[21]Brevard S. Childs, *Isaiah: A Commentary* (Louisville, KY: John Knox, 2001), 152.

[22]John Calvin mistakenly construed this image to speak of "maternal tenderness." See B. A. Gerrish, *Grace and Gratitude: The Eucharistic Theology of John Calvin* (Eugene, OR: Wipf & Stock, 2002), 40.

[23]R. N. Whybray, *Isaiah 40–66*, New Century Bible Commentary (London: Oliphants, 1975), 78.

roars are not just a "sudden burst of commotion," neither are they an ugly and distasteful way of signaling that "something new is about to be born." The groans of a woman in labor are powerful and fierce. For women, labor is a primal, instinctive experience. In this experience, all of a woman's physical and mental energy is focused on a single goal: delivering the child. In labor, and especially in unmedicated labor, women are warriors. In the combination of both masculine and feminine metaphors, Yahweh's power in judgment is not exclusively male or female. Rather, "stripped of its conventional connotations, [the birthing metaphor] ceases to be an image of fear and pain and becomes instead a new way of describing God's behavior and its awesome effects."[24]

A mother nursing her child. Just a few chapters later, the metaphor of Yahweh as a woman in labor gives way to that of a mother who nurses Israel at her breast and carries Israel in her womb (Is 49:14-15)—an image of Zion, Jerusalem, and a bereaved mother skillfully woven together. The physical distance of a father is distinguished from that of a mother, in that "the child has never drawn life from the father's body either in the womb or after. But, the attachment of a mother and child is direct, and thus almost mystical."[25] The love and care God gives Israel is even stronger than that of a nursing mother. In response to Zion's lament that "the LORD has forsaken me," Yahweh asks, "Can a mother forget the baby at her breast and have no compassion [Hebrew *rachem*] on the child [of her womb; Hebrew *bitnah*]? Though she may forget, I will not forget you!" (NIV). There are physical consequences of a mother withholding breastmilk from a hungry infant. A mother nursing an infant is a physical expression of her unique love for her child. It is almost inconceivable that she would forget the child at her breast, because her body sends powerful signals that are very difficult to ignore. Through this feminine metaphor, one learns that Yahweh's covenant bond with Israel is deep and foundational to God's divine character. Israel's covenant maker cannot transgress this bond so as to forsake God's people; indeed, to do so would be to go against the very essence of the threefold divine personhood. Indeed, "[a]s profound as the

---

[24]Katheryn Pfisterer Darr, "Like Warrior, Like Woman: Destruction and Deliverance in Isaiah 42:10-17," *CBQ* 49, no. 4 (1984): 564.

[25]Oswalt, *Book of Isaiah*, 305.

love of a human mother is for her child, Yahweh the Divine mother transcends even this."[26]

A mother nurturing her weaned child. Nursing imagery is also one way
of understanding Hosea 11:4, 8: "And I was for them like those who take a
nursling to the breast, and I bowed down to him in order to give him
suck. . . . How can I give you up, O Ephraim? How can I hand you over, O
Israel? . . . My heart recoils against me, my womb is utterly inflamed within
me."[27] Although Israel has been faithless to Yahweh, and the prophet
speaks words of coming wrath and judgment, ultimately Yahweh's mother-
love preserves and comforts Ephraim and Israel. Such an impulse for compassion is seated in Yahweh's womb, for "God is not only fatherly. God is
also [a] mother who lifts her loved child from the ground to her knee. The
Trinity is like a mother's cloak wherein the child finds a home and lays its
head on the maternal breast."[28]

Returning to the opening citation in this essay, King David writes, "I do
not concern myself with great matters or things too wonderful for me. But
I have calmed and quieted myself, I am like a weaned child with its mother;
like a weaned child I am content" (Ps 131:1-2 NIV). The child at this stage
"no longer wants to be nursed by the mother but merely desires her nearness and affection. It is a mark of maturity."[29] The tender imagery of this
Hebrew poem invites God's beloved children—at whatever stage of spiritual formation they may be—to an intimate, quiet, and safe place of rest in
God's presence, one that reflects growth into a deeper, soul-forming life.

Similarly, Isaiah 66:12-13 combines several motherhood images when
Yahweh speaks tenderly to Israel at her time of restoration: "I will extend
peace to her like a river, and the wealth of nations like a flooding stream;
you will nurse and be carried on her arm and dandled on her knees. As a
mother comforts her child, so will I comfort you; and you will be comforted over Jerusalem" (NIV). The comfort of a young child by his or her

---

[26]Carol A. Newsom, "Second Isaiah," in *The Women's Bible Commentary*, ed. Carol A. Newsom and
Sharon H. Ringe (Louisville, KY: Westminster John Knox, 1992), 176.

[27]Interpretive translation by Silvia Schroer and Thomas Staubli, *Body Symbolism in the Bible*, illustrated ed. (Collegeville, MN: Michael Glazier, 2001), 79.

[28]Mechtild of Magdeburg (thirteenth-century nun), cited in Matthew Fox, *Original Blessing* (New
York: Tarcher/Putnam, 2000), 221, 223.

[29]C. Hassell Bullock, *Psalms*, vol. 2, *Psalms 73–150*, Teach the Text Commentary (Grand Rapids,
MI: Baker, 2017), 446.

loving mother brings the genuine peace (Hebrew *shalom*) that uniquely comes from a relationship forged in her womb. In this text, Israel has been invited to return to this personal and intimate aspect of its covenantal relationship intended for it by God from its conception as God's people.

In sum, prophetic imagery in Isaiah, Jeremiah, Hosea—and elsewhere in the Old Testament—draws on the rich and unique, physical images of motherhood to communicate God's persistent, tender, yet fierce love for Israel. In human terms, this love is meant to be experienced from a child's inception until well after the child is weaned—indeed, even into adulthood. In the context of spiritual formation, God's love continues from our earliest experiences of divine grace, to a more mature—yet nonetheless intimate, safe, and consoling—relationship with our Creator, Redeemer, and Sustainer.

JESUS THE MESSIAH OF ISRAEL AS MOTHER

In addition to being many other things, Jesus of Nazareth is the motherly love of Yahweh incarnate. Again, this does not mean that Jesus the Son of God was female. Rather, the love and compassion revealed in the Old Testament in terms appropriate to motherhood are the same love and compassion manifested in the person and mission of Jesus, as he said, "Anyone who has seen me has seen the Father" (Jn 14:9 NIV). As such, Jesus represents the best of masculine and feminine strengths.[30]

Shortly before his passion week, and in the thick of arguments with Jewish religious leaders in the temple, Jesus laments, "Jerusalem, Jerusalem, the city that kills the prophets and stones those who are sent to it! How often have I desired to gather your children together as a hen gathers her brood under her wings, and you were not willing!" (Mt 23:37; Lk 13:34). Our Lord's lament is that of a distressed mother bird welcoming and inviting her children to draw near for her instinctively unifying and protective care.[31] Although Jesus is not quoting from an Old Testament text here, his words are evocative of Yahweh's mothering of Israel in Isaiah, alongside other Old Testament passages where Yahweh carries them on eagles' wings (e.g., Ex 19:4) and shelters them under his wings (e.g., Ps 17:8).

---

[30]Smith, *Is It Okay*, 68.
[31]R. T. France, *The Gospel of Matthew*, NICNT (Grand Rapids, MI: Eerdmans, 2007), 883.

Deuteronomy 32:9, 11 is perhaps the most comprehensive, where God
expresses his motherly love to "Jacob his allotted inheritance . . . like an
eagle that stirs up its nest and hovers over its young, that spreads its wings
to catch them and carries them aloft" (NIV). Our focus here is on the
context of Matthew's account of Jesus' words, though a similar argument
could be made from Luke's narrative.

In order to understand Matthew's hermeneutic, we must first come to
grips with his portrayal of Christ as "Immanuel, God with us."[32] This conviction causes him to read Isaiah's recurring theme of blindness in the face
of Yahweh's saving activity with new eyes conditioned by the Evangelist's
time with the Messiah. Perhaps, then, we are to understand the whole of
Matthew's gospel as the enactment of Yahweh's promises to Isaiah—
promises of justice and judgment that are couched in the language of
motherhood at key places in his writings, especially in Isaiah 42; 49.[33]

In Matthew 12 the Evangelist cites Isaiah 42:1-4 in order to cast Jesus
into the role of Isaiah's "servant" to "proclaim justice to the nations" (NIV).
It is difficult to know how much of Isaiah's text Matthew has in mind here,
but it is striking that here Yahweh the warrior's actions of judgment are
coannounced by Yahweh the birthing mother vocalizing labor pains.
There, God lays waste to the mountains and hills, leads the blind by paths
they do not know, and turns darkness into light before them. Yet by the
end of the passage, the servant is Israel, who is still blind and hard of heart.
This Gospel writer regularly casts Israel's religious elite into the role of
Isaiah's blind and hardhearted people. However, striking parallels also can
be seen between Yahweh's motherly activity in Isaiah 42; 49, and Jesus'
ministry in this Gospel account. As Yahweh is in travail for Israel, so Jesus
longs to gather Jacob's descendants to himself like a mother bird would do,
and yet in both instances Israel will not see.

There is no "hidden God" behind Jesus, for in his embodied personhood we see God as God is.[34] It is important for us to keep this in mind

---

[32]On Matthew's hermeneutic, see especially Richard Hays, *Echoes of Scripture in the Gospels* (Waco,
TX: Baylor University Press, 2016).

[33]For a compelling defense of Matthew's use of Isaiah's Christ that focuses particularly on Is 42:1-4, see
Richard Beaton, *Isaiah's Christ in Matthew's Gospel* (Cambridge: Cambridge University Press, 2002).

[34]On this point see T. F. Torrance, *The Christian Doctrine of God: One Being in Three Persons*
(London: Bloomsbury T&T Clark, 2016), 243.

when we read Jesus' lament in Matthew 23:37. Here he portrays himself as the mother hen of Jerusalem, like hens that instinctively gather their baby chicks for protection—implying a history between Jesus and the people of Jerusalem. A mother hen lays eggs, becomes broody, and sits on her eggs until they hatch. Only then can she gather her chicks under her wings. This is an image of devotion, nurture, and protection that is implicitly drawing from Isaiah 49:8-21, which speaks of Yahweh's mothering of Jerusalem. Here, Israel's covenant-keeping God pursues Zion with a fierce and loyal love, even when mother Zion is unfaithful to her own children. Jesus is Yahweh incarnate, and in his voice we hear echoes of Yahweh's fierce motherly love for God's people.

Jesus' words, "How often I have longed to gather your children," seem intentionally reminiscent of the prophet Isaiah's words, "Can a mother forget the baby at her breast and have no compassion on the child she has borne?" (Is 49:15 NIV). Although the "how often" in Jesus' lament seems otherwise out of place in Matthew's narrative, when taken in accordance with John's Gospel, it may imply that Jesus has visited Jerusalem several times previously. Or perhaps the Lord's words reflect a theme so prominently displayed in Isaiah. In other words, the mother-love of God incarnate is a manifestation of Yahweh's mother-love. His "how often" reaches back before the incarnation and connects with Yahweh's motherly love for Israel. The resonances between the two passages are striking and powerful.

In Matthew 23:38-39, Jesus' motherly lament over Jerusalem is also coupled with Psalm 118:26, a psalm of praise turned into the prediction: "For I tell you, you will not see me again until you say, 'Blessed is he who comes in the name of the Lord'" (NIV). This statement marks a turning point in Jesus' ministry. He has pronounced judgment on Israel's failed religious leaders, leading to the Olivet discourse, regarding the signs of Christ's coming (Mt 24). In short, the Messiah's lament over Jerusalem is the beginning of the end. Immanuel, in whom the motherly love of Yahweh has been brought down and given flesh, carries this love to its fullest expression in the cross.

In sum, we have observed in the Old Testament texts how bodily motherhood metaphors bring to the fore Yahweh's fierce, relentless, yet Old

Testament pursuit of Israel for judgment, deliverance, provision, and protection. Although these speak in terms of a mother's body, they do so through anthropomorphisms, for Yahweh does not have such physicality. In Jesus, however, Yahweh has come in the flesh as "God with us." Although Jesus is physically a man, he is no less the embodiment of a divine love that includes motherly love. Alongside other salient metaphors such as substitutionary atonement (Lev 16), Jesus' act of sacrifice is a physical instantiation of Yahweh as Mother, as there are striking parallels to the Old Testament motherhood metaphors in the sacrifice of Jesus' own body. For example, motherhood involves the giving of one's body on behalf of another; it involves the shedding of one's blood in order to bring new life. Likewise, Jesus sacrifices his body and sheds his blood to bring forth life in the new covenant. Certainly, the gift of Jesus' death and resurrection is much more than an expression of Yahweh's motherly love, yet it is equally certain that it is no less than that.

Jesus' comfort with using the imagery of motherhood to express his lament over Jerusalem carries implications for our own spiritual formation: "being conformed to the image of Christ for the sake of others."[35] First, in Jesus' ministry—as we will see in Galatians 4 and 1 Thessalonians 2— motherhood is an apt framework for ministry. Both men and women can minister out of motherly devotion, providing motherly care for a congregation, a small group, a family, a mentee, a spiritual directee, and so forth. Through our personal contemplation and our practice of living out the truths taught in Scripture, we too can cultivate motherly love that at the least gestures toward the motherly love of God.

Second, when Jesus relates to and utilizes a woman's experience of motherhood, he provides the church with the groundwork for cultivating mutual empathy and understanding between men and women. Moreover, this moves us away from speaking of rigid categories of "masculine" and "feminine" attributes. As the divine man, Jesus ministers in a motherly way. Though one might argue that Jesus is able to mother out of his divine nature and that other men are unable to emulate such mothering, this argument breaks down in Paul's emulation of Jesus' motherhood. We will,

---

[35]Mulholland, *Invitation to a Journey*, 15.

however, set this example aside for a moment as we turn first to the work of the Spirit.

THE HOLY SPIRIT AS MOTHER

We turn now to the imagery of motherhood found in the third person of the Trinity in John 3:1-8. Forms of the Greek word *gennaō* ("to be born") are used eight times here amid a discussion of wombs, flesh, water, and blood. The whole conversation is predicated on the analogous relationship between physical birth and spiritual rebirth. Thus, if one follows the metaphor where it leads, one discovers that the Spirit in this text is not merely an impersonal force but a birthing mother. Therefore, this passage is better read in light of Yahweh's crying out, gasping, and panting in labor (Is 42:13-15), where the covenantal God of Israel "will give birth to a new act of deliverance."[36] However, the connection between spiritual birth and physical birth is often obscured in contemporary readings. As Beth Stovell remarks, "Many commentaries speak of the childbirth in John 3 as simple and painless because it is spiritual rather than physical, as though a spiritual stork dropped the child off in a nice neat package."[37] If we attend to the parallels between spiritual and physical birth drawn out in the text, a much richer reading of John 3 emerges. Both physical birth and spiritual rebirth represent a point in time, yet both lead to a process of growth. In terms of spiritual formation, this process can be just as lengthy and challenging, joyous and painful—perhaps even more—as the process of physical and emotional maturing in our earthy lives.

In John 3:1-8, we find Nicodemus initiating a conversation with Jesus: "Rabbi, we know that you are a teacher who has come from God; for no one can do these signs that you do apart from the presence of God" (Jn 3:2). In response, Jesus begins a lengthy discourse by declaring, "No one can see the kingdom of God without being born from above" (Jn 3:3). This learned yet curious religious leader is understandably confused, even though he most certainly understands what childbirth entails. So, he asserts, "Surely

---

[36]Ben Witherington III, *Isaiah Old and New: Exegesis, Intertextuality, and Hermeneutics* (Minneapolis: Fortress, 2017), 204.

[37]Beth Stovell, "The Birthing Spirit, the Childbearing God: Metaphors of Motherhood and Their Place in Christian Discipleship," in *Making Sense of Motherhood*, ed. Beth Stovell (Eugene, OR: Wipf & Stock, 2016), 38.

they cannot enter a second time into their mother's womb to be born?"
(Jn 3:4 NIV). Nicodemus's words may reveal "a crass misunderstanding"
of *anōthen*, which can mean either "again" or "from above." Though Nicodemus may lack "the categories or insight to grasp Jesus's words, he is not
entirely off base in imagining that being born anew requires something
drastic and difficult, something deemed impossible from the human point
of view."[38]

It is also striking that, as Jesus continues, he does not say, "This is not
about childbirth." Rather, he says to Nicodemus, "No one can enter the
kingdom of God without being born of water and Spirit" (Jn 3:5). By dwelling on this metaphor, several important implications emerge. First, it is
striking in itself that Jesus is using a feminine birthing metaphor to describe
the activity of the Spirit. The womb of the Spirit is not overtly mentioned
but perhaps implied as a counterpart to Nicodemus's assertion. Being
brought forth in birth from the womb of the Spirit identifies the Spirit as
the source and sustainer of life, and the giver of motherly compassion.

Second, as Beth Stovell observes, "Jesus's clarification that this birth is
spiritual and not physical does not necessarily remove the metaphorical
implications of possible pain."[39] Notably, the only pain alluded to in John 3
is that of Jesus: God so loved the world that he "gave" his son, and the Son
of Man must be "lifted up." Thus, Nicodemus and his generic, universal-
izing, third-person "Surely *they* cannot enter a second time into their
mother's womb" (Jn 3:4 NIV, emphasis added) do not experience the pain
of childbirth. Rather, the Spirit's birthing pain is mapped on to the agony
of the cross. The Spirit is active in birthing children "from above," and
these children are transformed in the Spirit's womb from flesh to spirit by
the painful labor of the cross. Moreover, we as followers of Jesus enter into
this experience when we respond to the invitation on the way to his passion week in Jerusalem, "Whoever wants to be my disciple must deny
themselves and take up their cross and follow me" (Mt 16:24 NIV).

---

[38]Marianne Meye Thompson, *John*, New Testament Library (Louisville, KY: Westminster John
    Knox, 2015), 79.
[39]Stovell, "Birthing Spirit," 38.

MOTHERING MINISTERS: THE APOSTLE
PAUL AND SPIRITUAL FORMATION

There is an organic and instructive progression in the Bible from divine-motherhood metaphors to the appropriation of these metaphors by mothering ministers of the gospel—most notably the apostle Paul. His use of labor and birth imagery can function as a case study for what it might mean to be spiritually formed by the Bible's mothering metaphors. In the ancient world, the sights, sounds, and smells of childbirth were not nearly as separate from everyday life as they are in contemporary Western culture. Therefore, it should not surprise us that Paul was familiar with birth and breastfeeding, as he was steeped in the Hebrew Scriptures and undoubtedly influenced and formed by their metaphors of motherhood.

One example of this appears during a personal experience of Paul around AD 51–53, while he was on his second missionary journey. He is speaking to the people of Athens about the altar inscription, "TO AN UNKNOWN GOD." Using words familiar to them from their own poets, Paul bears witness to the one true God, who, he declares, "made the world and everything in it," who "gives everyone life and breath," and in whom "we live and move and have our being" (Acts 24–25, 28 NIV). Of this God, Paul argues, "We are his offspring" (Acts 17:28 NIV). In this metaphor, readers can hear Old Testament echoes of pregnancy and birthing, especially those experienced by an unborn child in their mother's womb, kept until the day on which she gives the newborn the experience of "life and breath."[40] This apostle to the Gentiles "understands the entire human race as living, moving, and existing within the cosmic womb of the One [true] God."[41]

Paul also emulates and embodies Yahweh's motherly love and care for his congregants, finding these apt metaphors for communicating his role as a mothering shepherd to his spiritual offspring in the province of Galatia as well as the cities of Corinth and Thessalonica. For example, Paul is once again in the pains of childbirth until Christ is formed in those believers scattered across the Galatian province (Gal 4:19). His language of labor and travail in this circulating letter is most closely associated with the

---

[40]Mollenkott, *Divine Feminine*, 16.
[41]Smith, *Is It Okay*, 57-58.

eschatological tension between the "already" and the "not yet." In this context, he experiences spiritual birth pangs, groaning in travail as he carries these congregations along, pressing ever forward toward the ultimate eschatological renewal at the Lord's return. But for Christ to be formed in them is more than a merely spiritual or moral development. It is "simultaneously their crucifixion with him, the eclipse of the old occurring among them."[42] Paul knew the experience of labor to be shockingly intense, even though he personally could not experience it. Moreover, he understood what it meant, using this metaphor to describe his ministry to them. Both ministry and labor have an immediacy, intimacy, and physicality to them—and Paul's use of this image connotes all of these things. In addition, by using an intimate image such as a laboring woman, Paul identifies the Galatians as his spiritual children, creating a familial bond between them and arguably—simply on the basis of its physicality—the most intimate of bonds: the bond between a mother and her children. By employing this metaphor, Paul skillfully combines pastoral devotion and intimacy with apocalyptic urgency.

In his first letters to the Thessalonians and to the Corinthians, respectively, Paul employs two different breastfeeding metaphors. To the Thessalonians he writes, "Just as a nursing mother cares for her children, so we cared for you. Because we loved you so much, we were delighted to share with you not only the gospel of God but our lives as well" (1 Thess 2:7-8 NIV). Shortly thereafter, he chastises them with these words: "I gave you milk, not solid food, for you were not yet ready for it. Indeed, you are still not ready" (1 Cor 3:2 NIV). In each of these passages the metaphor of a nursing mother assumes a profound intimacy between Paul and his audience. Also noteworthy in 1 Thessalonians is the lack of an appeal to his "apostolic authority." Paul is not the harshly demanding apostle of the opening chapters of Galatians, keen to defend his authority. Instead, in 1 Thessalonians he is like a gentle nursing mother, willingly giving of herself for the sake of her beloved congregation.[43]

---

[42]Beverly Roberts Gaventa, *Our Mother Saint Paul* (Louisville, KY: Westminster John Knox, 2007), 36.

[43]Abraham J. Malherbe, *The Letters to the Thessalonians*, AB (New Haven, CT: Yale University Press, 2004), 101.

"It is striking that none of these instances in which Paul uses maternal imagery can be read as referring to a single event that occurred at one moment in the past. Quite the contrary, when Paul uses maternal language, the image always requires the elapse of some extended period of time."[44] Motherhood, like Paul's ministry, is a process, not an event. Pregnancy is a nine-month commitment, nursing can last several years, and even when children are weaned, they are dependent on their mothers. It is precisely these biological ties between mothers and children that make labor and breastfeeding metaphors so appropriate for pastoral ministry. Moreover, in adopting motherhood metaphors alongside fatherhood metaphors, Paul tempers his position of authority. This kind of "maternal imagery becomes effective precisely because it plays on hierarchical expectations: Paul presents himself as the authority who does not conform to standard norms of authority."[45] This is a critically important lesson to learn for those of us who are privileged to serve in positions of leadership in the body of Christ.

CONCLUDING THOUGHTS

In keeping with the personal and practical tone of this chapter, we have chosen to conclude with five questions meant for the contemplation of our readers. We trust these will be helpful.

1. How might a deeper understanding and realization of God's motherly love change the way you minister out of this quality of love?

2. How might you approach the Communion table afresh, with a new understanding of Jesus' words, "This is my body, given for you"?

3. How could your awareness of the God who bends down to feed us—nourishing us by the Spirit, who birthed us to new life—be deepened and enriched as you care for others?

4. How might you care for others with greater gentleness, like that of a nursing mother, even as you travail and moan for them through seasons of spiritual darkness?

---

[44]Gaventa, *Our Mother Saint Paul*, 7.
[45]Gaventa, *Our Mother Saint Paul*, 14.

5. Finally, since these metaphors of motherhood in Scripture honor and dignify female experiences as equally reflective of God's person and character, how could you honor and include women more fully in your ministries for the nurturers, providers, and strong warriors that they are, while they labor side by side with their brothers for the sake of God's kingdom?

As we have acknowledged from the outset, Scripture clearly emphasizes the fatherhood of God most frequently, especially in the Old Testament. Yet, in similar ways it also confronts us with the motherhood side to God's nature that we as his spiritual children—sacred siblings—*must* not forget.[46] Only by allowing both fatherhood and motherhood images of the triune God to be fully represented in and incorporated into our quest to know God more fully and minister in that fullness can we become more radically biblical, more theologically sound, and more fully transformed into the image of Christ for the sake of others.

---

[46]Warren W. Wiersbe, *Be Comforted: Feeling Secure in the Arms of God*, Old Testament Commentary: Isaiah (Colorado Springs: David C. Cook, 1992), 145-46.

20

"EQUAL IN BEING, UNEQUAL IN ROLE"

CHALLENGING THE LOGIC OF WOMEN'S SUBORDINATION

Rebecca Merrill Groothuis

• • • • •

ACCORDING TO ARISTOTLE, the male is "by nature fitter for command than the female."[1] According to John Piper and Wayne Grudem, male authority and female submission are integral to the "deeper differences," the "underlying nature," and the "true meaning" of manhood and womanhood.[2] Men have the inherent right and responsibility to direct the affairs of others. Women are meant to be in submission, to have their affairs directed by men.[3] It seems that in both Aristotelian thought and evangelical patriarchy, the subordination of women to male authority follows from what is understood to be the created nature of maleness and femaleness.[4] Authority is deemed natural and fitting for men, and submission is deemed natural and fitting for women.

---

[1] Aristotle, *Politics* 1259.b.3.

[2] John Piper and Wayne Grudem, "An Overview of Central Concerns: Questions and Answers," in *RBMW*, 73-115; see 73-74, 108.

[3] Piper and Grudem, "Overview of Central Concerns," 107-8; John Piper, "A Vision of Biblical Complementarity: Manhood and Womanhood Defined According to the Bible," in *RBMW*, 40-63.

[4] In this essay the *nature* of a thing is understood to mean its inherent character, intended purpose, defining qualities, essence, or being.

Yet there is one respect in which evangelical patriarchy has departed from Aristotle—and from the Western theologians and philosophers who have followed in his intellectual footsteps.[5] Aristotle maintained that it is precisely *because* "the male is by nature superior, and the female inferior, [that] the one rules, and the other is ruled."[6] Historically, male superiority was assumed to inhere primarily in a natural male advantage in morality and rationality. But when evangelical patriarchalists today claim that male leadership is natural and fitting given the deeper differences of masculinity and femininity, they accompany this claim with protestations that women are not morally or rationally deficient with respect to men; rather, men and women are "equal in being" but "different" (that is, unequal) in "function" or "role."[7]

Aristotle's conclusion—that men are by nature fitter for command than women—has been retained. Aristotle's premise—that men are by nature morally and rationally superior to women—has been rejected (which leaves the rationale for the conclusion somewhat unclear). Today it is undeniable that many women *are* morally and intellectually qualified for leadership. Although some patriarchalists may wish to categorize such women as exceptions, the ban on women assuming "male" leadership roles is without exception. No matter how stellar a woman's spiritual and intellectual qualifications, this can *never* overrule the unalterable fact of her female nature, which dictates that in church and home she must not have authority over a man but must support and submit to man's authority over her.

But notice that in evangelical patriarchy a woman's subordination still follows—necessarily and permanently—from what she necessarily and

---

[5]In *The Less Noble Sex* (Indianapolis: Indiana University Press, 1993), Nancy Tuana develops the thesis that "Aristotle's conception of [woman as] the misbegotten man held sway in science, philosophy, and theology at least until the nineteenth century" (ix).

[6]Aristotle, *Politics* 1254.b.10.

[7]I will refer to nonegalitarian evangelicals as *patriarchalists* or in some cases *subordinationists*, since these terms identify most clearly the key concepts—male rule and female subordination—that distinguish this view from that of evangelical egalitarians. For the use of the term *patriarchy* to identify the doctrine of male leadership, see Steven Tracy, "Headship with a Heart: How Biblical Patriarchy Actually Prevents Abuse," *CT* 47, no. 2 (2003): 50-54. Tracy defines patriarchy as "the affirmation of male authority over females," which is the sense in which I use it here. The issue at stake in this debate is precisely the concept of patriarchy—and not of hierarchy or tradition or complementarity (all legitimate concepts in themselves). For further discussion of the terminology issue, see the introduction to the present volume.

permanently *is* by nature (namely, female). Her personal being decides and determines her subordinate status. Piper and Grudem concur: "Scripture and nature teach that personal manhood and womanhood are indeed relevant in deciding . . . who gives primary leadership in the relationship."[8] Men's authority and women's subordination are integral to "what true manhood and womanhood *are.*"[9] The essence of masculinity is a sense of leadership, and the essence of femininity is a disposition to submit to male leadership.[10] In other words, men are to lead because authority is a constitutive element of masculinity, and women are to submit to male leadership because submission is a constitutive element of femininity. A man is fit to lead by virtue of his male nature. A woman, by virtue of her female nature, is not.

Despite the rhetoric of "roles" and "equality," it seems that a fundamental similarity remains between Aristotle and the evangelical patriarchalists of today. Woman's subordinate status is—as it has always been—decided solely by woman's female being. Whether woman is deemed unable to rule because of her mental and moral inferiority (historic patriarchy) or whether just *being* female makes a woman unfit for authority or decision making (today's patriarchy), it appears to be on account of a prior assumption about the meaning and nature of womanhood that women are not expected or permitted to share authority equally with men. By virtue of her female being, a woman is fit to be subject to man's will and unfit to exercise her own will with the freedom and authority accorded a man. Nothing she *does* either confirms or negates this state of affairs. Aristotle would have agreed.

UNPACKING THE RHETORIC OF ROLES

Although evangelical patriarchy is similar to traditional patriarchy in key respects, it also trades heavily on the distinctive and historically novel claim that women are "equal in being but unequal in role." In other words, women are the equals of men spiritually and in their "being," but

---

[8]Piper and Grudem, "Overview of Central Concerns," 108. Conversely, they feel dismayed that "'manhood' and 'womanhood' as such are now often seen as irrelevant factors in determining fitness for leadership." See John Piper and Wayne Grudem, "Preface," in *RBMW*, 13.

[9]Piper, "Vision of Biblical Complementarity," 40, emphasis added.

[10]Piper, "Vision of Biblical Complementarity," 41.

when it comes to living out the meaning and purpose of manhood and womanhood, women must submit to male rule. This distinction between being and function—or ontology and role—is fundamental to the doctrine of male leadership today. The distinction between equal being and unequal role serves as the hermeneutical lens through which the biblical data are interpreted. It is the theoretical construct that permits evangelical patriarchalists to interpret the submission texts as universal statements on the creational roles of manhood and womanhood, while also acknowledging biblical teaching on the spiritual and ontological equality of man and woman.

The role relationship of woman's subordination to man's authority is typically presented as a matter of "complementarity," "mutual interdependence," and "beneficial differences" between the sexes, without any implication of woman's inferiority.[11] The carefully chosen terminology serves to make this position appear plausible and persuasive to modern ears. Who can deny that there must be different roles, functional distinctions, and a certain order in any human society? Or that male and female are complementary? Given the choice of rhetoric, it all sounds quite sensible and acceptable. As a result, many evangelicals find themselves perplexed by two antithetical interpretations of biblical teaching on gender relations—egalitarianism and patriarchalism—both of which appear to be plausible in some respects and problematic in other respects. It can seem to be a toss-up.

But what if it is not logically possible for the same person to be at once spiritually and ontologically equal *and* permanently, comprehensively, and necessarily subordinate? What if this sort of subordination cannot truthfully be described as merely a role or function that has no bearing on one's inherent being or essence?

I believe we can choose between the two biblical interpretations by assessing each one in light of two fundamental premises. The first premise is theological: according to Scripture, women and men are equal spiritually and ontologically—a point that is uncontested in the gender debate. The second premise is logical: the foundational and indisputable law of

---

[11]Piper and Grudem, "Preface," 14-15.

noncontradiction, which states that A and non-A cannot both be true at the same time in the same respect.[12] The law of noncontradiction is not a mere human construct that God's truth somehow transcends. Rather, it is necessary and fundamental to all meaningful discourse and communication—including God's revelation of his Word in Scripture. That is why biblical scholars who hold to the Bible's infallibility seek to resolve apparent contradictions in Scripture: it is axiomatic that if the Bible contradicts itself, then it cannot be true in all that it affirms.[13]

Evangelical patriarchalists contend that women are unequal in a different respect from the way they are equal. I will argue that given its nature and rationale, woman's unequal role entails woman's unequal being. Thus, it contradicts woman's equality in being and so renders contradictory (and therefore untrue) the evangelical patriarchal interpretation of Scripture that sees woman as equal but subordinate. This leaves only two logically tenable options. Either (1) women are created by God for perpetual subordination to men and so are not equal to men in their nature/being/essence, or (2) women are created equal with men and so cannot be permanently, comprehensively, and necessarily subordinate to men. But option 1 contradicts premise 1, which is that, according to Scripture, women and men are equal spiritually and ontologically. Since Scripture cannot contradict itself, option 2 is the only position that is both logically and biblically tenable.

In part one of the chapter it will be argued that the *equal being/unequal role* construct fails to defend the subordination of women against the implication of women's inferiority.[14] First, I will consider what is meant by spiritual equality and ontological equality (equality of being), and will show how evangelical patriarchalism fails to honor and acknowledge such equality. Although spiritual equality is entailed by ontological equality, I will address it separately because of its particular relevance to this debate. I will then consider the nature and significance of the different roles that

---

[12]Aristotle, *Metaphysics* Γ3.1005b.

[13]See Ronald H. Nash, *Life's Ultimate Questions: An Introduction to Philosophy* (Grand Rapids, MI: Zondervan, 1999), 194-201, 207.

[14]The material in this chapter will build on and develop ideas presented in Rebecca Merrill Groothuis, *Good News for Women: A Biblical Picture of Gender Equality* (Grand Rapids, MI: Baker Books, 1997), especially 27-83.

patriarchalists assign to women and men and will argue that these roles are not just about function but are fundamentally a matter of ontology or being. The purpose of these considerations will be to show that evangelical patriarchy neither respects women's equality nor limits women's subordination to a merely functional role. Instead, the nature of women's inequality in function implies, by logical necessity, women's inequality in being.

In part two of the chapter I will respond to key counterarguments—ways in which proponents of patriarchy have attempted to defend the efficacy and validity of the *equal being/unequal role* construct against objections to it.[15] This will include a brief critique of the analogy that patriarchalists draw between women's subordination in role and what they see as the eternal role subordination in the Trinity. I will argue that even if there were an eternal subordination of the Son to the Father, the analogy fails fundamentally.

PART 1

Equality in being. A biblical understanding of human equality should begin with Genesis 1:26-28, where women and men together and without distinction are declared to be created in God's image and are given authority over all creation. In both their being (the divine image) and their calling (authority and dominion), men and women are creationally equal. On the basis of this foundational text, as well as the overall teaching of Scripture, evangelical egalitarians affirm an equality of human worth and human rights between women and men; that is, whatever human rights there may be, they belong no less to women than to men (since women are no less human than men).[16] From this follows an equality of consideration,

---

[15]Less compelling counterarguments will be addressed in footnotes in part one.
[16]Nineteenth-century American feminists believed women's rights were simply the basic human rights applied equally to women. In the feminist and broader cultural ideologies of recent decades, the notion of rights has often been abused and overextended. This is not the sense in which I speak of rights here. Claiming one's right to something is not, in itself, an unbiblical concept. Paul, for example, occasionally spoke of having rights, such as the right to receive recompense for his labor or to take "a believing wife" along with him in Christian ministry (1 Cor 9:4-12). Another example is the Syrophoenician woman who argued her case with Jesus, claiming (in essence) her right to ask for healing for her daughter. Jesus applauded her response and granted her request (Mk 7:24-30).

In addition to the overall teaching of Scripture, relevant biblical texts are examined throughout the present volume; see especially part one of this volume, "Looking to Scripture: The Biblical Texts"; see also Groothuis, *Good News for Women*, especially chaps. 1, 4-8.

whereby women and men alike have opportunity to earn and attain the place in church and society that is appropriate for each individual's God-given abilities and calling.

While this understanding of human equality resembles that of classical (nineteenth and early twentieth century) liberal political philosophy, it is here grounded in and justified solely by the biblical revelation of God's creational design for male and female humanity. This happens to be one point at which secular culture got it right, doubtless due in large part to the West's Christian heritage (a more prevalent influence in earlier centuries than at present). A task of the biblical thinker is to agree with culture where it agrees with the Bible.[17]

Although there are variations in ability between individuals, the human equality between women (as a class) and men (as a class) assures that women are inherently able to participate equally with men in the various distinctively human activities.[18] Due to both cultural and biological factors, there are some generalizable differences in behavior between women and men, and these differences not only determine different sexual and reproduction functions but may also make certain social roles generally (although not universally) more suitable for one gender than the other. However, these differences do not warrant the traditional notion that women are deficient in rationality and so are suited to be subordinate to men. Rather, the generally different aptitudes and

---

[17]Some seem to have missed the point entirely, insisting—evidently on the basis of a similarity between the equality of classical liberalism—that biblical egalitarianism is invalid because it is not grounded primarily in Scripture but is dependent on extrabiblical political premises. See, e.g., Thomas R. Schreiner, review of *Good News for Women, Themelios* 23, no. 1 (1997): 89-90; Schreiner, "Women in Ministry," in *Two Views on Women in Ministry*, ed. James R. Beck and Craig L. Blomberg (Grand Rapids, MI: Zondervan, 2001), 187n16, 200; and Sarah Sumner, *Men and Women in the Church* (Downers Grove, IL: InterVarsity Press, 2003), 33, 277, 281, 291n16. Both Schreiner and Sumner misconstrue my remarks in Groothuis, *Good News for Women*, 46-47, where I simply describe the classical liberal understanding of equality (which nineteenth-century feminists put into practice) and not that this understanding of equality is the logical and ethically consistent outworking of fundamental *biblical* principles. Thus, the political philosophy serves as an illustration of—*not* as a justification for—the sort of equality that is most consistent with the tenets of Scripture. At no point is biblical gender equality grounded in or morally justified on the basis of classical liberalism or feminism. For a historical and cultural analysis of the relationship between biblical equality and feminism, see Rebecca Merrill Groothuis, *Women Caught in the Conflict: The Culture War Between Traditionalism and Feminism* (Grand Rapids, MI: Baker, 1994; repr., Eugene OR: Wipf & Stock, 1997).

[18]More on this below.

proclivities of male and female point to ways in which women and men can complement one another as they live and work together in the context of a full recognition of their essential equality in maturity, giftedness, and social and spiritual value.

It should be evident from these observations that egalitarians do not affirm an equality of identity or sameness between women and men. Male and female are not identical. Sexual differences exist, and these differences make a difference. Sexual roles, therefore, are not interchangeable between men and women.[19] Egalitarians and patriarchalists agree that women and men are not equal in the sense of being identical and that the differences between men and women are complementary and mutually beneficial. But there is considerable disagreement as to the nature, meaning, and significance of these differences.

There are a number of different ways in which people, or groups of people, can be said to be equal.[20] It seems that evangelical patriarchalists reject all types of equality between men and women, except equality in being (essence, nature, ontology) and human value. The question before us is whether the patriarchal paradigm in fact acknowledges female humanity to be fully human, equal in value to male humanity.

If women and men are both fully human, then women (as a class) and men (as a class) share equally in the distinctively human capacities, and no woman can be deemed inferior to a man in any such area solely on account of her womanhood. Distinctively human capacities are those that distinguish humans from other creatures. For example, higher intellectual functions such as rationality, ethical reasoning, and the ability to analyze abstract concepts are unique to humans.[21] Therefore it cannot be said that any given woman is any more or less likely than any given man to be fully equipped—in her God-given being—for such higher functions of the mind. More specifically, if women and men are equal in essence or being,

---

[19] A sexual role has to do with sexual functions (marriage, parenthood, etc.). Ministries such as teaching the Bible and shepherding a church are not sexual functions.

[20] See Groothuis, *Good News for Women*, 45-49, where different kinds of equality are explained and delineated.

[21] At least some angels are probably also endowed with such capabilities, but the comparison here is with earthly creatures. Some animals may have some rational function, but certainly not at the level of which humans are capable.

then female humanity does not, in and of itself, suffer from a net deficiency of the valuable qualities and inherent capacities distinctively characteristic of human nature and human behavior.[22]

Yet the doctrine of male rule presupposes that woman is uniquely designed by God *not* to perform certain distinctively human activities. In order to be true to her divine design and her God-given femininity, woman must not engage in these activities (which, per patriarchy, are no longer distinctively human but reclassified as distinctively masculine). By contrast, there are no uniquely human behaviors from which male humans must abstain in order to be true to their masculine being. No, masculinity is defined precisely in terms of certain distinctively human activities that only men are deemed fit to do—namely, the spiritual discernment and high-level cognitive/rational behaviors involved in making decisions, and directing and taking final responsibility for one or more other human beings.[23]

According to the patriarchal paradigm, women do have their own uniquely feminine activities not shared by men—for example, bearing and rearing their young and being submissive and obedient to the master of the home. But note that these activities are not unique to human beings; rather, childbearing and nursing are shared with females of all mammal species, and submission to the household master is shared

---

[22]Of course, some individuals, male or female, will be less gifted in certain distinctively human activities than other individuals, whether by difference in training or innate ability. But this is a matter of variation between individuals; the point at issue here is variation between womanhood and manhood. That is, is being female in and of itself sufficient to render a person inferior, or likely to be inferior, in uniquely human capacities?

[23]The question of women's inherent *ability* to perform these tasks can elicit considerable equivocation among patriarchalists. The historically traditional view—based (erroneously) on 1 Tim 2:14—is that women are constitutionally unfit for leadership because they are more easily deceived. This rationale for women's subordination is largely rejected today; but see Thomas Schreiner and Daniel Doriani, who have proposed a rationale similar to the traditional one, in *Women in the Church: A Fresh Analysis of 1 Timothy 2:9-15*, ed. Andreas Köstenberger, Thomas R. Schreiner, and H. Scott Baldwin (Grand Rapids, MI: Baker, 1995), 145-46, 262-67. For a response to their view, see Rebecca Merrill Groothuis, "Leading Him up the Garden Path: Further Thoughts on 1 Timothy 2:11-15," *PriscPap* 16, no. 2 (2002): 11-12. More recently, Robert Saucy also offers an ontological basis for male leadership when he suggests that the implications of the difference in "spirit" between maleness and femaleness (a notion he takes from M. Scott Peek) could provide a rationale for women's subordination to men. See Saucy, "The 'Order' and 'Equality' of Galatians 3:28," in *Women and Men in Ministry*, ed. Robert L. Saucy and Judith K. TenElshof (Chicago: Moody, 2001), 154.

(albeit in a different sense!) with a wide array of household pets.[24] Certainly, it is a privilege and joy for women to bear and rear children. The point is not to diminish the value of motherhood but to note that while childbearing and nursing are distinctively female capabilities, they are not, in and of themselves, among the distinctively human capabilities (such as high-level rationality).

Patriarchal men, for their part, govern their homes and churches—making decisions, teaching the whole body of believers, ascertaining and making final determinations of God's will for their families—and women do not. Furthermore, women *could* bear authority and responsibility for these things equally with men, but they do not because they are not permitted to do so. Men, by contrast, do not bear or nurse children, simply because they are not *able* to do so. The one is the "can't" of permission denied; the other is the "can't" of personal inability. This is not a case of equally dividing different opportunities and abilities between the sexes.

Nonetheless, those who insist that the woman must submit her mind and will to that of the man who is the master of the household also insist that the woman is equal to the man in her humanity and human value. But the full humanity of womanhood is not honored or recognized when what is deemed constitutive of femininity is shared by the lower species while what is deemed constitutive of masculinity is unique to the human species. This delineation of male-female difference fails to acknowledge the full humanity of woman. This is not to say that people with less ability in any of the distinctively human functions are somehow less human. However, when all women—purely by virtue of their womanhood—are denied opportunity to fully engage all the uniquely human capacities (to the degree of their ability), this logically implies that womanhood per se is characterized by a deficit of certain distinctively human traits.

Always, with patriarchy, it is the female human's *being* that is the decisive factor; it alone is sufficient to consign her to being subordinate. Because her human being is female, she is subordinate. As Raymond Ortlund puts it, "A man, just by virtue of his manhood, is called to lead for

---

[24]If this analogy seems a bit strong, it should be noted that Piper and Grudem draw a comparison between the woman and the animals in Gen 2, arguing that just as the animals were to be submissive to the man, so was the woman ("Overview of Central Concerns," 108).

God. A woman, just by virtue of her womanhood, is called to help for God."[25] So while woman is said to be equal in her essential being, she is deemed subordinate precisely because of her essential being. Yet the notion that woman is equal *in* her being yet unequal *by virtue of* her being is incoherent.

Could this inconsistency be reconciled by asserting that woman is equal in her *human* being but not equal in her *female* being? It seems not. There is, after all, no generic humanity; human being is either male or female. If I am equal in my human being, then I am equal in my female human being, because female is what my human being is. Or, conversely, human is what my female being is. At all times and in every respect, my "being" is essentially and intrinsically female and human. If I am unequal as a *female* human being, then I am unequal as a human being.

Given the above considerations, it seems warranted to conclude that patriarchy cannot fully acknowledge woman's human equality in being but rather implies her inferiority in being. This is even further in evidence when we examine woman's *spiritual* place in the patriarchal scheme of things.

Spiritual equality. The human spirit—that which enables us to know and communicate with God—is inherent in the divine image. This spiritual capacity is definitive of and unique to human beings, among all God's earthly creatures. Scripture is clear that women and men equally bear God's image and rule over God's creation (Gen 1:26-28). God, at creation, gave spirituality and authority to male and female alike. This is the divine, uncorrupted, creational design. Nowhere in the Genesis creation account is this qualified by any mention of different kinds of spirituality or different degrees of authority for man and for woman.[26]

If women and men are equal before God, then surely God desires the same sort of relationship with female believers that God desires with male believers. There is no reason to believe that God's treatment and expectations of women with respect to spiritual concerns should be significantly

---

[25]Raymond C. Ortlund, "Male-Female Equality and Male Headship: Genesis 1–3," in *RBMW*, 128.

[26]The fall did not normatively change the male-female equality established at creation; see Groothuis, *Good News for Women*, chap. 5; also Mary L. Conway, "Gender in Creation and Fall: Genesis 1–3" in this present volume.

different from God's treatment and expectations of men. By extension, we in the church have no basis for treating women as somehow less fit for certain spiritual gifts and ministries. Nor should we expect any woman to have a more distantly removed or "different" sort of relationship with God simply because she is a woman.[27] Equality before God means that every believer may approach God, and minister to God, on the same terms—through Jesus Christ alone, in submission to the Holy Spirit.

So, let us consider how the truth of spiritual equality fares in the context of woman's subordination to man's authority. In evangelical patriarchy today, the authority reserved exclusively for men is largely a *spiritual* authority. That is, within the contexts of marriage and the church, the exposition of God's Word and the discernment of God's will (and the decision making that follows such discernment) are deemed the final responsibility of men alone. Although there occasionally appears some general expression of concern that women not appear too authoritative (i.e., masculine) in everyday interactions in society at large—Piper, for example, wants to ensure that if a woman gives a man directions to the freeway, she does so in a properly feminine (submissive) manner—the primary concern appears to be the exercise of spiritual authority.[28]

Evangelical patriarchy teaches that the man is divinely charged with responsibility and authority to discern God's will on behalf of himself and his wife and children. Whether or not he gives consideration to his wife's insights, interests, and expertise (as patriarchal teaching typically urges him to do), his "final decision" concerning God's will for the family has binding authority.[29] As George Knight puts it, "Because the headship of the husband is established by God, the husband who fulfills that role does so as a servant of God, and the leadership given to him in this role expresses God's authority in the marriage." Given that the husband's authority over the wife represents the authority of God, a wife "should submit to her husband as she submits to the Lord." Such

---

[27]Individuals (both male and female) will, of course, have different kinds of relationships with God. But these differences will be due to a host of factors relating to the unique circumstances of each person; they will not be strictly on account of gender.

[28]Piper, "Vision of Biblical Complementarity," 44.

[29]See Wayne Grudem, "Wives like Sarah, and the Husbands Who Honor Them: 1 Peter 3:1-7," in *RBMW*, 266. However, the wife is exempted from obeying a decision that is overtly immoral.

submission is analogous to "the godly submission a Christian renders to the Lord Jesus."[30]

Patriarchal doctrine requires, in both marriage and the larger believing community, that men obey and hear from God directly while women obey and hear from God by hearing from and obeying the man or men in spiritual authority over them. A woman does not have direct authority under God but is under the spiritual authority of man, who mediates to her the Word and the will of God for her life. Woman's traditionally subordinate place within the social relationships of church and home is largely a consequence of the subordinate place in which she is believed to stand in the spiritual order. But note that this arrangement is not, as is often claimed, spiritual equality plus social inequality.[31] It is, quite simply, spiritual inequality.

According to key representatives of evangelical patriarchy, God has invested the man with the spiritual authority "to decide, in the light of Holy Scripture, what courses of action will most glorify God" for his family. The man is "finally responsible" for both his own and his wife's moral and spiritual condition. The husband's authority "expresses God's authority in the marriage." The man's role in the family has him "standing in the place of Christ," to "act *as* Christ" and "*for* Christ" with respect to his wife, obligating him to "protect [his family] from the greatest enemies of all, Satan and sin."[32] But if these things be true—if, indeed, only a man and never a woman can be deemed fit to serve as a stand-in for Christ, and if every married woman actually *needs* a man to serve in this capacity for her

---

[30]George W. Knight III, "Husbands and Wives as Analogues of Christ and the Church," in *RBMW*, 227.

[31]However, a fair description of the situation in the New Testament church *would* be spiritual equality with social inequality (due to the cultural patriarchy of ancient times). Nothing in the New Testament stipulates that a man must have authority over and responsibility for his wife's spiritual condition, as many patriarchalists today advocate. The apostle Peter commended Christian women who refused to submit to their husbands' false religious beliefs, yet urged these women to be submissive to the social roles of the time (1 Pet 3:1-6). Evangelical patriarchalists today actually invert the New Testament situation by advocating, in essence, an inequality in *spiritual* rights and responsibilities for women in a cultural context in which women generally experience equality in *social* rights and responsibilities. See Groothuis, *Good News for Women*, 36-39.

[32]Ortlund, "Male-Female Equality," 139-40, 586n50; Knight, "Husbands and Wives," 227; Piper, "Vision of Biblical Complementarity," 43-44; Piper and Grudem, "Overview of Central Concerns," 78-79. "Standing in the place of Christ" is qualified by the comment that a husband "must not be Christ to his wife."

(which must be the case if the man's headship is to be an act of love and service rather than presumption and condescension)—then it follows that men and women are not on the same spiritual level at all.

Nowhere does the Bible say that it is a man's job to discern the will of God, take responsibility for another person's spirituality, and protect others from Satan and sin. If God has given responsibility and dominion to both male and female (Gen 1:26-28), if we all stand on equal ground before God (Gal 3:26-28), if women are equal heirs of the grace of God (1 Pet 3:7) and if all believers together—both men and women—form God's new priesthood (1 Pet 2:5, 9; Rev 1:6; 5:10), then there is no reason for anyone to take this sort of spiritual responsibility for anyone else. If Jesus Christ is a female believer's Lord and Savior in the same way that he is a male believer's, then surely no Christian woman has need of a man to stand in the place of Christ for her.

Despite popular evangelical teaching, the New Testament never says the man authoritatively represents God as the priest of the home.[33] This teaching may derive from a misunderstanding of the analogy Paul draws in Ephesians 5:21-33 between a husband as "head" of his wife and Christ as "head" of the church. Patriarchalists readily perceive that Paul did not mean that the husband is like Christ in redeeming his wife from her sins, for this would contradict biblical teaching elsewhere. Yet neither did Paul mean that the husband—like Christ—has the authority to serve as a priestly mediator between God and his wife; for this contradicts biblical teaching that Christ is the one mediator between God and humans (1 Tim 2:5, see also Mt 11:27; Jn 14:6). What Paul *was* saying by means of this analogy is evident from his description of the husband's Christlike ministry of life-giving, self-giving love for his wife (Eph 5:25-30).[34] As Christ loves, nurtures, provides for, and sacrifices his own life and special (divine) prerogatives for the church, so should the husband for his wife; as

---

[33]Some go even further, proclaiming "the husband as prophet, priest and king." See the workshop by this title at the conference cosponsored by the Council on Biblical Manhood and Womanhood held March 20-22, 2000, in Dallas.

[34]There is no implication in the text that the husband has *spiritual* authority over his wife, although the husband's *civil* authority was assumed, given the culture of Paul's day. On the head metaphor, see Lynn H. Cohick, "Loving and Submitting to One Another in Marriage: Ephesians 5:21-33 and Colossians 3:18-19," in the present volume.

the church submits to the ministry of Christ (and as believers submit to one another, Eph 5:21), so should the wife to her husband.[35]

Under the new covenant, every believer is a representative of God (2 Cor 5:20) with direct access to God through Christ our high priest (Heb 4:14-16). Designating masculinity as a condition for the authoritative discernment and mediation of God's will denies the equal access to God through Christ that the new covenant provides to all believers.[36]

A male hierarchy of spiritual authority and command also violates the status and identity that every believer has in Christ. The New Testament teaches that God gives all believers the responsibility and prerogative to use their gifts, to preach the gospel, to teach other believers, to discern and obey the Word and will of God, to serve as priests unto God, to have the mind of Christ, to exercise spiritual authority in the name of Christ, and to represent Christ to the world at large. Yet patriarchalists alter the teaching of God's Word by denying to women a measure of each one of these God-given privileges and responsibilities, allocating to men the lion's share of what the Bible speaks of as the status and calling of all believers.[37]

Patriarchalists consign women to a permanently inferior status in a hierarchy of spiritual authority, calling, responsibility, and privilege, all the while insisting that women are not spiritually inferior to men but that women and men stand on equal ground before God. This position is logically incoherent and so cannot be true. Women do not stand on equal ground before God if God has permanently denied them spiritual opportunities and privileges to which every man has access.

Difference in role or function. To say that two people differ in function is not necessarily to say that one is personally superior to the other. Therefore, when we are told that men and women are equal yet have different functions, we can readily agree with the face value of that statement. There are many instances in which equals have different

---

[35]See Groothuis, *Good News for Women*, 152-55, 164-70, 180-82.

[36]See discussion of Gal 3:28 in Groothuis, *Good News for Women*, chap. 1.

[37]The spiritual authority that patriarchalists reserve exclusively for male believers actually goes beyond the biblical ministry of *all* believers in that the man's priestlike spiritual authority encroaches upon the unique mediatorial ministry of Christ. See Groothuis, *Good News for Women*, 115-17.

roles—even roles of subordination and authority—yet with no entailment of personal inequality.[38]

We can affirm that there are role differences between men and women
without necessarily affirming that spiritual authority belongs by divine
right to men. The latter belief does not follow from the former, and to
reject the latter is not to reject the former. This conceptual distinction
was not missed by respondents to a *Christianity Today* readers' poll on
gender issues. A significant number of people who agreed that men and
women are "equal in personhood and value but different in roles" also
rejected the idea that men should have primary leadership in churches
and homes.[39] The existence of gender role differences neither entails nor
justifies a permanent hierarchy of male authority.

Although functional differences often are compatible with personal
equality, this is not always the case. Advocates of male authority seem
to have difficulty acknowledging that the *reason* for the difference and
the *nature* of the function determine whether such a difference can
logically coexist with equality of being. As it happens, the reason for
and the nature of woman's subordination logically exclude woman's
equality.[40] The vocabulary of evangelical patriarchy reflects and reinforces this conceptual confusion. For example, woman's lifelong subordination to male authority is routinely referred to as merely a "role
difference" or "functional distinction." Semantic strategies such as
these subsume the disputed concept (woman's subordination) under a
larger—and largely undisputed—conceptual category (role differences,
functional distinctions), thereby appearing to legitimate the disputed
concept ipso facto.[41]

---

[38]There has been persistent misrepresentation and misunderstanding on this matter. Schreiner,
for example, asserts that "the basic point of Rebecca Merrill Groothuis's *Good News for Women*
is that one cannot logically posit both equality of personhood and differences in role" (Schreiner,
"Women in Ministry," 200). In fact, I affirm quite the opposite of this "basic point." See Groothuis, *Good News for Women*, 49-52, where I show that many types of role differences *are* compatible with personal equality.

[39]Agnieszka Tennant, "Nuptial Agreements," *CT* 46, no. 3 (2002): 61.

[40]This will be argued below. Also see Groothuis, *Good News for Women*, 49-56, 60-63.

[41]On rhetorical strategies of patriarchalists, see Rebecca Merrill Groothuis, "Strange Bedfellows:
A Look at Darwinists and Traditionalists and the Strategies They Share," *PriscPap* 14, no. 4
(2000): 3-9; see also Kevin Giles, *The Trinity and Subordinationism* (Downers Grove, IL:
InterVarsity Press, 2002), 187-90.

By these and other means, patriarchalists implicitly present their *equal being/unequal function* defense of woman's subordination in the following form:

1. Different function does not necessarily entail personal inferiority or superiority.

2. Woman's subordination and man's authority involve different functions.

3. Therefore the subordination of woman to man's authority has nothing to do with female inferiority or male superiority; these are male-female role differences, pure and simple.

The argument is invalid. The premises are correct, but the conclusion does not follow logically from them. While the notion that equal beings may have different roles is certainly legitimate, it is not applicable to, or descriptive of, the male-female authority relations prescribed by evangelical patriarchalists. Patriarchy involves different functions, to be sure, but the different functions are grounded in supposed differences in the nature, meaning, and purpose of manhood and womanhood. To describe as mere roles the different functions that follow from these ontological/teleological differences is to equivocate and obfuscate.

"Equal in being but subordinate in role" *can* accurately describe instances of functional subordination; however, it does not serve as a description of *every* relationship of subordination to authority, and it cannot accurately be applied to woman's subordination. Female subordination is not functional subordination; therefore, it cannot be justified on those grounds.

Functional subordination is typically determined either according to an individual's abilities (or lack thereof) or for the sake of expediency in accomplishing a specific task; therefore, such subordination is limited in scope or duration. An example of functional subordination for the sake of expediency would be a person who serves on a committee under the direction of a coworker who is otherwise her equal in the organization; her subordination is limited to the task at hand, and it ends whenever the committee completes its work or she leaves the committee. An example of functional subordination based on unequal ability would be a student who is subordinated to his teacher—but only in the context and for the duration of the class.

Functional subordination is not necessarily limited in both scope and duration. If the subordinate's deficiency in ability is permanent (if he either cannot or will not overcome the deficiency), then his subordination in that area of deficiency will be permanent. If the unequal ability is innate, then the resulting subordination does reflect the person's inherently inferior ability in that particular area. But it need not indicate the subordinate's inferiority as a person, because the subordination remains limited in scope to the area of deficient ability; the person may far excel the average person in even more important areas of function.[42]

Female subordination differs from functional subordination in its scope, duration, and criterion. The subordination of women is limited neither in scope nor in duration. It is not based on inferior ability or designed to accomplish a temporary task. It is comprehensive (encompassing all that a woman does), permanent (extending throughout the life of a woman and applying to all women at all times), and decided solely by an unchangeable aspect of a woman's personal being (femaleness). Although femaleness is, in fact, irrelevant to ascertaining a person's innate abilities in the higher human functions involved in leadership, decision making, and self-governance, these are precisely the functions from which women are permanently excluded; thus, the inferiority of female persons in these key areas is clearly implied.

When subordination follows necessarily *and justifiably* from the subordinate person's unalterable nature, the subordinate *is* inferior in at least some aspect of her being; in this case, the scope and duration of the person's subordination will reflect the extent and significance of the inferiority. Because the subordination that is demanded by women's unalterable (female) being is of comprehensive scope and permanent duration—excluding women from a wide range of high-level, distinctively human functions—it implies an extensive and significant personal inferiority. But in this case the subordination is *not* justifiable, because women are not, in

---

[42]See Groothuis, *Good News for Women*, 50-51. For an example of functional subordination with limited duration and unlimited scope, see section below titled "False Analogies."

fact, innately inferior in these distinctively human capabilities. Put more formally and succinctly:

1. If the permanent, comprehensive, and ontologically grounded subordination of women is justified, then women are inferior persons.

2. Women are not inferior persons.

3. Therefore women's subordination is not justified.[43]

Another way to distinguish functional subordination from female subordination is in terms of the concepts of necessity and contingency. Something that is contingent obtains (is the case) only in certain contexts or under certain conditions. It is thus dependent, or contingent, on these contexts or conditions; it is not always and necessarily true. Unlike functional subordination, female subordination is not contingent. Because a woman is always and necessarily female, she is always and necessarily subordinate. No condition or context in this life nullifies her subordination to male authority.[44]

Given evangelical patriarchy's theological premise that God designed man and woman at creation for a (benevolent) male-rule relationship, it is necessary for a woman to be subordinate to male rule if she is to be true to the divinely designed meaning of womanhood. Not to submit would be unnatural and unfitting. Her subordination to male authority is thus a moral necessity, rooted in ontology—in the way God made man and woman to be from the beginning. Philosophically speaking, this is a

---

[43]See Groothuis, *Good News for Women*, 44-45, 49-56, 60-63, 74-77, for further explanation of these issues. Robert Saucy tries to debunk my claim that woman's permanent subordination implies woman's inferiority by arguing that if woman is rendered unequal because her subordination is permanent, then the mere passing of time must make a person unequal (which is nonsensical; "'Order' and 'Equality,'" 153-54). However, I do not say that permanent subordination *necessarily* implies personal inequality. The issue is not simply permanence but whether the subordination is truly functional. Subordination can allow for equality of personhood *only* if it is a *functional* subordination—which female subordination is not; moreover, it *is* possible for functional subordination to be permanent (see Groothuis, *Good News for Women*, 50, 74-75). Saucy appears to attempt another *reductio ad absurdum* argument when he claims that I say subordination renders a person inferior only if the subordination is *not* based on inferior abilities (also nonsensical; "'Order' and 'Equality,'" 154). But my point is not that female subordination actually *renders* women inferior but that it logically *implies* women's inferiority, and that women's subordination is unjustified precisely because women are *not* inferior to men in leadership ability.

[44]Some patriarchalists believe the pattern of male leadership extends throughout the next life as well. See, e.g., Wayne Grudem, *Systematic Theology* (Grand Rapids, MI: Zondervan, 1994), 940.

hypothetical necessity, because it follows from a certain premise. *If* God created man to rule woman and woman to serve man, *then* a woman's submission to male authority obtains necessarily, solely by virtue of her womanhood. Her subordination is not contingent on her voluntarily taking on this role.[45]

Functional subordination, on the other hand, is dependent on limited contexts or occasional conditions. A blind person submits to the authority of his seeing-eye dog in the context of negotiating a busy street. A student is subordinate to her teacher, given the student's inferior ability in the subject being taught. In these cases, subordination is limited in scope or duration because it is contingent on conditions that do not always and everywhere obtain. But because female subordination is necessary (context independent), it is both permanent (enduring throughout a woman's life) and comprehensive (including all that a woman does; in all things she must be submissive).[46]

It should be evident from these observations that woman's subordination does not fit the definition of a role. A role is a part that is played or a particular function or office that is assumed for a specific purpose or period of time. Anyone with the requisite abilities can play the part. By definition, a role is not synonymous with or inexorably tied to who a person is. Yet the roles of male authority and female subordination are deemed essential to God's creational design for true manhood and womanhood. Indeed, Piper and Grudem state that their concern is not merely with "behavioral roles" but with the "true meaning" and "underlying nature of manhood and womanhood."[47]

---

[45]Saucy objects to my depiction of woman's subordination as necessary and not voluntary, insisting that it is indeed voluntary because nobody can force a woman to submit to her husband's authority (Saucy, "'Order' and 'Equality,'" 157-58). But this seems to equivocate on the meaning of *voluntary*. Normally an act is considered voluntary if one can choose either to do or not to do it without censure. But when something is the law—whether civil law or God's law—those who are under the law are obligated to obey it, and disobedience incurs some form of censure. (Referring to the biblical "command" for wives to submit, Grudem notes that "submission to one's husband is not optional for Christian wives" ["Wives like Sarah," 207].) Even more to the point, woman's subordination is grounded in her female being, not in her will. The rationale for women's subordination is not that they choose of their own volition to be subordinate but that they are created to be subordinate.

[46]Some milder forms of patriarchy today allow women to have authority over men so long as it is not "final authority" or spiritual authority. Nonetheless, a married woman must be submissive to her husband's authority in every area of her life.

[47]Piper and Grudem, "Overview of Central Concerns," 73-74.

A woman can have many roles in life—teacher, office administrator, physician, writer—but none of these roles is seen as *essential* to true womanhood. That is because these roles are truly roles—chosen or appropriate for some women but not for others. Submission to male authority is the only role that is deemed essential for every woman who would be truly feminine and fulfill the purpose for which God created womanhood. That is because this role serves the role of constituting the meaning of femininity, of identifying a woman as a *real* woman. Female submission to male authority, then, is a function only in the sense that it is a *necessary* function of a woman's true being.

That submission is considered to be inherent in what a woman is by nature (and authority inherent in what a man is by nature) is evident in the patriarchalists' slippery-slope argument that egalitarianism leads logically to acceptance of homosexuality.[48] Their thinking is that once we say gender is irrelevant for deciding who is to have "primary leadership," the next "logical" step is to say the gender of one's marriage partner is also irrelevant. Just as a woman is meant to marry a man and not another woman, so a woman is meant to be submissive to a man and not to share authority equally with a man. Patriarchalists believe that gender differences in status and authority are as natural and essential to manhood and womanhood as is heterosexuality. To eliminate the former entails eliminating the latter, because it consists of eliminating what is inherent and universally normative in the gender distinction. The elimination of a mere role would not evoke such comparisons and predicted consequences.

It should also be noted that although role theology has become central to evangelical patriarchy, nowhere does Scripture use the term *role* or any synonym for it with reference to the responsibilities of believers toward God or one another. At no point do we read that God designed us—and requires us—to play a role. No, God's concern is for each of us to *be* a righteous person and to use whatever gifts of the Spirit we have been given for the good of the church and the glory of God. The Bible's focused exhortation is that we are *all* to be Christlike, to follow the example of Jesus'

---

[48]See Piper and Grudem, "Overview of Central Concerns," 102-4. For a response to this change, see Ronald W. Pierce, "Gender Equality and Same-Sex Marriage" in this volume.

earthly life—in humility, faithfulness, submission to God, and spiritual authority (in Christ's name) over all the powers of evil.

The consistency and clarity of this biblical message stands starkly against the notion that women do not have direct authority under God and so must submit spiritually to men, who are the primary wielders of spiritual authority in the body of Christ. This doctrine of spiritual inequality posing as "gender role difference" simply does not fit with the Bible's clear, core message.

When "role" plays the role of being. Regardless of how patriarchal gender relations may be explained or masculinity and femininity defined, the fact remains that woman's subordinate role is determined exclusively and necessarily by her personal nature; that is, *solely* on account of her *being* female she *must* be subordinate. Therefore woman's role designates not merely what she does (or doesn't do) but what she is. She is female; she is subordinate.

It may sound quite plausible to insist that woman's subordination and man's authority are merely roles assigned by God and so do not entail woman's personal inferiority. Roles, by definition, do not necessarily bespeak qualities of personal being. But patriarchal gender roles are not roles in accordance with the usual definition. These roles have a one-to-one correspondence with being. Where the being is, there the role is also. Female being corresponds precisely to a role of subordination to male authority. The word *role* is used in a way that renders its meaning basically synonymous, or redundant, with *being*.

Female subordination and male authority may be semantically reduced to roles or functions, but in reality they serve as modes of being—permanent personal identities, built into each one's personal makeup by the Creator himself. Thus, when the man rules and the woman obeys, each is only doing what each is inherently designed to do.

As a blind person cannot generally negotiate unfamiliar territory as well as a sighted person on his own, so a woman is not fit to preach God's Word with authority or to discern God's will for her own life apart from her husband's spiritual authority over her. The female person and the blind person must each have someone do for them what they are not fit to do for themselves. However, the state of being blind does not bear the weight of ontological necessity or the implication of personal inferiority that woman's subordination does. Under patriarchy, a woman's deficiency in personal authority is regarded as ordained by God's creational decree. But a blind person—even if blind from birth—is not deficient in sight by virtue of God's creational design for humanity. His limitations are not intrinsic to and demanded by his essential, created nature. Nor are his limitations as deep or as wide as a woman's. He is deprived of a physical function; he is not denied a spiritual ministry or the governance of his own life under God. Moreover, blindness is not necessarily a life sentence; it can sometimes be reversed.

Could it then be accurate to say that a blind person's role is to be sightless? No, this is simply the way the person *is*; it is a mode of being, not a mode of behavior that is assumed for a specific purpose (as is a role). If a blind person's lack of sight cannot rightly be described as a role that has no bearing on his state of being or personal ability, then (a fortiori) neither can woman's creationally based lack of authority in key areas be accurately spoken of as a role that has no ontological entailment.

Thus, the theoretical distinction between woman's being and woman's subordinate role evaporates under scrutiny. Woman's lifelong subordination to man's authority is not merely a role that is independent of and ontologically isolated from her being. Rather, the role is determined by the being and obtains solely because of the being. Where there is female being, there must of necessity be subordinate function. When one's role is grounded in one's essential being and obtains in all things and at all times, one's role defines one's personhood. Women are subordinate persons—by nature and definition. Their subordination is constitutive of and essential to their personhood.[49] But this is not ontological equality. Nor is it merely a matter of playing a role; rather, it is about *being* what one intrinsically *is* by virtue of the God-ordained nature and meaning of one's sex.

The basis for women's subordination (God's design and purpose for womanhood), as well as the functions in which women are subordinate (spiritual discernment, decision making, and self-governance), is all about being. Woman's nature or ontology, her life purpose or teleology, her will,

---

[49]See the excellent discussion of role difference in Giles, *Trinity and Subordinationism*, 179-88.

intellect, and moral understanding, her spiritual responsibilities before God—these are matters as close to the heart of a person's being as anything ever could be. They define and characterize what a person *is*. The suppression of women (and not men) in these critical areas of personhood is not meaningfully described merely as women's different role.

The nature of and rationale for female subordination, then, make it fundamentally unlike functional subordination. Its nature (necessary, permanent, and comprehensive) and its rationale (God's creational design) place woman's subordination foursquare in the realm of being. In woman's "equal being and unequal role," the role is as much about woman's being as is the equality. Thus, evangelical patriarchy does not have woman being unequal in a different respect from the way she is equal. Rather, a woman is unequal (subordinate) in the same respect that she is equal—by virtue of her being, as a constitutive element and necessary consequence of her being. Therefore, woman's equality (as biblically defined) and woman's subordination (as defined by patriarchalists) cannot coexist without logical contradiction. Evangelical patriarchy's *equal being/unequal role* construct must be deemed internally incoherent.

PART 2

"But it's about God's will, not gender." Defenders of the *equal being/unequal role* distinction may insist that female subordination does not imply woman's inferiority because it is not determined by or grounded in a woman's female nature; rather, it is determined by and grounded in God's will alone. In other words, authority is not essential to manhood, nor is subordination essential to womanhood. Rather, women have a subordinate role and men have an authoritative role (or *office*, the term of choice for some). And women and men are assigned permanently to their roles not because of their gender but simply because God, for reasons of his own, has commanded that women function in a role of subordination to men.[50]

---

[50]Sarah Sumner offers an argument to this effect in *Men and Women in the Church*, 278. She calls this the Scotist view—that we cannot, nor need we, understand the reasons for God's commands. She claims Piper and Grudem hold this view; yet these men affirm that the nature, meaning, and deeper differences of manhood and womanhood are relevant to deciding who submits and who has authority, thus affirming an ontological basis for gender roles. But perhaps the Scotist perspective often serves more as an ad hoc argumentative strategy than as a principled conviction.

But if God has commanded subordination of all women and only women—such that femaleness is the necessary and sufficient criterion that decides a person's permanent and comprehensive subordination—then God has indeed decreed a subordination that is determined by female gender. That is, God has set up an arrangement whereby the question "Who is to be in charge, and who is to be subordinate?" is answered solely according to gender.[51]

A crucial point at issue here is whether God has in fact decreed such a thing. If God's Word makes it clear that women are not ontologically inferior to men, and if—as has been argued above—the permanent, comprehensive, and necessary subordination of women logically implies the ontological inferiority of the female gender, then we must conclude that God has *not* decreed such a thing and that biblical texts understood to convey such a decree have been wrongly interpreted.

Furthermore, the idea that woman's subordination is not in any sense determined by or grounded in what a woman *is* or what God designed her to *be* is contrary to the ways of God in that it separates God's will for creation from his design for creation. Ontology and teleology become detached, irrelevant to each other. In what other area of theology would this be asserted? Can the will of God be deemed to be at odds with the created nature of things? Would God require—has God ever required—of us anything for which he did not design us? God's decrees always tell us something about his character, our humanity, the very nature of things the way God created them. For example, God's ban on homosexual relationships tells us about—and is grounded in—the created nature of sexuality, its meaning, design, and purpose. Surely if God has banned women from leadership in key areas and consigned women to be subordinate to male leadership, this tells us something about the created nature of womanhood and manhood.

The idea that what women may and may not do is ontologically disconnected from what women can and cannot do is also contrary to the whole tenor of New Testament teaching—that whatever one has been given one

---

[51]This is precisely the case in determining authority in marriages. For church leadership, maleness is necessary but (unlike male rule in marriage) not sufficient; other qualifications must be met as well.

should use by investing it in and for the kingdom of God (e.g., 1 Pet 4:10-11). Being and function, fruit and gifts, personal character and public ministry are tandem expressions of faithful service and obedience to Christ. Biblically, one does not stop short of serving God's people in a way for which one has been divinely gifted and prepared, any more than one takes on a ministry role that one is not personally or spiritually equipped to handle.

At least one patriarchalist has a clear view of the fallacy of using role language to describe what it means to be a man or a woman. German theologian Werner Neuer writes:

> A person does not play the role of a man or a woman, but he is a man or she is a woman. Sex is no role that can be changed at will like stage roles, but is a fundamental aspect of human existence from which no one can escape. It carries with it quite definite tasks and modes of conduct. And language must reflect this state of affairs. . . . Sex is concerned with being and not with roles. . . . In the cause of truth we should therefore give up talking about the roles of the sexes.[52]

Neuer states the patriarchal position sans the role rhetoric: "The Christian view of the sexes starts from the premise that both men and women are in every respect God's creatures and of equal value, but that in their *being* they are fundamentally distinct. Consequently, they have different tasks to fulfill."[53] That is, the different functions or tasks (male authority and female subordination) are grounded in and determined by the ontologically distinct male and female beings.

Indeed, it seems the typical patriarchal view is not just that God has *willed* that women and men have these distinct functions but that, because God's creational design is for women to be subordinate to men, these roles are in some sense uniquely fitting expressions of personal manhood and womanhood. God has designed men and women such that true femininity inclines toward submissiveness and true masculinity inclines toward personal, directive leadership.[54] Few patriarchalists today

---

[52]Werner Neuer, *Man and Woman in Christian Perspective* (Wheaton, IL: Crossway, 1991), 29-30.
[53]Neuer, *Man and Woman*, 23, emphasis added. Neuer apparently does not acknowledge that such a difference or inequality in being implies women's inferiority in being.
[54]As noted earlier in this chapter, this is the view of Piper and Grudem, who are representative of many, especially those of the Council on Biblical Manhood and Womanhood.

consistently claim or believe that submissiveness does not in some sense fit with the nature of womanhood, or that men are not by virtue of their manhood more suited to be in authority than are women.

What many patriarchalists actually believe about the being (and not merely the function) of women is reflected not only in their discussions of the subject but also in their day-to-day interactions with women and men in churches and Christian ministries. What, I wonder, would the church look like if people consistently believed—in both theory *and* practice— that superior male function does not bespeak superior male being (but only God's apparently arbitrary will)? It is difficult to imagine, but it seems certain that women would not be treated the way they now are. If women were truly regarded as no less than men in their intrinsic capacities and inbuilt resources for leadership, decision making, and spiritual under- standing, then men in leadership would routinely utilize women's abilities fully in such areas as financial and administrative management, ministry to both men and women, moral and theological reasoning, spiritual gifts and insights, and biblical exegesis and exposition. Furthermore, women would not be consistently interrupted, dismissed, patronized, or ignored when they speak up in classrooms or staff/faculty/board meetings of Christian organizations. Rather, men would listen to, respect, appreciate, and seek out women's counsel and expertise in all the areas where gifted women stand to contribute to the important tasks of shepherding God's flock and sharing the gospel of Christ with the world at large.

People's actual treatment of women often belies their professed belief that only the role is inferior, not the person. It is, after all, not possible to live out an implausible belief. Role theology would have us believe that although the subordinate role is not demanded by the nature of the female person, a woman who is truly feminine will play the role of submission to male authority because God ordained at creation that this is to be the woman's permanent role, and only the woman who plays this role is fulfill- ing her purpose and true identity as a woman.

However, it is illogical to maintain that there is no basis for the role in the nature of the person when the role is one of moral necessity given the nature of the person, and when the role is perceived as defining one's per- sonal gender identity and as having been established by God at creation.

In what other area of life do we freight a mere *role* with such ontological significance? Creational design, personal nature, gender identity—this is the stuff of *being*, not of a mere role or function. The concept of role is simply playing the role of being!

The logical connection between woman's being and woman's subordinate role is attested not only by common sense but also by common experience—an experience all too common for countless women who have followed God's call into Christian ministry.

False analogies. Many attempts to defend woman's subordination against the implication of woman's inferiority resort to some kind of argument by analogy: that is, if other instances of role difference are compatible with equality in being, then woman's subordination in role is compatible with her equality in being. But are such analogies valid, or are they comparing apples and oranges? We have already seen that not all differences in function or role logically permit personal equality. Many of these arguments attempt to justify woman's subordination (which is incompatible with personal equality) by likening it to a role that *is* compatible with personal equality. In order to refrain from falling into such logical errors, one must have a keen eye for the critical differences between female subordination and functional subordination. Subordination is necessarily personal and not merely functional when (as in female subordination) its scope is comprehensive, its duration is permanent, and the criterion for its determination is one's unalterable ontology.

One argument-by-analogy often put forth is that if a child's subordination to a parent does not imply the child's inferiority in being, then neither does a woman's subordination to her husband imply that the woman is inferior in being.[55] But this is a classic case of false analogy. The child's subordination is *like* female subordination in that it is comprehensive and ontologically based; however, it is *unlike* female subordination in that its ontological basis—childhood—is a temporary condition. It is also unlike female subordination in that the child's parental governance follows justifiably from the child's lack of experience and inferior skills in decision making. The child's subordination ends when its

---

[55]Ortlund argues along these lines in "Male-Female Equality," 130-31.

purpose has been accomplished and the child is sufficiently mature to make independent decisions.

Because the nature of childhood warrants the child's subordination, and childhood is a temporary condition that all humans undergo, the subordination of child to parent does not imply the child's inferiority in fundamental personhood. The child, for that matter, could grow up to hold a position of authority over her own parents. (A woman can never "grow up" to have authority over—or even equal with—a man.) Of course, the grown child will still owe respect and honor to her parents as a permanent obligation. However, the point at issue is not whether a woman should respect and honor her husband (as she certainly should) but whether she should submit to his rule.

Space does not permit a response to all such spurious arguments-by-analogy.[56] The rest of this chapter will address two key theological analogies that are often advanced in order to justify woman's subordination.

The priests and the Levites. Some have argued that because God assigned the Levites, especially those in the Aaronic priesthood, to a special religious function from which other Israelites were excluded, this shows, by analogy, that the doctrine of male authority in marriage and ministry does not violate the essential equality of women and men.[57] This argument is flawed both analogically and theologically.

It is true that each arrangement grants to some people a religious status that is denied to others, based entirely on physical attributes of birth. However, the analogy fails at several key points. Unlike male authority and female subordination, the special role of the Levites did not meet all the characteristics of criteria, duration, and scope, which together render a superior-subordinate order fundamentally ontological rather than merely functional.[58]

Although the Levitical priesthood is roughly analogous to male authority in terms of its lifelong duration and its basis in unalterable physical being, its scope is a different matter. The scope of female subordination to male

---

[56]See Groothuis, *Good News for Women*, 49-52, 60-63, for additional examples and discussion.

[57]See, e.g., James B. Hurley, *Man and Woman in Biblical Perspective* (Grand Rapids, MI: Zondervan, 1981), 44-45; Schreiner, "Women in Ministry," 201.

[58]See previous section, "Difference in 'Role' or 'Function'"; see also chart in Groothuis, *Good News for Women*, 45.

authority is comprehensive. A married woman is subject to her husband's authority in every area of her life. There is no area in which a woman has any authority, privilege, or opportunity that a man is denied.[59] The male is consistently advantaged with respect to the female, and the female is consistently disadvantaged with respect to the male. The Levites, however, were not consistently advantaged with respect to the people; they were denied the right of the other tribes to own and inherit land (Num 18:20). In patriarchal agrarian societies, land ownership was deemed supremely desirable and a mark of social status—a right generally denied the less privileged classes (such as women and slaves). It was also denied the Levites. Thus, there remained a sense of equality or parity between the Levites and the other Israelites in that each group had its own advantages and disadvantages.

Furthermore, while God chose the Levites to perform a ministry of lifelong duration, it was not a permanent decree as is the (supposed) divine decree that women be subordinate to male authority. The authority/status difference between women and men is deemed an essential feature of God's creational design; thus, it is permanent not only in the sense that it endures throughout a person's lifetime but also in that it pertains to all men and women everywhere for all time. The Levites' role, by contrast, was not permanent but provisional, in that it pertained only to a temporary religious system at a particular time and for a particular purpose in history.

It should also be noted that men in the Levitical priesthood did not have the sort of spiritual authority over the people that men today are given over women in the church and home. In the Old Testament, spiritual authority in this sense—whereby certain individuals spoke for God and made the will of God known to others—was exercised less by the priests than by the prophets (among whom were women).

Moreover, there was a discernible purpose and reason for God's choosing the Levites for a special spiritual status. Intrinsic to God's rationale was that this arrangement was *not* permanent or inherent in creational design but served a specific and limited function until the new covenant in Christ. The Bible characteristically does not reveal God's universal commands without also revealing the moral or theological reasons for the commands. Yet there

---

[59]As noted in the "Equality in Being" section above, this is not effectively countered by the claim that there is functional parity between male and female because only women can have babies.

is no discernible reason why God would have chosen men for permanently superior spiritual status. The only possible *logical* rationale would be that all men are spiritually superior to all women—a supposition for which no evidence exists, and which today's proponents of male authority deny.

God chose the Levites to serve on behalf of all the firstborn sons of Israel, who by right belonged to Yahweh. In lieu of demanding the firstborn of every family, God set aside the Levites as his own (Num 3:11-13, 40-51). In this sense the Levites were playing a role. It was for symbolic, illustrative, and instructional purposes that God formally consecrated the priests and Levites for their special role of representing God's holiness to the people and representing Israel before God (Num 8). The Levitical priesthood was justified during the time of the old covenant, because God had ordained that certain individuals who possessed physical attributes and pedigrees deemed worthy by human standards should serve as an object lesson for the people, a visible picture of an invisible God who is utterly perfect and supremely worthy.[60] Furthermore, God's ultimate covenant purpose was for *all* his people to serve as his priesthood (Ex 19:6; Is 61:6). The representative ministry of the Levitical priesthood prevailed only until the new covenant instituted the high priesthood of Christ and the priesthood of all believers.

Everything that was prefigured in the Levitical priesthood has now been fulfilled forever in Jesus Christ, who is the firstborn of all creation (Col 1:15), the one mediator between God and humans (1 Tim 2:5), and our high priest forever after the order of Melchizedek, which supersedes the order of Aaron (Heb 6:19-20; 7:11-28). The perfect representation of God has now been given once and for all in the life, ministry, death, and resurrection of Jesus Christ (Jn 14:9; Col 1:15, 19; Heb 1:3), and this leaves no room for addition, development, or duplication in the form of men who believe they stand in the authority of Christ vis-à-vis women.

In the new covenant, physical distinctions such as race and gender no longer demarcate unequal levels of religious privilege (Gal 3:26-28). No one in the body of Christ is excluded from the priestly responsibilities of representing God's holiness to the world, offering spiritual sacrifices to God,

---

[60]See Groothuis, *Good News for Women*, 31-36.

representing God before other believers, and interceding for others before God. The failure to perceive and honor the pivotal difference between priesthood in the old covenant and priesthood in the new covenant is a fundamental theological flaw of evangelical patriarchy.[61] This point of confusion is reflected in the attempt to defend a special spiritual status for Christian men by comparing it to the Levitical priesthood of the old covenant.

The subordination of the Son to the Father. Support for the claim that woman's unequal role does not bespeak woman's unequal being is often sought in the analogy of the relationship of God the Son to God the Father.[62] It is argued that the Father and the Son are "equal in being," yet in all things and through all eternity they relate to each other according to a hierarchy of authority and obedience; thus the analogy of the "eternal functional subordination" within the Trinity illustrates and vindicates woman's permanent and comprehensive subordination to man's authority. As with the Levitical argument, I believe the trinitarian argument fails to hold up either analogically or theologically.

False analogy. Christian orthodoxy affirms that God and Christ are of the same substance and nature; they are not just equal in being but *one* in being. There is no difference between the divine nature of the Father and the divine nature of the Son.[63] Thus human nature is not analogous to divine nature. God (three persons sharing one divine nature) is a unitary being, while humanity (billions of persons sharing human nature) is a category consisting of a multiplicity of beings. There is a oneness in nature/essence/substance between the Father and the Son that is absent from any male-female relationship.

Therefore, any subordination of Christ to God would necessarily be fundamentally dissimilar to the subordination of woman to man, which is decided by and deemed essential to the "deeper differences" of manhood and womanhood. Unlike woman's subordination to man, the Son's subordination to the Father cannot be grounded in or determined by his "different" nature. Although subordinationists consider Christ's eternal subordination

---

[61]See Groothuis, *Good News for Women*, chaps. 1 and 4, especially 31-36, 115-17; also Stanley J. Grenz, "Biblical Priesthood and Women in Ministry," in the present volume.

[62]See, e.g., Grudem, *Systematic Theology*, 459-60.

[63]See Millard J. Erickson, *Christian Theology* (Grand Rapids, MI: Baker, 1985), 337, 339.

to be an inherent, unchanging element of the Godhead, it evidently obtains by virtue of Christ's relationship as Son to the Father, not by virtue of his nature being different from the Father's. (Yet here, too, they assume a false analogy. A son is not permanently subordinate in all things to his father.)

It has often been stated that one purpose of male leadership in marriage is to determine who makes the decision when husband and wife cannot agree. The properly submissive wife will act against her own best judgment if the husband's final decision is contrary to her will. But the members of the Trinity are always completely one in will.[64] Unlike the subordination prescribed for women, there could be no subordination in the eternal Trinity that would involve one divine person acting against his own preference or best judgment under orders issued from the contrary will of another divine person. When the Father sent the Son, it was not along the lines of an earthly father who says, "Well, son, here's what I'm going to have you do," at which point the son learns what he had better do or else. Rather, with Father, Son, and Holy Spirit of one mind on how to redeem sinful humans (as they always are on every matter), it was the Son's will to go as much as it was the Father's will to send him (Phil 2:5-11).

Moreover, in Christ's own description of his earthly ministry, he states that the Father has given him all judgment and authority (Mt 28:18; Jn 5:21-27; 17:2).[65] Even during his earthly incarnation, when Jesus did only the Father's will (Jn 5:30; 8:28-29), the relationship of Father and Son was not at all like that of husband and wife in a patriarchal marriage, where the husband holds final decision-making authority and is neither expected nor required to share this authority with his wife.

Even if there were an eternal subordination of the Son to the Father, it would fail to model the key elements of woman's lifelong subordination to

---

[64]Although Paul exhorts believers to be of one mind (Phil 2:2), this refers to unity and harmony in relationships, not to the complete and consistent oneness in will and desire that characterizes the members of the Trinity.

[65]Patriarchalist Steven Tracy acknowledges this aspect of the Father-Son analogy and says this should challenge men to "exercise biblical headship by giving women authority in various spheres of life and ministry." Males, however, must still retain "final decision-making authority" over females (Tracy, "Headship with a Heart," 53). This sort of arrangement, however, falls short of the analogy of the Father's giving "all judgment" to the Son. Note also that even in Tracy's benevolent construal of patriarchy, the woman has no direct authority under God; she has only the authority her husband decides to give her.

man. What would female subordination to male authority look like if it were truly analogous to a subordination of the Son to the Father? First, the authority of the man and the submission of the woman would not be decided or demanded by their different male and female natures. Second, there would never be an occasion in which the man's will would or should overrule the woman's will; the man therefore would "send" the woman to do only what was in accordance with her own will. Third, every husband would willingly and consistently share all authority with his wife, acknowledging her full authority to make judgments and decisions on behalf of both of them. In short, the oneness in being of the divine persons, which results in oneness of will, precludes invoking the Trinity as either illustrating or vindicating the doctrine of woman's subordination to man.

Theological problems. The oneness in nature and will of the divine persons not only renders any eternal functional subordination of the Son disanalogous to female subordination but also brings into question the logical coherence of the doctrine itself. What could be the logic of one person always functioning subject to the authority of another person without some cause or ground for this continuous subordination in the respective natures of the two persons? And how could there be a permanent, unilateral order of authority and obedience between persons who are always of one mind and will, who have the same perfect knowledge and understanding, the same perfectly righteous desires, the same infinite and inexhaustible wisdom and love? How could there even be any sense of purpose in such an arrangement?

Philippians 2:5-11 states that during his time on earth in human flesh, Jesus put human limitations on his equality with God by choosing to take on the role of a servant. He "became obedient" (Phil 2:8). The time of Christ's earthly incarnation was not business as usual for God the Son and God the Father; it was an epic—although temporally limited—change in their relationship. Hebrews 5:7-8 states, "although he was a Son, he learned obedience" while he was on earth in the flesh, and God heard his prayers "because of his reverent submission." Since this was the first time the Son needed to be obedient to the Father, he had to learn how to do it. It was not until his earthly incarnation that the Son "*became* obedient" and "*learned* obedience." There is no indication of an *eternal* order of the Son's obedience to the Father's authority.[66]

Furthermore, when Christ humbled himself to become human in order to redeem fallen humanity, it was not so much a demonstration of the Son's submission to the Father as a demonstration of the nature and being of the Father. As F. F. Bruce notes, "Nowhere is God more fully or worthily revealed as God than when we see him 'in Christ reconciling the world to himself' (2 Cor 5:19)."[67]

In the incarnation, the Son became functionally subordinate to the Father only with respect to his work as our Redeemer. Thus, Christ's subordination is limited in both scope and duration, since the work of redemption has a beginning and endpoint in time. But if, as patriarchalists typically argue, Christ's subordination is not limited temporally and functionally but pertains in all things throughout all eternity, then it is not a functional subordination; it is a personal subordination. Subordinate is what he always is, what he always has been, what he always will be; it necessarily defines and characterizes the person and identity of the Son throughout all eternity.

The idea that Christ's subordination is eternal yet merely functional (and thereby compatible with ontological equality) is incongruent. An eternal subordination of Christ would seem logically to entail his ontological subordination.[68] As Millard Erickson concludes, "A temporal, functional subordination without inferiority of essence seems possible, but not an eternal subordination."[69]

The doctrine of an eternal role subordination of the Son to the Father not only is rife with logical and theological difficulties but utterly fails as an analogy to woman's subordination. Thus, it serves neither to illustrate

---

[66]See Gilbert Bilezikian, "Hermeneutical Bungee-Jumping: Subordination in the Godhead," *JETS* 40, no. 1 (1997): 65.

[67]F. F. Bruce, *The Epistle to the Hebrews*, rev. ed. (Grand Rapids, MI: Eerdmans, 1990), 80.

[68]Those who affirm the Son's "eternal functional subordination" deny that the Son's subordination is ontological. Thus, my argument is not that these proponents of trinitarian subordination are heretical but that they fail to acknowledge this theological and philosophical entailment of their position. Robert Letham's ruminations illustrate how the notion of eternal functional subordination collapses into ontological subordination. See Letham, "The Man-Woman Debate," *WTJ* 52 (1990): 67-68. For a response, see Groothuis, *Good News for Women*, 57-58.

[69]Millard J. Erickson, *God in Three Persons* (Grand Rapids, MI: Baker, 1995), 309.

nor to vindicate the claim that woman's subordination and woman's equality can coexist without contradiction.[70]

IN CONCLUSION

Whether within a marriage or within the Trinity, subordination is not functional but ontological when it defines and characterizes a person in all his or her aspects, in perpetuity—when subordination is thereby inherent in the very identity of a person. To attempt to legitimize such subordination by declaring it to be a role that has no bearing on the "equality in being" of the subordinated person is a rhetorical sleight of hand. Saying it does not make it so—or even logically possible.

Truly functional subordination *can* logically coexist with equality of being. However, neither female subordination nor an eternal subordination of the Son to the Father fits the definition of functional subordination. Female subordination is not about performing a function as much as it is about being—*being* female, *being* submissive to male authority. Because women's subordination is not merely a function or a role but is fundamentally ontological, it contradicts the biblical teaching of the essential equality of women and men. Similarly, any eternal subordination of the Son would seem logically to entail the Son's ontologically inferior status and so to contradict biblical teaching on the oneness of God and the absolute equality in being of Father, Son, and Holy Spirit.

Woman's inferior role cannot be defended by the claim that it is ontologically distinct from woman's equal being. In female subordination, being determines role, and role defines being; thus, there can be no real distinction between the two. If the one is inferior, so must be the other. If, on the other hand, woman is *not* less than man in her personal being, then neither can there be any biblical or theological warrant for woman's permanent, comprehensive, and ontologically grounded subordination to man's authority.[71]

---

[70]For a detailed critique of the doctrine of Christ's subordination, see Kevin Giles, "The Trinity Argument for Women's Subordination," in the present volume.

[71]I am grateful to Douglas Groothuis and a half-dozen other writers and scholars who critiqued earlier versions of this chapter. For more on the philosophical debate concerning the concept of equal in being, unequal in function, see Steven B. Cowan, "Complementarianism Unfazed," *Philosophia Christi* 13, no. 1 (2011): 181-88; Adam Omelianchuk, "Ontologically Grounded Subordination: A Reply to Steven B. Cowan," *Philosophia Christi* 13, no. 1 (2011): 169-80; Steven B. Cowan, "Complementarianism Unfazed," *Philosophia Christi* 13, no. 1 (2011): 181-88.

PART III

ADDRESSING THE ISSUES

Interpretive and

Cultural Perspectives

21

INTERPRETIVE METHODS AND THE GENDER DEBATE

Cynthia Long Westfall

•••••

I TAUGHT CHURCH HISTORY for several years and have always been impressed by the time and attention that early church leaders devoted to formulating the orthodox view of the two natures of Jesus Christ. Each confession and doctrine was carefully weighed for inconsistencies that would compromise Christ's divinity or humanity. The time has come to focus the same critical and careful attention on a biblical theology of gender.[1]

Most of the passages that are central for the traditional theologies of gender and affect the church, home, and society are located in the collection of letters in the Pauline corpus (Romans, 1 Corinthians, 2 Corinthians, Galatians, Ephesians, Philippians, Colossians, 1 Thessalonians, 2 Thessalonians, 1 Timothy, 2 Timothy, Titus, and Philemon). We often think that the discussion of gender in the Pauline corpus is simply about "women in leadership," or issues that have been raised by feminists, but these texts about women belong to a much bigger context of Pauline texts that are concerned with issues such as the nature of male and female, the

---

[1] *Biblical theology* has several definitions. In this chapter it refers to the exploration of the coherence of the canonical witness. In includes detecting and tracing a theme through the Bible or through a corpus and discerning its coherence. See, e.g., Craig Bartholomew, *Out of Egypt: Biblical Theology and Biblical Interpretation*, Scripture and Hermeneutics Series 5 (Grand Rapids, MI: Zondervan Academic, 2011). In this chapter, *gender* refers to characteristics that are associated with male and female (or masculine and feminine) and that which differentiates the two.

image of God in humanity at creation, dominion in creation and the kingdom of God, the effects of the fall, the nature of spiritual authority, the spiritual obligations of all believers, and spiritual gifts and calling. Historically, Pauline scholars, biblical scholars, and the church have failed to carefully examine and resolve the contradictions and logical inconsistencies among commentaries, biblical theologies, and praxis concerning men and women with clear statements in Scripture, the general theology and orthodox confessions about human beings, Christians, and Christianity.

The traditional theologies of gender accumulated a lot of baggage with traditions of interpretation that are difficult or impossible to reconcile with Paul's gospel of salvation by faith, justification, grace, and freedom. In addition, the intellectual, spiritual, and moral inferiority of women and the ontological superiority of men has been assumed throughout the majority of church history. However, in the last forty years, there has been a marked tendency to jettison the clearly misogynistic elements of the theological traditions, and a strong shift to profess ontological equality in gender. At the same time, many attempt to maintain the same trajectory with the rest of the presuppositions, inferences, and consequent interpretations of passages that have been used to restrict women in the Christian community. If the analysis is legitimate, it is impossible to change such a foundational assumption in the interpretive process without affecting the outcome.

This chapter describes an approach to interpretation that provides a way forward in composing a coherent Pauline theology of gender.[2] It is a call to treat the texts and data that concern male and female in the Pauline epistles with consistent hermeneutics. We need specific and well-defined methodologies that attempt to compose a coherent Pauline theology of gender that is faithful to the texts and also coherent within the theology of the Pauline corpus, the narrative of Paul's life, the profile of Paul as a person, and the biblical contexts.

GENDER AND THE PAULINE CORPUS

One of the primary commitments of this volume is to the belief in the authority of the Bible as God's revelation to humanity. That should mean

---

[2]See an earlier discussion on this topic in Cynthia Long Westfall, "On Developing a Consistent Hermeneutical Approach to the Application of General Scriptures," *PriscPap* 24 (2010): 9-13.

that, at the very least, we adopt a canonical approach to the authority of the entire Pauline corpus in faith and practice. One of the major issues in the interpretation of texts that deal with gender is that scholarship has strongly challenged Pauline authorship in the books in which most of the passages occur that have been central to the gender discussion. How should we approach the passages that occur in the disputed Pauline corpus?[3] Most importantly for our topic, how do we approach the passages about gender in Ephesians, Colossians, and the Pastoral Epistles (particularly 1 Timothy and Titus)?[4] Much of the scholarly discussion of Paul's theology of gender has either omitted most of the texts that have been used to subjugate or restrict women as non-Pauline, or embraced traditional interpretations of these texts at face value, thus accentuating the alleged inconsistencies and contradictions of these texts with the rest of the Pauline letters.[5] Consequently, the state of scholarship has created strange bedfellows in that those who are committed to the rejection (or even the vilification) of these Pauline passages often support the traditional interpretations of these texts that are demonstrably atomistic, in that they are

---

[3]The issue of Pauline authorship has made the discussion of his theology of gender difficult and all but unworkable. Other than 1 Corinthians, some of the best-known Pauline passages that contain material on gender are in the disputed corpus: the prison epistles and the Pastoral Epistles. The apparent contradictions between 1 Corinthians and the Pastoral Epistles appear to support the alleged pseudonymous authorship of the Pastoral Epistles and would push against any attempt to find a coherent Pauline theology of gender. However, this would be tautological if there are valid interpretive options that create coherence. A benign explanation of pseudonymous authorship would be that the "real author" was attempting to write what he or she imagined that Paul would have written if he had the opportunity to address Gnosticism and consolidation of church structure. On the other hand, it is possible that the Pastoral Epistles were written to confront, contradict, correct, or adjust Pauline theology on gender in the undisputed letters. However, unless one wishes to find dissonance, if there is a sound interpretive option that is coherent within the rest of the corpus, it should be seriously considered. The burden of proof should be on those who claim that the Pastoral Epistles (for example) were written to correct Paul, given that all but the gender material is thought to be an addition to Pauline theology rather than a contradiction or correction. See E. E. Ellis, "Pastoral Letters," in *Dictionary of Paul and His Letters*, ed. Gerald F. Hawthorne and Ralph P. Martin (Downers Grove, IL: InterVarsity Press, 1993), 658-66. It is difficult to accept that an early, blatant attempt to hijack Pauline theology would be successful. Each interpreter comes to the text with certain assumptions and tends to select the interpretive options that are consistent and coherent with their own presuppositions about Paul, the text, and the context that frames it.

[4]For a summary of the discussion on the canonicity of Paul's letters, see A. G. Patzia, "Canon," in Hawthorne and Martin, *Dictionary of Paul*, 85-92.

[5]The consensus of scholars accepts Romans, 1 Corinthians, 2 Corinthians, Galatians, Philippians, 1 Thessalonians, and Philemon as Pauline (often referred to as the *haute Briefe*).

interpreted in isolation from the context of the passages in which they occur or the context of the Pauline corpus as a whole.

However, these epistles claim to be written by Paul and place themselves within a Pauline narrative. So, they should not be interpreted in an atomistic way apart from or against the contexts in which they occur or the context of the rest of the Pauline corpus if there are valid alternatives that better fit the contexts. The ways in which the letters place themselves in the life and writings of Paul indicate that these are the contexts in which the content is meant to be interpreted. Therefore, these contexts should be essential tools in determining the intended message and meaning of the text and what was being done with language, regardless of one's view on authorship. The starting point should be to explore the interpretation of the texts according to their own terms as part of the Pauline corpus, within the narrative of Paul's life and within a viable Pauline theology.[6] As part of the canon, these texts have been central in the discussion on gender, and they have been instrumental in practices related to gender. However, traditional atomistic interpretations of texts such as Ephesians 5:22-33 and 1 Timothy 2:12 have often been treated as the clearest teaching and starting point on gender and have been used by many as an interpretive grid for the rest of the Pauline corpus, indeed for the entire Bible, in regards to the function of gender in the church and society. This chapter suggests that we set apart the use of such interpretive grids since they are used to override other passages and create unnecessary contradictions within the Pauline texts. Our mission should be to explore alternate readings that are consistent with each other in theology and application in which we take the entire Pauline corpus into account.

GENDER AND THE "COMPOSITE PAUL"

If we are committed to the authority of Scripture, then the way forward is to develop a theology of gender of the "composite Paul" that emerges from

---

[6]This is not precisely the same as canonical criticism but has some resemblance to that and to narrative criticism, where one assumes the world the author creates in order to understand and interpret the literature. For a canonical approach, see Brevard S. Childs, *Old Testament Theology in a Canonical Context* (Minneapolis: Fortress, 1990). Alan Padgett argues for "the canonical sense of Scripture" in understanding the ethics of submission, gender roles, and servant leadership in the New Testament. See Padgett, *As Christ Submits to the Church: A Biblical Understanding of Leadership and Mutual Submission* (Grand Rapids, MI: Baker, 2011), 21-30. For an example of narrative criticism, see R. Alan Culpepper, *Anatomy of the Fourth Gospel* (Minneapolis: Augsburg Fortress, 1983).

the combined portrait of Acts and the canonical Pauline epistles.[7] However, people are often inconsistent and have unexamined double or conflicting standards both in their study of Paul and the Pauline theology of gender in which Paul is fragmented, and consequently they choose or support interpretive options of passages on gender that render Paul incoherent and theologically inconsistent. For instance, Paul would have been inconsistent in his theology of gender if he differed from traditional Jewish and Greco-Roman ideology concerning males only, but he did not differ from Jewish and Greco-Roman ideology concerning females.[8] Paul would have been inconsistent if he argued that salvation for men was by faith but that salvation for women was by some other means.[9] Paul would have been inconsistent to say that Jesus was reversing the effects of the fall for men while forcing women to pay a penalty for their role in the fall.[10] Paul would have been inconsistent if he brought freedom from the law and cultural customs for men while he enforced a stricter subjugation to women than the law required or depicted.[11] Paul would have been inconsistent if he

---

[7]Therefore, for those who dispute the Pauline authorship of any given epistle or set of epistles, this study of Paul can be compared to David Clines's study of the masculine Jesus in the canonical Gospels, which he distinguishes from the historical Jesus or the portraits of Jesus in the individual Gospels. See D. J. A. Clines, "*Ecce Vir*; or, Gendering the Son of Man," in *Biblical Studies/Cultural Studies: The Third Sheffield Colloquium*, ed. J. Cheryl Exum and Stephen D. Moore, JSOTSup 266 (Sheffield: Sheffield Academic, 1998), 352-75.

[8]For example, the benefits of not requiring circumcision are generally understood, though they are usually understood as benefiting all Gentiles rather than only Gentile males. The sweeping social and religious changes for Gentile males and the challenge and adjustment of the entitlement of Jewish males (see Rom 2) is understood to varying degrees. Paul's critique of the masculine values and concepts of authority of the Greco-Roman culture is often acknowledged, though in varying degrees. Whatever degree of change is acknowledged for males, it has been the consensus that the status quo of the Greco-Roman role for women was uncritically adopted by Paul in the churches.

[9]While salvation by faith is acknowledged as a central Pauline theme, the consensus of the interpretation of 1 Tim 2:15 has understood "Yet she will be saved through childbearing" as having a salvific meaning for women.

[10]While Christ's work on the cross has been understood to remove the penalty of sin and death for all men, 1 Tim 2:14 has been understood as a mandate to penalize all women for Eve's role in the fall. For example, Tertullian writes: "And do you not know that you are (each) an Eve? The sentence of God on this sex of yours lives in this age: the guilt must of necessity live too" (*On the Apparel of Women* 1.1.2).

[11]The application of freedom and grace for men in Paul's teaching on Jews and Gentiles was explicitly understood as greater subjugation and less freedom than women experienced under Judaism in the Catholic *Code of Canon Law*: "In the Old Testament much was permitted which today is abolished, through the perfection of grace. So if [in the Old Testament] women were permitted to judge the people, today because of sin, which woman brought into the world, women are

argued that all believers had certain privileges, obligations, goals, and ethical requirements and then restricted women in such a way that they were unable to fulfill those requirements.[12] These inconsistencies are systemic in the traditional interpretations and theologies that have guided the beliefs, policies, and practices based on gender. Up until now, for a variety of reasons, many churches and biblical scholars have been strangely comfortable to hold these contradictions in tension. Of course, it is always possible that Paul was inconsistent, but if we wish to have a high view of Scripture, should we not explore the possibility that the composite Paul's theology of gender could be consistent and coherent?

The central question is, Are these alleged contradictions really an issue of what the text actually says, or are they an issue of how the text has been interpreted with the extratextual inferences that have been projected on the text? This chapter suggests a robust exploration of interpretative options that are faithful to the text, consistent with Pauline theology, and consistent in hermeneutics. One should ruthlessly identify and strip down the extra information that has been assumed and has controlled interpretation, including misleading subtitles, extra words placed in translations that reverse the meaning of the Greek, questionable methods of lexicography that skew the meaning of key words, and other interpretive frames that have been placed on these texts.

GENDER AND THE PAULINE NARRATIVE

Given their internal arrangement and their probable placement within or after the book of Acts, the Pauline epistles are embedded in a Pauline narrative that must be taken seriously, even for those who are reluctant to take it literally or historically. One of the contexts in which we interpret the Pauline letters is the wider story of Paul's life and the story of each letter.[13]

---

admonished by the Apostle to be careful to practice a modest restraint, to be subject to men and to veil themselves as a sign of subjugation" (*Decretum Gratiani* Causa 2, question 7, princ.).

[12]The restriction of women exercising the verbal gifts in Rom 12:1-9 on the basis of 1 Tim 1:12 prohibits or inhibits gifted women from following the instructions in the passage, e.g., Rom 12:6: "We have gifts that differ according to the grace given to us: prophecy, in proportion to faith."

[13]For an explanation of Paul's theology in the context of the wider story of Paul's life, see F. F. Bruce, *Apostle of the Heart Set Free* (Grand Rapids, MI: Eerdmans, 1977). For the narrative world of an epistle, see Norman R. Petersen, *Rediscovering Paul: Philemon and the Sociology of Paul's Narrative World* (Eugene, OR: Wipf & Stock, 1985). For reading Paul in the context of the larger story of

Paul placed each of his letters in a story in which he had selected and arranged the relevant events. Between the events that Paul arranged to voice his point of view and the information that he shared with the recipient(s) of the letter, there is a coherent story that accounts for the contents of the letter. Norman Petersen writes:

> Regardless of "what happened" historically, we cannot understand what Paul says *did* happen prior to the sending of the letter apart from the total framework of the events he envisioned. Paul's motives, strategies, and expectations as an actor in his own story can only be comprehended in terms of the whole story as he envisioned it. Hence the importance both of our constructing that story as carefully as possible, and of our distinguishing between story and history.[14]

When we interpret Paul's letters, we try to recover the information that he shared with the recipient(s), and we reconstruct stories about Paul's life and the role the text played in Paul's life in which the text is coherent. This is a healthy corrective to atomistic readings of the text and readings that are more theological than contextual, which have tended to be the norm for the passages that concern gender and are often dogmatically asserted to be the plain teaching of Scripture.

GENDER AND PAUL THE MAN

Interpreters bring presuppositions about Paul as a person to the text. Once I heard a sermon open with the statement, "Paul never met a stereotype he didn't like!" However, the Paul of Acts and the Pauline epistles was an incredibly adaptable and innovative revisionist, demonstrated in his pioneering work in the gender-specific issue of circumcision.[15] Paul's theology concerning gender was formed by both his Hellenistic Jewish worldview and the Scriptures of ancient Israel. But his interpretation of the Scriptures was dramatically reconfigured by his experience of his own conversion, and his experiences with Gentile conversions in Antioch, and his Gentile

---

Israel, see J. R. Daniel Kirk, *Jesus Have I Loved, but Paul? A Narrative Approach to the Problem of Pauline Christianity* (Grand Rapids, MI: Baker, 2011).

[14]Petersen, *Rediscovering Paul*, 16.

[15]See Clarence E. Glad, "Paul and Adaptability," in *Paul in the Greco-Roman World*, ed. J. Paul Sampley (Harrisburg, PA: Trinity Press International, 2003), 17-41.

mission. We can observe Paul's relentless theological systemization of the ramifications of those changes—Paul shows that he is very interested in coherence and consistency, particularly in his letter to the Galatians. A Pauline theology for male Gentiles emerged that challenged central Jewish beliefs and practices, while his Hellenist Jewish ethics formed the core of his teaching on sexuality and confronted central features of the Greco-Roman gender ideology. The model of the incarnate servanthood and suffering of Jesus Christ opposed both Jewish and Greco-Roman ideologies.

A hermeneutic for gender that is consistent with what Paul modeled would apply the same relentless theological systemization of what should change in order to be coherent and consistent. Three key trajectories that are relevant for practice in the church are (1) that the change in the constructions of Jewish and Greco-Roman ideology for males changed the gender construction for females by definition, (2) that Paul's teaching on servanthood equalized all believers as slaves, and (3) that his identification of believers as members of the family of God equalized believers as children of God and co-heirs with Christ.

Paul's teaching on relationships within the church and the kingdom of God must be carefully distinguished from Paul's instructions on how believers should conduct themselves in the world, which included the overlapping domains of Greco-Roman homes and society, including the status and roles that individuals had in those domains. Paul's Gentile churches still existed in a rigidly hierarchical culture, and the structure of the household was political because it was considered to be a microcosm of the empire. Paul the missionary and the churches he planted needed to survive and carry out their mission within the context of the Greco-Roman culture. In accordance with the best missionary practices, Paul coached his churches to fit in with the culture in terms of their social roles in the household, but also adapted the meaning of those roles in the execution of his mission strategy so that it was ethically consistent with the gospel. Typically, interpreters (influenced by the anachronistic assumptions of Christendom, etc.) collapse Paul's teaching on home and society with the church, confusing the categories and particularly the extent of Paul's influence. Paul had no personal power to challenge or change the Greco-Roman culture and its oppressive structures; he could only model and teach churches to be light in the darkness (2 Cor 4:1-18), and give them dignity and motivation to function and survive under stringent conditions in which most had little or no choice.

GENDER AS MALE AND FEMALE

Most of the recent gender debates have not been about what Paul says about gender but have rather centered on what Paul says about women and their role in the church and home, and what one may infer from those verses. The role of men has even been primarily inferred from Paul's teaching on women, but the Pauline passages that directly concern men and male ideology often have not been understood as constructions of gender. The hermeneutics that Paul used when he changed gender ideology for Jewish and Gentile males in the issue of circumcision should inform his gender ideology for females. Galatians 3:28, which says that there is no male and female, should be interpreted in the context of his relentless argument establishing the trajectory that resulted from circumcision no longer being required for Gentile males—this one decision radically challenged and changed social practices and authority structures for males in the Christian community. The parallels between Jews and Gentiles, free and slave, and men and women in Galatians 3:28 indicate that the same hermeneutics that Paul applied to Gentile males should be applied to slaves and women.[16]

It is necessary to have a broader focus that reads the Pauline passages on women in the light of the Pauline passages on men so that they are brought into conversation with each other and interpret each other, and the same hermeneutics that are used to interpret and apply Scriptures to men are used for women. For example, the freedoms and equal rights enjoyed by all men in our democratic cultures and the characteristics associated with masculinity are vastly different from the lives of men in the Greco-Roman culture. The commands to men that reflect the harsh Greco-Roman social and familial hierarchy are relativized with democratic principles and modern realities—in fact, according to John Piper's teachings on male and female roles and teachings on headship in the context of

---

[16]See Cynthia Long Westfall's "Male and Female, One in Christ: Galatians 3:26-29," in the present book, in which Gal 3:28 is interpreted with this kind of hermeneutic.

Western culture, every man is meant to have authority and potentially be the equivalent of a *paterfamilias* of his nuclear family, though that was never the case in the first century, nor could it have been understood that way by the recipients of Paul's letters, particularly the male slaves.[17] However, the commands to women that reflect the Greco-Roman constraints of women, and beliefs about the Greco-Roman characteristics associated with femininity, are often taken to reflect absolute and universal biblical principles for all women in all cultures for all time.

GENDER WITHIN PAULINE THEMES

This chapter calls for the construction of a Pauline theology of gender that explores possible coherence of Pauline passages that concern gender with the dominant biblical themes of the Pauline corpus and the narrative of Paul's life, as well as in the literary context, the context of Greco-Roman culture, and the context of the Greek language.[18] Pauline constructions of gender should be examined in the context of larger themes in Pauline theology and mission. The exegesis of the passages on gender should be placed in the context of major Pauline themes and doctrines including creation, fall, eschatology, calling, and authority. The interpretive choices on gender passages for both males and females that create tensions or

---

[17]John Piper asserts that every man has a God-given responsibility for authority and leadership over a woman, which he extends in some form to all relationships between men and women. Consequently, women should nurture (and not compromise) this God-given authority, strength, and leadership in a total stranger in the manner in which she gives him directions. See John Piper, "A Vision of Biblical Complementarity: Manhood and Womanhood Defined According to the Bible," *RBMW*, 41, 59-61.

While many examples can be given of such teachings on headship, see how Raymond Ortlund understands and interprets headship in Gen 1–3 without reference to Pauline passages, though the terminology for headship is only found in the Pauline corpus and must be understood in a Greco-Roman cultural and linguistic context. He places headship in the context of a nuclear marriage in which neither the husband nor wife are answerable to any outside authority in their marriage. The way in which he depicts the husband as exercising primary responsibility and leadership assumes the authority that the *paterfamilias* had, but in fact, the married men in his extended household (free and especially slave) did not have this kind of authority over their wives. Most men in the Greco-Roman culture that Paul addressed were under a social and economic system of checks and balances on any power and authority that they may have. See Raymond C. Ortlund, "Male-Female Equality and Male Headship: Gen 1–3," in *RBMW*, 119-41.

[18]Judith Gundry-Volf asserts, "Paul's teachings on sexuality and gender are especially appropriate for conducting a test case of 'narrative coherence,' in that Paul's discourse on gender is, arguably, one of the most glaring examples of dissonance in the NT." See Gundry-Volf, "Putting the Moral Vision of the New Testament into Focus: A Review," *BBR* 9 (1999): 278.

contradictions within Pauline theology should be reexamined for alternate interpretive options. Conversely, presuppositions about gender should not determine our theology of the Trinity, but rather our understanding of the image of God should inform our theology of humanity as a whole. Interpreters need to be held accountable for the consequences and trajectories of their interpretive choices.

GENDER AND THE GREEK LANGUAGE

I have already made the point that the passages on males and females and the application of general teaching to males and females should use the same hermeneutics. It is unfortunate that some of the primary issues in the study of gender in biblical texts need to be conducted at technical levels that concern grammar, linguistics, and lexicography. While seminary students, pastors, and many academics may not be willing to devote the time to master complex theories of linguistics, the study of the texts that concern gender in the Pauline corpus ought to be continually sensitized and accountable to sound linguistic theory and methodology as much as possible. Every student of Scripture would benefit from developing more sophisticated exegesis that is informed by linguistics, and particularly for how to read texts in the larger context of the epistle in which they occur and how to determine the meaning of words.[19] So much of the gender discussion is controlled by atomistic readings and word studies that claim to be based on linguistic principles but lack sophistication in their approach and fail to use the tools that are available. In part, this may occur because many of the studies are essentially arguments in which scholars gather evidence to make their case rather than conduct

---

[19]Two helpful theories are (1) semantic domains, and (2) how the use of language and particular words varies according to registers. For semantic domains, see L&N 1:vi-xx. See also Cynthia Long Westfall, "Blessed Be the Ties That Bind: Semantic Domains and Cohesive Chains in Hebrews 1:1–2:4 and 12:5-8," *JGRChJ* 6 (2009): 199-216. For an introduction to register, see M. A. K. Halliday and R. Hasan, *Language, Context and Text: Aspects of Language in a Social-Semiotic Perspective* (Geelong, Australia: Deakon University Press, 1985), 36-39. The meaning of a given word is never a case of determining what it means in the majority of occurrences, regardless of the size of the sample. Words have meaning in context.

The study of the entire epistle can be informed by the use of discourse analysis. Discourse analysis cannot be reduced to a single methodology or approach. However, for an overview with an explanation of key concepts, see Cynthia Long Westfall, *A Discourse Analysis of the Letter to the Hebrews*, LNTS 297 (London: T&T Clark, 2005), 22-87.

investigations that utilize criteria and methodology based on sound practices of lexicography.[20] When analysis is properly driven by methodology,
one must be prepared to reach and embrace unanticipated conclusions.

Some who believe in the inspiration of Scripture confuse that doctrine
with "the inspiration of the languages used in the Bible." But biblical writers used human languages that are, according to contemporary linguistics,
embedded in and reflect the values and beliefs of the cultures that use
them. That means that the grammar and vocabulary of the ancient languages in which the Bible was written (Hebrew, Aramaic, and Greek) conveyed and preserved the patriarchal values of those ancient cultures.

There has been a great deal of debate surrounding the issue of grammatical gender and Bible translation, which is addressed in the chapter in
this volume by Jeffrey Miller, "A Defense of Gender-Accurate Bible
Translation."[21] The assumption should be that grammatical gender in the
New Testament language functions as it does in other gendered languages
where the masculine is the default gender, and thus it serves as the inclusive grammatical gender.[22] It should be assumed that the masculine plural
includes the feminine unless it is specifically excluded (or the context of
situation would exclude it), and masculine singular terms will tend to be
used for proverbial and general expressions that may have a feminine referent.[23] However, if women alone are the referents (excluding any men),

---

[20]See my critique of representative studies in Cynthia Long Westfall, "The Meaning of αὐθεντέω
in 1 Timothy 2:12," *JGRChJ* 10 (2014): 138-47, www.jgrchj.net/volume10/JGRChJ10-7_Westfall.pdf.

[21]See also, e.g., Mark Strauss, *Distorting Scripture?: The Challenge of Bible Translation and Gender
Accuracy* (Eugene, OR: Wipf & Stock, 2010); and for a defense of the inclusive use of the masculine grammatical gender in English translation, see Vern S. Poythress and Wayne A. Grudem,
The Gender-Neutral Bible Controversy: Muting the Masculinity of God's Words (Nashville: Broadman & Holman, 2000).

[22]Corbett calls this the "default agreement form," which is "pressing one of the regular gender/
number forms into service" to solve the problem of agreement. See Greville Corbett, *Gender*,
Cambridge Textbooks in Linguistics (Cambridge: Cambridge University Press, 1991), 205. However, the feminine gender exclusively refers to feminine referents. When Paul writes about
"everyone" or "all believers," women would be included as the referents. In general, "brothers"
refers to women as well in Pauline texts.

[23]The debates about *anēr* and *anthrōpos* do not play into this discussion to a great degree except
for certain translation choices. However, *anthrōpos* refers to a "person" or a "human," and the
masculine gender does not select maleness. The word *anthrōpos* has a similar semantic range to
man in English. It can be used generically or proverbially, but in general it conveys maleness
and the sense that male is prototypical for human. However, there is no theology conveyed by
its semantic range or its prototypical use—the Greek language system and the choices that it
offers the writer/speaker should not be treated as inspired.

the feminine will be used, and it will be marked (emphasized) as unusual. There is no theology conveyed in the structure of the Greek language, because the author is using a language system that was a "social semiotic" (a system of signs) embedded in the ancient Greek and Hellenist cultures, which were hardly a reflection of righteous Judeo-Christian values.[24] Rather, biblical theology is conveyed in the choices that apostolic language users make from the language system to create meaning.[25]

GENDER AND THE CULTURE(S) OF THE MEDITERRANEAN AND THE MIDDLE EAST

The significant contribution of social-scientific criticism to biblical studies should be central in understanding the meaning of gender in the Pauline corpus.[26] Within the past twenty-five years, there has been a substantial amount of work on the social systems in the Greco-Roman culture. The rich amount of information about the social structure, combined with linguistic theory and method that explains the relationship between the social structure and language, has proven to be productive.

The use of anthropology, or "demographic borrowing," has been very helpful where views about gender and gender behavior in other parts of the world are much closer to the cultures of the New Testament than the Western world.[27] For example, Islamic ideology and practice concerning gender in the Middle East has marked parallels with the Greco-Roman culture and rabbinic literature. Kenneth Bailey's books, articles, and

---

[24]Language as a social semiotic that is used and produced within a culture is one of the guiding principles of systemic functional linguistics, which is discussed in M. A. K. Halliday, *Language as a Social Semiotic* (London: Edward Arnold, 1978).

[25]One of the major principles of systemic functional linguistics is that meaning is made by the choice of the speaker/writer from the linguistic system (the linguistic system itself is not the meaning). See, e.g., M. A. K. Halliday, "Meaning as Choice," in *Systemic Functional Linguistics: Exploring Choice*, ed. L. Fontaine, T. Bartlett, and G. O'Grady (Cambridge: Cambridge University Press, 2013), 15-36.

[26]See, e.g., Wayne A. Meeks, *The First Urban Christians: The Social World of the Apostle Paul* (New Haven, CT: Yale University Press, 1983); Jerome H. Neyrey and Eric C. Stewart, eds., *The Social World of the New Testament: Insights and Models* (Peabody, MA: Hendrickson, 2008).

[27]See Moyer Hubbard, who describes "demographic borrowing" as a well-established practice among social historians, which is "drawing meaningful analogies between societies that appear to be similar in salient respects, but where one is well documented and the other is not." See Moyer Hubbard, "Kept Safe Through Childbearing: Maternal Mortality, Justification by Faith, and the Social Setting of 1 Timothy 2:15," *JETS* 55 (2012): 753.

scholarship have sensitized readers to "the imposition of Western cultural models and mental attitudes into a Middle Eastern cultural world."[28] Bailey points out that the supposed objective interpretation of Western scholars is actually subjective. However, the Middle Eastern cultural world is an alternate lens for reading first-century Middle Eastern texts, which is far closer to the first-century context of the New Testament. The significant amount of continuity indicates that we can find valid correlations and both correct and avoid misleading anachronisms projected on the text by Western culture. This particularly sheds light on the significance of the veil or head covering for men and women.

THE CONTEXT OF THE GOSPEL ORAL TRADITION AND THE OLD TESTAMENT

What is the relationship between Paul and the oral traditions of the Gospel and the teaching of Jesus that affect our understanding of gender and authority? What is the relationship between Paul and the Law, the Prophets and the Writings?

One of the more serious issues is the assumptions about the nature of authority and power that underlie the entire gender discussion. Paul has been used to support male-dominated authority structures that Jesus criticized, so that there appears to be dissonance between Paul and the teachings of Jesus in the theology and practice of authority. However, Paul demonstrates a great deal of knowledge of the oral tradition behind the Gospels. There are multiple and powerful ties between Jesus' example and teaching on authority and Paul's discussion of authority, submission, and humility in his letters. In understanding Pauline authority, it is better to begin with the Pauline ties to the oral tradition, and then interpret and organize the rest of the Pauline material on authority with Jesus' incarnate example of humility, service, and suffering. This will prove to be helpful

---

[28]Kenneth E. Bailey, "Informal Controlled Oral Tradition and the Synoptic Gospels," *Themelios* 20, no. 2 (1995): 4-11. In this article, Bailey states his methodology as applied to oral tradition: "We intend to present the concrete reality of our own experience of more than three decades of life and study in the Middle East among communities of great antiquity that still preserve in oral form much of what is important to them." See also Bailey, *Jesus Through Middle Eastern Eyes: Cultural Studies in the Gospels* (Downers Grove, IL: InterVarsity Press, 2008); Bailey, *Paul Through Mediterranean Eyes: Cultural Studies in 1 Corinthians* (Downers Grove, IL: InterVarsity Press, 2011).

in evaluating the tradition that equates male priority over women with the authority of the ascended Lord Jesus Christ and the "headship" of God the Father.

Furthermore, the examination of Paul's use of the Old Testament is crucial in understanding gender.[29] The intertextuality between the Pauline letters and the Genesis accounts of creation and fall in the Septuagint (LXX) is extremely important in the analysis of two of the most crucial passages on gender and their immediate context. The traditional interpretations of Paul's texts on gender have often been declared as the authoritative understanding of gender in creation and fall. However, the study of these texts should be used to interpret the Pauline passages and to mediate between interpretive options. Intertextuality within the Pauline corpus, such as the household codes, is also particularly relevant for the passages on gender. We may look at these texts again in the light of the Pauline narrative. In addition, intertextual ties between Paul and Second Temple literature can supply interpretive options, such as 1 Esdras 4.17, which throws light on how woman is the glory of man (1 Cor 11:7) because it clarifies that women's bringing glory to men indicates their superior power.

Another issue is understanding the influence of the history of interpretation that we have inherited.[30] The meaning of the Pauline passages on gender and sexuality changed when interpreters read Platonic dualism and Aristotelian philosophy into the texts. The interpretation of gender passages and passages on authority came to be controlled by privileged members of Western culture who held positions of hierarchical authority in the church and state and who came to have faith in their own modernist objectivity. We have inherited the entire history of conversation, which has changed the meaning of the text. However, the answer is not reader-oriented criticism but a healthy humility and an honest effort to understand

---

[29]For information on the study of the Old Testament in the New Testament, see S. E. Porter, ed., *Hearing the Old Testament in the New Testament*, McMaster NT Studies Series (Grand Rapids, MI: Eerdmans, 2006); J. M. Court, ed., *New Testament Writers and the Old Testament: An Introduction* (London: SPCK, 2002); Steve Moyise, ed., *The Old Testament in the New Testament: Essays in Honour of J. L. North* (Sheffield: Sheffield Academic, 2000).

[30]For an introduction to the theory of intertextuality, see Graham Allen, *Intertextuality* (London: Routledge, 2000). We do not assume all the presuppositions or goals of intertextuality but accept many of the observations of the nature of language as valid.

what the Pauline texts meant to communicate and what impact they were supposed to have when they were written.

CONSIDERING ALTERNATE OCCASIONAL CONTEXTS

There needs to be a commitment to interpreting the Pauline texts as part of the story in Paul's life and as part of a story that lies behind each letter. It has become progressively more apparent that sometimes texts are incoherent because of unexamined assumptions about the occasional context that lies behind a given passage, particularly in the passages that concern gender. Adjusting certain aspects of the occasional context may resolve incoherence. Such adjustments should be consistent with the signals in the text and with the social context. This is particularly relevant to 1 Corinthians 11:3-16 and 1 Timothy 2:8-15. If nothing else, this practice demonstrates the power of context in determining meaning and the deep significance of our exegetical choices in determining the outcome.

THE DOCUMENTS AND DOCTRINES OF
MEN VERSUS THE LIVES OF WOMEN

It is now generally acknowledged by evangelical scholars that interpreters bring their own presuppositions, background, bias, and purposes to the text. It is a major issue that the interpretation of biblical texts that involve gender issues has been controlled by male church authorities, ministers, and scholars. As a result, the traditional theologies are, in effect, examples of reader-oriented interpretation because they assume male experiences, priorities, and special interests by definition. By way of parallel, Jen Gunter, a physician who specializes in women's health, says, "Up until recently, all studies were done by men, and even if they had really great intentions, if you don't have any diversity in the people who are studying things, it's easy to have oversight."[31] What applies to women's health will even more apply to a biblical understanding of gender (characteristics that are associated with male and female, and what differentiates the two). We cannot expect to arrive at a coherent understanding of gender any more than we could expect to understand a coherent and biblical understanding of race if only

---

[31]Rani Sheen, "This Doctor Wants Us to Talk More About Our Vaginas," *The Hamilton Spectator*, August 27, 2019.

the dominant White culture interpreted the data and set the policies, while minorities were excluded from the interpretive process.

Another important issue that is often overlooked is the reality of people's lives that the texts were addressing. The texts should also be read as much as possible through the lens of first-century men's and women's experience, since they were the recipients of the letters. The study of the history of women's lives, views, and religious concerns has been neglected until recently and will illuminate passages that address or correct women. For example, what did the practice of veiling mean to women in the first century?[32] What was the role of Artemis in the lives of women in Ephesus, particularly in regard to childbirth? What did the process of childbirth mean to women in the first century? Did women ever exercise authority in the first-century culture? What were the experiences of women householders, slave owners, freedwomen, and slaves, and how did they fit in Paul's instructions? We may assume that Paul was attempting to communicate with real women and that he took their lives and situations into account.

Changed views on women over the last half of the twentieth century were based in great part on a combination of data, statistics, and experiences comparable to Paul's experiences in the Gentile revival at Antioch that led to the formulation of his theology of salvation by faith alone. Formerly, the ontological beliefs about gender in the church traditions generally remained consistent with the rhetoric of the Greco-Roman first-century culture. However, data and statistics together with the education of women have seriously challenged views on women and men that have been taken for granted for thousands of years, and have overturned many societal practices and strictures that restricted or disadvantaged women

---

[32]The interpretations of women's behavior in Corinth sound a lot like bra burning in the 1960s. As one man observed to me, "It has always seemed to me that the issue in 1 Corinthians 11 is the same as what I see with parochial school uniforms—the girls are always hiking up their skirts shorter, unbuttoning their blouses lower and wearing their sweaters tighter." But I argue in *Paul and Gender*, 34-36, assuming a rebellious flaunting of propriety among the women is an implausible presupposition historically, culturally, and textually. It renders 1 Cor 11:2-16 incoherent, especially 1 Cor 11:11, where Paul concludes that a woman ought to have authority over her head—this contradiction has led English translations to say the exact opposite: a woman ought to wear a symbol of authority (symbolizing their subjugation) on their head. See also Lynn Cohick's critique of similar ideas about the liberated "new woman" in Corinth in *Women in the World of the Earliest Christians: Illuminating Ancient Ways of Life* (Grand Rapids, MI: Baker Academic, 2009), 72-75.

on the basis of perceived inferiority in intellectual capacity, moral, and ethical facilities, and physical strength and stamina.

EGALITARIAN HERMENEUTICS AND
THE LGTBQ COMMUNITY

There has been a marked tendency among conservative believers to directly link the issue of the status of women to the issue of the status of individuals in the LGTBQ community in the kingdom of God, the church, home, and society. However, in the Pauline corpus, such a correlation does not exist. In the church, the status of women is parallel with the status of Gentiles in relationship to Jews, and the status of slaves in relationship to free. That is, the issue of gender (as male/female) collocates with race and social status, and there women are parallel to Gentiles, who were disadvantaged religiously, and slaves, who were disadvantaged socially. In the household, the function of wives is linked to but also contrasted with the status of two other groups that were disadvantaged in the power differential in the Greco-Roman home. These other groups were based on Aristotle's household code: children in relationship to parents, and slaves in relationship to masters.

The Pauline corpus (and the Old Testament) addresses sexual intercourse between those with the same biological gender, but the Bible does not address the full range of LGBTQ identities and issues that have been brought up in the current debate.[33] In the Pauline corpus, same-sex intercourse is placed into vice lists in Romans 1:26-27; 1 Corinthians 6:9-10; and 1 Timothy 1:10.[34] Therefore, the biblical questions that concern the status of those who participate in same-sex intercourse are distinctly different from the issue of the status of women in the kingdom of God, the church, home, and society. The nature, identity, and function of women is never

---

[33]Though the initials LGBTQ originally referred to lesbian, gay, bisexual, transgender, and queer (or questioning), the initials now represent a diversity of sexuality and gender-based cultures. The Bible addresses same-sex intercourse (Lev 18:22; 20:13; Rom 1:26-27; 1 Cor 6:9-10; 1 Tim 1:10) and cross-dressing, which may be an outward expression of noncisgendered person (Deut 22:5).

[34]For example, 1 Cor 6:9-10: "Don't you know that people who are unjust won't inherit God's kingdom? Don't be deceived. Those who are sexually immoral, those who worship false gods, adulterers, both participants in same-sex intercourse, thieves, the greedy, drunks, abusive people, and swindlers won't inherit God's kingdom" (CEB).

identified in the Pauline corpus with the qualities on the vice lists in a way that men are not. The Bible does not correlate women and their function in the church, home, and the kingdom of God with same-sex intercourse and ethical/moral issues.

One primary criticism is that both groups use the same hermeneutics to support their position.[35] Wayne Grudem names evangelical scholars Howard Marshall, Richard France, and David Thompson, who, he argues, are on a liberal trajectory that leads to "the approval of homosexuality."[36] However, these scholars are arguing that certain of Paul's instructions/commands to women are situational or cultural rather than universal, which is a valid application of a widely recognized principle of biblical interpretation. Their arguments more accurately parallel biblical arguments for the abolition of slavery—a parallel established by Paul in Galatians 3:28 and the household codes.[37] Other hermeneutics shared by egalitarian and affirming scholars deal with the mistranslation of words, word studies, the meaning of texts in the cultural context, and the meaning of texts in their literary context, all of which are standard exegetical practice. The use of standard principles of interpretation and hermeneutical approaches does not undermine the authority of Scripture; they rather challenge the authority of the traditional interpretations. Of course, the question must be whether a given argument is convincing, and there must be controls as to what counts for evidence. The Pauline instructions for women are laden with interpretive issues that render the traditional position open to question. In contrast, the consistent and specific ethical prohibitions of same-sex intercourse in the Old Testament and Paul's statements in the New Testament render a situational interpretation implausible and unconvincing. The validity of each scholar's interpretation and their application of

---

[35]Roy Clements writes, "Gay Christians are using exactly the same kind of hermeneutic tools [as egalitarians] to challenge tradition in regard to homosexuality." Quoted by Grudem with italics in *Evangelical Feminism: A New Path to Liberalism* (Wheaton, IL: Crossway Books, 2006), 238.

[36]Grudem, *Evangelical Feminism*, 237n1. He cross-references his comments with 59-60, where he names Thompson, France, and Marshall. The quotation "the approval of homosexuality" is taken from the chapter title on p. 237.

[37]Most evangelical Christians in North America reject slavery as unbiblical. They are compelled by scriptural statements, the biblical narrative, and the trajectory of Scripture.

the principles of biblical interpretation should be evaluated according to their own merits.[38]

CONCLUSION

Paul did not share the Greco-Roman view of women that the church later adopted, nor did he teach or wield hierarchical authority and power within his churches that was comparable to the authoritative power structures that developed in Christian traditions. I suggest that the impact of assumptions and new methodologies, together with the new information about the Greco-Roman social system, and the ontological nature of women, requires a robust reworking of the Pauline theology of gender. Not only do interpreters need to change their confessions about the ontological equality of genders, but biblical scholars and theologians need to also follow Paul's example and exegesis in a systematic deconstruction of the theological and interpretive systems that were built on assumptions of hierarchy and power inconsistent with Paul's teaching. The new wine needs some new wineskins.

---

[38]See the chapter in this volume by Ronald W. Pierce, "Biblical Equality and Same-Sex Marriage."

22

GENDER DIFFERENCES AND BIBLICAL INTERPRETATION

A VIEW FROM THE SOCIAL SCIENCES

M. Elizabeth Lewis Hall

*Men have broad and large chests, and small narrow hips,
and more understanding than women, who have but small and
narrow breasts, and broad hips, to the end they should remain
at home, sit still, keep house, and bear and bring up children.*

MARTIN LUTHER, *TABLE TALK*

• • • • •

WHAT DOES IT MEAN TO BE A MAN? What does it mean to be a woman? What is masculinity and femininity? What are the differences between men and women? Are we different? What implications do the answers to these questions have for our lives? These issues—never easy—have become ever more complicated in a society where the notion of gender is increasingly challenged. In this area, as in so many other areas where we seek to understand and live out God's will in our lives, we often try to piece together what we learn from our Bible with what we know to be true because of our engagement with the world around us. Christian thinkers throughout the centuries have encouraged this approach, arguing that truth, wherever it can be found, comes from God. Augustine, for example, affirmed that "every good and true Christian should understand that wherever he may find truth, it is his Lord's."[1] Despite the underlying unity of truth, the challenge comes in disentangling truth from error, whether that error be interpretive error in understanding God's Word or interpretive and methodological error in understanding God's world.

In the area of gender, this desire to connect what we learn from Scripture and what we learn (or intuitively know to be true) from the world around us is undoubtedly present. Throughout history, biblical interpretations of passages relevant to gender have been drawn together with observations about gender differences based on experience. For example, Aquinas saw the need for women to be subject to men because "their conduct is not based on solid reason, but easily swayed by feeling."[2] In a more contemporary example, Wayne Grudem argues for gender differences on the basis of what he calls "internal testimony from both men's and women's hearts." He presented as evidence his perceptions of differences in internal desires. According to Grudem, men desire to provide for their family, and women desire to depend on men. These presumed differences are explicitly tied to his own experiences. He states, "I have never met a man who does not feel some measure of shame at the idea of being supported by his wife in the long term. . . . I have never met a woman who did not want her husband to provide that sense of security for her." Later in the same book he makes the claim that "men in general are more aggressive and women in general are more relational; men tend to seek leadership roles and women tend to affirm and support men in those roles."[3] He does not specify the basis for these claims, suggesting that they, too, are based on his own perceptions of reality.

Often, these common sense observations are assumed to reflect enduring, changeless differences shared by all members of each sex, a view known as gender essentialism. Sometimes, in a form of gender

---

[1] Augustine, *On Christian Doctrine*, trans. J. Shaw (Oxford: Benediction Classics, 2010), 2.75.

[2] Thomas Aquinas, "Well Tempered Passion," *Summa Theologica* 44:21, trans. Thomas Gilby, quoted in Daniel Doriani, "A History of the Interpretation of 1 Timothy 2," in *Women in the Church: A Fresh Analysis of 1 Timothy 2:9-15*, ed. Andreas J. Köstenberger, Thomas R. Schreiner, and H. Scott Baldwin (Grand Rapids, MI: Baker, 1995), 231.

[3] Wayne Grudem, *Evangelical Feminism and Biblical Truth* (Sisters, OR: Multnomah, 2004), 45, 487.

essentialism known as biological reductivism, conclusions are reached about how men and women are different psychologically based on how they are different physically. This is exemplified in the quote from Martin Luther at the beginning of the chapter. Or, in a more contemporary variation, gender differences are believed to be "wholly and directly determined by genetic differences (e.g. the different sex chromosomes) between men and women."[4] Evidence of biologically based versions of gender essentialism can be seen in contemporary scholarship on gender debates. In this vein, John Piper cites, with approval, Emil Brunner's essentializing statement that "the physical differences between the man and the woman are a parable of psychical and spiritual differences of a more ultimate nature."[5]

The challenge to confirming certain interpretations with our own observations is that it is quite clear that we do not perceive the world—much less gendered others—in unbiased ways. I imagine most people reading this chapter would be uncomfortable with Luther's observations about gender differences, demonstrating how our perceptions of gender differences are influenced by factors such as culture and history. The psychological study of gender schemas demonstrates quite persuasively that one of our primary filters for interpreting the world is what Sandra Bem long ago called "gender lenses."[6] We see what we expect to see. Recent research has demonstrated that more sexist people tend to perceive greater gender differences.[7] Furthermore, our gender schemas act powerfully in our own lives, as we unconsciously adapt to the gendered expectations of others and internalize those expectations through socialization processes. One of the largest areas of gender difference is in the self-endorsement of sex-consistent stereotypical traits—even in the absence of documented gender

---

[4]K. Lippert-Rasmussen, "Gender Constructions: The Politics of Biological Constraints," *Distinktion: Scandinavian Journal of Social Theory* 11, no. 1 (2010): 74.

[5]John Piper, "A Vision of Biblical Complementarity: Manhood and Womanhood Defined According to the Bible," in *RBMW*, 39.

[6]Sandra L. Bem, "Gender Schema Theory: A Cognitive Account of Sex Typing," *Psychological Review* 88, no. 4 (1981): 354-64. For a more recent summary of this point, see C. N. Macrae and G. V. Bodenhausen, "Social Cognition: Thinking Categorically About Others," *Annual Review of Psychology* 51 (2000): 93-120.

[7]Ethan Zell, Jason E. Strickhouser, Tyler N. Lane, and Sabrina R. Teeter, "Mars, Venus, or Earth? Sexism and the Exaggeration of Psychological Gender Differences," *Sex Roles* 75 (2016): 287-300.

differences in these traits.[8] In a self-confirming process, the world we observe conforms to our expectations of it. Presumed gender differences become self-evident truths. A wealth of psychological studies confirms these points. Consequently, it is unwise to assume generalized differences between genders based on our own experience.

In more recent decades, as the more systematic methods of science have developed and given rise to ways of learning about the world that are less influenced by biases, these common sense observations about gender have often given way to the findings of science, especially the social sciences, with respect to gender differences. It has now become common to support biblical interpretations by appealing to ways in which these interpretations coincide with social-scientific findings about gender differences. Following cultural trends, this appeal to science is thought to be particularly strong when it is drawn from neuroscience. Appeals to brain differences between men and women are presented as evidence for creation design in gender differences.

In theory, it is a marvelous idea to attempt a more accurate understanding of truth by bringing together biblical teachings and the findings of science. If all truth is God's truth, we can learn a great deal from bringing God's Word and God's world into dialogue. It can actually be problematic to ignore social science findings, such as when the Bible is interpreted as indicating certain gender differences when social science finds no gender differences in that particular area. For example, Douglas Moo argued in an article on 1 Timothy 2:11-15 that women are more easily deceived than men and that "this susceptibility to deception bars them from engaging in public teaching."[9] However, psychological findings fail to confirm this gender difference.[10] Moo later retracted his claim.[11]

In practice, however, these attempts to integrate the findings of social science have been negatively affected by a number of factors. First,

---

[8]Ethan Zell, Zlatan Krizan, and Sabrina R. Teeter, "Evaluating Gender Similarities and Differences Using Metasynthesis," *American Psychologist* 70, no. 1 (2015): 15.

[9]Douglas Moo, "1 Timothy 2:11-15: Meaning and Significance," *Trinity Journal* 1, no. 1 (1980): 70.

[10]Alice H. Eagly and Linda L. Carli, "Sex of Researchers and Sex-Typed Communications as Determinants of Sex Differences in Influenceability: A Meta-Analysis of Social Influence Studies," *Psychological Bulletin* 90, no. 1 (1981): 1-20.

[11]Douglas Moo, "What Does It Mean Not to Teach or Have Authority over Men? 1 Timothy 2," in *RBMW*, 247.

limitations in the ability to understand the findings of the social sciences have resulted in misunderstandings and misuse of these findings. This problem has been further exacerbated by an overreliance on popular media depictions of the social-scientific findings, and by undue confidence being placed on neuroscientific findings. Second, high-level scholarly sources summarizing research in the area of gender are largely ignored, and the more dubious approach of selectively drawing on isolated studies to support points is used instead.

In this chapter, I will attempt to address these limitations in the following three ways. First, I will briefly provide information that is necessary for understanding the social science of gender differences and for accurately drawing implications from these studies. Second, I will review the most current and sophisticated findings on gender differences. Third, I will highlight some ways of moving forward in the integration of social-scientific findings with biblical interpretation of gender differences.

UNDERSTANDING SOCIAL-SCIENTIFIC FINDINGS

In this section I will cover a number of issues related to correctly interpreting scientific findings. I will illustrate these points by drawing on problematic interpretations in the existing literature on the gender-difference debates.

Categorical and average differences. Let us begin with what it means to say that there are gender *differences*. Biological sex (with some exceptions) is a *categorical* variable. In other words, it consists of two nonoverlapping categories. Most people intuitively think of all gender differences—not just biological sex—as categorical differences. In other words, they attribute certain characteristics to women as a group, and opposing characteristics to men as a group. As I noted above, people tend to be gender essentialists. "Men are rational; women are emotional." "Men are aggressive; women are nurturing." When popular media (including popular-level books distributed widely in Christian circles) discusses social science findings, it tends to misrepresent these findings by using this kind of categorical language. For example, one recent Christian book summarized men's and women's brain differences by stating, "The Creator's plan is that [his] brain is designed to truly love, honor, nourish, and cherish [his spouse] . . . and [her] brain is designed to truly respect, admire, and encourage [her spouse]."[12]

The problem is that, with the exception of biological sex characteristics, all documented gender differences are not categorical differences but *average* differences (most of them quite small—but more on that later) in *continuous* variables. The distribution of most continuous psychological variables takes the shape of a normal curve (see fig. 22.1).

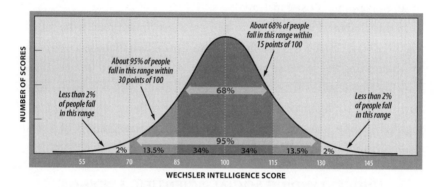

Fig. 22.1. The normal curve

Take the distribution of intelligence (a trait that most people consider gender neutral).[13] Without going into too much technical detail, the significant point is that most people are around the middle of the distribution; most people have an average level of intelligence. This is why the middle of the normal curve is the highest point. There are fewer people in the extremes. These are the people with very high intelligence or very low intelligence. Since there are fewer people in these categories, the ends of the bell curve are very low. When we want to compare men and women on some psychological trait, we can depict the gender differences through the use of two normal curves, one for men and one for women (see fig. 22.2).

---

[12]Walt Larimore and Barb Larimore, *His Brain, Her Brain: How Divinely Designed Differences Can Strengthen Your Marriage*, Kindle ed. (Grand Rapids, MI: Zondervan, 2008), 204-5.

[13]Although, ironically, nineteenth-century scientific opinion held that women were intellectually inferior, and attributed this to their smaller and lighter brains. See C. E. Russett, *Sexual Science: The Victorian Construction of Womanhood* (Cambridge, MA: Harvard University Press, 1989).

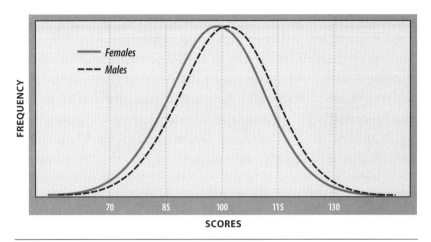

Fig. 22.2. Hypothetical trait distribution showing gender differences

One important thing to note is that, with average differences, there is not a clean difference between men and women—the difference is not categorical. Instead, the normal curves are overlapping. Consequently, we cannot draw conclusions based on these average differences about the differences between any particular man and any particular woman. So, one important point about gender differences is that, with the exception of biological sex, gender differences are *average* differences.

Significance and meaningfulness. A second area of confusion in understanding social-scientific results has to do with the word *significant*. In popular usage, *significant* means substantial, something that makes a real difference in the world. This is not the case in the social sciences. In statistical usage of the word, it simply means that the difference found between men and women has less than a 5 percent chance of being due simply to chance. In other words, it means that the chances are good that it is a stable difference, that it reflects an actual difference in the real world. However, the word has no implications for the size of the difference, or for the real-life importance of the finding. Whether significance is found depends substantially on the size of the sample. With large samples, even very tiny average differences may be statistically significant, a fact that is usually ignored by media accounts of scientific findings.

To understand whether significant statistical differences are actually meaningful differences in terms of real-life implications, we look to the *effect sizes.* I will not go into details here about the statistical details of effect sizes. It is sufficient to know that there are conventions within the social sciences for classifying effect sizes as small, medium, or large.[14] In the section that follows, I will discuss gender differences in terms of these established categories. For now, I simply note that most gender differences are small enough that the normal curves are almost entirely overlapping (as in fig. 22.2). The differences we find on any given trait are much larger *within* each sex than they are *between* the sexes. In practice, simply knowing that someone is a man or a woman will not give us any guidance with respect to how much they have a given trait. Consequently, it is simply misleading (and potentially deceptive) to make statements about meaningful differences between men and women based on most of these findings.

Examples of this kind of use of statistical results are rampant. For example, George Alan Rekers alludes to a number of gender differences in his chapter in *Recovering Biblical Manhood and Womanhood.*[15] He argues for strong gender differences and in a footnote outlines a number of gender differences based on "numerous research studies." The list includes mathematical skills, verbal skills, nurturance, sociability, and empathy. Unfortunately, none of these presented findings are nuanced with effect sizes, and all of these gender differences are in areas where only small gender differences have been found.

Choosing good sources. Individual psychological studies can be affected by the ways in which participants were recruited to participate, by biases introduced during the course of the experiment, or even by idiosyncrasies in the particular population from which participants are drawn. Consequently, the results of individual studies should be taken with a certain degree of caution. In addition, all of the research in a particular area should be taken into account so that we do not selectively choose the studies that support what we want them to support. When many studies exist in a certain area, it is possible to statistically aggregate the results of all the studies to arrive at an overall bottom line about the area in question. This technique is called *meta-analysis.* Meta-analyses are able to summarize the results of

---

[14]J. Cohen, *Statistical Power Analysis for the Behavioral Sciences,* 2nd ed. (Hillsdale, NJ: Erlbaum, 1988).
[15]George Alan Rekers, "Psychological Foundations for Rearing Masculine Boys and Feminine Girls," in *RBMW,* 2nd ed., 308, 522n57.

all available studies in a certain area, taking into account the size of each sample and the variability of scores in each sample, in order to arrive at an effect size for all of the studies together. When meta-analyses are available, they should be preferred over the results of individual studies.

Unfortunately, much of the social-scientific literature employed in the gender debates relies heavily on individual studies or fails to acknowledge existing meta-analyses. Gregg Johnson, for example, in his chapter in *Recovering Biblical Manhood and Womanhood*, bases all psychological claims about gender differences on a review of the literature by Eleanor Maccoby and Carol Nagy Jacklin—a review that was done in 1974, before meta-analyses were in widespread use in psychology.[16] Many of the conclusions reached in that review have been undermined by more recent meta-analyses (and had been undermined at the time Johnson published his chapter).

Certain popular social scientists also tend to be cited frequently in the gender debates.[17] The most common of these are psychologist Carol Gilligan's *In a Different Voice* and linguist Deborah Tannen's *You Just Don't Understand*. These books proposed important gender differences in moral reasoning and communication styles, respectively, and are often referenced in support of gender differences. For example, Timothy Keller cites Gilligan in defending his interpretation of what woman as "helper" actually means. "Women have a gift of interdependence, a 'receiving' gift. They are inwardly perceptive. They nurture."[18] However, a meta-analysis on gender differences in moral orientation found only small differences, undermining Gilligan's claims, and meta-analyses on traits such as empathy and helping have also failed to find substantial gender differences.[19] Similarly, several meta-analyses on communication have found no or small differences in communication styles, undermining Tannen's claims.[20]

---

[16]Eleanor E. Maccoby and Carol Nagy Jacklin, *The Psychology of Sex Differences* (Stanford, CA: Stanford University Press, 1974).

[17]John Gray's *Men Are from Mars, Women Are from Venus* will not be addressed here, as it is a popular-level book with no scientific backing that should not be brought into academic discussions.

[18]Timothy Keller, *The Meaning of Marriage: Facing the Complexities of Commitment with the Wisdom of God* (New York: Penguin Books, 2011).

[19]S. Jaffee and Janet S. Hyde, "Gender Differences in Moral Orientation: A Meta-Analysis," *Psychological Bulletin* 126, no. 5 (2000): 703-26.

[20]Janet Shibley Hyde, "The Gender Similarities Hypothesis," *American Psychologist* 60, no. 6 (2005): 583-84.

Creation design or consequence of the fall? Once we understand the statistical results, we are still left to figure out what the results mean. What can we conclude on the basis of social-scientific findings about gender differences? A common mistake is to interpret them as unequivocal evidence of creation design. This conclusion is not warranted for two reasons—one theological, and one psychological. First, social-scientific findings regarding gender differences are snapshots in time. They describe things as they are. From a theological perspective, this means that these findings reflect both our creation in the image of God and our fall into sin. Consequently, gender differences should not be taken as prescriptive. They tell us only what is, not what should be. We might hypothesize that certain differences reflect creation design or fall, but we cannot draw firm conclusions merely on the basis of social-scientific findings.

Second, these findings cannot give us a clear picture of creation design, because they reflect both nature and nurture, both our biological givens and the ways in which our biological givens interact in complex ways with our experiences. While men and women may not differ much in their traits, their lived experiences throughout the ages, and in our current context, do differ. This means that men and women are exposed to different shaping influences. These shaping influences begin as soon as we leave the womb (and perhaps even prenatally).[21] Research has demonstrated that we perceive and interact with babies differently beginning very early in life. A series of experiments was conducted in which adults were shown an unfamiliar infant, labeled as either a girl or a boy. These studies showed a number of differences in the ways adults interacted with the infants. For example, adults talked more to girls but encouraged motor activities with boys.[22] They described the girls as littler, softer, finer featured, and more inattentive than boys. These gendered experiences of the world, like the traits themselves, reflect the good and the bad of living in a world designed by God and affected by the fall.

Many instances of interpreting gender differences as evidence of God's intention for creation can be found in the gender debates. David Ayers, in

---

[21]Medora W. Barner, "Anticipatory Socialization of Pregnant Women: Learning Fetal Sex and Gendered Interactions," *Sociological Perspectives* 58, no. 2 (2015): 187-203.

[22]Marily Stern and Katherine Hildebrandt Karraker, "Sex Stereotyping of Infants: A Review of Gender Labeling Studies," *Sex Roles* 20, no. 9/10 (1989): 501-22.

a chapter in *Recovering Biblical Manhood and Womanhood*, makes the broad claim that "professionals in the biological and social sciences are generating findings that support the traditional viewpoint that healthy individuals and societies express, rather than deny, the complementary differences between the sexes."[23] He goes on to cite not academic sources, much less meta-analyses, but books on gender differences written for a popular audience. He summarizes these differences as follows: "The primary examples of universal male/female differences lie in the areas of male dominance, superiority in status achievement, and patriarchy."[24] I find it troubling that any Christian would see male domination and status as evidence of "healthy individuals and societies." These gender differences certainly are not consistent with biblical interpretations from either the complementarian or the egalitarian perspectives. Instead, these "universal male/female differences" seem to paint a picture of a broken world, a point to which I will later return.

Additional interpretive challenges with brain studies. Increasingly, neuroscientific findings touting differences in the brain are invoked in gender debates. For example, *Recovering Biblical Manhood and Womanhood* includes a chapter by Gregg Johnson, a biologist, on the biological basis for gender-specific behavior. In this chapter Johnson argues for a "divinely ordained and biologically rooted division of gifts between the sexes."[25] He then proceeds to review biological sex differences, including sex differences in the brain. Space precludes my giving an exhaustive critique of this chapter. The same cautions against overemphasizing small, average differences are in order with respect to the differences he covers in the chapter. One example would be his conclusions about differential use of both sides of the brain by men and women, as I will discuss more fully below. However, there are additional problems.

The tendency to see a kind of creation design in gender differences is particularly evident when discussing gender differences in the brain, as illustrated in Johnson's chapter. However, the same problems noted above

---

[23]David J. Ayers, "The Inevitability of Failure: The Assumptions and Implementations of Modern Feminism," in *RBMW*, 376.

[24]Ayers, "Inevitability of Failure," 377.

[25]Gregg Johnson, "The Biological Basis for Gender-Specific Behavior," in *RBMW*, 353.

apply to brain differences. Biological differences reflect the consequences of the fall. They also reflect the results of life experience, as we are increasingly learning that the plasticity of the brain—the capacity of the nervous system to change its organization and function over time—allows it to adapt in response to experiences. A gender difference in the brain in no way indicates that the difference is not learned; in fact, all learned behaviors will in some way change the brain. In other words, the results of brain studies are not *explanations* for gender differences and should not be used as such.[26]

The use of brain studies to argue for gender differences brings with it additional complexities for interpretation. In the first place, the popular preference for scientific findings that we can see, touch, and measure means that we tend to place unwarranted confidence in these kinds of studies, seeing them as somehow definitive. There is actually research on preferences for neuroscientific findings. In one study, participants were asked to evaluate psychology explanations that did or did not contain neuroscience information.[27] Participants with no neuroscience training found the psychology explanations with neuroscience information more satisfying. However, participants who were experts in neuroscience rated the explanations with neuroscience information as significantly less satisfying! A follow-up study found that including any mention of the brain in the explanation caused participants to lose the ability to distinguish between good psychological explanations and bad ones.[28] Clearly, neuroscientific findings must be interpreted carefully and with appropriate nuance.

Furthermore, Johnson's approach is subject to the same critiques as those leveled against more primitive forms of biological gender essentialism. If the argument is being made that men's and women's traits and behaviors are different in ways that make them suited for different roles, then simply identifying biological differences does not do the job. It must

---

[26]For additional reading on interpreting brain differences, see Diane M. Beck, "The Appeal of the Brain in the Popular Press," *Perspectives on Psychological Science* 5, no. 6 (2010): 762-66.

[27]Deena Skolnick Weisberg et al., "The Seductive Allure of Neuroscience Explanations," *Journal of Cognitive Neuroscience* 20, no. 3 (2008): 470-77.

[28]Deena Skolnick Weisberg, Jordan C. V. Taylor, and Emily J. Hopkins, "Deconstructing the Seductive Allure of Neuroscience Explanations," *Judgment and Decision Making* 10, no. 5 (2015): 429-41.

be demonstrated that these biological differences do, in fact, result in the kinds of gender differences in traits and behavior that are postulated, and it must be demonstrated that these biological differences are the cause, rather than the consequence, of the behaviors. This brings us back again to the social-scientific findings. Since Johnson recognizes that these psychological studies do not bear out his conclusions about essential biological differences, he attempts to discredit these studies, stating, "Although some studies have come to different conclusions than those represented in this chapter, most of the support for those conclusions appears to be based on psychological survey and test data that are more suspect than those underlying this survey."[29] However, there is no clear reason to think that the psychological studies are more suspect than the studies that he covers. If you state that women have biological differences that should make them more nurturing than men, but then find in psychological studies that women are not more nurturing than men, the inferences drawn from the biological studies should clearly be questioned. This discrepancy should lead us to question the assumption that these specific biological differences are, in fact, causal with respect to certain hypothesized psychological differences. In fact, little is still known about how neural structures contribute to complex psychological phenomena, making strong psychological claims based on brain differences inappropriate.[30] There simply is no one-to-one mapping between brain regions and psychological processes; human are too complex for this kind of mapping.

The importance of these problems can be illustrated by the often-cited claim that males are more strongly left-hemisphere dominant for language processing and right-hemisphere dominant for visuospatial processing, while females engage both hemispheres for these tasks. Given women's supposed use of both hemispheres, the claim is also made that the corpus callosum—the bundle of fibers that connects the hemispheres—is thicker in women. These differences are then provided as evidence for a number of claims about supposed psychological differences between men and

---

[29]Johnson, "Biological Basis for Gender-Specific Behavior," 353.

[30]Cordelia Fine, "From Scanner to Sound Bite: Issues in Interpreting and Reporting Sex Differences in the Brain," *Current Directions in Psychological Science* 19, no. 5 (2010): 280-83. See also C. Fine, *Delusions of Gender: How Our Minds, Society, and Neurosexism Create Difference* (New York: W. W. Norton, 2010).

women, including the claim that this makes men more logical and able to succeed in the sciences but less able to talk about their feelings, and makes women more empathic, more verbal, and better at multitasking. Johnson cites this research, basing his claims on several individual studies.[31]

This biologically based theory of gender differences has a number of problems. First, it should be noted that the most sophisticated approach to studying these brain differences (using meta-analysis, a technique described below) has not found sex differences in use of the brain hemispheres, nor in the thickness of the corpus callosum (taking into account absolute brain mass).[32] There simply is no such thing as a male brain distinct from a female brain. Second, these claims are made in spite of evidence that men and women do not actually differ on the psychological processes that are assumed to be associated with differential use of the brain hemispheres, as will be reviewed in the next section. Until we know much more about the brain, it might be best to simply leave brain studies out of the gender debate and focus on studies of actual psychological traits and behaviors.

HOW ARE MEN AND WOMEN DIFFERENT?

Fortunately, in the area of gender differences there are thousands of studies that have been summarized in many meta-analyses. Even more fortunately, in 2005 psychologist Janet Hyde published a landmark article in the leading publication in psychology, the *American Psychologist*. In this article, she summarized all existing meta-analyses at that point, encompassing hundreds of individual studies. Taking advantage of the wave of meta-analyses engendered by Hyde's seminal article, a second review of meta-analyses on gender differences was published in 2015, also in the *American Psychologist*, encompassing over twenty thousand individual studies.[33] We will briefly cover the findings of these two reviews here, as well as supplementing the conclusions of these reviews with a few more recent meta-analyses. In addition, given the many potential areas of gender differences, we will focus only on those that have implications for theological gender debates.

---

[31]Johnson, "Biological Basis for Gender-Specific Behavior," 361-64.

[32]I. E. Sommer et al., "Sex Differences in Handedness, Asymmetry of the Planum Temporale and Functional Language Lateralization," *Brain Research* 1206 (2008): 76-88.

[33]Zell et al., "Evaluating Gender Similarities and Differences," 2015.

Close-to-zero and small differences. Following conventions in the social sciences, Hyde divided the gender differences from the reviewed meta-analyses into categories based on their effect sizes: close-to-zero, small, moderate, and large differences. Of the 124 potential gender differences that she reviewed, 30 percent were in the close-to-zero range, and an additional 48 percent were in the small range. That is, 78 percent of the gender differences that she examined are small or close to zero. Ethan Zell and colleagues found that 85 percent of 386 potential gender differences were in this range. Figure 22.2 shows overlapping normal curves illustrating a small gender difference. Given the degree of overlap between the genders, it should be clear that differences that fall in this category are not meaningful differences between the sexes. On these variables, men and women are more alike than different.

What is striking about these gender differences in the close-to-zero and small effect size categories is that many of them are in areas that have typically been seen as areas of important differences between men and women. It is often claimed that men are more rational than women, emphasizing a difference in cognitive capacities. However, in mathematical performance, most areas have nonexistent or small differences. The ability to mentally rotate objects in space is the one domain where moderate differences are found. It is unclear whether this is a biologically based gender difference, since studies show that it is susceptible to environmental influences, as evidenced by a decline in the magnitude of the difference over time and with training.[34] Similarly, differences in verbal skills are nonexistent or small. In conclusion, men and women largely do not differ in their cognitive capacities.

A related claim is that women are more gullible.[35] To be gullible means to be "easily persuaded to believe something; credulous."[36] This claim has been tested multiple times. A meta-analysis examining whether women are influenced more by others than are men found only close-to-zero and small effects.[37] These included studies that examined attempts to persuade

---

[34]Janet Shibley Hyde, "Gender Similarities and Differences," *Annual Review of Psychology* 65 (2014): 382.

[35]Moo, "1 Timothy 2:11-15," 70.

[36]"Gullible," Oxford English Dictionary, https://en.oxforddictionaries.com/definition/gullible.

[37]Eagly and Carli, "Sex of Researchers."

participants and attempts to make participants conform under group-pressure situations. Similarly, in spite of widespread claims that men are more impartial in their moral reasoning and that women are more swayed by their relational commitments, gender differences in moral reasoning and moral orientation are small.[38]

What about in social and personality variables? Women are typically seen as more emotional than men, but there are no significant gender differences in emotionality or negative emotions, and only small differences in positive emotions, guilt, and shame, favoring women.[39] Men are perceived as being protectors. Consequently, one might expect to find gender differences in helping behaviors. A meta-analysis of helping behaviors showed only a small difference in helping behaviors, favoring men. Across studies, gender differences in helping were largest when onlookers were present and disappeared when no onlookers were present. Similarly, self-reported empathy shows a large difference favoring females, but when unobtrusive measures of empathy are used, sex differences disappear.[40]

Leadership variables are clearly of interest in theological gender debates. Meta-analyses show that men and women do not differ in leadership effectiveness, when either objective or subjective measures of effectiveness were used. With respect to leadership style, there are no gender differences in transformational leadership, a style in which the leader serves as a positive role model based on gaining the trust of the followers. In transactional leadership, there is a small difference favoring females with respect to reward-based approaches, and a small difference favoring men with respect to punishment-based approaches. Men are also slightly more likely to engage in laissez-faire leadership.[41]

In summary, in most psychological areas in which potential gender differences have been explored, these studies have failed to find differences

---

[38]Hyde, "Gender Similarities Hypothesis," 586.

[39]Zell et al., "Evaluating Gender Similarities and Differences," 2015; Hyde, "Gender Similarities and Differences," 383.

[40]Nancy Eisenberg and Randy Lennon, "Sex Differences in Empathy and Related Capacities," *Psychological Bulletin* 94, no. 1 (1983): 100-131; T. D. Wager et al., "Valence, Gender and Lateralization of Functional Brain Anatomy in Emotion: A Meta-Analysis of Findings from Neuroimaging," *NeuroImage* 19 (2003): 513-31. See also Kalina J. Michalskaa, Katherine D. Kinzlera, and Jean Decetya, "Age-Related Sex Differences in Explicit Measures of Empathy Do Not Predict Brain Responses Across Childhood and Adolescence," *Developmental Cognitive Neuroscience* 3 (2013): 22-32.

[41]Hyde, "Gender Similarities and Differences," 387.

or have found small average differences. Given the large degree of overlap in these areas, it is misleading to make claims about meaningful gender differences in these areas. Among areas in this category are cognitive abilities (except mental rotation), the ability to be persuaded by others, morality, emotionality, helping behaviors, and leadership.

Moderate and large differences. How about the moderate and large areas of difference, where we find 15 percent of the differences? In addition to the mental-rotation finding, mentioned above, the largest gender difference is in motor performance, especially in areas such as throwing velocity and throwing distance. These differences are more marked after puberty, when the gender gap in muscle mass and bone size widens.[42] Men also show a commensurately greater confidence in their physical abilities.[43]

A second area in which moderate gender differences are found is in some (though not all) measures of sexuality. A meta-analysis that compared men and women in thirty areas of sexuality found only four in the moderate range: frequency of masturbation, pornography use, number of sexual partners, and positive attitudes about sex in casual, uncommitted relationships, with men averaging higher in all these areas. Many other areas of sexuality, such as sexual satisfaction, show no gender differences.[44] Men also emphasize more the importance of beauty in mates.[45]

Third, aggression has repeatedly shown moderate gender differences. The gender difference in physical aggression is particularly reliable and is larger than the gender difference in verbal aggression. Later meta-analyses of relational aggression—a more indirect form of aggression that is aimed at harming peer relationships—show that women are more aggressive than men, although this is a small difference.[46]

While the differences in motor performance can clearly be tied to biological factors, the origins of the sexuality and aggression differences are more ambiguous. There is some evidence that both men and women are highly influenced by gender-role expectations, tending to respond in ways

---

[42]Hyde, "Gender Similarities Hypothesis."

[43]Zell et al., "Evaluating Gender Similarities and Differences," 15.

[44]J. L. Petersen and Janet Shibley Hyde, "A Meta-Analytic Review of Research on Gender Differences in Sexuality: 1993 to 2007," *Psychological* Bulletin 136 (2010): 21-38.

[45]Zell et al., "Evaluating Gender Similarities and Differences," 15.

[46]Hyde, "Gender Similarities and Differences," 385.

that conform to societal gender stereotypes. For example, in experimental situations where participants' identity as men and women is deemphasized, gender differences in aggression disappear.[47] Similarly, in experimental conditions where participants are connected to a fake lie detector, the gender difference in number of sexual partners disappears.

In addition to these well-established differences, there are a number of other areas in which gender differences hit the threshold of a moderate difference. However, these differences differ substantially among meta-analyses, suggesting the influence of developmental stage, time (as when older studies show differences that newer studies do not show), or culture. In children, girls score higher on inhibitory control, but a meta-analysis of effortful control in adults showed no gender differences. Men show more sensation-seeking than women. In terms of self-reported personality variables, men report being more assertive, and women report being more anxious and tender-minded—although these last two differences disappear in cultural contexts outside the United States. In addition, women did not differ from men in actual observed anxiety. Women report more interest in people over things and less interest in engineering and science.[48] It should be noted that these latter findings have to do with interest, not with ability, on which they do not differ (as noted above). Women smile more than do men, but the difference drops to a small difference when participants are not aware of being observed.[49]

CONCLUSION AND RECOMMENDATIONS

Given the unity of truth in a world created by God, it makes sense to bring together social-scientific research with our biblical interpretation in order to arrive at sound conclusions that are relevant to our everyday lives. I have argued in this chapter that in order to do this well, the social-scientific literature on gender differences must be interpreted carefully and correctly. The meaningfulness of the gender differences must be considered, rather than simply the existence of statistically significant differences. When meta-analyses are available, they should be preferred over individual

---

[47]Hyde, "Gender Similarities and Differences," 385.
[48]Hyde, "Gender Similarities and Differences," 383-85.
[49]Hyde, "Gender Similarities Hypothesis," 584.

studies. Books written for popular audiences should not be used as sources. The results should not be taken as unbiased evidence of creation design but must appropriately consider the reality of the fall, as well as the evidence for both nature and nurture in producing those differences. Special care should be taken in making use of neuroscience findings, given the ambiguity in correctly interpreting brain differences and our cultural bias to give undue weight to neuroscientific findings.

With those caveats in mind, I have reviewed existing meta-analyses on gender differences. These meta-analyses identify consistent and substantial differences in four areas: motor performance, sexuality, aggression (especially physical aggression), and mental rotation. Other areas, though moderate or large in effect, show more variability at different ages, across time, and across cultures. Consequently, it is less likely that these are enduring gender differences.

What are we to conclude from these gender differences? A first point is that there is little evidence for some kind of trait-based gender difference that would equip men and women for substantially different roles in life. Areas such as empathy and leadership do not show clear gender differences. Any interpretation of biblical gender roles that attempts to show role differences based on presumed differences in psychological traits is on very thin ice from a social-scientific perspective.

It should be noted that biblical interpretations need not rely on psychological gender differences to establish separate gender roles. It is possible to establish such differences entirely on the basis of other factors. For example, Sam Andreades, a complementarian, notes the relative absence of gender differences in the social-scientific literature and writes, "Let us rather applaud the wisdom of the Bible's teaching, not defining gender in terms of essential characteristics." Instead, he proposes that complementarity lies in individual relationships, in what men and women do for each other.[50] Other complementarians invoke God's choice, rather than innate gender differences, as the rationale for differences in roles. Abraham

---

[50]Sam A. Andreades, *enGendered: God's Gift of Gender Difference in Relationship* (Wooster, OH: Weaver, 2015), 59-61. However, he seems to suggest that we should cultivate stereotypical gender characteristics: "The more intimate the relationship, the more pronounced the gender distinction" (183).

Kuyper seemed to have taken this approach, writing in 1914 that, though women could practice medicine or law as well as men, God's ordained will was for women to limit their activities to the home, and men to the public arenas.[51]

A second point is that any interpretation about gender must take into account the gender differences that do exist. What kind of biblical narrative about gender can best account for a world in which men are stronger, more physically aggressive, and more indiscriminately sexual than women?[52] My own opinion is that this conforms very well to a view that sees current gender differences largely as a result of the fall. "To the woman [God] said . . . 'Your desire will be for your husband, and he will rule over you'" (Gen 3:16 NIV). Men want women sexually, and since they are bigger and stronger, they dominate women, "ruling over" them to get what they want. The fall has set up a pattern of gender relations across history in which men dominate, and women subject themselves to men to avoid harm and to seek protection. While women are the victims in patriarchy, this system is damaging to both men and women, limiting our ability to reflect God's image in our relationships with each other and hampering our ability to represent God in exercising appropriate dominion over creation.

A third point is that social-scientific literature might be useful in adjudicating between competing interpretations by rendering some more plausible than others. We find one example in the Genesis passage we just examined, which states, "her desire shall be for her husband." Most of the interpretations about this passage understand "desire" to be "desire to control or dominate." For example, George Knight III, in his chapter in *Recovering Biblical Manhood and Womanhood*, interprets this as meaning that women "will 'desire' to have mastery over their husbands."[53] Yet women as a group do not seem to be more controlling or dominating than men. Meta-analyses of issues relevant to this claim, such as

---

[51]Mary Stewart Van Leeuwen, "Abraham Kuyper and the Cult of True Womanhood," *Calvin Theological Journal* 31, no. 1 (1996): 97-124.

[52]I lay aside the findings about mental rotation since it is unclear what implications this finding might have for gender roles.

[53]George W. Knight III, "The Family and the Church: How Should Biblical Manhood and Womanhood Work Out in Practice?," in *RBMW*, 414.

dominance in communication, physical aggression, and statistics about the incidence of intimate partner violence do not support this claim.[54] In fact, when I look at the world around me, while certainly there are some controlling women and some controlled husbands, what I primarily see are women who are willing to put up with the most atrocious conditions for themselves and for their children in order to stay with their husbands. I do not know of many clinics that focus on battered husbands, but I know of many, many places that focus on helping women who are battered, or who have let their children be physically or sexually abused. The sad thing is that many times it is difficult for particular women to set appropriate boundaries with their abusive partners. They have a craving or longing for their husband that they have allowed to take a place that belongs only to God: "their desire is for their husband, and he rules over them." This alternate interpretation, articulated by Joan Burgess Winfrey in her chapter in an earlier edition of the present book as "an unreciprocated desire for intimacy on the part of the woman," is more consistent with what we learn from observing the world around us and from the social sciences.[55]

A fourth point is that social-scientific literature can be helpful to the gender debates in broader ways than in simply documenting gender differences. There is a wealth of information on gender schemas that helps us understand why we continue to hold to gender differences in spite of evidence to the contrary, and that explores how gender schemas influence us, often in limiting ways. There is research on differences between men and women in their lived experience, including things such as caregiving, housework, sexual objectification, violence, mental health, and other factors that differentially affect men and women. There is research on the relationship between patriarchal beliefs and violence against women, on the relationship between beliefs about gender differences and sexism, on the relationship between gender role ideology and mental health outcomes—the list goes on and on. The social sciences can provide many

---

[54]Hyde, "Gender Similarities Hypothesis," 583-84; "Statistics," National Coalition Against Domestic Violence, https://ncadv.org/statistics (accessed March 22, 2019).

[55]Joan Burgess Winfrey, "In Search of Holy Joy: Women and Self-Esteem," in *Discovering Biblical Equality: Complementarity Without Hierarchy*, ed. Ronald W. Pierce and Rebecca Merrill Groothuis (Downers Grove, IL: InterVarsity Press, 2005), 436.

useful insights into our lived realities as men and women that go far beyond the identification of gender differences.

Martin Luther's last, and possibly greatest work, *Commentary on Genesis*, was written over a ten-year period at the end of his life. By the time he wrote it, he had been married to Katharina von Bora for many years. It seems to have been a happy marriage. Luther admired Katharina's intellect, calling her "Doctora Lutherin."[56] She was an active partner in the marriage and contributed significantly to their income, managing their farm. The quote with which I began this chapter had been written many years before. It is clear that in the ensuing years, Luther had changed his mind about women. In his *Commentary*, he wrote, "Adam says concerning Eve, 'She shall be called . . . a man.' Because a wife is an heroic or man-like woman; for she does man-like things, and performs man-like duties . . . the husband differs from the wife in no other thing than in sex."[57] What is the truth about gender differences? As we strive to correctly interpret the biblical text and the social-scientific literature, we should follow Luther in allowing ourselves to humbly follow where truth leads.

---

[56]Larry D. Mansch and Curtis H. Peters, *Martin Luther: The Life and Lessons* (Jefferson, NC: McFarland, 2016), 289.

[57]Martin Luther, *Commentary on Genesis*, vol. 1, *Luther on the Creation*, trans. John Nicolas Lenker (Minneapolis: Luther, 1904), 184.

23

A DEFENSE OF GENDER-ACCURATE BIBLE TRANSLATION

Jeffrey D. Miller

• • • • •

ENGLISH-SPEAKING CHRISTIANS disagree on whether the gender-accurate translation efforts of certain versions, such as NRSV, NLT, TNIV, NIV 2011, and CEB, are faithful to Scripture. Those who disapprove often claim that such efforts change the tone and even the nature of the Bible by removing the "masculine feel" integral to the Scriptures. Consider, for example, the subtitle of one book on the subject: *Muting the Masculinity of God's Words*.[1]

The cultures in which the Bible came to be were patriarchal. Similarly, the Bible itself contains considerable androcentric language. Examples are easy to find. In 1 Corinthians 16:13, for example, when Paul tells his hearers, who included women, to be brave, he uses the word *andrizesthe*, which etymologically suggests "act like men." Nevertheless, the Bible is not wholly androcentric. Feminine images of God, for example, appear repeatedly (e.g., Num 11:12; Deut 32:18; Ps 123:2; 131:2; Is 42:14; 49:15; 66:13; Hos 11:3-4; Mt 23:37; Lk 13:34; 15:8-10; Jas 1:18).[2] Thus the Bible both abounds

---

[1] Vern Poythress and Wayne Grudem, *The Gender-Neutral Bible Controversy: Muting the Masculinity of God's Words* (Nashville: Broadman & Holman, 2000).

[2] See Heim and Pierce's treatment of these metaphors in chapter nineteen of this volume. The Bible also uses feminine metaphors for ministry, believers, and the church (the most well-known being the bride of Christ).

in and pushes back against androcentric language. Unfortunately, however, some English translations maximize the abundance and minimize the pushback.

This chapter will demonstrate that, in spite of the androcentric language in the Bible, the "masculine feel" that many English-speaking Christians attribute to the New Testament comes not primarily from the Greek text itself, but from translations such as KJV, RSV, NASB, HCSB, ESV, CSB, and pre-2011 editions of NIV.[3] In short, such translations are indeed more androcentric than the Greek text. As a result, gender-accurate translations have moved toward, rather than away from, the Greek text of the New Testament by expressing a lesser degree of masculinity than most English Bibles.

INSERTIONS OF *MAN* AND *MEN*

A striking example of English translators importing masculinity into the text of the Bible concerns the contrasting treatment of *man* and *woman*. Forms of *gynē* ("woman," "wife") occur 215 times in the Greek New Testament. Forms of the English words *woman* and *wife* occur 251 times in the KJV New Testament. This increase of thirty-six occurrences is understandable, for a translation must sometimes add words to bring across meaning. For example, one of the thirty-six is in Matthew 24:41, which says, "Two *women shall be* grinding at the mill" (KJV). KJV has "women shall be" in italics because these words are not in the Greek text.

Forms of *anēr* ("man," "husband") occur 216 times in the New Testament. In contrast, however, forms of *man* and *husband* occur 1,343 times in the KJV New Testament—an addition of 1,127! Thus, KJV has inserted forms of *man* about thirty times more than it has inserted forms of *woman*. Table 23.1 gives data for several translations.

---

[3]This chapter adds my voice to those who have argued similar points, such as Mark Strauss, *Distorting Scripture?: The Challenge of Bible Translation and Gender Accuracy* (Downers Grove, IL: InterVarsity Press, 1998); Strauss, "Current Issues in the Gender-Language Debate: A Response to Vern Poythress and Wayne Grudem," in *The Challenge of Bible Translation: Communicating God's Word to the World*, ed. Glen Scorgie, Mark Strauss, and Steven Voth (Grand Rapids, MI: Zondervan, 2003), chap. 4. Largely for the sake of space, I have limited my argument primarily to the New Testament. The Old Testament offers similar data, such as the inclusive meaning of *'adam* early in Genesis and the ESV's inconsistent translation of "sons/children of Israel."

Table 23.1. *Woman* and *man* in select translations

	Greek[a]	KJV 1611	NASB 1977	NIV 1984	NRSV 1989	HCSB 1999	ESV 2002	NIV 2011[b]	CEB 2011	CSB 2017
woman/ wife	215	251 (+36)	250 (+35)	259 (+44)	241 (+26)	239 (+24)	247 (+32)	99 (-116)	264 (+49)	249 (+34)
man/ husband	216	1356 (+1140)	1094 (+878)	1138 (+922)	536 (+320)	1082 (+866)	799 (+583)	93 (-123)	448 (+232)	684 (+468)

[a]UBS[5]/NA[28]
[b]The numbers in the NIV 2011 column reveal a different translation philosophy applied to gendered language. The salient feature of this column is the similarity of its numbers (99 and 93). These similar numbers suggest that NIV 2011 translators have applied the same translation tactics to masculine language as they have to feminine language.

The conspicuous disparity in several columns in table 23.1 results from certain translation tendencies. These tendencies include rendering *anthrōpos* ("person," "human") as "man," androcentric treatment of grammatically masculine words, and pure insertions of masculine language in spite of the lack of any corresponding Greek word.

TRANSLATING *ANTHRŌPOS* ("HUMAN") AND *ANĒR* ("MAN")

Many Bibles frequently translate *anthrōpos* as "man." The standard Greek-English lexicon for New Testament studies is the third edition of *A Greek-English Lexicon of the New Testament and Other Early Christian Literature*. It gives the gloss "human being, man, person" and then lists nine definitions. The first two definitions are both "human being."[4] The third is "a male person." The earlier 1957 and 1979 editions of this lexicon similarly give "human being" first place in their definition. Another lexicon states, "The NT has no trace of the curious misuse by which the principal difference between *anthrōpos* and *anēr* is ignored."[5] Challenges do indeed confront translators as they encounter specialized uses of *anthrōpos* (e.g., *huios tou anthrōpou*, "son of man, human being"). Nevertheless, the basic policy should be to render *anthrōpos* as "man" only when context supports it.

---

[4]BDAG's first definition is "a person of either sex, w. focus on participation in the human race, *a human being*." The second is "a member of the human race, w. focus on limitations and weaknesses, *a human being*."
[5]James H. Moulton and George Milligan, *The Vocabulary of the Greek Testament* (London, 1930), 44. Though they perhaps overstate the case, certain New Testament instances of *anthrōpos* meaning "male person" can be found, e.g., Mt 19:10; Mk 10:7 (quoting Gen 2:24).

Examples of increasing the masculine nature of a text by unnecessarily translating *anthrōpos* as "man" are abundant. In Mark 1:17 (cf. Mt 4:19; Lk 5:10), as a first example, we read, "I will make you to become fishers of men [*anthrōpōn*]" (KJV). Such language was standard in 1611. Numerous twentieth-century Bibles as well as some twenty-first-century Bibles, such as ESV, still use the phrase "of men." Happily, four hundred years after the KJV, the NIV 2011 instead reads, "I will send you out to fish for people."

A second and more striking example is 2 Peter 1:21. KJV reads, "For the prophecy came not in old time by the will of man [*anthrōpou*]: but holy men [*anthrōpoi*] of God spake." This translation, as well as others, including the pre-2011 NIV, HCSB, ESV, and CSB, includes both "man" and "men"—each time translating *anthrōpos*, even though *anēr* is absent from this verse. Contrast, for example, the gender-accurate wording of the CEB: "no prophecy ever came by human will. Instead, men and women led by the Holy Spirit spoke." How unfortunate that many translations here exacerbate the problem of ignoring the Bible's female prophets. The likelihood that a sermon or lesson will feature female prophets such as Miriam, Huldah, Anna, or Philip's daughters quickly declines when several translations of the verse used to define prophecy inaccurately call them men.

A third example is 2 Timothy 3:17. Paul's famous counsel in 2 Timothy 3:16-17 reads, in the ESV, "All Scripture is breathed out by God and profitable . . . that the man [*anthrōpos*] of God may be competent." In contrast, NIV 2011, for example, has "servant of God," and CEB has "person who belongs to God." Compare the German use of *Mensch* ("person") rather than *Mann* ("man") here. Similarly, Jerome's fourth-century Latin Vulgate has *homō* ("person") rather than *vir* ("man").

Consider, however, the ESV footnote on "man of God" here in 2 Timothy 3:17: "That is, a messenger of God (the phrase echoes a common Old Testament expression)." This expression mentioned in the ESV footnote occurs about seventy-five times in the Old Testament and uses the Hebrew word *'ish* (typically "a male") rather than *'adam* (typically "human, person"; e.g., Deut 33:1; 1 Sam 2:27; 1 Kings 12:22). If the ESV footnote is correct that 2 Timothy 3:17 echoes this Old Testament expression, we should note the following sequence: First, numerous Old Testament passages include the phrase using the word usually limited to males (*'ish* rather than *'adam*).

Then 2 Timothy 3:17 shifts to a word rarely limited to males (*anthrōpos* rather than *anēr*). Finally, ESV restores the full force of the expression's masculine aspect, which the New Testament author had muted.

In Hebrews 13:6, an Old Testament quotation displays a different sequence that nevertheless reveals the same ESV tendency. First, Psalm 118:6 uses *'adam* in the question, "What can mortals do to me?" (NRSV; cf. NIV 2011, "mere mortals," and CEB, "anyone"). Hebrews then renders *'adam* as *anthrōpos*, retaining the gender inclusivity of its source. Yet ESV uses "man," without footnote, in both Psalms and Hebrews.[6]

Even the word *anēr*, as opposed to *anthrōpos*, can occasionally convey a gender-inclusive meaning, thus reflecting the text's androcentric setting. In Acts 17:22, for example, Paul addresses the Areopagus philosophers as "men of Athens," yet those who respond favorably to his speech include Damaris, a woman (Acts 17:34). For other examples of *anēr* used inclusively, see Matthew 14:35; Romans 4:8; and James 1:7.

James 1:12 uses *anēr* inclusively, as we see in translations such as NIV 2011 and CSB, which begin, "Blessed is the one [*anēr*]." A few modern translations, such as ESV, persist with, "Blessed is the man." Though this verse has been debated, I accept the verdict of D. A. Carson: "although *anēr* most commonly means 'man,' that is, male human being, nevertheless both in the lexica and in texts some extension is occasionally found. In this instance, is James really saying that only male human beings are blessed if they persevere under trial?"[7]

ANDROCENTRIC TRANSLATIONS OF GRAMMATICALLY MASCULINE WORDS

The word *anthrōpos* occurs 550 times in the New Testament. Thus, even if every instance could fairly be translated "man" or "men," the copious insertions made by KJV, NIV 1984, HCSB, and ESV would still not be explained. A second way some translations have greatly increased the New Testament occurrences of *man* concerns words that, though masculine, do

---

[6]Other examples of *anthrōpos* wrongly rendered as masculine can be found in various translations of Mk 8:36-37; Lk 2:14; Jn 1:4, 9; 2:25; 16:21; Rom 3:28; 1 Cor 2:9; Col 3:9; 2 Thess 3:2; 2 Tim 2:2; Titus 1:14; 2:11; 3:2; Jas 2:20; Jude 4; Rev 13:13, 18.

[7]D. A. Carson, *The Inclusive Language Debate: A Plea for Realism* (Grand Rapids, MI: Baker, 1998), 161; see also 120-28.

not refer to men only. Many translations display this tendency, in part because English (like various other languages, such as Chinese and Turkish) exhibits only a minimal amount of grammatical gender. A person who speaks French, German, Italian, or Spanish, for example, is accustomed to the concept of grammatical gender. A person who knows only English, however, will likely struggle with the concept. The three biblical languages are highly gendered. As a result, it is essential to realize that all biblical authors and all people who were in their original audiences would have naturally understood grammatical gender.

A central feature of grammatical gender is that, when a gendered word describes a person, that word's gender does not inform us in any way about the character or personality of the person.[8] The New Testament itself frequently demonstrates this feature. In the Gospel of John, for example, Jesus famously self-identifies with seven "I am" claims. Only two of these titles are masculine (bread and shepherd). One is neuter (light), and six are feminine (door, resurrection, way, truth, life, vine). We can conclude nothing about Jesus from the gender of these titles. Similarly, in Hebrew and Aramaic, "spirit" (*ruah*) is often a feminine word, but in Greek "spirit" (*pneuma*) is always neuter. The Spirit of God did not change genders between the Testaments! Moving forward in church history, the Latin word *spiritus* is masculine. Jerome, translating the Vulgate, used a masculine Latin word to render a neuter Greek word that in turn translates a feminine Hebrew word, even though those words each describe the genderless Holy Spirit of God.

Having mentioned the genders of *ruah* and *pneuma*, it should be noted that modifiers of these words match their grammatical gender. Examples of neuter modifiers of *pneuma*, for example, are abundant.[9] An important example is John 14:17, in which none of the CSB's six masculine pronouns

---

[8]See, e.g., Bruce K. Waltke and M. O'Connor, *An Introduction to Biblical Hebrew Syntax* (Winona Lake, IN: Eisenbrauns, 1990), 99: "Grammatical gender does not primarily denote sex in animate beings and 'analogous' features of inanimates. Rather, gender is primarily a matter of syntax. . . . The error of the idea that gender is attached to an object according to certain perceived qualities is further illustrated by comparing the genders of words in one language with those in another."
[9]On this and related topics, see Marg Mowczko, "Why Masculine Pronouns Can Be Misleading in English Bibles and in the Church," September 11, 2014, http://margmowczko.com/masculine-pronouns-english-bible. For an investigation of the few exceptions to this pattern, see Daniel B. Wallace, "Greek Grammar and the Personality of the Holy Spirit," *BBR* 13, no. 1 (2003): 97-125.

that refer to the Spirit translate a masculine Greek word: "He is the Spirit of truth. The world is unable to receive him because it doesn't see him or know him. But you do know him, because he remains with you and will be in you."

Masculine plurals. One rule in many languages, including Koine Greek, is that grammatically masculine expressions regularly describe groups that include both men and women.[10] An example is Matthew 19:4, "he who created . . . made them male and female" (ESV). The word *them* here is a masculine plural pronoun, though it obviously refers to a man and a woman. The description of Zechariah and Elizabeth in Luke 1:6 provides another clear example: "Both were righteous before God, living blamelessly." The words *both, righteous, living,* and *blamelessly* are each masculine, though Elizabeth is one of the two referents.

The Beatitudes further demonstrate this rule. The thirteen occurrences of *makarioi* ("blessed") in Matthew 5 and Luke 6 are masculine plural adjectives. Clearly, however, neither Jesus nor either Evangelist intended these blessings only for men. Likewise, the numerous "one another" statements throughout the New Testament are masculine plural but not limited to men. Another widespread example is *hagioi* ("holy ones, saints"), which is always masculine but always refers to both men and women.

Romans 16 provides a string of examples of this rule. In Romans 16:16 the masculine plural exhortation to "greet one another with a holy kiss" comes in a context where several women are mentioned by name. Indeed, all New Testament holy-kiss commands are masculine plural (1 Cor 16:22; 2 Cor 13:12; 1 Thess 5:26; 1 Pet 5:14). Romans 16:7 begins, "Greet Andronicus and Junia," and goes on to describe this man and woman with several masculine plural words. A few verses later, masculine words refer to the households of Aristobulus and Narcissus, though they certainly included women. In Romans 16:15, "who are with them" is a wholly masculine phrase, yet two of the five Christians constituting "them" are women.

Shifting to a cluster of examples from the Gospels and Acts, in Mark 10:21, Jesus says, "go, sell all that you have and give to the poor" (ESV). Though "the poor" is masculine plural, Jesus surely did not limit the rich

---

[10]See, e.g., Herbert Weir Smyth, *Greek Grammar* (Cambridge, MA: Harvard University Press, 1920), §197 a.

young ruler's benevolence to male peasants. Mark 10:31 has five masculine plural words: "But many who are first will be last, and the last first" (ESV). Again, in Acts 12:12 the clause "many people had gathered and were praying" is grammatically masculine, though Mary (Acts 12:12) and Rhoda (Acts 12:13) are present. Acts 17:12 begins with the masculine plural *polloi* ("many") and then notes that these "many" included "not a few Greek women of high standing" (ESV).

Acts 8 heightens the impact of this rule of grammar. Both Acts 8:1 and Acts 8:4 refer to the scattering of persecuted Christians, each time using a masculine expression. Yet there is no reason to think only male believers scatter. We then read that these scattered ones "went about preaching the word" (Acts 8:4). Because *preaching* is a masculine word (*euangelizomenoi*), readers may be tempted to conclude that only men do this preaching. But because it is plural, its masculine gender does not require all these early evangelists to be men. In fact, the context (see Acts 8:3, "both men and women") strongly suggests that these persecuted preachers include men and women.

Another application of this rule, that masculine plurals describe groups of men and women, challenges the oft-heard claim that elders in the New Testament were always men. However, neither Paul nor Acts mentions *any* individual elder.[11] Instead, we read of elders in the plural and in the abstract. On the basis of grammar, therefore, we cannot say whether these plural references include women elders. So, for example, in Acts 14 Paul and Barnabas appoint elders, and in Acts 20 Paul summons the Ephesian elders. *Elders* in these contexts is a masculine plural adjective (*presbyteroi*) and does not imply they were all men.[12]

One final example, from a seemingly unending list of options, also concerns *presbyteroi*.[13] Hebrews 11:2 refers to "ancestors" (NRSV, CSB) or "the ancients" (NIV 2011) with this masculine term. The following catalogue of the faithful, however, includes women—Sarah in Hebrews 11:11 and Rahab

---

[11]Individual elders are mentioned in 2 Jn 1; 3 Jn 1; 1 Pet 5:1.

[12]This point about elders is expressed more fully in my "Asking the Wrong Questions," *PriscPap* 24, no. 3 (Summer 2010): 5. Similar arguments apply to "pastor" (*poimēn*) and "overseer" (*episkopos*).

[13]See also Mk 10:31; Lk 2:3; Jn 2:24; 20:29; 1 Cor 2:9; 12:13; 2 Cor 9:13; 1 Thess 5:8; 1 Tim 5:8; Jas 2:15; 1 Jn 2:17; Rev 13:15-16.

in Hebrews 11:13. Because the masculine plural here clearly refers to both men and women, even KJV ("the elders"), NIV 1984 ("the ancients"), HCSB ("our ancestors"), and ESV ("the people of old") use gender-inclusive translations. RSV and NASB, unfortunately, have "the men of old."

The words of Carson, commenting on *monous* ("only men," "only people") in the difficult and controversial 1 Corinthians 14:36, provide an apt conclusion to this section about masculine plurals: "The masculine . . . in 14:36 does not prove that Paul is addressing only the men of the congregation . . . and not the women. Rather, it refers to both the men and the women who constitute the church: the Greek regularly uses plural masculine forms when people (without distinction as to sex) are being referred to or addressed."[14]

Feminine plurals. In contrast, when feminine plural expressions refer to people, the reference is indeed to women only. In Luke 23:55-56, for example, I have italicized three feminine plural participles: "The women *who had come with him* from Galilee *followed* and saw the tomb and how his body was laid. Then *they returned* and prepared spices and ointments" (ESV).

Luke 8:1-3 provides a troubling example of a mishandled feminine plural expression: "The twelve were with him [Jesus], as well as some women . . . Mary, called Magdalene, from whom seven demons had gone out, and Joanna, the wife of Herod's steward Chuza, and Susanna, and many others" (NRSV). This text gives us a snapshot of a typical group of Jesus' companions. These companions include men (the Twelve), women (Mary, Joanna, Susanna), and "many others." Presented with essentially any English translation, the reader cannot conclusively determine whether these "many others" are men, women, or both. As a result, English readers tend to assume this paragraph presents Jesus' companions in Luke 8 as composed of twelve men, three women, and many other men—or, at best, many other people. But this is clearly not the case—the phrase "many others" (*heterai pollai*) is feminine plural and can in this context only mean "many other women." Yet it is surprisingly difficult to find an English translation that makes this clear. It is no surprise that we find this oversight in

---

[14]D. A. Carson, *Exegetical Fallacies*, 2nd ed. (Grand Rapids, MI: Baker, 1996), 39.

pre–twentieth century translations such as Tyndale's New Testament
(1534), Douay-Rheims Bible (1582), Bishops' New Testament (1595), the
Geneva Bible (1599), KJV (1611), Young's Literal Translation (1862), the
Revised Version (1881), and the Darby Bible (1884). Yet we continue to find
the genderless "many others" or its equivalent as we move forward in time:
ASV (1901), Moffatt (1913), NAB (1941), RSV (1946), Phillips (1958), *The
Living Bible* (1967), NASB (1971), NKJV (1979), NJB (1985), NRSV (1989),
NLT (1996), *The Message* (1993), HCSB (1999), ESV (2001), CEB (2011),
and CSB (2017). All editions of the NIV, including TNIV, have taken a
small step in the right direction. They add "these women" to the following
clause: "and many others. *These women* were helping to support them"
(italics added). The innovative and recent edition called *The Voice* (2012)
includes a similar expansion. One rare exception to this unfortunate trend
is *Today's English Version* (1966, also known as the Good News Bible),
which correctly renders *heterai pollai* here as "many other women."

Masculine singulars and pronouns. Returning to masculine expressions, a word need not be plural to refer to both men and women. Some
singular words and expressions function in a similar way. One such construction uses a singular masculine word as a hypothetical representative.
Acts 10:34-35 provides an example, and an ironic one indeed. KJV has
Simon Peter say, "God is no respecter of persons: But in every nation he
that feareth him, and worketh righteousness, is accepted with him." The
he in "he that feareth" does not translate a Greek word. Rather, it has been
inferred because the participle *feareth* is masculine in gender. This is a case
of the gender-inclusive masculine singular, as various modern translations,
including HCSB and CSB ("the person who fears") and ESV ("anyone who
fears"), have rightly noted (unlike NIV 1984, which inserts the word *men*).
Another example is James 1:13, where a masculine singular participle
causes ESV to include *he* in its translation: "Let no one say when he is
tempted." KJV inserts *man* twice here in James 1:13. This verse could begin,
"Let no one who is tempted say," and thus remove the gender bias.

Another example of this grammatical construction comes in 1 John 3:24.
This verse begins and ends with masculine singular words, hence the KJV
rendering, "And he that keepeth [masculine participle] his commandments dwelleth in him, and he in him [masculine pronoun]." In spite of

these two masculine words, even NIV 1984 and ESV grasp the gender-inclusive sense of the sentence, switching the final pronoun to *them*.

Because 2 Corinthians 9:7 begins with the masculine singular adjective *hekastos* ("each"), HCSB and ESV add *he* and *his*: "Each one must give as he has decided in his heart" (ESV). KJV and NIV 1984 have gone a step further by adding *man* as well as two masculine pronouns: "Each man should give what he has decided in his heart" (NIV 1984). This adjective *hekastos* appears also in 1 Peter 1:17, resulting in "each man's work" in NIV 1984 and "every man's work" in KJV. Notably, both ESV and HCSB are gender-accurate here.

When Peter refers in Acts 2:21 to "everyone who calls on the name of the Lord," both "everyone" (*pas*) and "who" (*hos*) are masculine singular, in spite of the proximate references to daughters (Acts 2:17) and female slaves (Acts 2:18). In 1 Peter 3:15, the adjective *pas* is again masculine singular, as is the adjacent participle, hence "everyone who asks." As a result, KJV reads "to every man that asketh." KJV here breaks its custom of italicizing inserted words. Fortunately, most other English translations recognize this masculine singular word as gender inclusive.

The indefinite pronoun *tis* ("someone," "a certain person") has prompted numerous presumptuous insertions of *man* and *he*. The forms of this pronoun do not distinguish between masculine and feminine. Thus, only context can determine whether an occurrence of this pronoun refers to men, women, or both. One important example is 1 Timothy 3:1, which reads in ESV, "If anyone [*tis*] aspires to the office of overseer, he [no corresponding word in the Greek text] desires a noble task." ESV's assumption that *tis* is masculine results in the insertion of *he*. The same is true in NIV 1984 and HCSB. The masculine insertion is even stronger in KJV, which includes *he* and also translates *tis* as "a man."

KJV is guilty of another double insertion in John 3:5: "Except a man [*tis*] be born of water and of the Spirit, he [no corresponding word in the Greek text] cannot enter into the kingdom of God." NRSV, NLT, NIV 2011, and CEB translate this sentence as gender inclusive. NIV 1984, ESV, HCSB, and CSB add *he*. Another example from John is in 6:51, where NIV 1984, ESV, HCSB, and CSB again insert *he*: "If anyone [*tis*] eats of this bread, he [no corresponding word in the Greek text] will live forever."

By their rendering of *tis*, many translations masculinize Paul's proclamation of a new creation in 2 Corinthians 5:17. This is again doubly true
in KJV, which inserts both *man* and *he*: "Therefore if any man [*tis*] be in
Christ, he [no corresponding word in the Greek text] is a new creature."
HCSB and ESV insert *he* in "he is a new creation" but do not also use *man*.
Various translations, including NRSV, NIV 2011, and CEB, have avoided
adding such masculine words to the verse.

Pure insertions. A third cause of accumulating masculine terminology
is that some Bibles regularly add words such as *man* and *he* when there is
no corresponding Greek word whatsoever. An example of these pure
insertions is in Romans 13:1, where NIV 1984 begins, "Everyone must submit himself to the governing authorities." The word *himself*, however, is not
in the Greek text.

Another example is Matthew 5:11, which in KJV begins, "Blessed are ye,
when *men* shall revile you," but no Greek word corresponds to *men* (hence
KJV's italics). The verb is third-person plural ("they revile"). Because
Greek verbs do not have gender, many translations rightly use a gender-
inclusive clause such as "when people revile you" (e.g., NIV 1984 and 2011,
NRSV, HCSB, ESV, CSB).

KJV includes *men* in John 4:20, though the Greek text offers no justification for its presence: "the place where men ought to worship." Like the
earlier example of 1 Peter 3:15, KJV here breaks its custom of italicizing
added words.

Revelation includes the list "tribe, language, people, nation" seven times
in varying forms. NIV 1984, with no Greek justification, inserts *men* into
two such lists (Rev 5:9; 11:9). For example, Revelation 11:9 reads, "men from
every people, tribe, language and nation" (cf. NIV 2011, "some from every
people," and HCSB, "representatives from the peoples"). Elsewhere in Revelation, NIV 1984 inserts *men* into Revelation 16:10, "Men gnawed their
tongues in agony," again without any corresponding Greek word.

First Timothy 5:8 provides another example of such an insertion. KJV
reads, "But if any provide not for his own, and specially for those of his
own house, he hath denied the faith." This translation includes three masculine pronouns, and various translations follow suit. NIV 2011 more faithfully follows the gender-inclusive Greek text. Consider also the NRSV:

"And whoever does not provide for relatives, and especially for family members." This verse is ripe for misunderstanding; uncountable Christians believe the Bible instructs the husband to be the breadwinner for a family. On the contrary, though many translations say this, it is not what Paul said.[15]

It is noteworthy that, in the Greek text, James 2:15 uses the phrase "a brother or sister" instead of the New Testament's ubiquitous "brothers": "Suppose a brother or sister [*adelphos ē adelphē*] is without clothes and daily food" (NIV 1984, 2011). James is clear that the poor are to be cared for without gender distinction. Though James here uses gender-inclusive wording, he has not anachronistically become politically correct. Perhaps the reason James here expands his wording with "or a sister" is that the chapter begins with his exhortation not to show favoritism. That is, he is practicing what he preaches! Similarly, later in this chapter, James 2:21-26 offers Abraham and Rahab as tandem examples of the inseparable bond of faith and works. Rahab comes second, and her commendation begins with "likewise," or "in the same way" (*homoiōs*)—again, James himself avoids showing favoritism.[16]

Unfortunately, not all translations practice what James preaches. NIV 1984, for example, reads: "Suppose a brother or sister is without clothes and daily food. If one of you says to *him*, 'Go, I wish you well; keep warm and well fed' but does nothing about *his* physical needs, what good is it?" (Jas 2:15-16, italics added). The two italicized words are each singular translations of a plural pronoun. Though the biblical author has explicitly included sisters, NIV 1984 has thwarted the author's intent by using *him* and *his* to describe these Christian sisters.[17]

Finally, two curious examples are worthy of brief notice. For no reason other than androcentrism, KJV has added (and thus italicized) *men* in Luke 17:34, "in that night there shall be two *men* in one bed." The supposedly literal NASB also has *men* here. Finally, it seems even the four living creatures surrounding the throne in the vision of Revelation 4 are not

---

[15]Furthermore, the prior context speaks of children caring for parents (specifically widows, 1 Tim 5:4), rather than vice versa.

[16]See Luke Timothy Johnson, "Gender in the Letter of James: A Surprising Witness," in *Brother of Jesus, Friend of God: Studies in the Letter of James* (Grand Rapids, MI: Eerdmans, 2004), 221-34.

[17]NIV 2011 has made the appropriate changes to "them" and "their" (*autois* in both cases).

immune to an assumption of masculine gender (in spite of "living creature" [*zōon*] being grammatically neuter), at least in KJV, in which Revelation 4:8 begins, "And the four beasts had each of them six wings about him." The word *him* here has no Greek counterpart.

KINSHIP TERMS

The numerous examples above demonstrate that certain translations have significantly increased the "masculine feel" of the New Testament, as compared to the Greek text, by inserting hundreds of occurrences of *man* and *men* and an even larger number of masculine pronouns. Such translations further add to the masculine vocabulary of the New Testament in the way they tend to render words that express family relationships. The word *brother*, ubiquitous in the New Testament, will be discussed below. Space constraints prevent similar treatment of vocabulary associated with other family relationships, such as husbands and wives, children and parents, and ancestors.

The noun *adelphos* (plural *adelphoi*) occurs 343 times in the Greek New Testament. A significant number of these occurrences (222) are plural. The standard New Testament lexicon's first definition describes a biological brother and goes on to note that the plural can mean "brothers and sisters."[18] It then cites Luke 21:16 as an instance where "there is no doubt" the plural *adelphoi* refers to brothers and sisters. CEB begins this verse, "You will be betrayed by your parents, brothers and sisters [*adelphoi*]." NIV 2011 is also gender inclusive here, unlike either NRSV or NLT.

Rendering the metaphorical use of the plural *adelphoi* as "brothers and sisters," "believers," or something similar became mainstream in 1989 with the publication of NRSV (e.g., Jn 20:17; Acts 11:29; Rom 1:13; Phil 3:1, 13; Jas 1:2, 19; 2:14; 1 Jn 2:10-11). NLT, CEB, NIV 2011, and CSB have continued this practice. The tendency is also present, though ambiguous, in nearly 140 ESV footnotes.[19] Though less common, singular *adelphos* sometimes also receives inclusive treatment. In 1 John 2:11, for example, NRSV renders *adelphos* as "another believer," and CSB has "a brother or sister."

---

[18]BDAG, s.v.; *LSJ* and L&N concur.

[19]For an assessment of these ESV footnotes, see Rebecca Card-Hyatt, "Footnoted: Was the Bible Written Only for Men? Part 1," Junia Project, November 29, 2013, http://juniaproject.com /footnoted-bible-written-for-men-part-1/.

While gender-inclusive rendering of *adelphoi* has been largely limited to metaphorical uses of the word, *adelphoi* should often be translated as "brothers and sisters" or "siblings," not only when it symbolizes a spiritual relationship but also when it is used of actual family members (as in the Lk 21:16 example above). Consider Luke 18:29: "there is no one who has left house or wife or brothers or parents or children" (ESV). Clearly, "brothers" should here be "siblings" or "brothers and sisters."

In Matthew 13:55-56, we have the fullest list of the holy family of Nazareth (see also the parallel Mk 6:3). Matthew 13:55 names Jesus' four brothers. Matthew 13:56 then adds, "Are not all his sisters with us?" Because of these sisters, some readers might wonder why most texts about Jesus' family only mention brothers (e.g., Lk 8:19-21; Jn 2:12 [see ESV note]; 7:3-10; and especially Mt 12:46-50). Such a question is misguided, however, for the plural *adelphoi* can indeed mean "brothers and sisters." The last phrase of Acts 1:14 is another example of a text where "siblings" or "brothers and sisters" is an appropriate translation: "All these [the eleven apostles] with one accord were devoting themselves to prayer, together with the women and Mary the mother of Jesus, and his brothers [*adelphois*]" (ESV). Regrettably, however, I cannot find an English Bible with a gender-inclusive translation of *adelphois* here in Acts 1:14.

THE CUMULATIVE EFFECT

Though the examples given above are numerous, they are a small fraction of the total number of places where masculine language has been unnecessarily included in, and sometimes added to, translations of the New Testament. While each individual example is of varying significance, it is essential to realize that such language does its damage largely by cumulative effect.

To illustrate this cumulative effect, my final example broadens to a longer passage, Romans 14. Table 23.2 collects four sets of data from eight translations. Column 2 shows the number of times a translation uses a form of the word "man." It is important to note that Romans 14 does not include *anēr* ("man"). Furthermore, *anthrōpos* occurs only twice in this chapter (meaning "people" in Rom 14:18 and "person" in Rom 14:20). Column 3 gives the number of times a translation renders *adelphos* as "brother" without an accompanying "sister." The Greek text has five occurrences of

adelphos in this chapter. Column 4 records the number of times a translation uses a masculine pronoun. For many of these, there is indeed a corresponding Greek masculine pronoun. The difference, however, as discussed above, is that Greek is a highly gendered language and English is
not. The far right column gives the resulting total number of times in
Romans 14 that unnecessary masculine words have been used—an alarming forty-five times in the KJV.

Table 23.2. Masculine terms in Romans 14

	"man," "men"	"brother"	"he," "him," etc.	Total
KJV (1611)	7	5	33	45
NIV (1984)	11	6	21	38
NRSV (1989)	0	0	0	0
HCSB (1999)	3	5	18	26
ESV (2001)	1	5	16	22
NIV (2011)	0	0	2	2
CEB (2011)	0	0	0	0
CSB (2017)	0	0	18	18

CONCLUSION

The claim that some translations minimize the inherently masculine
nature of the New Testament is misguided. Instead, the numerous examples above, which come from all New Testament documents except Philemon, demonstrate that certain translations, including the especially influential KJV and pre-2011 NIV, have given English Bible readers this false
impression. Efforts at gender-accurate Bible translation are thus to be
commended for taking an important step toward, not away from, fidelity
to the Greek text.

24

BIBLICAL EQUALITY AND SAME-SEX MARRIAGE

Ronald W. Pierce

• • • • •

INTRODUCTION

Students in my undergraduate Creation, Sexuality, and Gender course sometimes ask, "As an evangelical who affirms mutually-shared leadership for men and women in marriage and ministry, do you affirm same-sex marriage for Christians as well?"[1] Often my response is, "For me, it is not about hermeneutics as much as it is about the exegesis of the relevant passages in Scripture."[2] Consequently, the focus of this essay is exegetical. Moreover, I wish to address this sensitive topic in a respectful dialogue with fellow believers who arrive at a different answer to this question, one that is seasoned with a spirit of Christian kindness and academic inquiry.[3] To this end, the biblical passages relevant to sexual integrity and marriage

---

[1]The relevance of this question is underscored by the success of Marriage Equality USA, which advocated successfully from 1996–2017 for legalizing same-sex marriage at the state and federal levels. Because of the common usage of the label "marriage equality" in Western culture to endorse same-sex marriage, I usually qualify my view as marriage equality regarding leadership and decision making, or something to that effect.

[2]To be clear, I affirm the doctrinal basis of the Evangelical Theological Society, which is clear about the inerrancy of God's fully inspired and authoritative Word. For a discussion of hermeneutics, see Cynthia Long Westfall, "Interpretive Methods and the Gender Debate," in this volume.

[3]Two resources have helped set the tone of this essay: Ted Grimsrud and Mark Thiessen Nation, *Reasoning Together: A Conversation on Homosexuality* (Scottdale, PA: Herald, 2008); Barry H. Corey, *Love Kindness: Discover the Power of a Forgotten Christian Virtue* (Carol Stream, IL: Tyndale, 2016), esp. 75-90.

will remain my focus.[4] To this end, the most recent evangelical affirming and nonaffirming interpretations regarding same-sex marriage are summarized and compared.[5]

Although the term *evangelical* carries varying connotations in religious, secular, and political contexts, it is used more narrowly to mean a way of coming to the text that demonstrates a respect for the inspiration and authority of Scripture by paying careful attention to its historical, cultural, and literary contexts, while not dismissing its teachings as irrelevant to contemporary readers or showing disregard for the authorial intent. With this in mind, it is important to note that evangelicals generally share the following convictions regarding sexual integrity and marriage. First, God designed marriage as a lifelong, covenantal bond and as the only human relationship where sexual intimacy should be embraced.[6] Second, Jesus cites the biblical prescriptions to love God and neighbor as the two greatest commandments in Scripture on which hang "all the law and the prophets" (Mt 22:34-40; Mk 12:28-31; cf. Lev 19:18; Deut 6:4-5). Similarly, Paul argues that the command to "love your neighbor as yourself" fulfills the entire Old Testament law (Gal 5:14). Third, the reality that sexual orientation is not merely a choice is commonly accepted by most Christians.[7] And,

---

[4]Though I have focused here only on marriage, a similar argument could be made regarding the New Testament texts that speak to the question of women and men in ministry and leadership: 1 Cor 11:2-16; 14:34-35; 1 Tim 2:8-15.

[5]I use the term *nonaffirming* because it communicates most clearly the differences in the two main views at this time within evangelicalism. However, I might prefer the term *creational* for three reasons. First, too much emphasis has been placed on the prohibitive aspect of this view. Second, *creational* language flows naturally from the foundational creation accounts in Gen 1–2 throughout the New Testament texts. Third, *traditional* or *historical* language carries too much unnecessary and often unbiblical baggage in both of the marriage debates being addressed in this chapter.

My primary interlocutors include James V. Brownson, *Bible, Gender, Sexuality: Reframing the Church's Debate on Same-Sex Relations* (Grand Rapids, MI: Eerdmans, 2013); Robert Song, *Covenant and Calling: Towards a Theology of Same-Sex Relationships* (Norwich, UK: SCM Press, 2014); and Karen R. Keen, *Scripture, Ethics and the Possibility of Same-Sex Relationships* (Grand Rapids, MI: Eerdmans, 2018).

[6]Despite the fact that this conviction is held by most churches and Christian organizations, the increasing number of Christians involved in casual sex with multiple partners (hookups) is presenting a challenge for believers that carries ramifications equally as challenging as the topic discussed in this chapter.

[7]See Mark A. Yarhouse with Janet B. Dean, Stephen P. Stratton, and Michael Lastoria, *Listening to Sexual Minorities: A Study of Faith and Sexual Identity on Christian College Campuses* (Downers Grove, IL: IVP Academic, 2018), 25-59. This is also generally supported by a 2018 Gallup Poll, discussed by Lydia Saad, "More Say 'Nature' than 'Nurture' Explains Sexual Orientation," Gallup, May 24, 2018, https://news.gallup.com/poll/234941/say-nature-nurture-explains-sexual-orientation.aspx.

fourth, grace, forgiveness, and hope are readily available to any follower of Jesus with a history of or propensity toward any kind of sin, including sins that are sexually related. In this spirit Paul declares, "You were washed, you were sanctified, you were justified" (1 Cor 6:11). These issues need not be in dispute here.

A caveat regarding my personal journey in the area of gender studies and theology is also in order because human experiences tend to shape the way we interpret the Bible, regardless of how objective we seek to remain.[8] As I was born in the 1940s—fewer than twenty years after the beginning of the sexual revolution of the 1920s—my thinking was formed by both the backlash of traditional patriarchy in the 1950s and the second wave of the gender-equality movement in the 1960s. My study of gender began in earnest in the late 1970s, when I was still advocating for a male-leadership, roles-based model. Yet, just over a decade later I had changed my mind to a shared-leadership view as the better interpretation of Scripture.[9] At that time, one of my colleagues predicted that I would endorse same-sex marriage within ten years because of the "interpretive method" that led me to advocate for gender equality. This slippery-slope argument is still commonly heard—and for some this has been their experience.[10] In addition, my evangelical, Protestant convictions call me to remain open-minded to better understandings of Scripture on all theological questions. Nevertheless, my ongoing studies continue to lead me to a welcoming, yet non-affirming position.[11] Yes, I have changed my mind on one "gender question,"

---

[8]Most of the broadly read treatments on same-sex marriage begin with the author's personal narrative. For example, compare the affirming story of Matthew Vines in *God and the Gay Christian: The Biblical Case in Support of Same-Sex Relations* (New York: Convergent, 2014) with the creational narrative of David Bennett in *A War of Loves: The Unexpected Story of a Gay Activist Discovering Jesus* (Grand Rapids, MI: Zondervan. 2018); or that of Christopher Yuan, *Holy Sexuality and the Gospel: Sex, Desire, and Relationships Shaped by God's Grand Story* (Colorado Springs: Multnomah, 2018).

[9]See Ronald W. Pierce, "Evangelicals and Gender Roles in the 1990s: I Timothy 2:8-15: A Test Case," *JETS* 36, no. 3 (1993). For other prominent evangelicals who have similar stories, see Alan F. Johnson, ed., *How I Changed My Mind About Women in Leadership* (Grand Rapids, MI: Zondervan, 2010).

[10]Grudem sees the approval of homosexuality as "the final step" by evangelical feminism toward liberalism, including same-sex marriage: Wayne Grudem, *Evangelical Feminism: A New Path to Liberalism* (Wheaton, IL: Crossway, 2006), 237-49.

[11]I remain indebted to Stanley J. Grenz, *Welcoming but Not Affirming: An Evangelical Response to Homosexuality* (Louisville, KY: Westminster John Knox, 1998), though I do not agree with him on every point.

so why have I not done so on the other? This essay is my answer to that
lingering question.

AFFIRMING VERSUS NONAFFIRMING INTERPRETATIONS
RELATING TO SAME-SEX MARRIAGE

Biblical prescriptions regarding marriage. The prescriptive texts relevant
to the possibility of same-sex marriage include both the Old Testament
creation accounts (Gen 1–2) and the New Testament passages that cite the
"one-flesh" metaphor from Genesis 2:24 (Mt 19:4-6; 1 Cor 6:15-17; Eph 5:31).
I briefly summarize the pertinent content of each, after which I compare
affirming and nonaffirming interpretations. I should again note that book-
length treatments from affirming Christians address these texts. I briefly
summarize their arguments to show that both sides of this debate are critically engaging Scripture. Instead of levying the charge "affirming Christians just dismiss the Bible," I will show that this is not the case, and, like
so many egalitarians who have been accused of this same thing, I understand how hurtful such an accusation can be. I encourage readers to go to
these sources themselves to read the fuller arguments firsthand.

Genesis 1–2 describes humanity's creation in the divine image as male
and female (Gen 1:26-27). The man is formed from the ground, after which
the woman is taken from his side. Then, they unite as "one flesh" in sexual
intimacy so that Eve becomes "the mother of all the living" (Gen 2:24; 3:20;
cf. 1 Cor 11:8-12). The two share a unique relationship in that she is his
"bone" and "flesh" (Gen 2:23), forming a kinship bond that calls the man
to leave his parents and become one with his woman (Gen 2:24).[12] Eve's
formation specifically addresses Adam's aloneness (Gen 2:18), which prevents him from fulfilling the procreation aspect of the creation mandate.
She becomes a "corresponding helper" (*ezer kenegdo*; Gen 2:18, 20, my
translation) in that they are alike as human beings, yet they have different
anatomical and biological characteristics essential to this purpose.

The one-flesh metaphor from Genesis 2 is referenced in the New Testament in the words of Jesus, as well as in the writings of Paul. In

---

[12]This more literal translation should not be understood in the colloquial sense of a wife being
the husband's possession. Rather, it reflects the mutually corresponding language of "man and
woman" (Hebrew *'ish* and *'ishah*) in the passage.

Matthew 19:1-12 a group of Pharisees ask Jesus, "Is it lawful for a man to divorce his wife for any cause?" (Mt 19:3).[13] He responds by weaving together two threads, one from each creation narrative: "at the beginning the Creator 'made them male and female'" (Mt 19:4 NIV; see Gen 1:27), and "for this reason a man will leave his father and mother and be united to his wife, and the two will become one flesh" (Mt 19:5 NIV; see Gen 2:24). When the disciples challenge the difficulty of such a lifelong commitment, Jesus acknowledges that some may not be able to accept this. Then, he gives an illustration of "eunuchs," who because of birth, forced mutilation, or a personal choice "live like eunuchs for the sake of the kingdom of heaven" and may experience difficult lives when it comes to the question of marriage (Mt 19:12 NIV).[14] Perhaps Jesus has in mind the remarkably affirming statement in Isaiah 56:4-5 by Yahweh to "the eunuchs who keep my sabbaths, who choose the things that please me and hold fast to my covenant." They will have an everlasting name, better than sons and daughters, that will last forever. In the end, Jesus explains that "the one who can accept this word should" (Mt 19:12 NIV).

In 1 Corinthians 6:12-20, Paul responds to news that some in this church are asserting "the right" or "privilege" to eat whatever foods they wish— even those that are unclean or have been offered to idols. Building on this, he turns his readers' attention to the issue of sexual immorality (*porneia*), specifically a married man having sex with a prostitute—a practice common in Greco-Roman society.[15] Both eating food and having sex, he argues, constitute things we do with our bodies, which will be fully transformed in the end. In support of marital fidelity, he cites from Genesis 2:24, "The two shall be one flesh" (1 Cor 6:16). Then he adds, "Every sin a person commits is outside the body; but the fornicator sins against the body

---

[13]I have chosen the longer of the accounts, although the same case could be made from Mk 10:1-12.

[14]The Greek *eunouchos* could be translated, "bedroom guard," describing castrated males who guarded the women's living quarters. The term is used here to describe persons physically incapable (for whatever reason) of having male-to-female, penetrative sexual intercourse. For a helpful study on the intersex community by an affirming evangelical scholar, see Megan K. DeFranza, *Sex Difference in Christian Theology: Male Female, and Intersex in the Image of God* (Grand Rapids, MI: Eerdmans, 2015).

[15]For the question of whether this should be associated with cultic prostitution, see S. Donald Fortson III and Rollin G. Grams, *Unchanging Witness: The Consistent Christian Teaching on Homosexuality in Scripture and Tradition* (Nashville: B&H Academic, 2016) 365n34.

itself. . . . Therefore, glorify God with your body," which is a "temple of the Holy Spirit" (1 Cor 6:18-20). Regarding this, both sides of the evangelical same-sex-marriage debate agree that sexual sin against one's own body is serious and should not be taken lightly, as it too often is in the current "hookup" culture in Western society.[16]

Playing off of these remarks while at the same time referencing a letter he received from them, Paul pens his longest collection of remarks on marriage and singleness (1 Cor 7:1-40). Here, among twelve prescriptions for mutuality in a male-female marriage, he argues that celibate single-ness is equally as good a gift from God as marriage—*if not better*. In every instance throughout this passage, his language is gender inclusive yet differentiated, resulting in a strong and countercultural statement about mutuality in a male-female marriage.[17] In this context, Paul's con-cession that those who cannot control their lusts should marry (1 Cor 7:7-9) is especially relevant to the discussion of same-sex marriage. His reference to an individual "gift" (*charisma*) may infer a "special abil-ity" to remain single and celibate (as Paul chooses to do), or possibly, to God's "gift of marriage" to some and "gift of singleness" to others.[18] I will return to this below.

Paul also cites the one-flesh metaphor from Genesis 2:24 in Ephe-sians 5:15-33 in the context of his command to "be filled with the Spirit" (Eph 5:18), among other things as this is manifested in "be[ing] subject to one another out of reverence for Christ" (Eph 5:21).[19] He addresses wives and husbands alike regarding how this should be practiced in the context of Greco-Roman household codes. For the wife, no further instruction seems necessary regarding this commonly accepted practice, except to say

---

[16]Brownson, *Bible, Gender, Sexuality*, 101-4. See the analysis by Justin R. Garcia of this now com-monly accepted practice even in churches and other Christian organizations: "Sexual Hookup Culture: A Review," *Review of General Psychology* 16, no. 2 (2012): 161-76. Also see J. Robin Maxson with Garry Friesen, "Cohabitation: A Dangerous Liaison," in *Singleness, Marriage, and the Will of God: A Comprehensive Biblical Guide* (Eugene, OR: Harvest House, 2012).

[17]Paul speaks of man and woman, husband and wife, widowers and widows, brothers and sisters, unmarried men and virgin women, sometimes mixtures of the above—and, in one case, the gender-inclusive "each other" (*allēlous*, 1 Cor 7:5).

[18]Vines, *God and the Gay Christian*, 49-50; Kenneth Berding, *What Are Spiritual Gifts? Rethinking the Conventional View* (Grand Rapids, MI: Kregel, 2006), 60-61.

[19]The Greek has the participial form of *hypotassō* ("submitting") as the last of the five participles following the imperative "be filled with the Spirit" in Eph 5:18.

that this has not changed in Christ. In contrast, there is a radical, counter-cultural shift for the husband, who now is to love his wife sacrificially, just as Christ in sacrificial love died for his body, the church. This stronger emphasis for the husband is informed by the creation mandate for a man to "leave his father and mother and be united to his wife" so that "the two will become one flesh" (Eph 5:31; see Gen 2:24).

Summarizing and contrasting interpretations of the prescriptive passages. Affirming interpretations of Genesis 1–2 (especially the New Testament references to one flesh in Gen 2:24) focus on sameness in a kinship bond, mutual love, and covenant, as well as faithfulness and care between marriage partners, rather than sexed differences.[20] Although the pattern of marriage between a man and a woman continues to be the *norm*, they argue, it was not intended by God to be *normative*. Moreover, Jesus' emphasis on spiritual family over procreation in the new-covenant era (Lk 9:23; 14:26) allows for the possibility of divorce (Mt 19:9)—and he declares that marriage will disappear altogether in heaven (Mt 22:30; Mk 12:25).[21] Further, affirming evangelicals insist that requiring lifelong celibacy of people with a same-sex orientation who do not have the "gift" (1 Cor 7:7-9) is unreasonable and unnecessarily burdensome—perhaps even impossible.[22] In addition, they note, younger persons are leaving the church over this issue, and emotional trauma—even suicide—is resulting from making such demands.[23] Therefore, it is concluded, covenanted, Christian, same-sex marriages are not explicitly prohibited in Scripture and can accomplish the essential, biblical prescriptions for marriage just as well as male-female marriages.[24] Even the creational aspect of procreation can be addressed through a surrogacy, in vitro fertilization, and/or adoption.

---

[20]Keen, *Scripture, Ethics*, 30-31; Brownson, *Bible, Gender, Sexuality*, 29-34.

[21]Though written from a nonaffirming perspective, see Joseph H. Hellerman, *When the Church Was Family: Recapturing Jesus' Vision for Authentic Christian Community* (Nashville: B&H, 2009), 53-75.

    Evangelicals generally have come to make exceptions to Jesus' prohibition of divorce for sexual immorality, such as in cases of abuse.

[22]Brownson, *Bible, Gender, Sexuality*, 97-101; Vines, *God and the Gay Christian*, 49-50; Keen, *Scripture, Ethics*, 63-74.

[23]Mark Achtemeier, *The Bible's Yes to Same-Sex Marriage: An Evangelical's Change of Heart* (Louisville, KY: John Knox, 2015), 9-14.

[24]Brownson, *Bible, Gender, Sexuality*, 97-101.

In comparison, nonaffirming arguments emphasize marital unity with sexual diversity as part of God's design for humanity, who was created male and female (cisgendered), yet each as a whole and complete person in the divine image.[25] The man's physical aloneness—that is, without a woman—would have prevented him from fulfilling God's call to procreate.[26] When Jesus addresses divorce, he intentionally includes "male and female" language—even though it was not necessary to make his point— and includes the "one-flesh" reference as a symbol of this indissoluble male-female bond. For Jesus, it seems to be one man, one woman, one flesh, for one lifetime. Paul reflects the same reasoning in his call for sexual purity (1 Cor 6:16, 18), celibate singleness, and mutual submission in marriage (Eph 5:31). Therefore, the nonaffirming view asserts that the only two viable options are a faithful male-female marriage or celibate singleness— both made new in Christ. Either of these lifestyles is possible and reasonable with the empowerment of God's Spirit—though neither is easy. Moreover, human flourishing is equally attainable without marriage, children, or being sexually active.[27] In short, the full functioning of the gifts of the Spirit does not require a marital bond to enact. Moreover, for Paul, marriage is not God's "gift" (*charisma*) to everyone (1 Cor 7:7). Finally, only such a theology of marriage faithfully carries forward the long-standing tradition of the Christian church.[28]

Biblical prohibitions of same-sex intercourse. The prohibitive texts of Moses and Paul (Gen 19:1-10; Judg 19:1-30; Lev 18:22; 20:13; Rom 1:18-32; 1 Cor 6:9-11; 1 Tim 1:8-11) comprise the substance of the ongoing debate on same-sex marriage. Affirming arguments, often pejoratively, label these "clobber texts" or dismiss these as merely "fragments" of passages.[29] I have included these because we as evangelicals should not prejudge a portion of Scripture because of its harshly negative tone or exclude it from

---

[25]Yuan, *Holy Sexuality and the Gospel*, 88-90.

[26]Sean McDowell and John Stonestreet, *Same-Sex Marriage: A Thoughtful Response to God's Design for Marriage* (Grand Rapids, MI: Baker, 2014), 38-42.

[27]Song, *Covenant and Calling*, 18. He rightly makes this point, though he affirms same-sex "covenant partnerships" that are of a sexual nature.

[28]Wesley Hill, "Christ, Scripture and Spiritual Friendship," in *Two Views on Homosexuality, the Bible, and the Church*, ed. Preston Sprinkle (Grand Rapids, MI: Zondervan, 2016), 127-31.

[29]Steve Harper, *Holy Love: A Biblical Theology for Human Sexuality* (Nashville: Abingdon, 2019), 35; Achtemeier, *Bible's Yes to Same-Sex Marriage*, 75-102.

consideration due to its brevity. Therefore, as with the prescriptive texts above, the pertinent content of each is briefly summarized, after which affirming and nonaffirming interpretations are compared.

Many discussions of this topic still begin with two Old Testament stories that involve same-sex gang rape.[30] In Genesis 19:1-10, two angels appearing as men visit Lot in Sodom and are threatened with gang rape by "wicked men" from the city. Abhorrently, Lot offers his virgin daughters to the mob in their place, but they want the apparently male visitors.[31] Judges 19:1-30 contains a similar account where a traveling Levite faces this kind of situation at Gibeah, where "wicked men" surround the house where he is staying and demand the host send out his guest so they can rape him. Again, two virgin daughters are offered in their place, but this time the Levite's concubine is offered as well. The latter is taken and raped to death. Both sides of the debate acknowledge that these are cases of rape—not same-sex attraction. Most likely, this represents an expression of radically inhospitable behavior in ancient Near Eastern culture (see Abram and Lot; Gen 18:1-8; 19:1-3). Nineteen Old Testament and New Testament texts reference the Sodom narrative (none mention Judg 19), of which three are especially relevant: Ezekiel 16:49-50; 2 Peter 2:6-7; and Jude 5-7. Ezekiel is concerned with Sodom being "arrogant, overfed and unconcerned; they did not help the poor and needy, and were haughty and did detestable things" (*toebah*) before God. Similarly, Peter refers to their "sensual conduct" (ESV; Greek *aselgeia*). Finally, Jude notes their "sexual immorality and perversion" (ESV; *ekporneuō* and *sarkos heteras*; the latter might be translated more literally "different flesh," connoting that which is counter to the cultural norm).

Leviticus 18:22; 20:13; along with Deuteronomy 23, are the most relevant Old Testament texts because of their sexually related prohibitions, as well as their being referenced three times in the New Testament: Romans 1;

---

[30]It is acknowledged by both sides as common knowledge that rape has always been more about power and domination than sexual attraction, whether it is same-sex or opposite-sex and whether it occurs in ancient warfare or modern society.

[31]The terrifying reality of the way young girls and adult women were treated in the ancient world calls to mind the even more disturbing fact of the ongoing abuse experienced by them around our world today. See the compelling work by Elaine Storkey, *Scars Across Humanity: Understanding and Overcoming Violence Against Women* (Downers Grove, IL: IVP Academic, 2018).

1 Corinthians 6; and 1 Timothy 1. The nearly identical language from the two expressions of the Levitical law makes it possible to discuss Leviticus 18 and Leviticus 20 together.[32] Both laws refer to a "man" (*'ish*) lying sexually with a "male" (*zakar*) as he would with a "woman" (*'ishah*), and denounce this act as "detestable" (*toebah*).[33] The Levitical prohibition of male-to-male sex appears among a wide range of unlawful sexual behaviors, including incest, prostitution, adultery, bestiality, child sacrifice to the pagan god Molek, and having sex with a woman during her monthly menstrual period (Lev 18:6-23; 20:10-21).[34] In one list, this prohibition is situated between child sacrifice and bestiality (Lev 18:21-23); in the other, it appears between two incest laws (Lev 20:12-14).

Romans 1:18-32 rightly remains the most frequently referenced New Testament text for this debate, because it places the Levitical prohibition against male-to-male sex into a larger theological context, as well as being the only mention in the New Testament of women acting in a similar way (Rom 1:27). These verses are preceded by Paul's proclamation of the gospel: the power of a righteous God for salvation to everyone who believes (Rom 1:16-17). He continues by declaring God's wrath against the unrighteousness of sinful humanity (Rom 1:18; 3:20), which leads to an announcement of God's saving righteousness by faith in Christ and a call for righteous living throughout the rest of Romans.

The indictment of pagan Gentiles by the apostle to the Gentiles is made clear in Romans 1:18-32 in his appeal to "nature," as well as in his description of Greco-Roman forms of idolatry and same-sex behavior. His argument concerns their rejection of God and the divinely imposed consequences of their choice. Paul asserts that God's invisible attributes are made clear to all humanity through creation, rendering all without excuse. Because they exchanged the truth of God's glory in order to worship created things rather than the Creator, God "gave them over . . . to sexual impurity . . . , shameful lusts . . . , and a depraved mind" (NIV; *paredōken*,

---

[32]Lev 18:22 is a prohibitive command ("Do not . . ."), whereas Lev 20:13 is a case law ("If a man . . .").

[33]The Hebrew terms *'ish* and *'ishah* also appear in Gen 2:23-24, whereas *zakar* is used in Gen 1:27.

[34]Menstrual sex (Lev 18:19; 20:18) is widely considered safe and healthy today for both marriage partners. Most Old Testament scholars see this as being related to the significant place blood played in the Levitical holiness code. See John W. Kleinig, *Leviticus*, Concordia Commentary Series (St. Louis: Concordia, 2003), 463.

"to deliver over," appears three times in Rom 1:24-28).[35] The passage concludes with a lengthy vice list (Rom 1:29-31), after which Paul declares that persons who practice such things deserve to die—along with anyone affirming them (Rom 1:32). Although, in the New Testament era, the apostle is not calling for the execution of those indicted in this list, he still insists that they are *deserving* of that penalty. Therefore, it is difficult to soften the sharp edge reflected here—as much as we might prefer—except to recall once again his words, "And that is what some of you used to be. But you were washed, you were sanctified, you were justified in the name of the Lord Jesus Christ and in the Spirit of our God" (1 Cor 6:11).

The most frequently referenced statement in the same-sex marriage debate appears in Romans 1:26-27, where Paul criticizes the behavior of both "males and females."[36] He writes,

> Even their females exchanged the "natural use of sexual relations" [*physikēn chrēsis*] for that which is unnatural. In the same way [*homoiōs*] the males also abandoned "natural sexual relations" [*chrēsis*] with females and were inflamed with lust for one another. Males committed "shameful acts" [*aschēmosynē*] with other males, and received in themselves the due penalty for their error. (my translation)

Paul's longer statement regarding the males reflects the fact that male same-sex sexual behavior was more common in Greco-Roman culture at this time, and most commonly including pederasty, prostitution, and sex with slaves. However, the linking of the two sexes with "in the same way" makes it clear that Paul believed female same-sex sexual relations to be wrong as well.[37]

In addition to the vice list in Romans 1:29-32, similar references to male-to-male sex appear in 1 Corinthians 6:9-11 and 1 Timothy 1:8-11. Again, strong language introduces the 1 Corinthians list, declaring, "Do you not know that [the unrighteous; *adiakos*; cf. Rom 1:18, 29] will not inherit the

---

[35]Compare the use of this term in the LXX regarding Israel's sin and God "giving them over" to judgments (e.g., Lev 26:25; Judg 2:14; 6:1; 13:1).

[36]Paul uses the Greek terms *thēlys* and *arsēn*—instead of *gynē* and *andros/anēr*, perhaps indicating that he is referencing the LXX of Gen 1:27.

[37]For an analysis of female homoeroticism in Paul's time, see Bernadette J. Brooten, *Love Between Women: Early Christian Responses to Female Homoeroticism*, Chicago Series on Sexuality, History, and Society (Chicago: University of Chicago Press, 1998).

kingdom of God" (1 Cor 6:9; cf. Rom 1:32). At the least, this speaks to the seriousness of willful, persistent sin that prevents believers from fully realizing God's kingdom blessings in their lives (see 1 Cor 6:10). This involves a transformative process of coming fully under God's kingdom rule in this age in preparation for the age to come.[38] In 1 Corinthians 6:9, the terms *malakos* and *arsenokoitēs* seem to refer to the passive and active participants in male same-sex acts. Similarly, the occurrence of *arsenokoitēs* by itself in 1 Timothy 1:10 likely carries the more general meaning of "men who have sex with men." Because of this, these two New Testament texts are regularly treated together in this debate, as both reflect the Septuagint translation of Leviticus 18:22; 20:13. In the Old Testament texts, the verb *koimaōmai* (Lev 18:22) and the noun *koiten* (Lev 20:13), meaning "to go to bed with," appear with the noun *arsenos* ("a man or male person"). Paul combines these terms in a single word, *arsenokoites*, to describe "men who go to bed in a sexual sense with other men." In 1 Corinthians 6:9, *malakos* ("soft men") can connote effeminate behavior or a culturally perceived weakness of men.

Summarizing and contrasting interpretations of the prohibitive passages. Affirming interpretations point out that gang rape is at issue in the Genesis and Judges narratives. Moreover, it is argued, Jude's "different flesh" language (*sarkos heteras*) connotes difference rather than sameness, suggesting that *sarkos homoiōs* ("similar flesh") would have been more appropriate if Jude had intended to connote *homo*sexual behavior.[39] Similarly, the specific laws in Leviticus 18; 22 are taken to refer to Canaanite cultic prostitution, as neither mention same-sex intercourse in general. It is also noted that most Old Testament laws are no longer considered binding to New Testament believers, such as circumcision, kosher eating, and holy days (Gal 2:1-16; 4:8-11; 5:2-6).[40] This line of reasoning is reinforced by the New Testament emphasis on the spiritual family and discipleship rather than marriage and procreation (Lk 9:23; 14:26), leading to its disappearance altogether in heaven (Mt 22:29-30; Mk 12:24-25). Moreover, they

---

[38]Anthony C. Thiselton, *The First Epistle to the Corinthians: A Commentary on the Greek Text* (Grand Rapids, MI: Eerdmans, 2000), 438.

[39]Vines, *God and the Gay Christian*, 69.

[40]Justin Lee, *Torn: Rescuing the Gospel from the Gays-vs.-Christians Debate* (New York: Jericho, 2012), 174-78.

insist that even Jesus engages in "legal deliberations" on the law to set aside some Sabbath restrictions in order to heal a person experiencing a significant humanitarian need (Mt 12:9-13; Jn 5:5-9).[41]

Further, affirming interpreters understand Paul to be addressing four things in Romans 1:18-32: (1) excessive lust by those not content with heterosexual relationships; (2) shameful treatment of a man "as a woman" in a patriarchal society; (3) selfish and socially irresponsible relationships that were nonprocreative; and (4) a "natural order" (*physikēn*) in terms of "one's individual disposition."[42] These may suggest that Paul has in mind the well-documented sexual exploits and pagan orgies of emperor Gaius Caligula, who was assassinated about a decade before Paul wrote this letter. Moreover, they insist that the references to creation are too general to be connected directly with Adam and Eve. Therefore, this passage seems to be more likely addressing pagan idolatry and lustful excesses as a *sinful kind of* same-sex acts. Finally, the terms for "soft men" (*malakos*) and "male bedders" (*arsenokoites*) could refer simply to pederastic same-sex behavior or rape of slaves.[43] The conclusion would then follow that none of these texts addresses Christian covenanted same-sex marriage, which can be blessed by God today.

In contrast, nonaffirming interpretations emphasize that in the Sodom narrative (Gen 19) the angels appear as "men" (MT *'ish*; LXX *andros*; Gen 19:10-12).[44] Moreover, the commentary on this story elsewhere in Scripture uses language of "detestable things" (*toebah*; Ezek 16:50); "sensual conduct" (ESV; *aselgeia*; 2 Pet 2:7); and "sexual immorality and perversion" (ESV; *ekporneuō* and *sarkos heteras*; Jude 7)—the last connoting something "different" from what God intends for people. Radically inhospitable behavior is certainly part of this story, but it is not the writer's only emphasis. Similarly, the immediate contexts of the Levitical laws (Lev 18:22; 20:13) include long lists of sexual sins, most of which are still considered

---

[41]Keen, *Scripture, Ethics*, 64.

[42]Brownson, *Bible, Gender, Sexuality*, 156-61, 223-55, 266-67. He further contends that *physikos* can also connote in a positive sense the "natural order of traditions and customs" (1 Cor 11:14), as well as in a negative sense the natural desires of the body (Eph 2:3).

[43]These terms could possibly refer to nonsexual behavior. See Vines, *God and the Gay Christian*, 117-31.

[44]Since there is no place in Scripture where angels are described as having wings, these angels likely appear as men.

wrong by Christians today, including incest, prostitution, adultery, and bestiality. Although the reference to child sacrifice to Molek in these texts could possibly suggest cultic prostitution, the Levitical prohibition explicitly mentions only male-to-male sex. Moreover, more recent Old Testament scholarship has moved away from this interpretation.[45]

Further, Paul's four concerns in Romans 1:18-32 are better summarized as (1) the universal nature of the fall of humanity, (2) same-sex intercourse as a graphic embodiment of the spiritual condition leading to the failure to glorify God as Creator, (3) sexual sin as one among many sins in the vice list, and (4) same-sex behavior as its own punishment.[46] In addition, the references to "creation," "creature," and "Creator" (Rom 1:20, 25) make it adequately clear that Paul has the biblical creation accounts in mind, where sexual differentiation is associated with both creation and procreation. This provides a clue to the basic orientation for interpreting this passage.[47] In light of this, Paul's natural/unnatural argument more likely refers to biological differences, which is underscored by Paul's emphasis on same-sex acts—"men with men, and women with women" (Rom 1:26-27).

Concerning the vice lists, the terms for "soft or self-indulgent men" (*malakos*) and "male bedders" (*arsenokoites*) could possibly connote consensual sex between adult males.[48] Though pederasty or rape of slaves may be in view as well, Paul's language describes only male-to-male sex. Further, in Paul's use of the term *arsenokoites*—which he may have coined—an intentional link can be seen to Leviticus 18:22; 20:13 in Romans 1:32; 1 Corinthians 6:9; and 1 Timothy 1:10. Finally, Paul appeals to this Old Testament prohibition by citing the death penalty (Rom 1:32), as well as by combining the two terms used in the LXX that prohibit male-to-male sex (*arsen* and *koites*) when referring to "male bedders" (*arsenokoites*; 1 Cor 6:9; 1 Tim 1:10). If Paul had intended to specifically address the common practice of pederasty, he would have likely used the term *piderastēs* (from which the

---

[45]See Preston Sprinkle, *People to Be Loved: Why Homosexuality Is Not Just an Issue* (Grand Rapids, MI: Zondervan, 2015), 41-53, for a summary of the evidence.

[46]Richard B. Hays, "Homosexuality," in *The Moral Vision of the New Testament: A Contemporary Introduction to New Testament Ethics* (New York: HarperOne, 1996), 388.

[47]Song argues this point as it relates to Gen 1, though with an exclusive emphasis on procreation (*Covenant and Calling*, 62-67).

[48]Fortson and Grams, *Unchanging Witness*, 277-301.

English *pederasty* is derived).[49] These points better uphold male-and-female marriage as the God-designed context where sexual intercourse should occur.

Comparing affirming and nonaffirming interpretations. This broad, yet necessarily brief survey of the key biblical texts relevant to the question of same-sex marriage reveals several aspects of interpretation that are becoming more evident in this debate. Again, only evangelical arguments have been considered, though some of these issues are discernible as well across the broader range of biblical scholarship.[50]

First, a propensity to appear overly certain about one's conclusions on this matter—sometimes to the point of arrogance—thwarts a healthy and productive conversation that could lead to a better understanding of Scripture by all. Nonaffirming arguments have tended more often to exhibit this. On the other hand, affirming arguments tend to move in the opposite direction, frequently reflecting a hermeneutic of suspicion, uncertainty, and doubt—which might lead to the *possibility* of same-sex relationships, but not the *probability*. Most evangelicals need a better argument than this to change their definition of God's creational, male-female design for marriage that has endured until the last century.

Second, the idea of spirit versus letter of the law, and the call to love one another (Rom 13:8; 1 Jn 4:11; etc.) and to love our neighbor as the fulfillment of the law (Gal 5:14; see Lev 19:18; etc.), all need to be taken to heart, along with the very real challenges of requiring lifelong celibacy for persons with same-sex attractions. At the least, these require a deliberative and prayerful process of discerning humanitarian need, similar to what evangelicals use to allow for separation, divorce, and remarriage for Christian couples in continuing and unresolved instances of domestic abuse.[51] When the Pharisees boast about keeping the law, Jesus chides them with these words: "You . . . have neglected the weightier matters of the law:

---

[49]See David E. Garland, *1 Corinthians*, BECNT (Grand Rapids, MI: Baker Book House, 2003), 212-13.

[50]"Evangelical arguments" means interpretations that respect the inspiration and authority of Scripture, consider carefully the texts' historical, cultural, and literary contexts, and do not dismiss its teachings as irrelevant to contemporary readers or disregard the authorial intent.

[51]Keen, *Scripture, Ethics*, 63-74. Even the conservative organization Focus on the Family has recognized this. See Mary J. Yerkes, "Healing the Emotionally Abusive Marriage," February 1, 2007, www.focusonthefamily.com/get-help/healing-the-emotionally-abusive-marriage/.

justice and mercy and faith. It is these you ought to have practiced without neglecting the others" (Mt 23:23). This spiritually balanced approach prescribed by Jesus continues to serve as an example for his church today.

Third, the church must regain the lost virtue of cultivating nonsexual, yet deeply intimate and covenanted spiritual friendships—perhaps even ones that could be recognized in civil law as "partnerships" or "unions."[52] On the one hand, many holding a nonaffirming view fall short of showing an adequate appreciation for the emotional loneliness that can accompany lifelong celibacy. No one in our contemporary churches should have to go it alone, if we really believe the church is family. Moreover, we need a renewal of this core component of being Christ's church, one that would apply to persons of all sexual and gender orientations, or convictions on this debate.

On the other hand, some efforts toward finding the *possibility* of Scripture allowing for same-sex marriage seem driven by the desire for persons with same-sex attractions to fully express their sexuality. A comparison of what is possible versus impossible must be addressed further by affirming advocates. For example, Robert Song writes, "The overwhelming social, religious, pragmatic and rhetorical pressures [of Paul's day] would have made it all but impossible for him to have written differently than he did. But the fact that it would have been impossible for him does not mean that it is necessarily impossible for us who live in the space shaped by the story of which he was an apostle."[53] Similarly, Karen Keen concludes, "Evidence indicates that lifelong celibacy is not achievable for every person. Lifelong celibacy is possible for some, but traditionalists have not demonstrated that it is possible for every person."[54] In response, it seems that more consideration should be given to the statement of Jesus that "with God all things are possible" (Mt 19:26 NIV; Mk 10:27), as well as to the work of the Holy Spirit in our lives to empower us to resist sin and live more fully into God's will for our lives. Moreover, our churches need to embody what is means to be a family to support, live together with, and be a safe place for

---

[52]On friendships, see J. P. Moreland and Klaus Issler, *The Lost Virtue of Happiness: Discovering the Disciplines of the Good Life* (Colorado Springs: NavPress, 2006), chap. 8, "Cultivating Spiritual Friendships."

[53]Song, *Covenant and Calling*, 76.

[54]Keen, *Scripture, Ethics*, 103.

those with same-sex attraction, as well as to create more infrastructure (both internal and external) to see God do the seemingly impossible.

Fourth, questions of authorial intent and the nature of Scripture need to be examined specifically regarding this discussion. A small but growing number of evangelicals who affirm same-sex marriage suggest the necessity of "supplementing," "updating," and/or or "setting aside both the Levitical laws and Paul's prohibitions in the NT because of his 'pre-scientific' or 'limited, first-century understanding of human sexuality.'"[55] Because the full inspiration and authority of Scripture remains a core doctrine within evangelicalism (2 Tim 3:16), this necessity understandably raises legitimate concerns.[56]

Fifth, more work is still needed in important areas of theology and ethics—alongside exegesis and biblical background studies—as these important disciplines relate to this debate, especially for evangelical affirming arguments. The three strongest contributions to date are found in James Brownson's *Bible, Gender, Sexuality* (2013), Song's *Covenant and Calling* (2014), and Keen's *Scripture, Ethics and the Possibility of Same-Sex Relationships* (2018). Brownson provides the most comprehensive discussion of Romans 1:18-32, making the case for this text applying only to the excessive lust of Caligula's orgies—not to Christian, covenantal marriages. In comparison, Song appeals to the deemphasis on marriage in the New Testament church community (Lk 9:23; 14:26) to where it eventually disappears in heaven (Mt 22:29-30; Mk 12:24-25), allowing for a nonprocreative form of marriage that is distinctively Christian in this age of the already and not yet.[57] Finally, Keen asks her readers to consider more seriously (1) the overarching intent of biblical mandates for a good and just world, (2) a more deliberative process for applying biblical mandates to sexual ethics, and (3) evidence that lifelong celibacy is not achievable for every person.[58]

---

[55]See William Loader, "Homosexuality and the Bible," in Sprinkle, *Two Views on Homosexuality*, 45-48; also Keen, *Scripture, Ethics*, 106.

[56]See the Evangelical Theological Society's doctrinal basis, "About the ETS," Evangelical Theological Society, www.etsjets.org/about.

[57]Robert Song, "The Beginning and End of Marriage," in *Covenant and Calling*, 1-22.

[58]Karen R. Keen, "What Is Ethical? Interpreting the Bible like Jesus," in *Scripture, Ethics*, 54-67, and also 105-6. For a discussion and critique of Keen's primary arguments, see Preston Sprinkle, "Review of Karen Keen, *Scripture, Ethics, and the Possibility of Same-Sex Relationships*," Center

Although many evangelicals do not yet find these arguments fully compelling, their plausibility is sufficient to warrant further consideration of the role of theology and ethics in the debate between affirming and non-affirming evangelicals in an ongoing effort to better understand Scripture and its application to those created in God's image. The majority of evangelicals continue to choose spiritual friendship without a sexual component over same-sex marriages.[59]

Sixth, our core identity in Christ needs to play a more central and practical role in our understanding of the many identities we use to characterize who we are, including our personal gender or sexual identities.[60] This holds true whether it concerns the ethnic, socioeconomic, and gender oneness that we as believers share "in Christ" (Gal 3:26-29), or the nearly thirty aspects of being "in Christ" that Paul mentions in Ephesians 1–3 as the foundation for his references to "submit[ting] to one-another out of reverence for Christ" in Ephesians 5:21-32. As believers, this is who we are at our core, and as such must be related to the question of same-sex marriage. Sadly, this has been lacking in both affirming and nonaffirming arguments.

In the end, academic honesty calls us to acknowledge that nowhere in Scripture does Moses, Jesus, or Paul directly address same-sex marriage— although this should not be construed to imply that the idea was inconceivable to Paul. On the contrary, there is evidence to suggest consensual, same-sex relationships existed at his time—although such cases were seemingly rare.[61] Therefore, conclusions reached regarding the possibility of affirming Christian, monogamous, covenanted, same-sex marriages

---

for Faith, Sexuality and Gender, December 14, 2018, www.centerforfaith.com/blog/scripture -ethics-and-the-possibility-of-same-sex-relationships.

[59]See Wesley Hill, *Spiritual Friendship: Finding Love in the Church as a Celibate Gay Christian* (Grand Rapids, MI: Brazos, 2015).

[60]See Rankin Wilbourne, "A New Identity: Who Am I?," in *Union with Christ: The Way to Know and Enjoy God* (Colorado Springs: David C. Cook, 2016), 133-50. Also, for a comprehensive examination of this foundational principle, consult Constantine R. Campbell, *Paul and Union with Christ: An Exegetical and Theological Study* (Grand Rapids, MI: Zondervan Academic, 2012).

[61]For an accessible summary of the primary evidence, see Preston Sprinkle, "Did Adult Consensual Same-Sex Relationships Exist in Bible Times?," Center for Faith, Sexuality and Gender, www.centerforfaith.com/resources (accessed November 17, 2019). For a critique of James Brownson's claim to the contrary, see Branson L. Parler, "Worlds Apart?: James Brownson and the Sexual Diversity of the Greco-Roman World," *Trinity Journal* 38, no. 2 (2017): 183-200.

today continue to remain inferential.[62] Of course, this fact does not give us, as contemporary readers, license to do whatever we feel is right regarding this issue. Rather, our obligation as evangelicals is to discern with wisdom our most well-reasoned interpretations of Scripture, then to live our lives in its light with humility, compassion, and grace in Christ toward other believers—sacred siblings in Christ—who arrive at different conclusions.

CONCLUSION

This chapter began with a question from a college student asking whether the method of interpretating Scripture that led me to advocate for mutually shared leadership in marriage would logically lead me to affirm same-sex marriage. After a thorough reexamination of this question in preparation for this essay, my mind has not yet changed. Why? Although there is not one explicitly prohibitive passage in Scripture against mutually shared leadership in a Christian marriage, there are five prohibitive texts against same-sex sexual intimacy (discussed above).[63] These either confirm the creational model of marriage between a man and woman or prohibit same-sex intercourse.[64] Though it is true that none speaks directly to the question of a covenanted, monogamous, Christian, same-sex marriage, it is precisely the sexual component of such an intimate relationship that seems to be at issue in Scripture. Beyond that, covenanted and deeply intimate spiritual friendships that are not sexual in nature should be encouraged and celebrated between all believers—although these should not be called marriages. *is this what I'm trying to capture in my section?*

Further, although the new-covenant era has shifted the emphasis on marriage and procreation to that of disciple making, the creational model of male-female marriage consistently remains evident in the New Testament. Moreover, this human institution will only disappear completely in the age to come, when sexual desire between humans will no longer be a

---

[62]Scott B. Rae, *Moral Choices: An Introduction to Ethics*, 4th ed. (Grand Rapids, MI: Zondervan, 2018), 325.

[63]Even the call for wives to submit to their own husbands in Eph 5 appears in the immediate context of mutual submission. See in this volume the chapters by Lynn Cohick (on Col 3 and Eph 5) and Peter Davids (on 1 Pet 3) as these New Testament texts are discussed by Pierce and Kay (1 Cor 7) against the background of Paul's call for a mutual yielding of authority.

[64]Keen acknowledges this in *Scripture, Ethics*, 40.

concern but will be fulfilled in the mystery of divine love in union with the triune God.[65] Meanwhile, Scripture provides no other model for marriage in this age. Finally, regarding the crucial text in Romans 1, it is important to note that Paul's rhetorical purpose is to condemn self-righteous Jews by condemning all of humanity in terms of Gentile immorality—a condemning of the condemners. This should caution affirming and nonaffirming advocates—same-sex or opposite-sex attracted—to be more aware of their own shortcomings, often blinded by self-righteousness.

It has been the explicit substance and focus of each of the key passages relating to same-sex sexual intimacy—taken in their respective contexts— rather than a particular or unusual method of interpretation, that continues to lead me to a nonaffirming view of same-sex marriage. That said, the call to love one's neighbor and show compassion to those experiencing significant human need for relationship is clear in Scripture and must be taken more seriously by all who claim the name of Christ. Also, if the church is going to accommodate divorce (apart from instances of adultery or abuse) for believers who experience significant hardships, and encourage divorced Christians to remarry under any circumstances, we must better justify why this kind of accommodation cannot be allowed for same-sex marriage. This inconsistency has not yet been adequately addressed by nonaffirming scholars and church leaders.

In the end, as this important discussion and debate continues between Spirit-filled Christians who love God and his Word, I personally will continue to honor the fivefold commitment I make to my students every academic term: (1) to genuinely love all people with God's unconditional love—especially my spiritual siblings in Christ—demonstrating that love in a way they can feel, (2) to keep an open mind and heart toward this sensitive and important concern, (3) to regularly check my biases and prejudices as I watch for my own blind spots, (4) to pay careful attention to new research and thinking;[66] and (5) to allow God's Word and Spirit to continue to shape and reshape my sense of moral reasoning. Taken together, all of

---

[65]To explore this provocative area more fully, see Sarah Coakley, *God, Sexuality, and the Self: An Essay "On The Trinity"* (Cambridge: Cambridge University Press, 2013), 22-27, 308-34; also see Philip Seldrake, *Befriending Our Desires*, 3rd ed. (Collegeville, MN: Liturgical Press, 2016), 57-79.

[66]For example, see Darrin W. Snyder Belousek, *Marriage, Scripture, and the Church: Theological Discernment on the Question of Same-Sex Union* (Grand Rapids, MI: Baker Academic, 2021).

this can lead us one day to a better understanding of what God intends for his people regarding sexuality and gender, as well as singleness and marriage, in Christ. With this in mind, I close with Paul's prayer for the church at Philippi: "And this is my prayer: that your love may abound more and more in knowledge and depth of insight, so that you may be able to discern what is best and may be pure and blameless for the day of Christ, filled with the righteousness that comes through Jesus Christ—to the glory and praise of God" (Phil 1:9-11 NIV).

25

GENDER EQUALITY AND THE SANCTITY OF LIFE

Heidi R. Unruh and Ronald J. Sider

• • • • •

THE SANCTITY OF HUMAN LIFE

The biblical teaching about the unique status and equal dignity of every person appears powerfully from the beginning of Genesis: "God created humankind in his image, in the image of God he created them; male and female he created them" (Gen 1:27). Many biblical texts affirm that God cares about all of creation (e.g., Gen 9:8-11; Ps 36:6; Mt 10:29), but only women and men are described as bearing the very image of God. The psalmist exclaims that God has crowned persons with glory and honor, making them "a little lower than the angels" (Ps 8:5 NIV).[1] Clearly, humanity is set apart from the rest of creation by being connected with our Maker in a special way.

This unique status of human beings created in the image of God is the foundation for the prohibition against killing other persons: "Whoever sheds the blood of a human, by a human shall that person's blood be shed; for in his own image God made humankind" (Gen 9:6).[2] Throughout the

---

[1] Some biblical scholars note that a more accurate translation might read "a little lower than *God*," making the uniqueness of humanity even more forceful. See Claude Mariottini, "Rereading Psalm 8:5: In Search of a Better Translation," April 3, 2006, https://claudemariottini .com/2006/04/03/rereading-psalm-85-in-search-of-a-better-translation-2/.

[2] Scholars disagree whether this verse is prescriptive, meaning that God commands the execution of murderers, or descriptive, saying that people often do kill murderers. It is notable that God dealt with Cain, the first murderer, not by killing him but by giving him a protective mark so that

Old Testament, especially in the Law and the Prophets, God's people are enjoined to treat people made in the image of God with justice, extending special care and protection for those who are most vulnerable to oppression and violence.[3] We must imitate God's attention to "the foreigners, the fatherless and the widows" (Deut 14:29 NIV), whose marginalized status does not diminish their share in the *imago Dei*.

The New Testament strengthens and deepens this affirmation of the sanctity of human life. When the almighty Creator of the universe became an embryo in Mary's womb and then grew as a child and a man, God revealed in the most astonishing way that human persons have an innate worth and dignity. "We are no longer 'just' made in God's image, cared for in creation, delivered from our distress, protected by God's laws. . . . The incarnation elevates the status of every human being everywhere on the planet at every time in human history."[4] The most impoverished, oppressed persons in the world have the same nature that the Lord of all creation embraced by taking on human form (Phil 2:6-8).

Throughout his ministry, Jesus' loving, respectful treatment of marginalized people affirmed the unique, immutable value and dignity of every person. Children, lepers, despised Samaritans, beggars, and outcast women received the same invitation and teaching as the wealthy and politically powerful. Then Jesus took his love for humanity to the cross. The brutality of the crucifixion underlines that people have worth independent of their actions or qualities. At the moment when humans were acting as God's enemies, God in human form sacrificed all for their reconciliation (Rom 5:8-10). The "immeasurable, incalculable value of the human person" rests unshakably in God's own "immeasurably, uncalculatingly great love for human beings."[5]

The dignity and worth of every person is also powerfully underscored by the invitation to life eternal in the presence of our Creator. This loving

---

others would not take his life (Gen 4:13-16). Also relevant is that when Jesus was presented a case for which the explicit penalty in Mosaic law was capital punishment, Jesus did *not* support that action (Jn 8:3-11).

[3]See the numerous citations in chapter 3 of Ronald J. Sider, *Rich Christians in an Age of Hunger*, 6th ed. (Nashville: Thomas Nelson, 2015).

[4]David P. Gushee, *The Sacredness of Human Life* (Grand Rapids, MI: Eerdmans, 2013), 95.

[5]Gushee, *Sacredness of Human Life*, 96.

invitation has a comprehensive reach: "Your Father in heaven is not willing that *any of these little ones* should perish" (Mt 18:14 NIV). "God our Savior . . . wants *all people* to be saved. . . . [Jesus] gave himself as a ransom for *all people*" (1 Tim 2:3-6). Every person, regardless of the circumstance of their birth or the history of their life, is indelibly precious to God.

David Gushee summarizes the implications of this biblical understanding:

> Human life is sacred: this means that God has consecrated each and every human being—without exception and in all circumstances—as a unique, incalculably precious being of elevated status and dignity. Through God's revelation in Scripture and incarnation in Jesus Christ, God has declared and demonstrated the sacred worth of human beings and will hold us accountable for responding appropriately. Such a response begins by adopting a posture of reverence and by accepting responsibility for the sacred gift that is a human life. It includes offering due respect and care to each human being that we encounter. It extends to an obligation to protect human life from wanton destruction, desecration, or the violation of human rights. A full embrace of the sacredness of human life leads to a full-hearted commitment to foster human flourishing.[6]

The early church taught and lived this broad understanding of the sanctity of human life. Every single early Christian text that discusses the topic of killing says that Christians must not kill: whether in infanticide, gladiatorial contests, capital punishment, or war.[7] These early Christian writers included abortion in this list.[8] In the early fourth-century context of a violent Roman culture and widespread persecution of Christians, the theologian Lactantias asserted:

> When God forbids us to kill, he not only prohibits us from open violence, which is not even allowed by the public laws, but He warns us against the commission of those things which are esteemed lawful among people. Thus,

---

[6]Gushee, *Sacredness of Human Life*, 411.

[7]Ronald J. Sider, ed., *The Early Church on Killing* (Grand Rapids, MI: Baker Academic, 2012). This book gathers all extant texts and other documents related to what the early church said and did in regard to killing, up until the time of Emperor Constantine in the early fourth century.

[8]For example, early theologian Tertullian states: "In our case, murder being once for all forbidden, we may not destroy even the fetus in the womb." The Didache puts it bluntly: "You shall not murder a child by abortion." Cited in Sider, ed., *Early Church on Killing*, 166.

it will be neither lawful for a just man [a Christian] . . . to accuse anyone of a capital charge, because it makes no difference whether you put a person to death by word or rather by the sword. . . . Therefore with regard to this precept of God, there ought to be no exception at all but that it is always unlawful to put to death a person, whom God willed to be a sacred creature.[9]

As we hold this principle of the sanctity of human life against the harsh realities of our world, we see how it has been selectively and imperfectly applied. Throughout our history, not all people have been accorded full human status. Not all lives have been diligently protected and cherished. Not all violence against persons has been condemned. While these harms are not exclusive to one gender, we must recognize the many ways that women in our culture—and around the world—have struggled to have their humanity fully affirmed. The sanctity of their lives has been disrupted, both from overt violence and from the gender-based inequities deeply ingrained in the systems needed for life to flourish. And women in minority racial/ethnic groups have suffered compounded inequities, indignities, and loss.

A "full embrace of the sacredness of human life" provides a conceptual framework for Christians to address the many wrenching issues of our day. To be fully prolife means to intervene wherever the flourishing of human life is threatened. This threat may result either from direct actions that degrade and destroy life, such as war, human trafficking, and capital punishment; from lack of access to food, health care, and other life-giving necessities; or from the ruin of the environment on which all life depends. This holistic sense reclaims the meaning of the term *prolife* from the narrow, politicized mold into which it has been forced over the past few decades.

Abortion, which ends nearly one in five pregnancies in our country, is a prolife concern.[10] The death rate of one in twenty-five mothers in many developing nations from complications in pregnancy and childbirth (compared with one in fifty-six hundred women in the developed world) is a prolife concern.[11] Acute malnutrition suffered by fifty million children

---

[9]Sider, *Early Church on Killing*, 110.

[10]"Induced Abortion in the United States," Guttmacher Institute Fact Sheet, January 2019. An estimated 862,320 abortions were peformed in the US in 2017.

[11]See Sider, *Rich Christians*, 5, 7, 14-21, 162, for citations. Even in the US, however, maternal mortality rates for Black women are three to four times higher than for White women.

globally, taking the lives of six children every minute, is a prolife concern.[12] Political corruption that siphons resources intended for food and medicine is a prolife concern. One in four women experiencing severe abuse from an intimate partner—and churches looking the other way when perpetrators are "respectable" members—is a prolife concern.[13] Nearly half a million children in the foster-care system (disproportionately children of color), around seventeen thousand of whom will age out of the system annually without a permanent family, is a prolife concern.[14] Birth defects and illnesses inflicted on children by pollutants in the air and water is a prolife concern. And the hope-crushing poverty that leads many women to end a pregnancy they might otherwise have welcomed is a prolife concern.[15]

Wherever we see the sacred worth of human life challenged, as believers in the truth of Scripture and recipients of the grace of Jesus, we must resist and work toward restoration.

ABORTION

Every sanctity-of-life issue is contentious, but perhaps none more so than abortion. How do the biblical teachings on the sanctity of human life speak to abortion?

I (Ron) have revised my thinking on that question over my lifetime. In the early years of my teaching, in the late 1960s and early 1970s, I argued that since there is no biblical text clearly stating that the unborn is a person whose life must be protected, early-term abortion could be morally acceptable for various reasons, such as the laudable aim of slowing population growth. Nor was I alone. Several prominent evangelicals of that era agreed

---

[12]UNICEF, "Malnutrition Prevalence Remains Alarming: Stunting Is Declining Too Slowly While Wasting Still Impacts the Lives of Far Too Many Young Children," May 2018, http://data.unicef .org/topic/nutrition/malnutrition/#.

[13]"Domestic Violence Fact Sheet," National Coalition Against Domestic Violence, 2015, https:// ncadv.org/statistics.

[14]North American Council on Adoptable Children, "Foster Care Numbers Up for Fifth Straight Year," *Adoptalk* 4 (2018), www.nacac.org/2019/01/18/foster-care-numbers-up-for-fifth-straight-year.

[15]Lawrence Finer et al., "Reasons U.S. Women Have Abortions: Quantitative and Qualitative Perspectives," *Perspectives on Sexual and Reproductive Health* (September 2005): 110-18. In a sample of 1,160 women who had abortions, the reason "Can't afford a baby now" was selected by 73 percent of all respondents and 81 percent of those living under the poverty line.

publicly that abortion was sometimes morally permissible.[16] Then, in 1973, I was moved by reading Senator Mark Hatfield's long, impassioned speech condemning the Supreme Court's decision legalizing abortion. I admired Senator Hatfield as an evangelical Christian and a prominent leader in promoting peace and justice. His speech prompted me to rethink the issue and change my mind.

Since the value and dignity of human life originates with our Creator, it cannot be negated by any other factor. The image of God is not measured by qualities such as capacity for self-fulfillment, autonomy, quality of life, or social usefulness. No attribute belonging to a human—gender, age, physical or mental maturity or ability—affects their essential humanness and thus the sanctity of their life. Violence always dehumanizes.

This foundation, however, does not settle the question of abortion, because we are still faced with a crucial question: Are the unborn human?

Scripture nowhere teaches explicitly that the being in the womb is a person. But there are signs pointing in that direction. The Bible often uses words for the fetus that are normally applied to persons already born.[17] Thus Luke calls Elizabeth's unborn child a "baby" (*brephos*; Lk 1:41, 44). Biblical passages also frequently assume significant personal continuity between the unborn and the child after birth (e.g., Jer 1:5; Ps 51:5). Psalm 139:13-16 is perhaps the most striking example:

> For you created my inmost being; you knit me together in my mother's womb.
>
> I praise you because I am fearfully and wonderfully made. . . .
>
> My frame was not hidden from you when I was made in the secret place, when I was woven together in the depths of the earth.
>
> Your eyes saw my unformed body; all the days ordained for me were written in your book before one of them came to be. (NIV)

---

[16]For the documentation, see Ronald J. Sider, *Completely Prolife* (Downers Grove, IL: InterVarsity Press, 1987), 37.

[17]E.g.: Gen 25:22; 38:27-30; Job 1:21; 3:3, 11-19; 10:18-19; 31:15; Is 44:2, 24; 49:5; Jer 20:14-18; Hos 12:3. Technically, *embryo* is the term used for a developing baby from fertilization through the eighth week, when it becomes known as a *fetus*. In this essay we use the term *fetus* more generally to refer to the developing baby at any stage of pregnancy (though the majority of abortions actually take place during the embryonic stage).

The personal pronouns ("You knit *me* together in *my* mother's womb")
indicate that the psalmist assumed a direct link between himself as an
adult and the tiny being whom God had lovingly watched over in utero.

We must take care, however, not to press the biblical material beyond
what it clearly says. Although strongly opposed to abortion, a careful study
by the Orthodox Presbyterian Church insists "there is *no way to demon-*
strate, either from Scripture or from science or from some combination of
the two, that the unborn child *is* a human person from the point of
conception."[18] The Orthodox Presbyterian Church document considers
and rejects arguments adduced to prove that the fetus is a person based on
John the Baptist's leaping in the womb, the incarnation, and Psalm 51:5.[19]

Does the Bible provide any hint that the unborn child is *less* than a
human being? Some have found this suggestion in Exodus 21:22-24:
"When people who are fighting injure a pregnant woman so that there is
a miscarriage, and yet no further harm follows, the one responsible shall
be fined what the woman's husband demands, paying as much as the
judges determine. If any harm follows, then you shall give life for life, eye
for eye, tooth for tooth." Many commentators understand this difficult
text to mean that if the fetus is killed and a miscarriage follows, the penalty is a mere fine; but if the mother is hurt or killed, then the penalty is
commensurate. The consequent implication is that the fetus has less value
than the mother.

It does not follow from this passage, however, that abortion is permissible. This text talks only about accidental killing, which, if not assigned
the death penalty, is at least not condoned. "How can we defend the *inten-*
tional destruction of the unborn on the basis of a passage which condemns
even its *accidental* destruction?"[20] Furthermore, many scholars argue that
the wording of the Hebrew typically refers to the ordinary birth of a child
(meaning literally, "Her children came out") and is not used elsewhere in

---

[18]"Report of the Committee to Study the Matter of Abortion," in Minutes of the Thirty-Eighth
General Assembly, The Orthodox Presbyterian Church, Philadelphia, May 24-29, 1971, 146,
emphasis original. However, we note that after comprehensive analysis, this document concludes
that "abortion in nearly all cases must be regarded as murder." Similarly: John Jefferson Davis,
Abortion and the Christian (Phillipsburg, NJ: Presbyterian and Reformed, 1984), 61.
[19]"Report of the Committee," 146-48.
[20]"Report of the Committee," 141, emphasis original.

the Bible to mean a miscarriage.[21] The NIV is probably better: "If people are fighting and hit a pregnant woman and she gives birth prematurely but there is no serious injury, the offender must be fined." If the physical contact results in a premature birth, but baby and mother live, a fine is charged for the trauma.[22] If either the baby or mother suffers harm, an equivalent penalty is exacted. This translation would reinforce the equal status of the fetus. It also recognizes the justice claims of the mother.

Science likewise offers compelling insights though not definitive answers on the personhood of the unborn. Neonatal care is expanding the limits of fetal viability.[23] Clinical studies suggest when the fetus begins to differentiate the mother's voice or experience pain.[24] Detailed images of prenatal development illuminate every stage of the process, from the moment of fertilization through every stage of gestation, sometimes in the precision of three dimensions.[25] We can now literally peer into the "secret place" of Psalm 139 and watch the fetus being "woven together." While such images alone do not resolve the ethical questions, if nothing else, they imbue the phrase "sanctity of life" with a more tangible sense of awe and wonder.

Science can also tell us that from the moment of conception a genetically distinct human being exists, one that is fully contiguous with its postnatal

---

[21]See the argument in "Report of the Committee," 142-43; John Warwick Montgomery, *Slaughter of the Innocents* (Westchester, IL: Crossway Books, 1981), 98-101; C. F. Deil and Franz Delitzsch, *Biblical Commentary on the Old Testament: The Pentateuch*, vol. 2, trans. James Martin (Grand Rapids, MI: Eerdmans, n.d.), 134-35.

[22]It should be noted, however, that the word *prematurely* in the NIV translation is not in the Hebrew text of Ex 21:22. Both the NIV and the NRSV are, to some extent, interpretations.

[23]Viability means the point at which a fetus could survive with medical assistance outside the womb. When *Roe v. Wade* was decided in 1973, the threshold for fetal survival was twenty-four to twenty-eight weeks. Viability from twenty-three or even twenty-two weeks is now growing more possible. Fewer than 1.5 percent of abortions take place after this viability threshold. See Lucy Westcott, "Finding That Babies Born at 22 Weeks Can Survive Could Change Abortion Debate," *Newsweek*, May 7, 2015.

[24]Laura Flynn McCarthy, "What Babies Learn in the Womb," *Parenting*, www.parenting.com /article/what-babies-learn-in-the-womb (accessed May 17, 2019); Sara Miller, "Do Fetuses Feel Pain? What the Science Says," Live Science, May 17, 2016, www.livescience.com/54774-fetal -pain-anesthesia.html.

[25]See, e.g., the stunning images in Peter Tallack, *In the Womb* (Washington, DC: National Geographic Society, 2006); and Lennart Nilsson and Linda Forsell, *A Child Is Born* (New York: Bantam Books, 2020). See also Emma Green, "Science Is Giving the Pro-Life Movement a Boost," *The Atlantic*, January 18, 2018.

identity.[26] As French geneticist Jermoe LeJeune testified before a Senate subcommittee back in 1981: "To accept the fact that after fertilization has taken place a new human has come into being is no longer a matter of taste or opinion. The human nature of the human being from conception to old age is not a metaphysical contention, it is plain experimental evidence."[27] The physical form undergoes radical alteration from conception to birth, but it always belongs to a human. And because Scripture arguably teaches body-soul unity, it is reasonable to believe that the preborn human is also a spiritual being in some form and at some point.[28]

Mere biological continuity does not tell us, however, at what point the *imago Dei* is fully present. When should this prenatal human be considered a *person*, created in God's image, "crowned . . . with glory and honor" (Ps 8:5)? When would ending the pregnancy mean ending a person's life? Does the single-celled zygote, created in conception, share the same sanctity of life as you and I? Are any of the other distinct stages of development—implantation, brain stem activity, capacity to feel pain, viability—definitive signposts of the image of God?

Perhaps by probing the boundaries of the humanity of the being inside the woman, what we are really asking is, "When do we have to start considering the moral consequences of our actions toward this being?" In other words: When is the unborn our neighbor (Lk 10:25-29)?

As demonstrated by the wrangling over the interpretation of Exodus 21:22, Christians may in good conscience come to different biblical, philosophical, and public-policy conclusions on this question. Ecclesiastes 11:5 directs us to approach these matters with great humility and gravity: "As you do not know the path of the wind, or how the body is formed in a mother's womb, so you cannot understand the work of God, the Maker of all things" (NIV). Not knowing for certain, we ought to assume that the developing embryo *may* be truly a person made in the image of its Maker.

---

[26]See Oliver O'Donovan's discussion of the exception of identical twins, in *The Christian and the Unborn Child*, 2nd ed. (Bramcote, UK: Grove Books, 1975), 12-13.

[27]Testimony to Subcommittee on Separation of Powers, report to Senate Judiciary Committee, as quoted in Norman L. Geisler, *Christian Ethics: Options and Issues* (Grand Rapids, MI: Baker, 1989), 149.

[28]John W. Cooper, *Body, Soul, and Life Everlasting: Biblical Anthropology and the Monism-Dualism Debate* (Grand Rapids, MI: Eerdmans, 2000). In Gen 2:7, God gave the first human physical form before spiritual essence.

We ought to assume that, at some point in a pregnancy, an abortion would end an irreplaceable life sacred to God.

Uncertainties and controversies will remain. Our purpose in this essay is to offer a holistically prolife approach to the issue of abortion, in light of our calling to gender equality. We explore how the goal of authentic equality and mutual service for women and men is integral to affirming sanctity of life for the unborn.

FEMINISM AND ABORTION IN HISTORICAL PERSPECTIVE

The rallying cry "a woman's right to choose" shows how *prochoice* and *feminist* have become nearly synonymous.

A common interpretation among secular feminists is that the antiabortion movement emerged as an evangelical backlash against the women's movement, which gained strength from the legalization of abortion and which went hand in hand with the sexual revolution. This narrative holds that conservative Christians were uncomfortable with women's growing claims to self-determination. Thus, in this view, the evangelical wing of the church—led by (primarily White) men—has sought, then and now, to limit women's access to abortion as a tool of control over their bodies, their sexuality, and their lives.

While such motives have undoubtedly played a role, a closer look at the history of prolife activism reveals that it initially emerged out of the desire to empower women, not control them. The early feminists (though they did not necessarily call themselves such) of the nineteenth century embraced the rights of the unborn as a natural corollary of their struggle for the full and equal rights of women.[29] Rather than pitting the value of a woman's life against her unborn child's, as much of the abortion debate does today, early prolife advocates viewed these as interconnected. An extensive survey of the roots of prolife feminism concludes:

> The early feminists did celebrate motherhood as a uniquely female power and strength that deserved genuine reverence, while exposing the motherhood mystique as a cover-up for real-life degradations. Recognizing that women had creative capacities other than the womb's, early feminists fought

---

[29]Many of these feminist foremothers and their contribution to the prolife cause are profiled on the website of Feminists for Life, www.feministsforlife.org/herstory/ (accessed May 17, 2019).

for women's entrance into higher education and the professions. . . . Their perspectives on motherhood led naturally to their outspoken criticisms of prudery and the sexual double standard. . . . They regarded abortion as a violent wrong against *women* as well.[30]

Early feminists called attention to the ways male dominance hurt women, including how men pushed women toward abortions. Patriarchal norms enabled men to coerce sexual relationships, publicly shame pregnant unmarried women, pressure a woman to terminate her pregnancy, and withhold financial and social support needed to raise a child—all without social accountability. Renowned suffragist Susan B. Anthony decried in one of her passionate pieces against abortion: "Thrice guilty is he who, for selfish gratification, heedless of her prayers, indifferent to her fate, drove her to the desperation which impels her to the crime!"[31]

In *Defenders of the Unborn*, historian Daniel Williams calls attention to how arguments for abortion rights were appropriated by those seeking to maintain male, White hegemony.[32] Some saw it as a tool for limiting the population of social "undesirables," including people with disabilities. "It was a widespread belief among abortion-liberalization advocates . . . that society would be better off if fewer severely deformed babies were born." In the early 1900s, defense of abortions went hand in hand with support for "the eugenic use of birth control" to limit the reproductive capacity of women based on factors such as economic class, physical or mental ability, lifestyle, and race.[33] The continued use of abortion as a weapon of male domination is evident in the sex trade. One study of trafficked women found that over half had experienced at least one abortion, many of them under threat.[34]

---

[30]Mary Krane Derr, Rachel MacNair, and Linda Naranjo-Huebl, *ProLife Feminism: Yesterday and Today* (Bloomington, IN: Xlibris, 2006), 18, emphasis original. This argument is also developed in Brian Fisher, *Abortion: The Ultimate Exploitation of Women* (New York: Morgan James, 2014).

[31]Quoted in Frederica Mathewes-Green, "Susan B Anthony: Pro-Life Feminist," *Focus on the Family* magazine (January 2000).

[32]Daniel Williams, *Defenders of the Unborn: The Prolife Movement Before Roe v. Wade* (Oxford: Oxford University Press, 2016).

[33]Williams, *Defenders of the Unborn*. See also Ann Farmer, *By Their Fruits: Eugenics, Population Control, and the Abortion Campaign* (Washington, DC: Catholic University of America Press, 2008).

[34]Laura Lederer and Christopher Wetzel, "The Health Consequences of Sex Trafficking and Their Implications for Identifying Victims in Healthcare Facilities," *Annals of Health Law* 23, no. 1 (Winter 2014): 61-91.

To be clear, we do not believe that the mainstream of prochoice advocacy has been, or is now, driven by such abhorrent motives.[35] We also acknowledge that the prolife cause has sometimes been endorsed for equally wrong reasons, including the patriarchal impulse to control women's options and to shame women for their sexual activity (without reciprocal judgement on their male partners). Patriarchy and prejudice have from the beginning played a role in both sides of the abortion debate. So have sincere faith and compassion.

Against this checkered historical backdrop, we can trace a persistent strand of feminism that has merged passion for justice and equality with reverence for the sanctity of life. *ProLife Feminism* calls this a "new but old" approach to abortion: "Yesterday's prolife feminists practiced what today is called 'a consistent life ethic,' or respect for lives before, during, and after birth."[36] By emphasizing the inherent value and inalienable rights of the most vulnerable members of society—the unborn—early prolife advocates helped shape the concepts that were later used by civil rights activists and, ironically, prochoice feminists. Prochoice historian Carl Degler provides evidence for this trajectory:

> Seen against the broad canvas of humanitarian thought and practice in Western society from the seventeenth to the twentieth century, the expansion of the definition of life to include the whole career of the fetus rather than only the months after quickening is quite consistent. It was in line with a number of movements to reduce cruelty and to expand the concept of the sanctity of life. . . . The elimination of the death penalty, the peace movement, the abolition of torture . . . all represented steps in that centuries-long movement. The prohibiting of abortion was but the most recent effort in that larger concern.[37]

CONTEMPORARY PROLIFE FEMINISM

Since the 1960s, the prolife and prochoice positions have hardened into polarized, politicized, hostile camps.[38] For decades it has seemed

---

[35]For example, Kira Schlesinger, *Pro-Choice and Christian* (Louisville, KY: Presbyterian, 2017).
[36]Quoted in Derr, MacNair, and Naranjo-Huebl, *ProLife Feminism*, 16.
[37]Derr, MacNair, and Naranjo-Huebl, *ProLife Feminism*, 20.
[38]For a historical analysis of this schism, see Williams, *Defenders of the Unborn*; also Cynthia Gorney, *Articles of Faith: A Frontline History of the Abortion Wars* (New York: Simon & Schuster, 2000).

unthinkable that common ground could be forged across the abortion divide.[39] Yet there have always been those who did not feel wholly at home in either camp—those who have upheld the sanctity of life within the womb, while also caring deeply about the human rights and freedom of the mother and her access to health care, childcare, education, and economic support. Today, a growing number are claiming to be both pro-woman and prolife, redefining the established labels.[40] Rather than taking sides, they are changing the debate.

These prolife feminist groups tend to have quite a different vibe (and are far more likely to be led by women) than traditional, conservative prolife groups.[41] Younger activists in particular are more likely to draw on secular, humanitarian principles for the sanctity of life, "using the language of feminism, human rights, and the Black Lives Matter movement to make their case for a new culture of life."[42] The organization Secular Pro-Life points out that for millennials, unlike prior generations, concerns about abortion often go hand in hand with negativity toward religion (especially evangelicalism).[43] Yet some appear to be open to working with evangelicals on shared concerns.

Another attribute of many feminist prolife groups is less focus on single-issue political engagement. "The pro-life message is not about who is president or about legislation; it's about cultural change. . . . We have to humanize the child," says New Wave Feminists founder Destiny Herndon-De La Rosa. Legislative action on abortion is one strand in a web of support for vulnerable lives that extends "from womb to tomb." They see a direct link between empowering women and protecting pregnancies.

---

[39]As the founder of a group that works to defend abortion puts it, being a prolife feminist is like saying you are a vegan who likes chicken: "It's just not possible [to be feminist], if you don't believe a woman has the human right to make decisions about her body and her health care and her future." Quoted in Michael Alison Chandler, "How the 'Pro-Life Feminist' Movement Is Straddling the March for Life and Women's March," *Washington Post*, January 19, 2018.

[40]The majority of millennial women who identify as feminists consider themselves either prolife (18 percent) or *both* prolife and prochoice (37 percent). See Charlotte Gendron, "Less Than Half of Millennial Women Identify as 'Feminist,'" PRRI Spotlight Analysis, April 15, 2015, https://www.prri.org/spotlight/less-than-half-of-millennial-women-identify-as-feminist/.

[41]Ellen Duffer, "Where Do Pro-Life Feminists Belong?," *Religion & Politics*, June 27, 2017.

[42]Ruth Graham, "The New Culture of Life," *Slate*, October 11, 2016, www.slate.com/articles/double_x/cover_story/2016/10/the_future_of_the_pro_life_movement.html.

[43]Graham, "New Culture of Life." See also Lydia Saad, "Generational Differences on Abortion Narrow," Gallup Poll Report, March 12, 2010.

For example, a leader with Students for Life of America described an initiative that connects pregnant students with practical resources, peer encouragement, and academic support: "It's not just about her choosing life, although of course that is our passion. . . . But it's also about seeing her finish school, because we know the number one segment of our population that is at or below poverty level is single mothers."[44] Expanding access to resources, opportunity, and supportive relationships for women is a key prolife strategy.

Like their nineteenth-century forbears, the new generation of activists views abortion as a violent act that harms women as well as their unborn. They connect the goal of deterring individual abortions to the broader need to confront our culture of violence.

> The "unwanted child" who is made a victim of abortion is "unwanted" due to radically anti-life, materialistic values driving the entire culture. Thus, we wish to avoid scapegoating the women who abort in often desperate circumstances. It's not enough to say "choose life." We need to choose life, collectively, as a society, and make the choice of life a truly realistic one. We need to shift our thinking, and recognize the ways our entire culture is complicit in rejecting the most vulnerable among us, and work to correct this.[45]

Prochoice feminists equate restrictions on abortion with an attack on the autonomy of women. They assert that having the unique right to terminate a pregnancy is empowering to women, a necessary protection against the social forces arrayed to control women's lives. From this perspective, the unborn child may even appear as the aggressor: only a fetus can "make free, nonconsensual use of another living person's uterus and blood supply, and cause permanent, unwanted changes to another person's body. In the relationship between [fetus] and woman, the woman is granted fewer rights than a corpse."[46] But pitting women's needs and rights against those of the unborn perpetuates acceptance of hierarchical relationships and dominance over the weak. A sign made for a prolife march sums it up: "Abortion is the epitome of 'Might makes right.'"

---

[44]Graham, "New Culture of Life."

[45]"About Us," The New Pro Life Movement, www.thenewprolifemovement.com (accessed September 7, 2018).

[46]Sally Rooney, "An Irish Problem," *London Review of Books* 40, no. 10 (May 24, 2018), 16.

People such as Aimee Murphy, founder of Rehumanize International and the journal *Life Matters*, are reframing the conversation about power and rights.[47] Aimee was raped by an abusive boyfriend as a teen. He then threatened to kill her if she didn't get an abortion. "In that moment, something clicked," she now reflects. "I could not use violence to get what I wanted in life. I realized that if I were to get an abortion, I would just be passing oppression on to a child." She joins other prolife feminists in seeking to foster a culture of nonviolence, equality, compassion, and respect for human dignity.

Another common feature of prolife feminism is intersectionality. Intersectionality is the understanding that oppression and discrimination are compounded by multiple, overlapping aspects of social identity. An intersectional framework acknowledges that abortion is not only a women's issue but is also significantly affected by race, class, and culture.[48] This provides an inclusive lens for complex issues often reduced to bumpersticker simplicity. While traditional prolife leadership has been largely White and middle class, prolife feminist groups tend to be more culturally diverse. An intersectional approach to reducing abortion involves seeking empathy and working for justice across social divides.

For example, noting that abortion rates are up to five times higher for African American women than White women, Catholic feminist Kassie Iwinksi cautions against interpretations of this statistic rooted in racial stereotypes. Instead, she suggests,

> We can start by recognizing the impact that the intersection of racism and sexism plays in that statistic, and asking questions.
>
> *How is it influenced by systemic racism and generational poverty?*
>
> *How does the very real danger of simply giving birth in America as a woman of color play into that decision?*
>
> *How does our current approach to crisis pregnancy care and fertility awareness education center on White, middle-class women and families?*

---

[47]The mission of Rehumanize International: "We work to ensure that each and every human being's life is respected, valued, and protected. As such, we oppose all forms of aggressive violence, including but not limited to: abortion, unjust war, capital punishment, euthanasia, torture, embryonic stem cell research, assisted suicide, abuse, human trafficking, police brutality, etc." See www.rehumanizeintl.org.

[48]For a history of how racial oppression has impacted the abortion debate, see Dorothy Roberts, *Killing the Black Body: Race, Reproduction, and the Meaning of Liberty* (New York: Vintage, 1998).

By acknowledging the complexity of the issue, challenging our assumptions, and listening across social differences, Iwinksi says, we can "begin doing the work of fully living out the radical gospel of Christ."[49]

AN EVANGELICAL EGALITARIAN APPROACH

As evangelicals seeking to integrate biblical teachings on gender equality and the sanctity of life, what can we draw from the work of past and present prolife feminists? How should we engage with abortion and other threats to the sanctity of life, without repressing women? We suggest four distinctive contributions of an egalitarian, theologically orthodox approach.

First, as people who know we are created, loved, and saved by the Lord of all, we hold reconciliation at the heart of our engagement. This reconciliation has both a horizontal (with others) and vertical (with God) dimension.

Abortion may be a private decision, but it is inherently embedded in relationships. Too often, the decision to abort is made in a context of broken relationships with partners and close family members, in a climate of rejection, coercion, and fear. About half of women who had abortions cited relationship problems or a desire to avoid single motherhood as a factor; one in four did not want others to know they were pregnant; one in five indicated pressure from a partner or parent.[50] An abortion ends the pregnancy, but not the feelings of betrayal, anger, and resentment that may accompany it. According to psychiatrist Philip Sarrel: "Abortion is frequently a negative turning point in a relationship leaving scars which can undermine the future of the couple either together or as individuals."[51]

Relational brokenness is also internalized—abortion literally disrupts a woman's ties with her offspring. The research is not settled, but evidence indicates at least one quarter of postabortive women experience lasting guilt, sadness, or depression.[52] Certainly, messages of condemnation and

---

[49]Kassie Iwinksi, "Intersectionality and the Catholic Feminist," FemCatholic, February 16, 2018, www.femcatholic.com/intersectionality-catholic-feminist.

[50]Finer et al., "Reasons U.S. Women Have Abortions."

[51]Quoted in Priscilla Coleman, "The Decline of Partner Relationships in the Aftermath of Abortion," *Association for Interdisciplinary Research in Values and Social Change* 20, no. 1 (2007).

[52]Coleman, "Decline of Partner Relationships." The impacts of abortion are complex, and we caution against overgeneralizing. For example, some studies find the most common emotion women report after an abortion is relief. See Corrine Rocca, "Emotions and Decision Rightness over Five Years Following an Abortion," *Social Science & Medicine* 248 (March 2020).

shame exacerbate these negative impacts. Women who have had abortions often struggle to accept God's forgiveness and to forgive themselves.

Following Jesus offers a path to healing and restoration. Frederica Mathewes-Green's book *Real Choices* shares the stories of postabortive women, including "Sally's" experience at a Catholic church retreat:

> When the priest invited anyone who wanted to come up for confession, I thought, "Not me. What's the point?" But to my amazement my legs just stood me up and started walking forward. . . . Somehow I went and sat in front of [the priest]. When I looked at him and said, "I had an abortion," I thought he would be horrified. But instead he looked at me with such love. And the thing that he said that I'll never forget, the thing that really started my healing, was this: "When you were up on that table, Jesus was right there with you."[53]

Some feminists argue that the way to end negative emotions after an abortion is to normalize this choice: if religious people would just stop telling women abortion is wrong, they would not feel any burden of guilt. Truly, shaming women is not the answer. Not only does this drive people away from prolife options, but it heaps further pain on an already stressful experience. Rather, our message is that Jesus is good news for broken relationships with God, self, and others. We are all equal in our need for deep reconciliation and healing. And Jesus is "right there" with each of us.

A second key feature of an evangelical egalitarian approach is that it addresses reproductive issues not just as a woman's concern but as a two-parent concern. Our starting point is God's original intention that children be brought into the world in the context of loving, committed parents. In Genesis 2:24, this relationship is envisioned as two becoming "one flesh." This childbearing union—a lifelong, loving partnership of interdependent equals—is a far cry from most sexual connections on the road to an abortion.[54]

A study of postabortive women found a high prevalence of concerns involving partners:

---

[53]Mathewes-Green, *Real Choices* (New York: Multnomah Books, 1994), 95-96.

[54]Only one in seven women was married at the time of their abortion, according to Finer et al., "Reasons U.S. Women Have Abortions." To be fair, too many births take place in relationships that are far from ideal as well.

Relationship problems included the partner's drinking, physical abuse, unfaithfulness, unreliability, immaturity and absence (often due to incarceration or responsibilities to his other children). Many of these women were disappointed because their partner had reacted to the pregnancy by denying paternity, breaking off communication with them or saying that they did not want a child.[55]

All too often it is not safe, advisable, or even possible for women to consult the biological father about their reproductive choices.

However, if the father *is* open to some form of a healthy dialogue, God's two-parent ideal calls for his inclusion in the decision-making process. Unless her mental and physical health is at risk, is it right for a woman to contemplate terminating her pregnancy without the input (or perhaps without even the awareness) of the father?

The absence of men in prochoice rhetoric—*A woman's right to choose; Trust women; Not your uterus, not your business!*—points to a double standard that undermines gender equality. Legal abortion gives women the right to decide the reproductive outcome of their sexual activity; men have no such right. If a man impregnates a woman who decides to keep the baby, he is legally responsible for supporting his child, whether he wished to become a parent or not. "While for women genetic parentage (conception) does not entail social parentage (motherhood or caring for a born child), this is not the case for men. . . . Equality of the sexes can—and should— hold both sexes to the same high moral standard, not absolve both from moral responsibility."[56] This moral responsibility can only be fulfilled in a context of mutuality.

Prochoice feminism centers on the rights and needs of the woman. Prolife feminism adds to this a concern for the rights of the person inside the woman. Prolife egalitarians must also consider the personhood of the male in the picture. This does not mean enabling men to be irresponsible, oppressive, or abusive. But we must acknowledge that the father's life is also sacred.

---

[55]Finer et al., "Reasons U.S. Women Have Abortions."

[56]Sulia Mason and Karen Mason, "Feminism and Abortion," in *Biblical Equality: Complementarity Without Hierarchy*, 2nd ed., ed. Ronald W. Pierce and Rebecca Merrill Groothuis (Downers Grove, IL: InterVarsity Press, 2005), 424-25. Also see Keith Pavlischek, "Paternal Responsibilities and Abortion Logic," *Capital Commentary*, December 7, 1998.

Postabortion fathers can also experience a range of powerful emotions—helplessness, grief, resentment, guilt—which are rarely addressed. Male abortion pain is described as the loss of fatherhood and a "wound you cannot see or feel."[57] Removing fathers from the prolife equation feeds the cycle of relational brokenness. By no means are we calling for a return to the days of shotgun weddings! Yet if we want to move toward a more fully prolife, egalitarian future, then men must be viewed not just as disposable sperm donors or threats to women's autonomy, but as God's co-creative image bearers. We can more consistently offer fathers encouragement and accountability to live up to this high calling.

A third unique feature of prolife egalitarianism is the understanding that God designed us to flourish in community. Passages such as Isaiah 65:18-24 offer a vision for a community that promotes the preciousness of all life, especially children:

> I will create Jerusalem to be a delight and its people a joy. . . . Never again will there be in it an infant who lives but a few days, or an old man who does not live out his years. . . . My chosen ones will long enjoy the work of their hands. They will not labor in vain, nor will they bear children doomed to misfortune; for they will be a people blessed by the LORD, they and their descendants with them. (NIV)

God wants all people to enjoy good health, long life, meaningful work, economic sufficiency, stable families, safe neighborhoods, and relationship with their Lord, and to pass these blessings on to the next generation. This is the kind of community into which we must actively seek to welcome and raise the unborn. Without this broader scope of activism, we are open to the charge that we care only about the baby until it is born. As the Catholic theologian Joan Chittister puts it, holistic concern for quality of life is what makes the difference between being "pro-birth" and "pro-life."[58]

The abortion debate is typically framed by individual choices, rights, and responsibilities. From the perspective of biblical community, we also

---

[57] Art Shostak, *Men and Abortion: Lessons, Losses and Love* (New York: Praeger, 1984). See also Coleman, "Decline of Partner Relationships." Research on postabortive fathers is scant, but the prolife community offers some supportive resources, e.g., Guy Condon and David Hazard, *Fatherhood Aborted* (Carol Stream, IL: Tyndale House, 2001).

[58] Joan Chittister, interview with Bill Moyers, 2004.

examine our collective responsibility to one another. Abortion stories not only reveal an individual in crisis; they point to brokenness in the broader society. For example, in a study of women's reasons for having an abortion, the two cited as most important were "I'm not ready" and "I can't afford a baby now."[59] A perspective focused on the individual might applaud this reasoning for postponing parenthood as a responsible reproductive choice, or else condemn it as personal selfishness. But a community perspective asks, "Can we make different choices as a society to lessen this overwhelming anxiety about having children?" Without diminishing the weighty personal responsibility of procreation, we can also aim for a community that offers parents greater emotional and practical support to bring their child into the world. We can do more to promote loving adoptive families. We can seek a society closer to the biblical vision, in which no worker "labors in vain," no child is "doomed to misfortune," and no parent faces child-bearing alone.

We may disagree in good faith on the role of government and the best social policies to advance this biblical vision.[60] However, none of us can say that this is someone else's job. Unwanted pregnancies "call for the assumption of extraordinary responsibilities by extended family members, supportive friends and neighbors, churches, social service organizations, and/or public authorities."[61] Our congregations ought to lead the way in encircling parents with a "village" of loving care. This momentous calling requires the contributions of men and women of faith working in equal partnership.

The fourth quality of an egalitarian evangelical approach is a global reach. We dare not focus exclusively on the abortion issue within our own borders without extending our resources and energy to other countries where the fate of preborn children and their mothers is even more

---

[59]Finer et al., "Reasons U.S. Women Have Abortions."

[60]Beyond legislation directly addressing abortion, our priorities for a consistent life ethic cradle-to-grave public policy would include access to family health care (including contraception), affordable childcare, support for education and vocational training as a pathway to economic sufficiency, strong protection from abuse, and improved systems for adoption and foster care. We also need to address the systemic disempowerment of women of color, such as the wage gap, which contributes to entrenched poverty and to abortions. See the recommendations in Ronald J. Sider, *Completely Pro-life: Building a Consistent Stance* (Eugene, OR: Wipf & Stock, 2010).

[61]Center for Public Justice, "Guideline on Human Life" (2007), quoted in Vincent E. Bacote, *The Political Disciple: A Theology of Public Life* (Grand Rapids, MI: Zondervan, 2015).

precarious. For example, in Pakistan, more than one in ten pregnant mothers will suffer the unintended death of their baby before its first birthday.[62] God cares just as much about a miscarriage due to lack of maternal health care in Pakistan or sub-Saharan Africa as an abortion in America.

We recognize that global prolife advocacy must be linked with reforms to value, protect, and empower women. The link between abortion and the dehumanization of women is powerfully evident in countries such as China and India, where patriarchal norms justify widespread sex-selective abortions. "What emerges is an alarming picture of mass termination: prenatal offspring, aborted for no other reason than they happen to be female. . . . Female gendercide is perhaps the clearest statement of the low value and disposability of girls and women." One of the insidious results of female feticide is that there are not enough native women for men to marry. Thus India, for example, has experienced an annual 25 percent rise in trafficked women and children. The cycle of violence continues with sex slavery, rape, and domestic abuse.[63]

J. Godwin Prem Singh, author of *Millennium Development Goals*, laments, "The elimination of girl children, either through sex-selective abortion or infanticide, goes largely uncensored, undetected, unpunished and unmourned."[64] As people of God committed to the sanctity of life, we must notice and mourn. We must arrange our priorities so that our prolife work includes coming alongside global sisters and brothers where the need is greatest.[65]

---

[62]This statistic combines stillborn and infant deaths. See "Pakistan Key Demographic Indicators," UNICEF, https://data.unicef.org/country/pak/# (accessed September 6, 2018); also see Hannah Blencowe et al., "National, Regional, and Worldwide Estimates of Stillbirth Rates in 2015," *The Lancet Global Health* 4, no. 2 (February 2016): e98-108. This unintended death rate for the late pregnancy/newborn stage is nearly seven times that of the United States. However, to add perspective, women in the US abort their unborn at nearly *twice* this rate of unintended deaths in Pakistan: more than 18 abortions per 100 pregnancies.

[63]Elaine Storkey, "Violence Against Women Begins in the Womb," *CT*, May 2, 2018, www.christian itytoday.com/women/2018/may/violence-against-women-begins-in-womb-abortion.html. Adapted from Elaine Storkey, *Scars Across Humanity: Understanding and Overcoming Violence Against Women* (Downers Grove, IL: InterVarsity Press, 2018). It should be noted that the US has no federal prohibition against gender-based abortions. See Michelle Crotwell Kirtle, "Challenging Sex-Selective Abortion in the United States," *Capital Commentary*, February 7, 2014.

[64]Storkey, "Violence Against Women Begins."

[65]The principles set out in 2 Cor 8–9 for economic sharing between communities apply to resources for activism as well: "Our desire is not that others might be relieved while you are hard pressed, but that there might be equality" (2 Cor 8:13).

WEAVING GENDER EQUALITY AND SANCTITY OF LIFE

If we recognize the sanctity of the life of the unborn, it seems clear that we must reject blanket permission to destroy this life through abortion. Yet thorny ethical and public-policy questions remain. What exceptions should be allowed for the health of the mother? For rape and incest? For fatal fetal deformities? Is preventing abortion equally urgent at every stage, from conception on?[66] Do abortifacients (e.g., the morning-after pill) have the same moral weight as abortions later in the pregnancy? Can Christians endorse access to sex education and contraceptives in a way that prevents unwanted pregnancies, while upholding biblical perspectives on sexual activity?[67]

Should moral objections against abortion always be translated into laws against abortion? Should we give precedence to policies that make abortion illegal or to policies that make abortion rare? If abortion is restricted, how do we prevent women from resorting to unsafe "back alley" services? What priority should we give to a politician's stand on abortion as a voting issue, in relation to other holistically prolife issues?

We cannot here resolve all (or any!) of these contentious questions. We raise them to note that Christians who are fully committed to the sanctity of life may have honest disagreements about how best to promote it. We need to move beyond entrenched battles that fail to change minds and hearts, and worse, may be failing to protect lives.

A framework of biblical gender equality helps us navigate a new approach. Instead of debating the clash of individual rights, we can focus on *relationships of equal regard*. "The ethic of equal regard is a response to the feminist ideology and social science literature that stresses independence rather than mutuality and interdependence. . . . Making the best interest of the other a priority is the essence of the extraordinary way of the cross and covenant love."[68] This ethic considers

---

[66]While later-term abortions attract the most attention, about two-thirds of abortions are performed by the eighth week of pregnancy, and 90 percent are performed within the first trimester. See Tara Jatlaoui et al., "Abortion Surveillance—United States, 2014," *Surveillance Summaries*, November 23, 2018, 66.

[67]In Colorado, for example, the state provided free, long-acting birth control. After six years, there was a 40 percent drop in the rate of teen abortions. See Sabrina Tavernise, "Colorado's Effort Against Teenage Pregnancies Is a Startling Success," *New York Times*, July 15, 2015.

[68]Judith Balswick and Jack Balswick, "Marriage as a Partnership of Equals," in *Discovering Biblical Equality: Complementarity Without Hierarchy*, ed. Ronald W. Pierce and Rebecca Merrill Groothuis (Downers Grove, IL: InterVarsity Press, 2004), 449.

how relationships contribute to God's plan for the flourishing of life. As we emphasize that developing babies need the gift of birth, we can also urge mothers and fathers, and their community as a whole, to regard and serve this new life as a gift, rather than a burden or a threat. The goal of equal regard is not to coerce women into submissive motherhood, or to give men control over women's choices (or to deny them any influence), or to sacrifice offspring to the will of their parents. Rather, the ideal that we strive for is mutual submission in love, to the glory of God.

The pursuit of empathy is vital to building relationships of equal regard. Neither of us coauthors can put ourselves in the shoes of someone struggling with an unwanted pregnancy. I (Heidi) went to great lengths to become pregnant and then was at high risk of miscarriage. At only five weeks we had to go in for an emergency sonogram. We were vastly relieved and awed to see the image of the pulsating pea-sized blob. My husband reflects, "I don't know for sure when life begins, but that was the moment when my relationship with my child began."

Our culture holds individual autonomy as a supreme value. Having a meaningful bond changes the equation. When you love someone, you move mountains to ensure their well-being. The size, appearance and maturity of the fetus take a back seat to whether you have a relationship with this being as *your child*. We can change the dialogue from "How do we convince women to keep their babies?" to "How can we join women in fighting for a good life for their babies?"

What can we do to strengthen this vital sense of prenatal connection— especially when a pregnancy comes as an unwelcome surprise?[69]

This is where supportive community comes in (as modeled by many wonderful churches and pregnancy centers). Rather than inducing guilt, we can foster relationships with women built on empathy and unconditional love. The majority of postabortive women say their decision was motivated by a sense that "Having a baby would dramatically change my life." Without dismissing their concerns, perhaps we can help mothers

---

[69]Half of all pregnancies in the United States are unintended; of these, 43 percent end in abortion. See Adrienne D. Bonham, "Why Are 50 Percent of Pregnancies in the U.S. Unplanned?," *The Shriver Report*, October 21, 2013.

(and fathers) picture how including this new life could lead to a *good* kind of change. We can listen without judgment to their fears and goals. We can encourage their hope for a future in which a meaningful connection with their child brings joy—if not to them, to an adoptive parent. And we can extend our spiritual family to walk with fragile biological (and adoptive) families, helping them overcome obstacles toward that life-affirming future.

Translating this goal of equal regard into public policy is fraught with challenges. Whatever the current status of law, we can all choose the calling of Galatians 5:13, to "use your freedom to serve one another in love" (NLT). While posters, marches, and wise legislation do serve a vital purpose, we believe that hearts can be changed—and life affirmed—one mutual relationship, one family at a time.

ADVICE FOR CHURCHES

In addition to building relationships with pregnant parents and working to improve families' quality of life, churches can pursue an egalitarian pro-life impact in several other ways.

First, churches can give priority to ministry with children in poverty and their parents. The majority of women who have an abortion already have at least one child. Concern that a new baby would compromise their ability to care for older siblings, particularly among low-income mothers, is a significant factor in the decision to abort.[70] If the church is already involved with caring for their other children, parents may find the hope and resources needed to expand their family.

Second, churches can promote adoption and fostering.[71] This includes a range of engagement options, from recruiting forever families, to providing respite, emotional support, and tangible aid to caregivers, to embracing parents in the difficult decision to share their child with another family. Churches can also work for reforms to reduce the trauma and disparities associated with the child-welfare system. Fewer than 1 percent of women with unintended pregnancies opt for adoption—compared to about

---

[70]Finer et al., "Reasons U.S. Women Have Abortions."

[71]See Jenn Ranter Hook, Joshua Hook, and Mike Berry, *Replanted: Faith-Based Support for Adoptive and Foster Families* (West Conshohocken, PA: Templeton, 2019).

40 percent who choose abortion.[72] But by opening homes to children, as well as supporting family reunification wherever possible, we nurture a culture of cherishing life and connections.

Third, churches can be sensitive to the reality that one in five women has had an abortion by age thirty. Thus, most congregations will have members with this experience. Out of mutual love, we ought to talk about abortion not as an abstract sin committed by "them" but a painful reality for many of "us."

A postabortive Christian woman who kept silent about her abortion for many years writes to the church: "May I humbly ask that you remember us in the midst of your zeal to end abortion? Maybe a pause to think about who will see what you post before you post it, maybe a phone call or a text to see how your post-abortive friend is holding up. . . . Shouldn't our news feeds and our mouths be as full of the Gospel as they are with the horrors of abortion?"[73]

Fourth, the prolife and prochoice communities must persistently affirm one another's immeasurable dignity and worth. Advocacy should not depend on naming others as our enemy. We show love as we are willing to listen to one another's stories and perspectives, not primarily to persuade but to seek to connect on a human level. We may grow in understanding and respect for the cry of another's heart. We may even find common ground on shared values: respecting women's bodies and minds, empowering women to flourish, enabling more control over the timing of pregnancies, offering adoption as a viable choice, dedication to parenting postbirth children well, compassion for women facing pregnancies in unimaginably difficult circumstances. Who knows what we could accomplish if we found ways to work together on these causes?[74] The plea and prayer of the authors is to enlarge the compass of these values to include the unborn—but we cannot make progress by dehumanizing our prochoice (or prolife) neighbors.

---

[72]Olga Khazan, "Why So Many Women Choose Abortion over Adoption," *The Atlantic*, May 20, 2019.

[73]Patti Withers, "The Gospel Is for Baby-Killers," Immanuel July 29, 2015, https://immanuelky.org /articles/the-gospel-is-for-baby-killers/.

[74]See the story of one group in the 1990s that actually made headway toward collaborative initiatives: Barbara Brotman, "Two Sides in Abortion Debate Find Common Ground in the Chasm Between Them," *Chicago Tribune*, January 25, 1998.

What unites us is what we all want most deeply: life, to the fullest (Jn 10:10). This is the gift our Creator gives and Christ redeems. For each individual, female and male, womb to tomb, this life in its fullness is always deeply interwoven with the lives of others. We share the sanctity of God's image together.

PART IV

LIVING IT OUT

Practical Applications

26

HELPING THE CHURCH UNDERSTAND BIBLICAL GENDER EQUALITY

Mimi Haddad

• • • • •

TEACHINGS ABOUT THE SCRIPTURAL BASIS for the equality of men and women in the church and home have been circulating within Christendom for nearly five hundred years.[1] Yet many Christian churches are still practicing, either consciously or unconsciously, a men-preferred or male-only pattern of leadership and teaching. Why should this be true? Why has biblical gender equality not been more fully accepted?

While the reality that sinfulness operates even in the church must be acknowledged, another element in the gender debate has become clear. Sociological research suggests that it is not enough to present the biblical facts. There are other significant factors that influence thoughts and actions.

In *Diffusion of Innovations*, Everett Rogers notes that in the early days of long sea voyages, scurvy was a far more effective killer of sailors than war, pirates, or accidents. In 1601 an English sea captain conducted an experiment that proved that citrus juice or fruits added to the diet would prevent scurvy. Though sailors were informed of these findings, it was not

---

[1]Mimi Haddad and Alvera Mickelsen coauthored an earlier version of "Helping the Church: Understand Biblical Equality" in *Discovering Biblical Equality: Complementarity Without Hierarchy*, ed. Ronald W. Pierce and Rebecca Merrill Groothuis (Downers Grove, IL: InterVarsity Press, 2004). Alvera Mickelsen passed away before she could coauthor a revised chapter.

until two hundred years later—and thousands of needless deaths—that scurvy was finally conquered by the British Navy.[2]

This is a classic example of how simply telling the facts often does little to change behavior. What held back this simple and much-needed change in the behavior of sailors? Why did the sailors not consume citrus products when they knew it might save their lives? Why did their behavior remain unchanged?

This dilemma brings us to the science of diffusion—the study of what causes a new idea or change in practice or belief to take hold in a social system. Rogers outlines five basic elements needed for a new idea or change to be accepted. These principles are well worth the consideration of Christian leaders who want the church to embrace biblical teachings on gender equality. The diffusion of a new idea is facilitated when we

- speak the truths of the Bible in language like that of our Lord Jesus Christ—simple, direct, and rich in personal stories;

- show how life improves, in marriages and in the church, when gender barriers are broken;

- connect the message to the core beliefs of Christians;

- model the message in as many ways as possible; and

- find simple, safe ways for people to sample their freedom in Christ with no gender barriers.

I will deal with each of these in some depth.

ELIMINATE COMPLEXITY: THE IMPORTANCE OF UNDERSTANDABLE LANGUAGE

Rogers writes, "Complexity is the degree to which an innovation is perceived as relatively difficult to understand and use. The higher the complexity, the lower the rate of adoption." The degree of perceived complexity will directly affect how quickly a new gadget, idea, or behavior is embraced. For example, when home computers were first introduced into the market, they were fairly complex; therefore, engineers and those with a technical background were the first to purchase them. Technical hobbyists were not

---

[2]Everett M. Rogers, *Diffusion of Innovations*, 4th ed. (New York: Free Press, 1995), 7-8.

put off by the complexity of these early computers, but the "perceived complexity of the home computers was an important negative force in their rate of adoption" among the general population. As "home computers became more user friendly," however, their adoption rate increased among those outside the technical community.[3]

Many people find the biblical debate on gender to be as incomprehensible as early home computers. Although it is important for evangelical scholars, pastors, and leaders to be acquainted with the arguments and issues, few laypersons have the educational background, time, patience, or resources to learn the ancient languages or engage the complex principles of biblical interpretation and theology that are frequently taken up in the gender debate. Many people are unable or unwilling to sort through the maze of technical language and ideas used in discussions of these matters.

How can we help the average person in the pew? How do we communicate in a way that minimizes complexity while stating clearly and simply the truth of Scripture on gender that so many need to hear?

Some have discovered that complexity is best overcome by the use of simple language and many personal examples, as evidenced in the teaching style of Christ. Jesus knew that making matters personal helps everyone understand. Take the Lord's Prayer as recorded in Matthew 6:9-13. Here we see very profound ideas expressed in simple language. In English the entire prayer has fifty-eight words, and forty-six of them have only one syllable! Most of the teachings of our Lord are framed in similarly simple language. No wonder the masses of people followed him—they understood him.

When we discuss biblical gender equality, we often use words such as *complementarianism, hermeneutics, traditionalism, exegesis, hierarchical,* and *egalitarianism.* Many people have only vague concepts of what these words mean. To reach the average person in the church, we must use language that is comprehensible. For example, instead of using the term *egalitarianism,* we can speak of gift-based ministry.

Jesus said things such as, "Love your neighbor as yourself," "What God has joined together, let no one separate," "Many who are first will be last,

---

[3]Rogers, *Diffusion of Innovations,* 242-43.

and the last will be first." All of these teachings run counter to the way most of his hearers (and most of us) actually think and live, but the ideas are crystal clear. There is no ambiguity and no jargon.

When we teach about gender equality, we probably should put more emphasis on the clear and simple teaching of Scripture, such as Christ's call to love one's neighbor as oneself, or the teaching of Genesis 1 that men and women alike are made in the image of God and are to share responsibility for God's created world.

The call to love is very clear, just as is the call to care for God's created world. To fulfill our call as human beings created in God's image, we must care for the earth, the animals, and one another—all of the things that make this world habitable. In our society, that includes caring for children, providing for a well-governed society, and what we commonly call work. And it surely includes making known the message of God and our responsibility to God.

This must be done in ways that are easily understandable to our fellow human beings. I recently listened to a fourth-grade girl recite memory verses, including Titus 2:11, "For the grace of God has appeared, bringing salvation to all men" (NASB 1995).

I asked her, "Does that include you?"

She answered, "No."

Fortunately, she had a NRSV Bible with her, and I asked her to look it up in that translation. It read, "For the grace of God has appeared, bringing salvation to all." Then I repeated my question, "Does that include you?"

She answered, "Yes."

It was a clear illustration of how important language is and why we need gender-accurate translations in which the language does not need further translation and explanation.[4]

Or take 1 Corinthians 12, where we find clear teaching regarding God's gifts to all his people. God gives gifts as God chooses, and all believers are to use their gifts for the good of the body, his church. There is no suggestion that men get "leadership gifts" and women get "service gifts." Such passages are clear and do not need abstract theological language to explain

---

[4]See Jeffrey Miller's treatment of these translations in his chapter in this volume.

them. They fit the Genesis account of men and women alike being created in the image of God and sharing responsibility for God's world.

If we who are involved in this biblical debate will express complex ideas simply, using easy-to-understand examples and personal stories, we will take an important step toward reaching all Christians with a vital and life-transforming message.

SHOW THE RELATIVE ADVANTAGE: HOW BIBLICAL GENDER EQUALITY IMPROVES PEOPLE'S LIVES

Rogers writes, "The Relative Advantage is the degree to which an innovation is perceived as being better than the idea it supersedes."[5] Although the thought patterns of the Western academic world are dominated by rationalism, this is probably not so true of most ordinary people. Most of us are more interested in entering into people's lives and sharing their feelings. There is good reason that *Guideposts* magazine has survived for so many years. Every article is a personal experience piece. Much of *Reader's Digest* is devoted to personal stories.

A large portion of the Bible recounts the experiences of individuals or of the nation Israel. We have four accounts of the life of Christ, and most of the rest of the New Testament consists of letters from individuals to churches or other individuals. The Bible has often been called a case study of God's acts with human beings.

Therefore, *seeing* the success of churches and marriages that practice gender equality will probably persuade more people than will theological discussions. At the first CBE International marriage conference (2000), couples were greatly moved as they observed the joy and satisfaction of some whose marriages had been transformed by the practice of equality. Some remarked, "The Spirit of God was so present it was like a revival meeting."

One woman explained that she and her husband had been taught that wives were to submit to their husbands as "God's plan for marriage." They wanted to be in God's plan, so they revised their way of relating to each other so that the husband made most of the decisions and she

---

[5]Rogers, *Diffusion of Innovations*, 212.

became a "submissive wife." She said it almost destroyed their marriage, and she became very depressed. Not until they found CBE International and saw with new eyes God's message of mutual submission were they able to salvage their relationship and experience deep joy. Their honest, moving testimony was a powerful agent in changing the attitudes of many. When people see the relative advantage of living out the biblical message of biblical gender quality, theology moves into practice and lives are changed.

Conversely, we can show the relative *disadvantage* of hierarchical gender roles by asking: What kind of life do you want your talented, outgoing daughter to have? Or what kind of life do you want your talented, shy son to have? Will the traditional view of male leadership and female submission provide for the fullest development of the gifts God has given them? Not all men enjoy leadership or have the gift. Not all women are quiet followers. In a truly biblical marriage, or in a church where everyone uses their God-given talents, each contributes what gifts they have in mutual submission to one another. Insisting that only men be leaders and that only women be followers denies the great differences between individuals in God's creation.

Most churches are looking for more gifted leaders to take charge of their programs. Churches that open leadership doors to women double their potential supply. Furthermore, many women are skilled at enlisting and working with volunteers because of their wide experience in organizing social and family activities. Most churches run largely on volunteer work. Women often have more experience than men in training and encouraging others. Many are skilled teachers with experience in motivating and directing. What a shame to have all of this lost to the church because of tradition. Churches that deny opportunity to women leaders are working with one hand tied behind their backs. But where women and men demonstrate success and fulfillment in using their gifts in the church, we observe firsthand the relative advantage of gift-based ministries.

A significant problem with ministry that is gender based rather than gift based is that it overlooks the successes women have had in global missions. In mission fields around the world women have preached, married, buried, and baptized thousands; begun and administered hospitals, orphanages, and schools; and planted hundreds of churches. The women's missionary movement flourished between 1870 and 1920. It brought the good news of Christ to millions of people around the world—especially in countries such as India and Pakistan, where men could not teach or minister to women at all. Women have also been influential in building the church in countries such as China, South Korea, and Africa.

By rehearsing the successes women have had on the mission field, we take another step toward bringing the message to life; we show the advantage of biblical gender equality in a vital way. Once we demonstrate this, we can ask: What if women had not taken the initiative? Millions of people would never have heard the gospel. Were these women missionary leaders out of God's will?

In pointing out the relative advantage of permitting women to serve in leadership, we should also note the biblical examples of powerful and successful women chosen by God to be leaders, prophets, and evangelists. Deborah (Judg 4–5) was a judge (at that time the top leadership position in Israel), the commander in chief of the army, and a poet, singer, and prophet. God used her to deliver Israel from the tyranny of King Jabin of Canaan. The first evangelist in the New Testament was the Samaritan woman at the well. She was also the first person to whom Jesus revealed that he was the Messiah. Mary Magdalene was the first person to see the risen Christ. The list goes on and on.

Women were so active in the early church that Saul had them imprisoned along with men (Acts 9:1-2). Women participated in the day of Pentecost, received the gift of tongues, and proclaimed the risen Christ. Paul speaks of Euodia and Syntyche (Phil 4:2-3) as his coworkers who fought at his side in spreading the gospel.[6]

Freedom in Christ, including gender equality, furthers evangelism and missions. It brings joy and fruitfulness to those who practice and believe it. By showing the relative advantage of embracing biblical gender equality, we harness a powerful communication tool and help the church understand the biblical message that ministry should be based on gifts, not gender.

---

[6]For an in-depth discussion of women leaders in the Bible, see chapter four in this volume.

INCREASE COMPATIBILITY: CONNECTING TO
THE CORE BELIEFS OF CHRISTIANS

Rogers writes, "Compatibility is the degree to which an innovation is perceived as consistent with the existing values, past experiences, and needs of potential adopters." Health workers in Peru attempted to eliminate typhoid fever by teaching villagers to boil their drinking water. However, few adopted this practice. Had these health workers been familiar with Peruvian culture, they would have been aware of the common belief that "only the ill use hot water." Villagers had been taught from an early age to dislike boiled water.[7]

Old ideas die hard because they function as the "main mental tools that individuals utilize to assess new ideas." Rogers adds, "One cannot deal with an innovation except on the basis of the familiar, what is known."[8] Previous practices serve as the standard by which a new idea is evaluated and interpreted.

For centuries many Christians have been taught that the submission of women to men in church, home, and society is God's plan (even as some have observed how these teachings can lead to an abuse of authority).[9] Yet, as we introduce people to a new, more biblically faithful model of men and women working together as equal partners, most people will interpret this "new" teaching through the old. How, then, ought we to proceed?

Researchers suggest we can effectively communicate a new belief that would otherwise be perceived as suspect if we connect to the core values of those who do not yet hold the belief. By beginning with what we already share as Christians, we help others accept what might otherwise be rejected as incompatible. Thus, we need to begin by stating the values we hold in common.

Evangelicals who promote biblical equality can affirm the core values of fellow Christians who disagree with us on gender equality. What we have in common as Christians far outweighs our disagreements; we must

---

[7]Rogers, *Diffusion of Innovations*, 224, 3.
[8]Rogers, *Diffusion of Innovations*, 225-26.
[9]Katharine Bushnell, *Dr. Katharine C. Bushnell: A Brief Sketch of Her Life and Work* (Hertford, UK: Rose and Sons Salisbury Square, 1930), 11-12. See also Jimmy Carter, *A Call to Action: Women, Religion, Violence, and Power* (New York: Simon & Schuster, 2014), 3-4.

therefore rehearse our shared values frequently and clearly. For example, some who oppose gender equality say that egalitarians deny or diminish the authority of the Bible and other core beliefs of Christianity. This is not true. We do well to carefully and frequently communicate our belief in the authority of the Bible in all matters of faith and practice. Our differences lie in how we interpret certain passages of the Bible, not in our respect for the Bible.

Because some Christians fear that the message of biblical gender equality will undermine the sanctity of marriage and the well-being of the Christian family, egalitarians must regularly reiterate their support of healthy families and the responsibility of parents for their children. We believe that this responsibility is so great that it needs to be shared by fathers and mothers together, as well as the extended family.

The gospel message is so important that we can agree that all must work to share it with others whenever we can. Every Christian should be free to tell others of the love of Christ—regardless of factors such as gender, age, or race. The same goes for public preaching and teaching. Many agree that there are some basic differences between how men and women generally see and experience life. For that very reason, it is helpful for both men and women to hear the gospel from the perspective of the other gender. It enlarges our understanding of God and of the gospel of Christ. The history of the church and the witness of Scripture show that God uses men and women alike to proclaim him and to serve as leaders in his kingdom work.

Because most Christians have a strong desire to see the gospel message adopted by people around the world, we can also speak of the rich tradition of women throughout the history of the church who brought many to faith by using their gifts of preaching and teaching. Pastor David Yonggi Cho in Korea, who led the largest Protestant church in the world, says that his church began to grow when he released women to use their gifts. Similarly, Loren Cunningham, president of Youth with a Mission, notes that global missions grew rapidly once women began using their gifts in preaching the gospel worldwide.[10] By affirming the commitment to evangelism of women such as Lottie Moon, Frances Willard, Anne Hasseltine Judson, and the

---

[10]Loren Cunningham, David Joel Hamilton, and Janice Rogers, *Why Not Women?* (Seattle: YWAM, 2000), 68.

hundreds of female pastors of Cho's church, we help others embrace gift-based ministry as a successful model of spreading the gospel.

By pointing to our commitment to the authority of Scripture, the well-being of families, and the centrality of evangelism and missions, we connect to the core values of those who are otherwise apprehensive of biblical gender equality. By carefully establishing the enormous ground we have in common, we build sturdy bridges to those who are unsure of our message. On these bridges we lead our brothers and sisters into the promised land where all Christians are encouraged to use their God-given gifts to forward Christ's kingdom.

IMPROVE OBSERVABILITY: MODELING THE MESSAGE OF GENDER EQUALITY

Rogers writes, "Observability is the degree to which the results of an innovation are visible to others."[11] For people to accept a new idea or product, they must see it in use. How did cellphones become so popular? Cellphones were not introduced in the United States until 1983. At that time, they cost about three thousand dollars, and their use was limited to executives and CEOs. As the price dropped and quality improved, their use grew dramatically, not only in the United States but also especially around the world. Soon people began seeing cellphones everywhere. As a result, people realized that they were a highly useful product. They ceased being a novelty and became widely used.

Similarly, gender equality has made rapid strides, is widely visible in the secular world, and is a growing reality in the evangelical world. Those who are uncomfortable working for a woman are at a distinct disadvantage. Young women gain leadership experience in high school and college, where student-body presidents and club leaders are often women. When they reach adulthood, they are unaccustomed to the restrictions that may be placed on them in the church. Where can we find living models of biblical gender equality in the church?

There are, of course, women pastors in a growing number of churches. Many Christian colleges and seminaries have women chaplains,

---

[11]Rogers, *Diffusion of Innovations*, 244.

administrators, vice presidents, and faculty teaching Bible or theology or preaching in chapel services. These women serve as important role models to many. We cannot underestimate our need to observe women using their gifts in the church, as well as husbands and wives serving one another in mutual submission. Several practical ways to model the message of biblical equality are listed at the end of this section.

In churches that restrict women, modeling must begin gradually. Usually there is no difficulty with women teaching children in any church. Women leaders are often acceptable even for high school and college groups. The students rarely question this, since they have had women leaders and teachers in high school and college. Any objections usually arise from adults who have not been exposed to models of females working as equals with men.

The Scriptures provide many examples of women serving alongside men in the gospel. By pointing to these narratives, we allow the Bible to model the message of equality. When Jesus visited the home of Mary and Martha in Bethany, Mary sat at Jesus' feet to listen to his teachings, just as male disciples did. When Martha complained, Jesus rebuked her and took the side of Mary (Lk 10:38-42).

Paul mentions Priscilla and Aquila more often than anyone else except Timothy. In most instances, he names Priscilla first, although that was contrary to the customs of the day. When people quote a few passages of Paul, often in isolation from the context, they must be helped to see the meaning of these passages in light of what Paul himself actually practiced.

Paul's practical counsel to married couples in 1 Corinthians 7 models an approach to marriage that is based on mutuality and equality. Here he gives identical instructions to husbands and wives regarding marital relations, explaining that each has authority over the other's body and each should yield to the other (1 Cor 7:2-5).

Through both the examples in the Bible and living models of gender equality in our churches and our homes, ideas about equality come to life. This is an important part of communication. We all need models to understand an idea fully.

Practical ways of modeling the message in churches include the following:

1. Use couples to serve as both greeters and ushers at church. After that is accepted, a church may be willing to use single women or women whose husbands do not come to church.

2. Have women read aloud the Scripture in church, during Bible study groups, and at other church functions.

3. Encourage or assign women to pray publicly when opportunities arise.

4. Ask couples and women to serve on church committees for which they are qualified.

5. Have couples share leadership of house groups, Bible studies, and adult education. At times when the husband cannot be present (illness or business), the wife can lead or take over his duties. Or they can take turns. This prepares the way for greater equality.

6. Encourage women to participate in church business meetings or on committees of which they are a part. Every committee needs women on it!

The appeal for change should be on the basis of using those most qualified and available rather than on the basis of choosing women specifically. However, there are some instances in which the appeal for women on a gender basis may be acceptable. On a church building committee, women are often better qualified than men to plan kitchens, nurseries, restrooms, and childcare centers. Most men will agree to that! If a woman has an obvious gift the church is in need of, she should be encouraged to use that gift.

OFFER TRIALABILITY: SAFE, SIMPLE WAYS
TO SAMPLE BIBLICAL EQUALITY

Rogers writes, "Trialability is the degree to which an innovation may be experimented with on a limited basis. . . . The personal trying-out of an innovation is a way to give meaning to an innovation, to find out how it works under one's own conditions. This trial is a means to dispel uncertainty about the new idea."[12] Looking again at the example of cellphones,

---

[12]Rogers, *Diffusion of Innovations*, 243.

we can readily see how easy it was to try out a friend's cellphone. Because of this and other factors, cellphones quickly became part of everyone's life.

As new ideas are sampled on a trial or installment basis, they are often easier to embrace. By allowing an individual an opportunity to sample biblical equality, we give the message personal meaning, whereby one comes to understand how it works "under one's own conditions."[13] This is a critical step in the process of diffusion. The trying out of a new innovation is the last step toward making it our own.

By providing small, safe opportunities for others to take their first steps as egalitarians, we help Christians understand and embrace the joy of living as God intended. Some simple changes in behavior may offer a safe means of sampling equality in traditional situations.

How can equality be sampled in marriages where male leadership has been firmly taught and practiced? Husbands often consider certain tasks inherently male. One of these is the control of money. Yet practically speaking in America, if God intended men to be in control of money, he played a terrible trick on women. In our society, women on average outlive men by six or seven years, and husbands are usually a few years older than their wives. This means that a woman is likely to be a widow for eight to ten years.

Some men keep such control of money that their wives have little or no knowledge of their financial situation and no experience in making important financial decisions. Some do not know what the financial resources of the family are or where they are located. This can have tragic consequences. Men who love their wives should never let that happen.

Couples can learn to take turns or to share the tasks of keeping records, paying bills, and handling financial affairs. No important financial decisions should be made by either one without consultation and agreement of the other. After all, in America, both husband and wife must sign joint tax returns, and both are responsible for their accuracy.

Women can be equally controlling over areas perceived as theirs. They may not want to see their husband participate in childcare, school conferences, cooking, laundry, and the like. If the wife needs to visit a sick relative or becomes ill herself, the husband is severely handicapped in his ability

---

[13]Rogers, *Diffusion of Innovations*, 243.

to help either her or himself. Changes in these situations can be introduced without any appeal to equality—just to common sense.

Very often husbands and wives need safe, structured opportunities to make their first big decision as egalitarians. CBE International offers marriage conferences and materials to help couples experience new ways of working together, in mutual submission, using their God-given gifts.

Egalitarians can help others embrace biblical equality by encouraging them to identify and use their gifts in their own churches. Where churches are closed to gift-based ministry, Christians eager to take their first step as egalitarians can proceed by learning to identify and sharpen their spiritual gifts in service to the community. There are many fine books, such as *Equipped for Every Good Work: Building a Gift-Based Church*, that help Christians identify and use their God-given gifts. One's gifts often parallel the issues one feels strongly about.[14]

Egalitarians can help their brothers and sisters in Christ try out or sample the message by empowering them to use their gifts. While some churches may be closed to a woman's giftedness, the community at large is often open. Many organizations need mentors and volunteers. Women can serve others and fulfill God's intended purpose for them and their gifts by offering their services in schools, nonprofit ministries, short-term mission projects, shelters, and neighborhood groups.

God will open a way. Pray, watch, and get busy. You will know when the time comes. Perhaps God will even lead you to a church that is open to you and your gifts.

CONCLUSION

Changes in societal patterns are usually very slow and painful. This tends to be especially true in conservative churches. Change of any kind is often feared and considered to be "the way of the world." Because Christians value the Bible, the Bible is often misused to prevent needed change and development. Most Christians have never really studied the biblical passages on gender for themselves; they believe what their pastor or Christian leader says these passages mean.

---

[14]Dan R. Dick and Barbara A. Dick, *Equipped for Every Good Work: Building a Gifts-Based Church* (Eugene, OR: Wipf & Stock, 2011).

Meanwhile, like those sailors who died of scurvy although prevention was easily available, churches and individual Christians go on denying themselves the great joy and opportunity of serving the Lord in ways that are taught and modeled for us in Scripture, in history, and in the lives of respected Christians around the world. So, when we model the truths of biblical equality and encourage others to experience them in small ways, we can help thousands of talented Christians find new ways to use their God-given gifts—gifts that are desperately needed by the church of Jesus Christ. And through genuine equal-partnership marriages, we help marriages and families become stronger and happier.

What can we do to encourage the acceptance and practice of biblical gender equality? Apply the principles of diffusion:

- Eliminate complexity: speak about biblical gender equality in simple, direct terms without using theological jargon.

- Show the relative advantage: demonstrate how life is improved in marriages and in the church with gender equality.

- Increase compatibility: connect with the core beliefs of those with whom you are working to show how biblical gender equality affirms those beliefs.

- Improve observability: model your beliefs in every situation and open doors for others to do the same.

- Offer trialability: help those interested to find safe and easy ways to try out the concept of male-female equality in church and marriage.

These five principles have made significant inroads in eliminating disease and death worldwide. Intriguingly, Scripture itself employs the principles of diffusion, supremely in the life and teachings of Christ. As I show in "Human Flourishing: Global Perspectives," gender equality is essential to reaching basic humanitarian goals.[15] It is also an overarching biblical principle. For these reasons, we communicate the message of biblical gender equality in the clearest terms, so its life-sustaining message is made understandable and compelling to larger numbers in the church and beyond.

---

[15]See Mimi Haddad, "Human Flourishing: Global Perspectives," in this volume.

27

MARRIAGE AS A PARTNERSHIP OF EQUALS

Judith K. Balswick and Jack O. Balswick

*Two are better than one, because they have a good reward
for their toil. For if they fall, one will lift up the other;
but woe to one who is alone and falls and does not have
another to help. Again, if two lie together, they keep warm;
but how can one keep warm alone? And though one
might prevail against another, two will withstand one.
A threefold cord is not quickly broken.*

ECCLESIASTES 4:9-12

• • • • •

A NUMBER OF THE CHAPTERS in this book give exegetical understandings of Scripture and theological support for marital equality. In this
chapter we build on this foundation and focus on the practical aspects of
how marriage as a partnership of equals can be a life-giving reality.

LANGUAGING MARRIAGE

The central issue and dividing line between marital equality and inequality
is the authority issue. Much of the controversy over marital authority is

about the language used to describe marriage in Christian circles. That marriage is a partnership is widely held, although *partnership* is defined and practiced in a variety of ways. Three categories for describing and negotiating authority in the marital partnership are male leadership, mutual submissiveness, and equal regard. It should come as no surprise that each approach boasts the authority of Scripture when it comes to interpretation and application to the marital relationship.

Male-leadership proponents regard authority as inherent in the position of the husband. According to this view, decisions about marriage and family life are ultimately to be made by the husband. The corresponding implication is that the wife must take a submissive role. Is it possible, one might ask, for marriage to be a partnership of equals according to this view? Answering this question requires some understanding of how the concept of male leadership is used. At the risk of oversimplifying, we suggest that the male-leadership model comes in two varieties—hard patriarchy and soft patriarchy.

Patriarchy refers to a social structural system that gives husbands an assumed position of authority over their wives. In hard patriarchy, husbands make critical and final decisions, and wives willingly submit to the husband's authority over them. Soft patriarchy emphasizes a suffering-servant model of the husband's leadership. Christian husbands are to emulate servant leadership in relationship to their wives, just as Christ laid down his life for the church.

The mutual submissiveness model calls for husbands and wives to be subject to one another (Eph 5:21). This model is applicable to relationships in the body of Christ, but specifically to the marital dyad.

Don Browning, director of the Religion, Culture and Family Project, describes Christian marriage as a relationship of equal regard. The ethic of equal regard is a response to the feminist ideology and social-scientific literature that stresses independence rather than mutuality and interdependence. The expressed concern is that language of submissiveness and self-sacrifice opens the door to personal abuse of power. It is further reasoned that since the biblical view of marital love is mutuality, each spouse should regard the other as she or he wants to be regarded.

Browning is open to the concept of self-sacrifice in love if it is "derived from equal regard."[1]

While we agree with Browning in substance, we also affirm the concept of mutual submission and personal sacrifice. Circumstances such as sickness, absence, or incapacity require unequal sacrifice of one spouse. In this case one spouse is challenged to give much more than an equal share. Making the best interest of the other a priority is the essence of the extraordinary way of the cross and covenant love.

Perhaps it is not so much the language we use but our actions that speak louder than words. While attitudes and beliefs certainly influence perceptions about marital roles, what truly makes a difference is how spouses experience their relationship in the day-to-day encounter. This is where the rubber meets the road. Should we conclude then that language is unimportant? Not at all, for behavior is a direct reflection of how spouses define themselves and their roles. However, we hasten to add that how one is treated determines marital satisfaction. Therefore, the two things, role definition and behavior, go hand in hand.

In fact, couples may use any one of these terms (male leadership, mutual submissiveness, or equal regard) and practice inequality or equality in marriage. So authority must be understood in terms of how power is defined and used in each unique relationship.

POWER IN MARRIAGE

Power is the ability to influence. Spousal power can be either achieved or ascribed. Achieved power is based on personal resources that are valued by both spouses. Each spouse has personal and relational qualities—such as emotional stability, wisdom, compassion, spirituality, knowledge, relational sensitivity—that have significant influence in the relationship and are valued by the other spouse. The greater one's resources, the greater the potential influence (power) in the relationship.

In contrast, ascribed power "comes with the position." In a patriarchal system the husband has power over the wife simply because he is male. This is a position of power that is culturally endowed, solely by virtue of

---

[1]Don S. Browning et al., *From Culture Wars to Common Ground: Religion and the American Family Debate*, 2nd ed. (Louisville, KY: Westminster John Knox, 2000), 238-84.

gender. He has certain rights and privileges that go along with the position. He has not had to earn it or prove it; it is a given. In fact, he can do what he likes even if it is selfish. His wife may resent him because she is at his mercy, but she succumbs nonetheless. Ascribed power can also be thought of as contingency power, for it is dependent on both the husband's and the wife's acceptance of the belief system that assigns power to the husband. A certain amount of power may also be ascribed to the woman in the role of mother or wife. She has power over her children or even over her husband in certain situations.

One common misunderstanding about power in marriage can be seen in the secular social-exchange model, in which each partner tries to maximize their personal interest. This model views the marital relationship as a zero-sum game in which there is a set number of units of power available in any relationship. Power in marriage can be represented as one hundred units to be divided up between the husband and wife. If the husband has all the power (one hundred units), the wife has none (zero units). If the wife has slightly more power (sixty units), then the husband is less powerful (forty units). According to this marital model, fifty units must be carefully allocated to each spouse. Scott Bartchy points out how this ludicrous scenario puts the husband effectively in command if he has fifty-one power units in contrast to the wife's forty-nine units.[2] Spouses keep score in a rat race of vying for one unit of power. Instead of spending all that energy over a one-point edge, it makes more sense for both spouses to be 100 percent powerful. In a marriage of mutual submission, both spouses reach full potential and together double their relationship satisfaction.

DOMINANT HUSBANDS AND MANIPULATIVE WIVES

Marriages of mutual empowerment do not come naturally or automatically. The human tendency in marriage is to dominate in order to guarantee personal interests. The desire for power and self-preservation is obvious in the Genesis narrative. Adam and Eve act out of desire for power and disobey God's boundaries. When confronted by God, Eve points the finger

---

[2]S. Scott Bartchy, "Issues of Power and a Theology of the Family: Consultation on a Theology of the Family," seminar given at Fuller Theological Seminary, Pasadena, CA, 1984; Bartchy, "Issues of Power and a Theology of the Family," *Mission Journal* 21 (July–August 1987): 3-15.

at the serpent, while Adam says Eve made him do it and is even bold enough to blame God for bringing Eve into his life. They protect and defend themselves rather than admit their fault and face the consequences of their behavior.

Unbalanced marital power is based on self-interest and ascribed power. The dilemma it sets up is that the husband has most of the power and the wife has little power. The wife is automatically in the "one down" position and the husband in the "one up" position. Because the husband's power is ascribed, there is no way for a wife to have equal power. The tendency in any social system based on inequality is for the more powerful to coerce and the less powerful to manipulate. Whether inequality is based on race, age, or gender, persons in subordinate positions are given one of two options: either submit or influence in indirect ways. In the case of marriage, the wife may find subtle ways to influence her husband. For example, she may form a coalition with her children or extended family members to gain strength and power in her position.

The not-too-subtle intent of many women's books is to teach wives how to manipulate their husbands in order to get what they want. This approach views the husband as the weak link because the subordinate wife can easily outsmart him. She is taught to use sex to get her way. The sexy wife can reduce her husband to compliance through sweet talk and finesse. In knowing and unknowing ways, she goes to extremely superficial and dishonest lengths to influence her husband. In truth, a husband whose masculine security is based on his wife's submission places himself in the position of actually being under her control. By merely disobeying him or refusing him sex, or showing little interest in the relationship, she brings his masculine ego into question. At this point his power is effectively reduced to zero, leaving him alone and desperate.

THE INHERENT SUPERIORITY OF EQUAL-PARTNERSHIP MARRIAGES

In his classic book *Love and Will* Rollo May identifies five types of power: (1) exploitative (influence by brute force), (2) manipulative (influence by devious social-psychological means), (3) competitive (influence based on the possession and use of personal resources), (4) nutritive (influence like that of a parent on a child—this power eventually outlives its usefulness), and (5) integrative (the use of personal power for another's sake).[3] What May calls integrative power is clearly what we refer to as empowerment. May points to Jesus as an example of one who used integrative power. In stating his central message Jesus says, "I came that they may have life, and have it abundantly" (Jn 10:10).

The power of God is available in unlimited supply. Each spouse is given the fruit of the Spirit in full measure; each spouse is to be an imitator of Christ; every believer is to be filled with the Holy Spirit. God calls spouses to give of their life out of fullness, not out of deprivation. Spouses who are for each other want the best for each other. Both spouses have power, and neither has to lord it over, control, or manipulate the other in order to express their wishes. Mutual empowerment means that two persons reach their fullest potential as God intended. They mesh their lives as individuals and partners in marriage, work, coparenting, life goals, and service to the Lord.

In equal partnership marriages the locus of authority is placed in the relationship, not in one spouse or the other. Even though it may take longer to arrive at a joint decision, as the couple listens, honors, and respects each other's opinion, they move toward a united stance. It adds the dimension of "we-ness" and mutual accountability as each one takes a responsible role in decisions that are made.

Carmen Martin-Knudson and Anne Mahoney have developed a measurement of marital equality based on four criteria: partners hold equal status, accommodation in the relationship is mutual, attention to the other in the relationship is mutual, and there is mutual well-being of the partners.[4] Several studies indicate the importance of equality in marriage as a success factor. In a study of 135 elderly married couples, Wallace Reynolds and Rory Rerner found different measurements of equality all to be associated with marital satisfaction.[5] In a crosscultural study of 186 cultures,

---

[3]Rollo May, *Love and Will* (New York: W. W. Norton, 1969).

[4]Carmen Martin-Knudson and Anne Mahoney, "Language and Processes in the Construction of Equality in New Marriages," *Family Relations: Interdisciplinary Journal of Applied Family Studies* 47, no. 1 (1998): 81-91.

[5]Wallace Reynolds and Rory Rerner, "Marital Satisfaction in Later Life: An Examination of Equity, Equality and Reward Theories," *International Journal of Aging and Human Development* 40, no. 2 (1995): 155-73.

Lewellyn Hendrix found role sharing to be strongly related to marital equality.[6] Drawing on extensive research and personal interviews in the United Kingdom, the United States, and Israel, Claire Low Rabin found a correlation between marital inequality and marital distress.[7]

Living out mutual-submission principles in the marital relationship requires ongoing refining. Dialoging about disagreements, honoring differences, communicating honestly, and facing the challenges of parenting and married life is a transforming process. The marital encounter becomes a crucible of sorts in which spouses are changed through their interaction. Each spouse must be brave enough to express personal needs as well as consider the needs of the spouse. The anxiety that occurs when things heat up and solutions are not easily found is often stressful. In fact, in their study of 150 Israeli married couples, Rabin and Ofrit Shapira-Berman found that while equal role sharing and decision making were predictive of wives' marital satisfaction, these predicted marital *tension* for husbands.[8]

Working out an equal partnership takes time, effort, and energy. Heartache and disappointment will be part of the refining process of living and loving in relationship. Spouses will be challenged to face themselves in new ways in the context of the other and the marriage. Admitting mistakes, becoming aware of one's faults and shortcomings, and making honest apologies can be grueling. It is not always easy to smooth out the rough edges that occur, but the very process of working it through creates character, personal strength, and relationship growth. Transformation is the ultimate promise and hope for marriages that are sharpened on the grindstone of truthful interaction.

Behind the "two are better than one" scripture passage is the idea that two independent persons have unique strengths to offer each other and the relationship. Without two separate identities, interdependence is not possible. Some hold to the false notion that dependency or fusion is the

---

[6]Lewellyn Hendrix, "Quality and Equality in Marriage: A Cross-Cultural View," *Journal of Comparative Social Science* 31, no. 3 (1997): 201-25.

[7]Claire Low Rabin, *Equal Partners, Good Friends: Empowering Couples Through Therapy* (London: Routledge, 1996).

[8]Claire Low Rabin and Ofrit Shapira-Berman, "Egalitarianism and Marital Happiness: Israeli Wives and Husbands on a Collision Course?," *American Journal of Family Therapy* 25, no. 4 (1997): 319-30.

ideal: "I can't do it without you, and I must lean on you to be strong." Two overly dependent persons hanging onto each other for dear life have no solid ground on which to stand when things get difficult or an unexpected stress hits.

Empowerment occurs when two equal partners influence each other. Interdependence is the intent. Spouses who are secure and self-confident can express themselves honestly and directly. In doing so, they have an opportunity to listen and to know the deeper feelings and thoughts of their spouse so they can come to a decision out of mutual respect and regard. Individual power is translated into relationship strength. When each spouse is able to stand solidly on his or her own feet, using the personal resources and relational strengths that have been developed, mutual empowerment happens.

EQUAL-PARTNERSHIP PARENTING

In hierarchical marriages, the mother does most of the parenting. Yet few parents can do it well all by themselves. The Bible teaches the importance of both parents' involvement in the lives of their children. Nowhere does Scripture teach that mothering is more important than fathering. A healthy byproduct of marriage as an equal partnership is the emergence of a strong coparenting model. In fact, some researchers have identified the lack of fathers' involvement in the lives of their children as the source of major social problems today.[9] An accumulation of evidence demonstrates the benefits of coparenting to children and parents alike. When father and mother are jointly involved in parenting, a strong parental partnership enhances their leadership capacity. Together and separately, a mother and father can nurture as well as teach, equip, discipline, and give wise counsel.

A study by Diane Ehrensaft reported a number of advantages for coparented children.[10] They had a more secure sense of basic trust, were better able to adapt to brief separations from the mother, and had closer

---

[9]David Blankenhorn, *Fatherless America: Confronting Our Most Urgent Social Problem* (New York: BasicBooks, 1995).
[10]Diane Ehrensaft, *Parenting Together: Men and Women Sharing the Care of Their Children* (Chicago: University of Illinois Press, 1990).

relationships with both mother and father. Coparented children developed better social discrimination skills and displayed greater creativity and moral development. Having less animosity toward the other gender, they were better able to develop strong friendship bonds with opposite-gender children and displayed fantasies of sustained connection with others.

Not surprisingly, sons seemed to benefit especially from coparenting. Boys who had a strong bond with both their father and mother were better able to display empathy, affection, and nurturing behavior; they thought highly of the way they were parented and were more likely to state that they wanted to be a father when they grew up. Strong fathering had a positive effect on how boys developed relational skills. Boys who grew up with fathers who connected emotionally were more nurturing and rational.

Girls who were coparented had a greater sense of self and personal boundaries. Also, when a father in particular took an active interest in his daughter's achievements, she was likely to succeed in her career goals. Mothers who modeled assertiveness and self-confidence, in addition to nurturing behaviors, gave their daughters permission to set firm boundaries as well as to make emotional connections with others.

There is significant evidence to suggest that coparenting is beneficial to parents as well. The most obvious benefit is for working mothers whose husbands take the parenting role seriously. In these homes, working mothers are less likely to be enmeshed or overinvolved with their children. Fathers involved in the parenting process were more apt to develop their social-emotional and relational side. In contrast to the world of work outside the home, where decisions are largely based on rational rather than emotional skills, taking care of children inclined men toward personal and emotional issues. This inclination had a positive impact on the way they performed in work roles, since high empathy skills helped them relate better to coworkers.

Coparenting allows mothers and fathers to better understand and be involved with their children and to be more consistent and effective in discipline. In addition, it strengthens the marriage as they work in tandem as parents. Ideally, dual-earner parents will find ways to complement each other on a day-to-day basis throughout their parenting years. One parent may find helping with homework to be a special gift, while the other is best with activities. Dividing up parenting responsibility will ease the burden as long as both parents learn the needed skills, such as nurturing, setting rules, and setting boundaries. Dual parenting is a rewarding investment that pays off in the end, as it benefits fathers, mothers, children, and family life as a whole.

EQUAL-PARTNERSHIP DUAL-EARNER MARRIAGE

It is estimated that two-thirds of two-parent families with dependent children are dual-earner families today. Almost a third of working women (32 percent) have children under the age of eighteen. Approximately two-thirds of these women work full time year-round. Women with children under the age of six account for 67 percent of those working women with children, while 76 percent of those working women had children between the ages of six and seventeen according to the US Census Bureau in 2018.[11] When both spouses are working outside the home, division of labor within the home becomes a very important issue. In hierarchical marriages, wives spend much more of their time working in the home than do husbands.

Marriage partners who both hold equally high commitments to work and home life need the agility of an acrobat to meet demands in both arenas. Wanting to do it all, they find that sooner or later something gives, whether it is work, the marriage, parenting, or the emotional health of the acrobats.

To practice marital equality, dual-earner couples must be proactive in establishing and maintaining a rightful balance of work and family.[12] Rather than merely reacting to life circumstances and pressures, the couple must become intentional in forming an equal-participation marriage. Here are some important points:

- Establish a close relationship.

- Be flexible and adaptable to life circumstances.

---

[11]Gayle H. Kimball, *Empowering Parents: How to Create Family-Friendly Workplaces, Schools and Governments* (Chicago: Equality, 1998); Cheridan Christnacht and Briana Sullivan, "About Two-Thirds of the 23.5 Million Working Women with Children Under 18 Worked Full-Time in 2018," United States Census Bureau, May 8, 2020, www.census.gov/library/stories/2020/05/the-choices-working-mothers-make.html.

[12]Jack O. Balswick and Judith K. Balswick, *The Family: A Christian Perspective on the Contemporary Home* (Grand Rapids, MI: Baker, 2021).

- Agree on priorities.

- Focus on the essentials.

- Draw on all the resources you can muster to help meet the demands of parenting and family life.

Sometimes it is necessary to accommodate the individual strengths of each partner. One spouse pulls back from work commitments in order to give more time to family life at a particular family stage. Then, at another time, the other spouse makes adjustments by taking on more childcare and decreasing employment responsibilities. Whatever the arrangement, both spouses equally respect and honor each other's commitments to work and the home.

There are major benefits for both men and women in a dual-earner/dual role-sharing marriage. Based on responses to questionnaires from 815 dual-career couples, Janice Steil and B. A. Turetsky found that the greater the marital equality, the less wives reported negative psychological symptoms.[13] John M. Gottman reports that doing housework may prove to be good for husbands' health. He found a correlation between the amount of housework a man did and his physical health four years later. Another important aspect for the man was that his involvement in the home led to validation and appreciation. This contributed to a mutually satisfying relationship with his wife and children.[14]

Relaxing perfectionist household and parenting standards is especially important for the woman. The couple must agree on the standards so they can cooperatively achieve their goals. When the wife is able to let go of certain areas as her domain, she will be able to appreciate her husband's efforts without setting up unrealistic expectations. Drawing on research of Rabin and Pepper Schwartz, Gottman states, "When wives and husbands make what they both feel is a successful effort to divide chores fairly, both spouses benefit. Inequalities in household and childcare have

---

[13]Janice M. Steil and B. A. Turetsky, "Is Equal Better? The Relationship Between Marital Equality and Psychological Symptomatology," in *Applied Social Psychology Annual 7*, ed. Stuart Oskamp (Newbury Park, CA: Sage, 1987), 73-97.

[14]John Mordechai Gottman and Nan Silver, *Why Marriages Succeed or Fail: What You Can Learn from Breakthrough Research to Make Your Marriage Last* (New York: Simon & Schuster, 1994), 157-58.

profound consequences for marital satisfaction of women, which has to affect the quality of the marriage for the man as well."[15] The benefit of shared roles for the wife is that she can find fulfillment in work, marriage, and mothering.

A hard lesson for all dual-earner couples to learn or admit is that they cannot do everything. In prioritizing what needs to be done, they must learn to do a "good enough" job. By living in previously uncharted territories, dual-earner couples can represent marriage as a partnership of equals. They need support from family, friends, and community as they work toward a satisfying and meaningful family life.

THE RELATIONAL EMBEDDEDNESS OF MARITAL EQUALITY

Marital equality can best be understood in a wider biblical context based on how our Creator God relates to us, the created ones. We offer four relationship principles—covenant, grace, empowerment, and intimacy—as foundational to marriage as a partnership of equals.

The covenant principle. Marriage as a partnership of equals is based on covenant, a reciprocal, unconditional commitment. The vows exchanged in the wedding ceremony, "for better or worse, for richer or poorer, in sickness and health, till death do us part," have unconditional commitment as the focus. The couple makes a public covenant before God, family, friends, and a community of faith, fully intending to keep these promises.

God's love is seen in the Old Testament as a covenant established with Adam and Eve, Noah and his family, Abraham and Sarah, and the children of Israel: "I will make a covenant with you. I will be your God and you will be my people." God's unconditional commitment is given with an expressed desire that it be returned. God's faithful, steadfast, always-abounding love is sure and secure. God invites a response from those who are loved. God's love is perfect, but we are imperfect. After all, we are sinners saved by grace. Yet God desires a reciprocal love, waiting for a maturity of faith that makes giving back possible. In mature, marital love, we hope for a similar mutual, reciprocal love.

---

[15]Gottman and Silver, *Why Marriages*, 157.

Human love, however, is typically conditional. Most of us commit ourselves to loving under certain requirements and conditions. A secular
model of marriage is often based on a social-exchange or quid pro quo
model that promises love when one is loved back in equal measure. It is tit
for tat: "I give something if I get something," "I will love you when you do
this." Spouses who are invested in having and keeping power in a relationship find ingenious ways to increase their influence and lessen that of their
spouse. Their way to gain power is to diminish the spouse's power. This
battle puts the self at the center and the spouse at the periphery. A marriage that is based on conditional love soon turns into a deadly, legalistic
war of keeping score.

In contrast, the Bible commands Christians to extend their view far
beyond this self-focused perspective. Christians are directed to "do to others what you would have them do to you," "go the second mile," and "turn
the other cheek." This extraordinary way of the cross is the deepest challenge of Christian marriage. The biblical concept of love requires an
unconditional commitment given equally by both partners. Covenant love
serves as the solid foundation of security. It is the backbone and relational
strength of an equal-partnership marriage. Trust is the core reward that
develops when spouses regard each other with a mutual respect that puts
priority on the relationship, when each spouse treats the other as a cherished equal, one who is uniquely gifted as God's creation.

The grace principle. Equal-partnership marriage thrives on grace
shown through mutual acceptance and forgiveness. Valuing each other's
personality strengths as well as accepting differences brings a comforting,
peaceful atmosphere to the marriage. Since human love is imperfect, partners will disappoint, offend, and fail each other from time to time. However, grace allows spouses to approach marital differences and disappoint-
ments with confession and understanding that takes them beyond the
failure toward responsible change. When spouses fail or make mistakes,
forgiveness renews their spirit and gives them courage to make necessary
amends. Grace keeps the couple open to ongoing reconciliation, restoration, and renewal.

The opposite of a gracing response is a shaming one. This is the message
that the spouse is not "good enough." Whereas guilt is the feeling that one

has done a wrong, shame is the feeling that one *is* a wrong. Spouses who cannot admit they are wrong will generally shame, blame, or point the finger at the other. They have a hard time being accountable for their part or failure in any given situation.

Jack grew up in a shaming home and learned early on that being less than perfect meant there was something unacceptable about him. Obviously that made it hard for him to admit when he was at fault, so he conveniently blamed Judy when things went wrong. For example, whenever they got lost while driving, it became quite clear that it was Judy's fault. This tendency to blame dampened Judy's spirit and put distance between them.

When Judy spoke up about the pattern, however, Jack took another look at what was behind the blaming and took responsibility for his actions. He learned he could admit mistakes without jumping to the conclusion that he was a woebegone reprobate.[16] The dilemma of unequal partnership is that husbands carry the burden of having to know everything and always be right, while wives pretend not to know or suppress what they know is right.

Nonacceptance puts marriage on an unequal footing. It is a devastating way of keeping a spouse in a one-down position. Focusing on deficits draws out a critical spirit that breaks the connection. On the other hand, grace brings acceptance and appreciation for the spouse. Grace places value on how the spouse views things without judging their thoughts as inadequate or inferior. Therefore, it eliminates the need to change the spouse into what is more acceptable according to one's self-centered assumptions.

In a gracing marriage each spouse feels appreciated for who they are. The relationship has a person-centered quality: spouses enjoy each other. A gracing spouse accepts the other spouse as being as important as oneself, recognizes there is more than one way (my way) to approach life, and sees differences as complementary resources instead of deficits. Grace fosters equal partnership.

The empowering principle. Whereas the first two principles provide a solid foundation, the third principle—mutual empowerment—is the core

---

[16]Early in our marriage it was difficult for Jack to realize his shaming tendencies, since he would justify his blaming as "spiritual correction."

work of equal-partnership marriages. As we noted earlier, power is the ability of one spouse to influence the other. Power is based on resources, and resources are qualities valued by the other spouse. Power issues are inevitable in marriage, because each person is unique, and spouses must learn to negotiate all kinds of life decisions from different perspectives. This naturally brings tension in the marriage.

The most problematic aspect of empowerment is how power is used in the marital relationship. An underlying assumption of social-scientific research is that spouses will use power in controlling or manipulative ways to get what they want and maintain their position of influence. While power *is* often perceived this way, Jesus radically redefined power as giving oneself for the other. Mutual empowerment is described in 1 Corinthians 7 as a harmony that emerges when spouses listen to and consider each other when making decisions. We describe empowerment as a reciprocal process of building up, equipping, supporting, encouraging, affirming, and challenging the other.

Empowerment can be seen as the ability to envision and encourage a spouse to be everything God created him or her to be. This includes personality, giftedness, and reaching one's greatest potential. It is not simply yielding to the wishes of another person, nor is it giving up one's own power in the process of empowering the other. Rather, empowerment is an active, intentional process that affirms the spouse to be an effective and equal partner. Internal strength and relationship confidence come from knowing that your spouse believes in and desires your best, takes great delight in your development, encourages you to reach your full potential, and supports your personal goals and growth.

The empowering principle seeks the full potential of each spouse through a synchronous rhythm of interaction and interdependence. Mutual support in coparenting, housekeeping, and work roles enables both spouses to live out their purpose and calling. This partnership, unhampered by predetermined and restricted definitions of marital roles, is free to expand into something beyond what each can do alone—two are better than one.

A biblical model of empowerment can be seen in the person of Jesus Christ. What Jesus taught about power was central to his mission and meant to be imitated. Jesus modeled a new way of being personally power-ful. He rejected the use of power to control others but used power to serve others, to lift up the fallen, to encourage responsibility and maturity. When James and John ask to sit on his right and left hand in glory, Jesus replies, "Whoever wishes to become great among you must be your servant, and whoever wishes to be first among you must be slave of all. For even the Son of Man came not to be served but to serve, and to give his life a ransom for many" (Mk 10:43-45).

Jesus' relationship to his disciples is a perfect example of empowerment. Preparing them for his leaving, Jesus encourages them to look to the Holy Spirit, who will give them strength to accomplish their ministry (Jn 16). He assures them, "But you will receive power when the Holy Spirit has come upon you" (Acts 1:8). When Scripture asks ordinary spouses to respond in extraordinary ways, such as forgiving seventy times seven, being a suffering servant, loving unconditionally, caring enough to con-front, and practicing mutual submission, we need the empowerment of the Holy Spirit to do so. The power of God's Spirit gives strength to live out the extraordinary way of the equal-partnership marriage.

The intimacy principle. The fourth principle of an equal-partnership marriage is to know and be known through emotional, physical, spiritual, and intellectual intimacy. Marriages that are built on mutual uncondi-tional love and lived out in an atmosphere of grace and empowerment have the greatest capacity for mutual intimacy.

The model of two becoming one flesh does not eradicate the individual. In fact, an individual spouse becomes even more defined through self-discovery within a relationship as intimate as marriage. Intimacy is best achieved when each person has regard for the other, for the self, and for the relationship.

The deepest craving of every spouse is to be understood. There is great satisfaction in knowing that your spouse has truly listened and responded sensitively to what you have expressed. Intimate communication is not easily achieved. It takes an ongoing experience of making yourself avail-able to your spouse. It means you stay emotionally connected even during anxious or fearful expressions. It means creating an atmosphere of safety so the heart can be laid bare. It requires the ability to stay with the agenda of the spouse without attempting to change, convince, or fix him or her. It does not mean that you must betray your own views, but that you must set them aside for a time so your partner can fully express hers or his without fear or shame. In a profound way, intimate communication means giving up your life, dying to self, in order to be fully present to the spouse.

The bold action of receiving and giving to each other emotionally and sexually maximizes intimacy. The receiver is able to give up the familiar in order to understand the spouse's needs, wishes, and desires. It takes heart and mind to give full attention, respect, sensitivity, compassion, awareness, and understanding.

Only when spouses believe they will be understood will they dare to share their deepest pains, fears, dreams, and hopes. Only when spouses are vulnerable with each other will they discover themselves. Self-disclosure deepens self-knowledge. Internal self-esteem grows out of clarifying personal values, beliefs, and convictions. Intimate sharing helps spouses know themselves and the other in more profound and endearing ways. The intimate connection between spouses enhances a sense of belonging and secure attachment. To know and be known emotionally gives each a solid base to know and be known sexually.

We believe intimacy deepens marital bonding and sexual unity. "Men want sexual intimacy, women want emotional intimacy," goes the saying. A common belief is that men experience closeness mostly through sex, while women experience closeness mostly through emotional sharing. It does seem to be generally true that sexual intimacy helps men feel emotionally connected, while emotional connection opens women up to sexual intimacy. Every couple must find a good balance and create ways to achieve deeper intimacy in both areas.

Keeping both sexual and emotional intimacy alive in marriage increases the likelihood of mutual satisfaction, according to Jean Duncombe and Dennis Marsden.[17] They found that couples gain the best of both worlds by attending to both aspects of intimacy. When women realized that erotic

---

[17]Jean Duncombe and Dennis Marsden, "Love and Intimacy: The Gender Division of Emotion and 'Emotion Work': A Neglected Aspect of Sociological Discussion of Heterosexual Relationships," *Sociology* 27, no. 2 (1993): 221-41; repr. in *The Sociology of the Family: A Reader*, ed. G. A. Allan (Oxford: Blackwell, 1999).

energy moved their spouse toward deeper emotional connection and men made a stronger link between sexual and emotional intimacy, couples' intimacy increased. As Paul Ricoeur notes, "When Eros is mated with tenderness and fidelity, authentic happiness and spiritual fulfillment follow."[18]

Spouses who are able to engage and respond to their spouse find mutual interdependence to be crucially important in all aspects of intimacy. Steil and Turetsky, in a longitudinal study of 130 husbands and wives, found that equality was positively related to sexual intimacy.[19] Cheryl Rampage found that marital intimacy is most achievable when there is equality between partners, empathy for each other's experience, and willingness to collaborate in both meaning and action.[20]

In the most tender moments, it is indeed a sacred experience to be seen, heard, known, and responded to with love. In an equal partnership the spouse will be experienced as godly, as one who cares. The interdependency of mutual commitment, grace, empowerment, and intimacy creates a holy place of communion between two who have become one flesh.

A delicate balance between separateness and togetherness emerges in an interdependent union. Marriage offers a profound place of personal, spiritual, and relationship growth. As two unique persons support and commit themselves to each other throughout life's journey, they reap the deep rewards of equal partnership. Scripture promotes marriage as a union between two spouses who regard and relate to each other as equals. We believe that making the best interest of the spouse and the relationship a priority reflects God's design for marriage. Practicing equal partnership throughout marriage brings out the crucial essence of covenant commitment and bears the fruit of a grace-filled, mutually empowered, and intimate union.

Weaving two lives into a threefold cord that is not easily broken is possible when God is at the center. In Christ the potential for a vital and fulfilling equal-partnership marriage is at its height. Because intimacy, covenant, grace, and empowerment are based on biblical principles, marriages like this are a powerful witness to the world of God's love.

---

[18]Paul Ricoeur, *Oneself as Another*, trans. Kathleen Blarney (Chicago: University of Chicago Press, 1994), 73.

[19]Steil and Turetsky, "Is Equal Better?"

[20]Cheryl Rampage, "Power, Gender and Marital Intimacy," *Journal of Family Therapy* 16, no. 1 (1994): 125-37.

28

COMPLEMENTARIANISM AND DOMESTIC ABUSE

A SOCIAL-SCIENTIFIC PERSPECTIVE ON WHETHER "EQUAL BUT DIFFERENT" IS REALLY EQUAL AT ALL

Kylie Maddox Pidgeon

Being kind in an unjust system is not enough.

SISTER HELEN PREJEAN

• • • • •

INTRODUCTION

Complementarians deny that their theology and practice create or promotes domestic abuse; indeed, many complementarians express sincere dismay at any incidences of domestic abuse within their churches.[1]

---

[1] Hayley Gleeson and Julia Baird, "Anglican Diocese of Sydney Makes Apology to Victims of Domestic Violence," ABC News Australia, October 11, 2017, www.abc.net.au/news/2017-10-11 /anglican-diocese-of-sydney-apologises-to-abuse-victims/9038410.

Christians hold a range of views on the roles of women and men in marriage and the church. Egalitarians hold that roles in church and family life are filled according to giftedness, not gender; women and men hold equal responsibility and authority. In contrast, complementarians differ slightly from traditional patriarchy by arguing that men and women are equal in dignity and human personhood, but with differing roles in the home and in the church and sometimes in society. These different roles are always restrictive for women. Often considered a relic of patriarchal societies, some churches still enforce gendered hierarchies wherein women are prevented

However, the doctrine and culture of male authority and female submission, even when enacted with loving kindness, presents obvious risks to the safety, voice, and participation of women, as it grants permanent and unilateral authority to men.

Complementarian church governments are male-dominated by design, where men are automatically afforded greater decision-making authority than women, irrespective of commensurate gifting. A gender-skewed bias is therefore created in many arenas of church life, including leadership, spiritual formation, and pastoral care. Complementarians argue that this "equal but different" gendered structure is biblical and remains edifying to both women and men, since male headship is only to be enacted in Christ-like loving kindness.[2]

Yet, the United Nations states that gender equality "refers to the equal rights, responsibilities and *opportunities* of women and men."[3] Complementarianism, therefore, is a form of gender inequality where the opportunities available to a person in church and family life are predetermined according to gender. Gender inequality arises from prescribed gender roles, whether socially, culturally, or theologically constructed. This chapter will assert that the risks and dangers in the complementarian church and household are not sufficiently mitigated by the most commonly proclaimed defense of male headship: that it is only enacted in loving kindness. Gender inequality exists not only in attitudes, but in cultures, structures, prejudices, and biases. Gender inequality, even if benevolently intended, is a primary foundation for domestic abuse.

Complementarians argue that their doctrine *should not* promote domestic abuse and that abuse only occurs when their doctrine is misapplied. However, since we know that in many cases abuse *does* occur within

---

from occupying positions and roles of spiritual leadership, such as minister, elder, or preacher. Men therefore occupy the positions of greater power and public influence in a church and hold the offices charged with major decision making and oversight of the congregation. Women usually fill support roles of administration, teaching children's church, Bible reading during church services, or food preparation.

[2]"Equal but Different: Promoting Biblical Relationships for Women and Men," Equal but Different, www.equalbutdifferent.org/.

[3]"Gender Mainstreaming: Concepts and Definitions," UN Women: United Nations Entity for Gender Equality and the Empowerment of Women, 2001, www.un.org/womenwatch/osagi /conceptsanddefinitions.htm, emphasis added.

complementarianism, the examination of any possible link is required.[4] Many examples of the doctrine being used as justification for spousal abuse have recently been disclosed in Australian media. Disturbingly, a number of women have even disclosed that their husband and abuser is a member of the clergy.[5]

If male headship is enacted for the good of the women it leads, as complementarians assert, we would then expect to see greater flourishing from women in complementarian churches and marriages. However, there is no clear evidence to support this claim. There is however, an international, peer-reviewed, growing body of evidence suggesting that practices that discriminate on the basis of gender create poorer outcomes for women. The World Health Organization, a global organization dedicated to the holistic health of all people, specifically cites "community norms that privilege or ascribe higher status to men and lower status to women" as a risk factor for violence against women.[6] Other research shows that the most significant determinants of violence against women are "the unequal distribution of power and resources between men and women" and "an adherence to rigidly defined gender roles."[7] Discrimination against women, or, in complementarian language, "God wants us to honor his divine design by honoring the principle of male headship in our homes and church families," creates fertile soil for abuse and violence against women.

This chapter will draw on evidence from social sciences, including psychology, social epidemiology, and behavioral economics, to give an overview of domestic abuse, discuss the ways complementarian practices

---

[4]Hayley Gleeson and Julia Baird, "'Submit to Your Husbands': Women Told to Endure Domestic Violence in the Name of God," ABC News Australia, July 18, 2017, www.abc.net.au/news/2017-07-18/domestic-violence-church-submit-to-husbands/8652028. While egalitarianism does not guarantee an absence of domestic abuse, this chapter will focus on the parallel dynamics that exist between complementarianism and domestic abuse.

[5]Hayley Gleeson and Julia Baird, "Raped, Tracked, Humiliated: Clergy Wives Speak Out About Domestic Violence," ABC News Australia, November 23, 2017, www.abc.net.au/news/2017-11-23/clergy-wives-speak-out-domestic-violence/9168096.

[6]"Violence Against Women," World Health Organization, November 29, 2017, www.who.int/news-room/fact-sheets/detail/violence-against-women.

[7]"Australians' Attitudes to Violence Against Women," 2013 National Community Attitudes Towards Violence Against Women Survey, VicHealth, www.vichealth.vic.gov.au/-/media/ProgramsandProjects/DiscriminationandViolence/PreventingViolence/NCAS-Summary-Final.pdf?la=en&hash=470a0fc07695da1068400865aaaad43e57d2f9ed.

construct and parallel the dynamics of domestic abuse, and note some of the discriminatory biases and practices that complementarianism creates and fosters.

To be people of truth, the church must note evidence of whether complementarianism is as loving as it claims. To be people of love, the church must note the truth of whether "equal but different" is really equal at all.

DOMESTIC ABUSE

Domestic abuse is a problem that disproportionately affects women, children, people with disabilities, indigenous peoples, and other vulnerable groups.[8] Worldwide, almost one-third of women report that they have experienced some form of physical and/or sexual abuse by their intimate partner in their lifetime.[9] Domestic abuse claims the life of three women per day in America and one woman per week in Australia.[10] It is therefore an issue that demands thoughtful attention if Christians are to take seriously the biblical mandate to care for the vulnerable (Ps 82:3-4; Is 1:17) and if complementarians anticipate credibility in the arena of caring for women.

Disappointingly, the church is not at the forefront of preventing domestic abuse and caring for those who experience it. It was accepted for a time that Protestant men who attended church regularly were less likely to abuse their wives than their nonchurchgoing counterparts.[11] However, the data supporting that assertion were later found to have been

---

[8]Men can also be the victims of domestic violence; however, prevalence is minimal when compared with women as victims. Men are most likely to be the perpetrators of violence against men and women. See, "Facts and Figures," Our Watch, www.ourwatch.org.au/understanding-violence/facts-and-figures (accessed May 15, 2019).

[9]World Health Organization, Department of Reproductive Health and Research, London School of Hygiene and Tropical Medicine, and South African Medical Research Council, *Global and Regional Estimates of Violence Against Women* (Geneva: World Health Organization, 2013), 31, www.who.int/reproductivehealth/publications/violence/9789241564625/en/.

[10]"Facts About Domestic Violence and Physical Abuse," National Coalition Against Domestics Violence, 2015, www.speakcdn.com/assets/2497/domestic_violence_and_physical_abuse_ncadv .pdf; "Facts and Figures." Australian figures are reported by Our Watch: "2017 National Homicide Monitoring Program report by the AIC showed that over a 2-year period from 2012/13 to 2013/14, there were 99 female victims of intimate partner homicide." Further, while much of the data in this chapter is Australia-centric, the principles are comparable in comparable societies.

[11]Steven Tracy, "Patriarchy and Domestic Violence," *JETS* 50, no.3 (September 2007): 581, https:// mendingthesoul.org/wp-content/uploads/Tracy-JETS503.pdf.

interpreted in error. Experts now suggest that domestic abuse does not vary significantly between men who attend church regularly and those who do not.[12]

Recent work has found that domestic abuse is poorly understood within faith communities and, worse, that some church communities have enabled and concealed it.[13] Professionals working in the field have identified multiple and compounding reasons why churches are ill-equipped to recognize and respond effectively, including domestic abuse being a taboo topic; lack of understanding that domestic abuse is perpetrated in ways other than physical violence; emphasis on forgiveness rather than accountability; cultures of victim blaming, stigma, and shame surrounding divorce; rigid gender-role teaching where wives are expected to submit to their husbands; and a strong emphasis on the sanctity of marriage without a commensurate understanding that it is abuse that ends marriages, not divorce.[14]

One survey conducted in America found that 87 percent of pastors strongly agree with the statement "A person experiencing domestic violence would find our church to be a safe haven."[15] Yet a growing body of stories from abuse survivors suggests that pastors' confidence in their ability to provide safety is drastically overinflated. Story after story is emerging of churches being radically unprepared or unwilling to believe women's accounts of abuse.[16] Rachael Denhollander, who was famously shunned by her church after she disclosed sexual assault in elite

---

[12]Naomi Priest, Mandy Truong, and Nicholas Biddle, "Domestic Violence and Australian Churches: Why the Current Data Have Limitations," The Conversation, July 23, 2017, https://theconversation.com/domestic-violence-and-australian-churches-why-the-current-data-have-limitations-81467.

[13]Bianca Calabria et al., "New Study Finds Family Violence Is Often Poorly Understood in Faith Communities," The Conversation, April 17, 2019, https://theconversation.com/new-study-finds-family-violence-is-often-poorly-understood-in-faith-communities-115562?fbclid=iwar3uqklmhid z9rnjuaoyqkkpmf3um-73d_t56pe_omx-7lnuwwwscz18bf4; Julia Baird, "Domestic Violence in the Church: When Women Are Believed, Change Will Happen," ABC News Australia, May 22, 2018, www.abc.net.au/news/2018-05-23/when-women-are-believed-the-church-will-change/9782184.

[14]Paula Glassborow, "Unconscious Incompetence—Domestic Violence and the Church," Common Grace, April 17, 2018, www.commongrace.org.au/unconscious_incompetence_domestic_violence_and_the_church; Calabria et al, "New Study Finds Family."

[15]Bob Smietana, "Good Intentions, Lack of Plans Mark Church Response to Domestic Violence," Life Way News Room, February 20, 2017, https://blog.lifeway.com/newsroom/2017/02/20/good-intentions-lack-of-plans-mark-church-response-to-domestic-violence/.

[16]Baird, "Domestic Violence in the Church."

gymnastics and became an advocate for abuse survivors, says: "Church is one of the least safe places to acknowledge abuse because the way it is counselled is, more often than not, damaging to the victim. There is an abhorrent lack of knowledge for the damage and devastation that sexual assault brings. It is with deep regret that I say the church is one of the worst places to go for help."[17]

Domestic abuse can fall into two categories: acts of abuse and acts of neglect. Generally, acts of abuse are sins of commission, where a physical act such as shoving or a psychological act such as undermining is performed that harms or hurts the victim. Other abusive behaviors are types of neglect (sins of omission), where a person with a responsibility to care for another fails to properly do so, excludes the victim from a healthy environment, or prevents them from accessing equal opportunities. Acts of abuse are generally easier to pinpoint than acts of neglect. *Abuse* is commonly used as the general term to refer to both abuse and neglect. Domestic abuse exists where a family member or ex-partner exhibits "a pattern of abusive behavior through which a person seeks to control or dominate another person."[18] It includes the following:

- *emotional/psychological abuse:* insulting, threatening, gaslighting, undermining, humiliating, stonewalling, excluding from healthy environments, or prohibiting access to appropriate care, whether physical, psychological, spiritual, and so on

- *spiritual abuse:* preventing participation in cultural or religious activities[19]

- *social abuse:* restricting or controlling contact with friends or family, undermining the care of friends and family

---

[17]Morgan Lee, "My Larry Nassar Testimony Went Viral. But There's More to the Gospel Than Forgiveness," *CT*, January 31, 2019, www.christianitytoday.com/ct/2018/january-web-only/rachael-denhollander-larry-nassar-forgiveness-gospel.html.

[18]"What Is Domestic Violence," Domestic Violence Resource Centre Victoria, www.dvrcv.org.au/about-us/relationship-violence (accessed May 15, 2019).

[19]"What Is Family and Domestic Violence: Australian Government Department of Human Services," Australian Government Department of Human Services, January 11, 2021, www.human services.gov.au/individuals/subjects/family-and-domestic-violence/what-family-and-domestic-violence#a4.

- *financial/economic abuse*: controlling access to money, preventing work or study, or requiring excessive accounts of finances
- *sexual abuse*: being forced or coerced into unwanted sexual activities, including rape or pornography
- *physical abuse*: for example, hitting, pushing, bruising, strangling, restraining, or murdering

The impact of domestic abuse on the victim, her children, and her community is far-reaching. Our Watch, an Australian organization devoted to ending violence against women, states: "Violence against women and their children takes a profound and long-term toll on women and children's health and wellbeing, on families and communities, and on society as a whole."[20] Domestic abuse is the greatest health risk factor for women aged twenty-five to forty-four and a violation of human rights.[21] The burden of disease and injury resulting from domestic abuse includes fatality from murder or suicide, traumatic brain injury, fractures and sprains, cardiovascular disease, depression, anxiety, self-harm, alcohol abuse, and antenatal complications.[22] Domestic abuse is also the single largest driver of homelessness for women.[23] The economic costs to women include loss of wages, increased medical costs, and poorer work and study outcomes.[24]

Children and young people are also adversely affected by domestic abuse, whether they are the direct target of the violence or not. Exposure to domestic abuse negatively affects children's behavior, cognition,

---

[20]"Facts and Figures." While this chapter will give particular reference to Australian organizations, the contexts closely resemble that in other parts of the world. As such, the implications are reasonably generalizable.

[21]Australia Institute of Health and Welfare, *Family, Domestic and Sexual Violence in Australia 2018* (Canberra, AU: Australian Institute of Health and Welfare, 2018), www.aihw.gov.au/reports /domestic-violence/family-domestic-sexual-violence-in-australia-2018/contents/table-of-contents; "Violence Against Women."

[22]Australia's National Research Organization for Women's Safety Limited, *Horizons: Examination of the Burden of Disease of Intimate Partner Violence Against Women in 2011* (Canberra, AU: Australia's National Research Organisation for Women's Safety Limited, 2016), 10, https://dh2wp aq0gtxwe.cloudfront.net/s3fs-public/BoD%20Horizons.pdf.

[23]Australia Institute of Health and Welfare, *Specialist Homelessness Services Annual Report 2016–17* (Canberra, AU: Australian Institute of Health and Welfare, 2018), www.aihw.gov.au/reports /homelessness-services/specialist-homelessness-services-2016-17/contents/contents. Overall, 40 percent of clients seeking specialist homelessness services were experiencing domestic and family violence, with 91 percent of these being female.

[24]"Violence Against Women."

emotional development, social development, and attitudes toward vio-lence.[25] Children witnessing domestic abuse is tantamount to child abuse.[26]

Abuse is often a pattern of subtle behaviors through which the victim is coerced, manipulated, or threatened into a position they would not choose for themselves. Victims are usually silenced, undermined and unsup-ported by their abusers. Many victims do not know that they are being abused, due to their abuser's rhetoric that such treatment is warranted, deserved, or necessary.

THE PARALLEL DYNAMICS OF COMPLEMENTARIANISM AND DOMESTIC ABUSE

In 1983, a positive association was observed in male college students between traditional gender-role beliefs and beliefs that function to ratio-nalize, justify, and/or perpetuate men's violence against women. These associations were exacerbated by religious fundamentalism.[27] By 2017, indicators such as authoritarianism, social dominance, and nonegalitarian attitudes toward women were also reported to show positive association with beliefs that function to rationalize, justify, and/or perpetuate men's violence against women. A 2018 study found significant positive correla-tions between complementarian gender ideology and domestic-violence myth acceptance (the extent to which an individual adheres to stereotypes and prejudicial beliefs about family violence, with emphasis on attributing responsibility for the violence to the female victim).[28] Associations between these beliefs are thought to be a product of in-group/out-group thinking, where "us-them" and "superior-inferior" dynamics are perceived with regards to gender.

In recent years, following increasing disclosures of domestic abuse within Christian communities, churches have begun to publicly condemn

---

[25]"Violence Against Women."

[26]Kristy O'Brien, "Lifting the Domestic Violence Cloak of Silence," Australian Government: Aus-tralian Institute of Family Studies, June 30, 2016, https://aifs.gov.au/cfca/pacra/lifting-domestic -violence-cloak-silence.

[27]A. B. Bunting and J. B. Reeves, "Perceived Male Sex Orientation and Beliefs About Rape," Devi-ant Behavior 4 (1983): 281-95.

[28]Peter J. Jankowski et al., "Religious Beliefs and Domestic Violence Myths," Psychology of Religion and Spirituality 10, no. 4 (2018): 386-97, www.researchgate.net/publication/323947603_Religious _Beliefs_and_Domestic_Violence_Myths.

domestic abuse, with many denominations issuing statements of zero tolerance to domestic abuse of any kind.[29] However, stories being told by survivors suggest that, in practice, churches continue to have a great deal of tolerance for abuse in their midst, with some churches even enabling or concealing such behavior.[30]

The power dynamics at play in complementarian churches in many ways parallel the dynamics in abusive relationships. In both contexts, unilateral and permanent advantage is claimed by men (even if framed in the language of "servant leadership"), while women are required to submit to male authority, independent of its quality. In both spheres, men create the dominant and public discourse, and women are excluded from equal voice and participation. Both allow for male entitlement while females are restricted in their opportunities. Whether women are treated with respect or with abuse is largely dependent on men's agency.

Of course, many men who assume positions of leadership in the home and the church do so with good intentions. The problematic assumption that often follows is that these good intentions of loving kindness or Christlike leadership thoroughly and permanently mitigate against abuse, as though malice were the only risk factor. Intentions of loving kindness or servant leadership are insufficient to produce behaviors, systems, structures, and attitudes that ensure women are not harmed. Systemic injustice, neglect, incompetence, lack of accountability, multiple forms of bias, and failure to mitigate the many other risks inherent in male-only leadership can also lead to women being abused.

Publicly stating zero tolerance for domestic abuse while allowing unjust structures, attitudes, prejudices and biases to linger only functions to promote moral licensing, where the church's perception of their moral position remains intact, even while continuing to overlook, enable, or contribute to the immoral problem.

---

[29] Anglican Diocese of Sydney, *Responding to Domestic Abuse: Policy and Good Practice Guidelines* (Sydney, AU: Anglican Diocese of Sydney, 2018), www.sds.asn.au/sites/default/files/Responding%20to%20Domestic%20Abuse%20-%20Policy%20only.as%20at%2017Oct2018_final .pdf?doc_id=NTUyNjg=.

[30] "Her Story of Domestic Violence," Fixing Her Eyes, August 8, 2017, www.fixinghereyes.org /single-post/Her-Story-of-Domestic-Violence.

King David, a man after God's own heart (1 Sam 13:14), showed that even God's devoted followers and anointed leaders will cause grief and pain to those whom they unilaterally oversee. David's power in his position as king corrupted his godly judgment when he abused Bathsheba by taking her for himself, most likely raping her, and arranging for her husband, Uriah, to be killed (2 Sam 11). David demonstrates that even the godliest of male leaders will at times fail to serve and protect their charges, and instead will abuse and control them. God's anointed are not immune from the adage that "power tends to corrupt."[31] Each degree of power and privilege that a person holds adds more scope for abuse.

David's whims are enacted when he asks for Bathsheba to be brought to him, his sexual desires fulfilled as he sleeps with her, his commandments followed as his army is deployed to destroy the Ammonites and besiege Rabbah, and his instructions heeded when Uriah is placed in the fiercest part of the battle to be killed. David had the authority to mobilize servants and an army. Yet Bathsheba did not have equal authority. Bathsheba's words and decisions are not recorded in 2 Samuel 11, beyond her informing David, "I am pregnant." She did not hold equal decision-making authority in David's arena. Far from an isolated event, David and Bathsheba's story displays many of the same gender-skewed elements of modern complementarian churches. Ultimate authority, decision making, and execution of justice (and injustice) rest with men. Women are denied equal authority and instead are expected to comply.

Our Watch states, "the latest international evidence shows there are certain factors that consistently predict—or drive—higher levels of violence against women."[32] We see these elements operating in both the story of David and Bathsheba and modern complementarian churches. They are as follows:

---

[31]Kylie Maddox Pidgeon, "Complementarianism and Family Violence: The Shared Dynamics of Power and Control," Fixing Her Eyes, May 23, 2016, www.fixinghereyes.org/single -post/2016/05/23/Complementarianism-and-Family-Violence-The-shared-dynamics-of -Power-and-Control-1.

[32]Our Watch, Australia's National Research Organisation for Women's Safety (ANROWS), and VicHealth, *Change the Story: A Shared Framework for the Primary Prevention of Violence Against Women and Their Children in Australia* (Melbourne, Australia: Our Watch, 2015), 18, www .ourwatch.org.au/resource/change-the-story-a-shared-framework-for-the-primary -prevention-of-violence-against-women-and-their-children-in-australia.

- condoning of violence against women

- men's control of decision making and limits to women's independence in public and private life

- rigid gender roles and stereotyped constructions of masculinity and femininity

- male peer relations that emphasize aggression and disrespect toward women

Each of these will be examined in turn below.

Condoning of violence against women. While no church would sensibly condone explicit physical violence against women, many churches do allow and condone other types of violence in more subtle forms. An example of this is the discourse within many churches that "Bathsheba was an adulteress" rather than "David was a rapist." By victim-blaming Bathsheba and shifting focus to her being a seductress, David's sexual violence is condoned and justified. Condoning violence against women does not only take the form of championing physical violence. It also takes the form of shifting the narrative, deflecting responsibility, and failing to acknowledge the impact of more insidious acts of violence toward women, including male political and theological superiority and male sexual entitlement. Failing to protect women from domestic abuse, responding to disclosures in a way that compounds the trauma, or failing to hold the abuser to account could also be termed acts of condoning violence. More broadly, it could also be argued that condoning violence against women takes place every time women are denied equal opportunity with men.

Men's control of decision making and limits to women's independence in public and private life. Complementarian churches, by definition, enforce this driver of violence. One of the precepts of complementarianism is that men are responsible for governance and oversight. For example, men are usually understood to be the head of the home and are therefore the primary decision makers of matters relating to the family. Women, designated as subordinates or helpers, are categorized in direct relationship to their authoritative husband, necessarily limiting their independence. In a more extreme example, David demonstrated sole decision-making authority when he summoned Bathsheba to him, most likely raped her, and arranged for her husband to be killed. Bathsheba's right to refuse David's request or assert her independence from David's control (without threat of death) was clearly absent.

Rigid gender roles and stereotyped constructions of masculinity and femininity. Again, this driver of violence against women is a core tenet of complementarianism. Gender roles are strictly defined in complementarian churches and homes without regard for competence or giftings. Noted complementarian John Piper states: "The roles of leadership and submission in the marriage are not based on competence. God never said that the man is appointed to be head because he is more competent, or that the woman is appointed to submission because she is less competent. Competence is not the issue in whether a man is head and a woman is submitting."[33] Complementarians are clear that roles are prescribed according to gender, not competence or any other qualifying criteria. Men are taught to fulfill the stereotyped role of a leader and authoritative head. Women are taught to fulfill the stereotyped role of a joyfully submissive wife.[34] David was fulfilling the traditionally masculine role of being a king and military commander. Bathsheba was described according to her appearance and sexual appeal, which are stereotypical descriptions of femininity.

Male peer relations that emphasize aggression and disrespect toward women. Male peer relations that emphasize aggression are present throughout David's interactions in 2 Samuel 11. He sends his army to enact the ultimate act of aggression by destroying the Ammonites and besieging Rabbah (women included). He orders his servants (at least one of whom is male) to bring Bathsheba to him. He further disrespects Bathsheba and causes her pain by ordering another act of aggression when he orders her husband to be killed.

While aggression toward women is not as explicitly condoned in churches as in this example of David's actions, male peer relations in families and churches that encourage the exclusion of women from leadership perpetrate disrespect toward women simply by the decision to exclude. As

---

[33]John Piper, "What Does It Mean for a Man to Lead His Family," Desiring God, January 11, 2006, www.desiringgod.org/interviews/what-does-it-mean-for-a-man-to-lead-his-family-spiritually.

[34]Our Watch, ANROWS, and VicHealth, *Change the Story*, 25.

this chapter will later discuss, multiple biases that are disadvantageous and disrespectful to women are created by complementarian structures.

According to these four primary drivers of violence against women, complementarian churches and families construct environments where multiple drivers of violence against women are enforced. Our Watch further states that if we want a society, "we have to challenge the historically-entrenched beliefs and behaviors that drive it, and the social, political and economic structures, practices and systems that support these."[35]

While not limited to domestic abuse, the #ChurchToo movement has brought countless stories of abuse at the hands of (overwhelmingly male) church leaders to public attention, with (overwhelmingly female) victims sharing on social media platforms the varied ways that church leaders have abused, assaulted, raped, betrayed, or failed to believe and support them. One initiator of the #ChurchToo movement, Hannah Paasch, writes about the damage caused to her by the power discourses of men in roles of church leadership: "The deep cognitive dissonance of purity culture demands that women trust men as leaders, protectors and providers while blaming ourselves when our boundaries are inevitably crossed."[36]

In both complementarian homes and churches, a culture of male headship is pursued and esteemed. As a result, just recourse for a woman after an abusive event is deeply flawed. The adjudicator over matters of abuse is likely to be either the abuser themselves or contemporaries of the abuser with equal power, privilege, and bias to the abuser. Paasch writes: "I have followed the stories of survivors online, lived them myself, and held my friends as they waded through the aftermath of their abuse and trauma, while [also experiencing] a complete lack of care and often hostility from the faith communities that were supposed to care for, support and protect them."[37] It is little wonder that most acts of abuse go unreported.[38]

---

[35]Our Watch, ANROWS, and VicHealth, *Change the Story*, foreword.

[36]Hannah Paasch, "Sexual Abuse Happens in #ChurchToo—We're Living Proof," HuffPost, May 12, 2017, www.huffpost.com/entry/sexual-abuse-churchtoo_n_5a205b30e4b03350e0b53131.

[37]Lorraine Caballero, "#Churchtoo: Christian Victims Flood Social Media with Own Stories of Clergy Abuse," Christian Daily, November 25, 2017, www.christiandaily.com/article/churchtoo -christian-victims-flood-social-media-with-own-stories-of-clergy-abuse/61533.htm.

[38]Enrique Gracia, "Unreported Cases of Domestic Violence Against Women: Towards an Epidemiology of Social Silence, Tolerance, and Inhibition," *Journal of Epidemiology & Community Health* 58 (2004): 536, https://jech.bmj.com/content/58/7/536.

Shane Clifton speaks well to this issue in his essay "Spirit, Submission, Power, and Abuse":

> The issue at stake is one of power, since enablement and concealment are the products of power. And the problem for some sections of the church is that their teaching and structures are overwhelmingly oriented to buttress the power of men and to disempower women. It seems to me obvious—only complementarians do not find it so—that churches that do not ordain women, or that keep women out of the pulpit and away from decision-making bodies (such as local church eldership and denominational structures), create and sustain potentially dangerous, gendered, hierarchies of power. The problem is not only that women have few people within such male-centered hierarchies with whom they can talk, nor that women's concerns are rarely thought of by institutions whose authority structures are wholly and predominantly male (domestic violence is a problem for everyone, but it is more commonly experienced by women). The foundational issue is that the symbolic message of male power and female powerlessness are given divine warrant, which no ancillary teaching against violence, nor pastoral support for those subject to it, nor emphasis on self-sacrificial love . . . can overcome.[39]

Many still misunderstand domestic abuse to be a problem, at its root, of physical violence.[40] However, it is widely accepted in the social sciences that the heart of domestic abuse is the desire for power and control over others. The Duluth Power and Control Wheel (fig. 28.1) is commonly used to illustrate the varied ways that power and control can manifest in an abusive domestic relationship.[41]

---

[39]Shane Clifton, "Spirit, Submission, Power and Abuse," *St Mark's Review*, no. 243 (March 2018): 74.

[40]Calabria et al., "New Study Finds Family."

[41]Domestic Abuse Intervention Programs, Duluth, MN, "Understanding the Power and Control Wheel," 1984, www.theduluthmodel.org/wheels/. Reprinted with permission.

Fig. 28.1. The Duluth Power and Control Wheel

This model outlines some of the tactics perpetrators of domestic abuse use, including using children, male privilege, economic abuse, coercion and threats, intimidation, emotional abuse, isolation, and minimizing, denying, and blaming. More specific behavioral examples are listed under each type of abuse. Using male privilege, for example, can include treating a woman like a servant, making all the big decisions, acting like the "master of the castle," and being the one to define men's and women's roles.

Some of the particular abusive behaviors listed bear striking resemblance to the governance structures of complementarian churches, in particular "making all the big decisions" and "being the one to define men's and women's roles." "Preventing her from getting or keeping a job" could also apply to ministry roles in complementarian churches, where women are excluded from employment as ministers. Similarly, some aspects of the category of "using emotional abuse" are present in complementarian churches, such as "putting her down" or "making her feel bad about herself" when creating a culture of limiting and silencing women.

Refusal to acknowledge gender inequality as the basis of gendered violence is in itself an act of abuse, by minimizing or denying the body of evidence pointing to gender inequality as the primary driver of domestic abuse. For example, the Anglican Diocese of Sydney, a notoriously complementarian diocese, fails to acknowledge the gendered drivers and nature of domestic abuse in its Policy on Domestic Violence.[42]

In my work as a psychologist, Christian women regularly report their despair at not being heard or taken seriously by all-male church leadership teams. Ideas are ignored, giftings are overlooked, and issues important to women are not prioritized on the church agenda. Other women who have been abused by their partner or church staff regularly report that all-male leadership teams very rarely act in an impartial manner when making judgments about a complaint made by a woman against a man. The experience of women in complementarian churches is often similar to the "minimizing, denying and blaming" category, where complaints are not taken seriously, male leaders dismiss or downplay abuse that has occurred in their church, or, worse, a woman is blamed for a man's abusive behaviors. Other church leaders respond in ways bearing comparison to the "using coercion and threats" category when they advise women suffering domestic abuse to "remain with her husband and submit to his authority, as this is God's will." These types of responses by church leaders have been corroborated in recent research.[43] Stories of women being abused by their husbands and then being revictimized and similarly treated by their churches are common.

One comprehensive, theologically informed, and evidence-based resource to equip churches to prevent, recognize, and respond to domestic abuse in

---

[42]Anglican Diocese of Sydney, *Responding to Domestic Abuse: Provisional Policy and Good Practice Guidelines* (Sydney, AU: Anglican Diocese of Sydney, 2017), https://safeministry.org.au/wp -content/uploads/2017/11/Responding-to-Domestic-Abuse.Policy-And-Guidelines.Synod2017 .full-resources.pdf.

[43]Calabria et al., "New Study Finds Family."

their midst, called SAFER, has been published online by Common Grace.[44] SAFER recognizes domestic abuse as a gendered problem, outlines why domestic-abuse prevention and response is a key faith issue, notes prevalence in the church, and offers guidance for churches to respond effectively and be safe communities. It can be accessed for free at saferresource.org.au.

PRIMARY, SECONDARY, AND TERTIARY INTERVENTION TARGETING GENDERED VIOLENCE

Gendered violence is preventable, and many public health organizations employ a proven framework for social change that goes beyond addressing individual behaviors to consider the broader social context of the drivers of violence.[45] It incorporates primary prevention, secondary intervention, and tertiary postvention.

1. Primary prevention aims to prevent a problem before it occurs. Usually encompassing populations and cultures, primary prevention of gendered violence targets gender inequality, the systemic driver of violence, with the aim of inequality and violence not gaining a foothold.

2. Secondary intervention refers to specific communities seeking to address the risk of violence growing in frequency or severity according to local culture and context.

3. Tertiary postvention operates where violence has occurred and seeks to minimize its impact and prevent reoccurrence.[46]

According to this widely accepted framework, complementarian churches find themselves in the tricky position of driving violence against women at the primary and secondary levels by creating and theologically sanctioning gender inequality, while condemning the resultant tertiary abuse.

---

[44]"Safer: A Resource to Help Australian Churches Understand, Identify, and Respond to Domestic and Family Violence," Safer Resource, www.saferresource.org.au.

[45]"What Is Primary Prevention of Violence Against Women," Our Watch, August 22, 2017, www
.ourwatch.org.au/News-media/Latest-news/What-is-primary-prevention-of-violence
-against-wom.

[46]"Violence Against Women in Australia: Research Summary," VicHealth, www.vichealth.vic.gov
.au/media-and-resources/publications/violence-against-women-in-australia-research
-summary.

The ABC of Women Worker's Rights and Gender Equality, published by the International Labor Organization, offers a helpful definition of gender equality, which makes explicit the idea that gender equality is free from the limitations set by rigid gender roles:

> Gender equality, equality between men and women, entails the concept that all human beings, both men and women, are free to develop their personal abilities and make choices without the limitations set by stereotypes, rigid gender roles and prejudices. Gender equality means that the different behavior, aspirations and needs of women and men are considered, valued and favored equally. It does not mean that women and men have to become the same, but that their rights, responsibilities and opportunities will not depend on whether they are born male or female.[47]

The gender inequality practiced in complementarian churches and families is clear.

- Women are prevented or restricted from holding ministry, teaching, or preaching roles, and are therefore afforded less public influence.

- Women are underrepresented in decision-making forums.

- Women are given fewer opportunities to practice and develop their spiritual gifts of leadership, teaching, and preaching.

- Women encounter more barriers to theological education.

- Women encounter more barriers to employment in ministry roles.

- Women are less able than men to receive pastoral care by a minister of their own gender. This is especially important when the issues are specific to women, such as pregnancy, childbirth, or sexual issues.

- Single women experience even greater barriers to receiving pastoral care from all-male leadership teams, due to the often-enforced propriety of a man and a woman not being allowed to meet alone together.

- Women have fewer formal avenues for input regarding the direction of the church.

---

[47]International Labour Organization, *ABC of Women Workers' Rights and Gender Equality* (Geneva: International Labour Office, 2000), 48.

- Women's career opportunities are potentially limited due to restrictions on the roles women are permitted to occupy. This is according to beliefs about women's ability to lead men in the church or secular workplace.

- Women who have completed seminary training are afforded far fewer ministry opportunities than their male counterparts.

Women's earning potential is restricted if a woman is required to be the primary carer for children and elders. The resulting cultural formation of the church and family can include the following:

- Theological teaching and formation that has been skewed toward the male voice.

- "Women's ministries" are developed as special-interest ministries rather than as mainstream ministry to the people of the church.

- Women have fewer visible role models and mentors in areas of spiritual formation, resulting in slowed maturity and growth.

- The issues that affect women are either not prioritized or are removed entirely from the church's agenda.

Women can be taught that being complicit in their subjugation to men equates with godliness. But beyond these observable effects of gender inequality in churches and families, other subtle, insidious problems are bred by complementarian ideology, including unconscious bias, questions of competence, the confidence gap, conscious bias, affinity bias, and apprehended bias.

UNCONSCIOUS BIAS

The most important and insidious phenomenon that complementarian structures and cultures create is unconscious bias. Unconscious biases are automatic, learned attitudes that we all form by summarizing our observations of our environment. Our brain stereotypes and categorizes people according to familiarity and *does not differentiate according to accuracy or fairness*. Perhaps the most famous experiment to uncover the extent of unconscious bias was in the selection of musicians for a New York orchestra in the 1950s. In this experiment, when the gender of the auditioning musician was known to the orchestra selection panel, only 5 percent of musicians accepted were women. Yet when a simple curtain was added and the auditions became gender blind, the selection of women rose from 5 percent to near 35 percent.[48] Other research has shown gendered bias to surface when considering two equally qualified people for a promotion: one female, one male. Evidence suggests the male will be chosen based on no other criteria than his gender.[49]

In the complementarian church, unconscious bias is initiated and perpetuated when men are regularly seen to be the minister, preacher, congregational leader, or elder. An unconscious belief that men are more competent and credible than woman will form, even in the presence of a conscious belief that women are just as capable, just as gifted, and just as credible as men. This unconscious bias then has a flow-on effect to alter our understanding, decisions, and behaviors.

Unconscious bias tells us that people believe what is *seen* more than what is *said*. As the parable of the two sons illustrates, it is our *actions* that reveal the kingdom of God, not our *words* (Mt 21:28-31). Stating that women are equally competent and credible (even stating it regularly) *does not* overcome the bias. Sometimes it can even strengthen it by providing a mechanism to alleviate the guilt of the unconscious belief without having to shift the belief itself. Nor does stating that male headship is only enacted in loving kindness overcome the bias, as such a statement does not permeate unconscious beliefs. This means that women in complementarian churches are denied the opportunity not only to preach, teach, and lead, but also to have their competence viewed without undue unconscious bias.

Harvard Business Review continues to build the body of evidence surrounding unconscious bias and recently stated that, due to unconscious bias, we naturally give less recognition to women's ideas.[50] That is, women

---

[48]Claudia Goldin and Cecilia Rouse, "Orchestrating Impartiality: The Impact of 'Blind' Auditions on Female Musicians," Gender Action Portal, Harvard Kenney School: Women and Public Policy Program, September 2000, http://gap.hks.harvard.edu/orchestrating-impartiality-impact -"blind"-auditions-female-musicians.

[49]Corinne A. Moss-Racusina et al., "Science Faculty's Subtle Gender Biases Favor Male Students," PNAS, August 21, 2012, www.pnas.org/content/pnas/early/2012/09/14/1211286109.full.pdf; Stefanie K. Johnson, David R. Hekman, and Elsa T. Chan, "If There's Only One Woman in Your Candidate Pool, There's Statistically No Chance She'll Be Hired," *Harvard Business Review*, April 26, 2016, https://hbr.org/2016/04/if-theres-only-one-woman-in-your-candidate-pool-theres -statistically-no-chance-shell-be-hired.

[50]Sean R. Martin, "Research: Men Get Credit for Voicing Ideas, but Not Problems. Women Don't Get Credit for Either," *Harvard Business Review*, November 3, 2017, https://hbr.org/2017/11/research

get less credit for voicing the very same ideas that men voice. Similarly, when a woman and a man voice opposing ideas over the same issue, the male voice is afforded more credibility. Public examples of this are common in cases of abuse and assault, when a woman discloses abuse and the alleged perpetrator denies such abuse. It generally takes multiple female victims testifying against one male abuser in order to amass an equal amount of credibility.

This issue is particularly salient in the church when assessing or adjudicating matters of domestic abuse, as the belief that the male partner is more competent than the female partner is likely to skew belief toward his explanation of events. So, when clergy are more likely to believe the perpetrator than the victim, not only does spiritual abuse occur, but the cycle of men holding positions of power and control over women in the home and the church is reinforced.

Iris Bohnet's work in unconscious bias and gender equality has led to an increasing number of organizations naming unconscious bias in their ranks and working to prevent the resulting discrimination through strategic planning, education and training, and conscious inclusion of women and their ideas.[51] Churches would do well to follow suit.

THE QUESTION OF COMPETENCE

Complementarians regularly argue that male headship is not an issue of competence but rather an issue of "different roles." Unconscious bias demands that this argument be reviewed. Seeing men in roles of leadership and authority more often than women *creates* an issue of competence by instigating and perpetuating the belief in observers that women are less competent. This unconscious belief persists even in the presence of discourses arguing that both genders are equally competent.

Furthermore, issues of *actual* competence are created when women are given fewer avenues for training and practice in skills such as preaching and teaching when compared with men. A woman's ability to become

---

-men-get-credit-for-voicing-ideas-but-not-problems-women-dont-get-credit-for-either?utm _campaign=hbr&utm_source=twitter&utm_medium=social.

[51]Iris Bohnet, *What Works: Gender Equality by Design* (Boston: Belknap, 2016); Australian Government: Australia Public Service Commission, "Unconcious Bias," March 29, 2018, www.apsc.gov .au/unconscious-bias.

more competent is undermined due to lack of opportunity to develop her skills or gifting. Complementarians can thus feel justified in their belief that women should not teach or preach, when women would actually be equally as competent given equal opportunity. Issues of competence are therefore a byproduct of complementarianism, if not a cause.

THE CONFIDENCE GAP

Across countries and professions, it is widely documented that men consistently overestimate their abilities and performance and women consistently underestimate theirs, even when their performances do not differ in quality.[52] Many reasons are hypothesized for this, including male-dominated discourses that marginalize women and the socialization of women to be less assertive than men. One particularly relevant study measured the confidence of female students entering nine Canadian Bible colleges and compared their confidence to women in secular colleges. The confidence of women in secular institutions fell 7 percent behind their male counterparts. Astonishingly, the confidence of women entering Christian colleges fell 40 percent below their male counterparts. Not only was the confidence of Christian women lower than that of secular women, but the confidence of Christian men was 15 percent higher than secular men.[53] Something particular to Christian theology or culture sees the confidence of men elevated and the confidence of women diminished.

AFFINITY BIAS

Affinity bias, a particular type of unconscious bias, is the tendency to hire, mentor, and champion "people like me." It has been one of the bedeviling factors in movement toward gender equality in predominantly male workplaces. Affinity bias in the church means that, as long as men are the ones recruiting and promoting church leaders, they are more likely to promote and recruit men, even if male and female candidates are equally suitable for the role.[54] One way to overcome this bias is to remove names and

---

[52]Katty Kay Shipman and Claire Shipman, "The Confidence Gap," *The Atlantic*, August 26, 2015, www.theatlantic.com/magazine/archive/2014/05/the-confidence-gap/359815/.

[53]David Neff, "Women in the Confidence Gap," *CT* (July 22, 1991), 13.

[54]Johnson, Hekman, and Chan, "If There's Only One Woman."

genders from resumes before they are given to a selection panel. Of course, in communities where selectors and candidates are already well known to each other, this strategy is insufficient to eliminate bias. This strategy will also fall short in communities where a belief is held that only male applicants are welcome to apply for particular roles.

CONSCIOUS BIAS

Another phenomenon is conscious bias. As the name suggests, conscious bias is a deliberate and overt bias against a person or group. In complementarian churches, this takes the form of believing that women should not hold particular roles or positions in the church. While this type of discrimination against women is theologically and culturally constructed and sanctioned, it nonetheless has obvious problems: it defines merit in a biased manner that provides justification for discrimination.[55] It results in gender inequality through discriminatory actions against women, barriers being erected for women, and women's voices and gifts being quieted or silenced.

A growing body of evidence suggests that diverse teams (including gender-diverse teams) perform better than homogenous teams. Teams with diverse members are more successful in a range of outcomes than homogenous ones, with results indicating diverse teams demonstrate greater factual accuracy, greater innovation, and less bias.[56] If complementarian church and family leaders seek to love and serve those whom they lead, it seems fitting that leadership teams incorporate both genders in order to achieve better outcomes for the group.

APPREHENDED BIAS

Often used in legal spheres, apprehended bias is the perception that a judge or adjudicator is unable to perform their role without significant bias. It may refer to racial prejudice against one party in a legal proceeding, resulting in biased proceedings and judgments. Or it may refer to a judge's

---

[55]Eric Luis Uhlmann and Geoffrey L. Cohen, "Constructed Criteria Redefining Merit to Justify Discrimination," *Psychological Science* 16 (2005): 478.

[56]David Rock and Heidi Grant, "Why Diverse Teams Are Smarter," *Harvard Business Review*, March 19, 2019, https://hbr.org/2016/11/why-diverse-teams-are-smarter.

vested interest, such as holding shares in a mining company while assessing and granting mining licenses.

Churches where governance structures are composed exclusively or predominantly of men are likely to demonstrate apprehended bias where the perceived neutrality of their adjudication is compromised. A poignant question regarding apprehended bias was raised during recent public discussions about domestic abuse in the church: "Is an all-male hierarchy even capable of responding effectively to gendered violence?"[57]

If these and other phenomena are indeed true of complementarian structures (and a growing body of international evidence suggests they are), then the "equal" aspect of the "equal but different" complementarian doctrine demands review. Perhaps it may be more accurate for complementarians to adopt wording that makes the insidious harm done to women more explicit. For instance, a more honest assessment of complementarian orthodoxy and orthopraxy is well stated by George Orwell in *Animal Farm*: "All animals are equal, but some animals are more equal than others."[58]

CONCLUSION

It is no longer credible to simply state from the pulpit that complementarianism, due to its loving kindness, does not facilitate gendered violence. It is by definition a system of permanently unequal power distribution with rigidly defined gender roles. These are some of the conditions under which abuse is known to flourish. Complementarianism, even if it could be enacted in perfect loving kindness, creates not only systemic discrimination but implicit and explicit biases that disadvantage women.

Domestic violence and complementarianism both involve men holding positions of power over women, men holding primary decision-making roles, and men restricting women's equal voice and participation. Power and privilege afforded to one group, to the exclusion of another, creates and perpetuates biases, prejudice, and discrimination. While many

---

[57]Hayley Gleeson, Julia Baird, and Rocco Fazzari, "'Their Cross to Bear': The Catholic Women Told to Forgive Domestic Violence," ABC News, November 4, 2017, www.abc.net.au /news/2017-11-04/cross-to-bear-catholic-church-domestic-abuse/8680158.

[58]George Orwell, *Animal Farm* (Blairgowrie, UK: Guidelines, 1989), 112.

complementarian churches condemn domestic abuse, they are clearly perpetuating the gender inequality that is a primary driver of that violence.

Dan Allender in his book *Leading with a Limp* describes how Jesus-like leaders use their position to ensure that power is used fairly within their sphere, essentially giving their power away.[59] Church leaders truly modeling the self-sacrificial love of Jesus will actively invite the voice and equality of all people. In the context of gender, this means understanding and overcoming any biases at play, actively prioritizing women's needs, and pursuing a culture of gender equality. To be truly opposed to domestic abuse requires repenting of and dismantling any form of gender inequality, which is the primary driver for violence against women. As Ruth Bader Ginsburg says, "Women belong wherever decisions are being made."[60]

---

[59]Dan B. Allender, *Leading with a Limp: Take Full Advantage of Your Most Powerful Weakness* (Colorado Springs: WaterBrook, 2011), 61.

[60]Ruth Bader Ginsburg, cited in "Justice Ginsburg to Welcome Sotomayor," CNN Politics, June 16, 2009, http://edition.cnn.com/2009/POLITICS/06/16/sotomayor.ginsburg/index.html.

29

WHEN WE WERE NOT WOMEN

RACE AND DISCOURSES ON WOMANHOOD

Juliany González Nieves

> *Little attention has been given women's nature in*
> *Euro-centric ontologies, and Black Women have been excluded*
> *most of all. If humankind has been conceived as "man,"*
> *to the exclusion of women, woman has been conceived as*
> *white women to the exclusion of woman of African descent.*

KAREN BAKER-FLETCHER, "WOMANISM, AFRO-CENTRISM,
AND THE RECONSTRUCTION OF BLACK WOMANHOOD"

• • • • •

OFTEN, DISCUSSIONS AMONG EVANGELICALS in the United States about womanhood and gender roles in society, the church, and the household are silent about the existence, realities, and values of Black women, indigenous women, and other women of color. These conversations are characterized by being White centered and male dominated, and often reflective of a privileged socioeconomic class.[1] A general review of the

---

[1]Whiteness is a sociological construct, and it is at the core of the myth of race. Whiteness preaches in word and deed the presumed (g)od-given superiority of Euro-American aesthetics, theologies,

literature demonstrates this. Consider who the defining voices in the conversation are, which authors are seriously engaged, and which voices are excluded. Terms such as *women* and *womanhood* are used without qualification and with the pretension of universality, a-culturality, and homogeneity. These terms are used as if we do not live in a historically racialized and classist society, a country founded on the idea of White exceptionalism, the broken and displaced bodies of indigenous women and communities, and the backs and exploited wombs of women of African descent.[2] As if the notions of woman and womanhood in this country have not been conceived and defined exclusively as White and middle class. As if Sojourner Truth never had to assert herself and ask, "Ain't I a woman?"

In this chapter, I examine a specific complementarian theological discourse and its convergence with the nineteenth-century "cult of true womanhood," a discourse that placed White, middle-class Christian women on a pedestal while denying the womanhood of poor women, Black women, and other women of color. The structure of this chapter is fourfold. First, I provide a description of what I identify as a comprehensive complementarian discourse, whose main proponents include John Piper and Wayne Grudem. Second, I analyze their construal of femininity, which I suggest is organized around three categories—the body, demeanor, and virtue—and delineate the convergence with the antebellum South's cult of true womanhood. Third, I discuss how the construal of the "true woman" was

---

cultures, and ways of life and thinking, locating everything and everyone in a spectrum that grants degrees of privilege based on their proximity to the baptized idol of the White man. The mythology of race, with its heresies of White supremacy and patriarchy (the belief that men are intrinsically superior to women), has become the cornerstone on which many nations and institutions—including Christian ones—have been built. That is a heritage that shapes the way dialogues are designed and approached. Hence, I call for a decentering of Whiteness. That is, to move away from ideas and practices that prioritize Euro-American cultures and their concerns, while moving toward a truly catholic approach, which is multisectorial, multiethnic, multiracial, multilingual, and inevitably intersectional (i.e., considers the intersections between socioeconomic class, gender, race/ethnicity, etc.). See also my blog post: Juliany González Nieves, "Building a Longer Table: Decentering Whiteness in Our (Re)conciliation Conversations," Legacy Disciple, July 7, 2019, https://legacydisciple.org/index.php/2019/07/30/building-a-longer-table-decentering-whiteness-in-our-reconciliation-conversations/.

[2]See Mark Charles and Soong-Chan Rah, *Unsettling Truths: The Ongoing, Dehumanizing Legacy of the Doctrine of Discovery* (Downers Grove, IL: InterVarsity Press, 2019); Jemar Tisby, *The Color of Compromise: The Truth About the American Church's Complicity in Racism* (Grand Rapids, MI: Zondervan, 2019); and Richard Twiss, *Rescuing the Gospel from the Cowboys: A Native American Expression of the Jesus Way* (Downers Grove, IL: InterVarsity Press, 2015).

inherently the misconstrual of the femininity of women of color around the very same categories of body, demeanor, and virtue. Last, I point out how correlated codified racio-linguistics between the comprehensive complementarian discourse and the nineteenth-century "true woman" ideal de facto render the notion of womanhood as Anglo and middle class. Hence, "true women" excluded indigenous women, Black women, and other women of color. I note that discourses on the feminine and nonfeminine are not neutral. They do not stand alone. For not only have they emerged in the context of a racialized society, but throughout history they have often been weaponized to perpetrate and perpetuate the exploitation of racialized bodies, with women of color being the most affected.

WHAT THIS CHAPTER DOES NOT DO

This chapter does not argue exclusively for one position or another. It does not put all complementarians in the same bucket, and it does not absolve egalitarians from their very own White-centeredness. I believe that rather than a binary, this conversation entails a spectrum of positions with nuances. I also believe that contextually informed applications of both complementarian and egalitarian views that have done the work of decentering Whiteness and maleness can result in the flourishing of communities. As a biblical scholar once told me, "You were not called to serve a tribe. You were called by God to serve the church." I hope this ethos is seen through this chapter as I call attention to a reality many within US evangelicalism prefer to ignore.

A (COMPREHENSIVE) COMPLEMENTARIAN
DISCOURSE ON WOMANHOOD AND FEMININITY

What does it mean to be a woman? What does it mean to be feminine? In *Recovering Biblical Manhood and Womanhood: A Response to Evangelical Feminism*, John Piper provides the following description of womanhood: "At the heart of mature femininity is a freeing disposition to affirm, receive and nurture strength and leadership from worthy men in ways appropriate to a woman's differing relationships."[3] Piper goes on to elaborate on each

---

[3]John Piper, "A Vision of Biblical Complementarity: Manhood and Womanhood Defined According to the Bible," in *RBMW*, 54.

component of his statement, including what he means by the phrase "mature femininity." Initially, he does not define the term *femininity*; rather, he argues that there are distortions of it. He refers to the work of Ronda Chevrin, who in her book *Feminine, Free and Faithful* shares two lists of what participants in her workshops have commonly considered positive and negative feminine traits. The participants described women embodying positive feminine traits as being

> responsive, compassionate, empathetic, enduring, gentle, warm, tender, hospitable, receptive, diplomatic, considerate, polite, supportive, intuitive, wise, perceptive, sensitive, spiritual, sincere, vulnerable (in the sense of emotionally open), obedient, trusting, graceful, sweet, expressive, charming, delicate, quiet, sensually receptive (vs. prudish), faithful, pure.[4]

Contrastingly, women exhibiting negative feminine traits were characterized as "weak, passive, slavish, weepy, wishy-washy, seductive, flirtatious, vain, chatter-box, silly, sentimental, naïve, moody, petty, catty, prudish, manipulative, complaining, nagging, pouty, smothering, spiteful."[5] Chevrin provides examples of women representatives for each list; however, Piper only makes a selection of examples from the positive list: "Ruth, Naomi, Sarah, Mary (Jesus' mother), Cordelia of *King Lear*, Melanie in *Gone with the Wind*, Grace Kelly, and Mother Teresa of Calcutta." Ultimately, he defines his use of "mature femininity" as referring to "what God willed for [womanhood] to be at its best." And although he does not present the lists of positive and negative feminine traits as definite characterizations of what he considers to be distortions brought about by the fall, there seems to be an implicit connection.[6]

Soon after this definition, Piper clarifies that he understands femininity as "a disposition rather than a set of behaviors or roles" due to the diversity of situations, relationships, and cultures. That is, a disposition "to affirm, receive and nurture strength and leadership from worthy men." But his initial parameter of "worthy men" quickly expands to simply "men" when he states, "She will affirm and receive and nurture the strength and leadership of men *in some form* in all her relationships with men." Womanhood

---

[4]Ronda Chevrin, *Feminine, Free and Faithful* (San Francisco: Ignatius, 1986), 15.
[5]Chevrin, *Feminine, Free and Faithful*, 15.
[6]Piper, "Vision of Biblical Complementarity," 54.

then is conceptualized as inherently related to serving men in different forms. This, consequently, raises up a particular concern regarding women who find themselves in leadership roles over men. He mentions multiple instances in which this is the case, including when a woman serves as prime minister, school principal, staff doctor, lawyer, judge, police officer, and legislator. Although in his view, "one or more of these roles might stretch appropriate expressions of femininity beyond the breaking point," he believes "there are ways for a woman to interact even with a male subordinate that signal to him and others her endorsement of his mature manhood." It all comes down to "her demeanor—the tone and style and disposition and discourse of her ranking position." He illustrates, "It is simply impossible that from time to time a woman not be put in a position of influencing or guiding men. For example, a housewife in her backyard may be asked by a man how to get to the freeway. At that point she is giving a kind of leadership. She has superior knowledge that the man needs and he submits himself to her guidance." Hence, when Piper thinks about femininity, he has in mind a demeanor, a tone, and a style in which women ought to relate to men. His selections of examples and illustrations throughout the chapter serve to materialize his idea of femininity to some extent: the housewife in her backyard, Cordelia of *King Lear*, Melanie in *Gone with the Wind*, and Grace Kelly. Furthermore, Piper's idea of femininity extends to the woman's body, classifying some women's body types as feminine and others as nonfeminine. This is evident in his illustration of "a muscular, scantily clad young woman pumping iron in a health club" who is presented in a negative light, accused of "[attempting] to assume a more masculine role by appearing muscular and aggressive."[7]

Piper is not the only voice shaping how femininity is understood within complementarian circles. Nancy Leigh DeMoss is an influential voice in the True Woman movement.[8] She is the author of multiple works, including *Lies Women Believe: And the Truth That Sets Them Free*, and

---

[7]Piper, "Vision of Biblical Complementarity," 47, 55, 59-61.

[8]The True Woman movement is described in its website as "a worldwide, grassroots movement" originated in 2008 at the Revive Our Hearts first True Woman Conference in Chicago. It started as a response to feminism, both secular and religious. The website reports that "over 27,000 women have attended the five True Woman national women's conferences." For more information, visit www.reviveourhearts.com/true-woman/about/.

coauthor of *True Woman 101—Divine Design: An Eight-Week Study on Biblical Womanhood*. In the latter, DeMoss, along with her coauthor, Mary A. Kassian, proposes four elements that constitute "the core of what it means to be a woman." The first one is "softness," which they describe by referring to the dictionary definition of the term: "not hard; yielding readily to touch, flexible, pliable; delicate, graceful; not loud; quietly pleasant; calm, gentle, kind, tender, compassionate, and sympathetic." Interestingly, this definition seems to touch on various elements often associated to femininity, including the aspect of demeanor. DeMoss and Kassian connect this understanding of softness to the New Testament use of the term *weaker*, noting that "women are physically and emotionally more tender, and are thus more susceptible to being hurt."[9] The following quote from Elisabeth Elliot serves as an anchor to the authors' elaboration of softness as a core element of the meaning of femaleness: "Yours is the body of a woman. What does it signify? Is there invisible meaning in its visible signs—the softness, the smoothness, the lighter bone and muscle structure, the breasts, the womb? Are they utterly unrelated to what you yourself are? Isn't your identity intimately bound up with these material forms?"[10] As it was the case with Piper's, DeMoss and Kassian's idea of femininity entails the woman's body beyond sexual differentiation. The idea of softness is conceived not only as an internal characteristic but as a physical one, and has been historically and socially almost exclusively ascribed to White women. I will return to Elliot's bodily conception of softness below.

The second element the authors present as being at the core of what it means to be a woman is "forming deep relational bonds." They argue women have a "unique bent toward relationships" that emerges from "being created for someone." They write, "Being created 'for someone' indicates that God created the female to be a highly relational creature. In contrast to the male, her identity isn't based on work nearly as much as on how well she connects and relates to others." In other words, there is

---

[9]Mary A. Kassian and Nancy Leigh DeMoss, *True Woman 101—Divine Design: An Eight-Week Study on Biblical Womanhood* (Chicago: Moody, 2012), 70-71.

[10]Elisabeth Elliot, *Let Me Be a Woman* (Carol Stream, IL: Tyndale House, 1976), 61. Also quoted by DeMoss and Kassian on page 68.

an ontological attribution of relationality to women. The third and fourth core elements of womanhood listed are "having a receptive or responsive spirit" and "creating a place to beget a nurture life." DeMoss and Kassian elaborate on the latter, "God wired man to be connected to work in a way woman is not, so He wired woman to be connected to home and relationships in a way man is not." This location of women's bodies in distinctive spheres is characteristic of the comprehensive complementarian discourse on womanhood. It relegates women to the domestic space, while men are placed outside the home. Toward the end of the book, DeMoss and Kassian adopt a tripartite understanding of how femininity ought to be modeled—that is, "by exhibiting a distinctive modesty, responsiveness, and gentleness of spirit." In summary, for Kassian and DeMoss, to be a woman is to be "the soft one—the relater, the responder, the nurturer." It is "to be man's helper."[11] Femininity is ultimately defined by the authors not solely in terms of characteristics but in terms of roles in relation to men. For this reason, it should come as no surprise that a significant portion of the conversation on womanhood and femininity revolves around marriage and motherhood.

Based on his understanding of Genesis 1–2, George Knight argues women's roles in the household are those of wife and mother, while man's main calling is "the responsibility of breadwinner and provider for his wife and family." Knight quickly categorizes this view as "the perspective God has given and not some 'Victorian' or 'traditional view' that has grown up out of some society or culture and been adopted unwittingly as the Biblical norm."[12] This understanding of gender roles within marriage and parenting is widespread within the complementarian spectrum at different levels. Knight clearly states that wives and mothers can work outside the home, as long as it is for the benefit of the family and does not take away from their main callings as wives and mothers. However, there is an imbalance in the emphasis on marriage and stay-at-home motherhood. Take, for instance, the Christian college subculture of "ring by spring" or the stereotypes and jokes about women getting their "Mrs. degrees" and not their

---

[11]Kassian and DeMoss, *True Woman 101*, 73-74, 80, 84-85, 214.

[12]George W. Knight III, "The Family and the Church: How Should Biblical Manhood and Womanhood Work Out in Practice?," in *RBMW*, 416.

academic degrees.[13] Or consider Dorothy Patterson's following statement, "In the Scriptures, the concern of godly women was not discrimination in vocation but rather the barrenness of the womb. Women were not pining away, pleading with the Almighty to be priests or prophets. They were praying for the blessing of bearing children." Patterson also passionately asserts, "There is no greater need for the coming years than a revival of interest in the responsibilities of motherhood. We need mothers who are not only family-oriented but also family-obsessed."[14]

These "family-obsessed" wives and mothers are expected to embody the kind of womanhood described by Piper, DeMoss, Kassian, and Knight. They are to be submissive, gentle, meek, obedient, reverent, pure, and morally upright, and have a quiet spirit.[15] Ultimately, they ought to be "femininely" virtuous. Carolyn Mahaney touches on this in her book *Feminine Appeal*. She argues that true feminine appeal is attained when "the seven feminine virtues" delineated in Titus 2 are exhibited by a wife and mother. She writes,

> Consider the loveliness of a woman who passionately adores her husband, who tenderly cherishes her children, who creates a warm and peaceful home, who exemplifies purity, self-control, and kindness in her character and who gladly submits to her husband leadership. . . . I dare say there are few things that display the gospel jewel with greater elegance. This is true *feminine appeal*.[16]

The aforementioned writers are proposing more than an ecclesial complementarianism. They are advocating a comprehensive, maximal, or societal complementarianism. For analytical purposes, I suggest this type of complementarianism construes femininity around at least three major categories: the body, demeanor, and virtuosity—all of which have been conceptualized around Whiteness.

---

[13]See Liam Adams, "'Ring by Spring': How Christian Colleges Fuel Students' Rush to Get Engaged," *Chronicle of Higher Education*, November 21, 2017, www.chronicle.com/article/Ring-by-Spring-How/241840; and Stacy Keogh George, *Ring by Spring: Dating and Relationship Cultures at Christian Colleges* (Eugene, OR: Cascade Books, 2019).

[14]Dorothy Patterson, "The High Calling of Wife and Mother in Biblical Perspective," in *RBMW*, 2nd ed., 369, 373.

[15]Wayne Grudem, "Wives like Sarah, and the Husbands Who Honor Them: 1 Peter 3:1-7," in *RBMW*, 268.

[16]Carolyn Mahaney, *Feminine Appeal: Seven Virtues of a Godly Wife and Mother* (Wheaton, IL: Crossway Books, 2003), 28-29.

CONSTRUALS OF FEMININITY:
BODY, DEMEANOR, AND VIRTUOSITY

The body. "The body remains a highly contested category," writes Mayra Rivera. "The body names the physicality of human existence. . . . It is described as 'natural' yet shaped by social practices and representations—biological and ideological." Conceptions about the body in theological discourses are not a-contextual. They do not emerge out of sterilized, a-cultural, nonideological milieus. To the contrary, they are directly and indirectly shaped by the sociological and cultural space, and the fears and hopes of those constructing the theological discourse. Consequently, these theological discourses in their hermeneutical spiral in turn affect the expectations and dynamics of the context, affecting how bodies are perceived and relate. For when we talk about the body, we are not just simply talking about the body. We are addressing the body and its relationship to the world. As Rivera states, "All bodies are constituted in relation to the world, but they do not encounter it in the same ways."[17]

It must be noted that I have no intention of arguing against the distinctiveness of biologically sexed female and male bodies. Rather, in this section, I want to punctuate how this complementarian discourse on womanhood and femininity describes, categorizes, locates, represents, and assigns roles to women's bodies.

First, women's bodies are often described as being soft. As I quoted in part earlier:

> Yours is the body of a woman. What does it signify? Is there invisible meaning in its visible signs—the softness, the smoothness, the lighter bone and muscle structure, the breasts, the womb? Are they utterly unrelated to what you yourself are? Isn't your identity intimately bound up with these material forms? Does the idea of you—Valerie—contain the idea of, let's say, "strapping" or "husky?"[18]

In *Let Me Be a Woman*, Elliot points to the body as a witness to the God-created distinctiveness between men and women. However, her

---

[17]Mayra Rivera, *Poetics of the Flesh* (Durham, NC: Duke University Press, 2015), 7, 12.
[18]Elliot, *Let Me Be a Woman*, 61.

description of "feminine" corporality goes well beyond "the breasts" and "the womb." It depicts in detail a soft and smooth skin almost palpable to the reader, and a lighter bone and muscle structure evocative of what would be considered a "delicate" figure. The question "Isn't your identity intimately bound up with these material forms?" then presumes what that identity should be. The body should be soft, smooth, and slender. That body is the only material form a woman is allowed to instantiate and remain "woman." These notions of "softness" and delicacy are then juxtaposed to bodies considered "strapping" and "husky," that is, body types that are big, strong, and with heavier muscular structure. In this way, Elliot's statement, intentionally or not, nevertheless inevitably puts forth a particular body image and type as that which is to be considered normative feminine, while also categorizing others as nonfeminine.

Second, Piper ties the image of musculature to masculinity and hence to that which is "nonfeminine." He writes,

> Consider what is lost when women attempt to assume a more masculine role by appearing physically muscular and aggressive. It is true that there is something sexually stimulating about a muscular, scantily clad young woman pumping iron in a health club. But no woman should be encouraged by this fact. For it probably means the sexual encounter that such an image would lead to is something very hasty and volatile, and in the long run unsatisfying. The image of a masculine musculature may beget arousal in a man, but it does not beget several hours of moonlight walking with significant, caring conversation.[19]

There are multiple elements worth noting in this quote. First, Piper accuses women who appear physically muscular of "attempting to assume a more masculine role." Second, he associates the physical attribute of musculature to aggressiveness. Third, he sexualizes the female muscular body, asserting that the image of "a muscular, scantily clad young woman pumping iron in a health club" is sexually stimulating. Fourth, he draws a connection between this image and unsatisfying, volatile, and very hasty sex. Last, he creates a false dichotomy between muscular women's body types and meaningful social interactions with men. Consequently, Piper

---

[19]Piper, "Vision of Biblical Complementarity," 47-48.

advocates a particular body image and type as the truly or prototypical feminine model: the figure with lighter muscle structure.

Piper's construal of the "feminine" body is concerning to say the least. It categorizes muscular women's body types as usurpers of a different role and as nonfeminine, also associating them with aggressiveness. Consequently, Piper seems to believe that a woman's body shape is responsible for superficial sexual experiences and detrimental for significant relationships with men. The pretentiousness of this fixation on prescribing even women's muscle tone as a controlling factor in their social life oozes of patriarchy. In fact, one of the benefits of men's locating themselves under the gaslighting of a virtuous biblical discourse is that they keep enjoying the privilege and power to judge what is true, beautiful, and feminine, and what is not. One obvious danger lies in that perceiving women as aggressive often leads to violence against them and their exploitation. Moreover, sexual objectification of bodies can only take place when there is an underlying dehumanization in the statement that allows for that objectification.

Third, women's bodies are also frequently located in the domestic sphere. Different bodies inhabit different spaces for different reasons. However, those reasons at a foundational level always have to do in some way or another with access, and access presumes power. In a racialized and gendered society such as the United States, some bodies are given power on the basis of sex and race, while others are destitute of it. Those who are given the power are then the ones who establish social arrangements through their words (e.g. law, denominational policies, theological discourses, etc.), locating bodies in specific spheres.

The theological complementarian discourse here described emphatically locates women's bodies in the domestic sphere, while men's bodies are located primarily outside the home. For instance, consider DeMoss and Kassian's statement,

> The Lord created man out in the field that he would one day work (not until after his creation was he placed in the garden). The location of man's creation seems to be connected to his distinct sphere of responsibility. The woman, on the other hand, wasn't created out in the field. She was created within the boundaries of the garden—the "home" where God had placed

her husband. This detail is intriguing, since Scripture indicates that managing the household is a woman's distinct sphere of responsibility.[20]

There is a relationship between bodies, location, and roles. Namely, roles assigned to gendered bodies determine the spheres they inhabit and vice versa. DeMoss and Kassian's quote delineates a complementarian understanding of the arrangement of this relationship. The authors place the female body in the household, while the male body is located outside it. These are the domestic and public spheres respectively. Additionally, these spheres are described as "distinct"—that is, assigned to a gender, although not in an exclusive way—and connected to the notion of responsibility. It is important to note that this specific arrangement of gendered bodies, locations, and roles is framed in this quote in association with the creation account.

For DeMoss and Kassian, "God wired man to be connected to work in a way woman is not," and "He wired woman to be connected to home and relationships in a way man is not." But what happens when women decide to carry out roles and inhabit spaces outside their "distinct" sphere of responsibility? That is, what happens when women decide to leave "the garden" and work "out in the field"? They become transgressive bodies whose femininity and womanhood is categorized as improper. The latter is what underlies DeMoss and Kassian's use of Proverbs 7:11 to argue that Scripture "casts in a negative light women whose hearts are inclined away from the home—those whose 'feet' are not centered there."[21] The use of this text to further their position inevitably results in an association between sexual impurity and women who inhabit the public sphere. Hence, in this case, the categorization goes beyond proper and improper femininity, and extends to an attribution of purity. Piper's belief that some "roles might stretch appropriate expressions of femininity beyond the breaking point" also points to the improper/proper femininity categorization. In summary, the masculinization of the public sphere in this complementarian discourse does not necessarily codify female bodies inhabiting it as nonfeminine; however, their femininity and virtuosity is inevitably put on trial.

---

[20]Kassian and DeMoss, *True Woman 101*, 80.
[21]Kassian and DeMoss, *True Woman 101*, 80-81.

Demeanor. A second category around which the discourse on woman-hood and femininity is built is demeanor. The idea of demeanor refers to a way of conceptualizing how a woman's femininity should be perceived in outward appearance and behavior. Here, talk about a woman's demeanor is a way of speaking about traits that are appropriate or fitting for a woman in her self-expression and communication, including aspects ranging from her physicality, clothing, and attitudes to her mannerisms, posture, and tone. Hence, the notion of demeanor is woven throughout the whole discourse about womanhood, touching on all aspects of it. For instance, consider Piper's discussion about "mature femininity" vis-à-vis what he considers to be distortions of it, and the implicit connection to the lists of positive and negative feminine traits. These traits inevitably evoke a particular demeanor, which is also culturally mediated and con-ditioned, and belong to specific social imaginaries and narratives of the feminine and nonfeminine, or of positive and negative femininity. Simi-larly, demeanor is in view in Piper's and Elliot's quotes regarding the female body, especially in their uses of terms such as *soft, muscular, husky, strapping*, and the images these elicit. Piper directly refers to demeanor when he writes,

> There are ways for a woman to interact even with a male subordinate that signal to him and others her endorsement of his mature manhood in rela-tionship to her as a woman. I do not have in mind anything like sexual suggestiveness or innuendo. Rather, I have in mind culturally appropriate expressions of respect for his kind of strength, and glad acceptance of his gentlemanly courtesies. Her demeanor—the tone and style and disposition and discourse of her ranking position—can signal clearly her affirmation of the unique role that men should play in relationship to women owing to their sense of responsibility to protect and lead.[22]

Here Piper identifies three defining elements of what he considers to be proper feminine demeanor, particularly in the context of women's relation to male subordinates. These are respect, a posture of receptivity with an attitude of delight, and affirmation. Piper also details what he means by demeanor by listing four specific aspects. Those are tone, style,

---

[22]Piper, "Vision of Biblical Complementarity," 60.

disposition, and discourse. It is worth noting that all these aspects in some way or another pertain, although not exclusively, to the woman's voice and her attitude.

Knight also touches on demeanor when he discusses "the correlation of role and attitude." He points out that the apostles not only "reiterate the mandate of God" about man's headship and woman's submission, but that they also "demand attitudes and actions that will seek to overcome the sinful tendencies that work against the proper functioning of these roles."[23] When talking about women in the context of the household, Knight posits that the biblical text calls for their submission to correspond to a demeanor characterized by respect and a gentle and quiet spirit. Additionally, drawing from his reading of Ephesians 5:27 and Colossians 3:18, he argues women's submission should be done with a distinguishing disposition, that is, "as to the Lord."

It is worth asking in this discussion, Who determines the parameters of what is respectful and what is not? Moreover, who gets to define what "a gentle and quiet spirit" is? How is it defined? How is it to be embodied? Who sets the rules of proper feminine demeanor? In this case, it is obvious who is defining these aspects of womanhood: White males in the Reformed Baptist tradition who assume a maximalist version of complementarianism. For even when complementarian women are reflecting on womanhood, they are dependent on the biblical and theological judgments of many of these male scholars, as their bibliographies show.

Furthermore, it becomes evident how culturally and socioeconomically mediated these discourses are, although that is not acknowledged. Maximal complementarians in our discussion insist on portraying their work as a universally binding discourse with an impressive naiveté in regards to its own culturally conditioned perspectives on women. From subtitles such as "The Universal Rightness of a Wife's Submission to Her Husband" to Knight's statement that the delineation of the man as breadwinner and of the woman as wife and mother "is the perspective God has given," the discourse has the pretension of coming from a God's-eye view.[24] And although the authors seem to think they speak from a point

---

[23]Knight, "Family and the Church," 415.
[24]Grudem, "Wives like Sarah," 264; Knight, "Family and the Church," 416.

of nowhere, the reality is that it is impossible for them to engage independently from their location in a culture and society that is racialized and classist. In the best of scenarios, this is simply a crass historical blind spot. In the worst case, it is a reiteration of gender mores anchored in the conventions of conservative Anglo Christian cultures. Either way, to present one's culturally and historically conditioned discourse on femininity and its proper demeanor without admission of its contextual contours will inevitably result in the marginalization of other cultural expressions of womanhood and in labeling those expressions as nonfeminine and nonbiblical.

Virtuosity. "Who can find a virtuous woman? for her price is far above rubies" (Prov 31:10 KJV). The third category around which the discourse on femininity and womanhood is construed is virtuosity, which regards aspects of morality and character. The True Woman Manifesto provides a list of virtues emphasized by the complementarian discourse on womanhood when it states, "Seek to glorify God by cultivating such virtues as purity, modesty, submission, meekness, and love."[25] This list is reminiscent of the "four cardinal virtues" of the nineteenth century's cult of domesticity and true womanhood: "piety, purity, submissiveness and domesticity."[26] Also, it is not coincidental that purity is preeminent on both lists. For, although purity should not be reduced to matters of sexuality, it certainly entails them. Women's sexuality is indeed a central component in this complementarian discourse. Consider, for instance, George Alan Rekers's description of "true femininity":

> It is true femininity to experience sexual intimacy in the protective confines of marriage with one's husband; extramarital promiscuity of the Playboy-bunny image is pseudofemininity. It is true femininity to conceive and bear a child in marriage; it is unfeminine to expose oneself to pregnancy out of wedlock. It is true femininity and motherhood to protect the unborn child from outside harm from tobacco or alcohol use; it is unfeminine and contrary to true motherhood to deliberately abort a child.[27]

---

[25]Kassian and DeMoss, *True Woman 101*, 215.

[26]Barbara Welter, "The Cult of True Womanhood: 1820–1860," *American Quarterly* 18, no. 2, part 1 (Summer 1966): 152.

[27]George Alan Rekers, "Psychological Foundations for Rearing Masculine Boys and Feminine Girls," in *RBMW*, 2nd ed., 306.

Here, Rekers delineates a sexual ethic for women, presented as a set of comparisons of actions that are categorized as corresponding to "true femininity" and "true motherhood" or to "pseudofemininity" and "non-femininity." The issue with this categorization is one I have pointed out already. It is problematic to categorize women's behaviors as "unfeminine" or "pseudofeminine" because it does not fit one's construal of femininity and womanhood. In fact, this can easily evolve from a categorization of behavior to a categorization of the person.

However, Rekers's language is not new. Rather, it is on brand with the nineteenth-century true womanhood discourse on purity. Barbara Welter writes, "Purity was as essential as piety to a young woman, its absence as unnatural and unfeminine. Without it she was, in fact, no woman at all, but a member of some lower order."[28] Michelle Lee-Barnewall also provides an insightful historical account of the connection between women (read Anglo and middle-class women) and virtue in the United States, which deserves to be quoted at length. She writes,

> Industrialization and urbanization caused a significant shift in the structure of the family. Men became more distant from domestic activities as they began to work outside the home, and the household became primarily the woman's realm. Since women were no longer as involved in economic production, their work concentrated on child rearing, housework, and making the home a "refuge" for men when they returned home from work. In this way industrialization and urbanization helped to create a distinction between the genders, with each being associated with a "separate sphere of activity and expertise." Women were the keepers of the home and domestic sphere, and men were linked with the realm of business, labor, and politics. . . . The view of woman's sphere has been called the "cult of true womanhood," in which there was a "sharp dichotomy between the home and the economic world outside that paralleled a sharp contrast between female and male natures, the designation of the home as the female's only proper sphere, the moral superiority of women, and the idealization of her function as mother." In the cult of true womanhood, women became associated with virtues such as "purity, piety, and domesticity."[29]

---

[28]Welter, "Cult of True Womanhood," 154.
[29]Michelle Lee-Barnewall, *Neither Complementarian nor Egalitarian: A Kingdom Corrective to the Evangelical Gender Debate* (Grand Rapids, MI: Baker Academic, 2016), 20.

The striking similarity between this historical account about mid-nineteenth-century White middle-class US society and the comprehensive complementarian discourse on womanhood should not be ignored. From the arrangement of bodies, gender roles, and locations to the tendency of categorizing women's bodies, demeanor, and character as unfeminine or feminine, proper or improper, there is a common thread: a conspicuous convergence with the cult of true womanhood, which "originated as a white cultural ideal" that generally devalued, if not entirely excluded, poor women and women of color.[30]

THE CULT OF TRUE WOMANHOOD: RACIST AND CLASSIST

The nineteenth-century concept of the true woman was the idealization of the "fragile, submissive, and sexually pure" woman who fulfilled her assigned role and embraced the domestic sphere as her proper place.[31] Any deviation from this ideal was considered "unwomanly," "unfeminine," and "unnatural." However, as Venetria Patton notes, "only white middle-class women could hope to embody it."[32] Tyson further explains,

> The Victorian definition of the "true woman" excluded African American women and poor women of all races, whose survival required hard physical labor and who, because their jobs took them out of the home, were vulnerable to rape and to sexual exploitation in the workplace. In other words, a woman whose racial or economic situation forced her to perform physical labor and made her the victim of sexual predators was considered unwomanly and therefore unworthy of protection from those who exploited her. Also, because the "cult of 'true womanhood'" originated as a white cultural ideal, women of color, no matter how feminine their attire or behavior, were generally devalued, if not entirely excluded from the definition, on racial grounds.[33]

The cult of true womanhood was a racially coded and classist sociocultural and theological discourse that placed White, middle-class Christian women on a pedestal while denying the womanhood of poor women,

---

[30]Lois Tyson, *Learning for a Diverse World: Using Critical Theory to Read and Write About Literature* (New York: Routledge, 2001), 89.

[31]Tyson, *Learning for a Diverse World*, 89.

[32]Venetria K. Patton, *Women in Chains: The Legacy of Slavery in Black Women's Fiction* (Albany: State University of New York Press, 2000), 29-30.

[33]Tyson, *Learning for a Diverse World*, 89.

Black women, and other women of color. This should come as no surprise, as this ideal partially emerged in the context of the antebellum South. There, the idea of the true woman coexisted with and reinforced myths and narratives about poor women and women of color, but in particular about Black women, whose enslavement was "rooted in the assumption of white superiority and the elevation of white flesh."[34] Although, the nineteenth-century discourse on true womanhood was not the genesis of the discursive dehumanization of Black women, it was undoubtedly an extension of it. The construal of the true woman was inherently the misconstrual of the femininity of women of color. It was the further "unfeminization" of their bodies and demeanor, and the denial of their virtuosity.

> *The Body*
> our backs
> tell stories
> no books have
> the spine to
> carry
> —"women of color"[35]

Strong bodies. The "unfeminization" of the bodies of indigenous women, Black women, and other women of color began way before the nineteenth century. In contexts of *conquista*, colonization, and empire building, women's bodies become an extension of the land. They were claimed by those in power as loci where their rule ought to be exerted. The notion of the true woman was an iteration of the discourse that presented "the European body as the scientific, philosophic, and cultural ideal."[36] It became the norm against which femininity and womanhood was judged, ascribed, and denied. Furthermore, it became a tool of White supremacy via which the exploitation of nonwhite bodies, especially Black women's bodies, was justified.

Referring to how Black women's bodies were perceived, historian Jemar Tisby writes, "In contrast to white women, who were viewed as delicate and in need of protection, Black women were perceived as strong and durable.

---

[34]Charles and Rah, *Unsettling Truths*, 88.
[35]Rupi Kaur, "women of color," in *Milk and Honey* (Kansas City, MO: Andrews McMeel, 2015), 171.
[36]Eboni Marshall Turman, *Toward a Womanist Ethic of Incarnation: Black Bodies, the Black Church, and the Council of Chalcedon* (New York: Palgrave Macmillan, 2013), 60.

Even when they were pregnant, it was expected that they should work in the fields, often up until the very moment of birth."[37] This perception that Black women's bodies were and are stronger did not arise from a positive narrative. Rather, it originated from the project of slavery and the commodification of Black women's bodies as "objects of property, production, reproduction, [and] of sexual violence."[38] Furthermore, it was the result of what bell hooks deems the masculization of the Black female. She writes,

> In colonial American society, privileged white women rarely worked in the fields. Occasionally, white female indentured servants were forced to work in the fields as punishment for misdeeds, but this was not a common practice. In the eyes of colonial white Americans, only debased and degraded members of the female sex labored in the fields. And any white woman forced by circumstances to work in the fields was regarded as unworthy of the title "woman." . . . Transplanted African women soon realized that they were seen as "surrogate" men by white slavers.[39]

Black women's bodies were "reduced to instruments of labor" and inevitably became physically stronger compared to those of White, middle-class women staying at home. Black women were not afforded to have "soft" bodies. The strong and—might I dare to say—muscular bodies of Black women stood as opposites of the idealized fragile and delicate figure of the true woman. They were automatically rendered as unfeminine.

Located in the field. While White, middle-class women embraced their distinctive domestic sphere, their "garden," the bodies of Black women were forcefully located in "the field." M. Shawn Copeland writes, "Black women and men worked from sunup to sundown, usually, six days each week, and sometimes for several hours on Sundays. . . . When it came to heavy labor in the field, there was little gender differentiation."[40] As mentioned earlier, different bodies inhabit different spaces due to different reasons. However, those reasons at a foundational level always have to do in some way or another with access, and access presumes power. In a racialized and gendered society such as the United States, some bodies are

---

[37]Tisby, *Color of Compromise*, 61.
[38]M. Shawn Copeland, *Enfleshing Freedom: Body, Race, and Being* (Minneapolis: Fortress, 2010), 29.
[39]bell hooks, *Ain't I a Woman: Black Women and Feminism* (New York: Routledge, 2014), 22-23.
[40]Copeland, *Enfleshing Freedom*, 32.

given power on the basis of sex and race, while others are destitute of it. Those who are given the power are then the ones who establish social arrangements through their words, locating bodies in specific spheres. In the nineteenth-century antebellum South, the relationship between Black bodies, forced labor, and the field was arranged and determined by White men with means for their profit. Black women were forced to be in the field. White supremacy and greed made that their "distinct sphere."

Demeanor. As stated earlier, "because 'the cult of true womanhood' originated as a White cultural ideal, women of color, no matter how feminine their attire or behavior, were generally devalued, if not entirely excluded from the definition, on racial grounds." This exclusion was in itself a categorization of Black women and other women of color as "unwomanly" and "unfeminine." The latter came together with the imposition of a stereotype that, as Tyson notes, survives until today—that is, the image of the woman who is "loud, brassy, promiscuous, and unattractive to men except as sexual objects."[41] In the eyes of White society, women of color could never attain feminine demeanor, for it was construed as an exclusive characteristic based on gender, race, and class, ascribed solely to White women with means.

No virtuosity ascribed. The cult of true womanhood's discourse on virtuosity, particularly as it regards purity, was articulated in racially coded terms. Consider for instance the "analogies used to describe virginal women: delicate as lilies, spotless as doves, polished as alabaster, fragile as porcelain—but above all, pure as the driven snow."[42] This racial mythology that equated purity to Whiteness coexisted and reinforced the myth of the promiscuous and sensual Black woman. While White, middle-class women were viewed as delicate and borderline asexual, Black women were generally considered "destitute of virtue or intelligence . . . , fit only to perpetuate the race."[43] This false narrative was designed to serve a dual purpose—that is, to justify the use of Black women's bodies by White men as objects of reproduction and sexual violence, while maintaining White men's innocence. Shirley Yee touches on this when she writes,

---

[41]Tyson, *Learning for a Diverse World*, 89.
[42]Catherine Clinton, quoted in Patton, *Women in Chains*, 30.
[43]Shirley Yee, *Black Women Abolitionists: A Study in Activism, 1828–1860* (Knoxville: University of Tennessee Press, 1992), 42.

The presence of racially mixed slave children on plantations forced whites to acknowledge that sexual intercourse occurred between white men and Black women. To admit white men's culpability, however, would have undermined notions of white moral superiority. Thus, rather than perceiving slave women as victims of sexual abuse, whites blamed them for initiating sexual relations with white men and, as a result, portrayed Black women as seducers.[44]

The imposition of the image of the seductress on Black women was not casual. It was instrumental. While White middle-class women's purity was protected, Black women's purity was not. While the virtuosity of White women with means was honored, Black women's virtuous resistance was met with whips and brutal punishments.[45] While virtue was basically equated to Whiteness, Blackness was considered its antonym.

CORRELATED CODIFIED RACIO-LINGUISTICS

The convergence between the discourses on biblical womanhood pontificated by comprehensive complementarians and the nineteenth-century cult of true womanhood does not necessarily entail causality. At the same time, this type of discourse has a long history of correlated codified raciolinguistics—that is, modes of speech that belong to a particular demographic in which "the other" is racialized and constructed in relationship to a standard.[46] Although the comprehensive complementarian discourse does not codify femininity in terms of White, middle-class womanhood de jure, it is rendered in those terms de facto. Without an intersectional approach, this discourse cannot get away from duplicating its raciolinguistic logic. Consider the following questions: Which women of color are writing programmatically in favor of this version of complementarianism? Who are the main proponents of this discourse? In our present socioeconomic reality, what demographic can hope to embody biblical womanhood and manhood?

---

[44]Yee, *Black Women Abolitionists*, 42-43.

[45]Copeland, *Enfleshing Freedom*, 35.

[46]See Samy H. Alim, John R. Rickford, and Arnetha F. Bail, eds., *Raciolinguistics: How Language Shapes Our Ideas About Race* (Oxford: Oxford University Press, 2016); Jonathan Rosa and Nelson Flores, "Unsettling Race and Language: Toward a Raciolinguistic Perspective," *Language in Society* 46, no. 5 (2017): 621-47.

Theological discourses on the feminine and nonfeminine are not neutral. They do not stand alone. For not only have they emerged in the context of a racialized society, but throughout history they have often been weaponized to perpetrate and perpetuate the exploitation of racialized bodies, with indigenous women, Black women, and other women of color the most affected. The evangelical conversation about gender cannot keep ignoring its racialized context and the need for an intersectional approach. Not doing so will perpetuate White-centeredness in a society and a church that still has to grapple with its legacy of White supremacy.

Views of women of color vis-à-vis Anglo women are not a thing of the past. The myths and stereotypes imposed on us as unfeminine throughout history are alive and well. The commodification of the bodies of Latinas as objects of production and sexual violence, which allow the White gaze to only conceive of us as maids or sexual bombshells without agency, is a testament to this. Another example is the narrative of the "welfare queen" imposed especially on "inner-city Black women."[47] However, one clear piece of evidence of the persistence of the "true woman" ideal as White and middle or upper class is a 2016 drawing by cartoonist Ben Garrison. In it, he portrays Michelle Obama "as a muscular, angry woman pitted against a more feminine and smiling Melania Trump with the caption 'Make the First Lady Great Again.'"[48] These narratives are not innocent, and the church is not exempt of them. Unless there is an intersectional approach to decenter Whiteness and maleness from the theological discourse on womanhood and femininity, the conversation will continue to perpetuate the logic of true womanhood as Anglo and middle class.

A WORD TO EGALITARIANS AND THE NEITHERS

It might be tempting for some White egalitarians and neithers, especially women, to have a sense of self-righteousness in this discussion.[49] However, it is imperative for us to remember that White egalitarians and neithers can

---

[47]Tisby, *Color of Compromise*, 168.

[48]Leona Allen, "Here's Why This Michelle Obama/Melania Trump Cartoon Is Despicable," *Dallas Morning News*, May 18, 2016, www.dallasnews.com/opinion/commentary/2016/05/18 /here-s-why-this-michelle-obama-melania-trump-cartoon-is-despicable/.

[49]Here *neithers* refer to people who do not identify themselves with either complementarianism or egalitarianism. See Lee-Barnewall, *Neither Complementarian nor Egalitarian*.

still be committed to White-centeredness. This was and still is the critique of womanist and *mujerista* theologians to White feminist theology.[50] In the words of Jacquelyn Grant, "The seriousness of the charge White feminists make regarding inappropriate male universalism is undercut by the limited perspective which presumes the universality of women's experience. White feminism does not emerge out of the particularity of the majority of women's experience."[51] The assumption of White women's experiences, concerns, and values as the norm is not exclusive to complementarian circles. Rather, this characteristic is also present in US evangelical egalitarianism. For US evangelical egalitarianism also emerged in the context of a racialized society that has consistently predicated womanhood in terms of Whiteness. Consider who the leading egalitarian voices are. Is their approach a robust intersectional one? How are they, especially White women, dealing with the legacy of White women's participation in racism? The lens of gender is not enough to construct a true egalitarian position. Intersectionality is required.

A LAST WORD

The gospel brings about a reconfiguration of the values we live by in society as fellow image bearers. It brings about a reversal, a decentering and rejection of ideas and practices that exclude or half-affirm the dignity of people based on racial constructs, gender, socioeconomic status, ethnicity, and so on. There is also a recentering. The gospel liberates, dignifies, and challenges us as followers of Christ to embody the values of the kingdom of God in the presence of the antikingdom. Our dialogue tables should be shaped by the eschatological vision of Revelation: all the nations gathering together at the table of the Lamb.

---

[50]Womanist theology emerged in the 1980s "as a form of reflection that places the religious and moral perspectives of Black women at the center of its method." Its approach is intersectional and serves as a corrective to Black theology and feminist theologies that do not consider how race intersects with the realities of gender, socioeconomic class, and other factors. Alice Walker coined the term *womanist*. See Emilie M. Townes, "Womanist Theology," in *Encyclopedia of Women and Religion in North America* (Bloomington: Indiana University Press, 2006), 1165. *Mujerista* theology emerged in the 1990s, centering the liberation of US Latinas and the struggle tied to it. The late Cuban theologian Ada María Isasi Díaz is considered one of the pioneers of this theological movement.

[51]Jacquelyn Grant, *White Women's Christ and Black Women's Jesus: Feminist Christology and Womanist Response* (Atlanta: Scholars Press, 1989), 6.

30

HUMAN FLOURISHING

GLOBAL PERSPECTIVES

Mimi Haddad

• • • • •

THE FACE OF POVERTY, illiteracy, disease, starvation, and abuse is predominantly female. Robert Seiple, former US ambassador and president of World Vision, observes:

> From birth to the grave, throughout much of our allegedly "modern" world, violence marks the lives of those born girls. We should not be surprised when girls are used, at best, as human workhorses, and at worst as human shields in time of war. We should not be surprised at attempts to intentionally destroy or limit female hopes in upward strides for a better life.[1]

For decades, Christian humanitarians have exposed the abuse of females and searched for root causes. Jimmy Carter writes,

> The most serious unaddressed worldwide challenge is the deprivation and abuse of women and girls, largely caused by a false interpretation of carefully selected religious texts and a growing tolerance of violence and warfare. . . . In addition to the unconscionable human suffering, almost embarrassing to acknowledge, there is a devastating effect on economic prosperity caused by the loss of contributions of at least half the human beings on earth. This is not just a women's issue. It is not confined to the poorest countries. It affects all of us.[2]

---

[1]Robert A. Seiple, "A Rent in the Human Garment," *Washington Forum* (1998): 9.
[2]Jimmy Carter, *Call to Action: Women, Religion, Violence, and Power* (New York: Simon & Schuster, 2014), 3.

Stunningly, the #MeToo movement has drawn widespread attention to gender-based violence.[3] A global reckoning, #MeToo and #ChurchToo reveal not only the abuse of girls and women globally but also the long-standing beliefs that fuel their suffering.

In tracing economic disparities, Nobel Prize–winning economist from India Amartya Sen found that more than one hundred million females had vanished.[4] Sen pointed to a gender holocaust—a mass-scale abuse and slaughter of females.[5] As a result of Sen's research, patriarchy is increasingly viewed as one of the most malicious and debilitating forces in history.[6]

While secular researchers in the 1990s scrutinized communities where men held "a disproportionately large share of power," concerns about feminist ideology prompted new evangelical efforts to assert male authority with renewed force.[7] By 1998, proponents of male headship gained control of the Southern Baptist Convention—the largest, wealthiest Protestant denomination in the United States, with an extensive missionary presence worldwide. Despite its legacy of supporting women missionaries and church planters, complementarians within the Southern Baptist Convention pressed the denomination to remove women pastors, academics, and leaders on global mission fields.[8] These events created enormous spiritual and humanitarian upheaval given that, as missiologists note, women missionaries were consistently in close relationship with those who suffer, especially women and children. Women missionaries "believed they had

---

[3] See "#MeToo: A Timeline of Events," *Chicago Tribune*, June 13, 2019, www.chicagotribune.com /lifestyles/ct-me-too-timeline-20171208-htmlstory.html.

[4] Amartya Sen, "More than 100 Million Women Are Missing," *New York Review of Books*, December 20, 1990, www.nybooks.com/articles/1990/12/20/more-than-100-million-women-are-missing/. Today the number of missing females may be as high as two hundred million.

[5] Nicholas Kristoff and Sheryl WuDunn, *Half the Sky: Turning Oppression into Opportunity for Women Worldwide* (New York: Knopf, 2009), xiv-xx.

[6] Bina Agarwal, Jane Humphries, and Ingrid Robeyns, "Exploring the Challenges of Amartya Sen's Work and Ideas: An Introduction," *Feminist Economics* 9, nos. 2-3 (2003): 3-12.

[7] See "Patriarchy," Merriam-Webster Online, www.merriam-webster.com/dictionary/patriarchy (accessed March 19, 2019).

[8] "Battle for the Minds," PBS, http://archive.pov.org/battlefortheminds/film-description (accessed June 1, 2019). Paige Patterson became president of the Southern Baptist Convention in 1998 and was fired in 2018 for his mistreatment of abused women. See Scott Neuman, "Seminary Votes to Fire Paige Patterson After Ousting Him as President," WBUR, May 31, 2018, www.wbur.org /npr/615711743/seminary-votes-to-fire-paige-patterson-after-ousting-him-as-president.

a special calling or sanction to aid the helpless and the oppressed."[9] Proof of these women's significance is evidenced by the fact that governments, journalists, and health workers have relied on local women and their missionary allies for information on humanitarian concerns.[10]

Recognizing the importance of women in humanitarian work, secular development organizations such as the World Bank, the International Monetary Fund, and the United Nations Commission on the Status of Women prioritize gender equality as a key lever in accomplishing their humanitarian goals.[11] Hence, the yearly conferences of the United Nations Commission on the Status of Women evaluate and amplify the status of the world's girls and women and publish significant data.[12] The following summary explores not only gender-based violence and the marginalization of girls and women from education, economic, and political representation, but also women's initiative in upending oppression and building a more just world where everyone flourishes.

Significantly, violence against females is the longest ongoing war in history. Thirty-five to seventy percent of the world's girls and women have experienced sexual abuse. Worldwide, 650 million females were forced to marry before age eighteen.[13] Over two hundred million women and girls today have undergone female genital mutilation, most before age fifteen.[14] Of the estimated 40.3 million slaves today, 99 percent are girls and women exploited by the commercial sex trade.[15] Approximately six hundred

---

[9]Diana Magnuson, "Swedish Baptist Women in America, 1850–1914: the 'High Calling' of Serving Christ in the Life of the Church," *The Baptist Pietist Clarion* 8, no. 1 (2009): 19.

[10]See Dana Robert, *American Women in Missions: A Social History of Their Thought and Practice* (Macon, GA: Mercer University Press, 2005), 126-88. Dr. Virginia Patterson, retired missionary with Sudan Interior Mission and former president of Pioneer Clubs, told me how she had been interviewed by government officials on the humanitarian concerns facing children where she served in Africa.

[11]"The World Bank in Gender," World Bank, www.worldbank.org/en/topic/gender (accessed March 19, 2019); "Gender and the IMF," International Monetary Fund, www.imf.org/external /themes/gender/ (accessed March 19, 2019).

[12]"Introduction," UN Division for the Advancement of Women, www.un.org/womenwatch/daw /CSW60YRS/index.htm (accessed March 19, 2019).

[13]"Facts and Figures: Ending Violence Against Women," UN Women, November 2020, www .unwomen.org/en/what-we-do/ending-violence-against-women/facts-and-figures.

[14]"Female Genital Mutilation," World Health Organization, January 31, 2018, www.who.int/news -room/fact-sheets/detail/female-genital-mutilation.

[15]"What Is Modern Slavery?," Anti-Slavery, www.antislavery.org/slavery-today/modern-slavery/ (accessed February 15, 2019); see also "Forced Labour, Modern Slavery and Human Trafficking,"

million women live in countries without laws against sexual violence—the most underreported crime worldwide.[16] All forms of violence against women increase during war, disaster, and displacement.[17]

Defeating gender-based violence is consistently a woman-led initiative. Consider the nonviolent peacemaking of Liberia's Leymah Gbowee and Ellen Johnson Sirleaf, both 2011 Nobel Peace Prize recipients. After fourteen years of civil war, Gbowee led an army of women peacemakers whose weapons were prayer and fasting. Rain or shine, women assembled in plain view of their country's dictator. Risking assassination, they also filled his offices and refused to move until peace was negotiated. In solidarity with abused women and children, Gbowee shouted, "We the women of Liberia will no more allow ourselves to be raped, abused, misused, maimed and killed. . . . Our children and grandchildren will not be used as killing machines and sex slaves!"[18] When she threatened to disrobe, Gbowee's demands for peace became reality.[19] Ellen Johnson Sirleaf later became Liberia's first female president, in 2006. Liberia was "one of the most diverse countries in the world" with a "history of ethnic conflict." Sirleaf doubled the number of women ministers, and her cabinet began to look more like the country. As a result, Liberia's gross domestic product increased from 1 percent to 4 percent.[20] Sirleaf made elementary school both free and mandatory. She also adopted a zero-tolerance policy against corruption.[21]

International Labour Organization, http://www.ilo.org/global/topics/forced-labour/lang--en /index.htm (accessed February 15, 2019).

[16]Paula Tavares and Quentin Wodon, "Ending Violence Against Women and Girls: Global and Regional Trends in Women's Legal Protection Against Domestic Violence and Sexual Harassment," World Bank, March 2018, http://pubdocs.worldbank.org/en/679221517425064052/End ingViolenceAgainstWomenandGirls-GBVLaws-Feb2018.pdf; see also "Global Challenge 11," Millennium Project, 2017, www.millennium-project.org/challenge-11/.

[17]"Facts and Figures: Humanitarian Action," UN Women, May 2017, www.unwomen.org/en /what-we-do/humanitarian-action/facts-and-figures.

[18]Tamasin Ford, "Leymah Gbowee—Profile," *The Guardian*, October 7, 2011, www.theguardian .com/world/2011/oct/07/leymah-gbowee-profile.

[19]Seizing shame as a political tool, Gbowee threatened to disrobe before government officials unless they agreed to a ceasefire. She recognized that Liberian men could not watch an older woman strip naked in their presence. It was a brilliant and successful political move.

[20]Susan Perkins and Katherine W. Phillips, "Research: Are Women Better at Leading Diverse Countries than Men?," *Harvard Business Review*, February 7, 2019, https://hbr.org/2019/02/research -are-women-better-at-leading-diverse-countries-than-men.

[21]Esther Addley, "Ellen Johnson Sirleaf, Leymah Gbowee and Tawakkul Karman Win Nobel Prize," *The Guardian*, October 7, 2011, www.theguardian.com/world/2011/oct/07/johnson -sirleaf-gbowee-karmen-nobel.

Sirleaf's commitment to educate girls makes enormous humanitarian and economic sense. Eliminating gendered educational barriers lowers infant mortality and stimulates economic growth by up to 50 percent.[22] Yet five million fewer girls worldwide attend primary school than boys.[23] As a result, women represent two-thirds of the world's illiterate (about 750 million adults).[24] In Kenya, 50 percent of girls lack menstrual products, causing some to miss "up to 20% their education."[25] Kenya's secretary of gender affairs, Margaret Kobia, provided one million sanitary pads to girls in 2018.[26] In the words of the 2019 Oscar-winning documentary *Period. End of the Sentence*, a period should end a sentence—"not a girl's education."[27]

Female leaders such as Kobia and Sirleaf not only prioritize the needs of girls and women, but they also collaborate more successfully across party lines, especially on children's and gender concerns.[28] Consider how Arab Islamic and Christian feminists worked across faith traditions to promote research and initiatives for women's empowerment. Risking imprisonment, women denounced selective readings of history and religious texts that foster gender essentialism, male authority, and the marginalization of women from public leadership. These 2015 conversations generated strategies for challenging "biology as destiny," reframing women as integral to leadership in any sphere.[29]

---

[22]"Facts and Figures: Economic Empowerment," UN Women, July 2018, www.unwomen.org/en/what-we-do/economic-empowerment/facts-and-figures; see also Sonia R. Bhalotra and Damian Clarke, "Does Women's Education Reduce Rates of Death in Childbirth," UNU-Wider, November 2016, www.wider.unu.edu/publication/does-women%E2%80%99s-education-reduce-rates-death-childbirth.

[23]"Why Girls Around the World Are Still Denied an Equal Chance of Education," Theirworld, July 26, 2017, https://theirworld.org/news/why-girls-are-still-denied-equal-chance-of-education.

[24]"International Literacy Day 2017," UNESCO, January 9, 2017, https://en.unesco.org/commemorations/literacyday/2017.

[25]"History of Pads4Girls," LunaPads, https://lunapads.com/pages/pads4girls (accessed February 15, 2019); see also Charlotte Clarke, "Free Sanitary Towels for Kenya's Schoolgirls," ActionAid, June 23, 2017, www.actionaid.org.uk/blog/news/2017/06/23/free-sanitary-towels-for-kenyas-schoolgirls.

[26]Rael Ombuor, "Kenya Seeks to Boost Girls' Education by Providing Free Sanitary Products," VOA News, June 19, 2018, www.voanews.com/a/kenya-seeks-to-boost-girls-education-by-providing-free-sanitary-products/4445900.html.

[27]"Oscars 2019: 'Let's Go Change the World'—What India-Set *Period. End Of Sentence* Producer Said After Win," *NDTV*, February 25, 2019, www.ndtv.com/entertainment/oscars-2019-what-india-set-period-end-of-sentence-producer-tweeted-after-win-1998740.

[28]"Facts and Figures: Leadership and Political Participation," UN Women, January 2019, www.unwomen.org/en/what-we-do/leadership-and-political-participation/facts-and-figures.

[29]Key leaders of this project were arrested for addressing the equality of women.

Yemen's Tawakkul Karmān also challenged antidemocracy and religious conservative advocates to raise women's marriageable age to seventeen.[30] Known as Yemen's reforming "iron woman," Karmān gained wide support for women's rights. She received the 2011 Nobel Peace Prize beside Sirleaf and Gbowee for her "non-violent struggle for the safety of women and for women's rights to full participation in peace-building work."[31]

Achieving greater political representation during the US's 2018 midterm elections, women voted in record numbers to gain five new congressional seats.[32] Prior to this election, women worldwide made up less than 24 percent of all national legislative bodies, with the US ranking at 41 out of 107 countries surveyed. Rwanda and Bolivia held first and second place.[33]

Women's leadership is also good for business. Though women comprise less than 20 percent of business governing boards, their presence improves productivity and ethical practices.[34] Companies with three or more women in senior management demonstrate greater organizational effectiveness.[35] Women's equal participation in agriculture would increase yields by 30 percent, reducing starvation by 150 million people per year![36] Though women comprise 40 percent of agricultural workers, less than 20 percent of landholders worldwide are female.[37] Further, women dominate unpaid work and most return home to housework and caretaking—the "second shift." At best, women earn 23 percent less than men for similar

---

[30]Aakanksha Gaur, "Tawakkul Karman," Britannica Online, March 30, 2016, www.britannica.com /biography/Tawakkul-Karman.

[31]"The Nobel Peace Prize 2011: Tawakkul Karmān, Facts," www.nobelprize.org/prizes/peace/2011 /karman/facts/ (accessed March 30, 2019).

[32]Li Zhou, "It's Official: A Record-Breaking Number of Women Have Won Seats in Congress," Vox, November 7, 2018, www.vox.com/policy-and-politics/2018/11/7/18024742/midterm-results -record-women-win.

[33]"Facts and Figures: Leadership and Political Participation."

[34]"Facts and Figures: Economic Empowerment"; see also Director Search LLC, "Women Comprise 12% of Public Company Boards, Globally," December 1, 2017, Cision PR Newswire, www .prnewswire.com/news-releases/women-comprise-12-of-public-company-boards-globally -300565331.html.

[35]"Facts and Figures: Economic Empowerment."

[36]"Women Hold the Key to Building a World Free from Hunger and Poverty," Food and Agriculture Organization of the United Nations, December 16, 2016, www.fao.org/news/story/en /item/460267/icode/.

[37]"Facts and Figures: Poverty and Hunger," UN Women, www.unwomen.org/en/news/in-focus /commission-on-the-status-of-women-2012/facts-and-figures (accessed February 15, 2019); see also "Gender Equality and Women's Empowerment," USAid, November 8, 2017, www.usaid.gov /what-we-do/gender-equality-and-womens-empowerment.

work.[38] When race, ethnicity, and gender are considered, the pay gap is greatest between White men and women of color.[39] While 70 percent of women prefer paid work, only 49 percent have it, compared to 75 percent of men.[40]

In Pakistan, where the illiteracy rate among women over percent hovers near 59 percent, two cousins changed the economic lives of women in their community. Cheated out of fair pay, Ameer decided to learn how to read. The only woman in her region with a high school diploma was her cousin Shazia. As Shazia began educating local girls and women, literacy increased for females in their village, and so did their confidence, economic capacity, and equity.[41]

The story of Shazia and her cousin Ameer is a picture of how women empower women globally. Because women invest in their families and communities at over twice the rate men do, supporting their education and businesses produces a virtuous cycle.[42] For this reason, the World Bank and the International Monetary Fund incorporated gender equality into their long-term goals.[43] Founded in 1945 and governed by nearly two hundred member countries, the International Monetary Fund acknowledges that despite gains, labor markets reflect a steep gender divide, with significant wage gaps for women that leave many in the informal sector— without government oversight or without paid work, thus placing women among the desperately poor. The International Monetary Fund's first female managing director, Christine Lagarde, is working to ensure "women

---

[38]"Facts and Figures: Economic Empowerment."

[39]See "Data: Historical Income Tables: People," US Census Bureau, September 15, 2020, www .census.gov/data/tables/time-series/demo/income-poverty/historical-income-people.html.

[40]"The Gender Gap in Employment: What's Holding Women Back?," ILO, December 2017, www .ilo.org/infostories/en-GB/Stories/Employment/barriers-women#global-gap.

[41]Asif Raza, "Pursuing Equal Access to Education for Girls and Women," World Vision, October 8, 2014, www.worldvision.org/gender-equality-news-stories/world-vision-educating-women-girls.

[42]"Get the Facts," Women Deliver, https://womendeliver.org/infographics/ (accessed March 21, 2019); "Women's Work: Driving the Economy," Goldman Sachs, April, 2013, www.goldmansachs .com/insights/investing-in-women/research-articles/womens-work.pdf.

[43]"Gender Empowerment: Advancing Our Commitment," World Bank, March 22, 2016, www .worldbank.org/en/events/2016/03/22/gender-empowerment-advancing-our-commitment; Katrin Elborgh-Woytek et al., "Women, Work, and the Economy: Macroeconomic Gains from Gender Equity," International Monetary Fund, December 1, 2013, www.imf.org/en/Publications /Staff-Discussion-Notes/Issues/2016/12/31/Women-Work-and-the-Economy-Macroeconomic -Gains-from-Gender-Equity-40915.

play a larger role in the economy."[44] Because an equal world is a better one, the Bill and Melinda Gates Foundation is also committed to lifting "the barriers that make women and girls less equal and more impoverished." The Gates Foundation has learned that expanding opportunities for girls and women benefits boys and men too.[45]

Despite the humanitarian advantages of investing in girls and women, pernicious obstacles to women's flourishing persist, chiefly "violence against women, unpaid care work, limited control over assets and property, and unequal participation in private and public decision-making."[46] Again, women-led change is at the forefront of toppling gender-based violence, especially in regions where activism is costly.

Rural women from Syria and northern Iraq for decades decried the Islamic State of Iraq and the Levant's violent abuse of their girls and women. While most turned a deaf ear, Jimmy Carter gave these women a platform at the Carter Center's Human Rights Defender Forum. He also ensured their concerns were included in his annual report sent to Washington. Even so, the Islamic State of Iraq and the Levant perpetrated a Yazidi genocide and made three thousand Yazidi girls and women sex slaves in 2014.[47] Nadia Murad escaped and became a symbol of courage and liberation. Breaking the silence on sexual violence during war, Murad overturned sexist social codes to win the respect of her people. Beside renowned international human rights lawyer Amal Clooney, they are working to bring the Islamic State to justice, beginning with the United Nations. Murad became the first United Nations Goodwill Ambassador for the Dignity of Survivors of Human Trafficking and later received the 2018 Nobel Peace Prize beside Denis Mukwege, a physician advocate of sexual-abuse survivors in the Democratic Republic of the

---

[44]"IMF Managing Director Christine Lagarde Announces Specific Actions on Women's Economic Empowerment," International Monetary Fund, September 22, 2016, www.imf.org/en/News /Articles/2016/09/22/PR16420-Lagarde-Announces-Specific-Actions-on-Womens -Economic-Empowerment.

[45]"Gender Equality: Strategic Overview," Bill and Melinda Gates Foundation, www.gatesfounda tion.org/What-We-Do/Gender-Equality/Gender-Equality (accessed January 21, 2021).

[46]"UN Women Position on the Post-2015 Development Agenda," UN Women, https://lac .unwomen.org/en/que-hacemos/post-2015/un-women-position (accessed January 21, 2021).

[47]Robert Guest, "Nadia Murad's Fight to Bring Islamic State to Justice," *The Economist 1843 Magazine* (February/March 2017), www.1843magazine.com/features/nadia-murads-fight-to-bring-islamic -state-to-justice.

Congo.[48] Murad and Mukwege drew needed attention to war crimes perpetrated against women and girls.

Women's everyday acts of courage are essential to balance the scales of power for girls and women. Saudi women fearlessly demanded the right to drive in dismantling guardianship laws; many are now exiled, imprisoned, sexually harassed, and tortured, even after winning the right to drive in 2018.[49] Nevertheless, women activists remain stunningly committed to their fight for gender equality.

Consider the courage and creativity of Lebanese women working to end colonial-era laws that protect rapists who marry their victims. Dressed in wedding gowns and covered with blood-soaked bandages, Lebanese women demonstrated outside Parliament in 2017. They also hung wedding dresses by nooses, filling the capital with images of abuse. Reframing rape survivors as marriageable, they challenged both the impunity of rapists and families who practice honor killings.[50]

In their fight to flourish, women activists often advocate for gender equality beside secular humanitarians. Both recognize women leaders as essential in attaining humanitarian goals. But what about Christian churches and organizations opposed to gender equality but committed to humanitarian causes? Can complementarian Christians address human suffering while supporting a power imbalance between men and women?

In the Democratic Republic of the Congo, known as the rape capital of the world, physician and 2011 Opus Prize–winner Lyn Lusi allied with survivors of wartime sexual violence. Lusi begged churches to embrace, rather than excommunicate, rape survivors. Tragically, the Christian community too often supports the belief that survivors are to blame for their rape—a view that ostracizes survivors from the very communities where they had hoped to find empathy, comfort, and healing.[51]

---

[48]"The Nobel Peace Prize for 2018," www.nobelprize.org/prizes/peace/2018/press-release/ (accessed February 21, 2019).

[49]Maya Oppenheim, "Brother of Saudi Women's Rights Activist 'Being Tortured in Prison' Fears Her Treatment Is Getting Worse," *The Independent*, February 22, 2019, www.independent.co.uk/news/world/middle-east/saudi-arabia-prison-torture-womens-rights-loujain-al-hathloul-walid-a8781851.html?amp&__twitter_impression=true.

[50]Rothna Begum, "Middle East on a Roll to Repeal 'Marry the Rapist' Laws," Human Rights Watch, August 24, 2017, www.hrw.org/news/2017/08/24/middle-east-roll-repeal-marry-rapist-laws.

[51]"HEAL Africa Co-founder Lyn Lusi Announced as Winner of Prestigious Opus Prize," HEAL Africa, October 27, 2011, http://archives.healafrica.org/co-founder-lyn-lusi-2011-opus-prize-winner-p-165.html;

In the same country, five years later, a prominent Christian nongovernmental organization had similar challenges supporting the recovery of rape survivors, where rape as a weapon of war left deep scars on two hundred thousand females. Because of the region's honor-shame culture, women languish in disgrace when they hold perpetrators accountable. In bringing hope and healing to beleaguered humanitarian staff and those they serve, a Kenyan Christian organization led biblical gender-equality training.[52] The impact of egalitarian teachings of Scripture had a significant impact and convinced executives in their headquarters to lead additional trainings despite their CEO's complementarian views.

Churches in Cambodia, a center for sex trafficking, also struggle in welcoming survivors of sexual exploitation. Their cultural view is that survivors can never be pure again. Theological patriarchy furthers the sexism noted in the Cambodian proverb, "'Men are gold, women are white linen.' . . . If gold becomes dirty, it is easily washed off; but if a white cloth becomes dirty, it will never be the same again."[53] Though this proverb reflects attitudes toward females throughout Southeast Asia, Christian organizations such as Chab Dai and Precious Women are reframing sexist narratives through both biblical gender-equality reentry programs and a systematic attack on trafficking through predator mapping and awareness.[54] CBE International has partnered with these leaders because shame and a lack of confidence remain significant elements fueling reentry. As Christian organizations and churches challenge patriarchy, culturally and theologically, the confidence survivors gain helps lower the rate of reentry into the sex industry.

Christian organizations such as World Relief and Tearfund have incorporated gender equality into their development programs, while World Vision created curriculum, Channels of Hope for Gender, to promote

---

Katherine Marshall, "The Modest Heroine of the 2011 Opus Prize: Lyn Lusi," HuffPost, November 8, 2011, www.huffingtonpost.com/katherine-marshall/lyn-lusi-opus-prize_b_1077963.html.

[52]Ekklesia Foundation for Gender Education.

[53]"Men Are Gold, Women Are Cloth," WomanStats, August 8, 2013, https://womanstats.word press.com/2013/08/08/men-are-gold-women-are-cloth/.

[54]*Reentry* refers to resuming life as a sex worker. See Gretchen Clark Hammond and Mandy McGlone, "Entry, Progression, Exit, and Service Provision for Survivors of Sex Trafficking: Implications for Effective Interventions," *Global Social Welfare*, March 22, 2014, https://link .springer.com/article/10.1007/s40609-014-0010-0.

gender equality as a Christian ideal.[55] I was invited to evaluate Channels of Hope for Gender in its early stages of development and later assessed its impact in rural South Africa. There I met Muneer, an energetic high school student with a contagious smile and magnetic personality.[56] Muneer spoke passionately about how Channels of Hope for Gender's curriculum convinced him to carry water for his sister—a practice considered shameful for males. "Why should my sister spend every evening carrying water, preparing dinner and cleaning up while I play soccer and study for exams? She has the talent to go to college, not me!" After he started assisting her with domestic work, Muneer's sister gained several more hours of study each night. Far from inciting ridicule, his popularity and love for his sister influenced others. Soon his male friends began carrying water too. One leader can change a village for girls and women.[57]

One outcome of changing attitudes regarding women's dignity and equality is men's willingness to help with domestic work. This in turn furthers girls' education. As more girls and women remain in school, child and mother mortality rates drop, and the outlook of their local economy improves. To further the virtuous cycle, CBE International's egalitarian curriculum is available in more than twenty languages.[58] Its use in East African communities has decreased patriarchal attitudes among men and women by up to 41 percent. Following one session, a girl admitted that her mother

> gave birth only to girls, so my father married a second woman because he wanted a male child. . . . When my stepmother gave birth to a boy, Father treated us (girls) as nothing. . . . I hated being a girl because I saw myself as of no value. . . . I didn't want to go home after school. But the message you

---

[55]"Our Mission," World Relief, https://worldrelief.org/ (accessed February 21, 2019); Tearfund, www.tearfund.org/; "Channels of Hope for Gender," World Vision, www.wvi.org/church-and -interfaith-engagement/channels-hope-gender (accessed February 21, 2019). See also Raising Voices, an organization that offers SASA Faith, a gender-equality curriculum for Christian and Muslim communities, available at http://raisingvoices.org/sasa-faith-guide/.

[56]Name changed.

[57]For Channels of Hope for Gender impact stories, see Mimi Haddad, "From Mourning to Dancing: Experiencing God's Delight in South Africa," CBE International, September 15, 2014, www .cbeinternational.org/blogs/mourning-dancing-experiencing-god%E2%80%99s-delight -south-africa.

[58]Janet George, Still Side by Side, www.cbeinternational.org/content/side-side-book.

taught about women's value has changed me. I started believing in myself, as I learned that God created male and female as equals.[59]

After using CBE International's curriculum in Uganda, men challenged sexism by hosting a cooking contest. One observer said, "it was an unbelievable experience for men to cook, as in this culture, men do not cook or even enter the kitchen. Children wondered to see their father cooking, as they have not ever seen that."[60] This event powerfully undermined attitudes that thwart human flourishing for men and women and children.

Ultimately, balancing power differentials that truncate human flourishing must address flawed Bible translations and interpretations. In some rural communities without access to Scripture, patriarchal attitudes persist through teachings that argue, for example, that Adam was farming when the serpent tempted Eve. Bible distribution is desperately needed around the world, but so are pastors who are ready to correct faulty readings of Scripture. As trusted leaders, pastors can also demonstrate the dignity and equality of girls and women by their example, by addressing abuse, and in challenging long-standing traditions that demean women, such as female genital mutilation, child marriage, dowry, and polygamy— all practiced by Christians.[61] Further, sex traffickers look for communities with gendered power differentials because these are least likely to resist the sale of their children.[62]

While achieving humanitarian goals is furthered by advancing women's equality, a 2019 study of prominent Christian nongovernmental organizations showed that where data was available, women were 29.6 percent of total board members, 16.7 percent of CEOs and presidents, 31.1 percent of vice presidents, and 41.1 percent of other senior leadership. Only two of twelve at the highest level of leadership were women. While Christian

---

[59]This comment was noted during a CBE International–cosponsored conference in 2018 in Uganda and distributed to CBE International supporters in "Upcoming Pentecostal Churches Network's September Gender Equality Conference Report," October 2018. To protect the safety and privacy of the sponsors and their community, the quote is not available online.

[60]"Upcoming Pentecostal Churches."

[61]I. El-Damanboury, "The Christian and Jewish View of Female Genital Mutilation," *African Journal of Urology* 19 (2013): 127-29.

[62]Kemi Fisayo Oyebanji, "Human Trafficking Across a Border in Nigeria: Experiences of Young Women Who Have Survived Trafficking," University of the Western Cape, March 14, 2018, http://etd.uwc.ac.za/xmlui/handle/11394/5939.

nongovernmental organizations had more equitable representation than organizations focused on traditional missionary work, the percentage of women declined at higher levels of leadership. The same study found that missionary organizations sent more women than men into the field, yet men held 76.1 percent of board positions and made up 94.4 percent of CEOs and presidents, 82.2 percent of vice presidents, 82.4 percent of other senior leadership, and 75 percent of field directors.[63] Gender power imbalances are steeper among Christian mission organizations than Christian nongovernmental organizations, which are more likely to support more gender equality in their leadership. Even so, secular non-governmental organizations are reticent to partner with Christian orga-nizations because of entrenched organizational sexism believed to hinder humanitarian objectives.[64]

Institutional barriers and economic disparities remain persistent obsta-cles to women in the United States. Women with college degrees still "earn 80 cents on the dollar" for similar work done by men.[65] When women earn roughly the same as men, it usually requires an additional degree.[66] Rec-ognizing economic and workplace bias is more challenging for Christian men than Christian women, with evangelicals being the most incredulous of "barriers for women in the workplace."[67] Yet, the more men dominate a field, the more women colleagues are marginalized and demeaned, espe-cially in conservative Christian contexts.

Consider the Evangelical Theological Society. Only 6 percent of its approximately forty-five hundred members are female—the most skewed gender ratio among evangelicals. Since the organization's founding in 1949,

---

[63]Chesna E. Hinkley conducted original research for this paragraph in February 2019.

[64]Michael Bodakowski et al., "Faith Inspired Organizations and Global Development: A Back-ground Review 'Mapping' Social and Economic Development Work in South and Central Asia," Berkley Center for Religion, Peace, and World Affairs and the World Faiths Development Dia-logue, Georgetown University, 2011. See also Tara R. Gingerich et al., "Local Humanitarian Leadership and Religious Literacy: Engaging with Religion, Faith, and Faith Actors," Harvard Divinity School Religious Literacy Project and Oxfam, March 2017.

[65]Janet Napolitano, "Women Earn More College Degrees and Men Still Earn More Money," Forbes, September 4, 2018, www.forbes.com/sites/janetnapolitano/2018/09/04/women-earn -more-college-degrees-and-men-still-earn-more-money/#38d3334a39fl.

[66]Kaitlin Mulhere, "Women Need One More Degree than Men to Earn the Same Average Salary," Money, February 27, 2018, http://money.com/money/5176517/gender-pay-gap-college-degrees/.

[67]"What Americans Think About Women in Power," Barna, March 8, 2017, www.barna.com /research/americans-think-women-power/.

no woman has been elected to the executive committee. A 2014 study of women's experiences at the Evangelical Theological Society uncovered a hostile atmosphere that marginalized women and actively excluded their participation.[68] This study helped raise men's consciousness of women's being demeaned, a problem not isolated to Christian environments.

Research shows that men significantly underestimate the level of sexual harassment women experience. A 2012 survey in Denmark "found 80% of women had experienced some form of sexual harassment," while men estimated women's rate of harassment at 31 percent. In lower-paid jobs, harassment and abuse are normalized. There is a significant cost to speaking out, and most women do not believe the effort will prove advantageous.[69]

Abusive systems and relationships are characterized by dominance, an absence of empathy, impunity, and gender roles.[70] Strikingly, pornography diminishes empathy and normalizes abuse. According to Barna, pornography feeds a narcissistic urge to control and dominate for self-pleasure.[71] In pornography, male domination, gang rape, strict gender roles, and sexual violence perpetrated on younger and younger females elicit sexual arousal. This creates a demand for sex trafficking, because rape of trafficked youth is choreographed, filmed, and sold on the dark web, a massively lucrative industry with nearly all male users.[72] Persons who participate in the porn industry are complicit in sex trafficking.

Generating $6 billion in 2018, porn is the "fastest-growing business of organized crime in the world, receiving more visitors each month than

---

[68]Emily Zimbrick Rogers, "A Question Mark over My Head: The Experiences of Women ETS Members at the 2014 ETS Annual Meeting," *A Special Edition Journal of Christians for Biblical Equality* (2015): 4-10, www.cbeinternational.org/resources/article/other/question-mark-over-my-head.

[69]Pamela Duncan and Alexandra Topping, "Men Underestimate Level of Sexual Harassment Against Women—Survey," *The Guardian*, December 6, 2018, www.theguardian.com/world/2018 /dec/06/men-underestimate-level-of-sexual-harassment-against-women-survey.

[70]See William Wan, "What Makes Some Men Sexual Harassers?," *Pittsburgh Post-Gazette*, December 31, 2017, www.post-gazette.com/opinion/Op-Ed/2017/12/31/What-makes-some-men-sexual -harassers/stories/201712310300.

[71]David Kinnaman, "The Porn Phenomenon," Barna, February 5, 2016, www.barna.com/the -porn-phenomenon/#.VqZoN_krIdU.

[72]Marlo Safi, "The Porn Industry and Human Trafficking Reinforce Each Other," *National Review*, August 1, 2018, www.nationalreview.com/2018/08/porn-human-trafficking-reinforce-each- other/; Daniel Mutzel, "Meet the Hacker Who Busts Child Pornographers on the Dark Net," Motherboard, November 8, 2017, https://motherboard.vice.com/en_us/article/ywbmyb /meet-the-hacker-who-busts-child-pornographers-on-the-dark-net.

Netflix, Amazon, and Twitter combined."[73] More than 60 percent of US men are porn users.[74] Christians and non-Christians use porn at the same rate, with more women using porn now than ever before.[75] Porn users are less likely to enjoy mutual and intimate relationships; they also experience higher rates of extramarital sexual activity and a greater probability of divorce.[76] The sexual dehumanization of women in porn fuels their subordination in other areas of life.

CONCLUSION

The authority and dominance of men established, legitimized, and reinforced by cultural and religious teachings create a power imbalance that wreaks havoc on human flourishing. Vastly prevalent throughout history and exceedingly violent in nearly all communities today, the toxic force of patriarchy aims to diminish women's dignity, capacity, and agency to normalize gender-based violence. The ubiquitous presence of patriarchy today also dulls our attentiveness to its presence and impact, and in this way it shields perpetrators, obstructs justice, and demeans survivors. For too many, the devastating consequence of sin—the "he shall rule over you" (Gen 3:16)—is elevated to a prescription that is part of God's plan, rather than a description of the result of human sinfulness that Christ is redeeming, healing, and restoring through the shared governance of men and women, which is God's ideal and the bedrock of human flourishing (Gen 1:26-28).

---

[73]Ross Benes, "Porn Could Have a Bigger Economic Influence on the US than Netflix," *Quartz*, June 20, 2018, https://qz.com/1309527/porn-could-have-a-bigger-economic-influence-on-the-us-than-netflix/; Safi, "Porn Industry."

[74]"New Survey of Porn Use: Men and Women Watching in Startling Numbers," Church Militant, January 18, 2016, www.churchmilitant.com/news/article/new-survey-of-porn-use-shows-startling-stats-for-men-and-women. See also Grant Hilary Brenner, "When Is Porn Use A Problem?," *Psychology Today*, February 19, 2018, www.psychologytoday.com/us/blog/experimentations/201802/when-is-porn-use-problem.

[75]Penny Starr, "Pornography Use Among Self-Identified Christians Largely Mirrors National Average, Survey Finds," CNS News, August 27, 2015, www.cnsnews.com/news/article/penny-starr/pornography-use-among-self-identified-christians-largely-mirrors-national.

[76]Amanda M. Maddox, Galena K. Rhoades, and Howard J. Markman, "Viewing Sexually-Explicit Materials Alone or Together: Associations with Relationship Quality" *Archives of Sexual Behavior* 40:2 (2011): 441-48, www.ncbi.nlm.nih.gov/pmc/articles/PMC2891580/; Samuel L. Perry and Cyrus Schleifer, "Till Porn Do Us Part? A Longitudinal Examination of Pornography Use and Divorce," *Journal of Sex Research* 55, no. 3 (2018): 284-96, www.tandfonline.com/doi/full/10.1080/00224499.2017.1317709.

31

TOWARD RECONCILIATION

HEALING THE SCHISM

Alice P. Mathews

• • • • •

RECONCILIATION IS A TERM VERY MUCH in vogue these days. In our litigious society, costly and destructive lawsuits have come to characterize the way even Christians handle differences. Yet the Bible shows us a better way.[1] Reconciliation is the Christian alternative for handling disputes between two parties who find themselves positioned against each other.[2]

Several decades of acrimonious labeling and infighting among Christians over the place of women in the church and the home has led to what appears to be a hopeless chasm of difference between those who advocate gender equality and those who maintain hierarchical structures for male and female relationships. Can those who hold such opposing views be reconciled?

A REAL AND SIGNIFICANT DIFFERENCE

If there is to be reconciliation, it must begin with the realization that the chasm between the two sides is real and significant. We must see and

---

[1]This is the heart of 1 Corinthians, especially 1 Cor 6:1-11. It is also integral to our worship. In Mt 5:23-24 Jesus regards reconciliation with any Christian who has something against us as essential before we can carry out our acts of worship to God.

[2]Resources for those who seek legal reconciliation include the Association of Christian Conciliation Services and the Christian Legal Society (PO Box 1492, Marrifield, VA 22116). See also Ken Sande, *The Peacemaker: A Biblical Guide to Resolving Personal Conflict* (Grand Rapids, MI: Baker, 1991).

respect this conflict for what it is: a struggle for truth. No one in that struggle can dismiss opponents merely by labeling them—whether as power-hungry defenders of the status quo or as pawns of contemporary culture who are willing to compromise Scripture for the sake of a social agenda. Truth is on the line for God-fearing Christians on both sides of the chasm. When we fail to respect those who hold views that call our own beliefs into question, we miss the valid and ongoing struggle for truth. But in the effort to respect those with whom we disagree, we are faced with the painful necessity of doing so without abandoning this struggle.

This, of course, is not the first time in the history of the church that contrary understandings of biblical truth have faced the people of God. The great councils in the early centuries remind us that God-fearing Christians disagreed vigorously and often separated over core issues.[3] Later, in the sixteenth century, Martin Luther opposed certain teachings and practices of the Roman Catholic Church, launching the Reformation when he nailed his Ninety-Five Theses to the Wittenberg door. Out of that act, more than a hundred years of military warfare between Catholics and Protestants erupted in Europe.[4]

More recently, Christians were divided over the issue of slavery, some using Scripture to defend the practice of owning other human beings and others using it to abolish that practice. Willard Swartley has helped us understand the ways the Bible has been used by groups opposing each other on this issue as well as on others, such as war and peace, Sabbath keeping, and the subject of this book—the relationship between men and women in the home and the church.[5]

---

[3]Most twenty-first-century Christians assume that the church was clear about the nature of Christ from its earliest days. But it took the Council of Nicaea in 325 to formalize the church's understanding of Christ's divine nature (that God and Christ are of the same essence) and the Council of Chalcedon in 451 to formalize the understanding of the relation between the divine and human natures of Christ (one person in two natures). Long and bitter infighting over these doctrines led to permanent schisms in the church.

[4]After Luther's bold move and the quick formation of crowds of protesting followers around him, the Roman Catholic Church called the Council of Trent (1545, 1563) to deal with this new threat to its hegemony. Numerous wars based on this religious conflict broke out as Catholic governments tried to stop the spread of Protestantism in their countries: civil war in France (1562–1598), rebellion in the Netherlands (1565–1648), war between Spain and England (1585–1604), and the Thirty Years' War (1618–1648).

[5]Willard Swartley, *Slavery, Sabbath, War and Women* (Scottdale, PA: Herald, 1983).

Even as I write in the twenty-first century, deep chasms exist between those who hold to an open theism and those who oppose it, and between those who believe all of the gifts of the Spirit should be operative in the church today and those who see some of those gifts as having been given to Christians in the first century only. All of this is to say that the church is no stranger to fracturing divisions in the name of truth.

Puzzled by the meaning or necessity of these fissures, we may ask why "the other side" cannot see what appear to us to be the *real* issues. Thomas Kuhn, examining the structure of scientific revolutions, concludes:

> The proponents of competing paradigms practice their trades in different worlds. . . . [They] see different things when they look from the same point in the same direction. Again, that is not to say that they can see anything they please. Both are looking at the world, and what they look at has not changed. But in some areas they see different things, and they see them in different relations one to the other. That is why a law that cannot even be demonstrated to one group of scientists may occasionally seem intuitively obvious to another.[6]

The extensive literature supporting male leadership and gender equality presents us with such competing paradigms.

Historian Anne Firor Scott, looking at the omission of women's accomplishments by earlier historians, reports: "It is a truism, yet one easy to forget, that people see most easily things they are prepared to see and overlook those they do not expect to encounter. . . . Because our minds are clouded, we do not see things that are before our eyes. What clouds our minds is, of course, the culture that at any time teaches us what to see and what not to see."[7] Our culture grinds the lens through which we look at all we see.

We may ask ourselves how people reading the same Scripture, and taking it as inspired and authoritative, can hold positions or paradigms as diverse as those represented by male-leadership and gender-equality views today. Or, to borrow Kuhn's words, we wonder why a position that cannot

---

[6]Thomas Kuhn, *The Structure of Scientific Revolutions*, 2nd ed. (Chicago: University of Chicago Press, 1970), 150.

[7]Anne Firor Scott, "On Seeing and Not Seeing: A Case of Historical Invisibility," *Journal of American History* 71, no. 1 (1984): 7, 19.

even be demonstrated to one group of sincere Christians seems intuitively obvious to another group of equally sincere Christians.

What is true for scientists and historians can also be true for theologians and biblical scholars. David Scholer puts his finger on a central problem for scholars in his discussion of starting points and the balance of texts. *The biblical text one chooses for one's starting point in the study of a doctrine or issue in Scripture becomes the lens through which one looks at all other texts.*[8] If, for example, an interpreter chooses 1 Timothy 2:12 as the starting point, then other texts will be evaluated and interpreted (consciously or unconsciously) in the light of Paul's restrictive statement. On the other hand, if Galatians 3:28 is chosen as the starting point, texts such as 1 Timothy 2:12 will be read with Paul's declaration of no distinctions in mind.

If the starting text sets the boundaries or limits for what one is able to see in other texts, then the issue is more hermeneutical than exegetical. What, then, determines which texts are to function as starting texts? Scholer suggests that "our theological traditions tend to select our 'windows' for us."[9] Indeed, our particular culture and subculture have ground the lens through which we look at the Bible. As a result, a commentary written by a hierarchicalist will emphasize female subordination to male leadership, focusing almost exclusively on texts that appear to support subordination. On the other hand, those advocating gender equality focus on texts that their evangelical opponents often consider irrelevant.

When both groups use the same texts, it is often with a way of "seeing" that supports opposing views. For example, in discussions of Genesis 2, Stephen Clark sees the male as central to the narrative and therefore as the "head," whereas Perry Yoder argues that woman is the climax of the narrative, giving her an equal or even more important role.[10] We see what our lenses allow us to see.

---

[8]David Scholer, "1 Timothy 2:9-15 and the Place of Women in the Church's Ministry," in *Women, Authority and the Bible*, ed. Alvera Mickelsen (Downers Grove, IL: InterVarsity Press, 1986), 193-219.

[9]David Scholer, "Feminist Hermeneutics and Evangelical Biblical Interpretation," *JETS* 30, no. 4 (1987): 417.

[10]Stephen B. Clark, *Man and Woman in Christ: An Examination of the Roles of Men and Women in the Light of Scriptures and the Social Sciences* (Ann Arbor, MI: Servant, 1980), 14. In this passage Clark cites three reasons that the partnership between man and woman should be understood as hierarchical: (1) "man is the center of the narrative," (2) "it is the man who is called 'Man' or

One of the myths of modernity, accepted by physical and social scientists alike, was logical positivism—the idea that the investigator of any phenomenon could come to the investigative task with objectivity, uninfluenced by personal or cultural values. Well into the twenty-first century, researchers in the natural and social sciences have come to understand that the way they personally view their world affects how they frame their questions. Those questions, in turn, determine the direction of their research. In effect, their assumptive world sets the limits for what they can or cannot see.

Theologians, too, bring their assumptive world to the questions they ask. Those who have spent their lives in service to Jesus Christ bring theological assumptions from their early training that continue to determine what they can and cannot see. Moreover, they are convinced that their assumptions are grounded in Scripture. Yet the history of the church should serve as a cautionary tale about assumptions that in fact were based at times more in political or social realities than in the core teachings of Scripture.

Therefore, we must step back and ask ourselves hard questions about our assumptions.[11] As John Piper and Wayne Grudem acknowledge, "We have a thousand ways to justify with our brains the biases of the soul."[12] This is a good reminder to all who are concerned about women's roles in the home and church.

'human' and not the woman," and (3) man is created first, giving him as firstborn a natural precedence by birth. This synopsis of Clark is taken from Swartley, *Slavery, Sabbath, War and Women*, 154; Perry Yoder, "Woman's Place in the Creation Accounts," in *Study Guide on Women*, ed. Herta Funk (Newton, KS: Faith and Life, 1975), 10-11. I am indebted to Swartley for the contrast in emphasis between Clark and Yoder (*Slavery, Sabbath, War and Women*, 154).

[11]Lewis Wirth, in his introduction to Karl Mannheim's *Ideology and Utopia*, comments that "the most important thing that we can know about a man [sic] is what he takes for granted, and the most elemental and important facts about a society are those that are seldom debated and generally regarded as settled" ([San Diego, CA: Harcourt Brace Jovanovich, 1936], xxiii). More recently, Huston Smith expands on the importance of understanding our unexamined assumptions: "The dominant assumptions of an age color the thoughts, beliefs, expectations, and images of the men and women who live within it. Being always with us, these assumptions usually pass unnoticed—like the pair of glasses which, because they are so often on the wearer's nose, simply stop being observed. But this doesn't mean they have no effect. Ultimately, assumptions which underlie our outlooks on life refract the world in ways that condition our art and our institutions: the kinds of homes we live in, our sense of right and wrong, our criteria of success, what we conceive our duty to be, what we think it means to be a man or woman, how we worship our God or whether, indeed, we have a God to worship." See Smith, *Beyond the Post-modern Mind*, 2nd ed. (Wheaton, IL: Theosophical Publishing House, 1989), 3-4.

[12]John Piper and Wayne Grudem, "Charity, Clarity, and Hope," in *RBMW*, 492.

At the same time, we cannot ignore our differences. If we are committed to truth as the controlling principle, we must accept the reality that ideas divide people. When we know that we are to love one another, yet we have strong differences over crucial issues, the resulting cognitive dissonance may tempt us to try to paper over the chasm that divides us from our brothers and sisters in Christ. This can be dangerous to our commitment to truth.

Truth is not merely the content of a series of discourses or arguments; it also includes being true to oneself and to what is true in one's opponent.[13] When we discard what we have come to accept as propositionally true merely to lower our cognitive dissonance, we do violence to the integrity of our own mind and heart. When we ignore or downplay serious differences in beliefs about propositional truth with someone who opposes us, we diminish or even nullify the worth of that person's mind and heart. As pompous old Polonius noted in Shakespeare's *Hamlet*, "To thine own self be true, and it follows as the day the night, thou canst not then be false to any man."

Truth can be a casualty when differences are trivialized in other ways as well. One means of trivializing real differences is to change nomenclature. For example, when the term *complementarian* was chosen to replace earlier designations of those who accept as biblical a hierarchical structure in male-female relationships, many people's perception of the debate changed. In defining their position, Piper and Grudem reject the terms *traditionalist* and *hierarchical*, arguing that *complementarian* is preferable because it "suggests both equality and beneficial differences between men and women."[14] This sounds like a significant change in the traditional position and, as such, a move toward reconciliation. But soon the reader discovers that the crux of the issue for complementarians is difference rather than equality, and that *difference* refers primarily to an inequality in authority between women and men. The nomenclature misleads, and truth is trivialized.

---

[13]Jesus refers to himself in Jn 14:6 as "the way, and the truth, and the life." Integral to living as the truth in first-century Palestine was being true not only to propositional truth but to his *being* God incarnate. It was his refusal to shade the truth of his being that put him on a collision course with the religious leaders.

[14]John Piper and Wayne Grudem, "Preface," in *RBMW*, 15.

As James Beck and Craig Blomberg note, "It is not clear that the idea of men and women playing complementary roles inherently suggests that certain roles are altogether prohibited for one gender. Some egalitarians have complained, rightly it seems, that their view can equally be described as complementarian," because they too reject unisex theories of gender development.[15]

The differences between opposing positions can also be trivialized by what Charles Long calls *significations*.[16] To signify is to name, and often by attaching pejorative names to movements or individuals, we can so color the perception of our opponents that it becomes impossible to carry on meaningful dialogue. For example, when an evangelical who supports gender equality is called a *feminist* without any further qualification (and sometimes in the tone and temper of an expletive), that naming confers a reality on the receiver that may not be true at all. It is a false generalization that makes further discourse more difficult, if not impossible. It trivializes the issue by ignoring the actual content of the argument and removing the other person from inclusion in the conversation.

In a powerful essay on the abuse of language, German theologian Josef Pieper examines the purposes of human language and the words we use: "Word and language form the medium that sustains the common existence of the human spirit. . . . If the word becomes corrupted, human existence itself will not remain unaffected and untainted."[17] Because words convey reality, when we name or identify someone or something, we communicate a quality of reality to that person or thing.

But Pieper insists that a lie (outright or implied) can never be taken as true communication because "it withholds the other's share and portion of reality, to prevent his participation in reality." It is a corruption of one's relationship to reality. A person who thus corrupts language can give fine speeches but is to a significant degree incapable of dialogue. This is a form

---

[15]James R. Beck and Craig L. Blomberg, "Introduction," in *Two Views on Women in Ministry*, ed. James R. Beck and Craig L. Blomberg (Grand Rapids, MI: Zondervan, 2001), 17.

[16]Charles Long, *Significations: Signs, Symbols and Images in the Interpretation of Religion* (Philadelphia: Fortress, 1988). Long's book is particularly germane for any reader pursuing a deeper understanding of the racial epithets or "namings" that demean and divide.

[17]Josef Pieper, *Abuse of Language, Abuse of Power*, trans. Lothar Krauth (San Francisco: Ignatius, 1988), 15.

of deceptive verbal artistry: superbly crafted, perfectly worded, brilliantly formulated, strikingly written, and at the same time false in its thrust and essence.[18] This is illustrated by a prominent Christian author who, in order to support her point, cites the first half of 1 Corinthians 7:4 ("The wife does not have authority over her own body but yields it to her husband") while omitting the second half of the same verse ("In the same way, the husband does not have authority over his own body but yields it to his wife"). This is patently dishonest no matter how elegantly stated.[19] Similarly, she offers two lists of "biblical commands" to husbands and to wives, in which she mingles loosely reworded biblical statements with other statements that are not found in Scripture.[20]

Our commitment to truth demands that we speak what is true and that we use language honestly. When we do this, we may discover that what we hold as true divides us from those who hold opposite views. If we are committed to truth as the controlling principle, then we must accept the reality that ideas can divide people.

Thus, a genuine problem exists, and it is *our* problem. Jesus is clear in Matthew 5:23-24 that if we are in the family of God, we have an obligation before God to do all that we can to be reconciled to anyone in God's household who "has something against" us. Note that the text is not about our behavior when we have something against someone else. It is about our behavior when others have something against us. The problem belongs to all of us in the family of God, and it cannot be ignored.

Whether we are egalitarians or hierarchicalists, there are people who hold things against us. In the process of acting to defend their paradigm, people hurt other people within the body of Christ. In the pursuit of truth, we demonstrate an un-Christian priority system when the idea becomes more important than the people holding that idea. We have only to scan the history of the church to discover how many paid dearly, often with their lives, as they found themselves caught in the crossfire of competing paradigms.

---

[18]Pieper, *Abuse of Language*, 16, 19.

[19]Elisabeth Elliot, *The Mark of a Man* (Old Tappan, NJ: Fleming H. Revell, 1981), 84.

[20]For example, she includes in the list of commands for wives the statement "Their role is to be receptive" (*Mark of a Man*, 84). By rephrasing quotations from Scripture in her own words, she implies that all of the statements have come from the Bible.

The chasm is real. Even more important, the way we often respond to it is a scandal to the church and a point of ridicule for the world. Jesus' prayer in John 17 shows us why this chasm is such a scandal. Crying out to the Father only hours before his trial and crucifixion, he prayed for the unity of all those who would follow him, then and in the ages to come, asking "that all of them may be one, . . . *so that the world may believe that you have sent me*" (Jn 17:21 NIV, emphasis added).

Do we understand that our oneness with each other and our mission of evangelism in the world are inseparable? Jesus' prayer was not a spiritual abstraction. Our unity is not simply for its own sake or because it would be pleasant or nice. In a profound way in this prayer our Lord links our unity with the success of our mission in the world. As J. Ramsey Michaels notes, "The unity of Jesus' followers challenges the world to believe."[21] This puts the matter of our unity in a different light. Yet the chasm is there, often using up time and energy and frequently diverting our attention from the fundamental mission of the church.

WHAT THEN MUST BE DONE?

We acknowledge that the chasm is real and that it comes from a struggle for truth. For these reasons we cannot trivialize it or water it down semantically. We attend to Jesus' prayer, and as his followers we acknowledge that the chasm often diverts us from the mission he gave us; moreover, it diverts nonbelievers from taking our Lord seriously. What, then, must we do?

First, we all must continue to explore honestly the competing paradigms, using the tools of biblical theology, logic, and courtesy. All Christians defending or forwarding one of the competing paradigms face the temptation of devoting their time to shoring up their own arguments while giving little attention or respect to the arguments of their opponents. We must adamantly resist this temptation.

A paradigm is like a closed box. Inside it are all of the pieces that make it a compelling explanation for the way things are or ought to be. To the extent that we enclose ourselves within the box, we fail to see the anomalies to our paradigm. Anomalies are like rocks piling up against the outer sides

---

[21]J. Ramsey Michaels, *John*, NIBC (Peabody, MA: Hendrickson, 1984), 299.

of our box. Kuhn has shown that we experience a *paradigm shift* only when the cumulative weight of anomalies pressing on the sides of the paradigm box forces it to collapse. All the major scientific discoveries of past centuries came about not because scientists were looking for a new theory but because significant anomalies overwhelmed their reigning paradigms.

What are the anomalies pressing against the sides of the respective paradigms? This book explores the anomalies pressing against the sides of the male-leadership paradigm, just as the contributors to Piper and Grudem's *Recovering Biblical Manhood and Womanhood* explored anomalies pressing against the sides of the gender-equality paradigm. Every paradigm has its anomalies.

Until we have explored the anomalies threatening both paradigms, we have not completed our task. This calls for the best efforts of our best scholars, as well as our best people working with women and men in the church and in wider society. It means reviewing the biblical and theological studies to see what may still need to be explored. It involves listening to people in the pew and on the street. It includes hearing insights from the social sciences (historians, anthropologists, sociologists, psychologists, and culture analysts). It means looking squarely at issues of abuse (sexual abuse, battering, and the abuse of power in church and home). It means examining our own accommodations to the godless culture around us. When we thoroughly understand the anomalies as well as the paradigms, we can move to the next step.

Second, we are obligated to explain the competing paradigms at many levels. Just as educators develop textbooks adapted to the needs of various ages, audiences, and educational levels, so must we develop tools that enable people at all levels to understand the issues at stake. What are the fundamental ideas in each of the paradigms? Where did these ideas come from? How long have they been with us? And most important, if we accept these ideas and adopt a particular paradigm as truth, what are the *implications* for the future?

Some would argue that such efforts have already been made. We can applaud the solid exegetical and hermeneutical work made available to wide audiences by biblical scholars and theologians. We are grateful for the Christian social scientists who have also helped us understand some of the implications of both paradigms for families and individuals in the home or church. But much remains to be done. As Kuhn observed, what is intuitively obvious to some is still opaque to others. How can we move beyond this impasse?

As the task of explaining the competing paradigms goes forward, the temptation is always to simplify issues to the point of being simplistic, to strip down the paradigms to such a point that the necessary nuancing of arguments disappears, resulting in a mere caricature of the paradigm. This happens, for example, when a young couple is frightened away from an egalitarian marriage by warnings of deadlock in decision making if one party (the husband) does not have the final word. Likewise, it happens when a pastor warns that having a woman in a leadership role in the congregation starts that church down the slippery slope into a godless accommodation to the culture.

Proponents of either paradigm must understand both paradigms inside and out and know the anomalies pressing against the sides of each paradigm box. Then they must develop adequate, truthful, simple (but not simplistic) ways to communicate the paradigm to others to whom it is unfamiliar.

Third, while the first two steps are being carried out, we must acknowledge the chasm between the paradigms and embrace as fellow believers those on the other side of the chasm. We cannot ignore the existence of the chasm or minimize its significance with semantic games. If, in fact, our paradigm has emerged in a struggle to find the truth about men and women in the home and church, we are dishonest with ourselves (as well as with others) if we attempt to water down the points of disagreement. This places us in a state of cognitive dissonance.[22] We cannot pretend the differences do not exist. Yet our Lord calls us to unity. We are admonished to speak the truth in love (Eph 4:15).

Leon Festinger, in his work with cognitive dissonance, concludes that when we experience this tension we typically do two things. We try to reduce the dissonance, and we "actively avoid situations and information

---

[22]This term was coined by Leon Festinger to describe the frustration or disequilibrium we experience when we are faced with inconsistencies between what we believe to be true and what we experience. See Festinger, *A Theory of Cognitive Dissonance* (Evanston, IL: Row, Peterson, 1957), 3.

that would likely increase the dissonance."[23] The issue of truth concerns not only the truth we embrace but also our difficulty in living with the tension between truth and love. We actively avoid information and situations that increase the tension or dissonance between what we believe and what we experience in our lives.

Does this begin to explain how something that is intuitively obvious to one remains opaque to another? In view of this tendency, how can we maintain an awareness of the chasm between the two paradigms even as we embrace those whose ideas we reject?

THE GOSPEL AS THE BASIS OF OUR RELATIONSHIP

Again, we recall Jesus' prayer that we may be one "so that the world may believe that you have sent me" (Jn 17:21 NIV). The unity for which he prayed in those last hours before dying on a Roman cross is not merely an agreement to sweep our differences under the carpet as if they did not matter. Nor is it a conformity that one group imposes on another in an effort to present an aura of unity. Jesus is clear about both the nature and the purpose of this unity. Just as the Father is in the Son and the Son is in the Father, so are we to be one in them. Our unity is in God, and the power to hold truth in love for one another lies first in our relationship to God. Reconciliation begins here.

Only the gospel has the power to convert our dissonance into consonance. But how does the gospel work to overturn our natural inability to hold the truth in love? The doctrine of reconciliation is clearly stated by Paul in 2 Corinthians 5:17-19:

> Therefore, if anyone is in Christ, the new creation has come. The old has gone, the new is here! All this is from God, who reconciled us to himself through Christ and gave us the ministry of reconciliation: that God was reconciling the world to himself in Christ, not counting people's sins against them. And he has committed to us the message of reconciliation. (NIV)

Thus, reconciliation brings together in love and friendship those who have been enemies. God was in Christ reconciling us to himself, not counting our trespasses against us. Then he gave to us the evangelistic task of

---

[23]Festinger, *Theory of Cognitive Dissonance*, 3.

bringing other people into a relationship to himself through Jesus Christ. God knew the truth about us yet reached out to us in the atoning death of his Son to bring us into a relationship of love with him. God demonstrates how truth and love can coexist in our relationship to him. But can it coexist in our relationships to others with whom we disagree?

The pursuit of truth can never be a substitute for nurturing relationships within the body of Christ. We are called to care for the brother or sister with whom we disagree while at the same time holding to the truth as we understand it. The tension between the two is inherent, and the resulting discomfort may persuade us that it is not merely difficult to achieve but morally wrong to marry the two. We think we cannot hold to the truth we have embraced while nurturing relationships with those with whom we disagree. Yet our Lord calls us to truth *and* to oneness in him. He does not tell us it is easy, but he is clear that it is necessary.

On the eve of Jesus' crucifixion "a dispute . . . arose among [the disciples] as to which of them was to be regarded as the greatest" (Lk 22:24). Jesus intervened, reminding them that his followers should not use power or authority in the manner of the "kings of the Gentiles." That dispute seemed minor, but Jesus knew that the spirit behind the dispute was the serpent's poison. It had the potential to destroy the work of God in the world. He could not ignore it and thus responded with a solemn rebuke. Why? Their oneness was essential to their work in the world for God's kingdom.

Paul faced factions tearing apart the believers in Corinth (petty infighting, sexual immorality, believers taking other believers to court, issues of relationships in and outside marriage, legalisms about eating and drinking, abuses of relationships at the Lord's Table, flaunting of spiritual gifts, etc.)— many seemingly intractable issues. While he ruled on or counseled certain attitudes and behaviors in each of the problem areas, he repeatedly pointed the Corinthians to Jesus Christ. When we talk about reconciliation, this is the only point of true unity. We are to be one in Christ even as the Father and the Son are one (Jn 17:20-23).

Working with mathematical set theory, anthropologist and missiologist Paul Hiebert offers a means of imaging how Jesus' prayer for oneness is realized in human life.[24] In set theory, a set is a kind of worldview, a way to understand what is or ought to be true in life. If you imagine a set as a circle, it has a circumference (boundary) and a center (target or goal).

Some people have what Hiebert calls bounded sets. They focus on the *boundary* of their set, its circumference. A person with a bounded set believes what is most important is to maintain the boundaries of truth. Bounded sets are fundamental to our understanding of order, and in a bounded set the definition of righteousness and justice is to live within the law (the boundary) but not necessarily to live in harmony with one another.

A different kind of set is the centered or relational set. Here the focus is not on maintaining the boundaries but on the *relationship* of everyone and everything to the center—the target or goal. Some are far from the center but are moving toward it. That makes them part of the set. Others may be near the center but are moving away from it. Thus, they are no longer seen as part of the set. The direction of movement toward or away from the center determines who is in and who is out.

In centered-set thinking, more emphasis is placed on strengthening the relationship to the center than on maintaining the boundary. The boundary exists by virtue of the members' relationship to the center. Hiebert sees Hebrew culture as a centered set in which the people were in covenant relationship to God first, then to one another as they moved toward the center. The theological worldview of Jesus and Paul was also a centered set. How else could they envision and speak of all believers as forming one body?

We are one in Jesus Christ. Yes, we know the boundaries of our paradigms. But as Christians wrestling with issues of gender limits or liberties in the church, we know that the focus cannot be on boundaries. So, we move from the image of a box (our own paradigm) to the image of a circle (a centered or relational set). Why? Because Jesus placed a priority on right relationships as absolutely integral to our mission in the world.

It is never easy to care deeply for the brother or sister with whom we disagree and at the same time to hold faithfully to the truth as we understand it. It can easily throw us into such cognitive dissonance that we either

---

[24]Paul Hiebert, *Anthropological Reflections on Missiological Issues* (Grand Rapids, MI: Baker, 1994); see chap. 6 on bounded sets.

let go of the truth we have embraced or let go of any obligation for relationship with a disagreeing (and possibly disagreeable) brother or sister in Christ. It is a strange but hopeful reality, however, that we most often grow and develop spiritually as we live within the tensions of the Christian life.[25]

If we are serious about healing the real schism between hierarchicalists and egalitarians, we will refuse to sacrifice the mission of the church (endangered by our lack of unity) for the sake of the paradigm we embrace. But we will also refuse to sacrifice the truth we have embraced, because we believe it is God's truth for the welfare of his people. In the midst of the tension between the two, we will find a way to live within this tension as we stay focused on Christ, our center. And we will discover that as we move toward him as center, we move closer to others who are moving in the same direction. Even if we disagree about women's place in the home and church, we will at least be close enough to show love and care for those with a competing paradigm.

It is not a neat vision with a simple list of things to do that will guarantee unity. It has about it the raw and messy look of reality. But if the focus is on Christ, by his Spirit we can be one—and we will see things we had not seen before. We may even discover a completely different paradigm replacing both of the existing paradigms. But we can never make such discoveries as long as we insist on a bounded set with a focus on the boundaries. It becomes possible only when we are part of a centered set, with Christ and his kingdom as our priority, as we *all* move toward our center.

There is an arrogance to which we are all liable. It is the arrogance of thinking that only we have the truth. God's truth may well be greater than all of our "truths." Until we come into that larger truth, we must be true to the truth we have embraced. But even as we embrace our paradigm, may God help us move toward an understanding of his true and perfect paradigm—which may well swallow up all earthly paradigms for the relationship of men and women in the church and home.

---

[25]I am indebted to Old Testament professor John Worgul (Bethel Seminary of the East), who has helped me—and many of his students—come to grips with this paradoxical reality.

CONCLUSION

RONALD W. PIERCE, CYNTHIA LONG WESTFALL, AND CHRISTA L. McKIRLAND

• • • • •

AS WE CONCLUDE THIS EDITION OF *Discovering Biblical Equality*, it seems appropriate to provide our readers with a brief summary of the volume's overall argument along with a look toward the future of this important evangelical dialogue.

SUMMING IT UP

A wide range of evangelical scholars have joined their voices here in defense of biblical gender equality in the home, church, and society. While each essay provides an in-depth discussion of a specific text or topic, a coherent summary of this book's main argument will help us to avoid missing the view of the forest because of a large tree standing just in front of us.

Part I: Looking to Scripture: The Biblical Texts. Against the backdrop of the gender-equality movement throughout church history—especially since the Reformation era—our study of the most relevant biblical passages has demonstrated a theme of mutuality that runs through the Bible from Moses to Jesus to the early apostolic church. This is clear from the God-intended mutuality and harmony in the creation accounts, through the fall of humanity and the challenging lot of women under the law and even into the New Testament era. For millennia godly women have served their Lord in leadership roles as effective prophets, deacons, and apostles. Moreover, they were blessed by Jesus and affirmed by both Paul and Peter.

Just over a decade after the resurrection of Jesus, Paul affirmed an equitable mutuality between Gentiles and Jews in both salvation and church practice, then applied this revolutionary principle to slave and free, as well as to male and female—all without qualification (Gal 3). Further, he elaborates on this kind of biblical gender equality, whether people choose marriage or singleness, by calling for a voluntary yielding of authority in marital intimacy, influencing one another spiritually, being faithful in marriage, and even choosing celibate singleness in order to serve Christ more effectively (1 Cor 7). Though respecting cultural norms regarding the appearance and behavior of men and women in public worship—especially women who were not as well educated as their male counterparts—Paul encourages women prophets to speak out in public worship with appropriate authority (1 Cor 11; 14).

Toward the end of his life, an imprisoned apostle Paul prescribes mutual submission and love in Christian marriages that mirror Christ's relationship with his bride, the church—one that is a direct result of the pouring out of God's Spirit on his sons and daughters, as well as the filling of the Spirit in the lives of all believers (Eph 5; Col 3; Acts 2). Though he often speaks specifically to men and women, his admonitions to pray, to dress modestly, to learn with respect, to avoid authoritarian teaching, and to trust Christ in the most pressing challenges in life are clearly applicable across gender lines (1 Tim 2). Likewise, by the end of the first century AD, the apostle Peter calls citizens, slaves, wives, and husbands to the same kind of submission for the sake of a Christian witness to a nonbelieving world in which the church is increasingly being dispersed. Indeed, this is a submission patterned after Christ's yielding to unjust suffering that ultimately led to his crucifixion (1 Pet 2–3).

In sum, even though leadership in the early church was predominantly male, neither Paul nor Peter endorses the hierarchies of either the prevailing Jewish or Roman cultures—including patriarchy—by telling husbands to exercise a gender-exclusive leadership in either the family or the church. Nowhere in God's inspired and authoritative Word is this kind of patriarchy prescribed.

Part II: Thinking It Through: Theological and Logical Perspectives. The Holy Spirit's gifting for Christian ministry must be made a priority over today's church structures, offices, and traditions. Within such a context, the nature of authority needs to be reconsidered with an emphasis on God's authority through the Spirit and the Word, rather than on anyone's individual rights or assumed responsibilities. Moreover, the shared image of God given in creation forms the basis for New Testament transformation into the image of Christ—one that all believers are privileged to share in. The error of gender essentialism must be abandoned in this light. These truths, along with the priesthood of all believers (a benchmark of the Reformation) and the analogy of gender equality with Scripture's critique of the institution of slavery (especially in Philemon), speak out strongly against any human-imposed church or family hierarchies.

Further, historical Christian orthodoxy has always denied the eternal subordination of the Son to the Father—until the complementarian movement of the twentieth century. Thankfully, this novel argument for the subordination of women is now crumbling under the weight of biblical and theological scholarship. Similarly, there is a long tradition in church history of recognizing and acknowledging the biblical metaphors for God as mother and their impact on Christian spirituality. This needs to be practiced and encouraged in the current revival of the lost art of spiritual formation, especially in Protestant contexts where it has been neglected for far too long. Finally, the illogical notion of women as equal in being, yet unequal in role precisely because of their being—to an extent the definition of complementarianism—fails to meet the test of rigorous philosophical examination. This, in concert with the theological issues discussed above, demonstrates that an egalitarian reading of the relevant biblical texts should be embraced by evangelicals today.

Part III: Addressing the Issues: Interpretive and Cultural Perspectives. The argument for gender equality is the result of essentially the same kind of rigorous methodology that is embraced across the evangelical academy. The relevant passages are explained in their biblical, historical, and cultural contexts, paying attention to authorial intent and seeking to apply the principles taught in each of these to the lives of believers in today's church. Specific texts are considered integratively alongside truths learned from other academic disciplines such as the social sciences for the purpose of understanding God's Word. This includes utilizing the best methods of translation so as to render the original texts most accurately in other languages. It also includes considering the now-contemporary questions of sanctity of life and a creational model for Christian marriage or celibate singleness. Finally, a defense of biblical equality does not require the endorsement of abortion on demand or affirming same-sex intimate relationships for Christians.

Part IV: Living It Out: Practical Applications. The message of biblical equality needs to be taken clearly and responsibly from academic debates (such as those offered in this volume) to the broader church in a way that is understandable and applicable. Models of healthy egalitarian marriages need to continue to demonstrate how a partnership of equals can best honor God by mirroring the divine mandate in creation. Evangelicals need to speak out prophetically against racial discrimination and domestic abuse, especially as the latter is often perpetuated under the cloak of so-called benevolent male leadership. We need to demonstrate more fully than ever how a biblical gender equality can lead to human flourishing, not just flourishing related to women and girls. Finally, for the sake of a better witness to the watching world, both complementarians and egalitarians must embrace the challenge of moving toward a genuinely Christian reconciliation, despite the significant differences that continue to divide us, as we all move toward a better understanding of God's will for us as men, women, and intersex persons fully sharing the divine image.

WHERE TO GO FROM HERE?

Where the discussion stands. We want to close with an evaluation of where the evangelical gender debate stands at this time and where it is going. First, it must be acknowledged that to date this discussion has largely been conducted in the evangelical churches and in the Evangelical Theological Society in the United States, which have been primarily complementarian, with significant contributions from the United Kingdom and Canada, which have been primarily egalitarian. As we are concluding this new edition of *Discovering Biblical Equality*, certain developments have emerged in the evangelical community in the United States that reveal that the discussion of women's role in the church is enmeshed in a greater polarizing schism of hostility and anger that extends far beyond a single issue, in which the uncivil discourse surrounding this topic is most likely a symptom of the nature of the American evangelical culture rather than a cause.

Egalitarians are distinguished by four relevant commitments in this divide: we are committed to the authority of Scripture, we are devoted to the lordship of Christ manifested by costly obedience, our identity is evangelical, and we are committed to local, denominational, and global unity in the body of Christ. This is the reason we stay in this conversation in our churches, denominations, and the Evangelical Theological Society, and attempt to nurture those relationships. The attempts of egalitarian men and women to practice and speak what we understand to be truth that is faithful to the Scriptures have involved costly and painful obedience to our calling, particularly for those of us who are now senior citizens, who broke new ground. One sustaining image has been drawn from a memorable word picture in the homeschooling movement: "We lie down in the mud and let the next generation walk on us." The younger generations of women have greater moral support and growing opportunities for education and ministry that older women lacked—though there clearly remains work to be done. That is to say, this journey has involved a participation in cruciformity that has been far more costly than profitable. No one's life displays this more clearly than Rebecca Groothuis, the coeditor of the first two volumes. She was a brilliant and gifted writer and editor who suffered from a debilitating illness that was destroying her body as she labored toward the goal of publication in 2004. The progression of her illness led to early-onset dementia, which destroyed her mind and ended her life. Her sacrifice was pivotal to produce this volume.

At its core, the egalitarian position is characterized by a costly commitment to biblical unity, servant leadership, service, mutuality, humility, love, responsibility, the example of Christ, and the upside-down values of the kingdom of God. Wherever this volume or we as individuals have fallen short in our exegesis, character, or behavior, we must be committed to repent and hold each other accountable as we move forward, because these are our standards and they have been so from the beginning. We have committed ourselves to a call to biblical equality, as determined by Scriptures such as Philippians 2:1-10, that must guide us, distinguish us, and constrain us from other notions of equality.

Looking forward. We also want to look to the future of this discussion, for much remains to be discussed. *Gender equality* is rapidly meaning something very different from what the original contributors to this volume could have envisioned. In future works, more will need to be done to develop a robust theology of sexuality that not only addresses crucial topics such as gender fluidity and gender identity, but also develops a life-giving conversation concerning an overarching biblical understanding of sexuality. We need to think more deeply about how masculinity and femininity might be conceived of in ways that do not lead to stereotypes and gender roles, but rather are culturally rich expressions of the goodness of being male and female—as well as addressing how intersex persons can be included in these formulations. Further, it is vital that we develop strategies together that effectively address pervasive challenges such as sexual immorality, pornography, domestic abuse, and body image.

In the introduction there is a statement that we believe in authority, but the emerging dialogue has indicated an imperative necessity of clarifying the biblical practice and character of power and authority in the church, home, and society. In regard to the church, it would appear that our argument that women are equal to serve has been heard, interpreted, and processed by many as arrogant demands for self-fulfillment through seizing power and control. This leads us to entertain the question of whether professional positions in the church and parachurch ministries are considered by many evangelicals to be equivalent to the kind of secular authority that Jesus roundly condemns in Matthew 20:25-28. If the qualification for professional ministry is to become a slave, no one can justifiably be excluded unless the metaphor of headship is turned on its head. This leads to an examination of the dynamics of power in our structures, exegesis, theology, and rhetoric. It clarifies the necessity of exploring and carefully defining the biblical relationship between the church, the home, and society/culture in a way in which the categories are not collapsed, as they are so often in both exegesis and theology.

As we said above, the majority of those engaging in this conversation have been the evangelical community in the United States, but the role of cultural diversity and globalization must be considered. What are these masculinities and feminities, especially from non-Western contexts, and how might multiple cultures enter into this conversation? The egalitarian movement needs to examine how it has centered Whiteness. The vision for biblical equality is for all women and men, so how do we hear from more voices who have been decentered throughout this debate? Moreover, how will the church respond to these concerns?

We hope you now have a better understanding of a faithful approach to Scripture that yields a resounding affirmation of women's gifts and callings to be used however and wherever the Spirit leads. Pastorally, we hope you are better equipped to discuss marital and leadership equality while also thinking globally about how much this matters for women and men's full flourishing. May God bless his church as we faithfully continue to seek to understand what Scripture teaches and apply it in our lives and communities.

LIST OF CONTRIBUTORS

• • • • •

Jack O. Balswick received his MA and PhD from the University of Iowa. He is senior professor of sociology and family development at Fuller Theological Seminary. His publications include *The Reciprocating Self: Human Development in Theological Perspective* and *Men at the Crossroads*. In addition, he has coauthored with his wife, Judy, *The Family: A Christian Perspective on the Contemporary Home*; *Authentic Human Sexuality: An Integrated Christian Approach*; *Family Pain: Getting Through the Hurts of Family Life*; *The Dual-Earner Marriage: The Elaborate Balancing Act*; and *A Model for Marriage: Covenant, Grace, Empowerment, Intimacy*.

Judith K. Balswick received her MA from the University of Iowa and EdD from the University of Georgia in counseling and human development. She is senior professor in the School of Psychology & Marriage and Family Therapy at Fuller Theological Seminary, and has been a licensed therapist and supervisor for over thirty years. Her publications include *Relationship-Empowering Parenting*, as well as the coauthored books *Life Ties* and *Then They Leave Home*, along with numerous coedited publications with her husband, Jack (see above). Judy and Jack are members of Pasadena Covenant Church. They have two married children and six grandchildren.

Linda L. Belleville received her MA from Trinity Evangelical Divinity School and PhD from St. Michael's College, University of Toronto. She previously taught at Calvin College, North Park Theological Seminary, and Bethel University. She is an adjunct professor of New Testament at Grand Rapids Theological Seminary. Her publications include *2 Corinthians* (IVP New Testament Commentaries), *1 Timothy* (Cornerstone), *Philippians* (Cascade), *Women Leaders and the Church* (Baker), *Two Views on Women in Ministry* (Zondervan), and numerous articles and essays on the issue of biblical teaching about women's roles in the church, society, and the family.

Lynn H. Cohick received her PhD from the University of Pennsylvania and is provost and dean of academic affairs at Northern Seminary. Lynn was professor of New Testament at Wheaton College and also taught for three years at Nairobi Evangelical Graduate School of Theology in Nairobi. Her publications include *The Letter to the*

Ephesians; Christian Women in the Patristic World: Their Influence, Authority, and Legacy in the Second Through the Fifth Centuries (coauthored with Amy Brown Hughes); *Philippians* in the Story of God Commentary; *Ephesians* in the New Covenant Commentary; and *Women in the World of the Earliest Christians*.

Mary L. Conway received her MTS from McMaster University and PhD from McMaster Divinity College, where she is now an associate professor of Old Testament. Her published articles include "Daughter Zion: Metaphor and Dialogue in the Book of Lamentations," in *Daughter Zion: Her Portrait, Her Response*. She has recently published *Judging the Judges: A Narrative Appraisal Analysis*, which involves an adaptation of appraisal theory to Hebrew narrative in order to evaluate characters and determine authorial stance, and has also coauthored a new discourse-based commentary on *Judges* (Zondervan Exegetical Commentary on the New Testament). Mary enjoys teaching adult classes in her local church.

Peter H. Davids received his MDiv from Trinity Evangelical Divinity School and PhD from the University of Manchester. He has taught at seminaries and universities in the United States, Canada, and a number of European countries. Starting as a Plymouth Brethren, he was an Episcopal priest for thirty-four years, but served Christian and Missionary Alliance, Vineyard, Baptist, Brethren, and nondenominational institutions. He was ordained a Catholic priest in 2014 and is currently chaplain to the Dominican Sisters of Mary, Mother of the Eucharist in Georgetown, Texas. His publications include *A Commentary on the Epistle of James; The First Epistle of Peter*; half of the New Testament part of *Hard Sayings of the Bible*; and *A Theology of James, Peter, and Jude*. He is married to Judith L. Davids, who is a spiritual director and counselor.

Gordon D. Fee received his MA from Seattle Pacific University and PhD from the University of Southern California. He is professor emeritus of New Testament studies at Regent College as well as an ordained minister with the Assemblies of God. His publications include *How to Read the Bible for All Its Worth; How to Read the Bible Book by Book; New Testament Exegesis: A Handbook; God's Empowering Presence: The Holy Spirit in the Letters of Paul; Listening to the Spirit in the Text; Jesus the Lord According to Paul the Apostle;* and commentaries on *1 Corinthians; 1 & 2 Thessalonians; Philippians; 1 & 2 Timothy; Titus;* and *Revelation*. He and his late wife, Maudine, have four married children.

Kevin Giles received his BD from Moore Theological College, Sydney, Australia, his MA from Durham University, UK, and his ThD from the Australian College of Theology. He served as an Anglican parish minister for more than forty years. His publications include *Women and Their Ministry; Created Woman; What the Bible Actually Teaches About Women; The Headship of Men and the Abuse of Women: Are They Related in Any Way?; The Trinity and Subordinationism: The Doctrine of God and the Contemporary Gender Debate; Jesus and the Father: Modern Evangelicals Reinvent the Doctrine of the Trinity; The Eternal Generation of the Son: Maintaining Orthodoxy in*

Trinitarian Theology; *The Rise and Fall of the Complementarian Doctrine of the Trinity*; and over forty journal articles as well as several chapters in collections of essays and a number of articles in theological dictionaries. Kevin and his wife, Lynley, a marriage educator and counselor, have four children and eleven grandchildren. They live in Melbourne, Australia.

Juliany González Nieves received her MDiv from Trinity Evangelical Divinity School and a BSc in Biology from the University of Puerto Rico, Río Piedras. Her main area of interest is Caribbean and Latin American theologies at the intersection of race, ethnicity, and gender across geographical and linguistic lines. She has collaborated with projects and initiatives from institutions such as the University of St Andrews, Scotland, and Trinity Evangelical Divinity School, such as Logia, the Sueña Initiative, Mosaic Ministries, and the Paul G. Hiebert Center for World Christianity and Global Theology. She currently works at Trinity International University, Florida.

Stanley J. Grenz received his MDiv from Denver Seminary and DTheol from the University of Munich, Germany. He was Pioneer McDonald Professor of Theology at Carey Theological College, Vancouver, and an ordained minister with the Baptist Union of Western Canada. His publications include *The Social God and the Relational Self: A Trinitarian Theology of the Imago Dei*; *Renewing the Center: Evangelical Theology in a Post-theological Era*; *Theology for the Community of God*; *What Christians Really Believe . . . and Why*; *The Moral Quest: Foundations for Christian Ethics*; *A Primer on Postmodernism*; and, coauthored with Denise Muir Kjesbo, *Women and the Church: A Biblical Theology of Women in Ministry*.

Rebecca Merrill Groothuis was a freelance writer, poet, editor, and a member of Mensa. Her publications include the award-winning *Women Caught in the Conflict: The Culture War Between Traditionalism and Feminism* and *Good News for Women: A Biblical Picture of Gender Equality*, as well as articles and reviews in *Christian Scholar's Review*, *Christianity Today*, *ReGeneration Quarterly*, *Perspectives*, *Priscilla Papers*, *Christian Counseling Today*, *Christian Ethics Today*, *Eternity*, and the *Denver Post*.

Mimi Haddad earned a MATS from Gordon Conwell Theological Seminary (summa cum laude) and a PhD from the University of Durham, England. Serving as president of CBE International, she teaches at Fuller Theological Seminary. A founding member of the Evangelical Theological Society's Evangelicals and Women, she has served as a gender consultant for Christian nongovernmental organizations. An Evangelical Press Association award winner, she has published over one hundred articles in journals such as *Ashland Theological Journal*, *The Campbellsville Review*, *Catalyst*, *Christian Ethics Today*, and *Evangelical Fellowship of India Commission on Relief*. She is a contributor to sixteen books, recently *Created to Thrive* (CBE International, 2021), *Is Women's Equality a Biblical Ideal?* (CBE International, 2021), and *Women in Pentecostal and Charismatic Ministry* (Brill, 2016). Mimi lives in Saint Paul with her husband, Dale.

M. Elizabeth Lewis Hall received her MA and PhD degrees in clinical psychology from Rosemead School of Psychology, Biola University. She is professor of psychology at Biola as well as maintaining a small clinical practice. She has published over one hundred articles and book chapers on issues at the intersection of psychology and Christianity on topics such as gender, embodiment, and meaning making in suffering, and she has received numerous awards for her scholarship. She is a fellow of the American Psychological Association and associate editor of *Psychology of Religion and Spirituality*. She is married to Todd and has two young-adult sons: Brennan and Aiden.

Erin M. Heim earned a BMus from the Univesity of Minnesota, an MA in New Testament from Denver Seminary, and a PhD from the University of Otago. In 2019 she received the Manfred T. Lautenschläger prize for her published doctoral thesis, *Adoption in Galatians and Romans* (Brill, 2017). She has authored numerous articles and essays on Pauline theology, theological interpretation of Scripture, and metaphor in the Bible. Erin is also a cohost of the popular biblical studies and theology podcast OnScript.

Elizabeth A. Kay received her MA in biblical exposition from Talbot School of Theology at Biola University in 2017. She served for several years as research and teaching assistant for several undergraduate Bible and theology courses, including Theology of Gender, and is currently the course materials manager at the Biola Store.

Craig S. Keener received his MA and MDiv from the Assemblies of God Theological Seminary and PhD from Duke University. He is F. M. and Ada Thompson Professor of Biblical Studies at Asbury Theological Seminary and has authored thirty-two books, with more than a million copies in circulation; six have won awards in *Christianity Today*. These include works on Bible background, the work of the Spirit, women in ministry, and many commentaries, most notably a four-volume commentary on Acts. He has also served as president of the Evangelical Theological Society (2020). Craig is married to Dr. Médine Moussounga Keener, who survived war in Congo (a story recounted in their book *Impossible Love*).

Walter L. Liefeld received his PhD from Columbia University and Union Theological Seminary. He is distinguished professor emeritus of New Testament at Trinity Evangelical Divinity School in Deerfield, Illinois. He has held several pastorates and interim pastorates, most recently serving as senior pastor of Christ Church in Lake Forest, Illinois. Among his several books are *New Testament Exposition*; *Interpreting the Book of Acts*; and, cowritten with Ruth Tucker, *Daughters of the Church*. He and his wife, Olive, have three grown children and seven grandchildren.

Kylie Maddox Pidgeon received her bachelor of social science in psychology (honors) from Charles Sturt University in Australia and works in private practice as a registered psychologist and associate member of the Australian Psychological Association. She is an adjunct lecturer at St. Mark's National Theological Centre in Canberra and has recently coauthored a chapter on play therapy in *Psychotherapy and Counselling:*

Reflection on Practice. Kylie has special interest in the integration of theology and psychology, especially as it regards domestic violence in Christian communities.

Alice P. Mathews received an MA in clinical psychology from Michigan State University and a PhD in a cross-disciplinary program in religion and social change from the Iliff School of Theology and the University of Denver. She is now retired after thirty years in theological education, having held the Distinguished Chair in Women's Ministries and Educational Ministries, as well as serving as academic dean, at Gordon-Conwell Theological Seminary. In addition, for twenty-three years she was a regular participant in the daily radio program Discover the Word (RBC Ministries). She is also the author of nine books, including *Preaching That Speaks to Women*; *Marriage Made in Eden*; *Gender Roles and the People of God*; and *Woman of Strength*. Prior to her academic career, Alice and her husband, Randall, spent seventeen years as missionaries in Europe. They are the parents of four adult children, six grandchildren, and ten great-grandchildren.

Christa L. McKirland is a lecturer in systematic theology at Carey Baptist College. She holds a BA in philosophy and women's studies from the University of Georgia; an MA in Bible exposition and a ThM in systematic theology, both from Talbot School of Theology, Biola University; and a PhD in exegetical and analytic theology from the University of St Andrews, Scotland. She enjoys bringing this rich diversity of disciplines together to speak into what it means to flourish. Christa is also founder and executive director of Logia International, an organization that encourages women to pursue postgraduate divinity education for the sake of the academy and the church. Logia seeks to highlight the excellence of women who are already established in their fields, while also developing the next generation of women scholars who will lead the way in theology, philosophy of religion, and biblical studies.

Jeffrey D. Miller holds bachelor's degrees in pastoral ministry and church music, an MDiv, and a PhD in biblical interpretation. He teaches biblical studies at Milligan University, in view of the Blue Ridge Mountains of eastern Tennessee. He is editor of *Priscilla Papers*, the academic journal of CBE International. He has published academic articles in *The Bible Translator*, *Priscilla Papers*, *Restoration Quarterly*, and *Stone-Campbell Journal*, as well as popular pieces in publications such as *Christian Standard*, *Didaktikos*, *Leaven*, and *Mutuality*. He and his wife, Dana, serve in a variety of ministry roles, mainly through their local congregation. They have two married daughters and five delightful grandchildren.

Ronald W. Pierce received his MDiv and ThM from Talbot School of Theology and a PhD from Fuller Theological Seminary. He is professor of Old Testament in the Talbot School of Theology at Biola University, as well as an ordained minister with Converge International and a spiritual director with SoulFormation. A founding member of Evangelicals and Women—a section of the Evangelical Theological Society—his publications include numerous academic articles. He served as coauthor and contributor to earlier editions of this volume and wrote *Partners in Marriage and Ministry* and a commentary on the book of Daniel. Ron and his wife, Pat, reside in Fullerton, California, and have two married children and four grandchildren.

Stanley E. Porter received his BA from Point Loma College, an MA from Claremont Graduate School, an M. from Trinity Evangelical Divinity School, and his PhD from the University of Sheffield. He is president, dean, and professor of New Testament, and holder of the Roy A. Hope Chair in Christian Worldview, at McMaster Divinity College, Hamilton, Ontario. Porter has written on many if not most areas of New Testament Studies. The author of over thirty books and editor of over ninety, he has recently published *When Paul Met Jesus: How an Idea Got Lost in History*; *Sacred Tradition in the New Testament*; *The Apostle Paul: His Life, Thought, and Letters*; *The Letter to the Romans: A Linguistic and Literary Commentary*; and, with Jason Robinson, *Active Hermeneutics: Seeking Understanding in an Age of Objectivism*.

Ronald J. Sider received his PhD from Yale University and is Distinguished Professor Emeritus of Theology, Holistic Ministry, and Public Policy at Palmer Theological Seminary at Eastern University and president emeritus of Evangelicals for Social Action. He has published more than forty-five books. His *Rich Christians in an Age of Hunger* (6th ed., 2015) was recognized by *Christianity Today* as one of the one hundred most influential religious books of the twentieth century and named the seventh most influential book in the evangelical world in the last fifty years. His more recent books include *Just Politics: A Guide for Christian Engagement*; *The Early Church on Killing: A Comprehensive Sourcebook on War, Abortion, and Capital Punishment*; *Nonviolent Action: What Christian Ethics Demands, but Most Christians Have Never Really Tried*; and *If Jesus Is Lord: Loving Our Enemies in an Age of Violence*. He is married to Arbutus Lichti Sider and has three children and seven grandchildren.

Aída Besançon Spencer received her MDiv and ThM from Princeton Theological Seminary and PhD from Southern Baptist Theological Seminary. She is senior professor of New Testament at Gordon-Conwell Theological Seminary and an ordained Presbyterian minister. She also serves as founding pastor of an organization with Pilgrim Church, Beverly, Massachusetts. Her publications include *Beyond the Curse: Women Called to Ministry*; *Paul's Literary Style*; and commentaries on *2 Corinthians*; *1 Timothy*; and *2 Timothy and Titus*. With her husband, William David Spencer, she has also written and coedited *The Global God*; *Joy Through the Night*; *The Goddess Revival*; and *Christian Egalitarian Leadership*. Aída and William have one grown son, Stephen.

Heidi R. Unruh received an MA in theology and public policy from Palmer Seminary. She is a ministry consultant and coach, equipping churches and nonprofits to move faithfully and effectively from principles to action. Her focus is faith-based engagement with poverty, vulnerable families, and asset-based community development. Her writings include coauthoring *Churches That Make a Difference*; *Hope for Children in Poverty*; *Saving Souls, Serving Society*; *The Salt & Light Guidebook*; and

Real Connections, along with numerous practical tools and training resources. She also coaches authors through Shine Writing Services. Heidi and her husband, Jim, a pastor, are raising their family in Hutchinson, Kansas.

Cynthia Long Westfall received an MA from Northern Arizona University, an MDiv from Denver Seminary, and a PhD from the University of Surrey Roehampton. She is associate professor of New Testament at McMaster Divinity College. Her areas of focus include Paul and gender, Bible translation, linguistics and discourse analysis, the book of Hebrews, the General Epistles, Revelation, and issues concerning biblical social justice including poverty, power, gender, and biblical interpretation by marginalized people groups. Her recent publications include *Paul and Gender* and *A Discourse Analysis of Hebrews*. She was also the associate Greek editor and a translator for the Common English Bible.

NAME INDEX

• • • • •

SUBJECT INDEX

•••••

SCRIPTURE INDEX

• • • • •